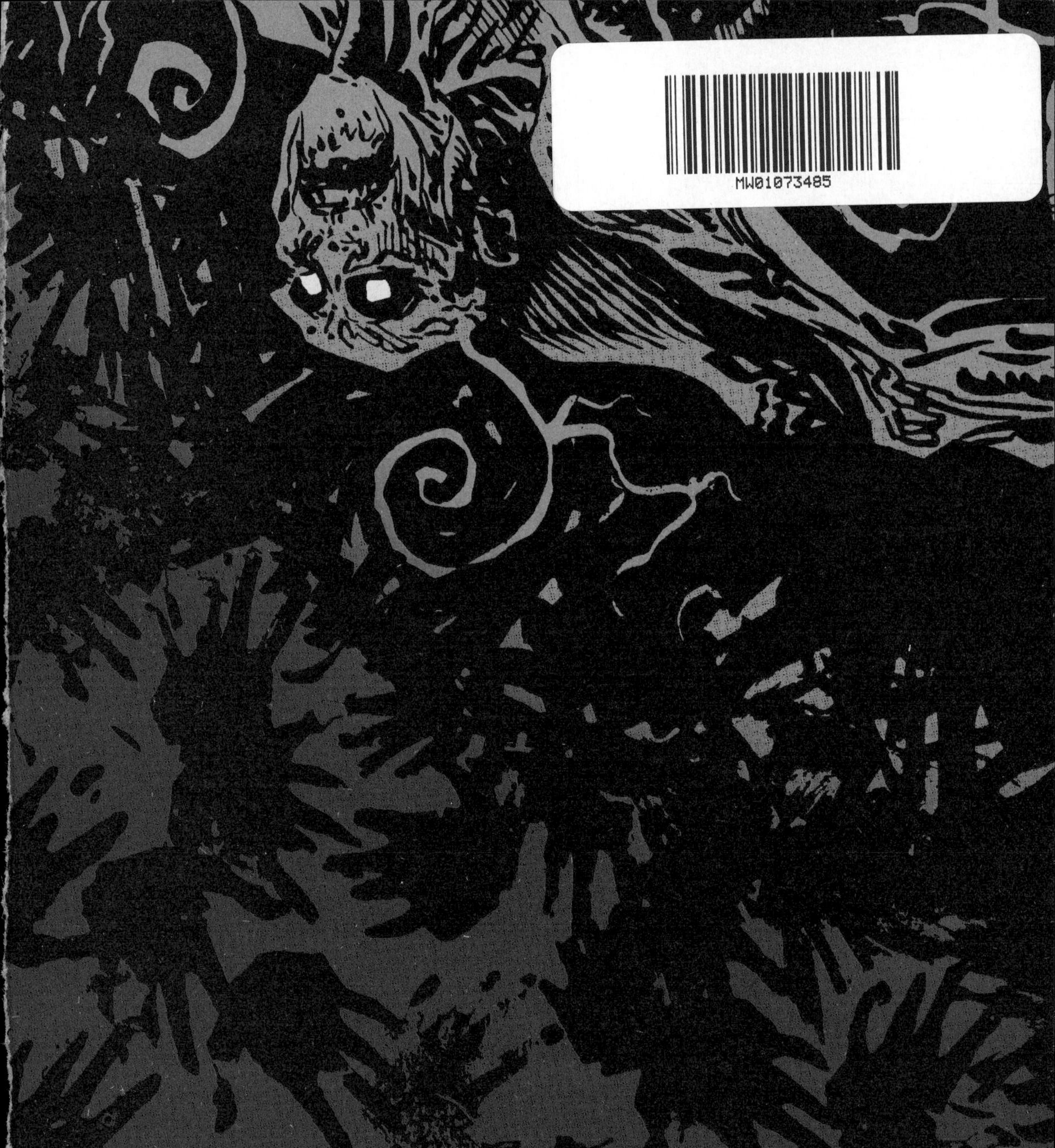

SWAMP THING:
THE ROOT OF ALL EVIL

Grant Morrison Mark Millar Writers
Phil Hester Kim DeMulder Artists
Tatjana Wood Colorist
Richard Starkings/Comicraft Letterer
John Mueller Cover Art and Original Series Covers
Swamp Thing created by Len Wein and Bernie Wrightson

Stuart Moore Editor – Original Series
Julie Rottenberg Assistant Editor – Original Series
Scott Nybakken Editor
Robbin Brosterman Design Director – Books
Louis Prandi Publication Design

Shelly Bond Executive Editor – Vertigo
Hank Kanalz Senior VP – Vertigo & Integrated Publishing

Diane Nelson President
Dan DiDio and Jim Lee Co-Publishers
Geoff Johns Chief Creative Officer
Amit Desai Senior VP – Marketing & Franchise Management
Amy Genkins Senior VP – Business & Legal Affairs
Nairi Gardiner Senior VP – Finance
Jeff Boison VP – Publishing Planning
Mark Chiarello VP – Art Direction & Design
John Cunningham VP – Marketing
Terri Cunningham VP – Editorial Administration
Larry Ganem VP – Talent Relations & Services
Alison Gill Senior VP – Manufacturing & Operations
Jay Kogan VP – Business & Legal Affairs, Publishing
Jack Mahan VP – Business Affairs, Talent
Nick Napolitano VP – Manufacturing Administration
Sue Pohja VP – Book Sales
Fred Ruiz VP – Manufacturing Operations
Courtney Simmons Senior VP – Publicity
Bob Wayne Senior VP – Sales

SWAMP THING: THE ROOT OF ALL EVIL

Published by DC Comics. Compilation Copyright © 2015 DC Comics.
All Rights Reserved.

Originally published in single magazine form in SWAMP THING 140-150.
Copyright © 1994, 1995 DC Comics. All Rights Reserved. All characters,
their distinctive likenesses and related elements featured in this publication
are trademarks of DC Comics. VERTIGO is a trademark of DC Comics. The
stories, characters and incidents featured in this publication are entirely
fictional. DC Comics does not read or accept unsolicited submissions of
ideas, stories or artwork.

DC Comics, 4000 Warner Blvd., Burbank, CA 91522
A Warner Bros. Entertainment Company.
Printed in the USA. First Printing.
ISBN: 978-1-4012-5241-0.

Library of Congress Cataloging-in-Publication Data

Morrison, Grant.
  Swamp Thing : the root of all evil / Grant Morrison, Mark Millar ;
illustrated by Phil Hester.
      pages cm
  ISBN 978-1-4012-5241-0 (paperback)
  1. Graphic novels. I. Millar, Mark, author. II. Hester, Phil, 1966-
illustrator. III. Title.
  PN6728.S93M75 2015
  741.5'973—dc23
                                2015008051

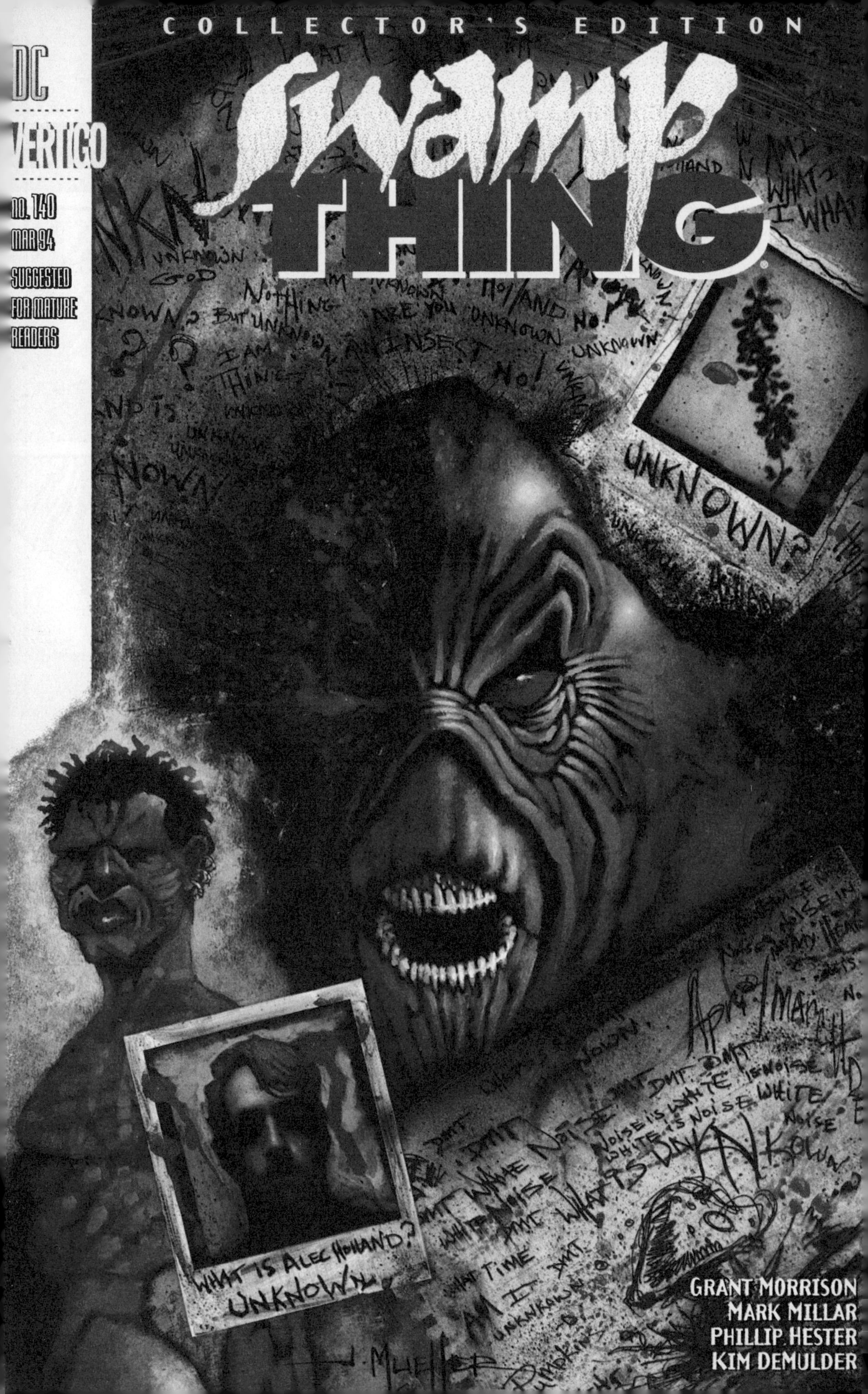
COLLECTOR'S EDITION
DC
VERTIGO
SWAMP THING
no. 140
MAR 94
SUGGESTED FOR MATURE READERS
UNKNOWN?
WHAT IS ALEC HOLLAND?
UNKNOWN
GRANT MORRISON
MARK MILLAR
PHILLIP HESTER
KIM DEMULDER

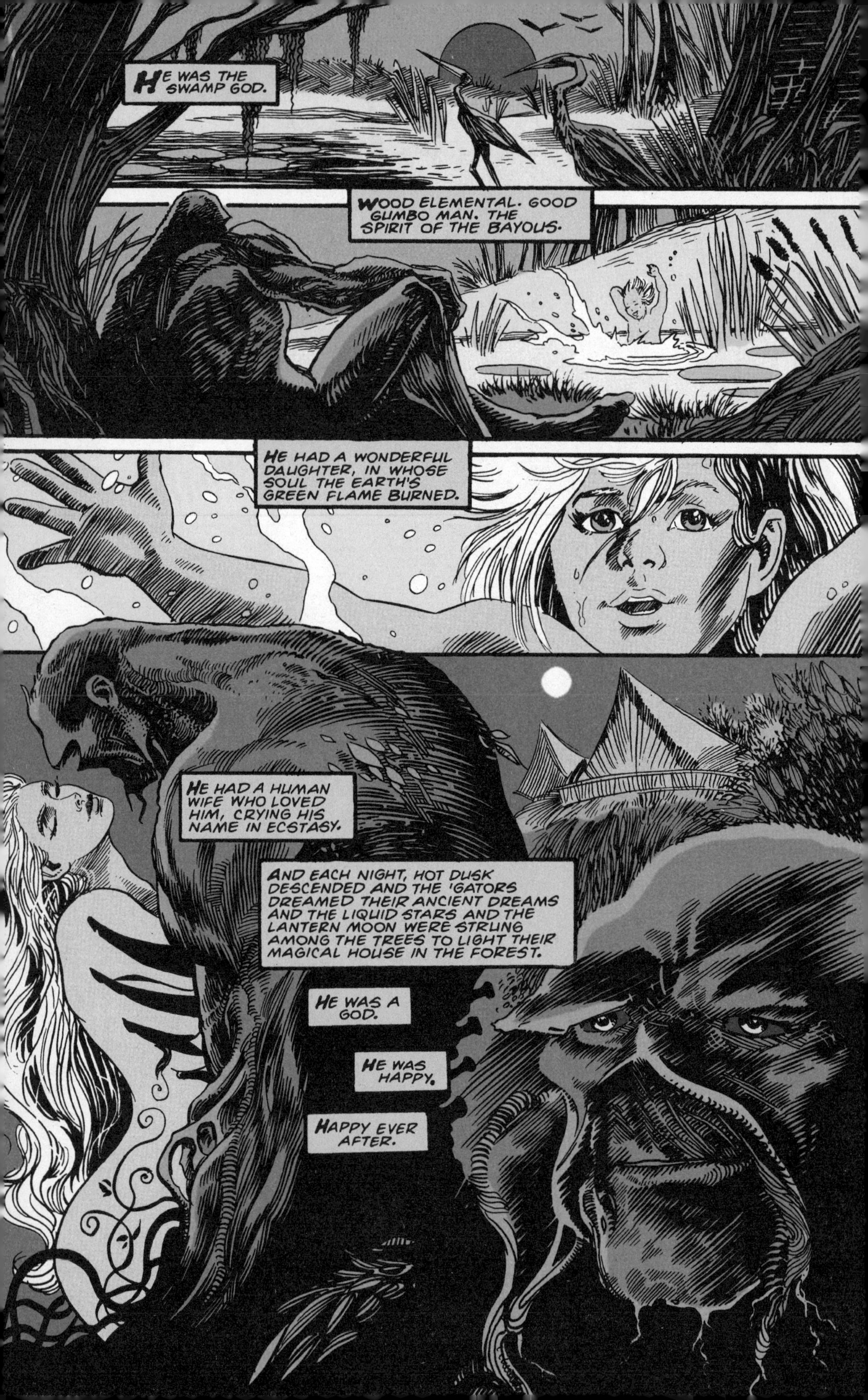
HE WAS THE SWAMP GOD.
WOOD ELEMENTAL. GOOD GUMBO MAN. THE SPIRIT OF THE BAYOUS.
HE HAD A WONDERFUL DAUGHTER, IN WHOSE SOUL THE EARTH'S GREEN FLAME BURNED.
HE HAD A HUMAN WIFE WHO LOVED HIM, CRYING HIS NAME IN ECSTASY.
AND EACH NIGHT, HOT DUSK DESCENDED AND THE 'GATORS DREAMED THEIR ANCIENT DREAMS AND THE LIQUID STARS AND THE LANTERN MOON WERE STRUNG AMONG THE TREES TO LIGHT THEIR MAGICAL HOUSE IN THE FOREST.
HE WAS A GOD.
HE WAS HAPPY.
HAPPY EVER AFTER.

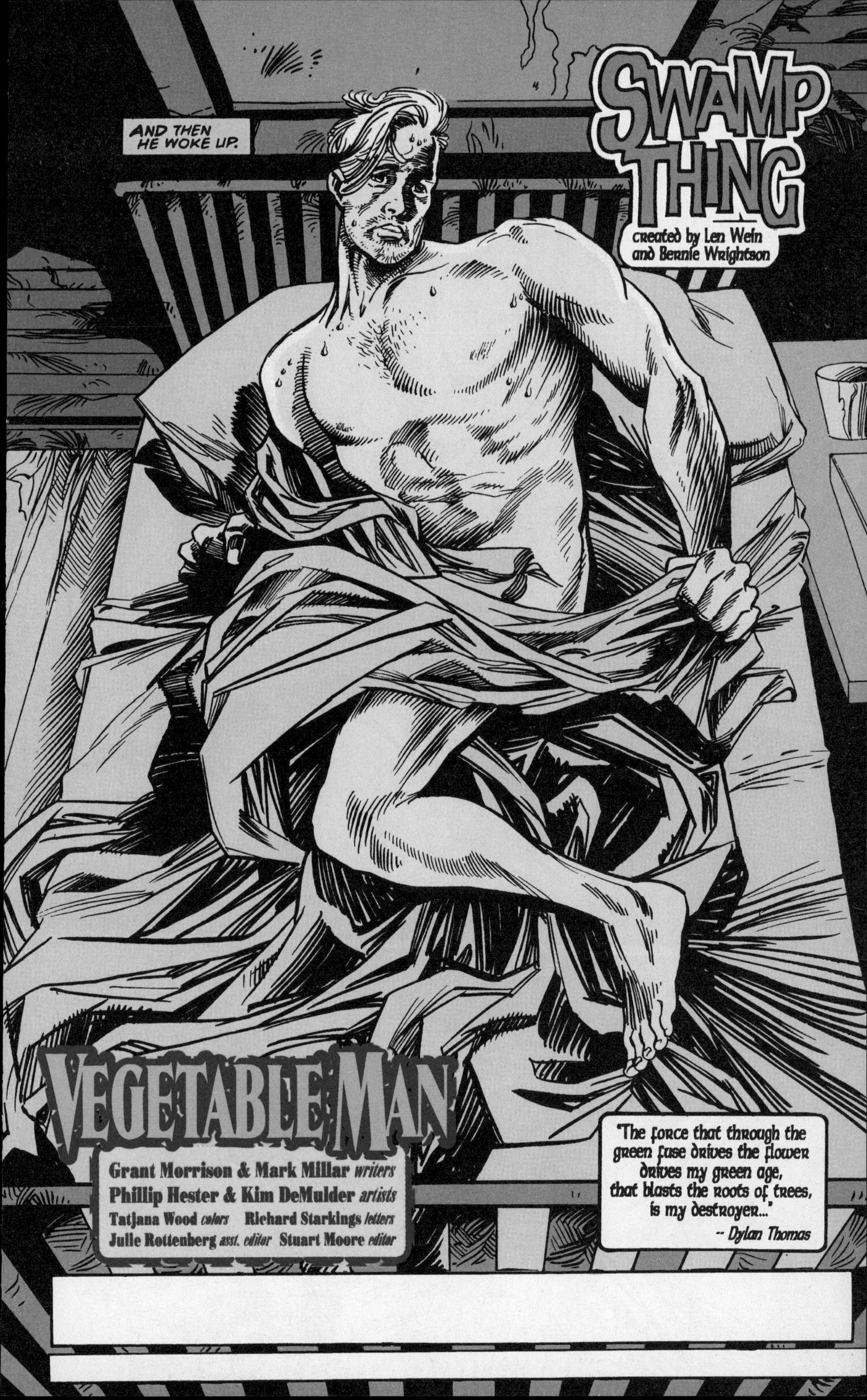
AND THEN HE WOKE UP.
SWAMP THING
created by Len Wein and Bernie Wrightson
VEGETABLE MAN
Grant Morrison & Mark Millar writers
Phillip Hester & Kim DeMulder artists
Tatjana Wood colors Richard Starkings letters
Julie Rottenberg asst. editor Stuart Moore editor
"The force that through the green fuse drives the flower drives my green age, that blasts the roots of trees, is my destroyer..."
-- Dylan Thomas

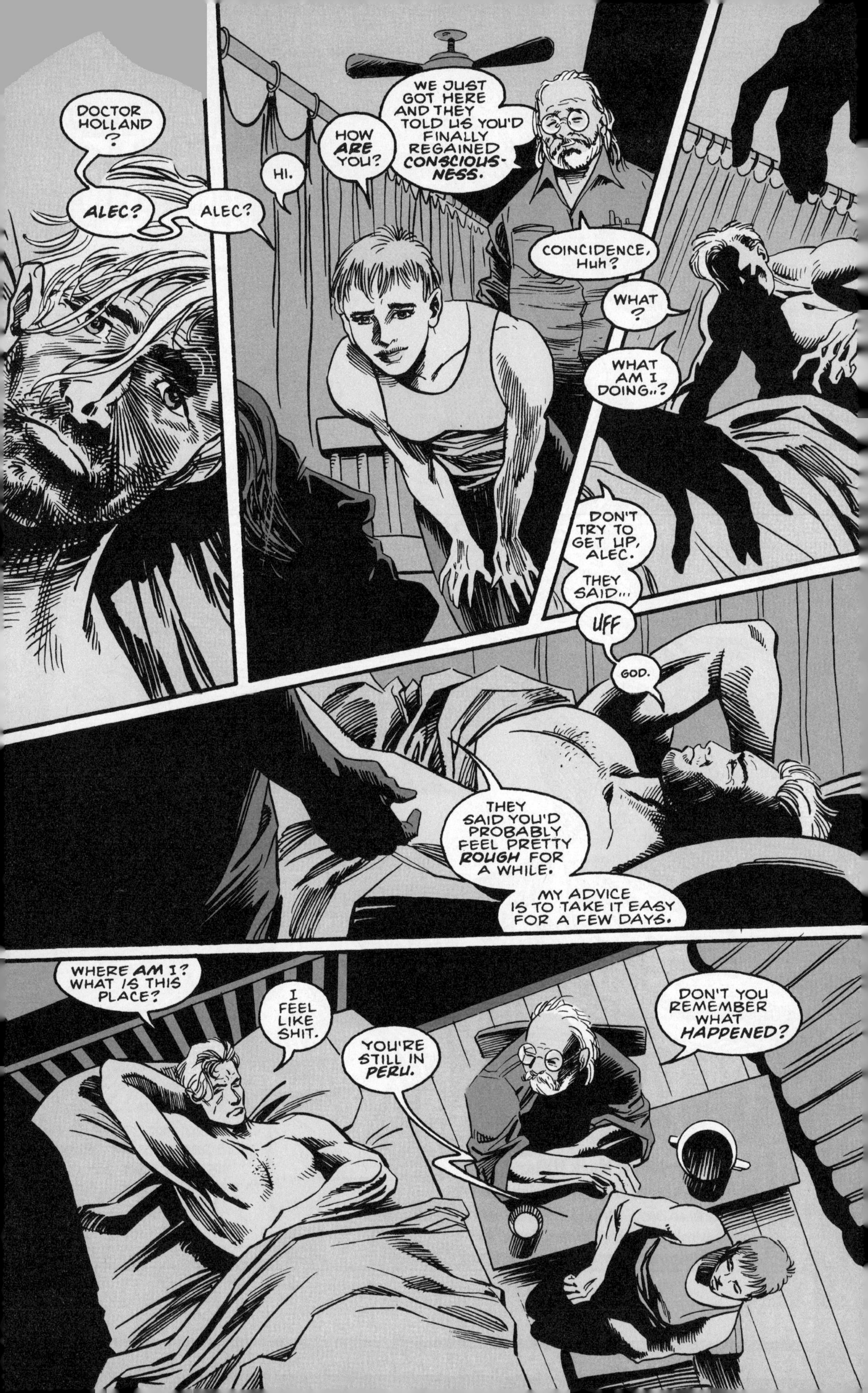
DOCTOR HOLLAND ?
ALEC?
ALEC?
HI.
HOW ARE YOU?
WE JUST GOT HERE AND THEY TOLD US YOU'D FINALLY REGAINED CONSCIOUSNESS.
COINCIDENCE, Huh?
WHAT ?
WHAT AM I DOING..?
DON'T TRY TO GET UP, ALEC.
THEY SAID...
UFF
GOD.
THEY SAID YOU'D PROBABLY FEEL PRETTY ROUGH FOR A WHILE.
MY ADVICE IS TO TAKE IT EASY FOR A FEW DAYS.
WHERE AM I? WHAT IS THIS PLACE?
I FEEL LIKE SHIT.
YOU'RE STILL IN PERU.
DON'T YOU REMEMBER WHAT HAPPENED?

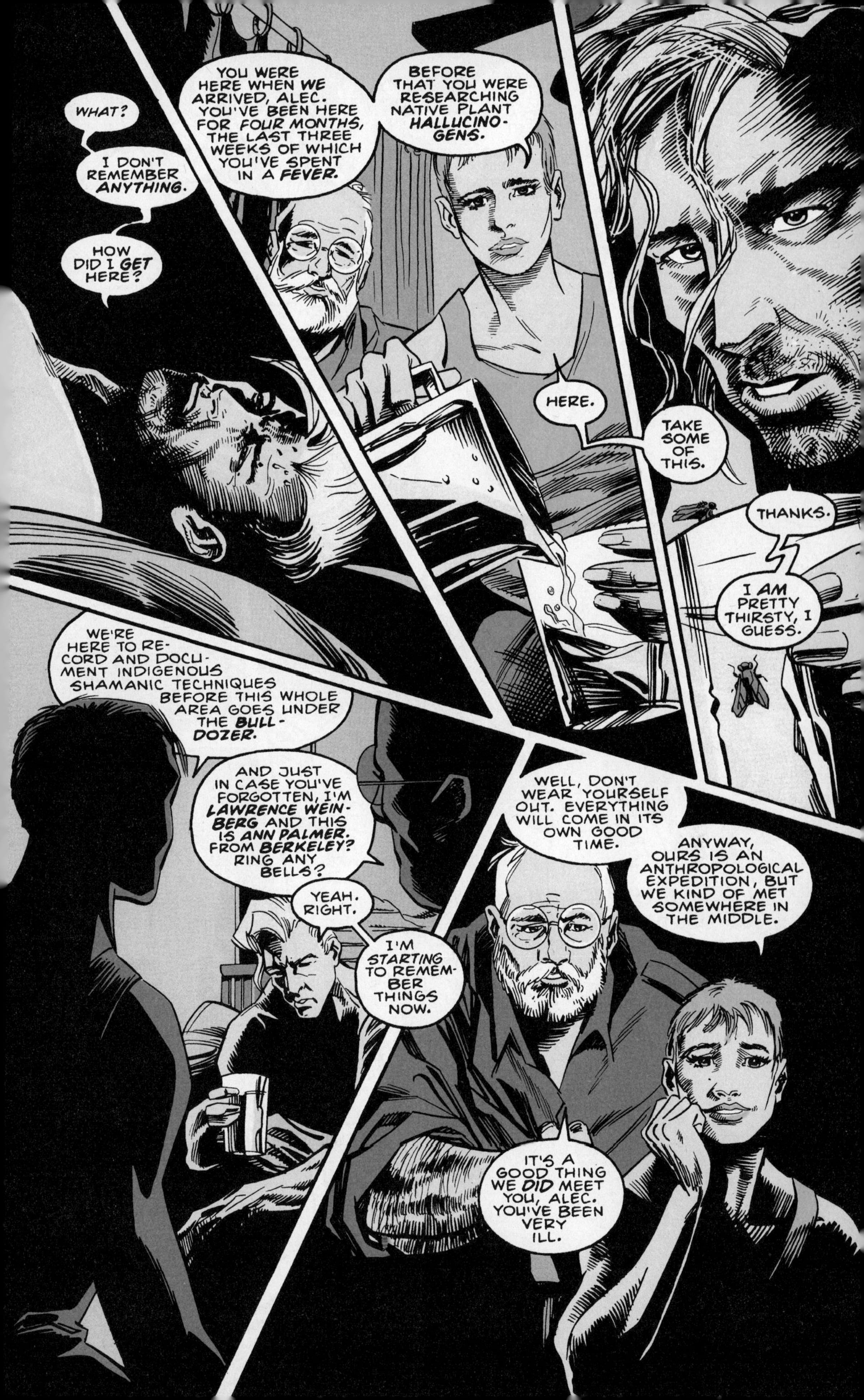
WHAT?
I DON'T REMEMBER ANYTHING.
HOW DID I GET HERE?
YOU WERE HERE WHEN WE ARRIVED, ALEC. YOU'VE BEEN HERE FOR FOUR MONTHS, THE LAST THREE WEEKS OF WHICH YOU'VE SPENT IN A FEVER.
BEFORE THAT YOU WERE RESEARCHING NATIVE PLANT HALLUCINOGENS.
HERE.
TAKE SOME OF THIS.
THANKS.
I AM PRETTY THIRSTY, I GUESS.
WE'RE HERE TO RECORD AND DOCUMENT INDIGENOUS SHAMANIC TECHNIQUES BEFORE THIS WHOLE AREA GOES UNDER THE BULLDOZER.
AND JUST IN CASE YOU'VE FORGOTTEN, I'M LAWRENCE WEINBERG AND THIS IS ANN PALMER. FROM BERKELEY? RING ANY BELLS?
YEAH. RIGHT.
I'M STARTING TO REMEMBER THINGS NOW.
WELL, DON'T WEAR YOURSELF OUT. EVERYTHING WILL COME IN ITS OWN GOOD TIME.
ANYWAY, OURS IS AN ANTHROPOLOGICAL EXPEDITION, BUT WE KIND OF MET SOMEWHERE IN THE MIDDLE.
IT'S A GOOD THING WE DID MEET YOU, ALEC. YOU'VE BEEN VERY ILL.

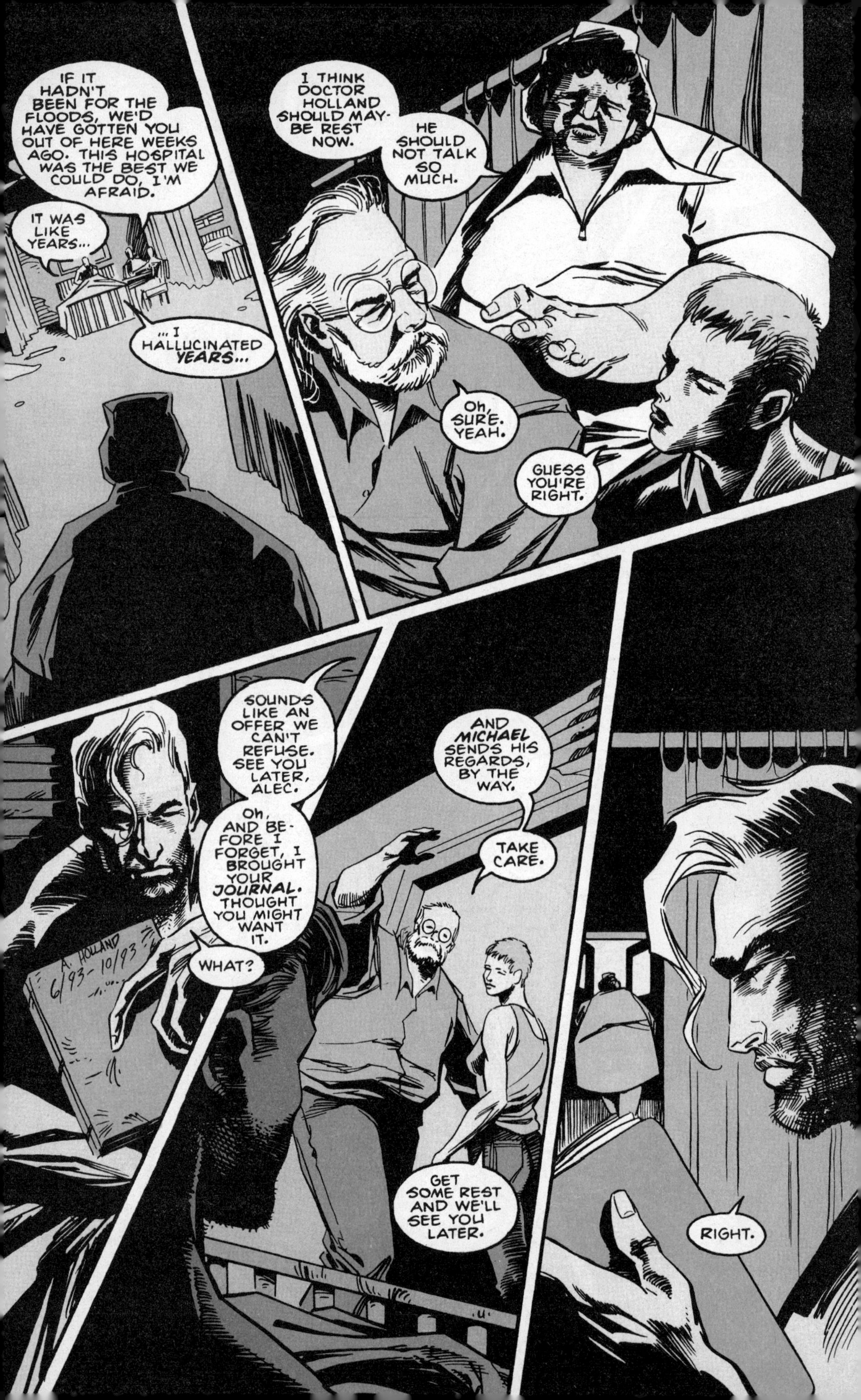
IF IT HADN'T BEEN FOR THE FLOODS, WE'D HAVE GOTTEN YOU OUT OF HERE WEEKS AGO. THIS HOSPITAL WAS THE BEST WE COULD DO, I'M AFRAID.
IT WAS LIKE YEARS...
...I HALLUCINATED YEARS...
I THINK DOCTOR HOLLAND SHOULD MAY-BE REST NOW.
HE SHOULD NOT TALK SO MUCH.
Oh, SURE. YEAH.
GUESS YOU'RE RIGHT.
SOUNDS LIKE AN OFFER WE CAN'T REFUSE. SEE YOU LATER, ALEC.
Oh, AND BE-FORE I FORGET, I BROUGHT YOUR JOURNAL. THOUGHT YOU MIGHT WANT IT.
WHAT?
A. HOLLAND
6/93 - 10/93
AND MICHAEL SENDS HIS REGARDS, BY THE WAY.
TAKE CARE.
GET SOME REST AND WE'LL SEE YOU LATER.
RIGHT.

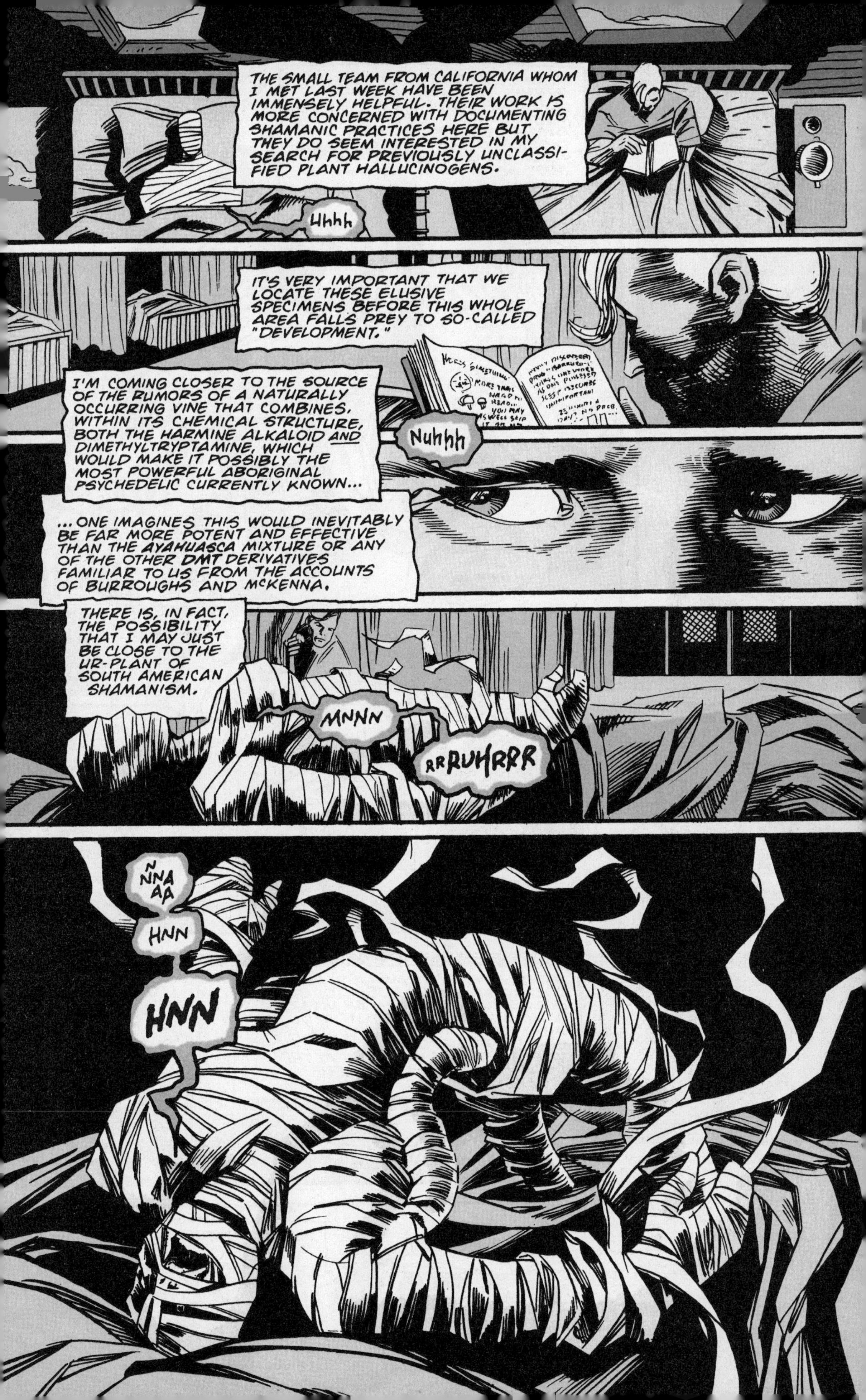
THE SMALL TEAM FROM CALIFORNIA WHOM I MET LAST WEEK HAVE BEEN IMMENSELY HELPFUL. THEIR WORK IS MORE CONCERNED WITH DOCUMENTING SHAMANIC PRACTICES HERE BUT THEY DO SEEM INTERESTED IN MY SEARCH FOR PREVIOUSLY UNCLASSIFIED PLANT HALLUCINOGENS.
Uhhh
IT'S VERY IMPORTANT THAT WE LOCATE THESE ELUSIVE SPECIMENS BEFORE THIS WHOLE AREA FALLS PREY TO SO-CALLED "DEVELOPMENT."
I'M COMING CLOSER TO THE SOURCE OF THE RUMORS OF A NATURALLY OCCURRING VINE THAT COMBINES, WITHIN ITS CHEMICAL STRUCTURE, BOTH THE HARMINE ALKALOID AND DIMETHYLTRYPTAMINE, WHICH WOULD MAKE IT POSSIBLY THE MOST POWERFUL ABORIGINAL PSYCHEDELIC CURRENTLY KNOWN...
Nuhhh
...ONE IMAGINES THIS WOULD INEVITABLY BE FAR MORE POTENT AND EFFECTIVE THAN THE AYAHUASCA MIXTURE OR ANY OF THE OTHER DMT DERIVATIVES FAMILIAR TO US FROM THE ACCOUNTS OF BURROUGHS AND McKENNA.
THERE IS, IN FACT, THE POSSIBILITY THAT I MAY JUST BE CLOSE TO THE UR-PLANT OF SOUTH AMERICAN SHAMANISM.
MNNN
RRRUHRRR
N NNA AA
HNN
HNN

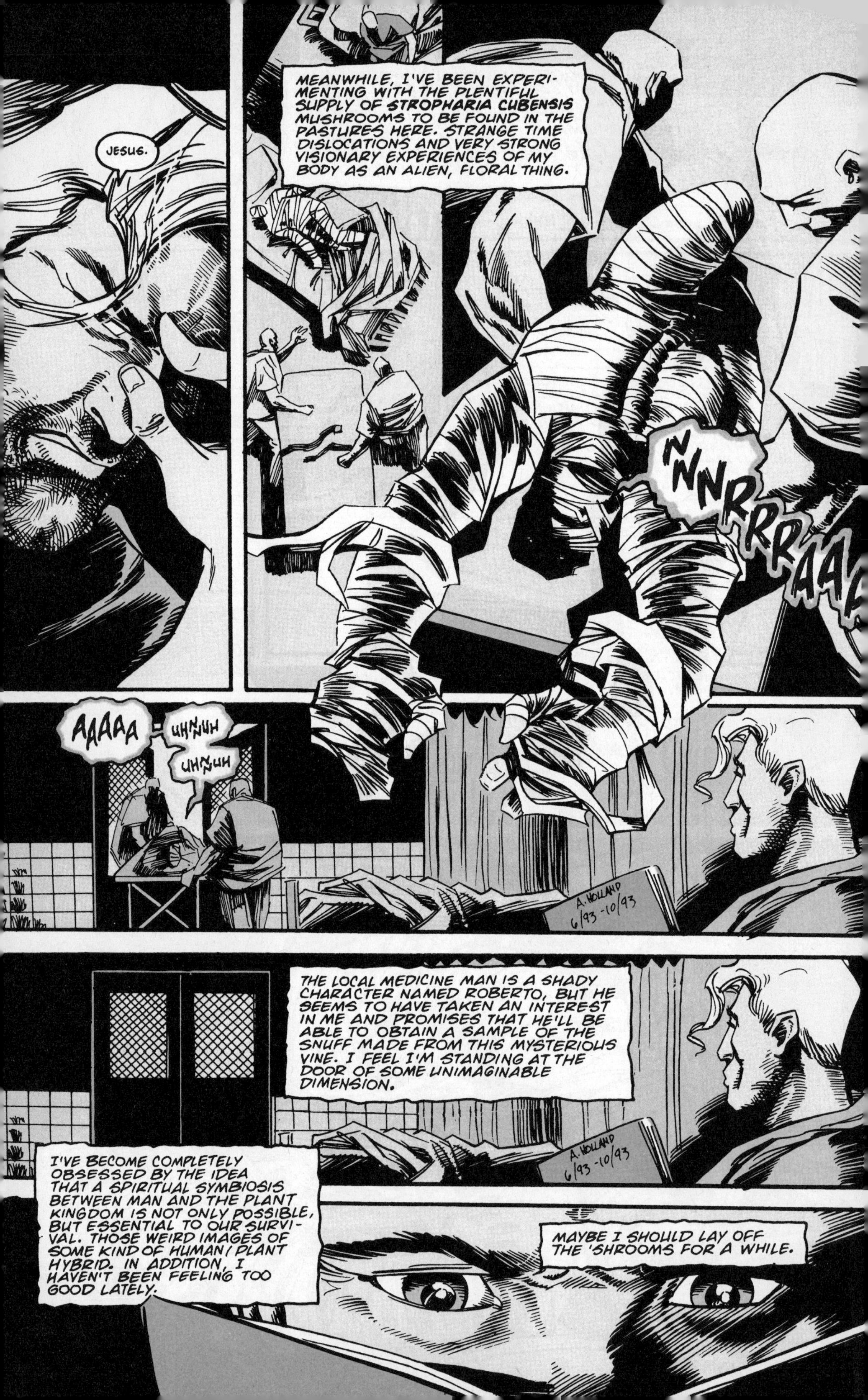
MEANWHILE, I'VE BEEN EXPERIMENTING WITH THE PLENTIFUL SUPPLY OF STROPHARIA CUBENSIS MUSHROOMS TO BE FOUND IN THE PASTURES HERE. STRANGE TIME DISLOCATIONS AND VERY STRONG VISIONARY EXPERIENCES OF MY BODY AS AN ALIEN, FLORAL THING.
JESUS.
NNNRRRAAA
AAAAA
UHNNUH
UHNNUH
A. HOLLAND 6/93 -10/93
THE LOCAL MEDICINE MAN IS A SHADY CHARACTER NAMED ROBERTO, BUT HE SEEMS TO HAVE TAKEN AN INTEREST IN ME AND PROMISES THAT HE'LL BE ABLE TO OBTAIN A SAMPLE OF THE SNUFF MADE FROM THIS MYSTERIOUS VINE. I FEEL I'M STANDING AT THE DOOR OF SOME UNIMAGINABLE DIMENSION.
A. HOLLAND 6/93 -10/93
I'VE BECOME COMPLETELY OBSESSED BY THE IDEA THAT A SPIRITUAL SYMBIOSIS BETWEEN MAN AND THE PLANT KINGDOM IS NOT ONLY POSSIBLE, BUT ESSENTIAL TO OUR SURVIVAL. THOSE WEIRD IMAGES OF SOME KIND OF HUMAN/PLANT HYBRID. IN ADDITION, I HAVEN'T BEEN FEELING TOO GOOD LATELY.
MAYBE I SHOULD LAY OFF THE 'SHROOMS FOR A WHILE.

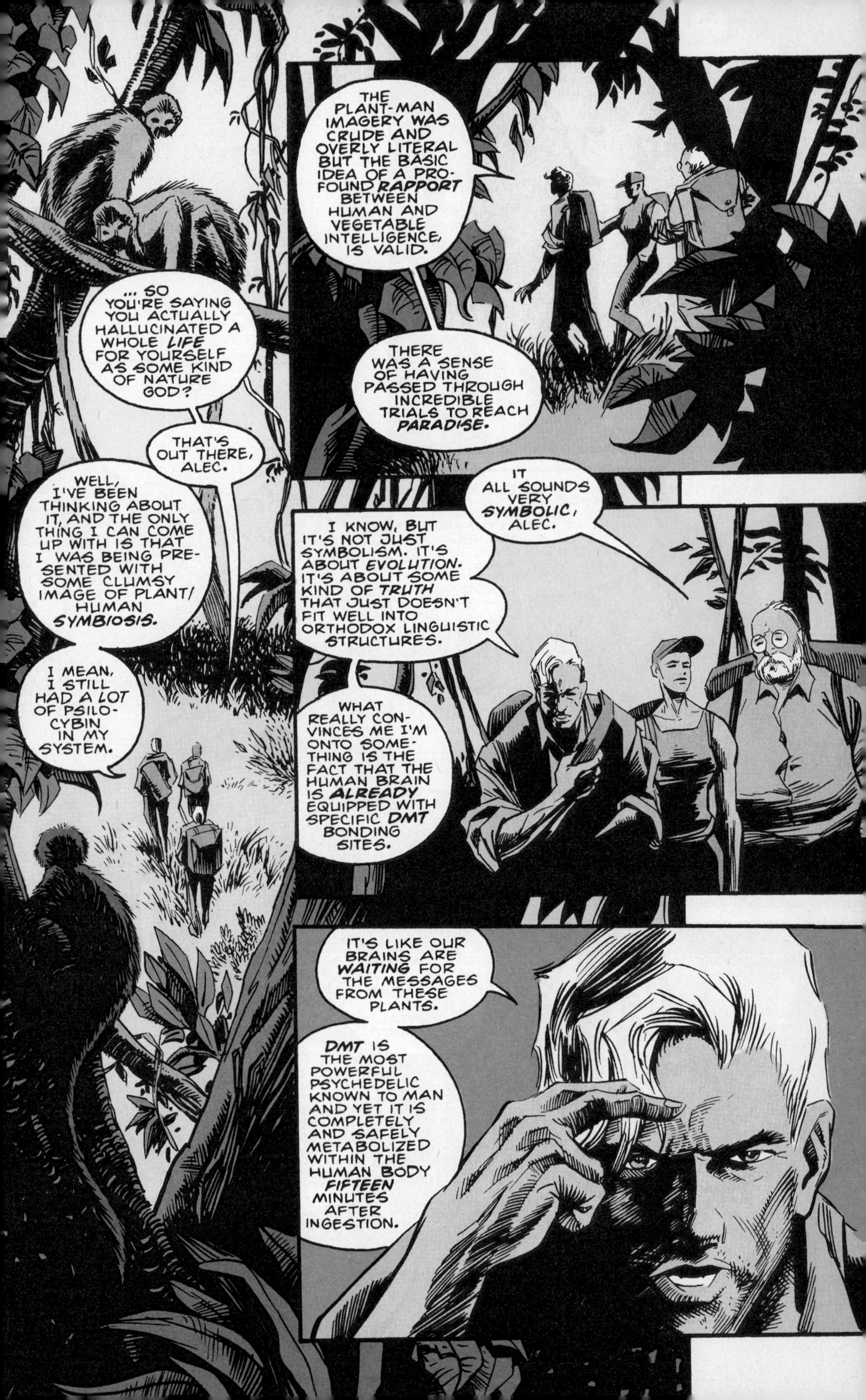
... SO YOU'RE SAYING YOU ACTUALLY HALLUCINATED A WHOLE *LIFE* FOR YOURSELF AS SOME KIND OF NATURE GOD?
THAT'S OUT THERE, ALEC.
WELL, I'VE BEEN THINKING ABOUT IT, AND THE ONLY THING I CAN COME UP WITH IS THAT I WAS BEING PRESENTED WITH SOME CLUMSY IMAGE OF PLANT/ HUMAN ***SYMBIOSIS.***
I MEAN, I STILL HAD A *LOT* OF PSILOCYBIN IN MY SYSTEM.
THE PLANT-MAN IMAGERY **WAS** CRUDE **AND** OVERLY LITERAL BUT THE BASIC IDEA OF A PROFOUND ***RAPPORT*** BETWEEN HUMAN AND VEGETABLE INTELLIGENCE, IS VALID.
THERE WAS A SENSE OF HAVING PASSED THROUGH INCREDIBLE TRIALS TO REACH ***PARADISE.***
IT ALL SOUNDS VERY ***SYMBOLIC,*** ALEC.
I KNOW, BUT IT'S NOT JUST SYMBOLISM. IT'S ABOUT *EVOLUTION.* IT'S ABOUT SOME KIND OF *TRUTH* THAT JUST DOESN'T FIT WELL INTO ORTHODOX LINGUISTIC STRUCTURES.
WHAT REALLY CONVINCES ME I'M ONTO SOMETHING IS THE FACT THAT THE HUMAN BRAIN IS ***ALREADY*** EQUIPPED WITH SPECIFIC ***DMT*** BONDING SITES.
IT'S LIKE OUR BRAINS ARE ***WAITING*** FOR THE MESSAGES FROM THESE PLANTS.
DMT IS THE MOST POWERFUL PSYCHEDELIC KNOWN TO MAN AND YET IT IS COMPLETELY AND SAFELY METABOLIZED WITHIN THE HUMAN BODY ***FIFTEEN*** MINUTES AFTER INGESTION.

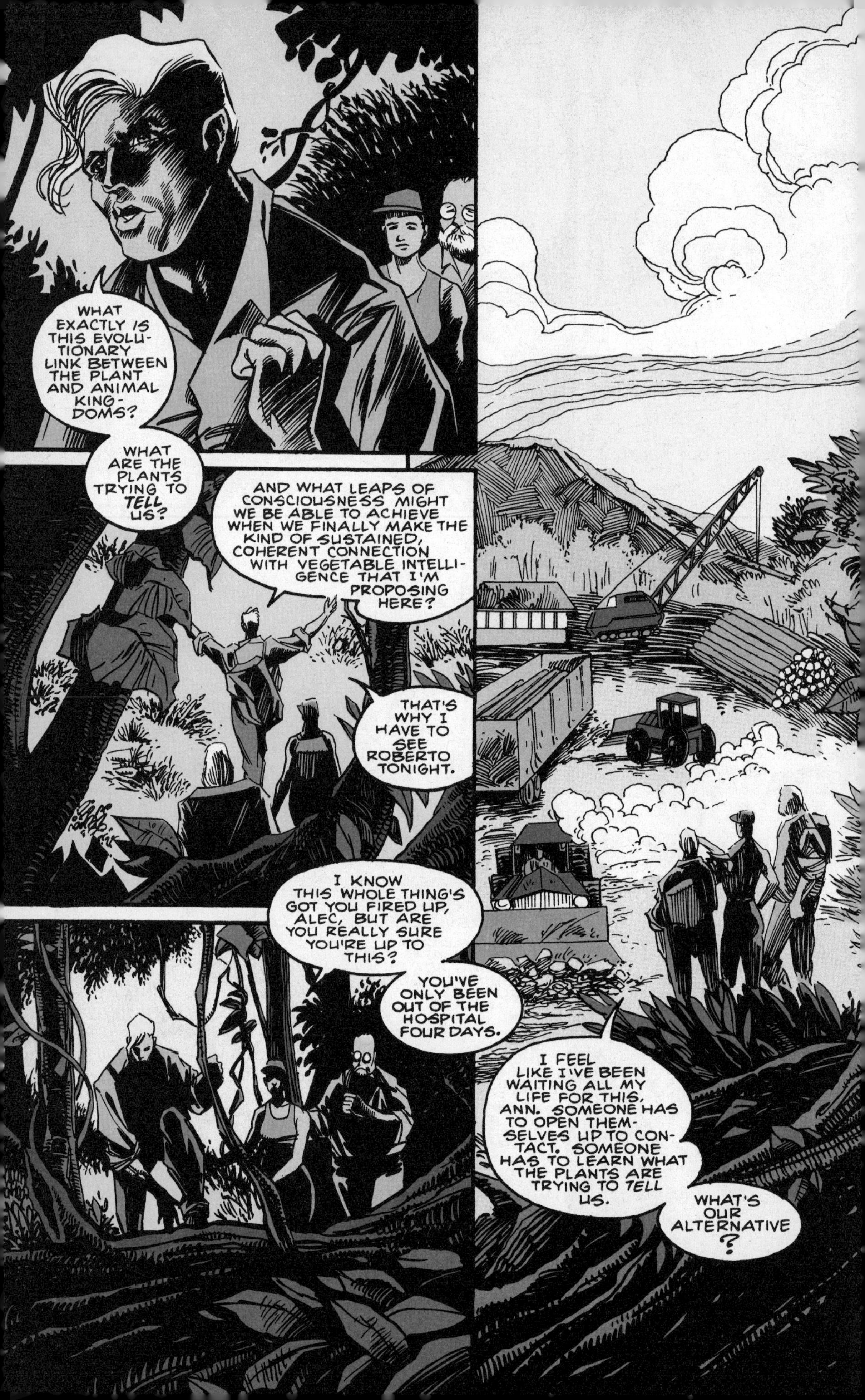
WHAT EXACTLY IS THIS EVOLUTIONARY LINK BETWEEN THE PLANT AND ANIMAL KINGDOMS?
WHAT ARE THE PLANTS TRYING TO TELL US?
AND WHAT LEAPS OF CONSCIOUSNESS MIGHT WE BE ABLE TO ACHIEVE WHEN WE FINALLY MAKE THE KIND OF SUSTAINED, COHERENT CONNECTION WITH VEGETABLE INTELLIGENCE THAT I'M PROPOSING HERE?
THAT'S WHY I HAVE TO SEE ROBERTO TONIGHT.
I KNOW THIS WHOLE THING'S GOT YOU FIRED UP, ALEC, BUT ARE YOU REALLY SURE YOU'RE UP TO THIS?
YOU'VE ONLY BEEN OUT OF THE HOSPITAL FOUR DAYS.
I FEEL LIKE I'VE BEEN WAITING ALL MY LIFE FOR THIS, ANN. SOMEONE HAS TO OPEN THEMSELVES UP TO CONTACT. SOMEONE HAS TO LEARN WHAT THE PLANTS ARE TRYING TO TELL US.
WHAT'S OUR ALTERNATIVE?

THIS VINE, DON ROBERTO: WHAT DO YOU CALL IT?

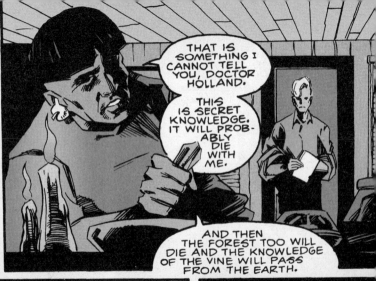

THAT IS SOMETHING I CANNOT TELL YOU, DOCTOR HOLLAND.

THIS IS SECRET KNOWLEDGE. IT WILL PROBABLY DIE WITH ME.

AND THEN THE FOREST TOO WILL DIE AND THE KNOWLEDGE OF THE VINE WILL PASS FROM THE EARTH.

I HOPE THAT DOESN'T HAPPEN.

IT IS ALREADY HAPPENING.

MY PEOPLE ARE POOR. YOUR PEOPLE OFFER THEM WORK AND MONEY TO BUY THE THINGS THEY SEE ON TELEVISION.

THEY'RE NOT MY PEOPLE. I DON'T WANT TO BELONG TO THEM.

WHAT WILL HAPPEN TO ME? I'M FAMILIAR WITH THE MUSHROOMS AND WITH THE YAGE MIXTURE...

THIS IS DIFFERENT.

WE FOLLOW THE VINE THROUGH THE DOOR IN THINGS, TO THE OTHER SIDE, TO THE WORLD'S SPIRIT.

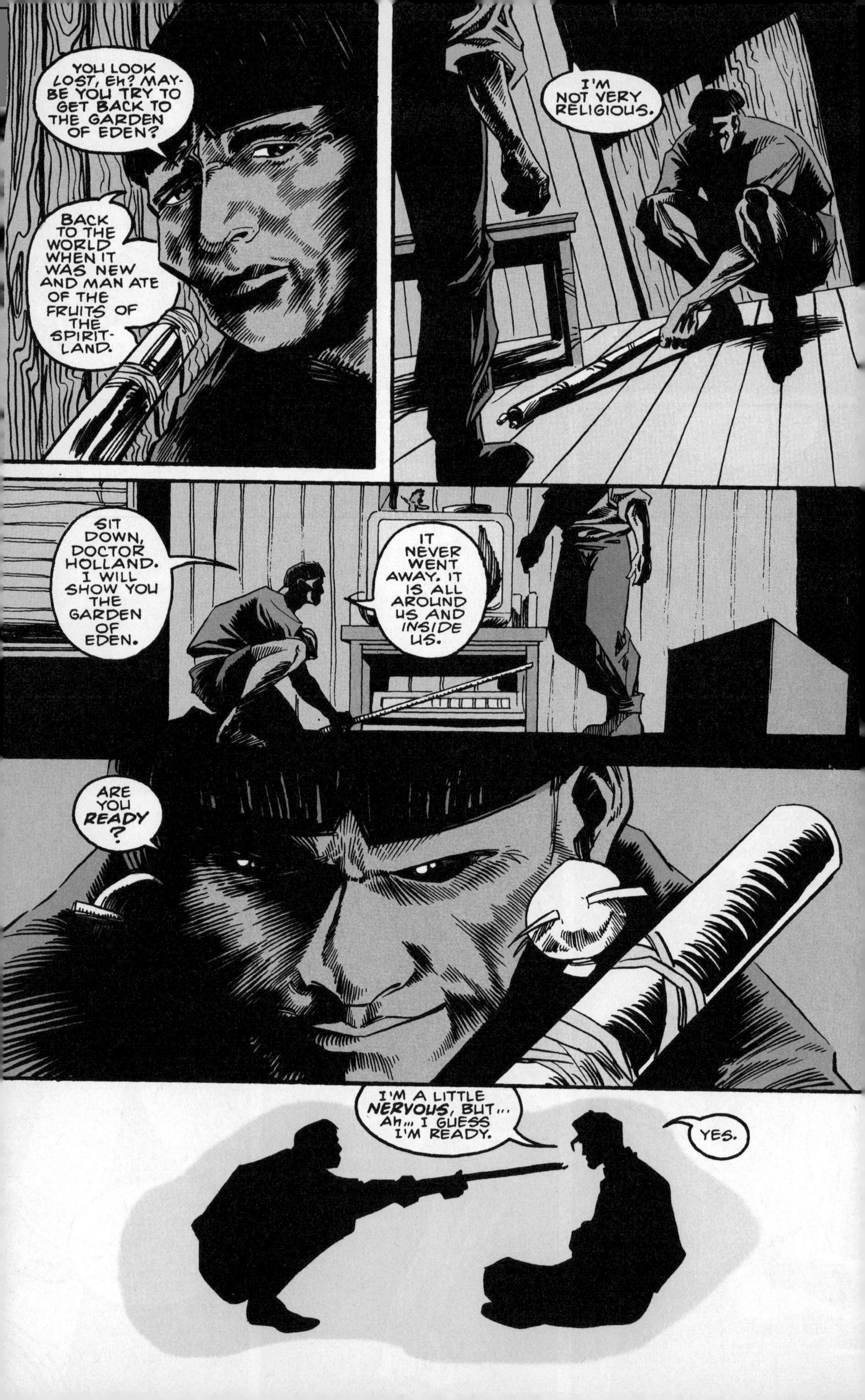
YOU LOOK LOST, EH? MAY-BE YOU TRY TO GET BACK TO THE GARDEN OF EDEN?
BACK TO THE WORLD WHEN IT WAS NEW AND MAN ATE OF THE FRUITS OF THE SPIRIT-LAND.
I'M NOT VERY RELIGIOUS.
SIT DOWN, DOCTOR HOLLAND. I WILL SHOW YOU THE GARDEN OF EDEN.
IT NEVER WENT AWAY. IT IS ALL AROUND US AND *INSIDE* US.
ARE YOU *READY*?
I'M A LITTLE *NERVOUS*, BUT... AH... I GUESS I'M READY.
YES.

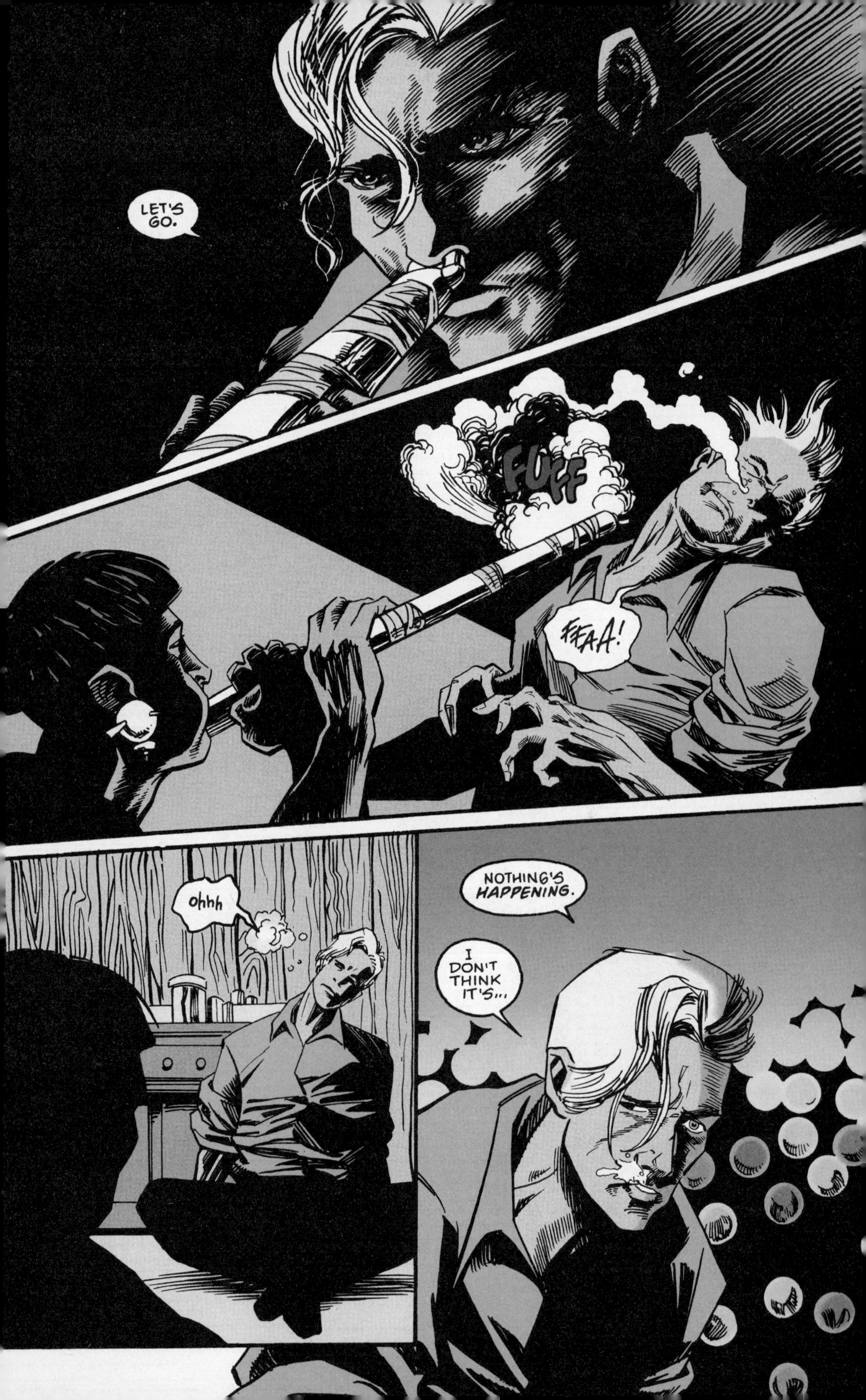
LET'S GO.
FUFF
FFEAA!
ohhh
NOTHING'S HAPPENING.
I DON'T THINK IT'S...

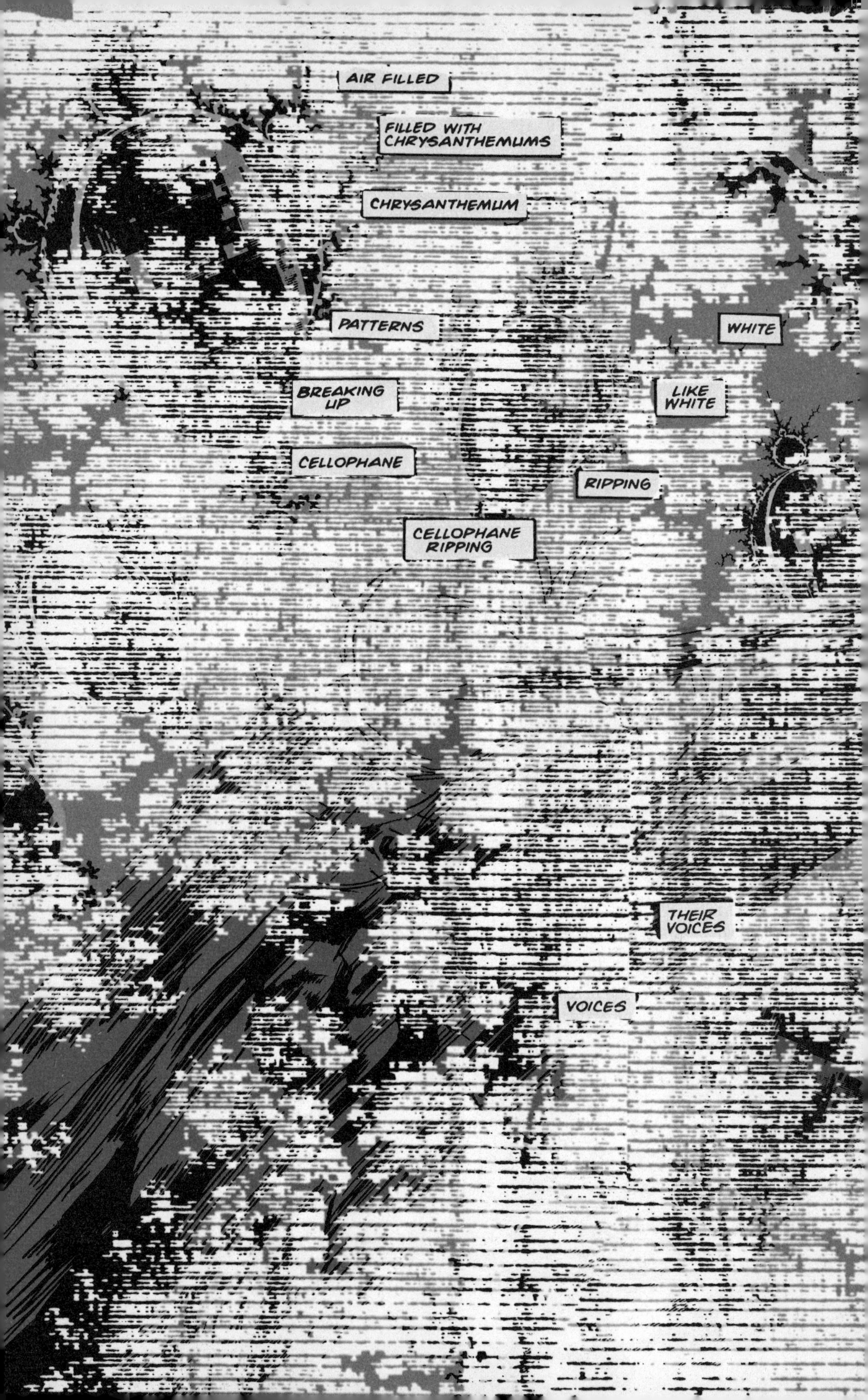
AIR FILLED
FILLED WITH CHRYSANTHEMUMS
CHRYSANTHEMUM
PATTERNS
BREAKING UP
CELLOPHANE
CELLOPHANE RIPPING
RIPPING
WHITE
LIKE WHITE
THEIR VOICES
VOICES

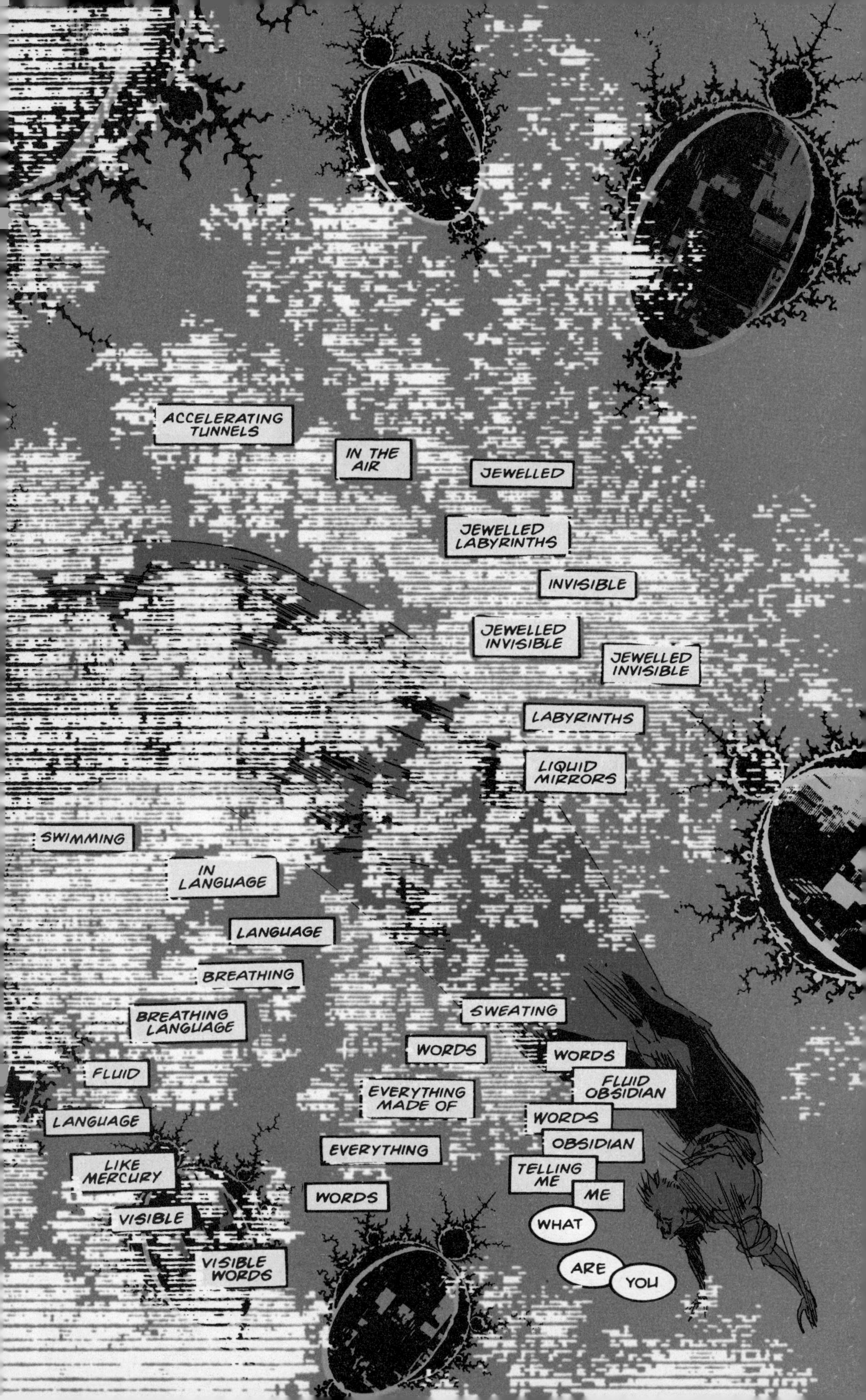
ACCELERATING TUNNELS
IN THE AIR
JEWELLED
JEWELLED LABYRINTHS
INVISIBLE
JEWELLED INVISIBLE
JEWELLED INVISIBLE
LABYRINTHS
LIQUID MIRRORS
SWIMMING
IN LANGUAGE
LANGUAGE
BREATHING
BREATHING LANGUAGE
FLUID
LANGUAGE
LIKE MERCURY
VISIBLE
VISIBLE WORDS
SWEATING
WORDS
EVERYTHING MADE OF
EVERYTHING
WORDS
WORDS
FLUID OBSIDIAN
WORDS
OBSIDIAN
TELLING ME
ME
WHAT
ARE
YOU

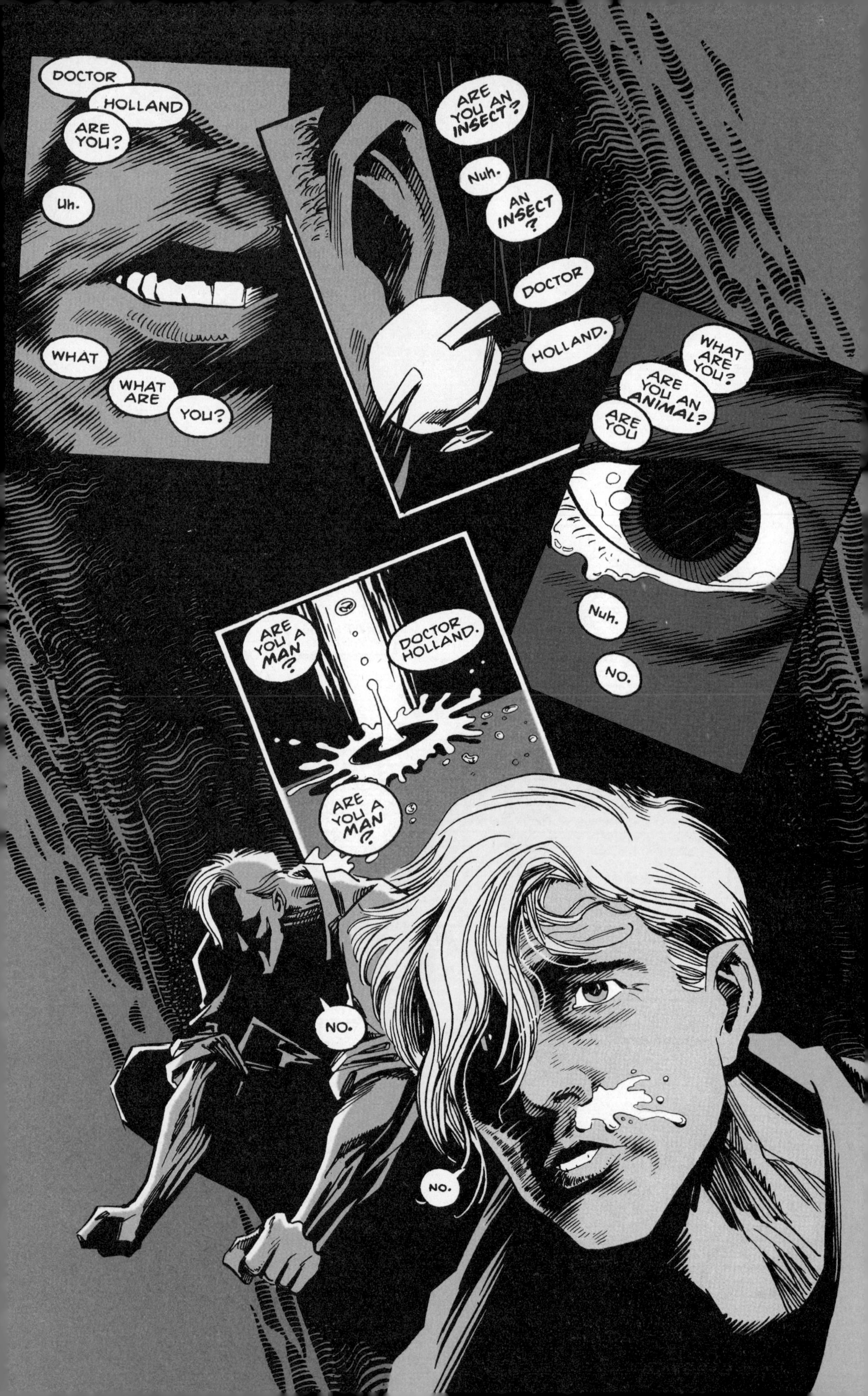
DOCTOR
HOLLAND
ARE YOU?
Uh.
WHAT
WHAT ARE
YOU?
ARE YOU AN INSECT?
Nuh.
AN INSECT?
DOCTOR
HOLLAND.
WHAT ARE YOU?
ARE YOU AN ANIMAL?
ARE YOU
Nuh.
NO.
ARE YOU A MAN?
DOCTOR HOLLAND.
ARE YOU A MAN?
NO.
NO.

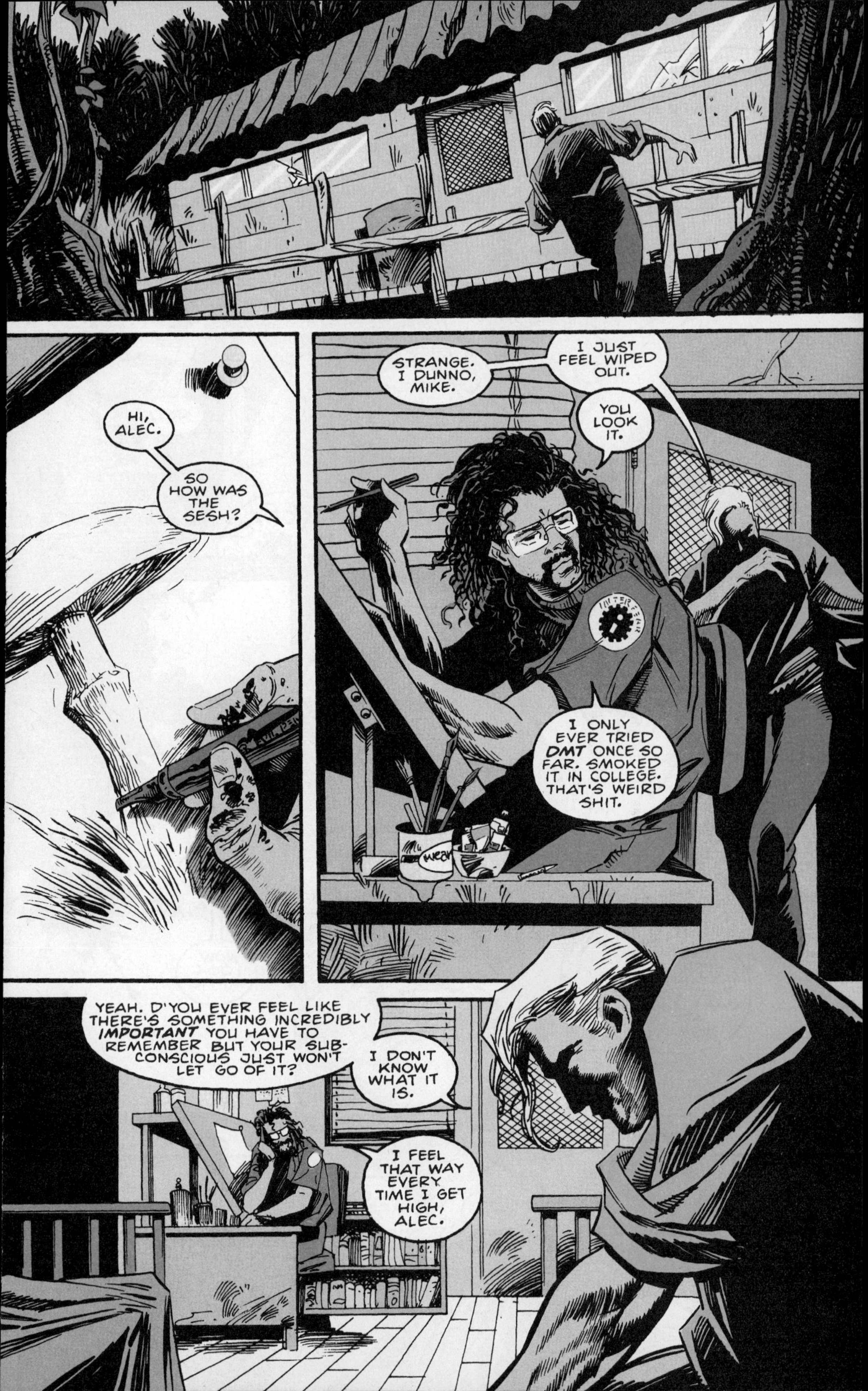
HI, ALEC.
SO HOW WAS THE SESH?
STRANGE. I DUNNO, MIKE.
I JUST FEEL WIPED OUT.
YOU LOOK IT.
I ONLY EVER TRIED DMT ONCE SO FAR. SMOKED IT IN COLLEGE. THAT'S WEIRD SHIT.
YEAH. D'YOU EVER FEEL LIKE THERE'S SOMETHING INCREDIBLY IMPORTANT YOU HAVE TO REMEMBER BUT YOUR SUB-CONSCIOUS JUST WON'T LET GO OF IT?
I DON'T KNOW WHAT IT IS.
I FEEL THAT WAY EVERY TIME I GET HIGH, ALEC.

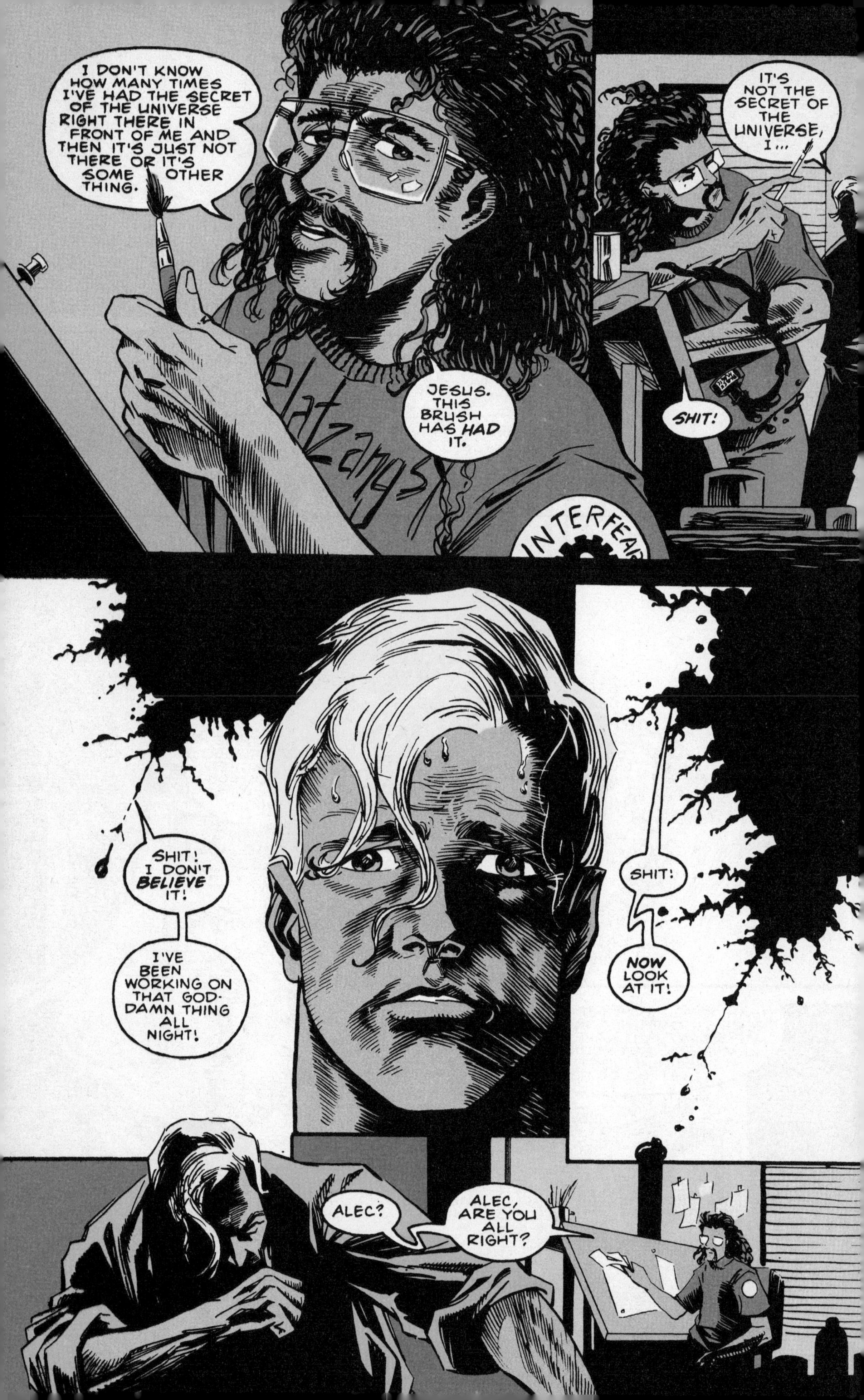

I DON'T KNOW HOW MANY TIMES I'VE HAD THE SECRET OF THE UNIVERSE RIGHT THERE IN FRONT OF ME AND THEN IT'S JUST NOT THERE OR IT'S SOME OTHER THING.
JESUS. THIS BRUSH HAS HAD IT.
IT'S NOT THE SECRET OF THE UNIVERSE, I...
SHIT!
INTERFEAR
SHIT! I DON'T BELIEVE IT!
I'VE BEEN WORKING ON THAT GOD-DAMN THING ALL NIGHT!
SHIT!
NOW LOOK AT IT!
ALEC?
ALEC, ARE YOU ALL RIGHT?

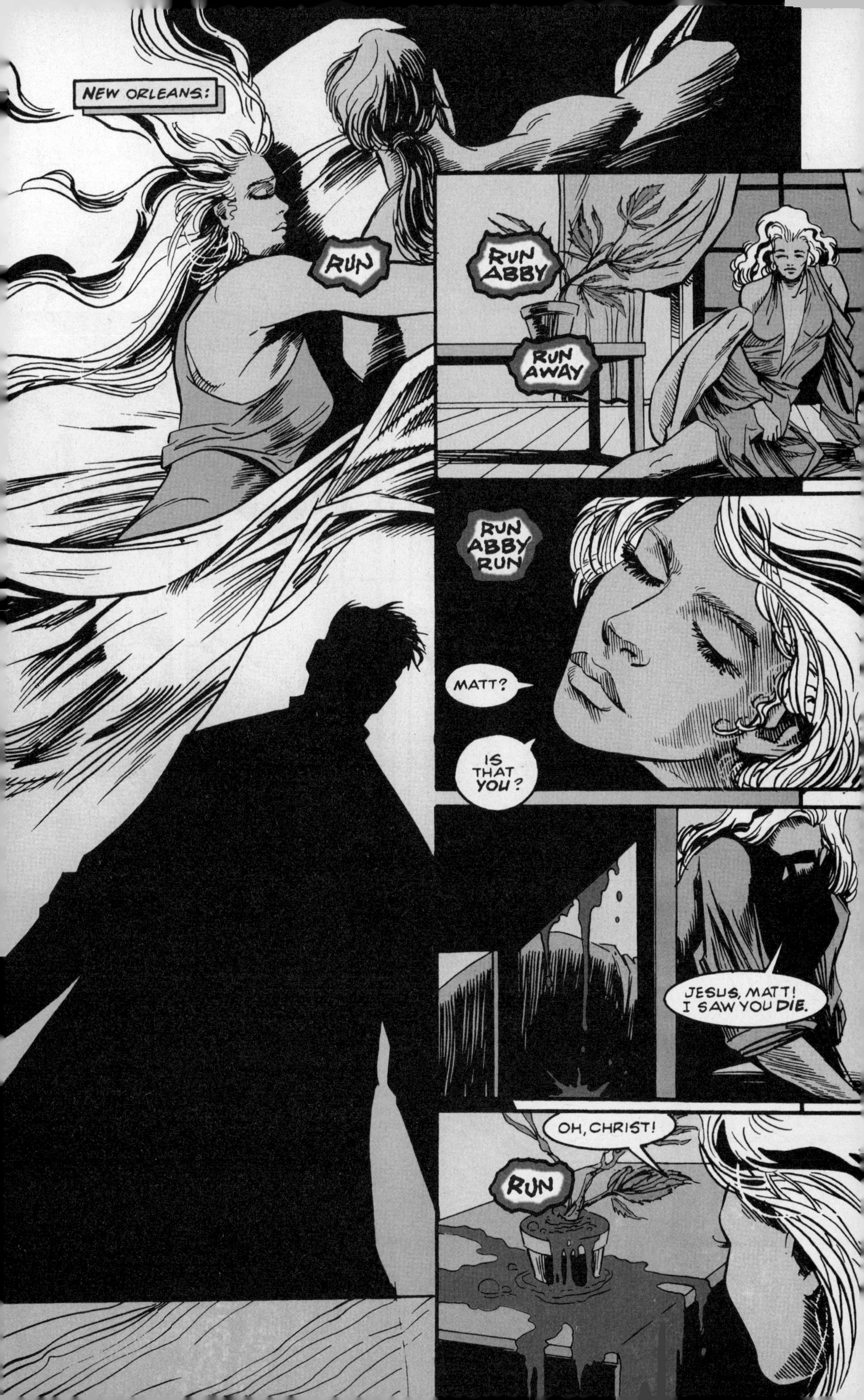
NEW ORLEANS:
RUN
RUN ABBY
RUN AWAY
RUN ABBY RUN
MATT?
IS THAT YOU?
JESUS, MATT! I SAW YOU DIE.
OH, CHRIST!
RUN

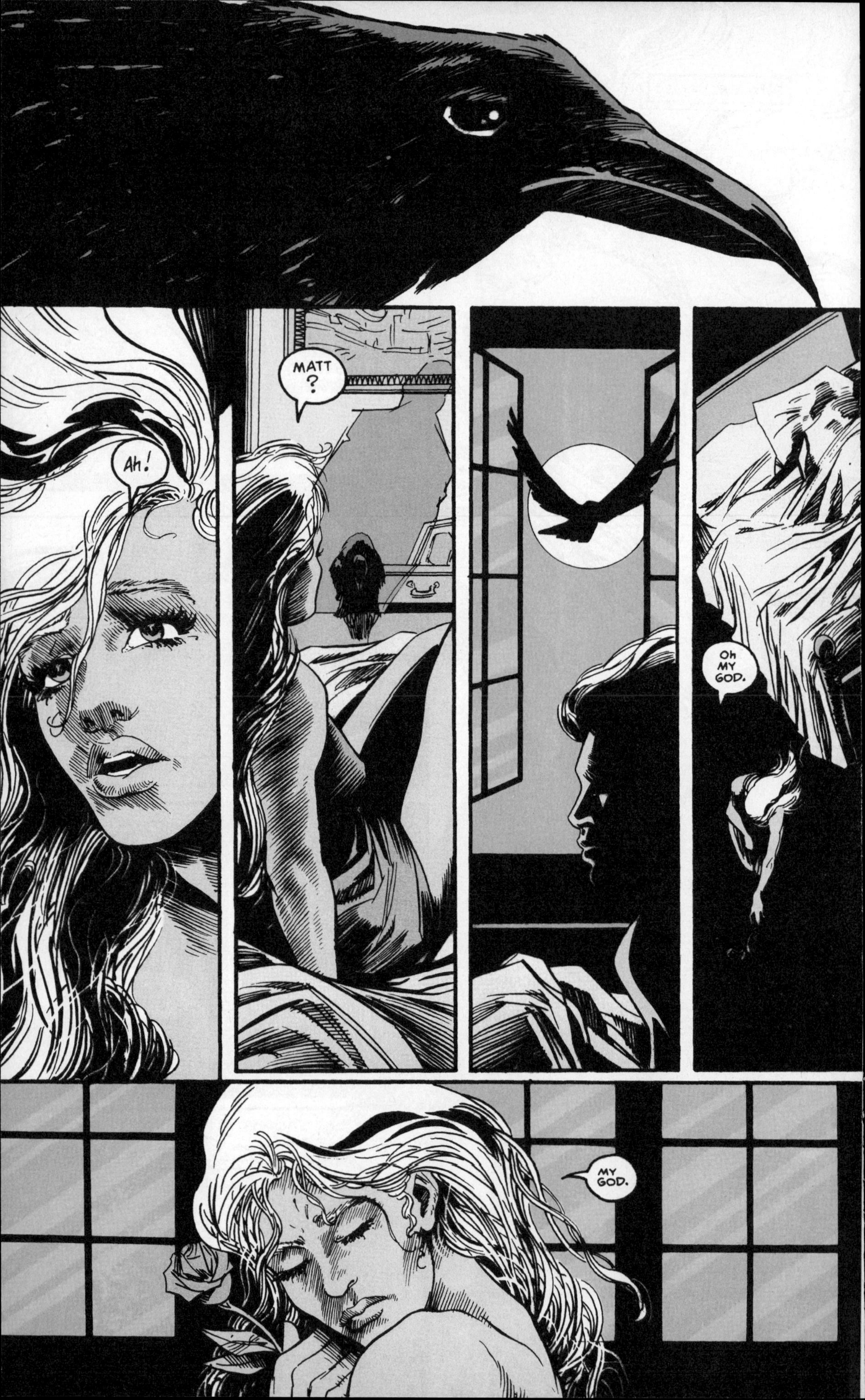
Ah!
MATT ?
Oh MY GOD.
MY GOD.

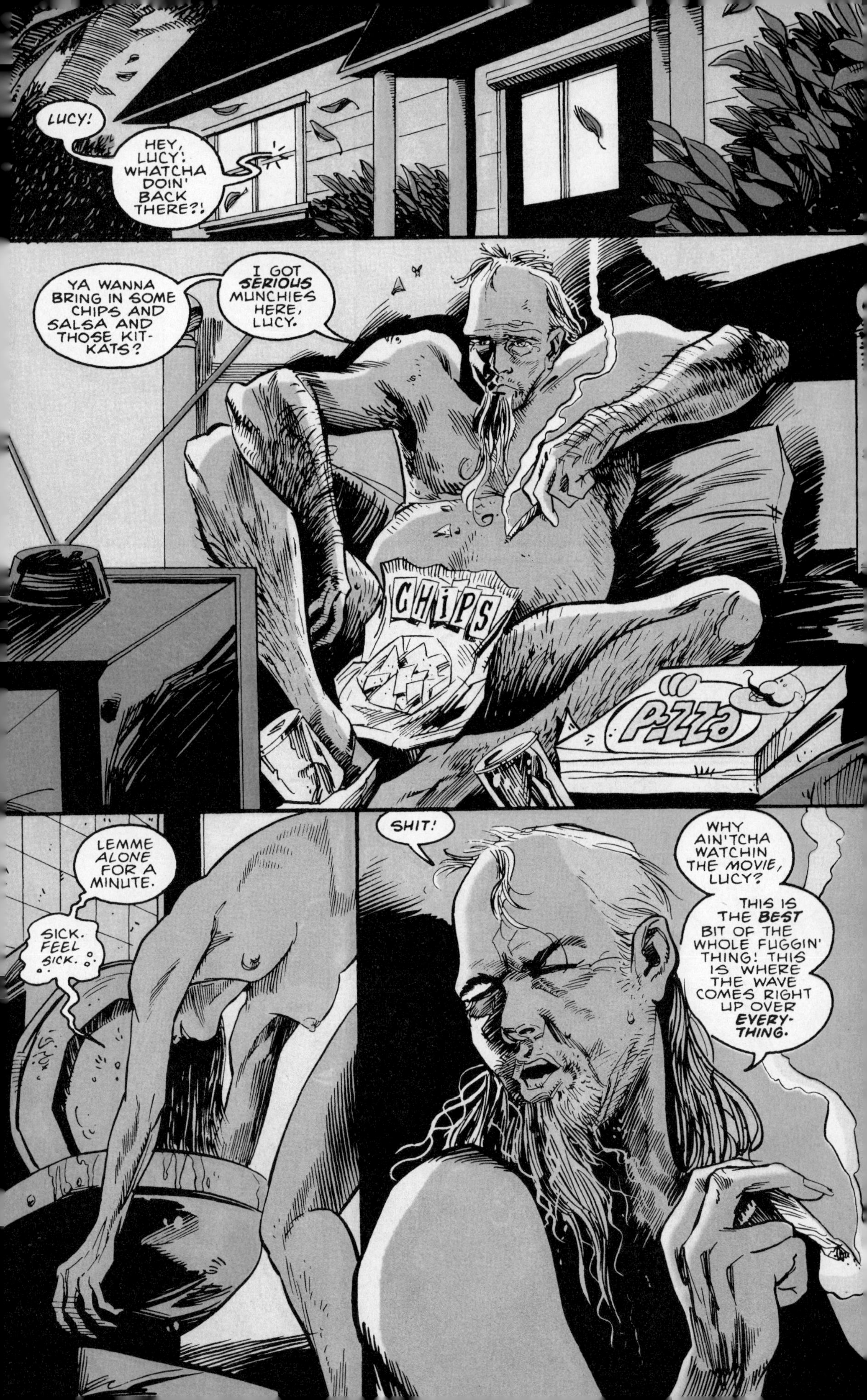
LUCY!
HEY, LUCY! WHATCHA DOIN' BACK THERE?!
YA WANNA BRING IN SOME CHIPS AND SALSA AND THOSE KIT-KATS?
I GOT SERIOUS MUNCHIES HERE, LUCY.
CHIPS
PIZZA
LEMME ALONE FOR A MINUTE.
SICK. FEEL SICK.
SHIT!
WHY AIN'TCHA WATCHIN THE MOVIE, LUCY?
THIS IS THE BEST BIT OF THE WHOLE FUGGIN' THING! THIS IS WHERE THE WAVE COMES RIGHT UP OVER EVERYTHING.

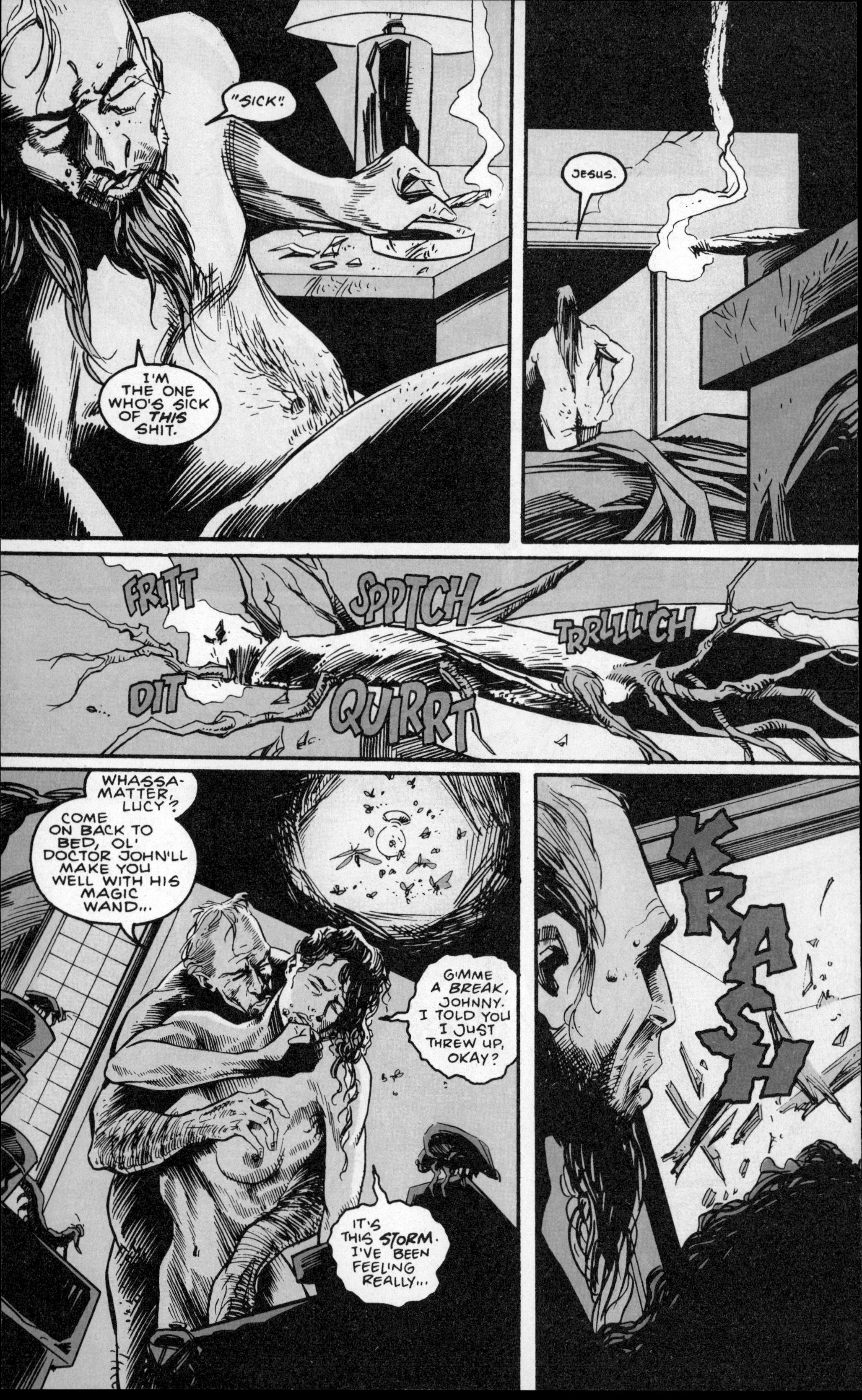
"SICK"!
I'M THE ONE WHO'S SICK OF THIS SHIT.
JESUS.
FRITT
SPPTCH
TRRLLLTCH
DIT
QUIRRT
WHASSA-MATTER, LUCY? COME ON BACK TO BED, OL' DOCTOR JOHN'LL MAKE YOU WELL WITH HIS MAGIC WAND...
GIMME A BREAK, JOHNNY. I TOLD YOU I JUST THREW UP, OKAY?
IT'S THIS STORM. I'VE BEEN FEELING REALLY...
KRASH

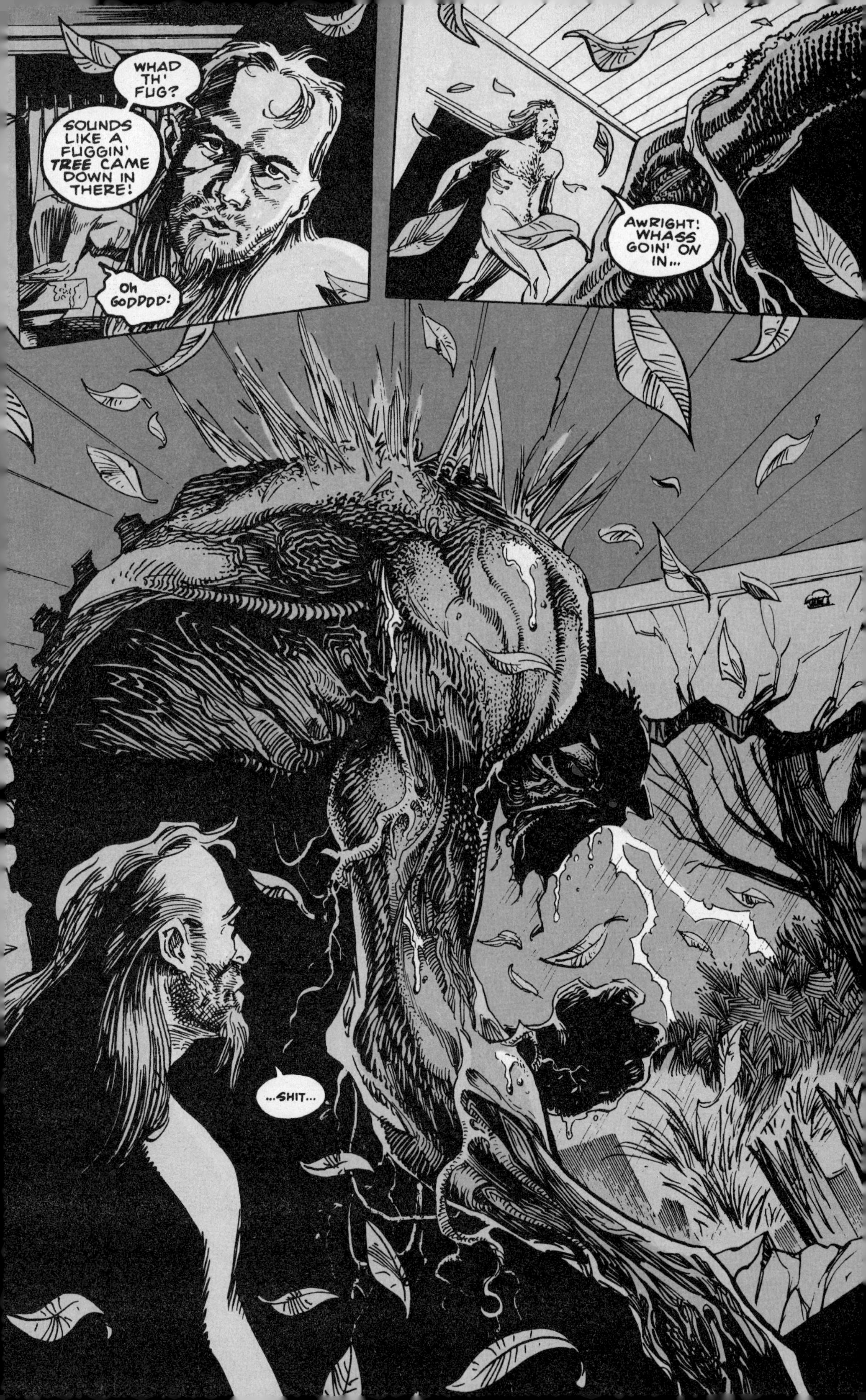
WHAD TH' FUG?
SOUNDS LIKE A FUGGIN' TREE CAME DOWN IN THERE!
Oh GODDDD!
AWRIGHT! WHASS GOIN' ON IN...
...SHIT...

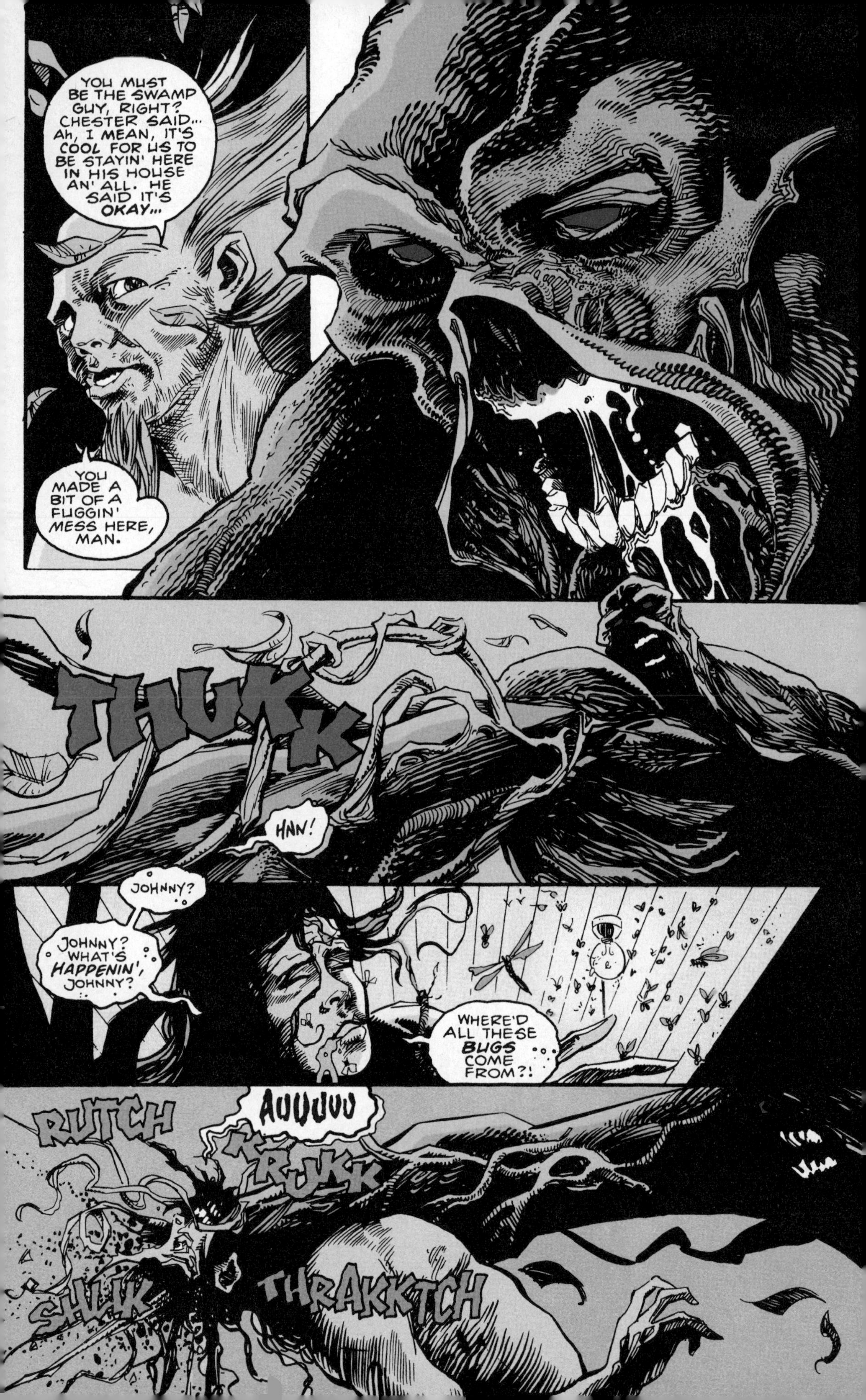
YOU MUST BE THE SWAMP GUY, RIGHT? CHESTER SAID... Ah, I MEAN, IT'S COOL FOR US TO BE STAYIN' HERE IN HIS HOUSE AN' ALL. HE SAID IT'S OKAY...
YOU MADE A BIT OF A FUGGIN' MESS HERE, MAN.
THUKK
HNN!
JOHNNY?
JOHNNY? WHAT'S HAPPENIN', JOHNNY?
WHERE'D ALL THESE BUGS COME FROM?!
RUTCH
AUUUUU
KRUKK
SHLIK
THRAKKTCH

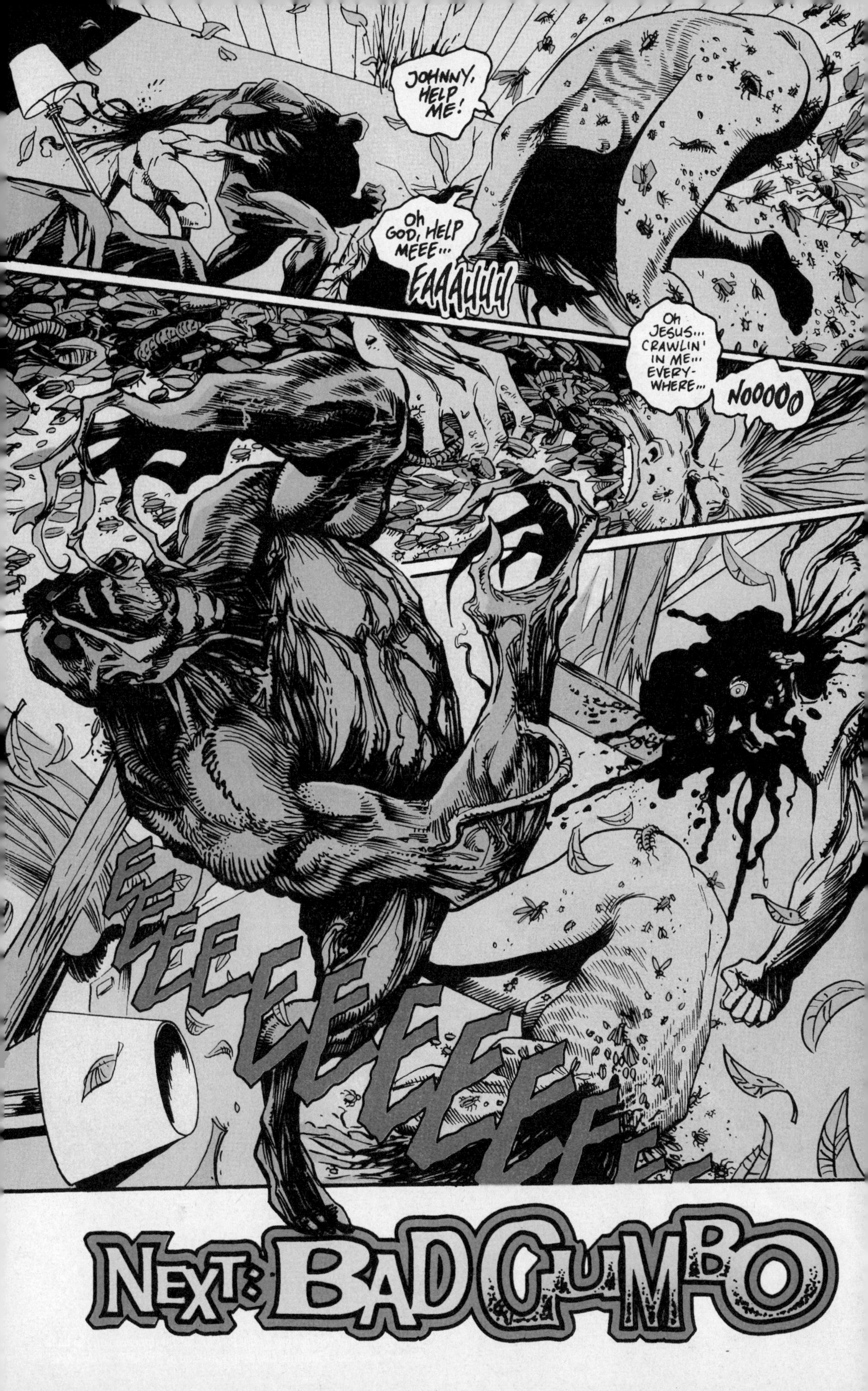
JOHNNY, HELP ME!
Oh GOD, HELP MEEE... EAAAUUU
Oh JESUS... CRAWLIN' IN ME... EVERY-WHERE...
NOOOOO
EEEEEEEEEE
NEXT: BAD GUMBO

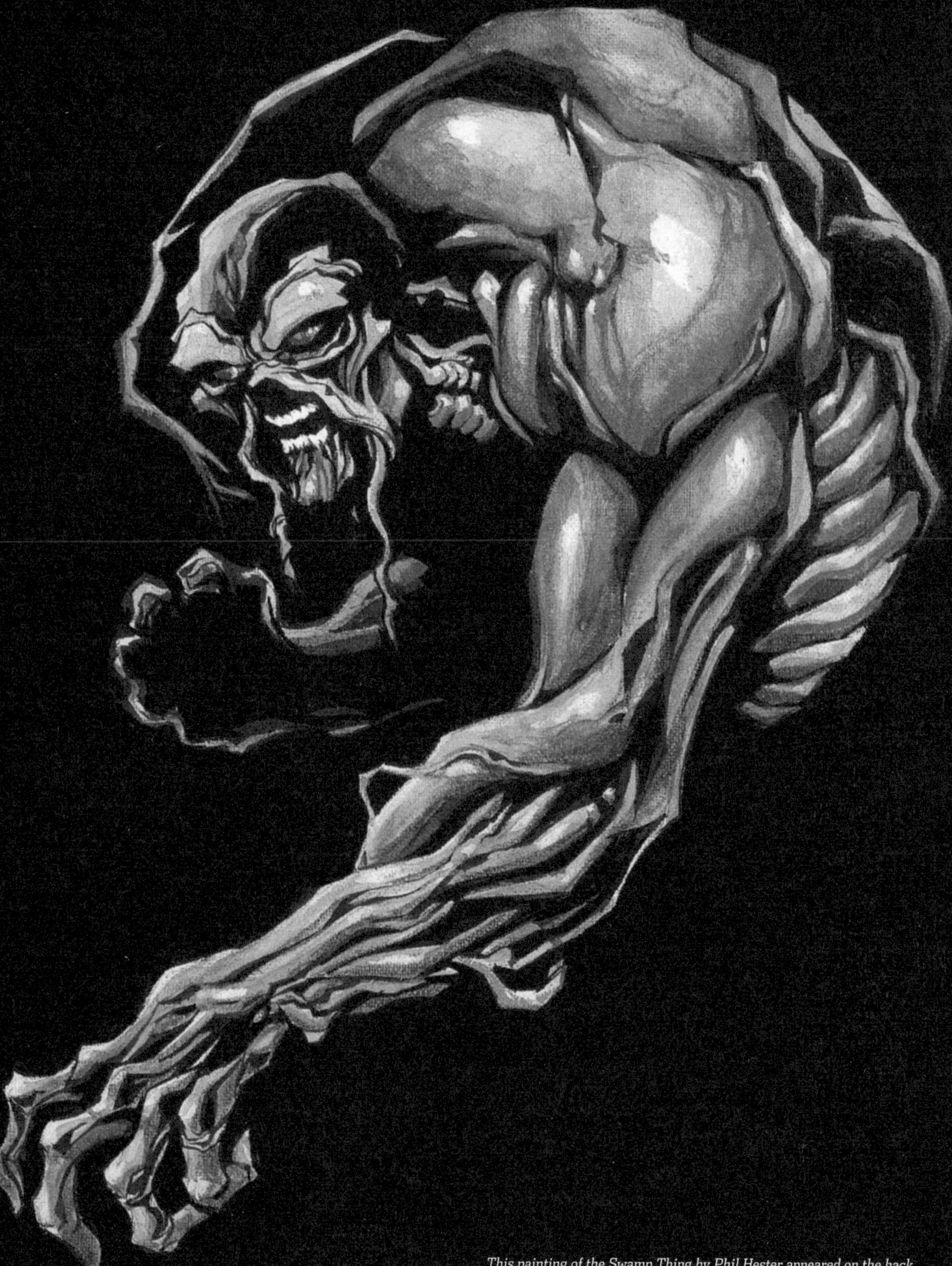

This painting of the Swamp Thing by Phil Hester appeared on the back cover of a special Platinum Collector's Edition of SWAMP THING #140.

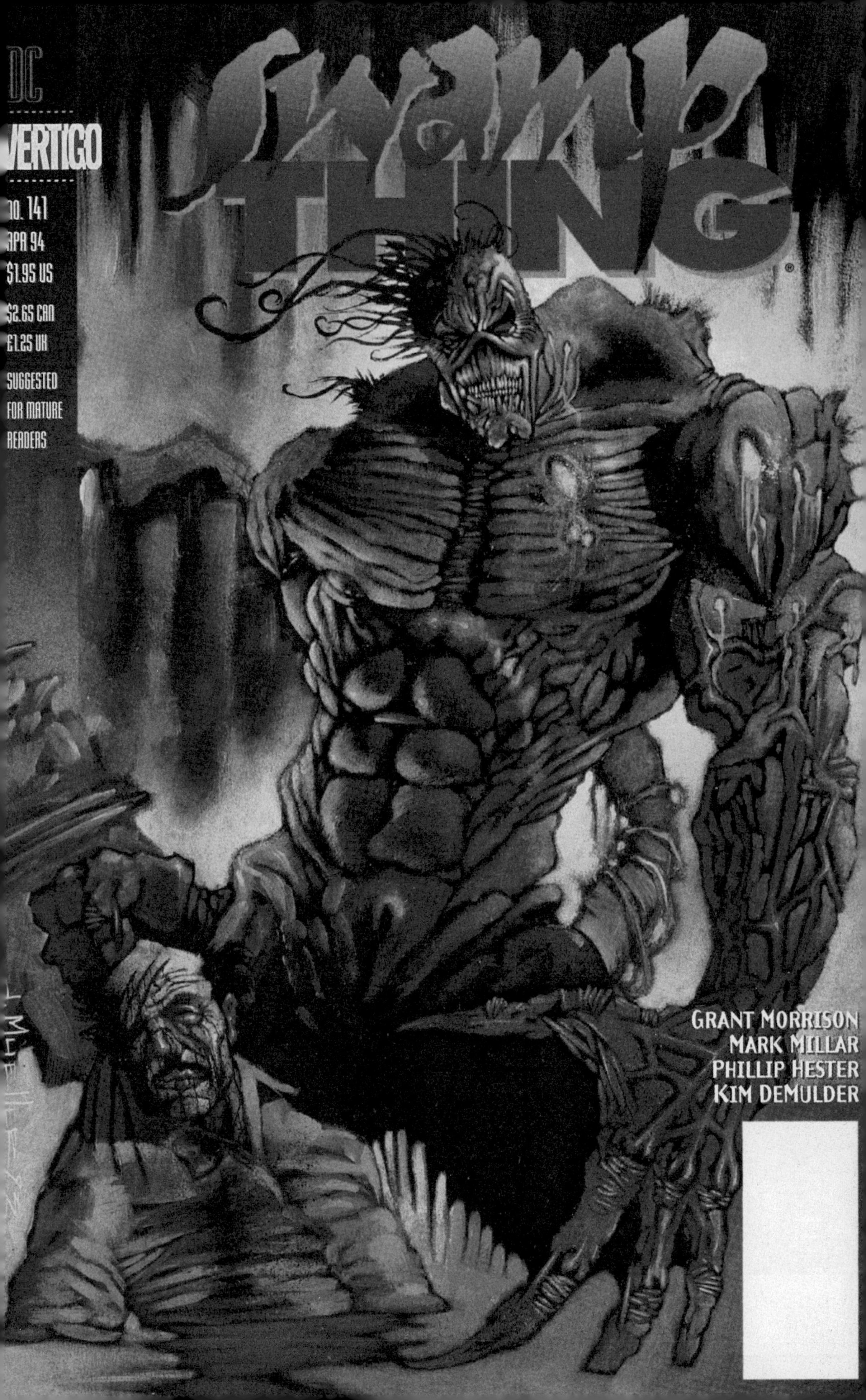
DC
VERTIGO
NO. 141
APR 94
$1.95 US
$2.65 CAN
£1.25 UK
SUGGESTED FOR MATURE READERS
Swamp THING
GRANT MORRISON
MARK MILLAR
PHILLIP HESTER
KIM DEMULDER

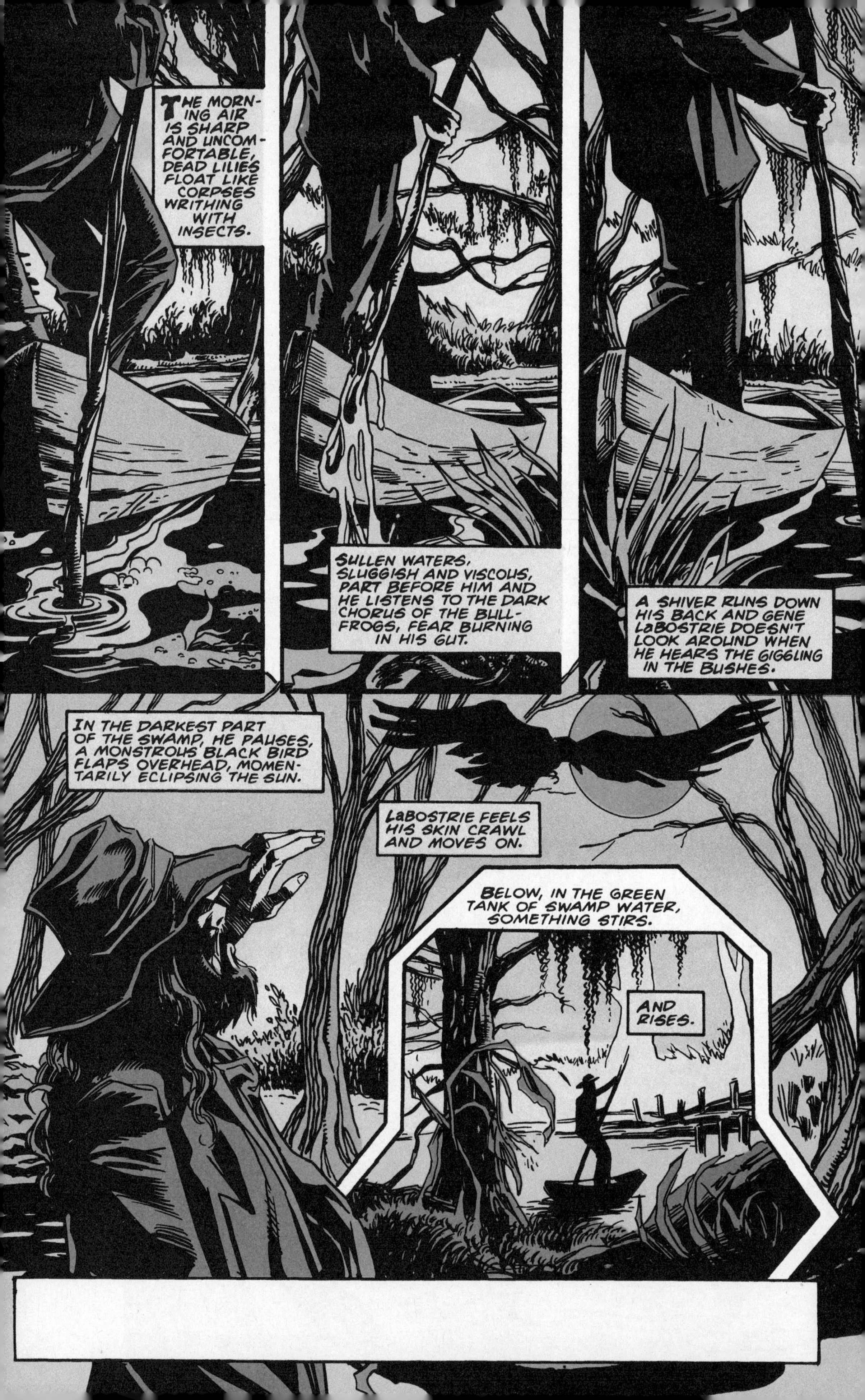
THE MORNING AIR IS SHARP AND UNCOMFORTABLE, DEAD LILIES FLOAT LIKE CORPSES WRITHING WITH INSECTS.
SULLEN WATERS, SLUGGISH AND VISCOUS, PART BEFORE HIM AND HE LISTENS TO THE DARK CHORUS OF THE BULLFROGS, FEAR BURNING IN HIS GUT.
A SHIVER RUNS DOWN HIS BACK AND GENE LaBOSTRIE DOESN'T LOOK AROUND WHEN HE HEARS THE GIGGLING IN THE BUSHES.
IN THE DARKEST PART OF THE SWAMP, HE PAUSES, A MONSTROUS BLACK BIRD FLAPS OVERHEAD, MOMENTARILY ECLIPSING THE SUN.
LaBOSTRIE FEELS HIS SKIN CRAWL AND MOVES ON.
BELOW, IN THE GREEN TANK OF SWAMP WATER, SOMETHING STIRS.
AND RISES.

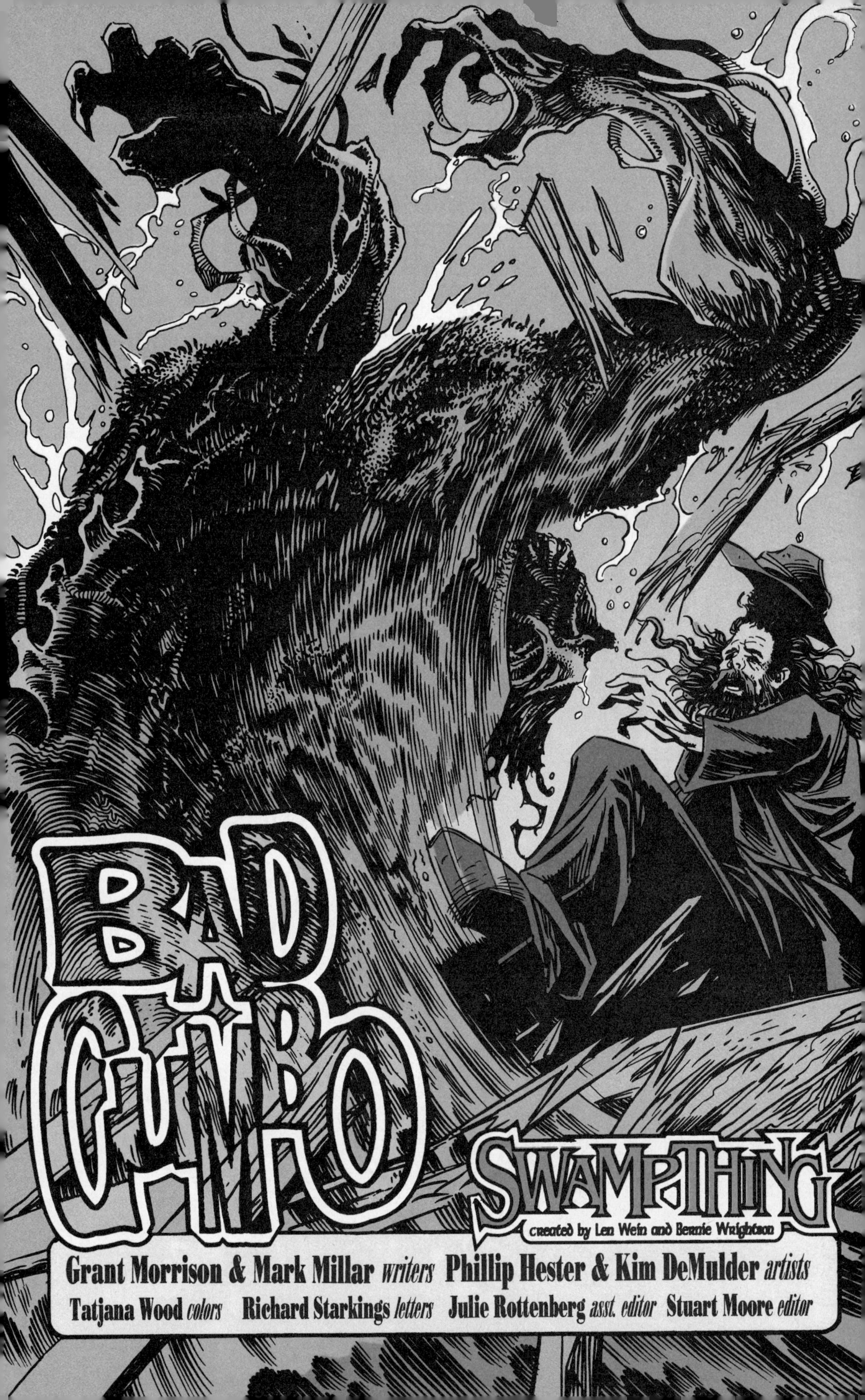
BAD GUMBO
SWAMP THING
created by Len Wein and Bernie Wrightson
Grant Morrison & Mark Millar *writers* Phillip Hester & Kim DeMulder *artists*
Tatjana Wood *colors* Richard Starkings *letters* Julie Rottenberg *asst. editor* Stuart Moore *editor*

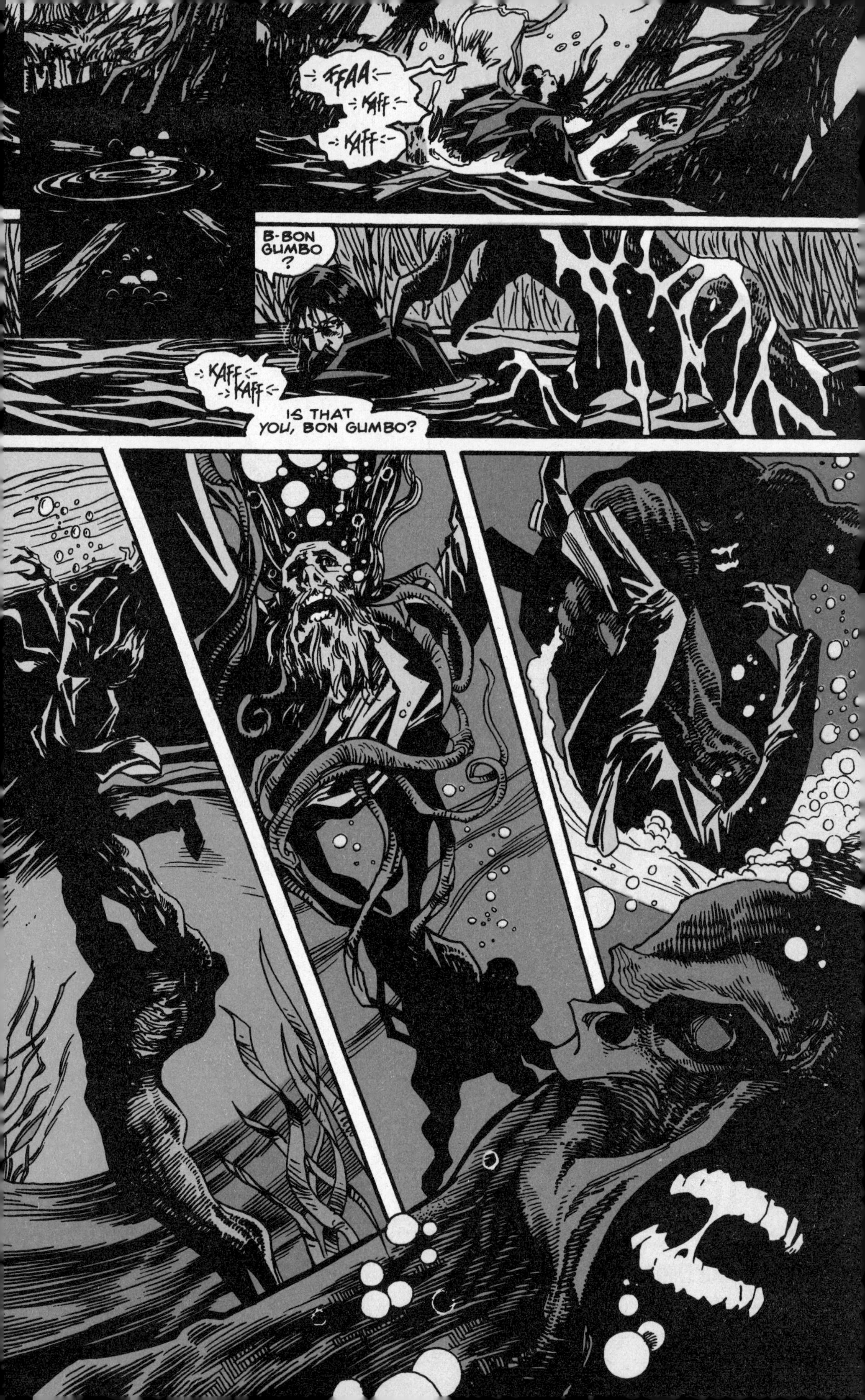
FFAA
KAFF
KAFF
B-BON GUMBO ?
KAFF KAFF
IS THAT YOU, BON GUMBO?

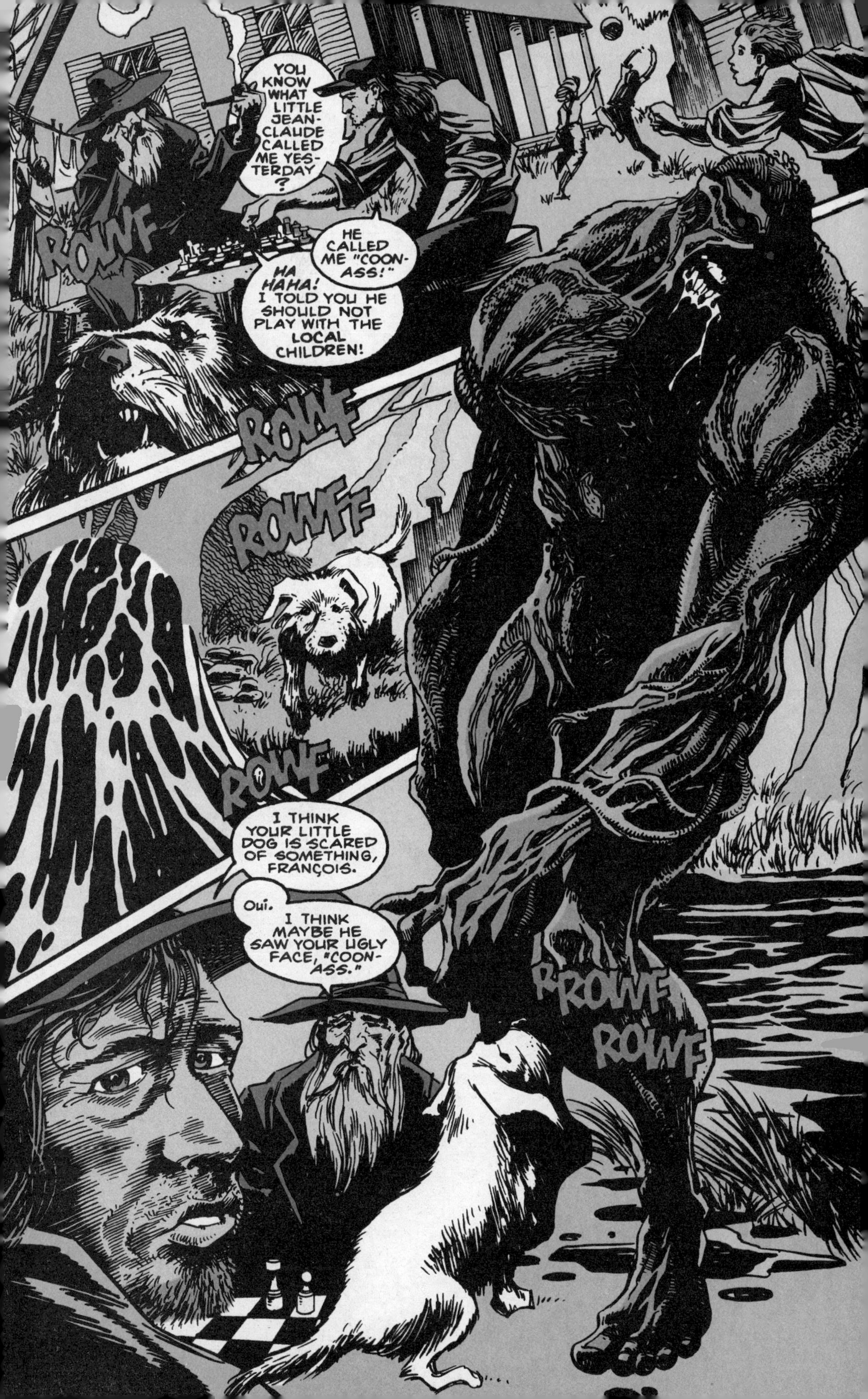
YOU KNOW WHAT LITTLE JEAN-CLAUDE CALLED ME YESTERDAY?
ROWF
HE CALLED ME "COON-ASS!"
HA HAHA! I TOLD YOU HE SHOULD NOT PLAY WITH THE LOCAL CHILDREN!
ROWF
ROWFF
ROWF
I THINK YOUR LITTLE DOG IS SCARED OF SOMETHING, FRANÇOIS.
Oui. I THINK MAYBE HE SAW YOUR UGLY FACE, "COON-ASS."
RROWF
ROWF

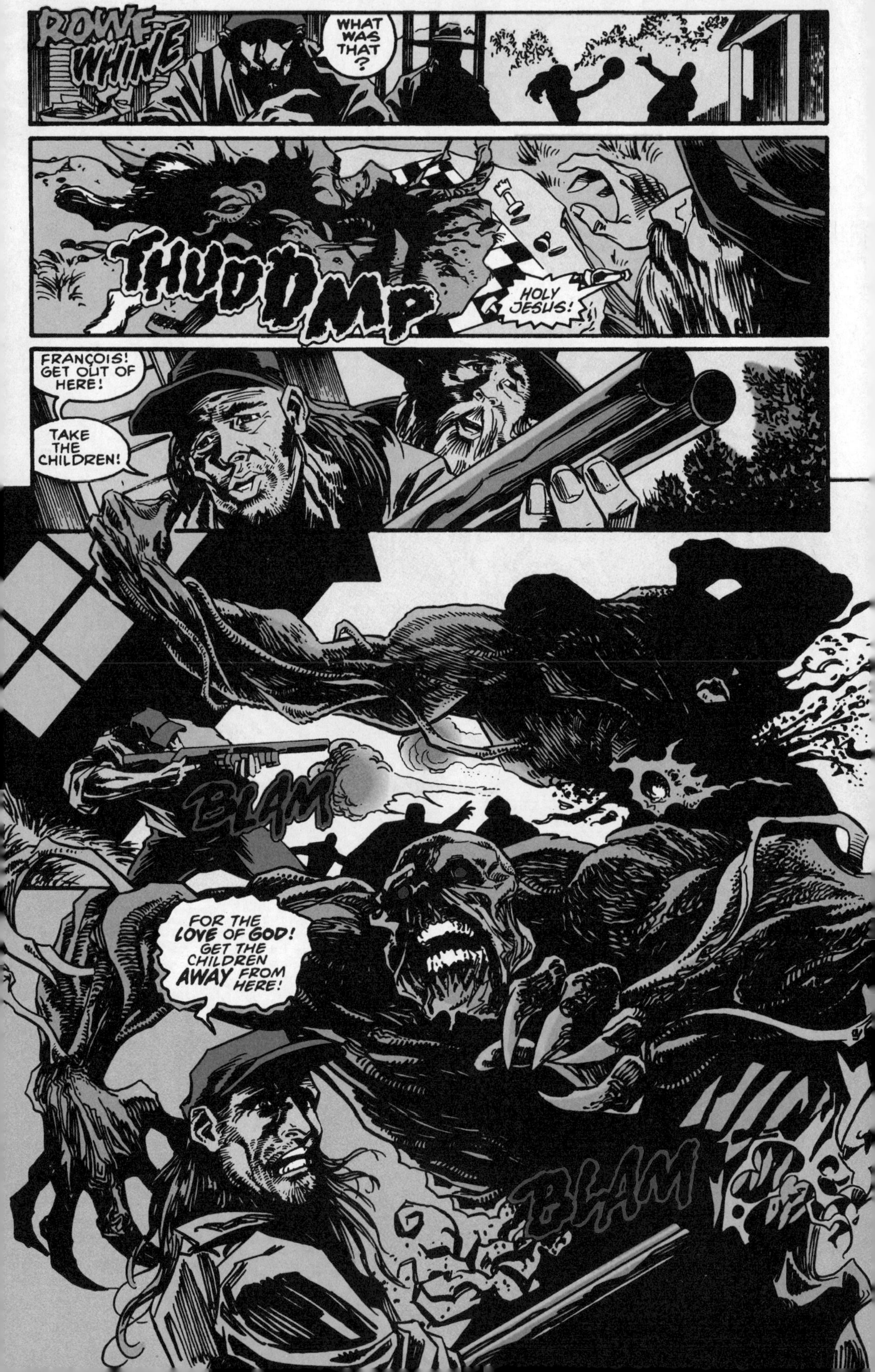
ROWF
WHINE
WHAT WAS THAT?
THUDDMP
HOLY JESUS!
FRANÇOIS! GET OUT OF HERE!
TAKE THE CHILDREN!
BLAM
FOR THE LOVE OF GOD! GET THE CHILDREN AWAY FROM HERE!
BLAM

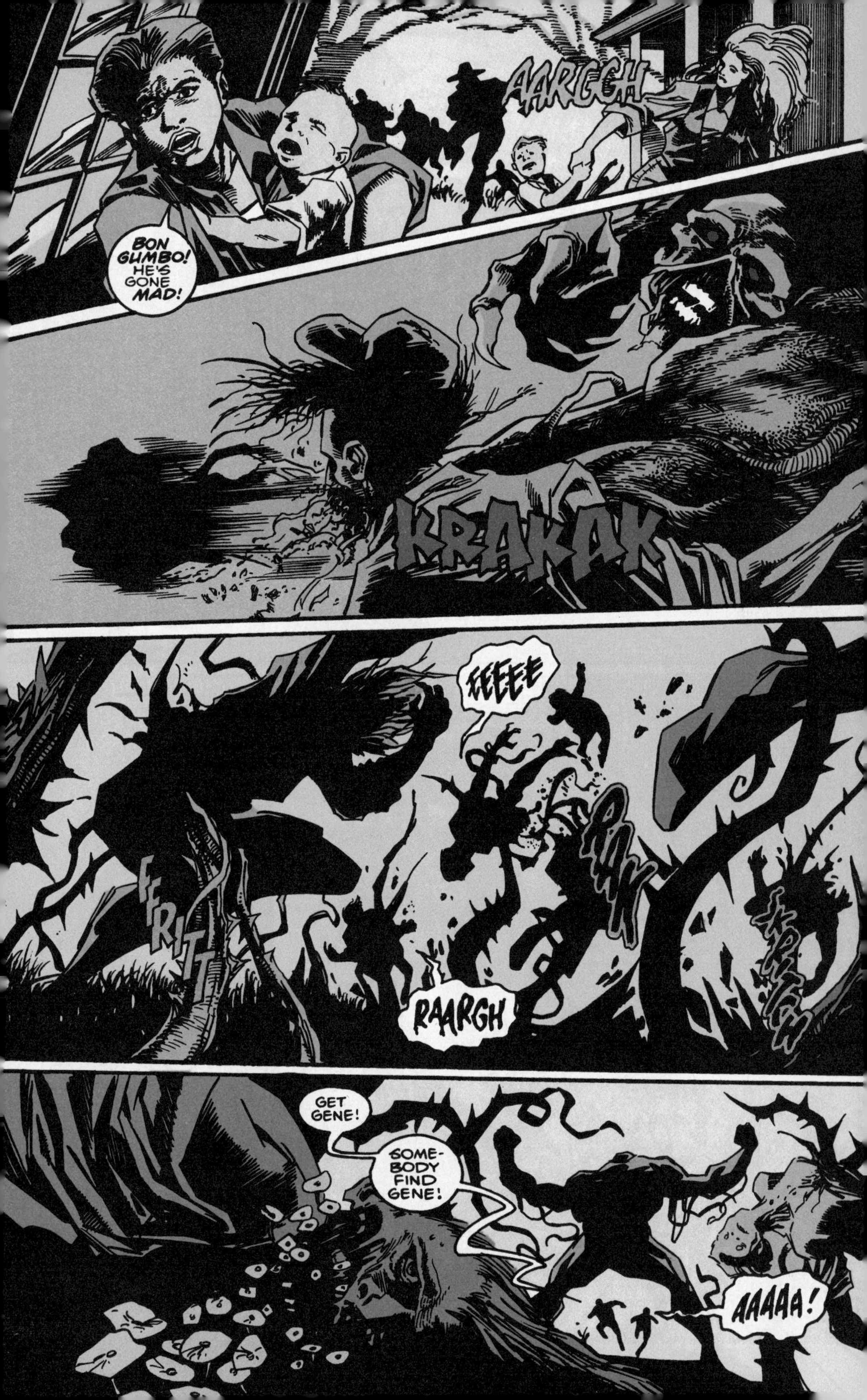
AARGGH
BON GUMBO! HE'S GONE MAD!
KRAKAK
EEEEE
FFRITT
RAARGH
SKRITCH
GET GENE!
SOME-BODY FIND GENE!
AAAAA!

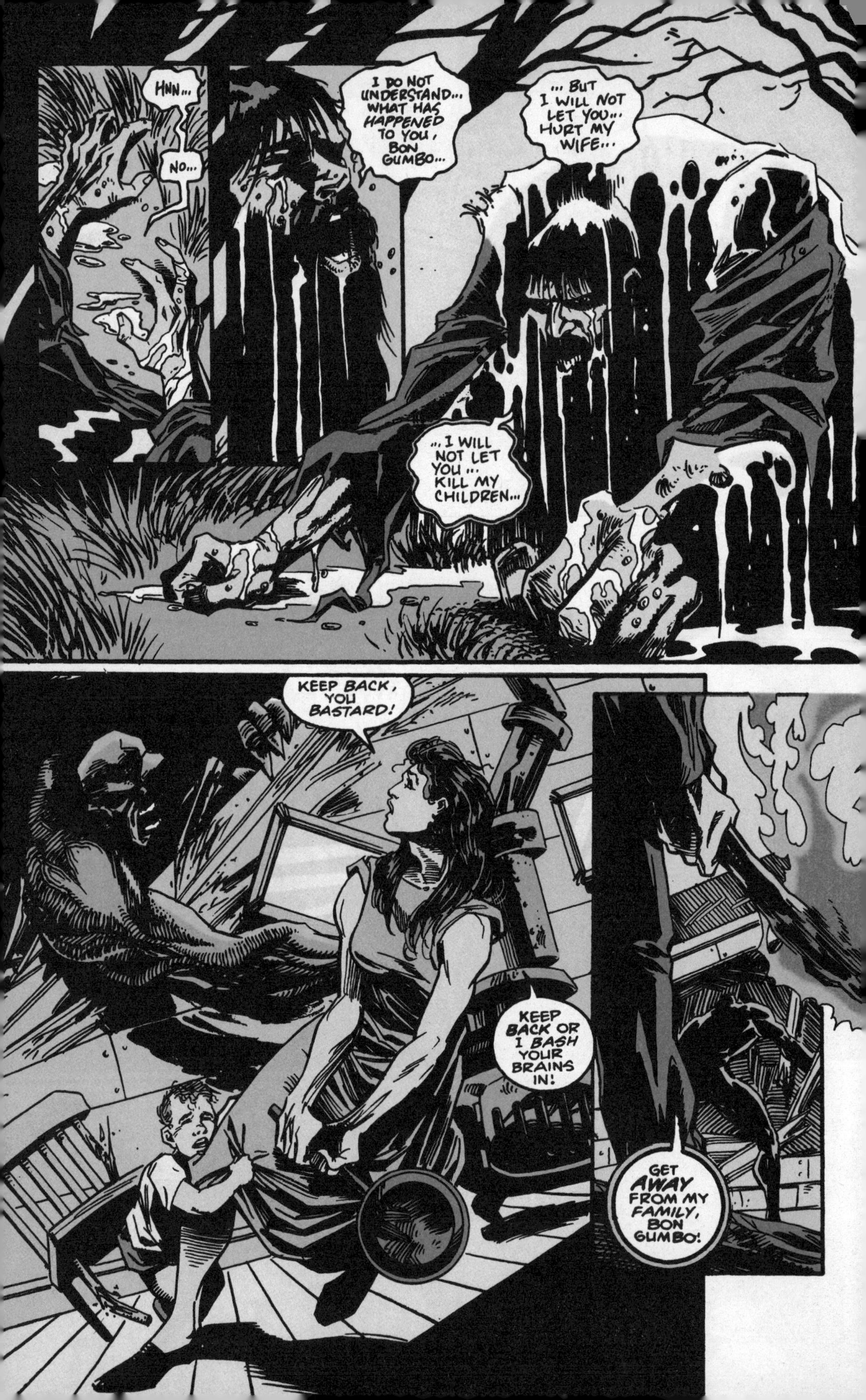
HNN...
NO...
I DO NOT UNDERSTAND... WHAT HAS HAPPENED TO YOU, BON GUMBO...
...BUT I WILL NOT LET YOU... HURT MY WIFE...
...I WILL NOT LET YOU... KILL MY CHILDREN...
KEEP BACK, YOU BASTARD!
KEEP BACK OR I BASH YOUR BRAINS IN!
GET AWAY FROM MY FAMILY, BON GUMBO!

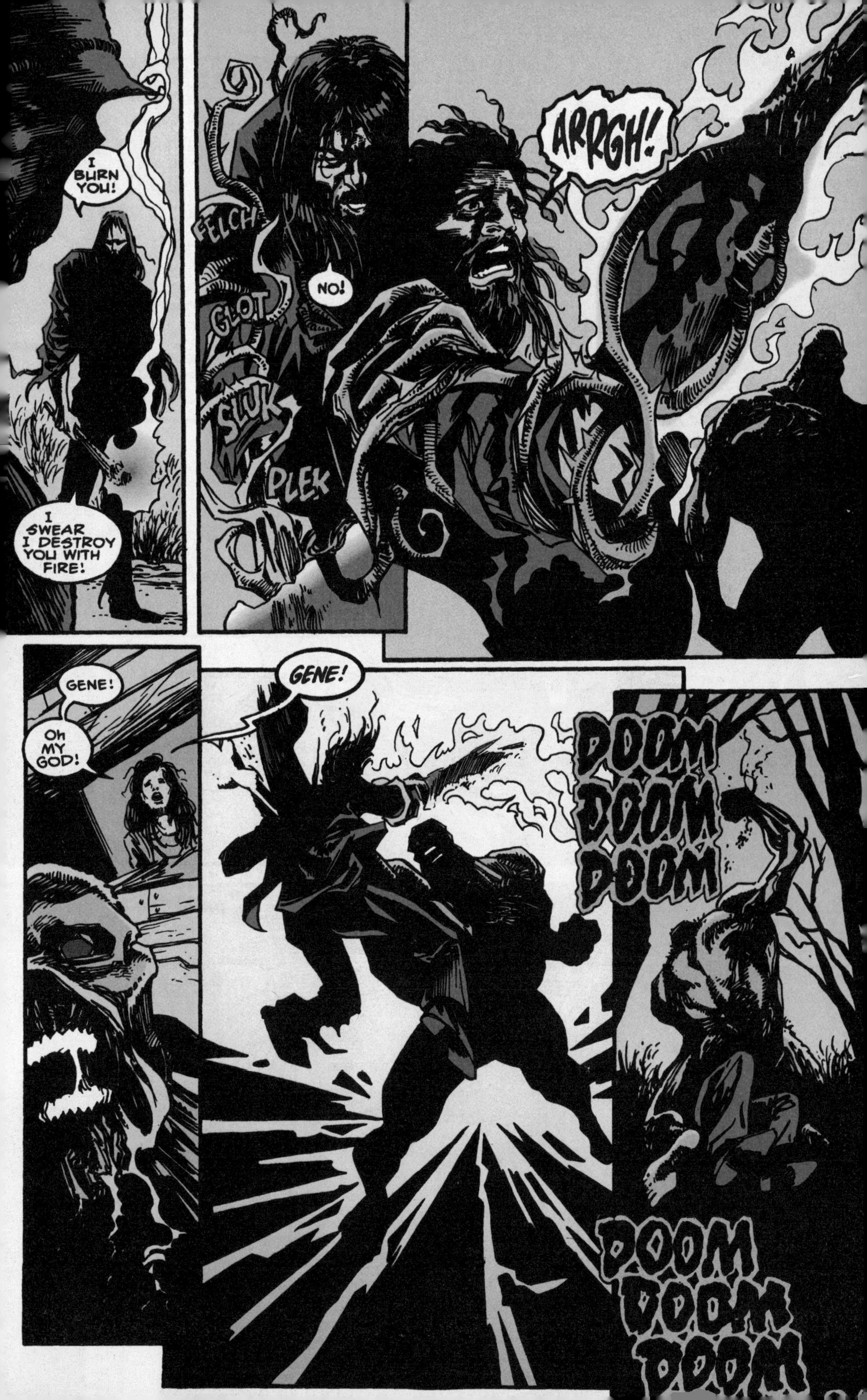
I BURN YOU!
I SWEAR I DESTROY YOU WITH FIRE!
FELCH
GLOT
SLUK
PLEK
NO!
ARRGH!
GENE!
Oh MY GOD!
GENE!
DOOM DOOM DOOM
DOOM DOOM DOOM

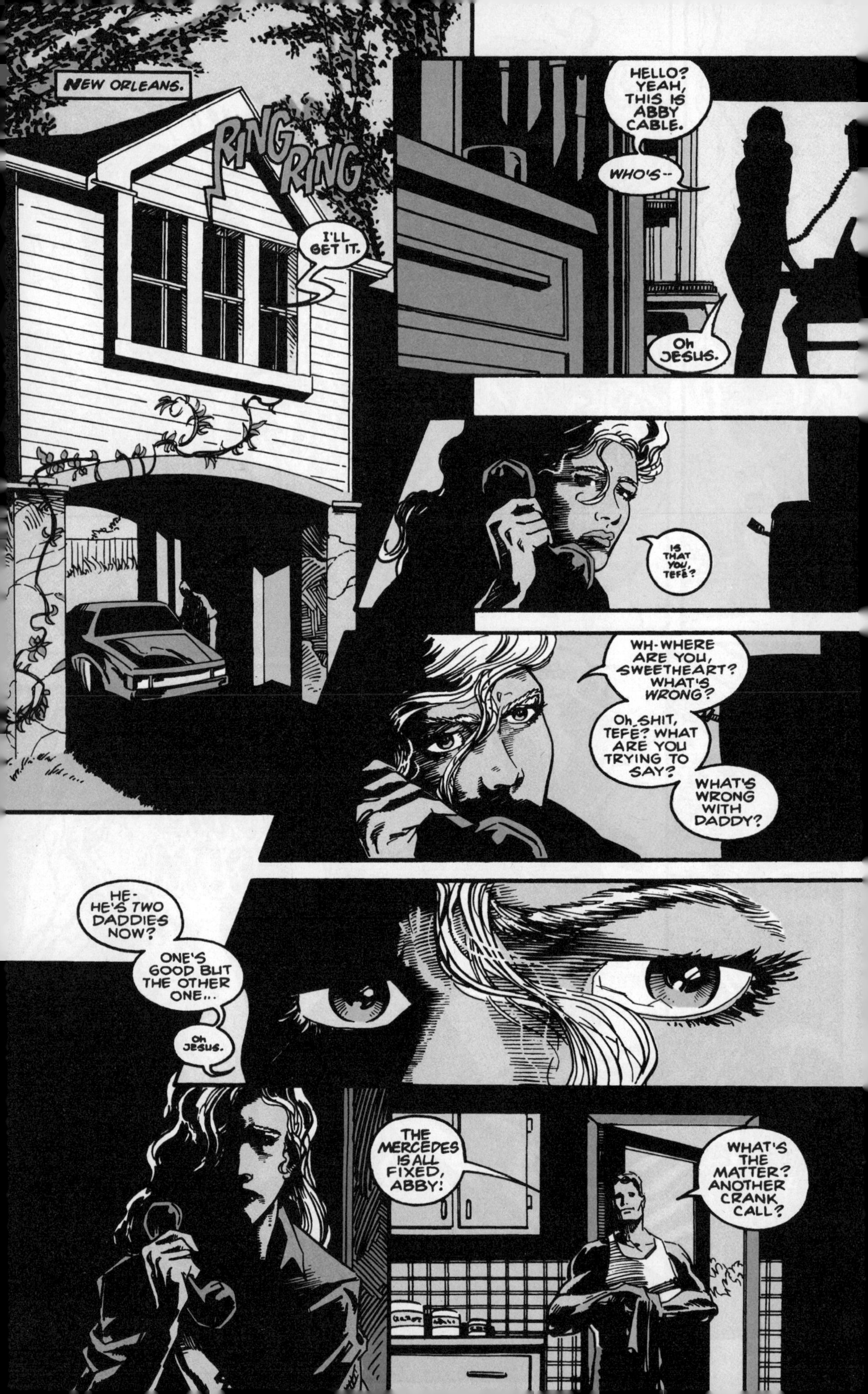
NEW ORLEANS.
RING RING
I'LL GET IT.
HELLO? YEAH, THIS IS ABBY CABLE.
WHO'S--
Oh JESUS.
IS THAT YOU, TEFÉ?
WH-WHERE ARE YOU, SWEETHEART? WHAT'S WRONG?
Oh, SHIT, TEFÉ? WHAT ARE YOU TRYING TO SAY?
WHAT'S WRONG WITH DADDY?
HE- HE'S TWO DADDIES NOW?
ONE'S GOOD BUT THE OTHER ONE...
Oh JESUS.
THE MERCEDES IS ALL FIXED, ABBY!
WHAT'S THE MATTER? ANOTHER CRANK CALL?

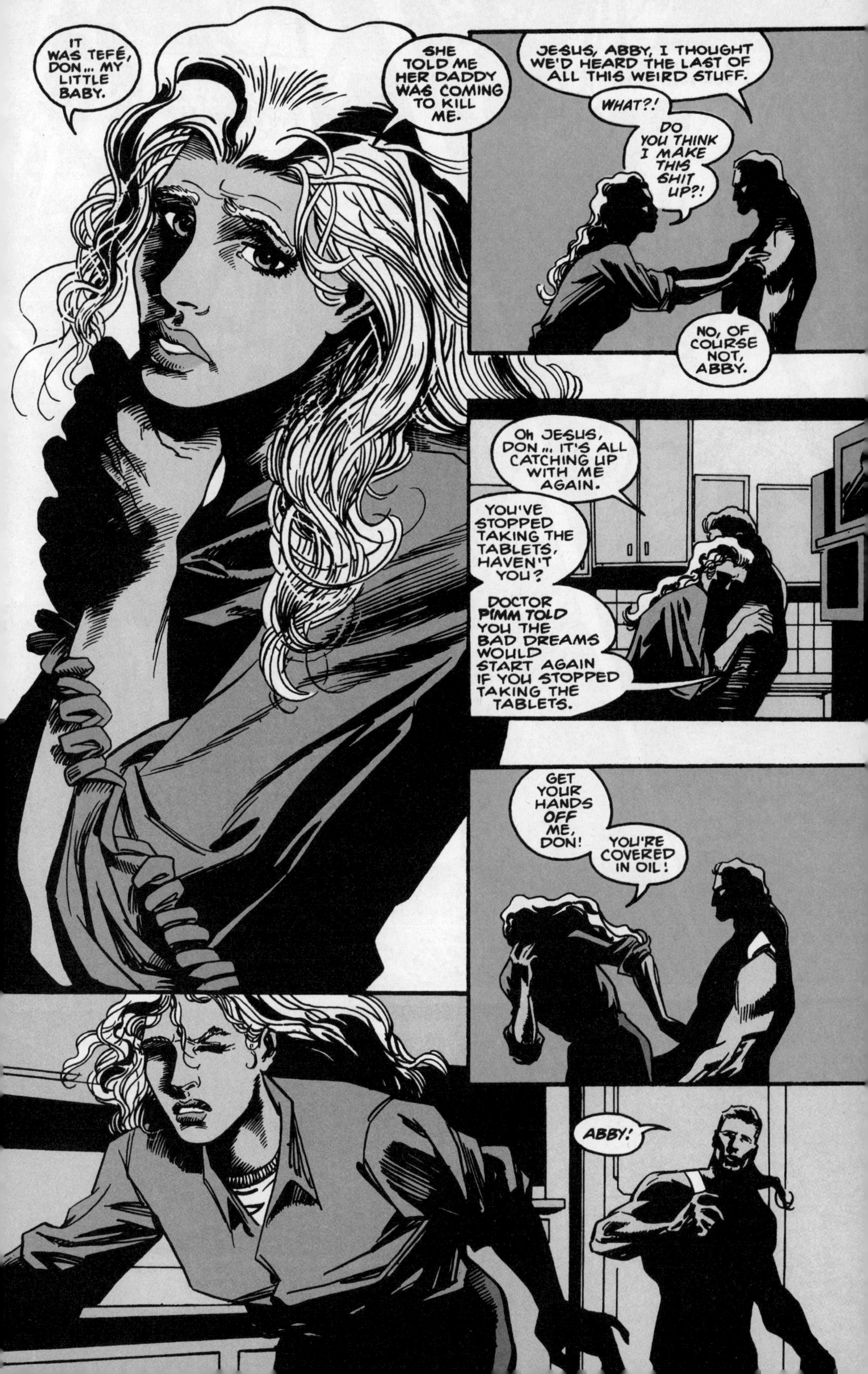
IT WAS TEFÉ, DON... MY LITTLE BABY.
SHE TOLD ME HER DADDY WAS COMING TO KILL ME.
JESUS, ABBY, I THOUGHT WE'D HEARD THE LAST OF ALL THIS WEIRD STUFF.
WHAT?!
DO YOU THINK I MAKE THIS SHIT UP?!
NO, OF COURSE NOT, ABBY.
Oh JESUS, DON... IT'S ALL CATCHING UP WITH ME AGAIN.
YOU'VE STOPPED TAKING THE TABLETS, HAVEN'T YOU?
DOCTOR PIMM TOLD YOU THE BAD DREAMS WOULD START AGAIN IF YOU STOPPED TAKING THE TABLETS.
GET YOUR HANDS OFF ME, DON!
YOU'RE COVERED IN OIL!
ABBY!

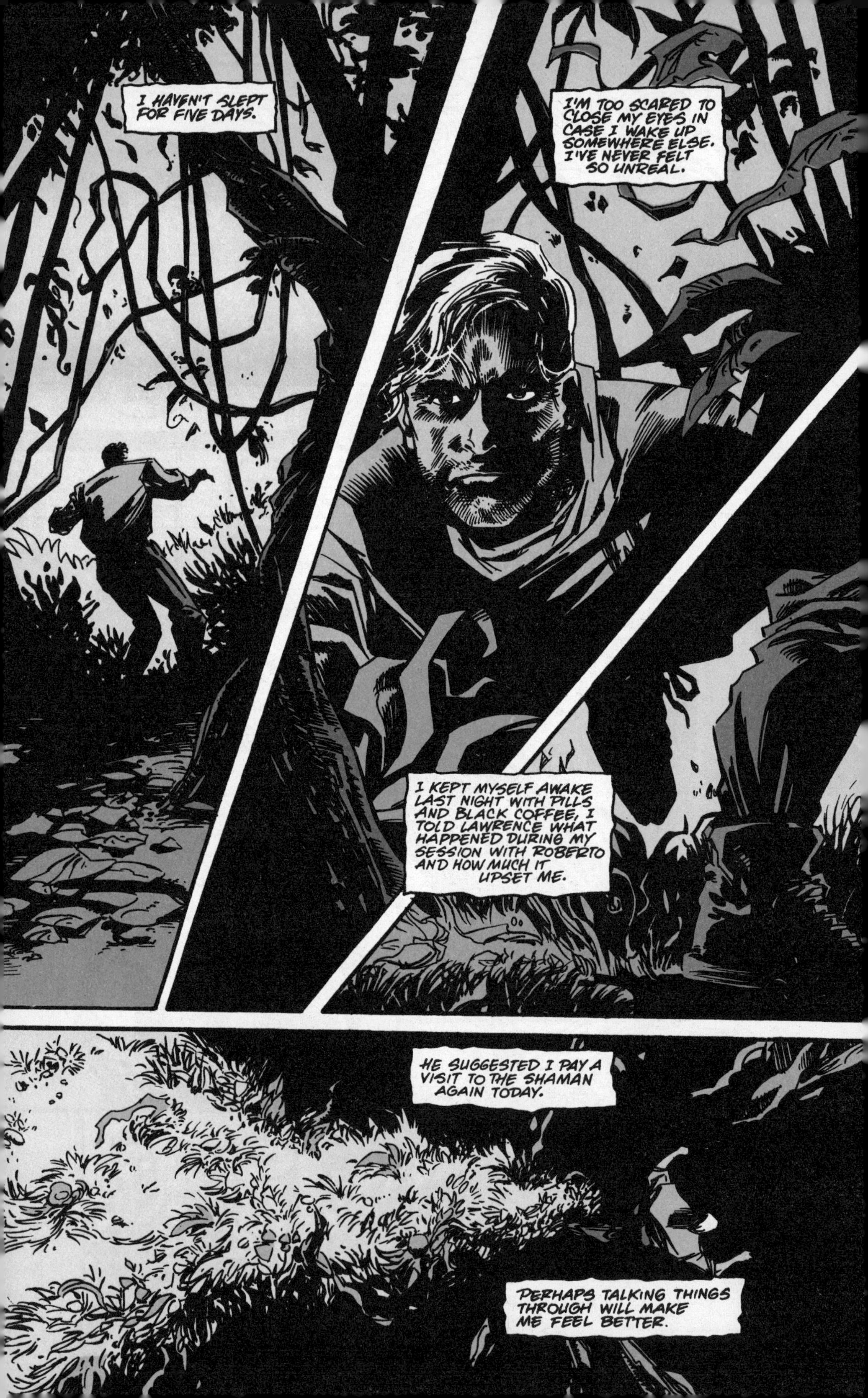
I HAVEN'T SLEPT FOR FIVE DAYS.
I'M TOO SCARED TO CLOSE MY EYES IN CASE I WAKE UP SOMEWHERE ELSE. I'VE NEVER FELT SO UNREAL.
I KEPT MYSELF AWAKE LAST NIGHT WITH PILLS AND BLACK COFFEE, I TOLD LAWRENCE WHAT HAPPENED DURING MY SESSION WITH ROBERTO AND HOW MUCH IT UPSET ME.
HE SUGGESTED I PAY A VISIT TO THE SHAMAN AGAIN TODAY.
PERHAPS TALKING THINGS THROUGH WILL MAKE ME FEEL BETTER.

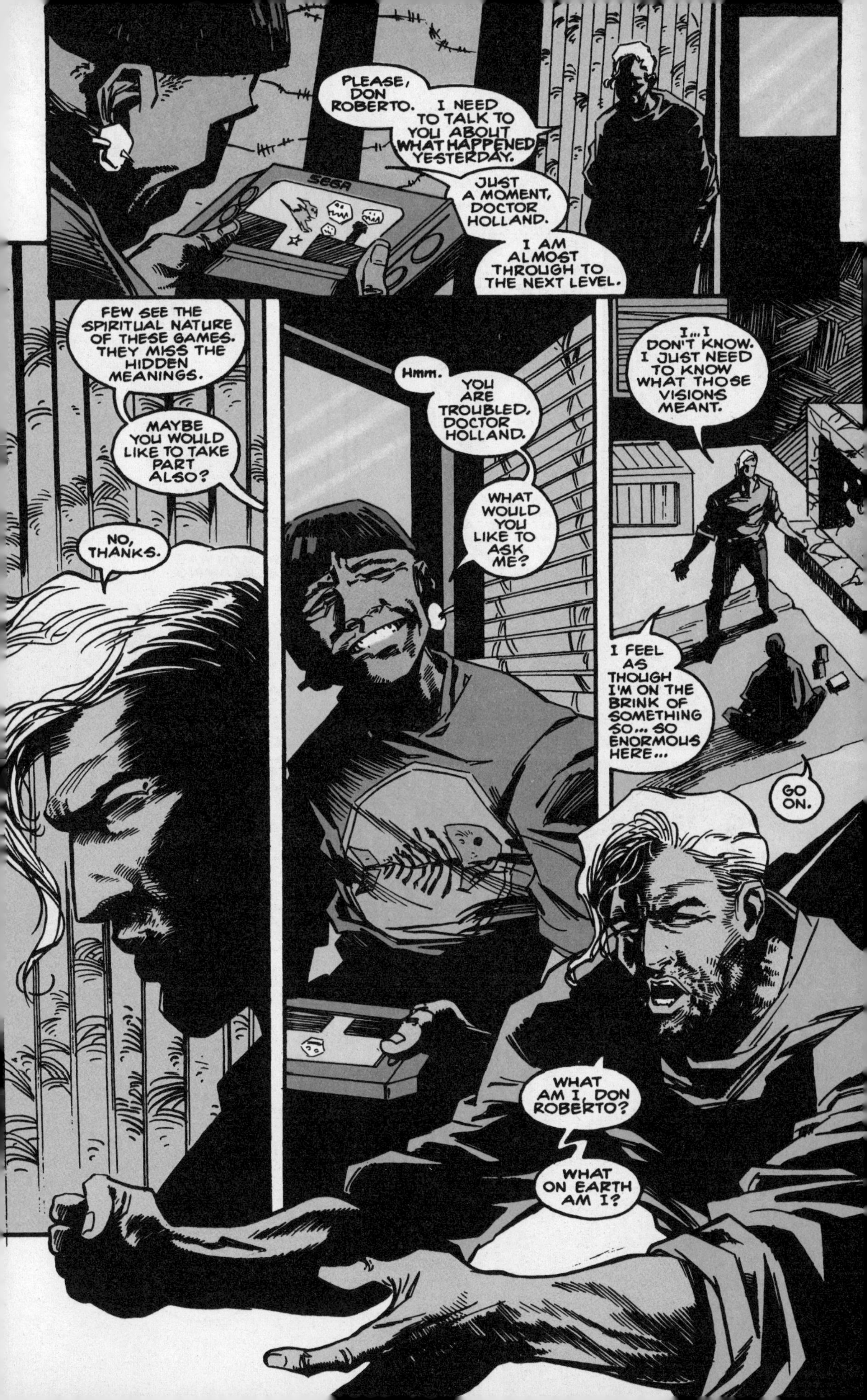
PLEASE, DON ROBERTO. I NEED TO TALK TO YOU ABOUT WHAT HAPPENED YESTERDAY.
SEGA
JUST A MOMENT, DOCTOR HOLLAND.
I AM ALMOST THROUGH TO THE NEXT LEVEL.
FEW SEE THE SPIRITUAL NATURE OF THESE GAMES. THEY MISS THE HIDDEN MEANINGS.
MAYBE YOU WOULD LIKE TO TAKE PART ALSO?
NO, THANKS.
Hmm.
YOU ARE TROUBLED, DOCTOR HOLLAND.
WHAT WOULD YOU LIKE TO ASK ME?
I...I DON'T KNOW. I JUST NEED TO KNOW WHAT THOSE VISIONS MEANT.
I FEEL AS THOUGH I'M ON THE BRINK OF SOMETHING SO... SO ENORMOUS HERE...
GO ON.
WHAT AM I, DON ROBERTO?
WHAT ON EARTH AM I?

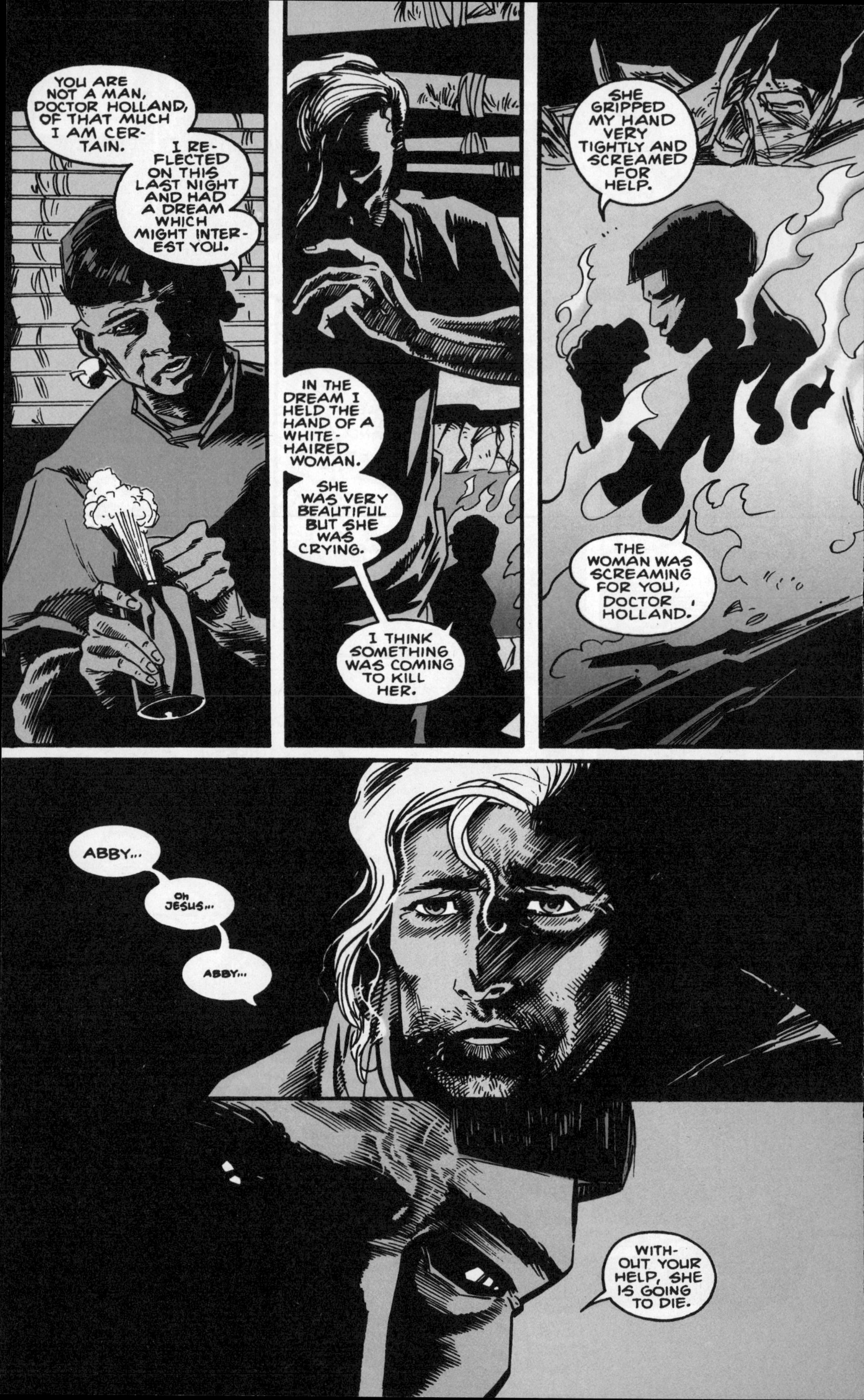
YOU ARE NOT A MAN, DOCTOR HOLLAND, OF THAT MUCH I AM CER-TAIN.
I RE-FLECTED ON THIS LAST NIGHT AND HAD A DREAM WHICH MIGHT INTER-EST YOU.
IN THE DREAM I HELD THE HAND OF A WHITE-HAIRED WOMAN.
SHE WAS VERY BEAUTIFUL BUT SHE WAS CRYING.
I THINK SOMETHING WAS COMING TO KILL HER.
SHE GRIPPED MY HAND VERY TIGHTLY AND SCREAMED FOR HELP.
THE WOMAN WAS SCREAMING FOR YOU, DOCTOR HOLLAND.
ABBY...
Oh JESUS...
ABBY...
WITH-OUT YOUR HELP, SHE IS GOING TO DIE.

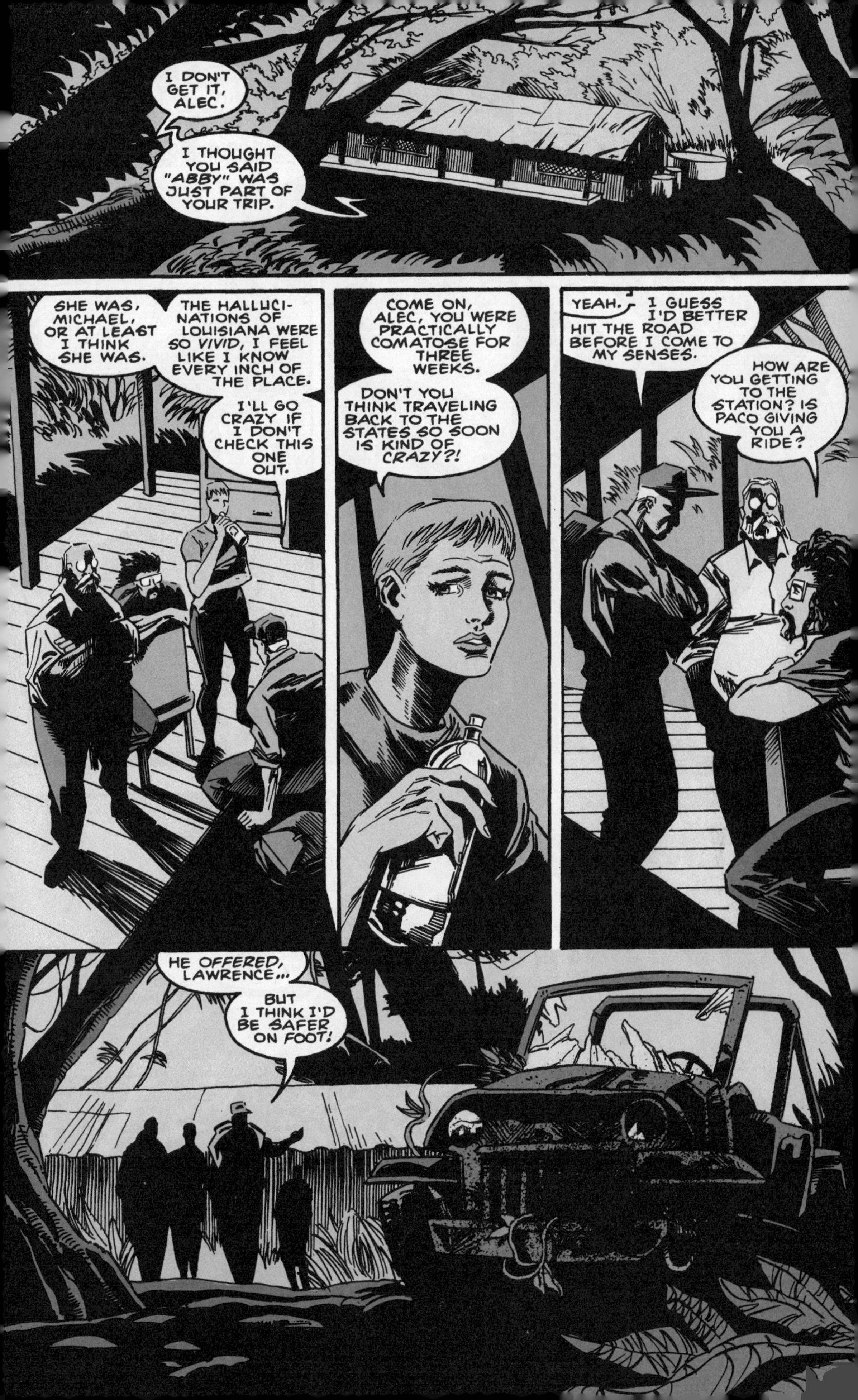
I DON'T GET IT, ALEC.
I THOUGHT YOU SAID "ABBY" WAS JUST PART OF YOUR TRIP.
SHE WAS, MICHAEL, OR AT LEAST I THINK SHE WAS.
THE HALLUCINATIONS OF LOUISIANA WERE SO VIVID, I FEEL LIKE I KNOW EVERY INCH OF THE PLACE.
I'LL GO CRAZY IF I DON'T CHECK THIS ONE OUT.
COME ON, ALEC, YOU WERE PRACTICALLY COMATOSE FOR THREE WEEKS.
DON'T YOU THINK TRAVELING BACK TO THE STATES SO SOON IS KIND OF CRAZY?!
YEAH.
I GUESS I'D BETTER HIT THE ROAD BEFORE I COME TO MY SENSES.
HOW ARE YOU GETTING TO THE STATION? IS PACO GIVING YOU A RIDE?
HE OFFERED, LAWRENCE...
BUT I THINK I'D BE SAFER ON FOOT!

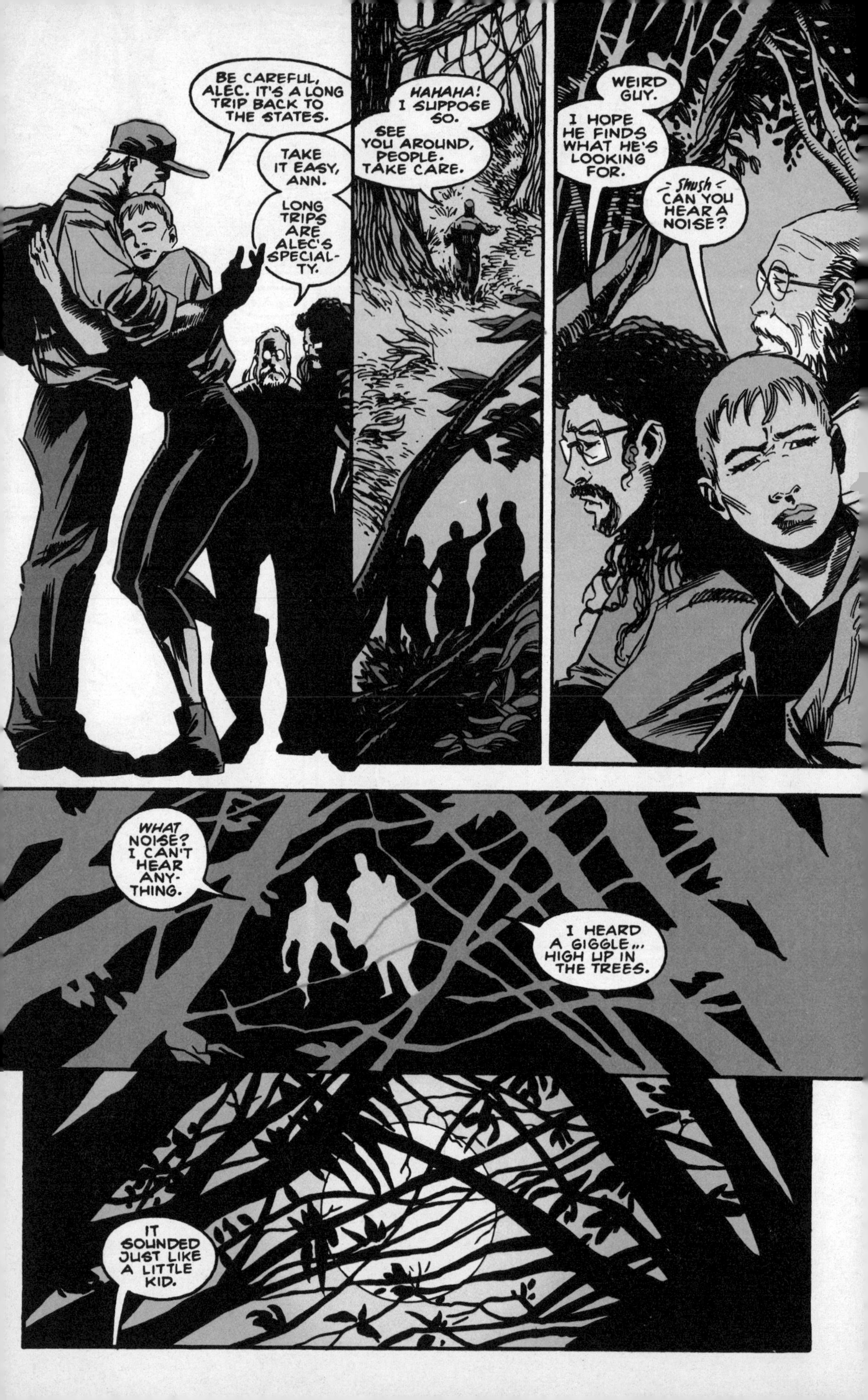
BE CAREFUL, ALEC. IT'S A LONG TRIP BACK TO THE STATES.
TAKE IT EASY, ANN.
LONG TRIPS ARE ALEC'S SPECIAL-TY.
HAHAHA! I SUPPOSE SO.
SEE YOU AROUND, PEOPLE. TAKE CARE.
WEIRD GUY.
I HOPE HE FINDS WHAT HE'S LOOKING FOR.
-Shush- CAN YOU HEAR A NOISE?
WHAT NOISE? I CAN'T HEAR ANY-THING.
I HEARD A GIGGLE... HIGH UP IN THE TREES.
IT SOUNDED JUST LIKE A LITTLE KID.

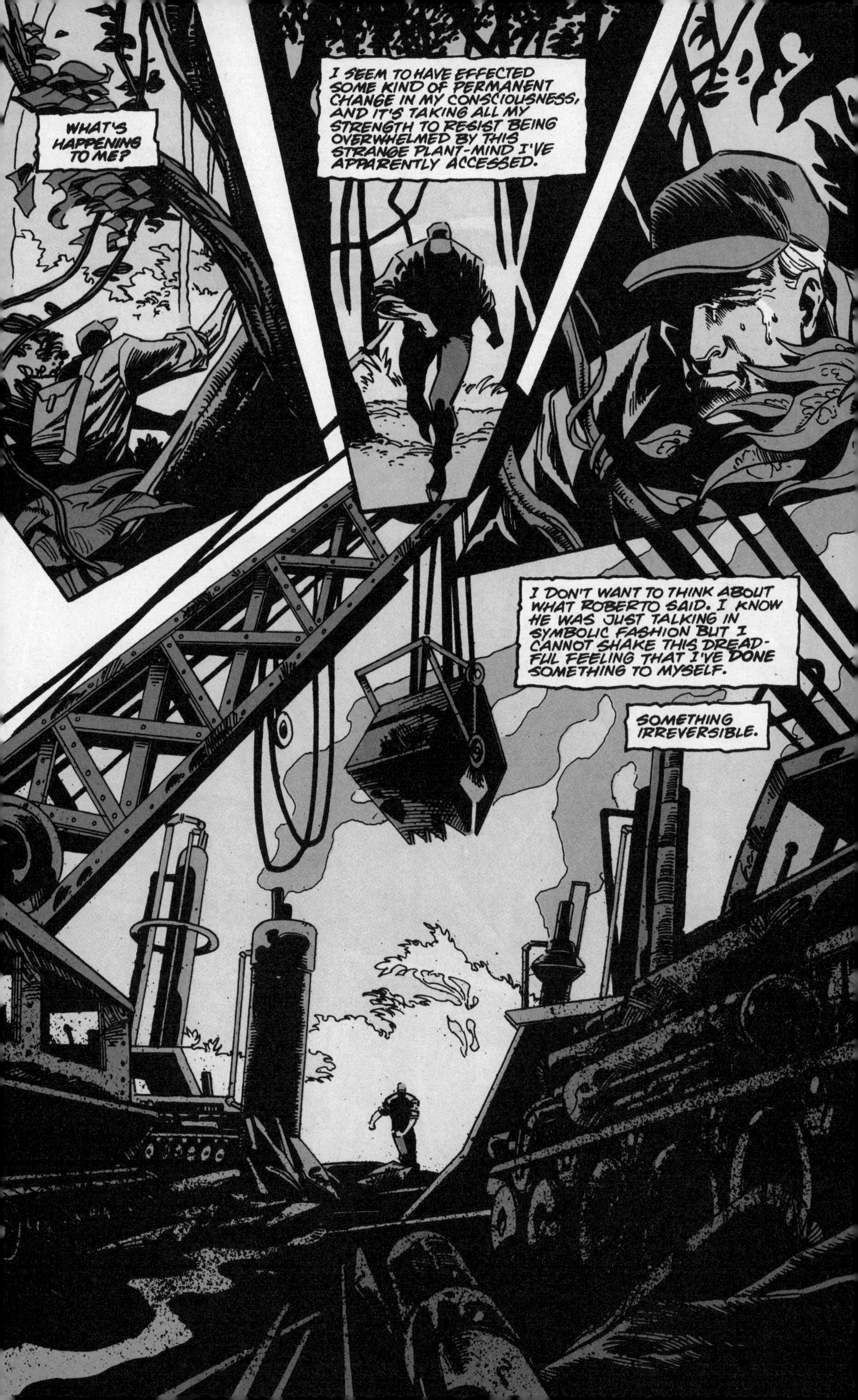
WHAT'S HAPPENING TO ME?
I SEEM TO HAVE EFFECTED SOME KIND OF PERMANENT CHANGE IN MY CONSCIOUSNESS, AND IT'S TAKING ALL MY STRENGTH TO RESIST BEING OVERWHELMED BY THIS STRANGE PLANT-MIND I'VE APPARENTLY ACCESSED.
I DON'T WANT TO THINK ABOUT WHAT ROBERTO SAID. I KNOW HE WAS JUST TALKING IN SYMBOLIC FASHION BUT I CANNOT SHAKE THIS DREAD-FUL FEELING THAT I'VE DONE SOMETHING TO MYSELF.
SOMETHING IRREVERSIBLE.

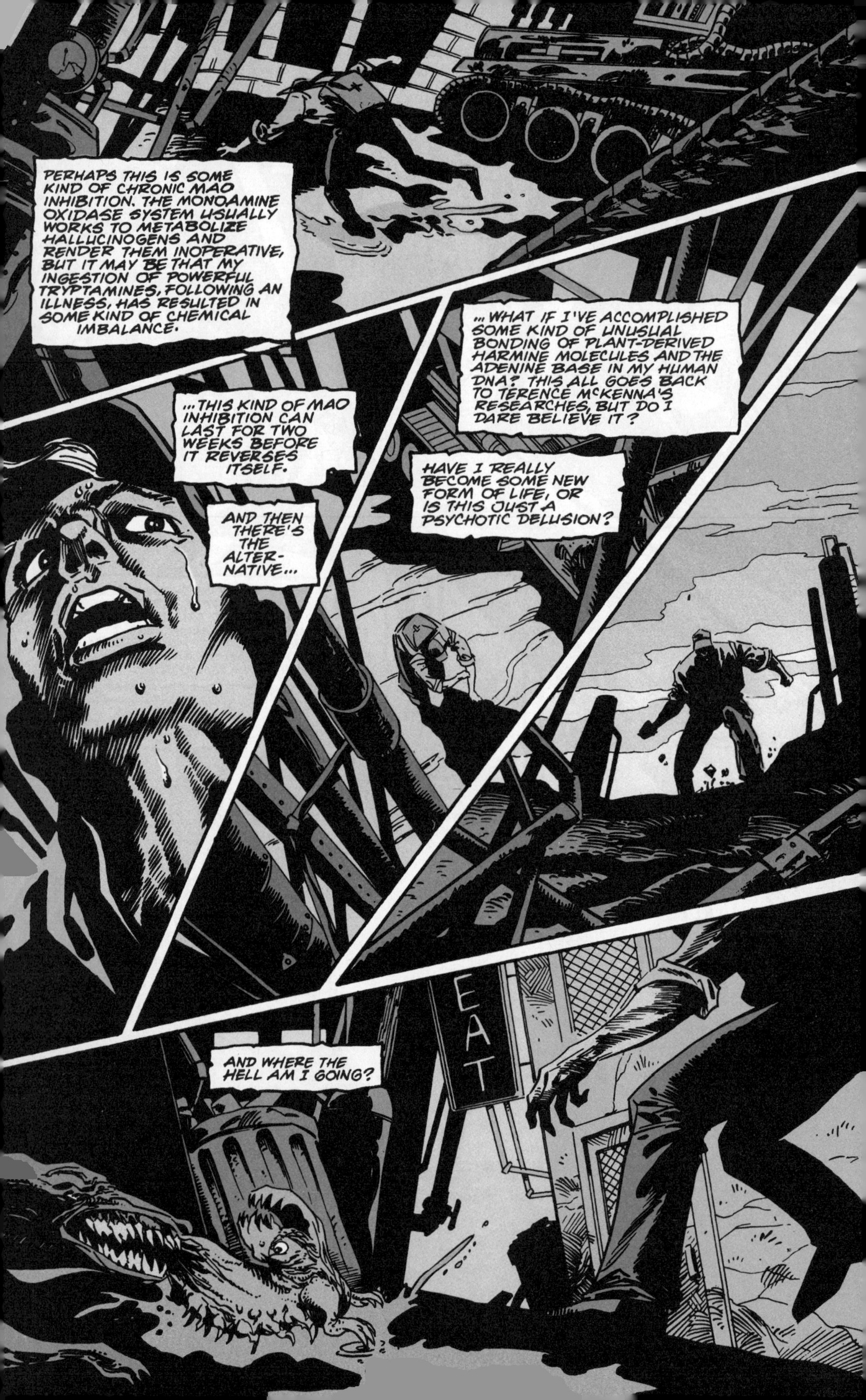
PERHAPS THIS IS SOME KIND OF CHRONIC MAO INHIBITION. THE MONOAMINE OXIDASE SYSTEM USUALLY WORKS TO METABOLIZE HALLUCINOGENS AND RENDER THEM INOPERATIVE, BUT IT MAY BE THAT MY INGESTION OF POWERFUL TRYPTAMINES, FOLLOWING AN ILLNESS, HAS RESULTED IN SOME KIND OF CHEMICAL IMBALANCE.
...THIS KIND OF MAO INHIBITION CAN LAST FOR TWO WEEKS BEFORE IT REVERSES ITSELF.
AND THEN THERE'S THE ALTER-NATIVE...
...WHAT IF I'VE ACCOMPLISHED SOME KIND OF UNUSUAL BONDING OF PLANT-DERIVED HARMINE MOLECULES AND THE ADENINE BASE IN MY HUMAN DNA? THIS ALL GOES BACK TO TERENCE McKENNA'S RESEARCHES, BUT DO I DARE BELIEVE IT?
HAVE I REALLY BECOME SOME NEW FORM OF LIFE, OR IS THIS JUST A PSYCHOTIC DELUSION?
AND WHERE THE HELL AM I GOING?
EAT

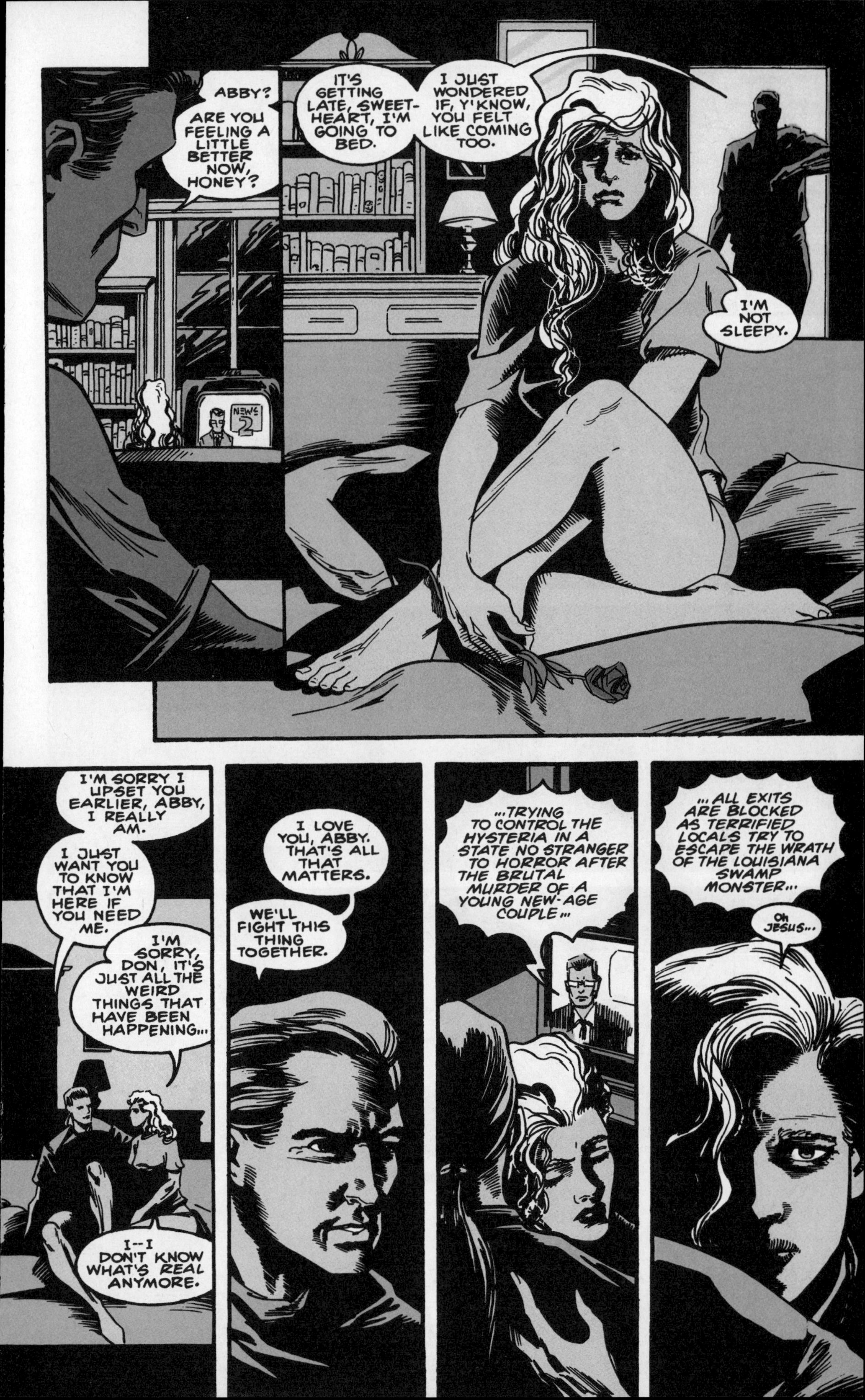
ABBY?
ARE YOU FEELING A LITTLE BETTER NOW, HONEY?
IT'S GETTING LATE, SWEET-HEART, I'M GOING TO BED.
I JUST WONDERED IF, Y'KNOW, YOU FELT LIKE COMING TOO.
I'M NOT SLEEPY.
I'M SORRY I UPSET YOU EARLIER, ABBY, I REALLY AM.
I JUST WANT YOU TO KNOW THAT I'M HERE IF YOU NEED ME.
I'M SORRY, DON, IT'S JUST ALL THE WEIRD THINGS THAT HAVE BEEN HAPPENING...
I--I DON'T KNOW WHAT'S REAL ANYMORE.
I LOVE YOU, ABBY. THAT'S ALL THAT MATTERS.
WE'LL FIGHT THIS THING TOGETHER.
...TRYING TO CONTROL THE HYSTERIA IN A STATE NO STRANGER TO HORROR AFTER THE BRUTAL MURDER OF A YOUNG NEW-AGE COUPLE...
...ALL EXITS ARE BLOCKED AS TERRIFIED LOCALS TRY TO ESCAPE THE WRATH OF THE LOUISIANA SWAMP MONSTER...
Oh JESUS...

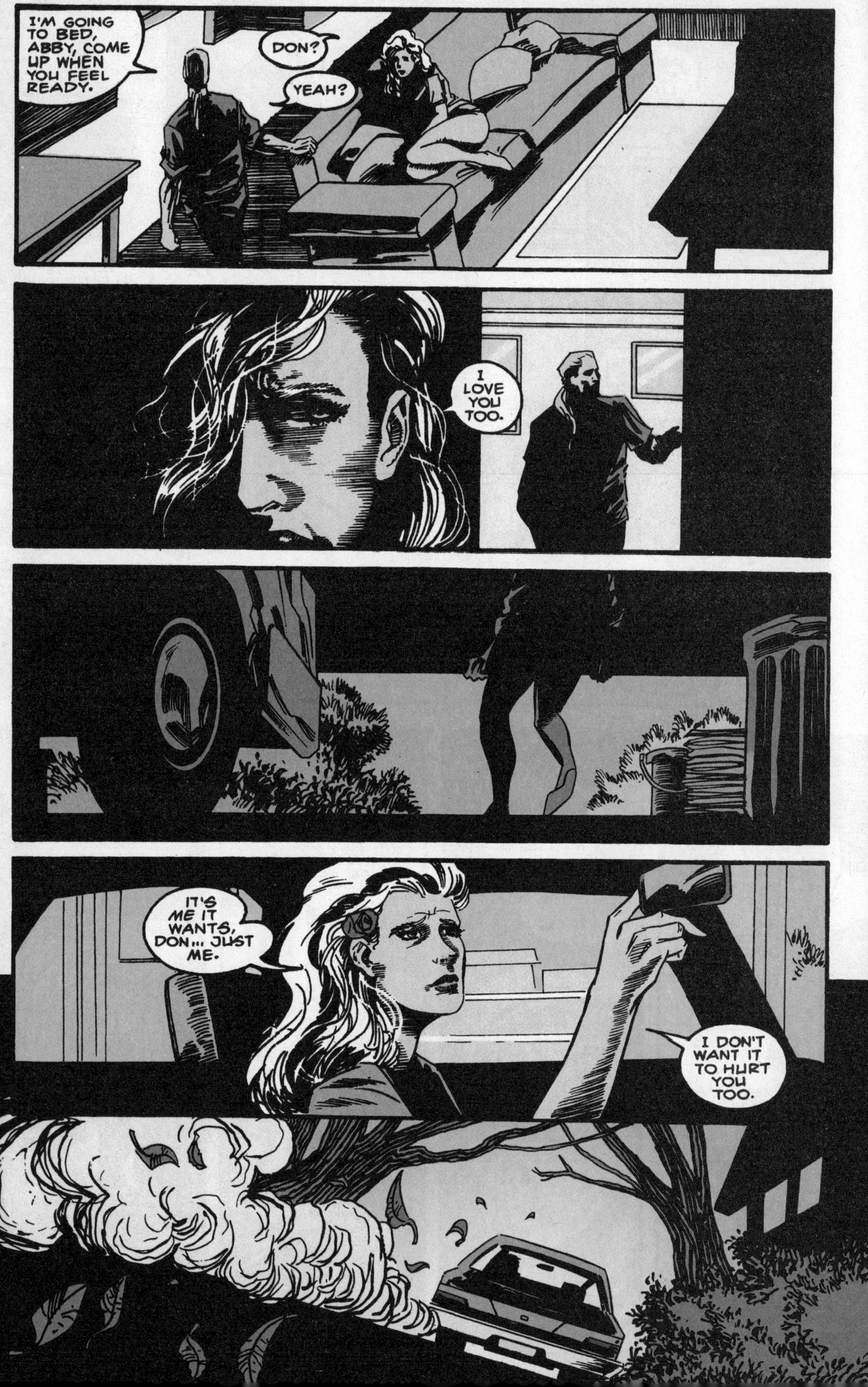
I'M GOING TO BED, ABBY, COME UP WHEN YOU FEEL READY.
DON?
YEAH?
I LOVE YOU TOO.
IT'S ME IT WANTS, DON... JUST ME.
I DON'T WANT IT TO HURT YOU TOO.

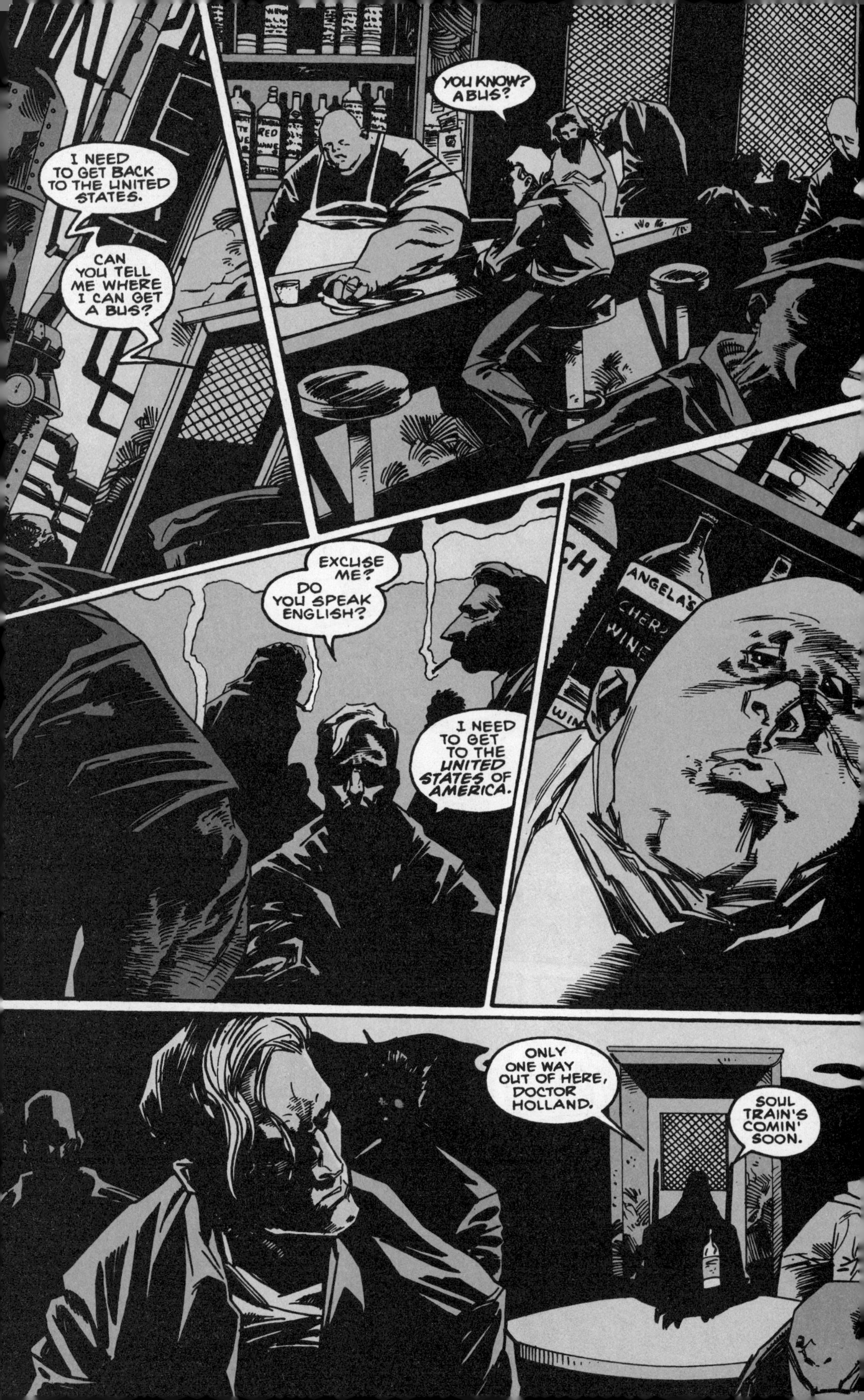

I NEED TO GET BACK TO THE UNITED STATES.
CAN YOU TELL ME WHERE I CAN GET A BUS?
YOU KNOW? A BUS?
EXCUSE ME? DO YOU SPEAK ENGLISH?
I NEED TO GET TO THE UNITED STATES OF AMERICA.
ANGELA'S
ONLY ONE WAY OUT OF HERE, DOCTOR HOLLAND.
SOUL TRAIN'S COMIN' SOON.

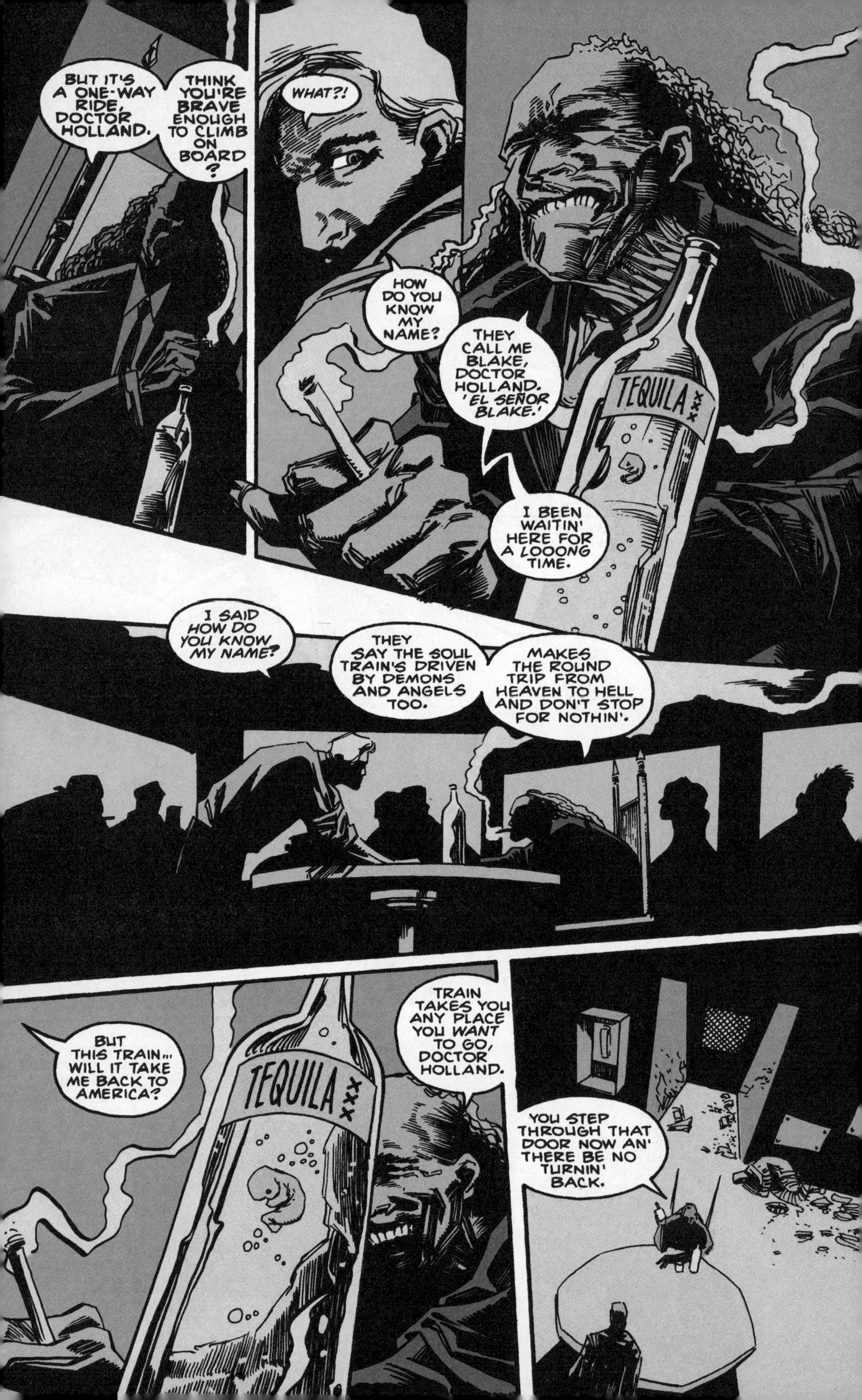
BUT IT'S A ONE-WAY RIDE, DOCTOR HOLLAND.
THINK YOU'RE BRAVE ENOUGH TO CLIMB ON BOARD?
WHAT?!
HOW DO YOU KNOW MY NAME?
THEY CALL ME BLAKE, DOCTOR HOLLAND. 'EL SEÑOR BLAKE.'
TEQUILA XXX
I BEEN WAITIN' HERE FOR A LOOONG TIME.
I SAID HOW DO YOU KNOW MY NAME?
THEY SAY THE SOUL TRAIN'S DRIVEN BY DEMONS AND ANGELS TOO.
MAKES THE ROUND TRIP FROM HEAVEN TO HELL AND DON'T STOP FOR NOTHIN'.
BUT THIS TRAIN... WILL IT TAKE ME BACK TO AMERICA?
TEQUILA XXX
TRAIN TAKES YOU ANY PLACE YOU WANT TO GO, DOCTOR HOLLAND.
YOU STEP THROUGH THAT DOOR NOW AN' THERE BE NO TURNIN' BACK.

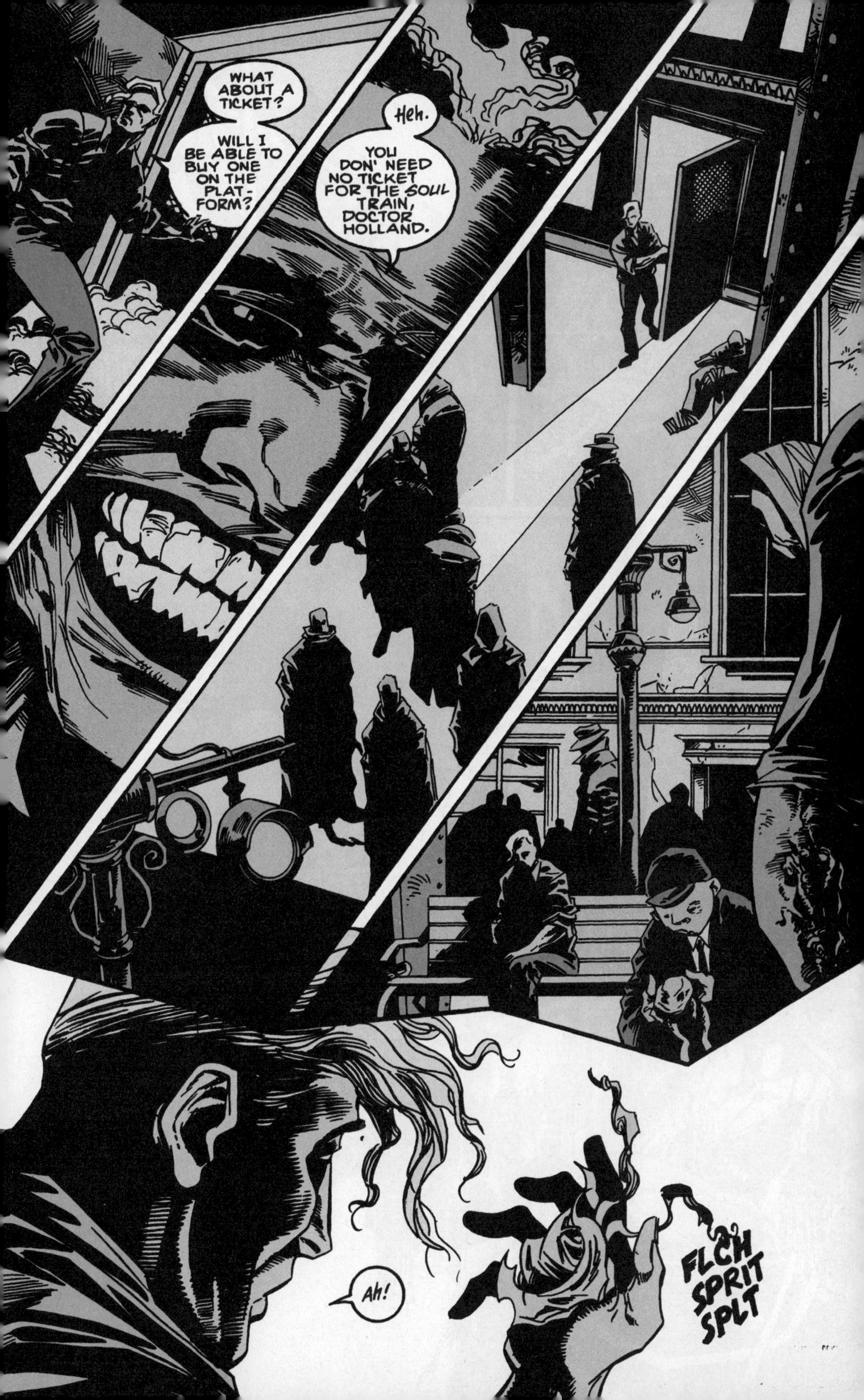
WHAT ABOUT A TICKET?
WILL I BE ABLE TO BUY ONE ON THE PLAT-FORM?
Heh.
YOU DON' NEED NO TICKET FOR THE SOUL TRAIN, DOCTOR HOLLAND.
Ah!
FLCH SPRIT SPLT

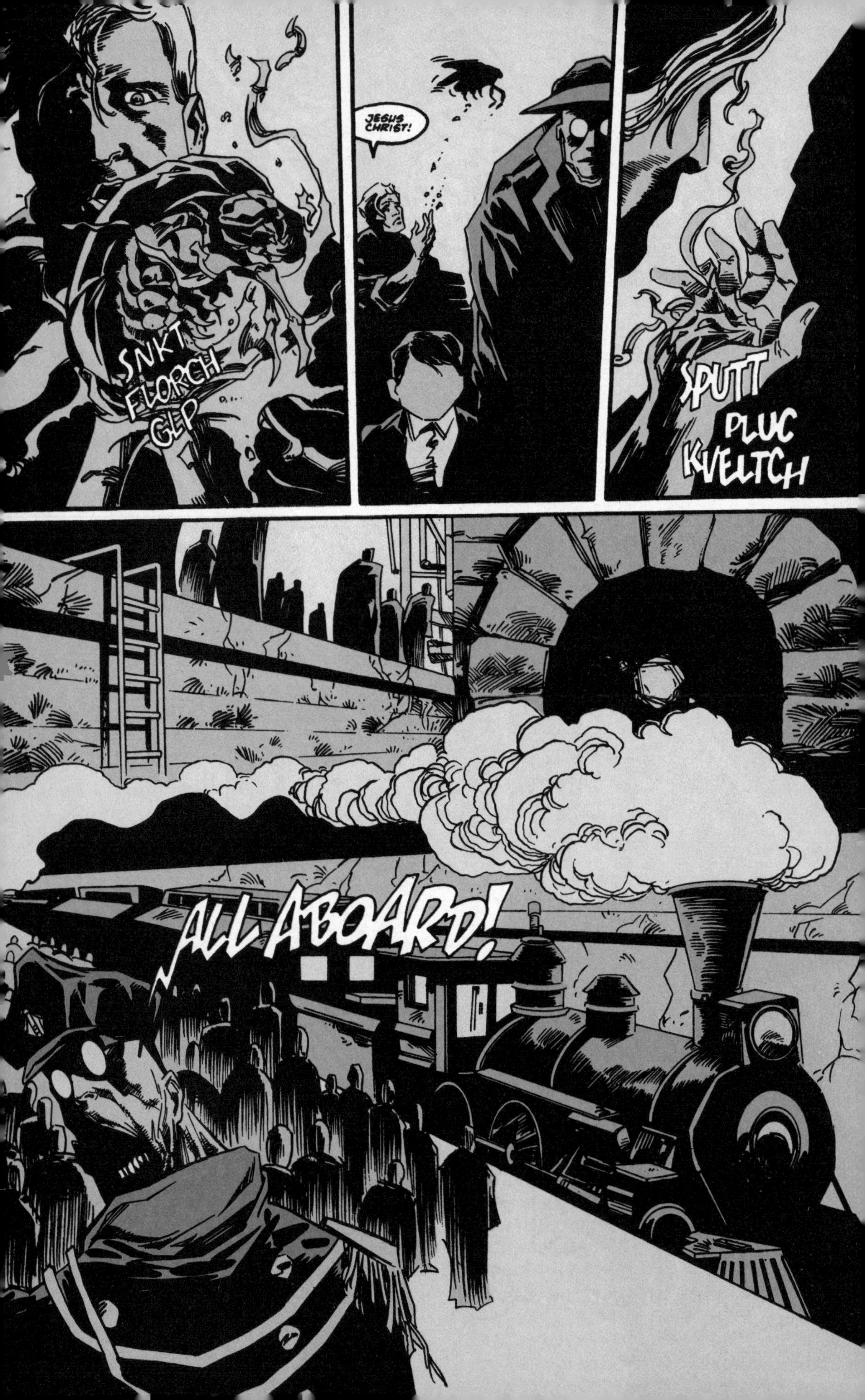
SNKT
FLORCH
GLP
JESUS CHRIST!
SPUTT
PLUC
KVELTCH
ALL ABOARD!

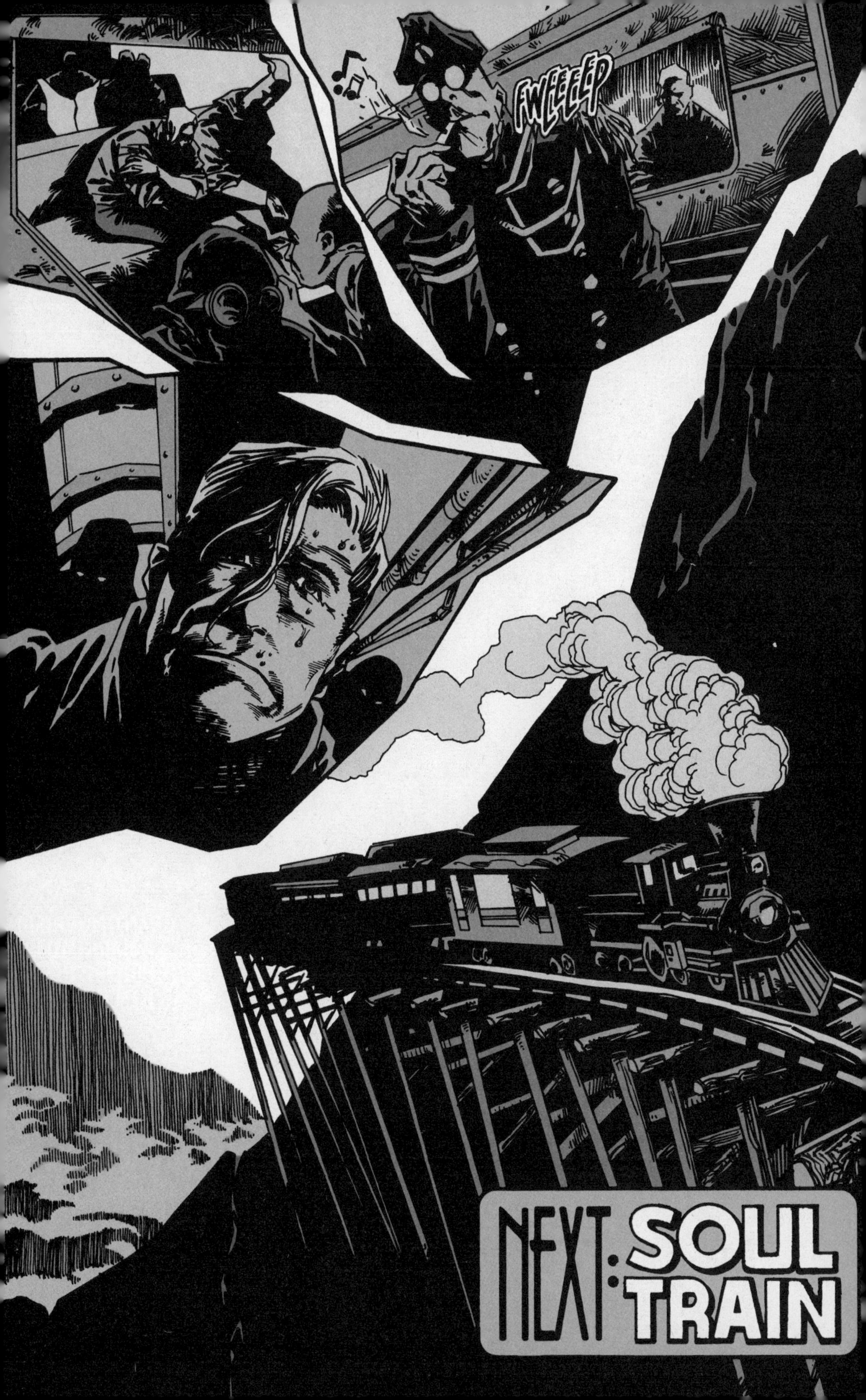
FWEEEEEP
NEXT: SOUL TRAIN

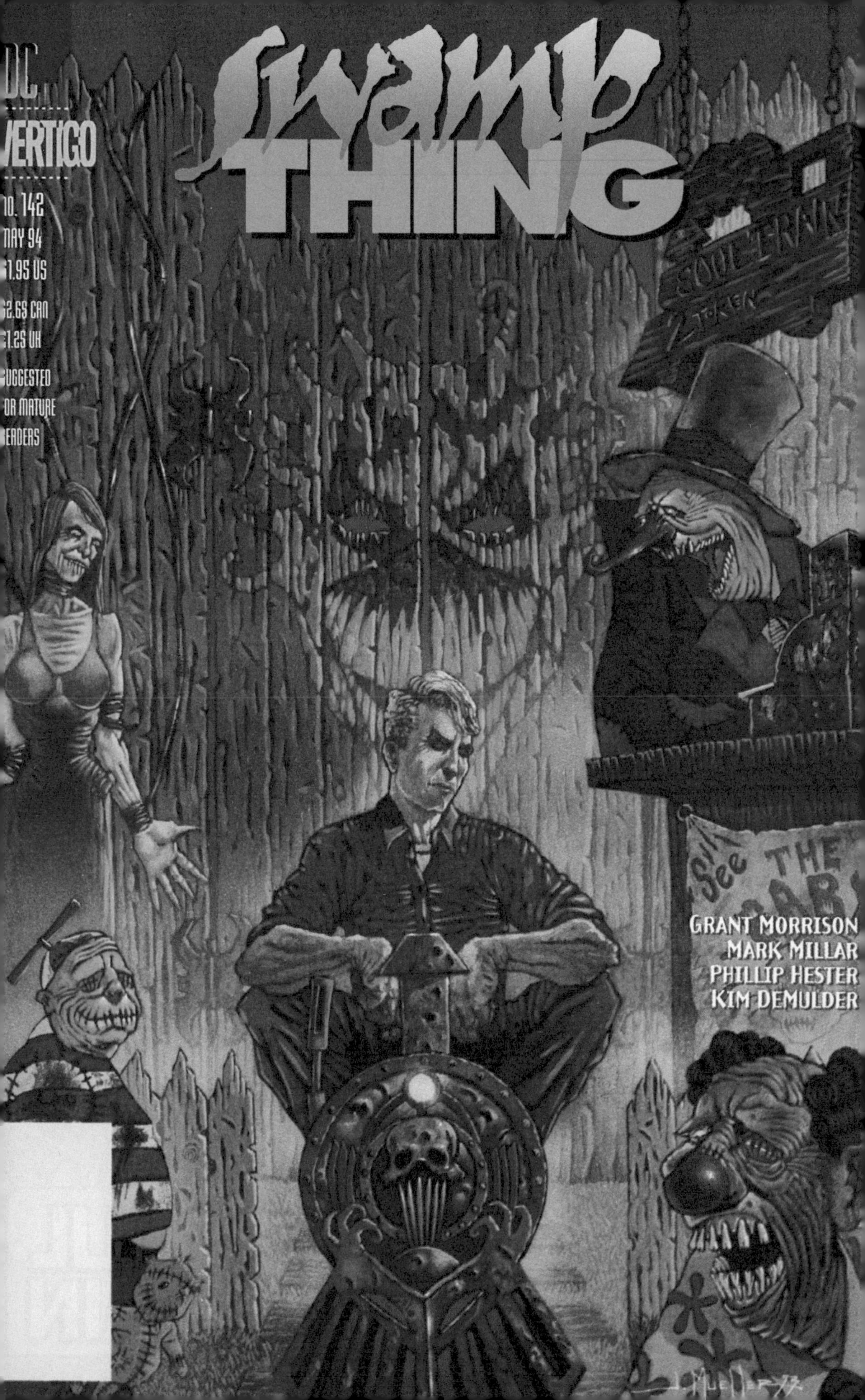

DC
VERTIGO
142
MAY 94
Swamp THING
See THE
GRANT MORRISON
MARK MILLAR
PHILLIP HESTER
KIM DEMULDER

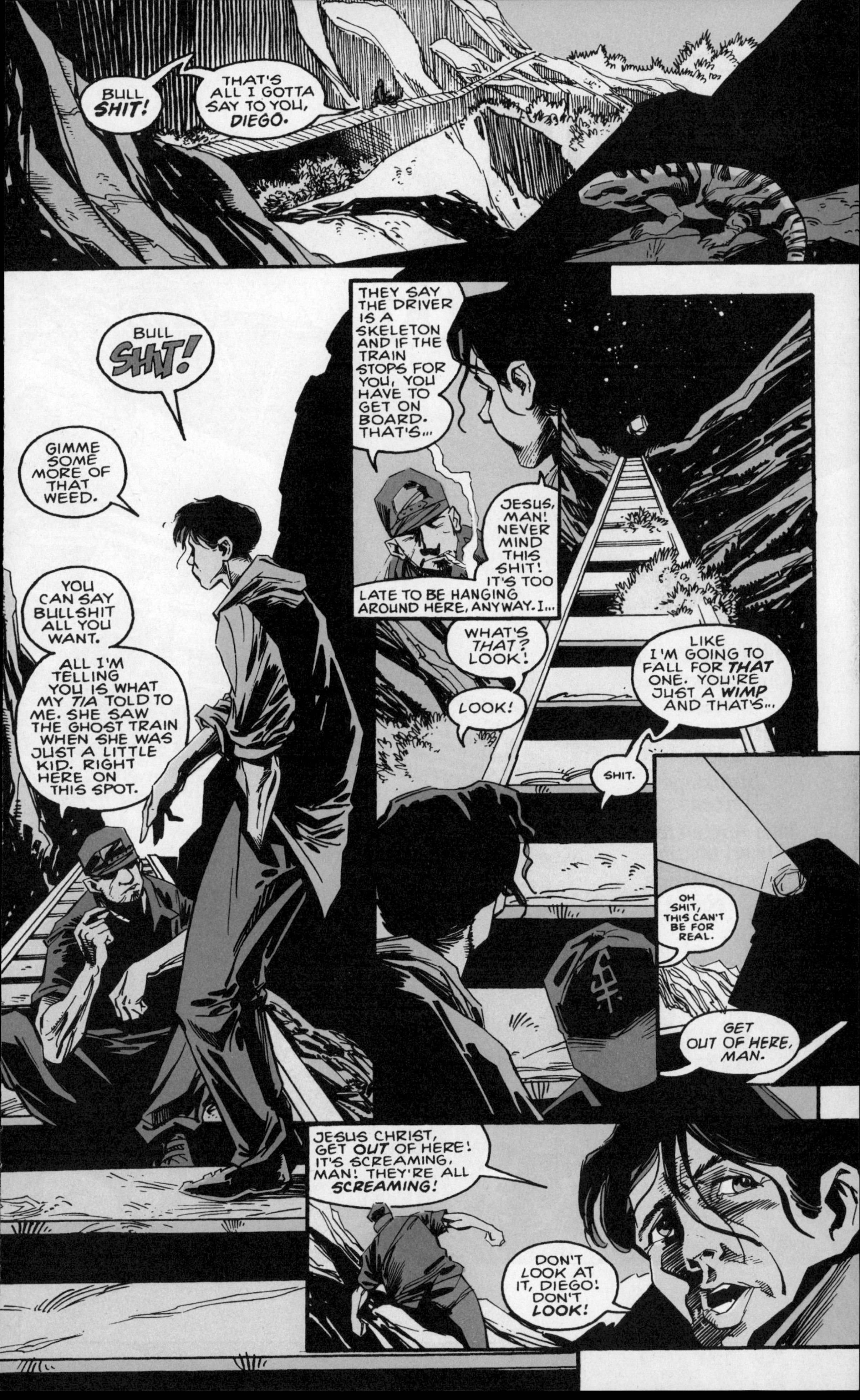
BULL SHIT!
THAT'S ALL I GOTTA SAY TO YOU, DIEGO.
BULL SHIT!
GIMME SOME MORE OF THAT WEED.
YOU CAN SAY BULLSHIT ALL YOU WANT.
ALL I'M TELLING YOU IS WHAT MY TIA TOLD TO ME. SHE SAW THE GHOST TRAIN WHEN SHE WAS JUST A LITTLE KID. RIGHT HERE ON THIS SPOT.
THEY SAY THE DRIVER IS A SKELETON AND IF THE TRAIN STOPS FOR YOU, YOU HAVE TO GET ON BOARD. THAT'S...
JESUS, MAN! NEVER MIND THIS SHIT! IT'S TOO LATE TO BE HANGING AROUND HERE, ANYWAY. I...
WHAT'S THAT? LOOK!
LOOK!
LIKE I'M GOING TO FALL FOR THAT ONE. YOU'RE JUST A WIMP AND THAT'S...
SHIT.
OH SHIT, THIS CAN'T BE FOR REAL.
GET OUT OF HERE, MAN.
JESUS CHRIST, GET OUT OF HERE! IT'S SCREAMING, MAN! THEY'RE ALL SCREAMING!
DON'T LOOK AT IT, DIEGO! DON'T LOOK!

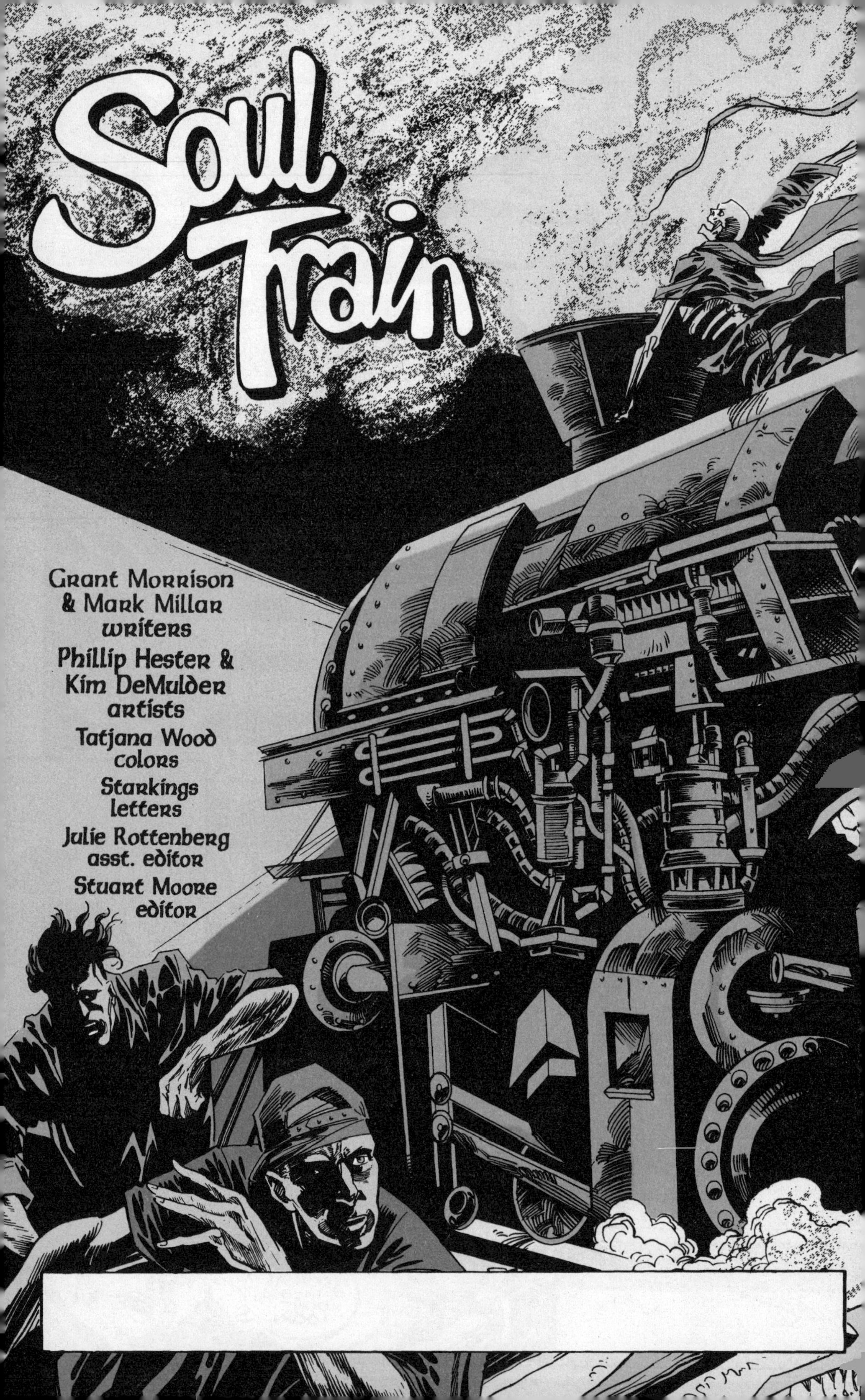
Soul Train
Grant Morrison
& Mark Millar
writers
Phillip Hester &
Kim DeMulder
artists
Tatjana Wood
colors
Starkings
letters
Julie Rottenberg
asst. editor
Stuart Moore
editor

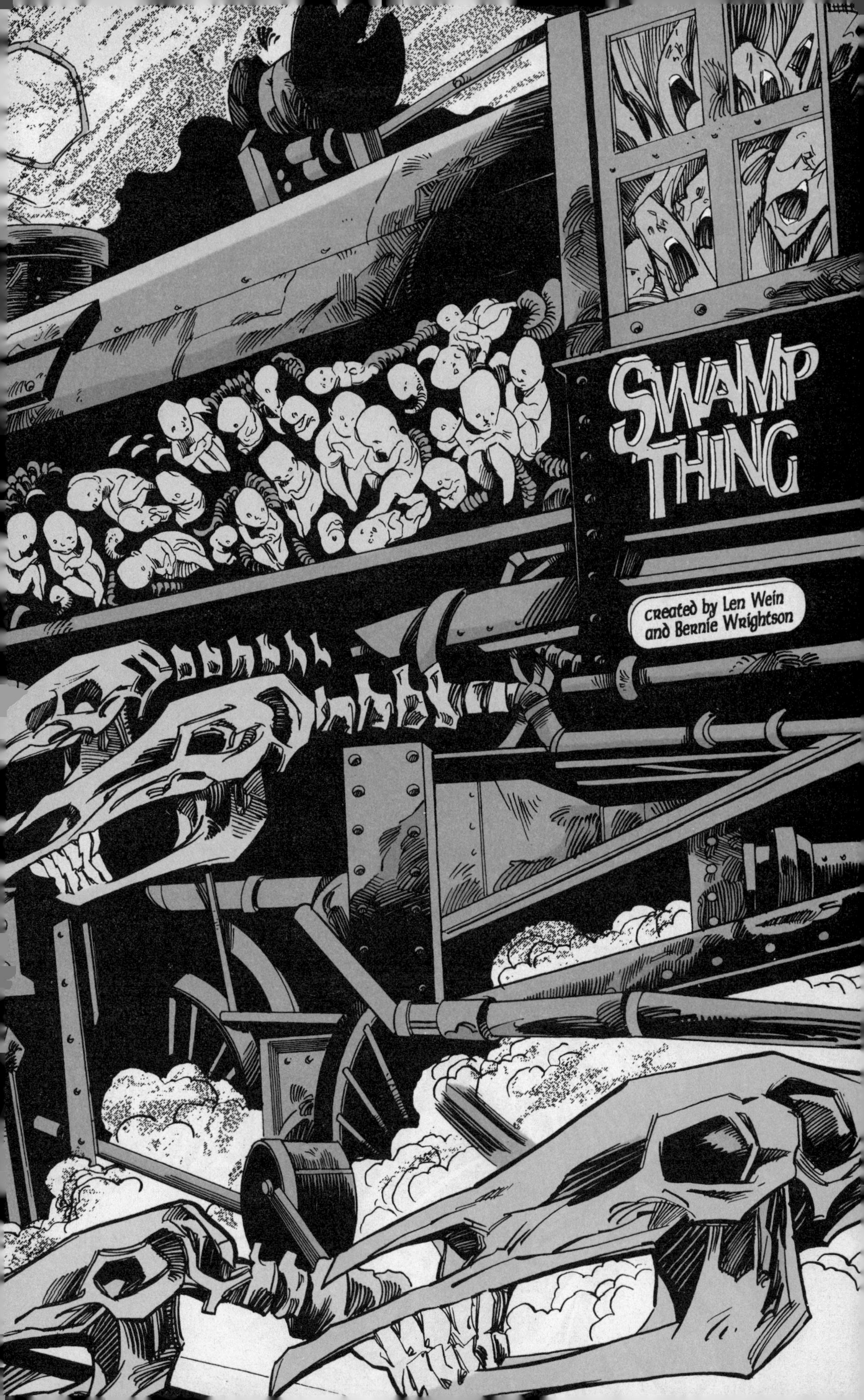
SWAMP THING
created by Len Wein and Bernie Wrightson

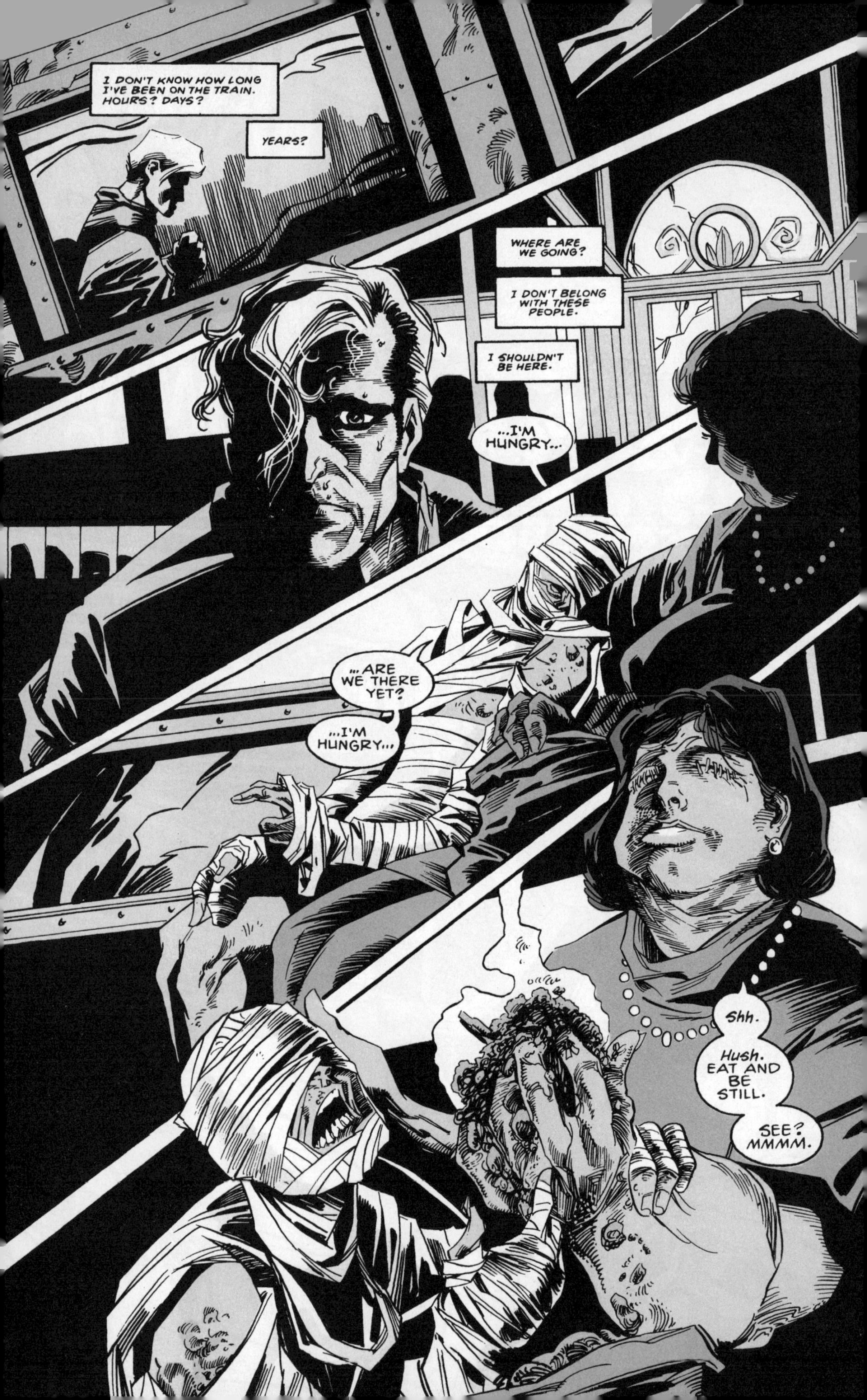
I DON'T KNOW HOW LONG I'VE BEEN ON THE TRAIN. HOURS? DAYS?
YEARS?
WHERE ARE WE GOING?
I DON'T BELONG WITH THESE PEOPLE.
I SHOULDN'T BE HERE.
...I'M HUNGRY...
...ARE WE THERE YET?
...I'M HUNGRY...
Shh.
Hush. EAT AND BE STILL.
SEE? MMMM.

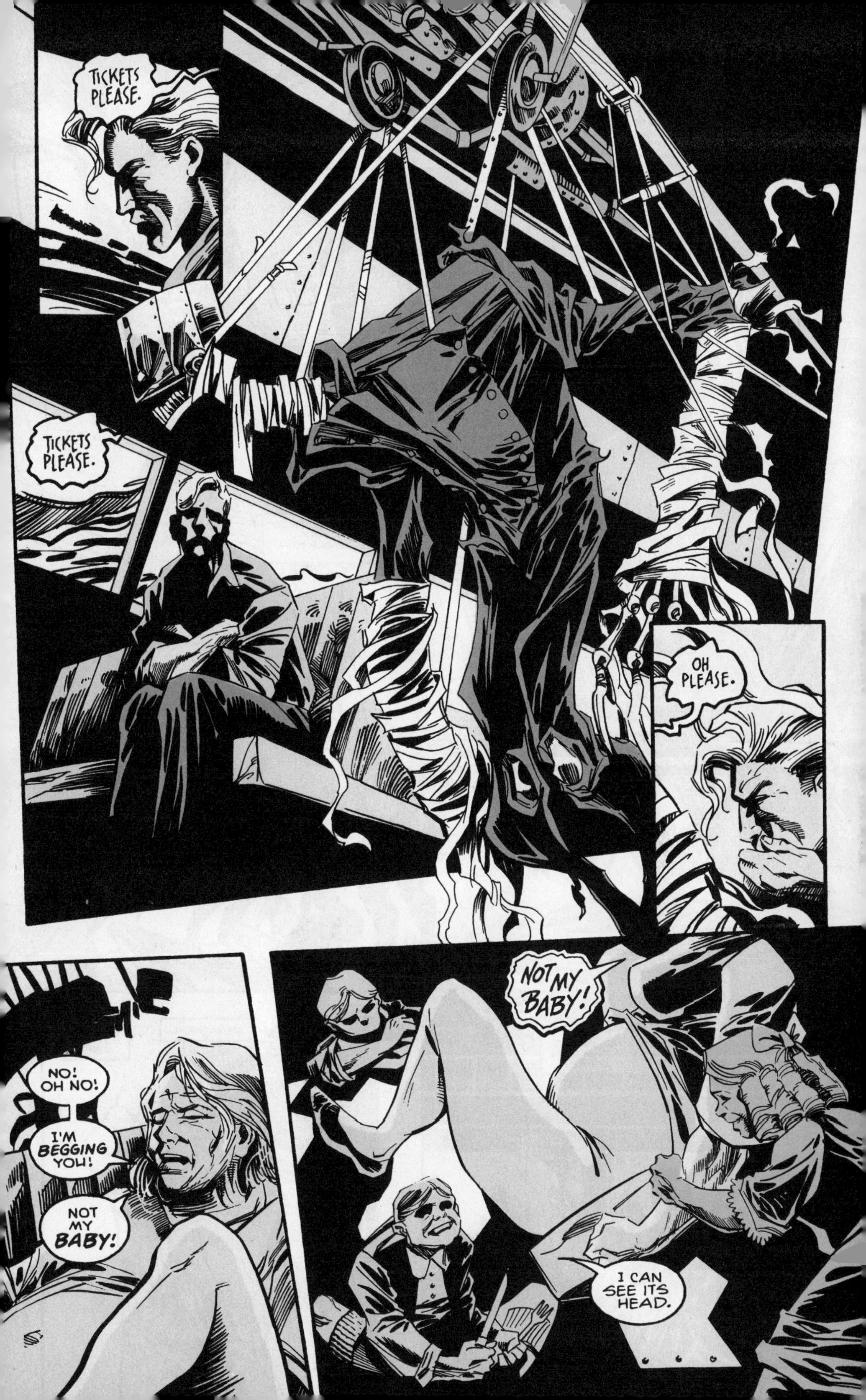
TICKETS PLEASE.
TICKETS PLEASE.
OH PLEASE.
NO! OH NO!
I'M BEGGING YOU!
NOT MY BABY!
NOT MY BABY!
I CAN SEE ITS HEAD.

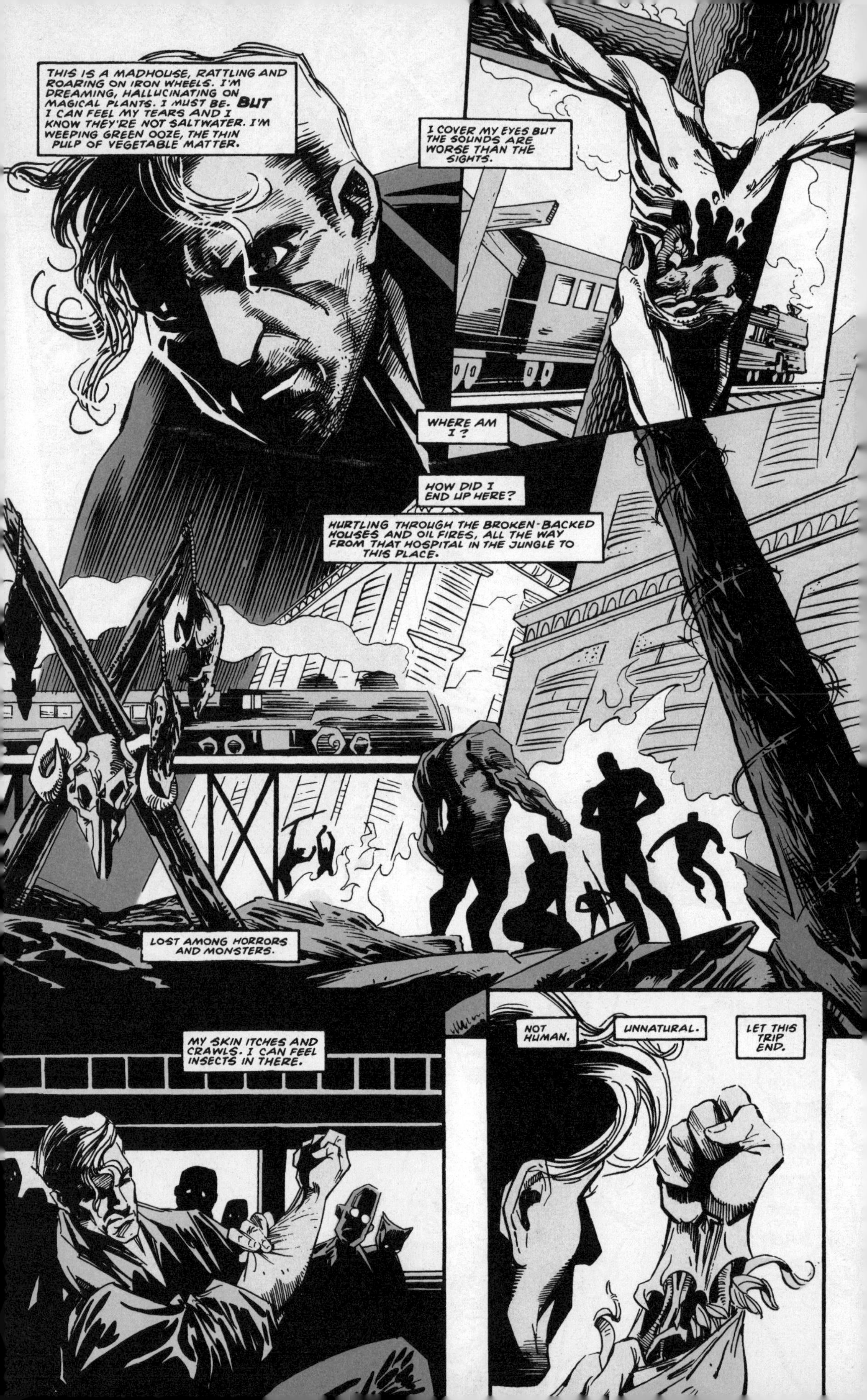
THIS IS A MADHOUSE, RATTLING AND ROARING ON IRON WHEELS. I'M DREAMING, HALLUCINATING ON MAGICAL PLANTS. I MUST BE. BUT I CAN FEEL MY TEARS AND I KNOW THEY'RE NOT SALTWATER. I'M WEEPING GREEN OOZE, THE THIN PULP OF VEGETABLE MATTER.
I COVER MY EYES BUT THE SOUNDS ARE WORSE THAN THE SIGHTS.
WHERE AM I?
HOW DID I END UP HERE?
HURTLING THROUGH THE BROKEN-BACKED HOUSES AND OIL FIRES, ALL THE WAY FROM THAT HOSPITAL IN THE JUNGLE TO THIS PLACE.
LOST AMONG HORRORS AND MONSTERS.
MY SKIN ITCHES AND CRAWLS. I CAN FEEL INSECTS IN THERE.
NOT HUMAN.
UNNATURAL.
LET THIS TRIP END.

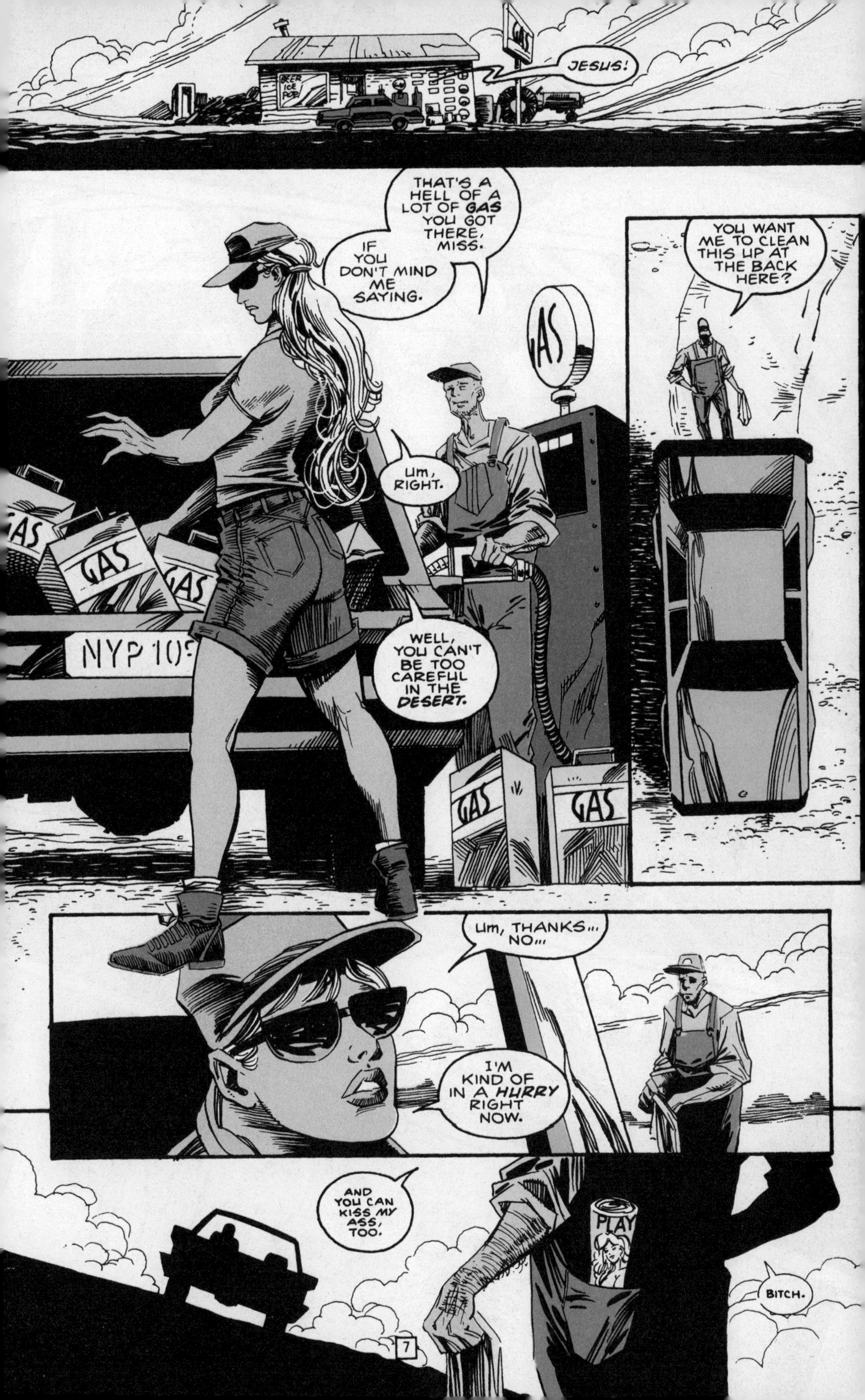
JESUS!
THAT'S A HELL OF A LOT OF GAS YOU GOT THERE, MISS.
IF YOU DON'T MIND ME SAYING.
YOU WANT ME TO CLEAN THIS UP AT THE BACK HERE?
GAS
UM, RIGHT.
GAS
GAS
GAS
NYP 10
WELL, YOU CAN'T BE TOO CAREFUL IN THE DESERT.
GAS
GAS
UM, THANKS... NO...
I'M KIND OF IN A HURRY RIGHT NOW.
AND YOU CAN KISS MY ASS, TOO.
PLAY
BITCH.

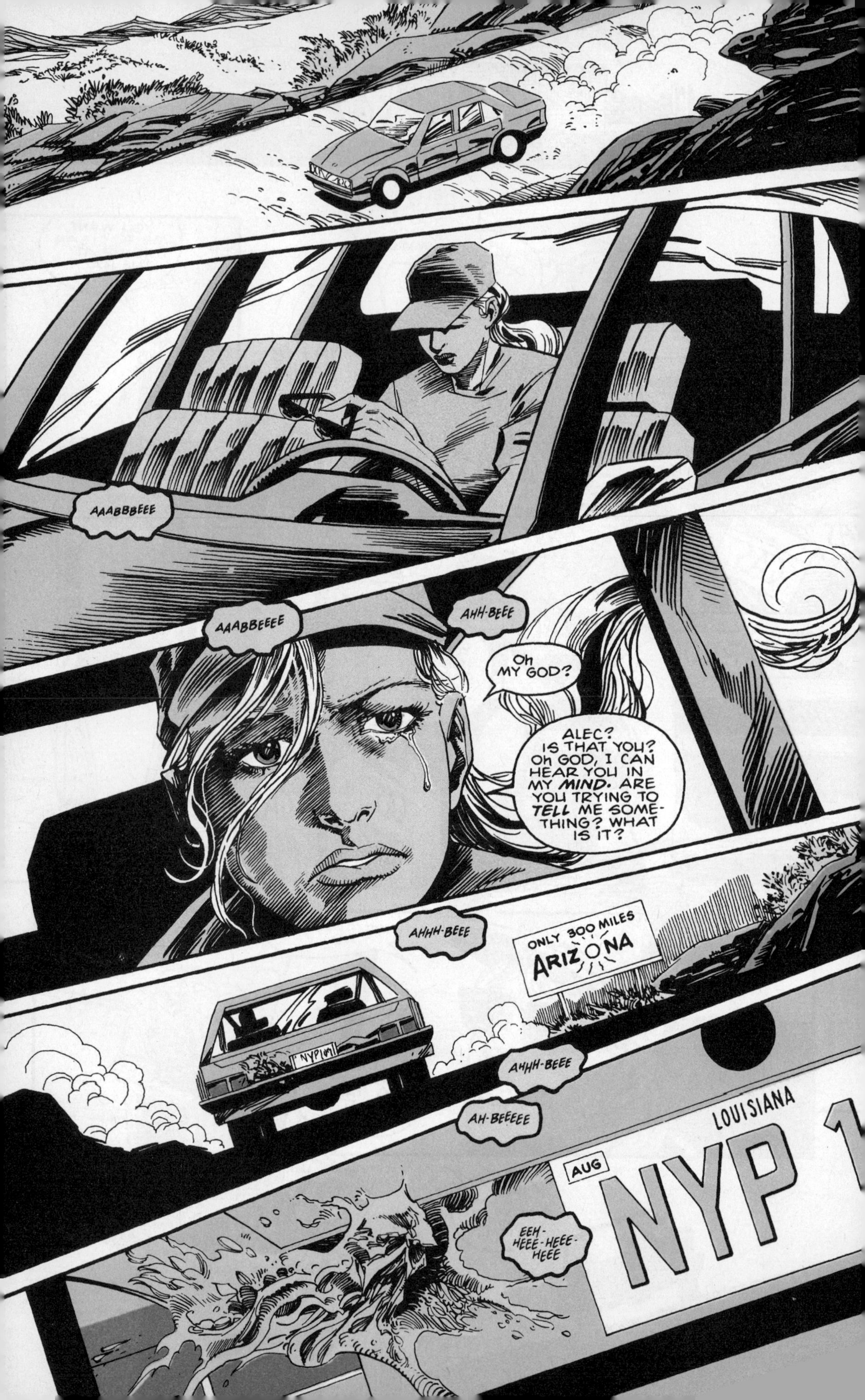
AAABBBEEE
AAABBEEEE
AHH-BEEE
Oh MY GOD?
ALEC? IS THAT YOU? Oh GOD, I CAN HEAR YOU IN MY *MIND.* ARE YOU TRYING TO *TELL* ME SOME-THING? WHAT IS IT?
AHHH-BEEE
ONLY 300 MILES
ARIZONA
AHHH-BEEE
AH-BEEEEE
LOUISIANA
AUG
NYP 1
EEH-HEEE-HEEE-HEEE

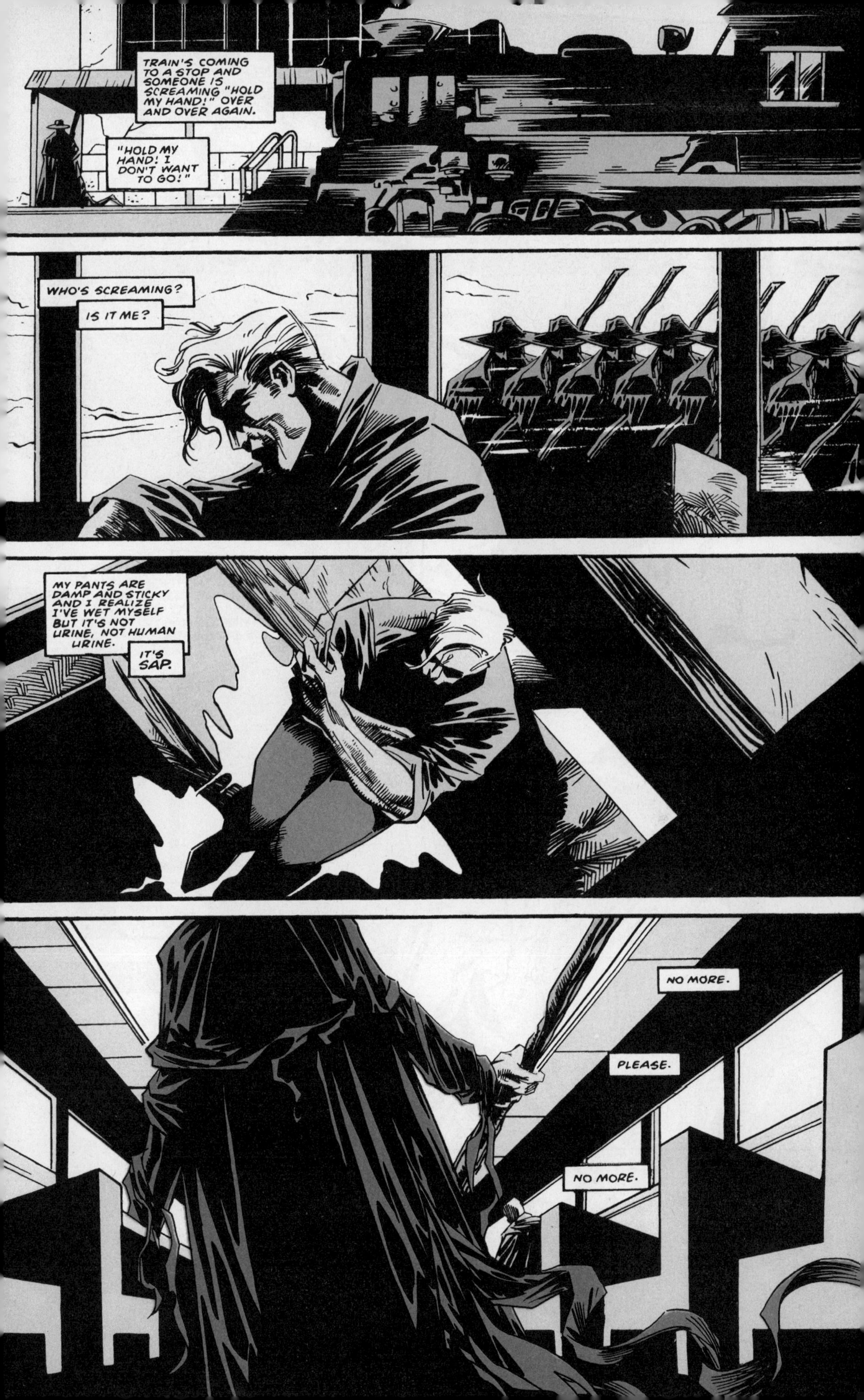
TRAIN'S COMING TO A STOP AND SOMEONE IS SCREAMING "HOLD MY HAND!" OVER AND OVER AGAIN.
"HOLD MY HAND! I DON'T WANT TO GO!"
WHO'S SCREAMING?
IS IT ME?
MY PANTS ARE DAMP AND STICKY AND I REALIZE I'VE WET MYSELF BUT IT'S NOT URINE, NOT HUMAN URINE.
IT'S SAP.
NO MORE.
PLEASE.
NO MORE.

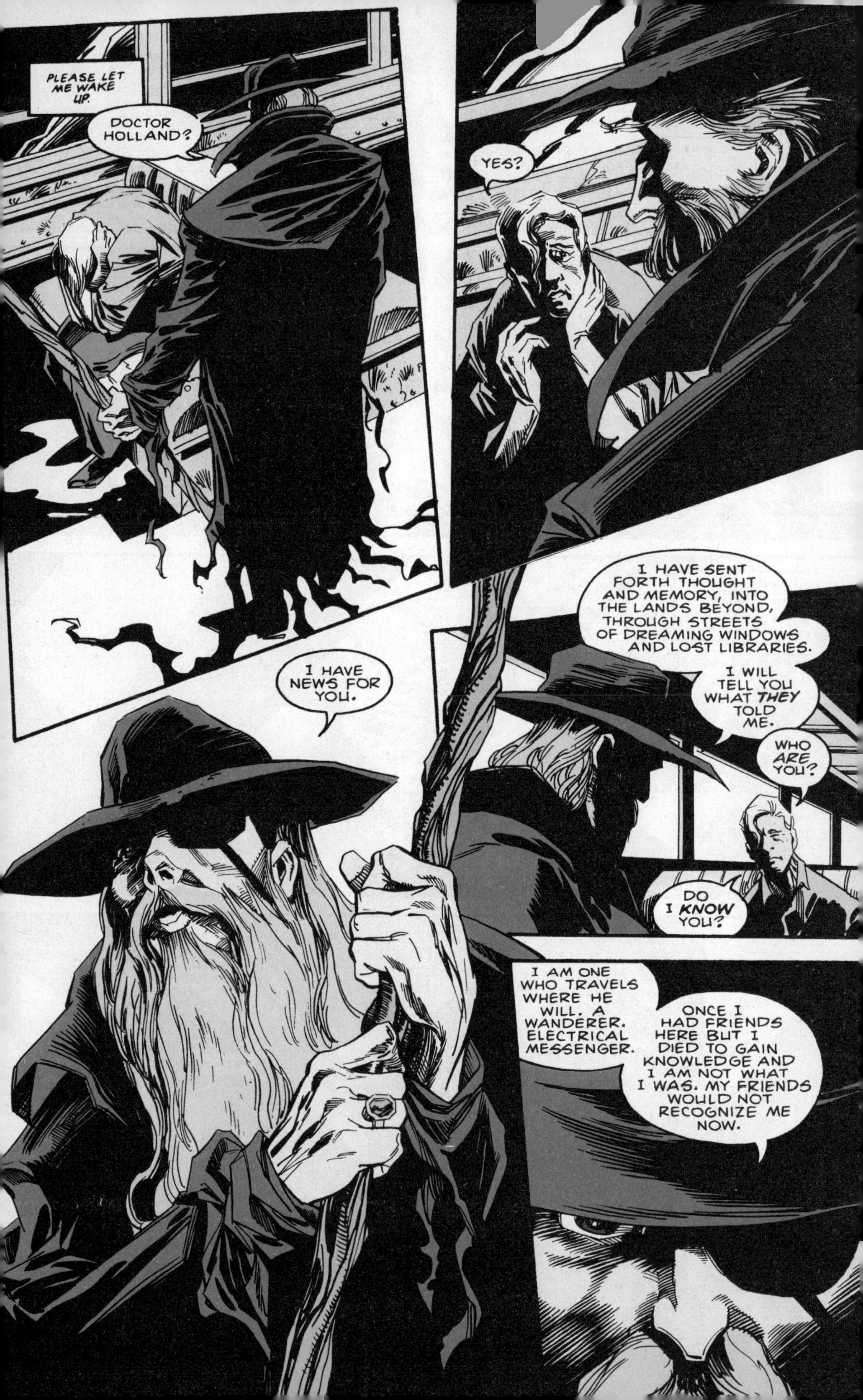

PLEASE LET ME WAKE UP.
DOCTOR HOLLAND?
YES?
I HAVE NEWS FOR YOU.
I HAVE SENT FORTH THOUGHT AND MEMORY, INTO THE LANDS BEYOND, THROUGH STREETS OF DREAMING WINDOWS AND LOST LIBRARIES.
I WILL TELL YOU WHAT THEY TOLD ME.
WHO ARE YOU?
DO I KNOW YOU?
I AM ONE WHO TRAVELS WHERE HE WILL. A WANDERER. ELECTRICAL MESSENGER.
ONCE I HAD FRIENDS HERE BUT I DIED TO GAIN KNOWLEDGE AND I AM NOT WHAT I WAS. MY FRIENDS WOULD NOT RECOGNIZE ME NOW.

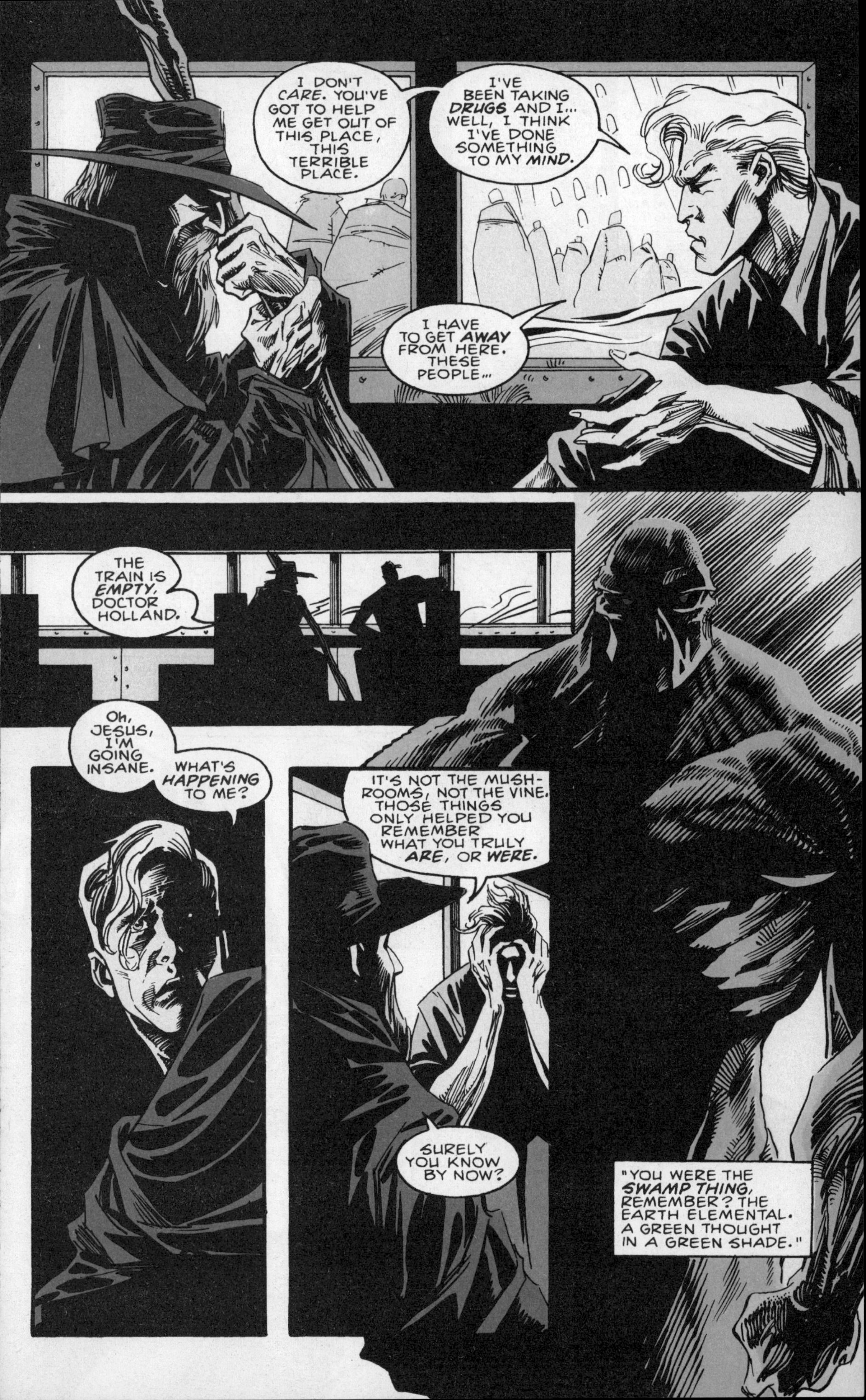
I DON'T CARE. YOU'VE GOT TO HELP ME GET OUT OF THIS PLACE, THIS TERRIBLE PLACE.
I'VE BEEN TAKING DRUGS AND I... WELL, I THINK I'VE DONE SOMETHING TO MY MIND.
I HAVE TO GET AWAY FROM HERE. THESE PEOPLE...
THE TRAIN IS EMPTY, DOCTOR HOLLAND.
Oh, JESUS, I'M GOING INSANE.
WHAT'S HAPPENING TO ME?
IT'S NOT THE MUSH-ROOMS, NOT THE VINE. THOSE THINGS ONLY HELPED YOU REMEMBER WHAT YOU TRULY ARE, OR WERE.
SURELY YOU KNOW BY NOW?
"YOU WERE THE SWAMP THING, REMEMBER? THE EARTH ELEMENTAL. A GREEN THOUGHT IN A GREEN SHADE."

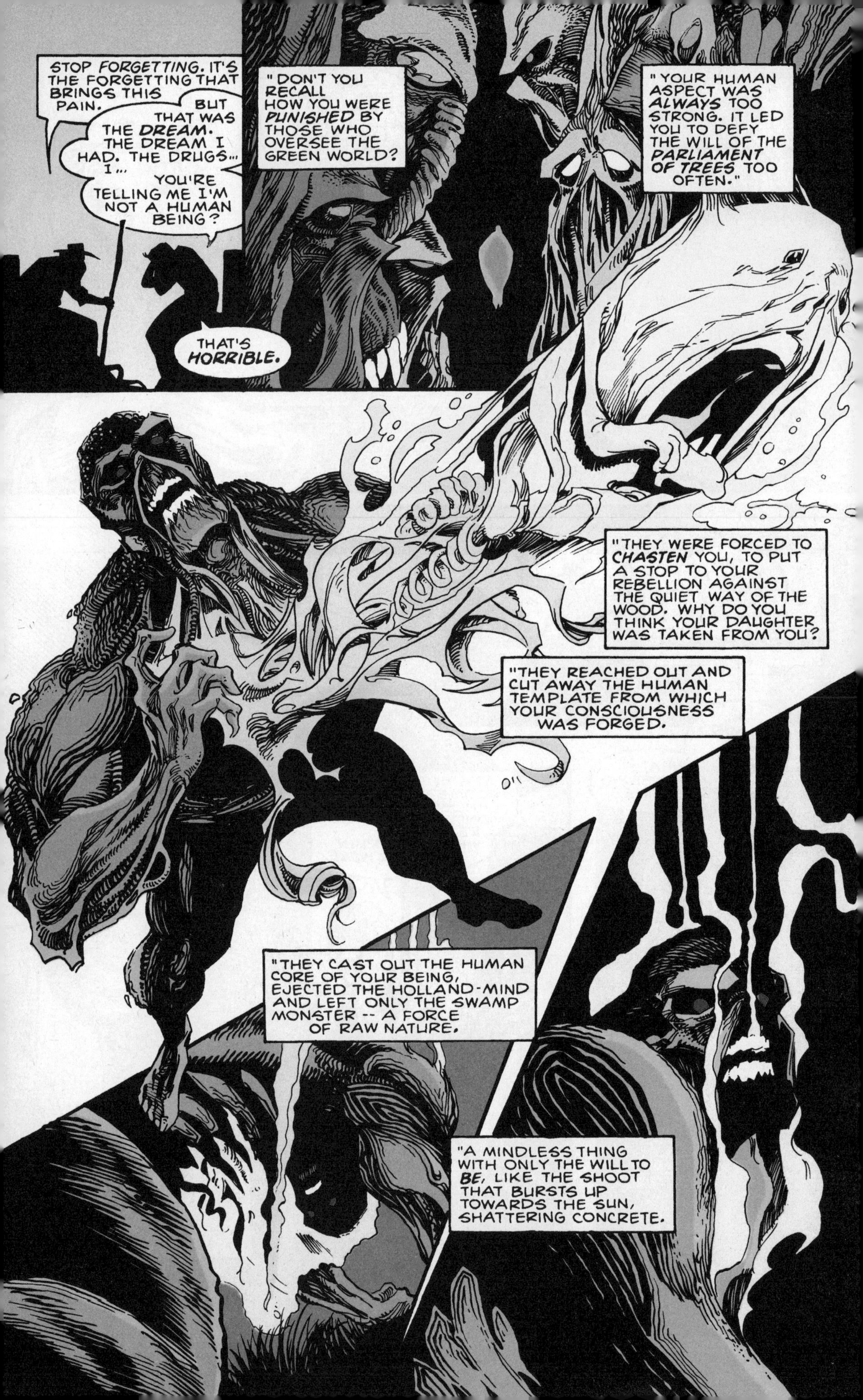
STOP FORGETTING. IT'S THE FORGETTING THAT BRINGS THIS PAIN.
BUT THAT WAS THE DREAM. THE DREAM I HAD. THE DRUGS... I...
YOU'RE TELLING ME I'M NOT A HUMAN BEING?
"DON'T YOU RECALL HOW YOU WERE PUNISHED BY THOSE WHO OVERSEE THE GREEN WORLD?
THAT'S HORRIBLE.
"YOUR HUMAN ASPECT WAS ALWAYS TOO STRONG. IT LED YOU TO DEFY THE WILL OF THE PARLIAMENT OF TREES TOO OFTEN."
"THEY WERE FORCED TO CHASTEN YOU, TO PUT A STOP TO YOUR REBELLION AGAINST THE QUIET WAY OF THE WOOD. WHY DO YOU THINK YOUR DAUGHTER WAS TAKEN FROM YOU?
"THEY REACHED OUT AND CUT AWAY THE HUMAN TEMPLATE FROM WHICH YOUR CONSCIOUSNESS WAS FORGED.
"THEY CAST OUT THE HUMAN CORE OF YOUR BEING, EJECTED THE HOLLAND-MIND AND LEFT ONLY THE SWAMP MONSTER -- A FORCE OF RAW NATURE.
"A MINDLESS THING WITH ONLY THE WILL TO BE, LIKE THE SHOOT THAT BURSTS UP TOWARDS THE SUN, SHATTERING CONCRETE.

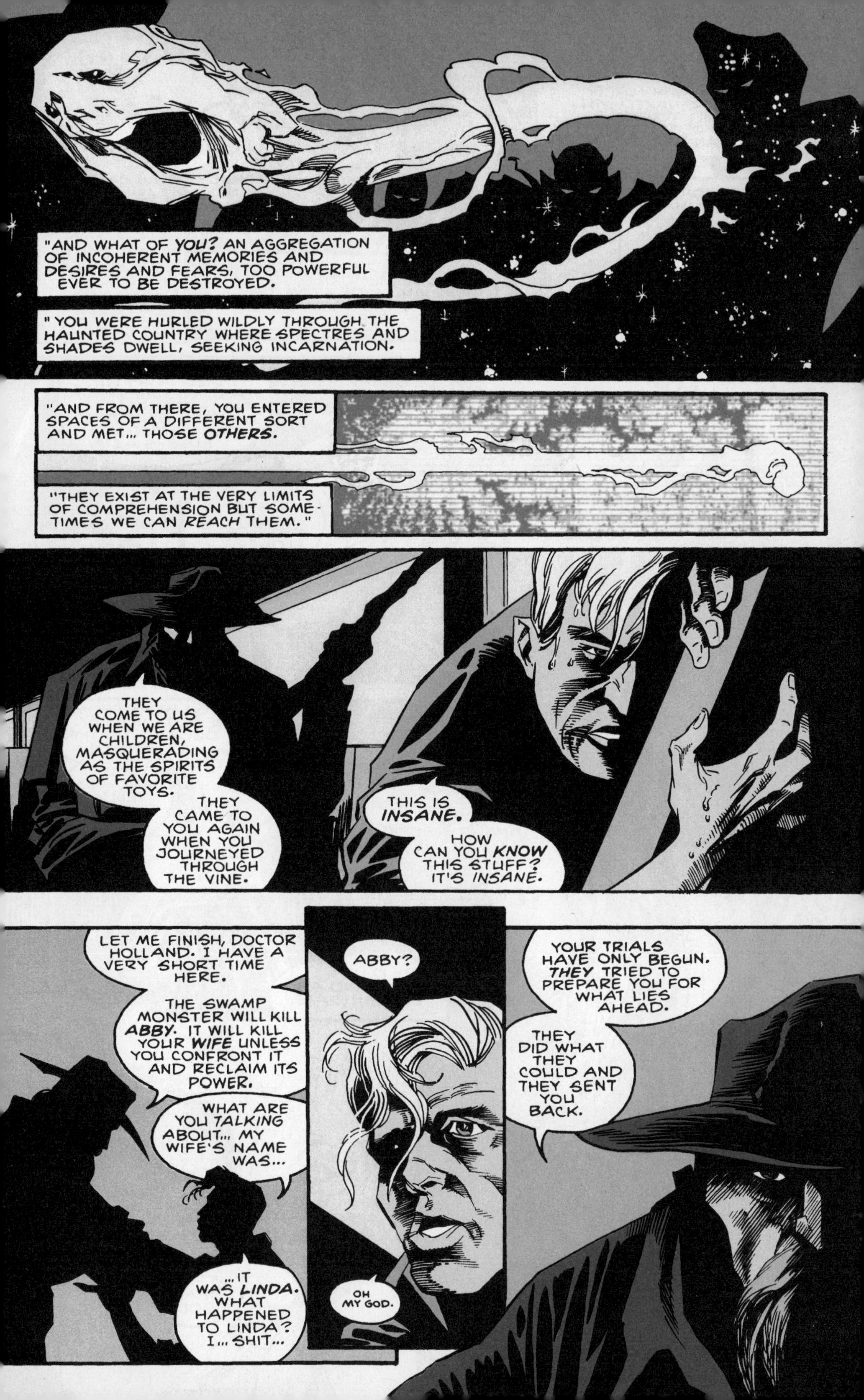
"AND WHAT OF YOU? AN AGGREGATION OF INCOHERENT MEMORIES AND DESIRES AND FEARS, TOO POWERFUL EVER TO BE DESTROYED.
"YOU WERE HURLED WILDLY THROUGH THE HAUNTED COUNTRY WHERE SPECTRES AND SHADES DWELL, SEEKING INCARNATION.
"AND FROM THERE, YOU ENTERED SPACES OF A DIFFERENT SORT AND MET... THOSE OTHERS.
"THEY EXIST AT THE VERY LIMITS OF COMPREHENSION BUT SOMETIMES WE CAN REACH THEM."
THEY COME TO US WHEN WE ARE CHILDREN, MASQUERADING AS THE SPIRITS OF FAVORITE TOYS.
THEY CAME TO YOU AGAIN WHEN YOU JOURNEYED THROUGH THE VINE.
THIS IS INSANE.
HOW CAN YOU KNOW THIS STUFF? IT'S INSANE.
LET ME FINISH, DOCTOR HOLLAND. I HAVE A VERY SHORT TIME HERE.
THE SWAMP MONSTER WILL KILL ABBY. IT WILL KILL YOUR WIFE UNLESS YOU CONFRONT IT AND RECLAIM ITS POWER.
WHAT ARE YOU TALKING ABOUT... MY WIFE'S NAME WAS...
...IT WAS LINDA. WHAT HAPPENED TO LINDA? I... SHIT...
ABBY?
OH MY GOD.
YOUR TRIALS HAVE ONLY BEGUN. THEY TRIED TO PREPARE YOU FOR WHAT LIES AHEAD.
THEY DID WHAT THEY COULD AND THEY SENT YOU BACK.

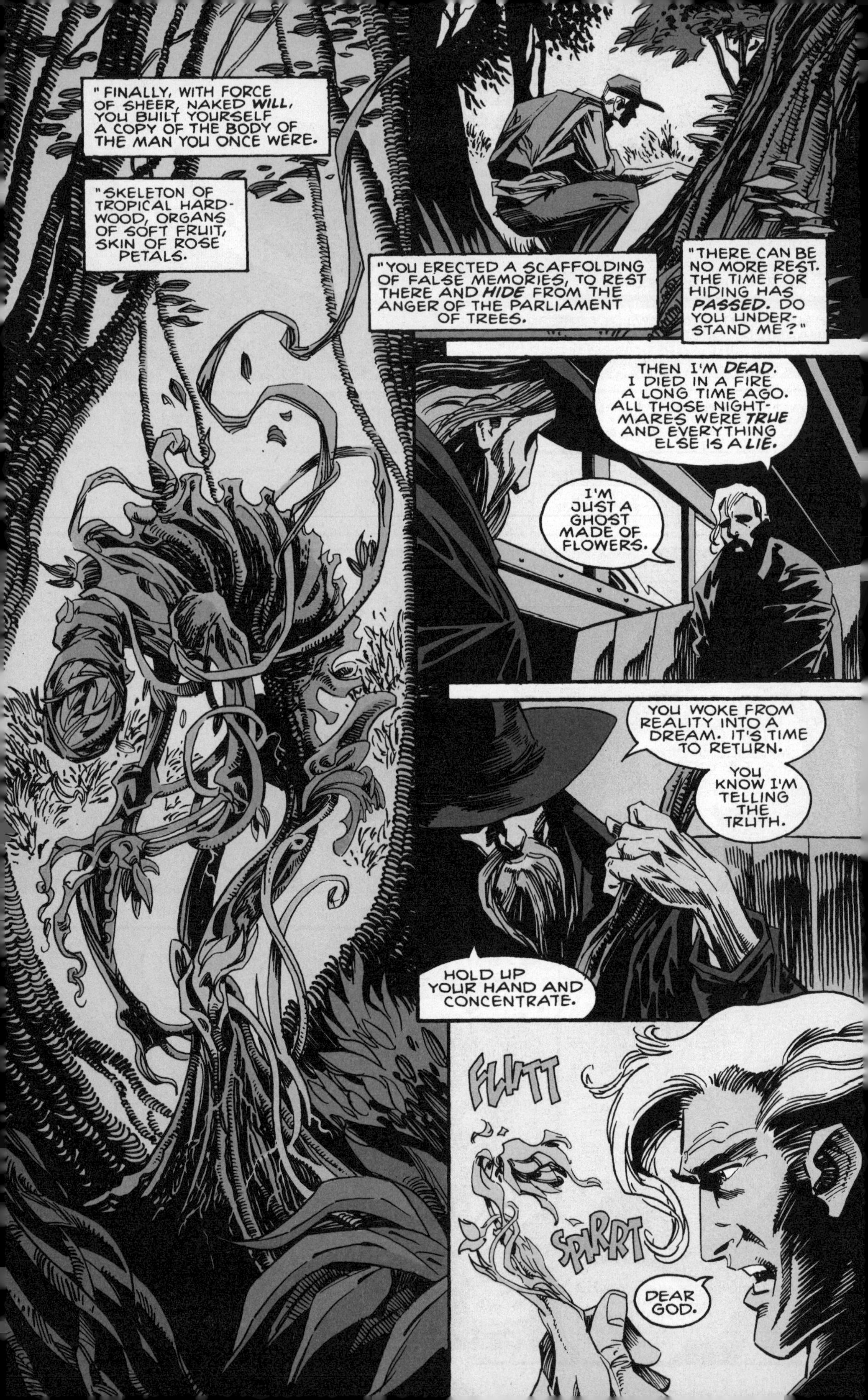
"FINALLY, WITH FORCE OF SHEER, NAKED WILL, YOU BUILT YOURSELF A COPY OF THE BODY OF THE MAN YOU ONCE WERE.
"SKELETON OF TROPICAL HARD-WOOD, ORGANS OF SOFT FRUIT, SKIN OF ROSE PETALS.
"YOU ERECTED A SCAFFOLDING OF FALSE MEMORIES, TO REST THERE AND HIDE FROM THE ANGER OF THE PARLIAMENT OF TREES.
"THERE CAN BE NO MORE REST. THE TIME FOR HIDING HAS PASSED. DO YOU UNDER-STAND ME?"
THEN I'M DEAD. I DIED IN A FIRE A LONG TIME AGO. ALL THOSE NIGHT-MARES WERE TRUE AND EVERYTHING ELSE IS A LIE.
I'M JUST A GHOST MADE OF FLOWERS.
YOU WOKE FROM REALITY INTO A DREAM. IT'S TIME TO RETURN.
YOU KNOW I'M TELLING THE TRUTH.
HOLD UP YOUR HAND AND CONCENTRATE.
FLUTT
SPIRRT
DEAR GOD.

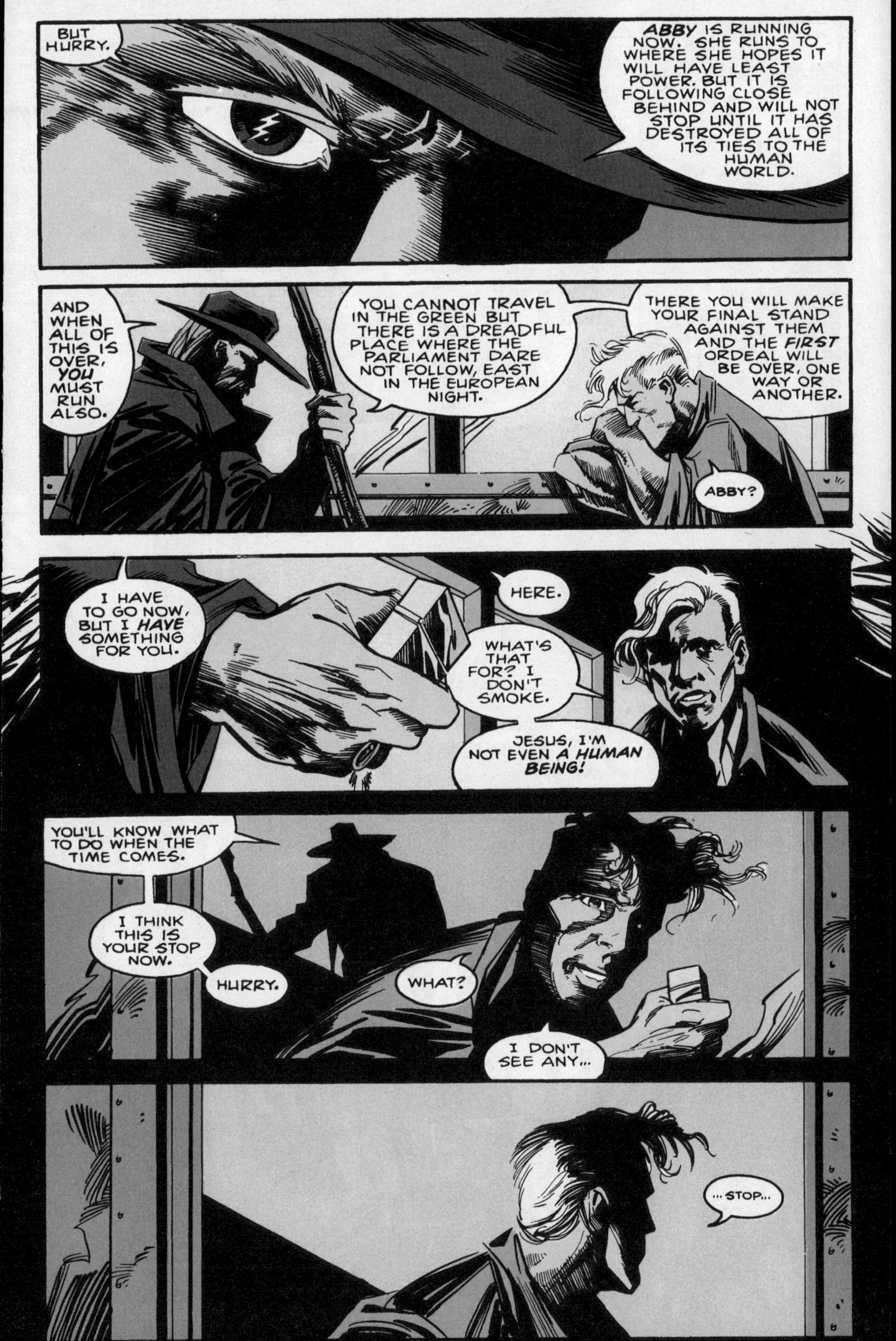
BUT HURRY.
ABBY IS RUNNING NOW. SHE RUNS TO WHERE SHE HOPES IT WILL HAVE LEAST POWER. BUT IT IS FOLLOWING CLOSE BEHIND AND WILL NOT STOP UNTIL IT HAS DESTROYED ALL OF ITS TIES TO THE HUMAN WORLD.
AND WHEN ALL OF THIS IS OVER, YOU MUST RUN ALSO.
YOU CANNOT TRAVEL IN THE GREEN BUT THERE IS A DREADFUL PLACE WHERE THE PARLIAMENT DARE NOT FOLLOW, EAST IN THE EUROPEAN NIGHT.
THERE YOU WILL MAKE YOUR FINAL STAND AGAINST THEM AND THE FIRST ORDEAL WILL BE OVER, ONE WAY OR ANOTHER.
ABBY?
I HAVE TO GO NOW, BUT I HAVE SOMETHING FOR YOU.
HERE.
WHAT'S THAT FOR? I DON'T SMOKE.
JESUS, I'M NOT EVEN A HUMAN BEING!
YOU'LL KNOW WHAT TO DO WHEN THE TIME COMES.
I THINK THIS IS YOUR STOP NOW.
HURRY.
WHAT?
I DON'T SEE ANY...
...STOP...

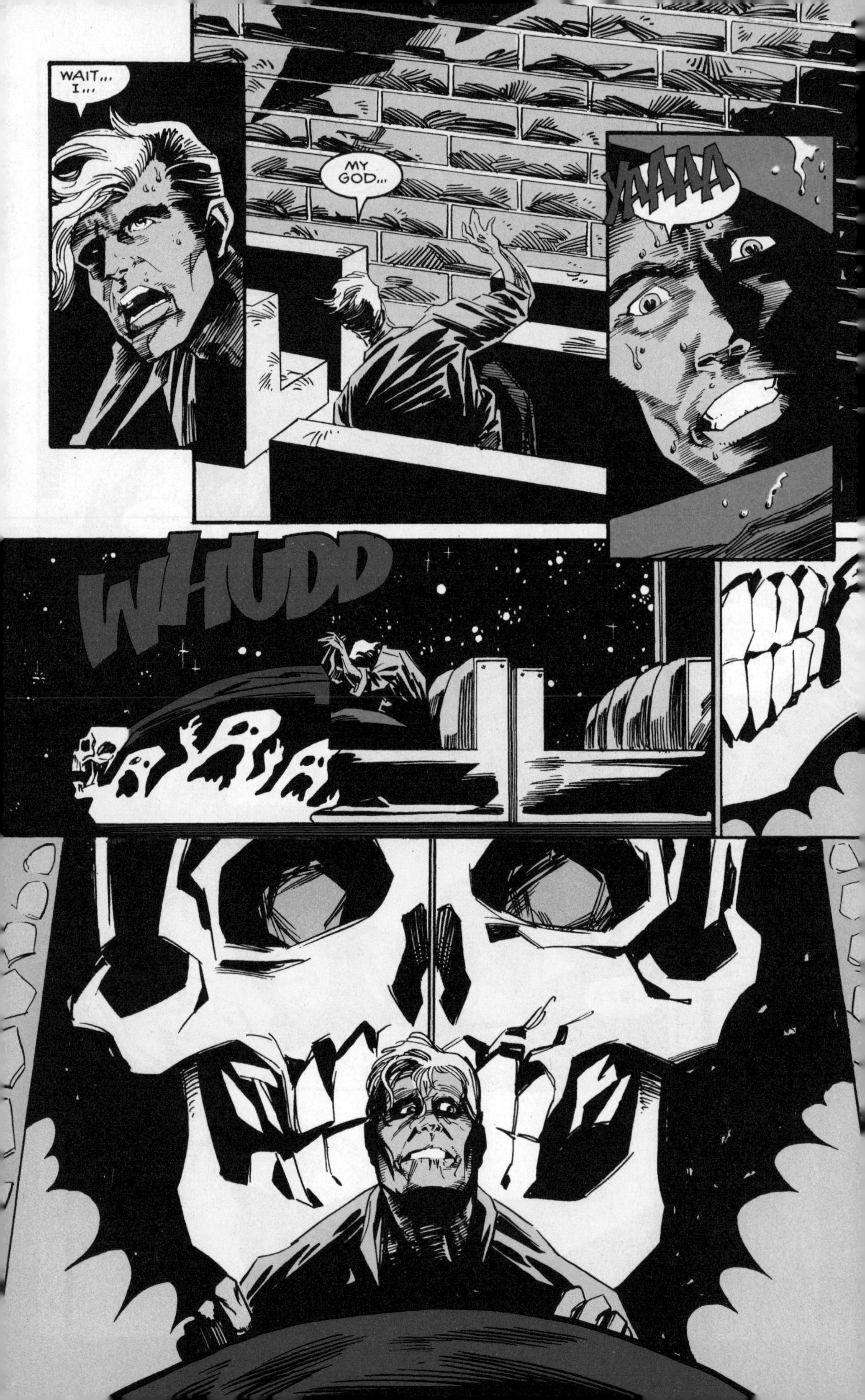
WAIT... I...
MY GOD...
YAAAAA
WHUDD

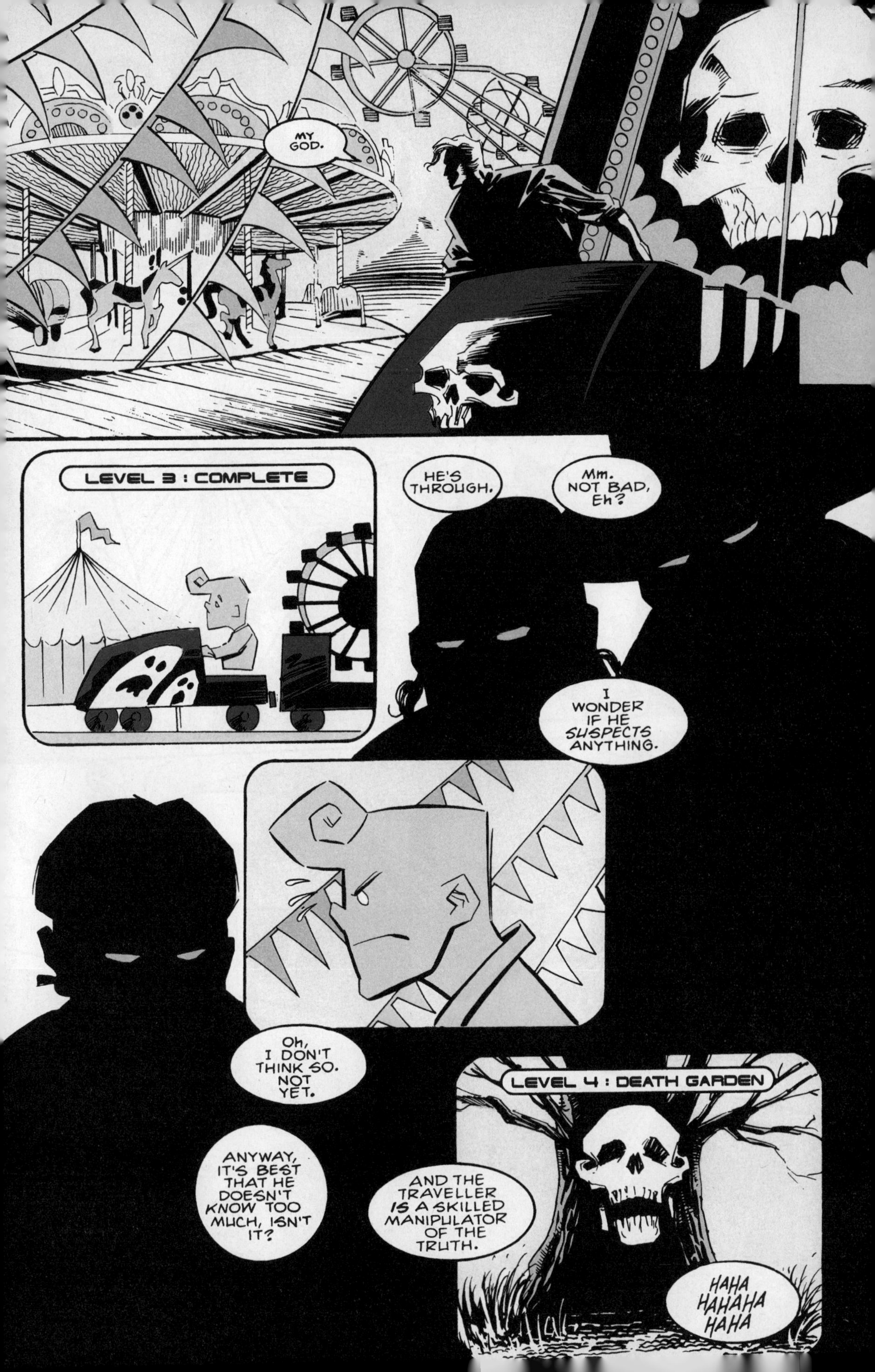
MY GOD.
LEVEL 3 : COMPLETE
HE'S THROUGH.
Mm. NOT BAD, Eh?
I WONDER IF HE SUSPECTS ANYTHING.
Oh, I DON'T THINK SO. NOT YET.
ANYWAY, IT'S BEST THAT HE DOESN'T KNOW TOO MUCH, ISN'T IT?
AND THE TRAVELLER IS A SKILLED MANIPULATOR OF THE TRUTH.
LEVEL 4 : DEATH GARDEN
HAHA HAHAHA HAHA

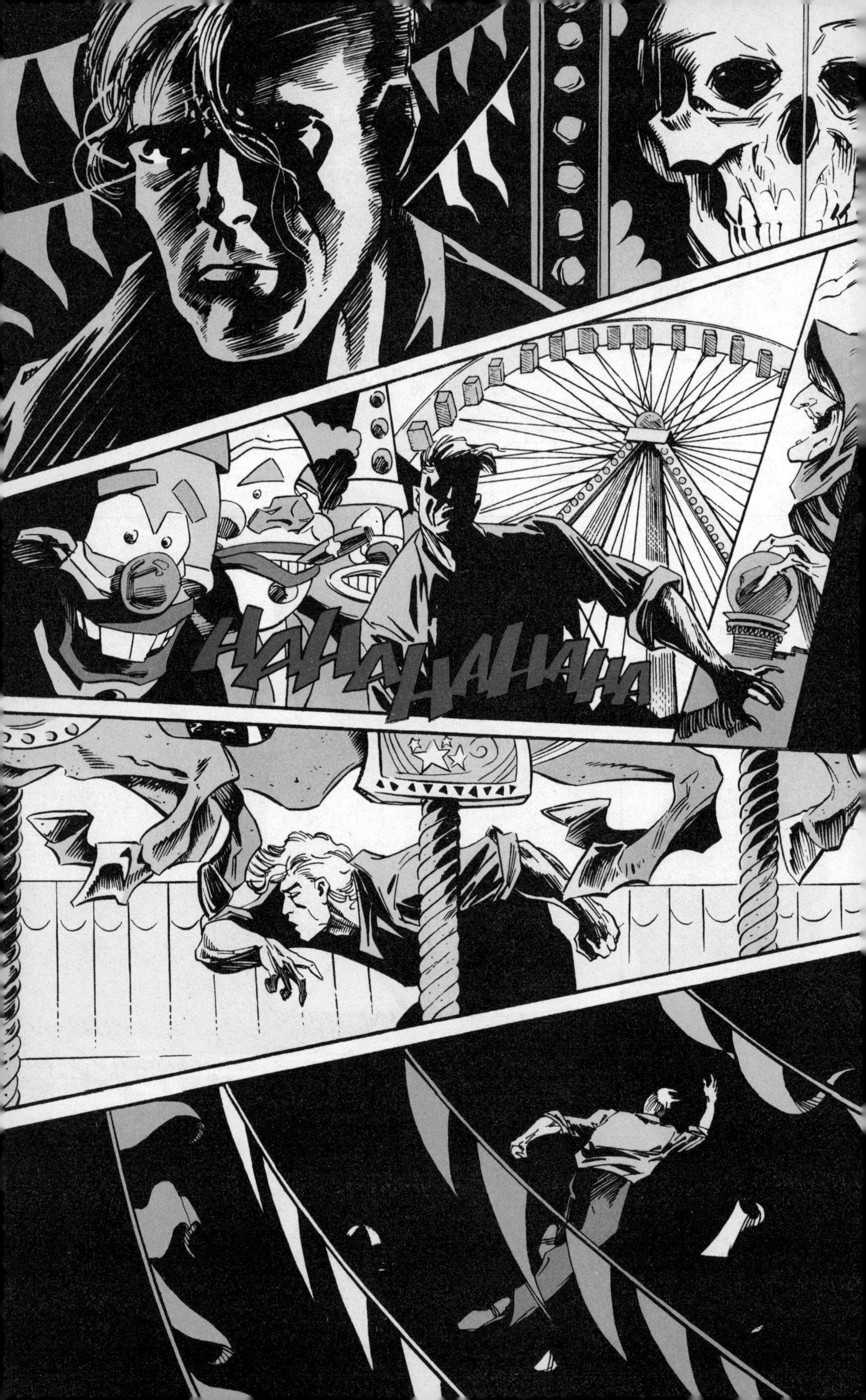
HAHAHAHAHAHA

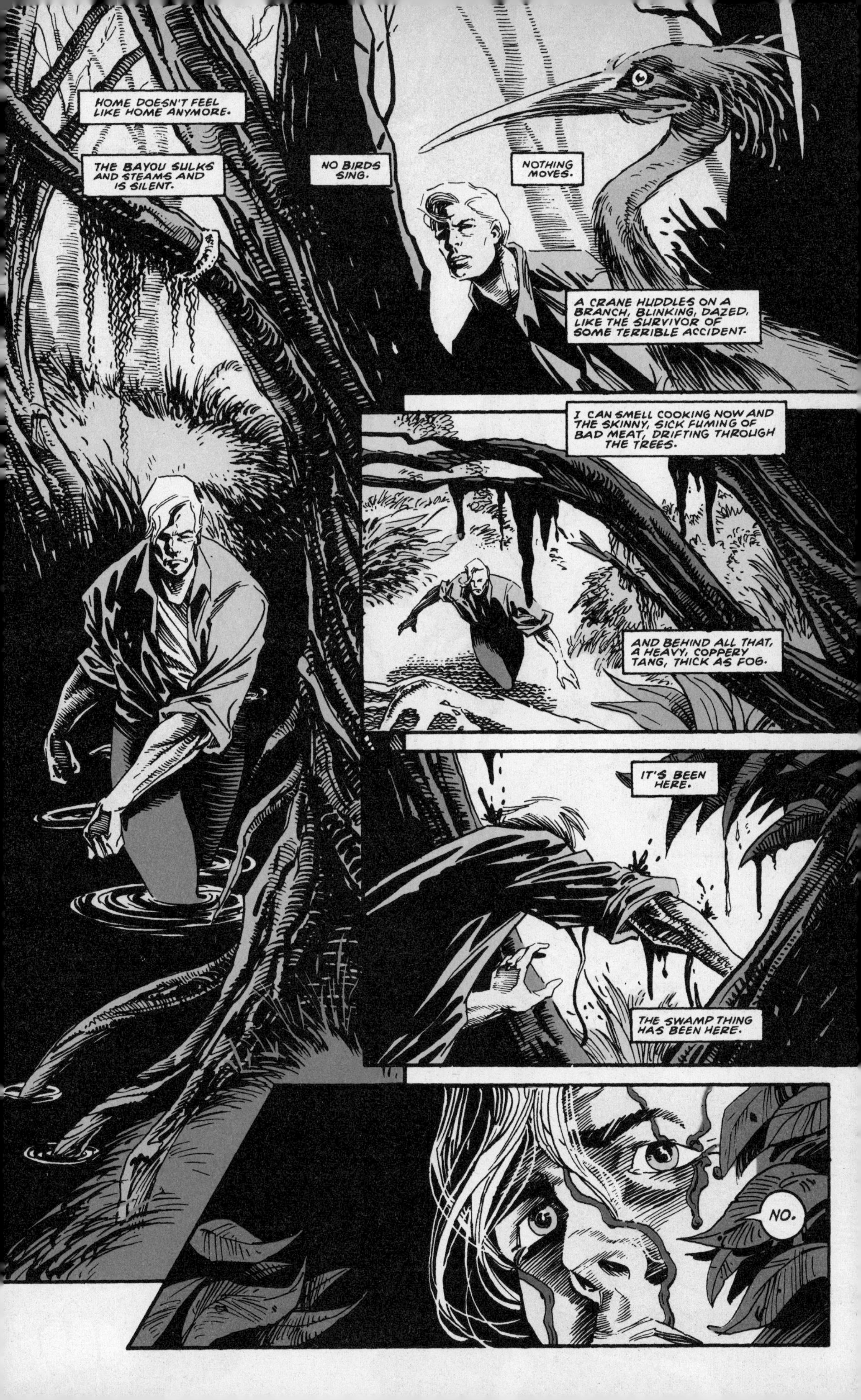
HOME DOESN'T FEEL LIKE HOME ANYMORE.
THE BAYOU SULKS AND STEAMS AND IS SILENT.
NO BIRDS SING.
NOTHING MOVES.
A CRANE HUDDLES ON A BRANCH, BLINKING, DAZED, LIKE THE SURVIVOR OF SOME TERRIBLE ACCIDENT.
I CAN SMELL COOKING NOW AND THE SKINNY, SICK FUMING OF BAD MEAT, DRIFTING THROUGH THE TREES.
AND BEHIND ALL THAT, A HEAVY, COPPERY TANG, THICK AS FOG.
IT'S BEEN HERE.
THE SWAMP THING HAS BEEN HERE.
NO.

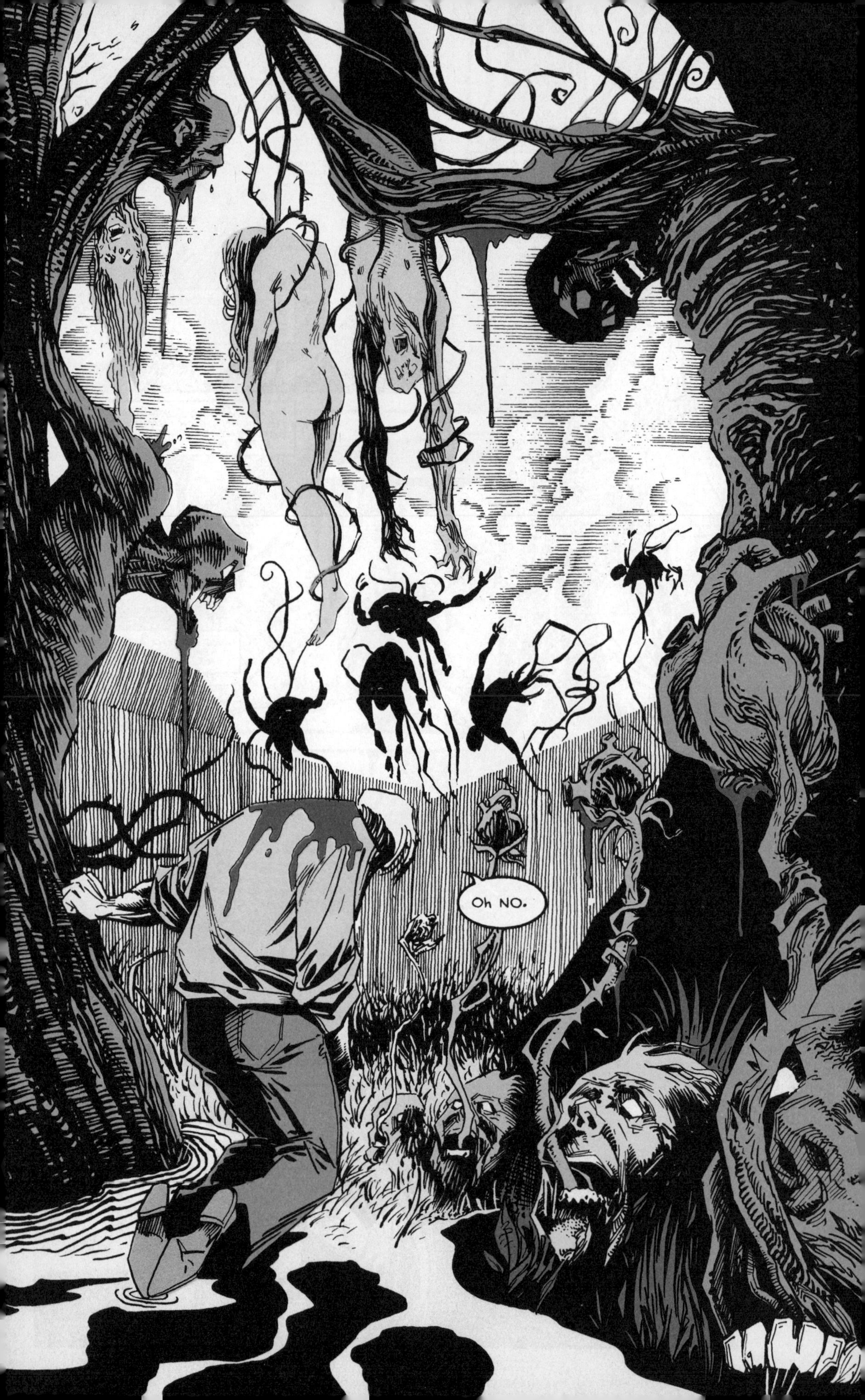
Oh NO.

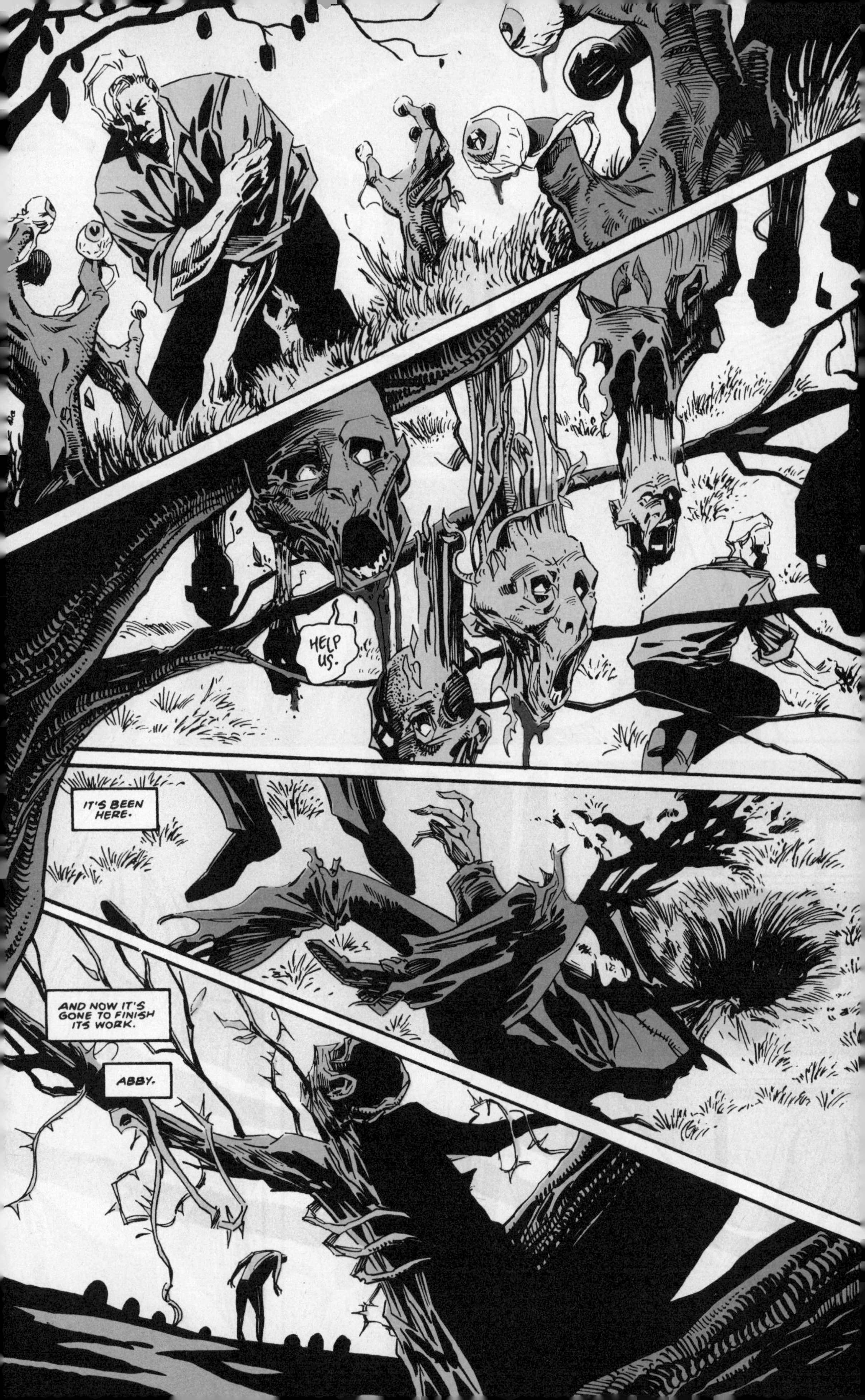
HELP US.
IT'S BEEN HERE.
AND NOW IT'S GONE TO FINISH ITS WORK.
ABBY.

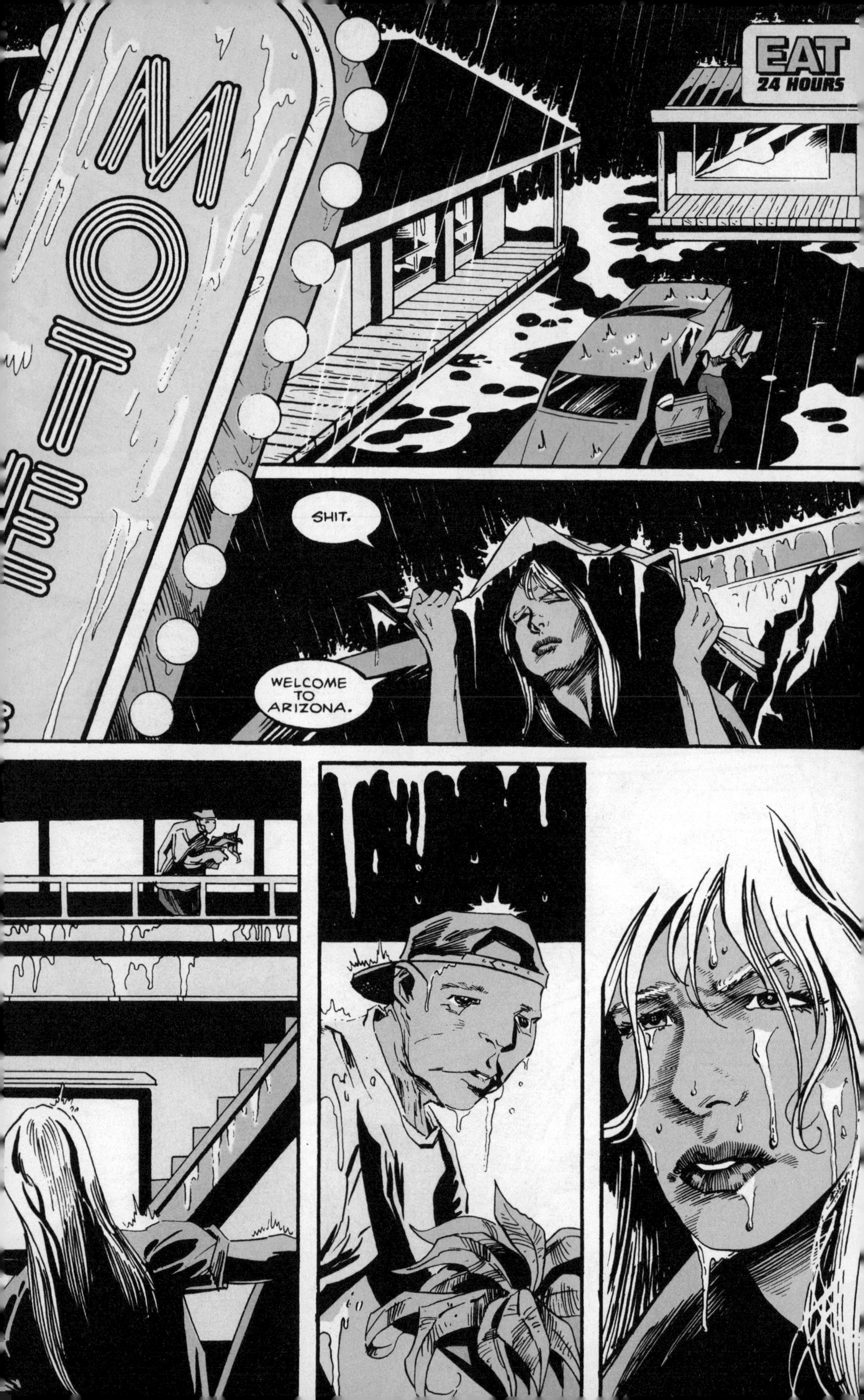
MOTEL
EAT
24 HOURS
SHIT.
WELCOME TO ARIZONA.

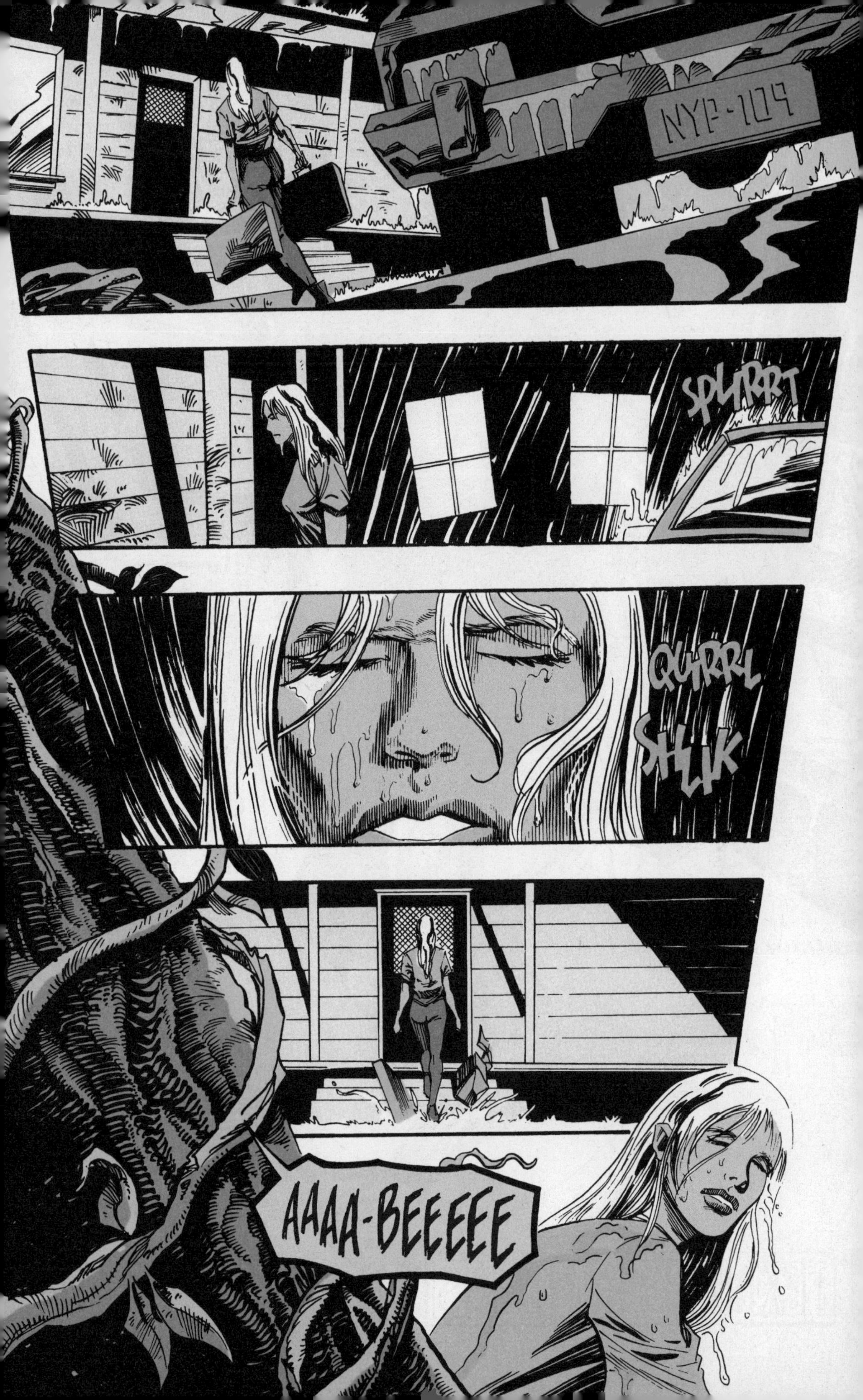
NYP-109
SPLRRRT
QURRRL
SHLIK
AAAA-BEEEEE

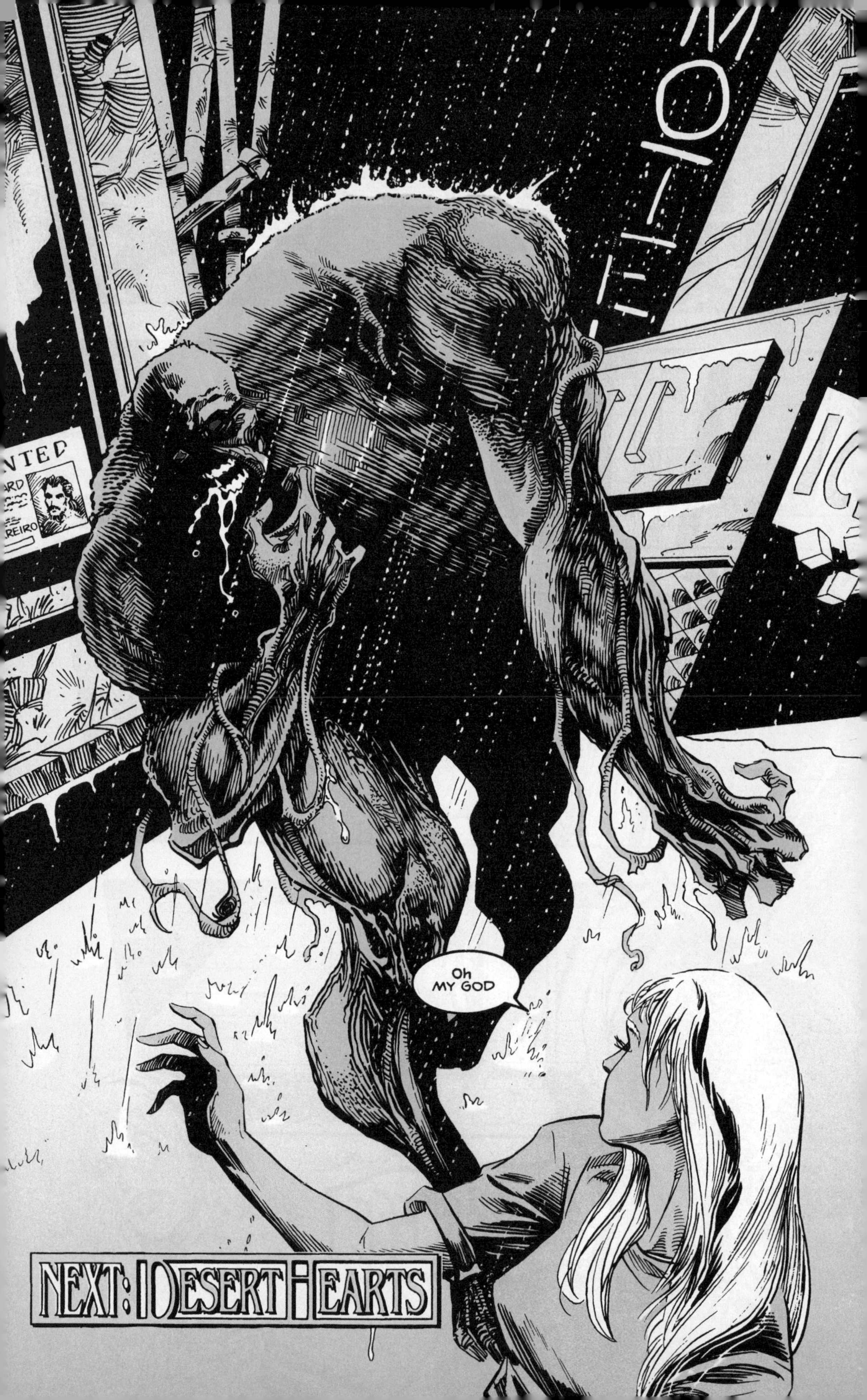
Oh MY GOD
NEXT: DESERT HEARTS

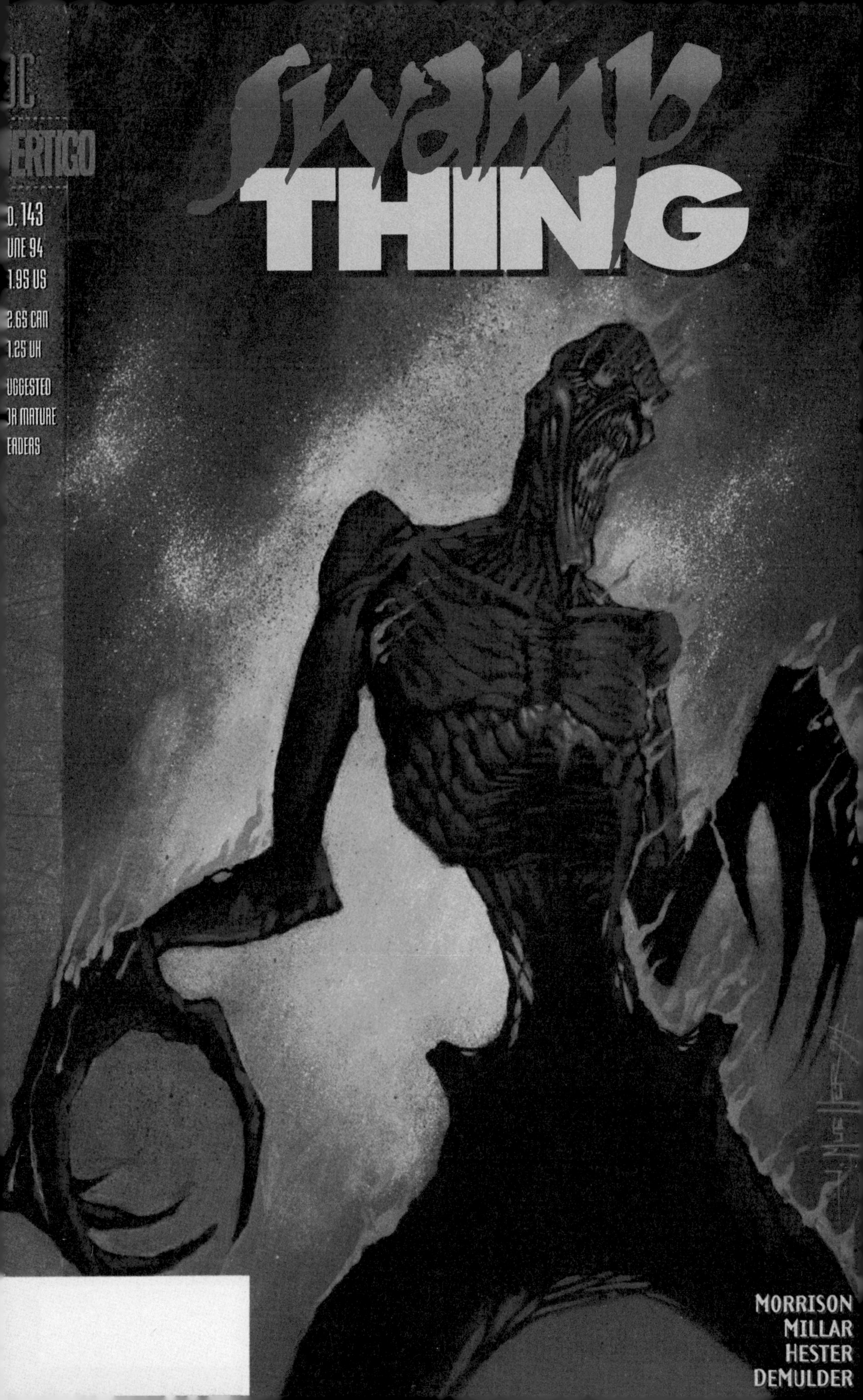
Swamp
THING
MORRISON
MILLAR
HESTER
DEMULDER

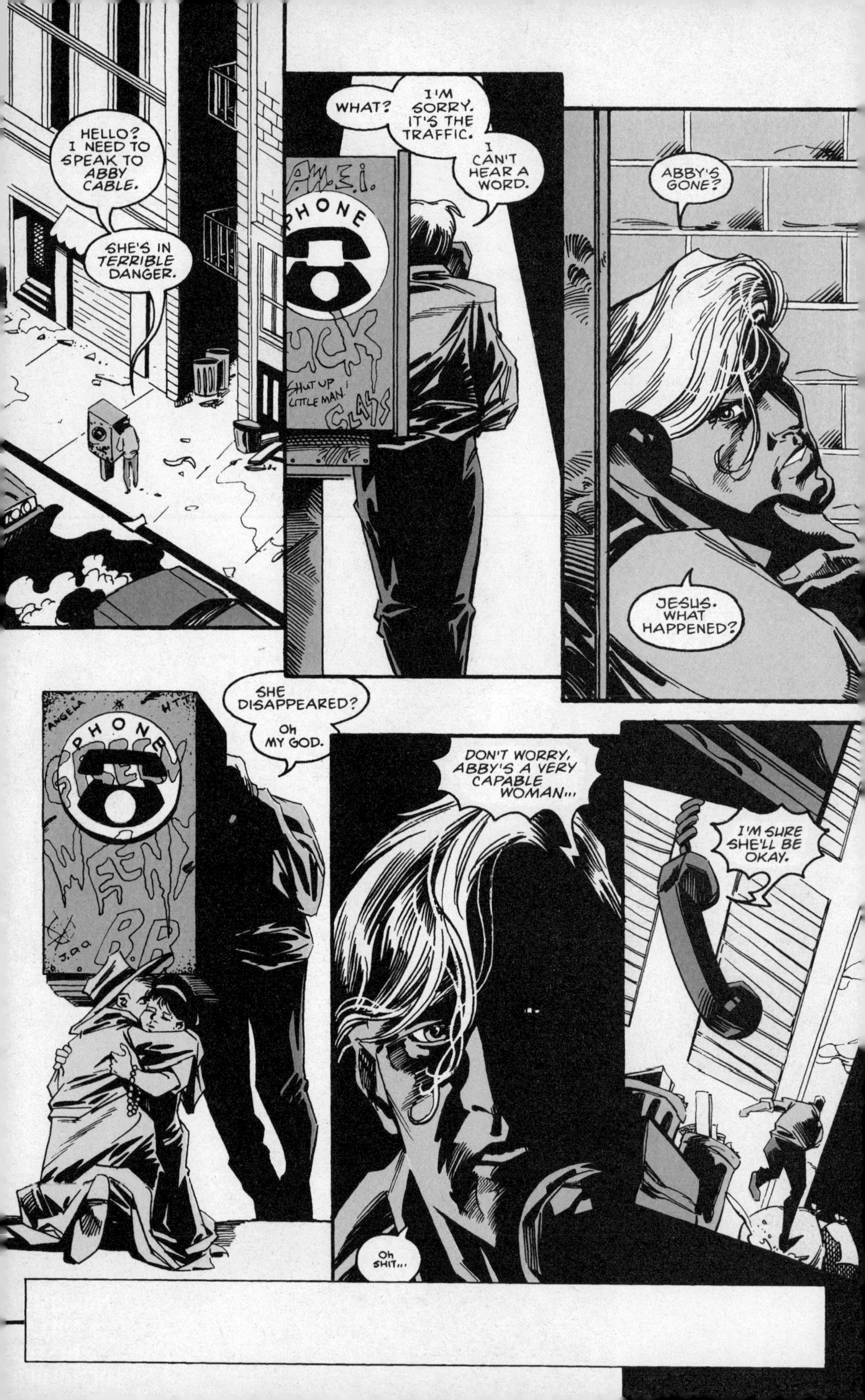
HELLO? I NEED TO SPEAK TO ABBY CABLE.
SHE'S IN TERRIBLE DANGER.
WHAT?
I'M SORRY. IT'S THE TRAFFIC.
I CAN'T HEAR A WORD.
PHONE
SHUT UP LITTLE MAN!
ABBY'S GONE?
JESUS. WHAT HAPPENED?
SHE DISAPPEARED?
Oh MY GOD.
PHONE
DON'T WORRY, ABBY'S A VERY CAPABLE WOMAN...
I'M SURE SHE'LL BE OKAY.
Oh SHIT...

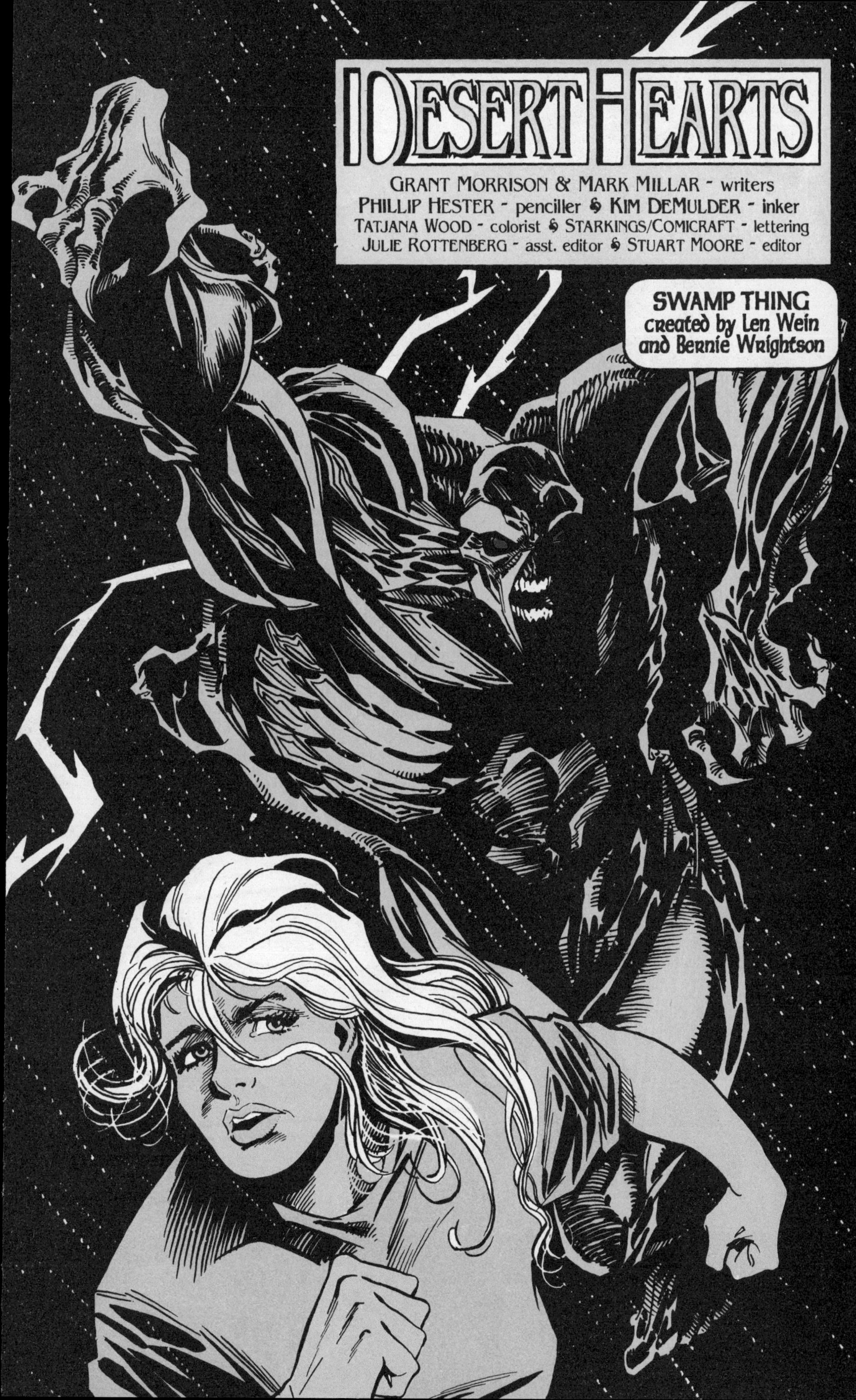
DESERT HEARTS
GRANT MORRISON & MARK MILLAR - writers
PHILLIP HESTER - penciller & KIM DEMULDER - inker
TATJANA WOOD - colorist & STARKINGS/COMICRAFT - lettering
JULIE ROTTENBERG - asst. editor & STUART MOORE - editor
SWAMP THING created by Len Wein and Bernie Wrightson

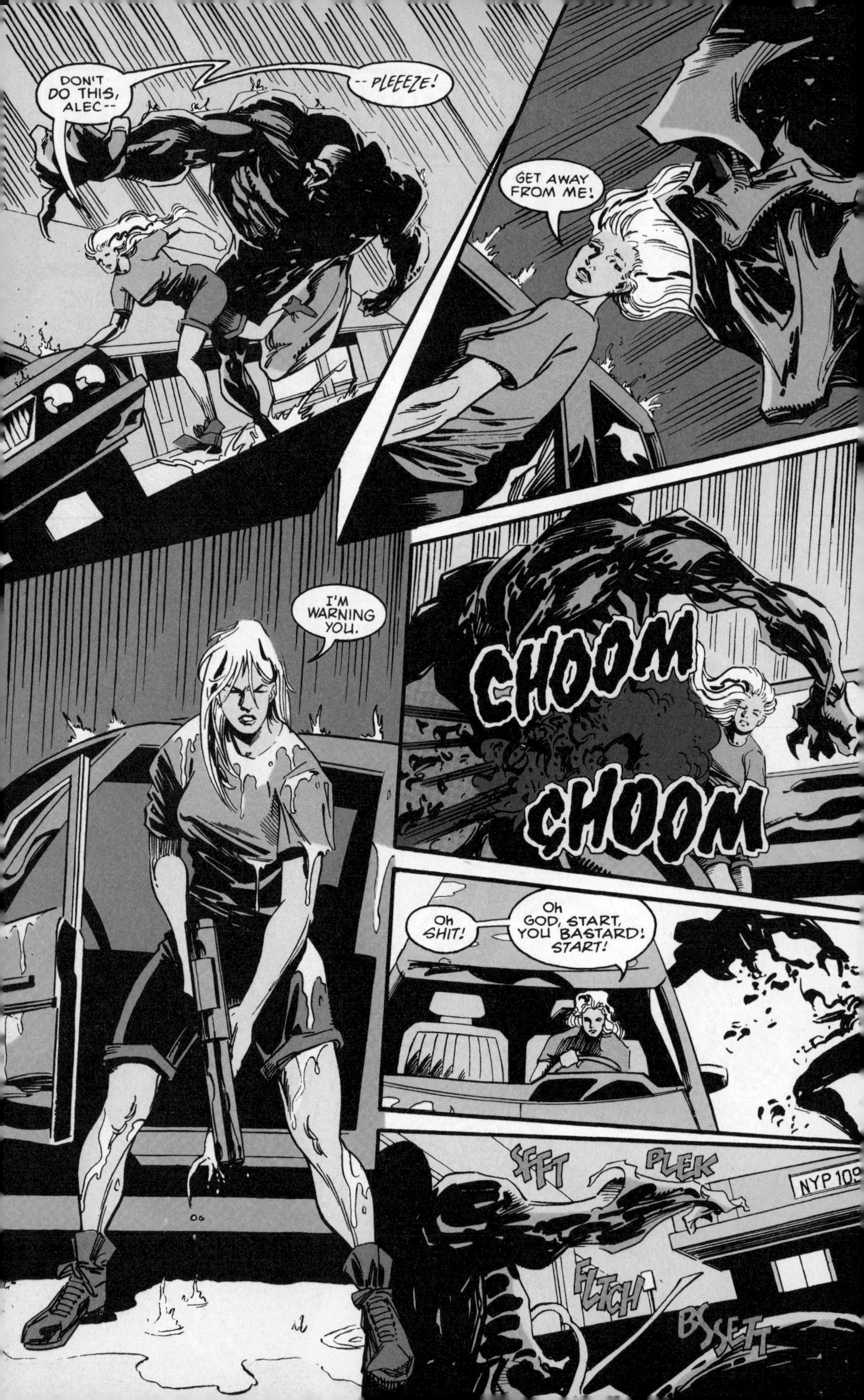
DON'T DO THIS, ALEC--
-- PLEEEZE!
GET AWAY FROM ME!
I'M WARNING YOU.
CHOOM
CHOOM
Oh SHIT!
Oh GOD, START, YOU BASTARD! START!
SFFT
PLEK
NYP 109
FLTCH
BSSEFT

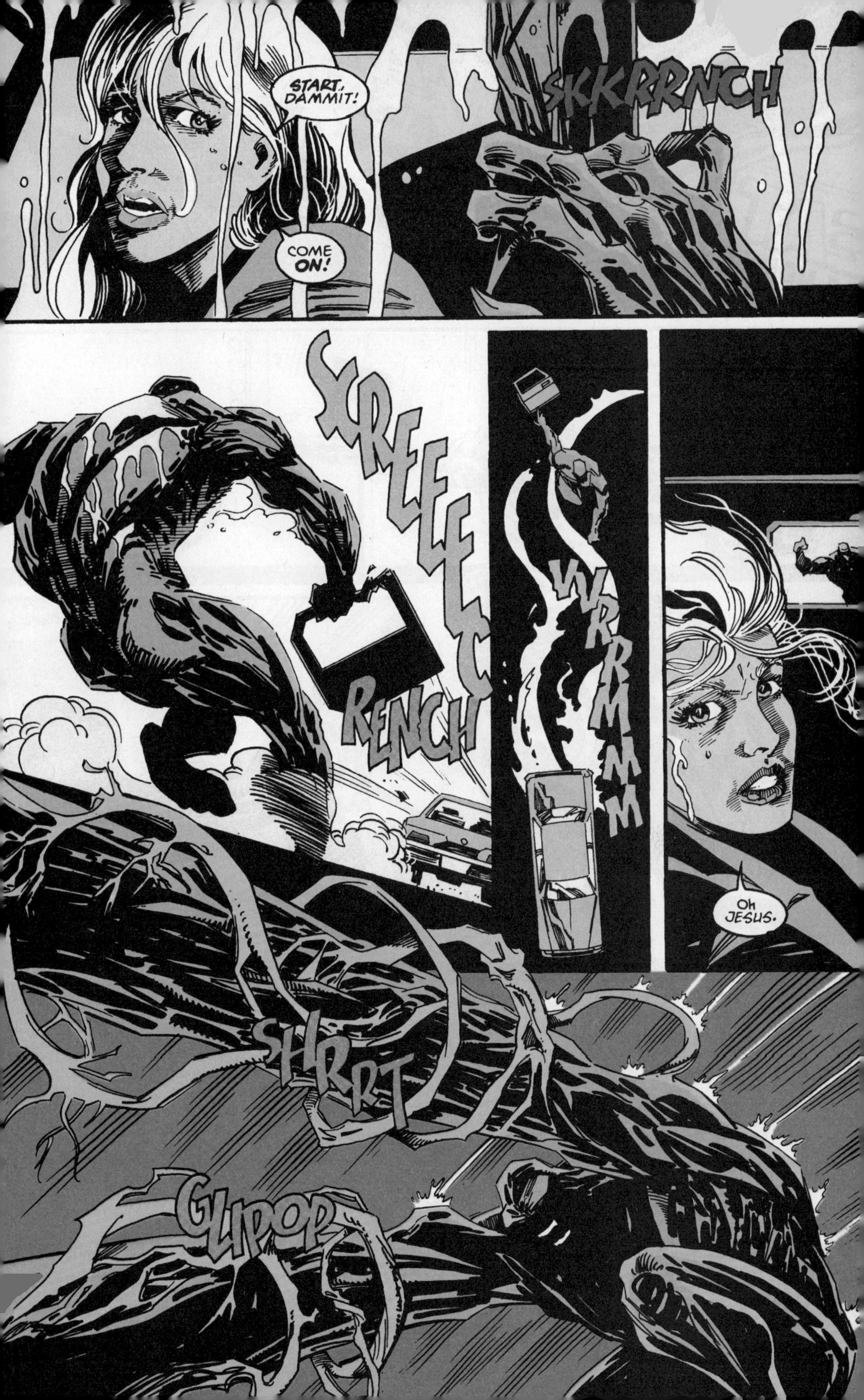
START, DAMMIT!
COME ON!
SKKRRRNCH
SCREEEEEC
RENCH
WRRRMMMM
Oh JESUS.
SHRRRT
GLIPOP

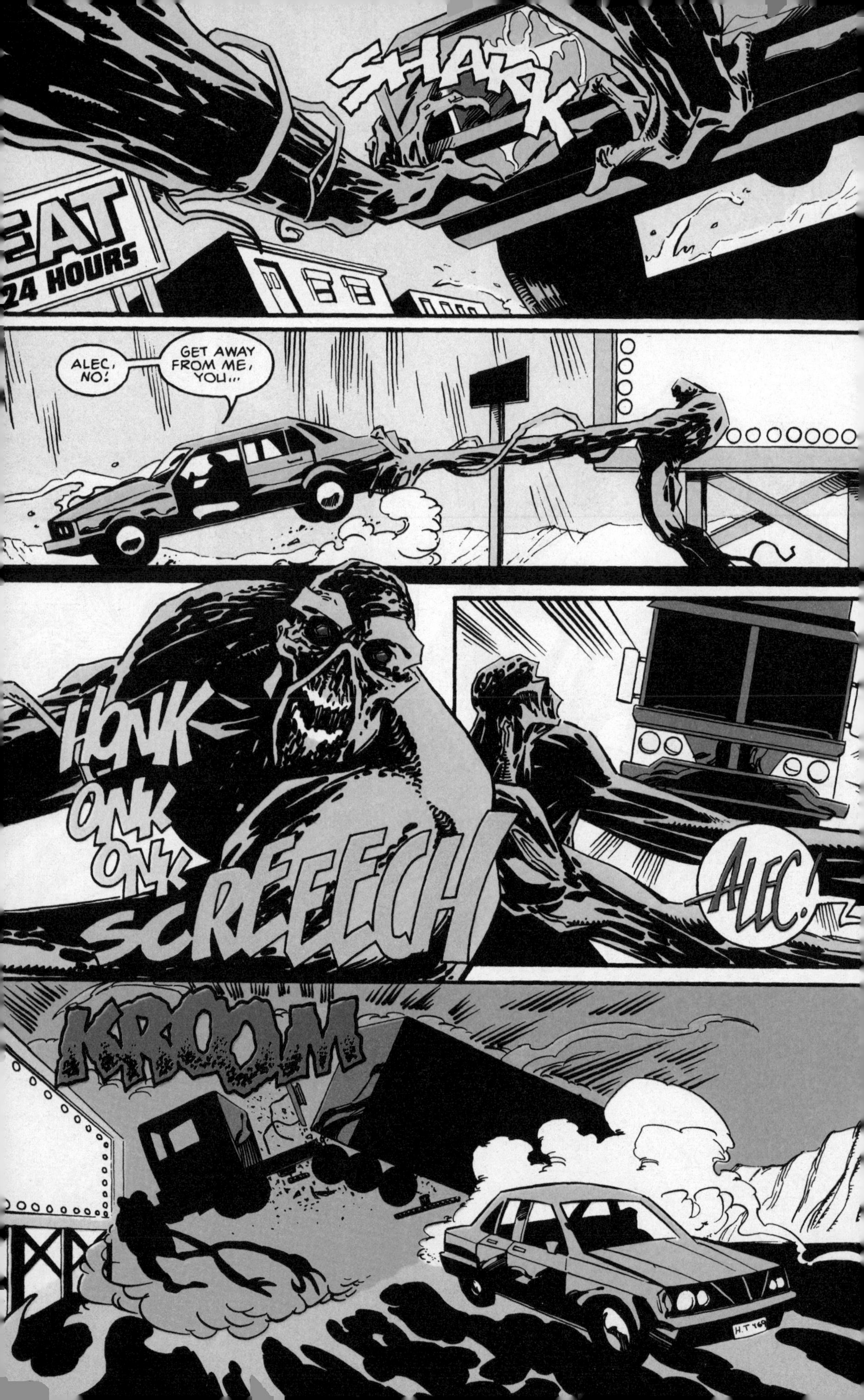
SHAKK
EAT
24 HOURS
ALEC, NO!
GET AWAY FROM ME, YOU...
HONK
ONK
ONK
SCREEECH
ALEC!
KROOM

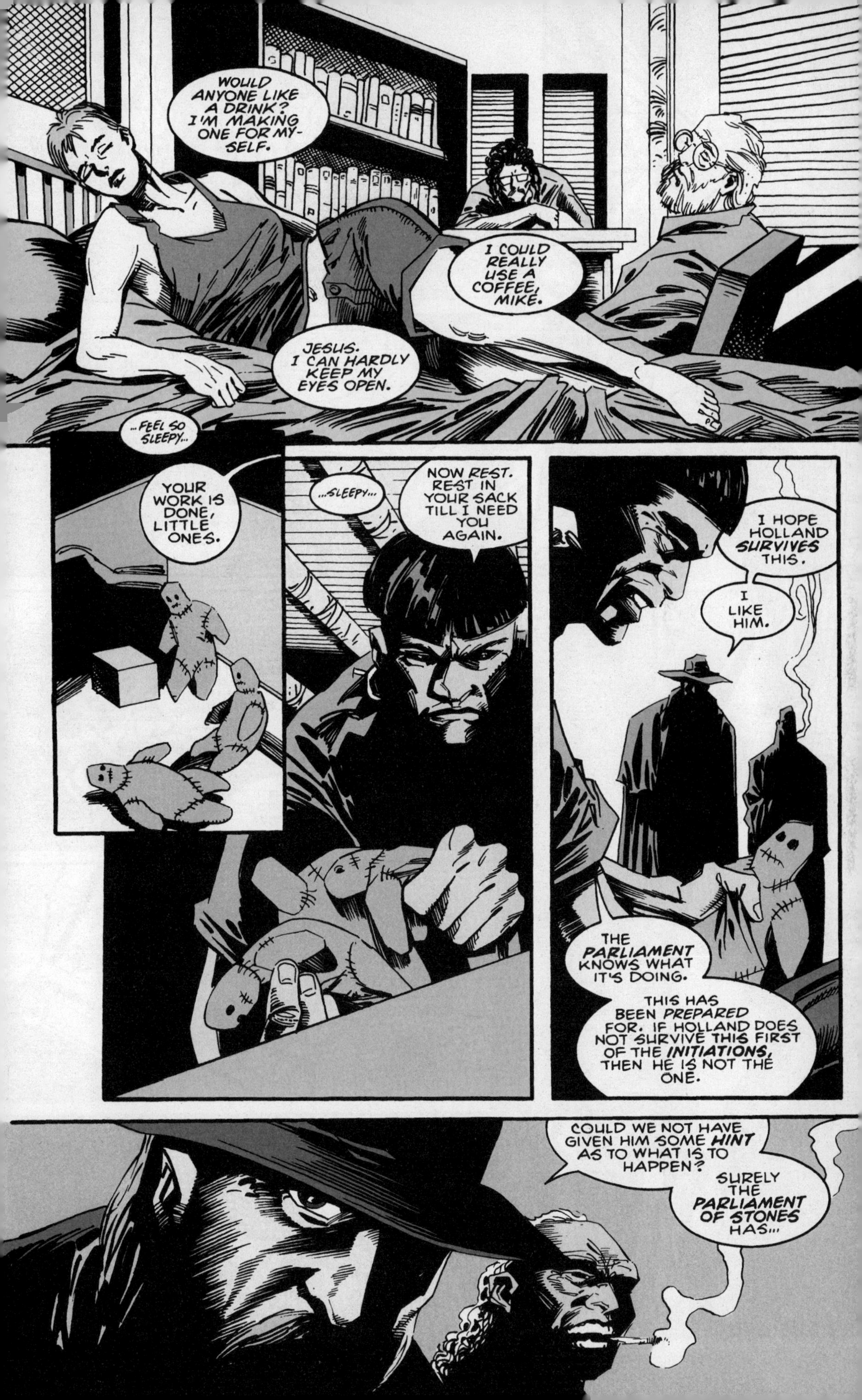
WOULD ANYONE LIKE A DRINK? I'M MAKING ONE FOR MY-SELF.
I COULD REALLY USE A COFFEE, MIKE.
JESUS. I CAN HARDLY KEEP MY EYES OPEN.
...FEEL SO SLEEPY...
YOUR WORK IS DONE, LITTLE ONES.
...SLEEPY...
NOW REST. REST IN YOUR SACK TILL I NEED YOU AGAIN.
I HOPE HOLLAND SURVIVES THIS.
I LIKE HIM.
THE PARLIAMENT KNOWS WHAT IT'S DOING.
THIS HAS BEEN PREPARED FOR. IF HOLLAND DOES NOT SURVIVE THIS FIRST OF THE INITIATIONS, THEN HE IS NOT THE ONE.
COULD WE NOT HAVE GIVEN HIM SOME HINT AS TO WHAT IS TO HAPPEN?
SURELY THE PARLIAMENT OF STONES HAS...

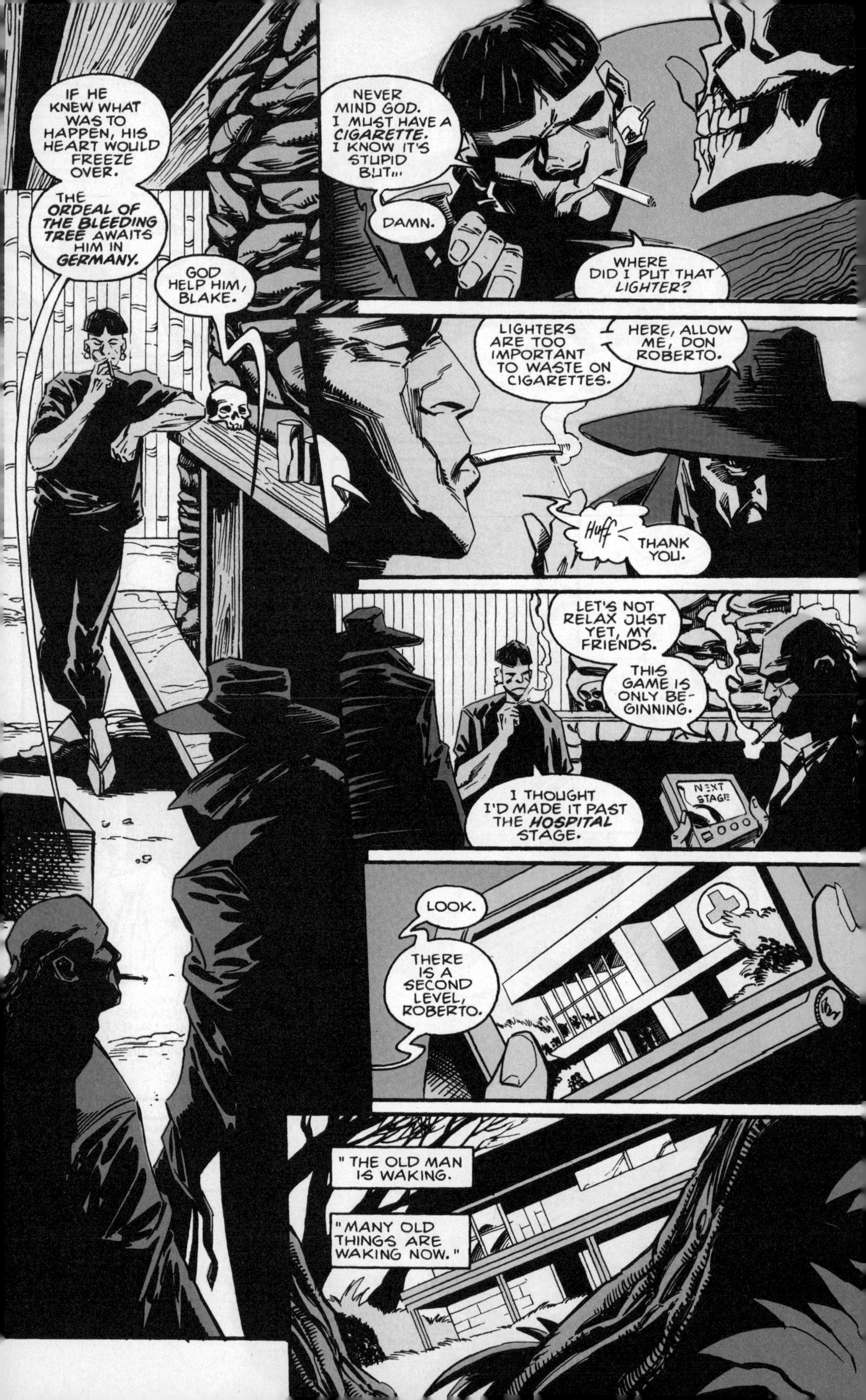

IF HE KNEW WHAT WAS TO HAPPEN, HIS HEART WOULD FREEZE OVER.
THE ORDEAL OF THE BLEEDING TREE AWAITS HIM IN GERMANY.
GOD HELP HIM, BLAKE.
NEVER MIND GOD. I MUST HAVE A CIGARETTE. I KNOW IT'S STUPID BUT...
DAMN.
WHERE DID I PUT THAT LIGHTER?
HERE, ALLOW ME, DON ROBERTO.
LIGHTERS ARE TOO IMPORTANT TO WASTE ON CIGARETTES.
Huff
THANK YOU.
LET'S NOT RELAX JUST YET, MY FRIENDS.
THIS GAME IS ONLY BE-GINNING.
NEXT STAGE
I THOUGHT I'D MADE IT PAST THE HOSPITAL STAGE.
LOOK.
THERE IS A SECOND LEVEL, ROBERTO.
"THE OLD MAN IS WAKING.
"MANY OLD THINGS ARE WAKING NOW."

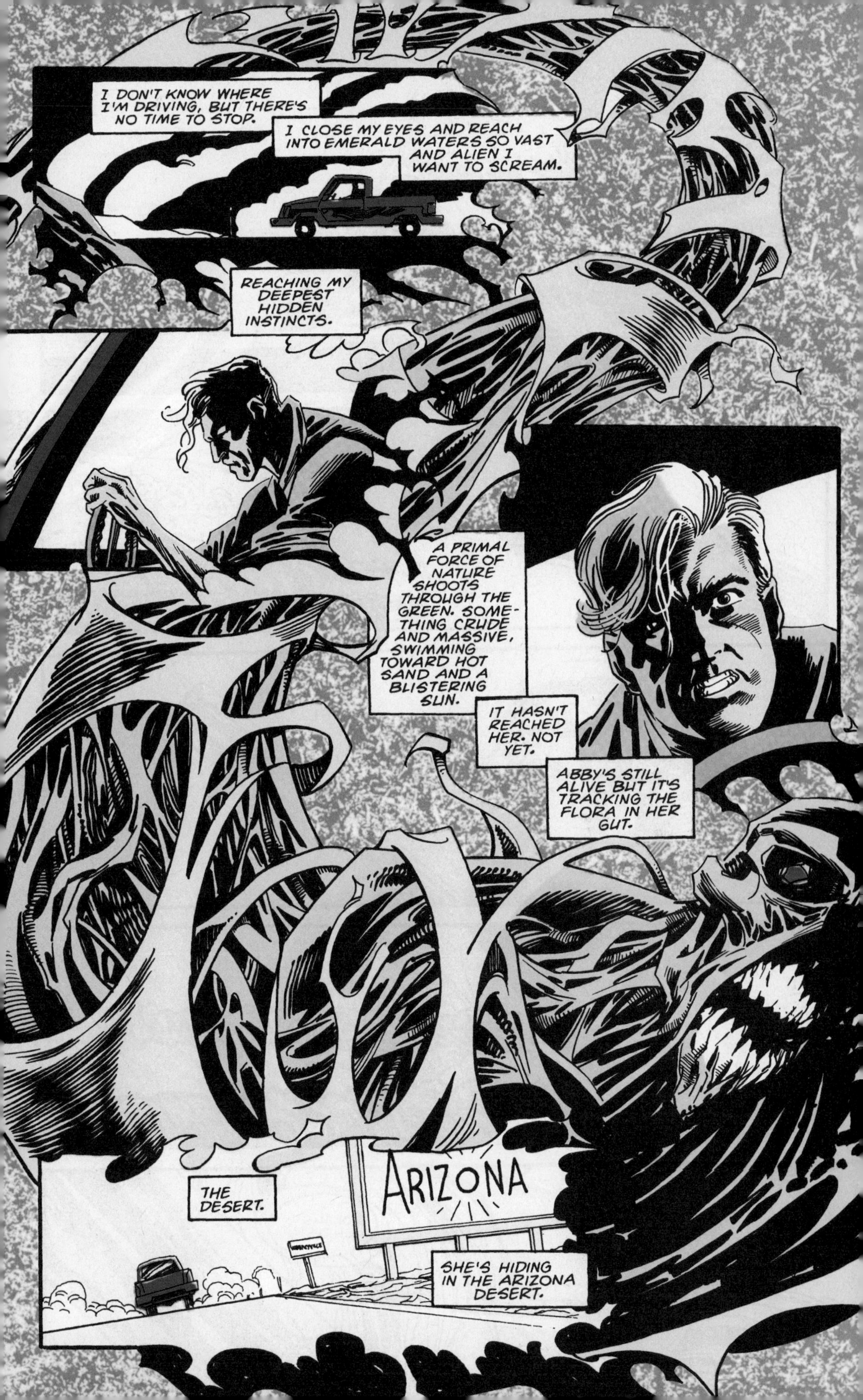
I DON'T KNOW WHERE I'M DRIVING, BUT THERE'S NO TIME TO STOP.
I CLOSE MY EYES AND REACH INTO EMERALD WATERS SO VAST AND ALIEN I WANT TO SCREAM.
REACHING MY DEEPEST HIDDEN INSTINCTS.
A PRIMAL FORCE OF NATURE SHOOTS THROUGH THE GREEN. SOMETHING CRUDE AND MASSIVE, SWIMMING TOWARD HOT SAND AND A BLISTERING SUN.
IT HASN'T REACHED HER. NOT YET.
ABBY'S STILL ALIVE BUT IT'S TRACKING THE FLORA IN HER GUT.
THE DESERT.
ARIZONA
SHE'S HIDING IN THE ARIZONA DESERT.

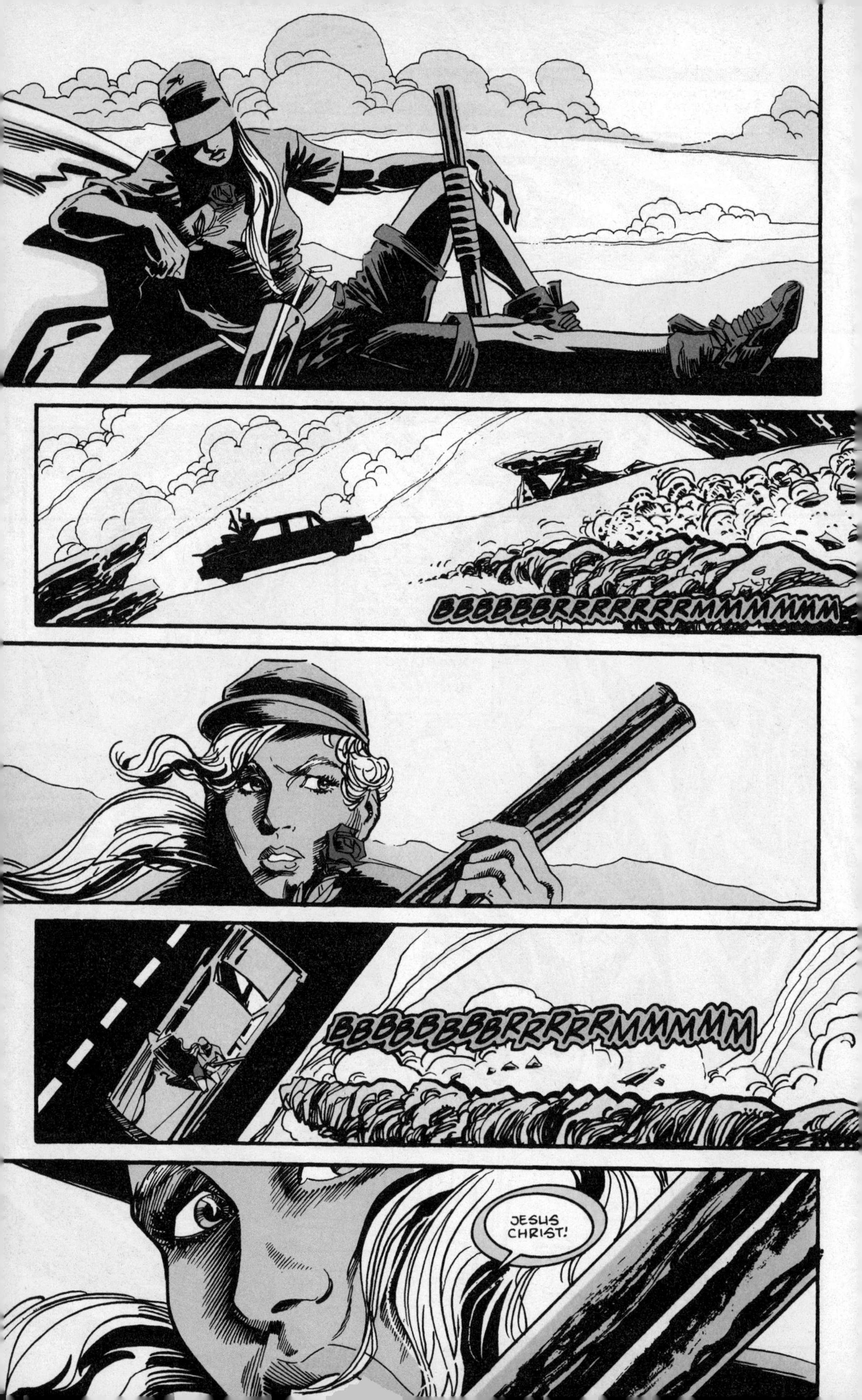
BBBBBBRRRRRRRMMMMMM
BBBBBBBBRRRRRMMMMMM
JESUS CHRIST!

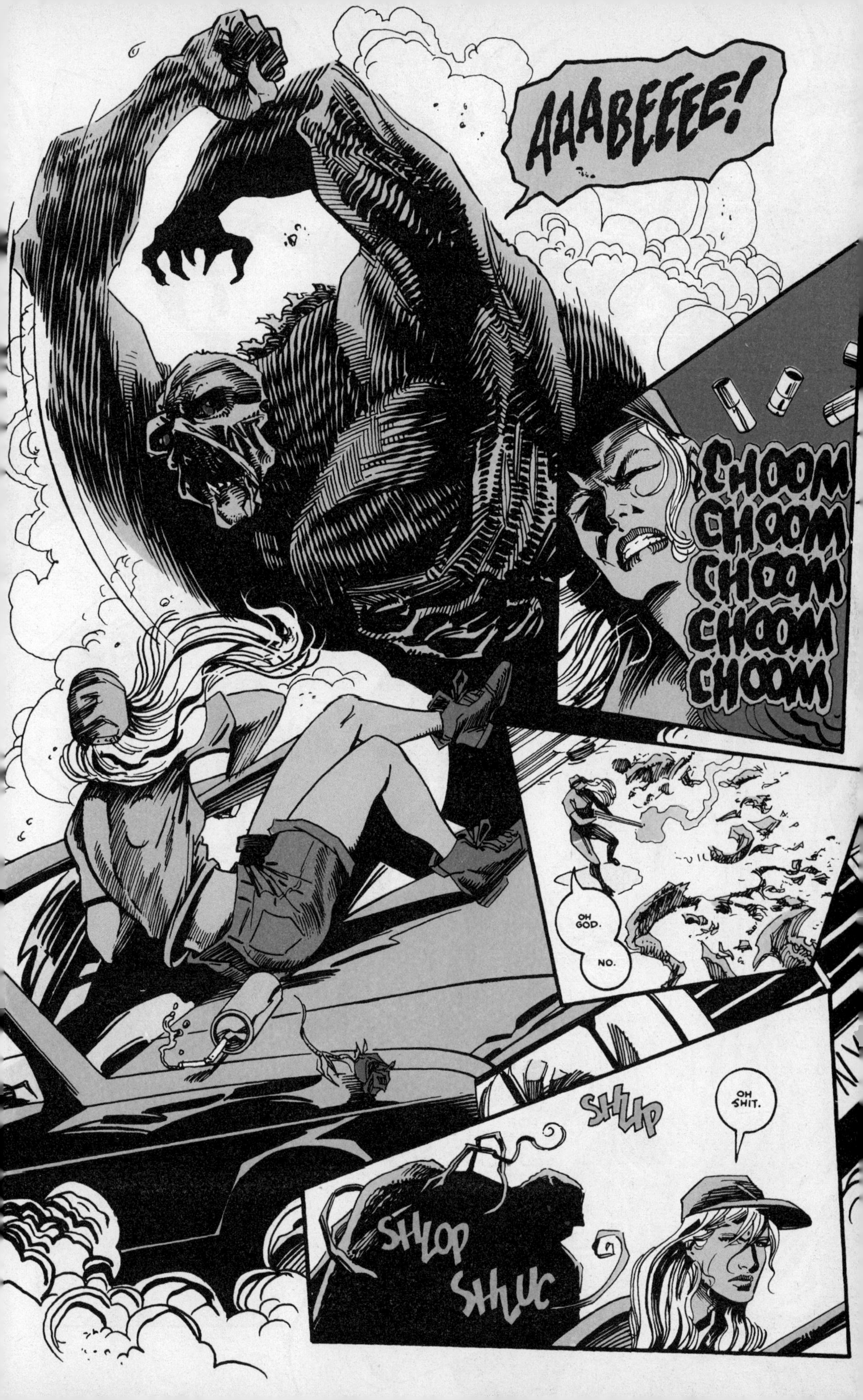
AAABEEEEE!
CHOOM
CHOOM
CHOOM
CHOOM
CHOOM
OH GOD.
NO.
SHLUP
OH SHIT.
SHLOP
SHLUC

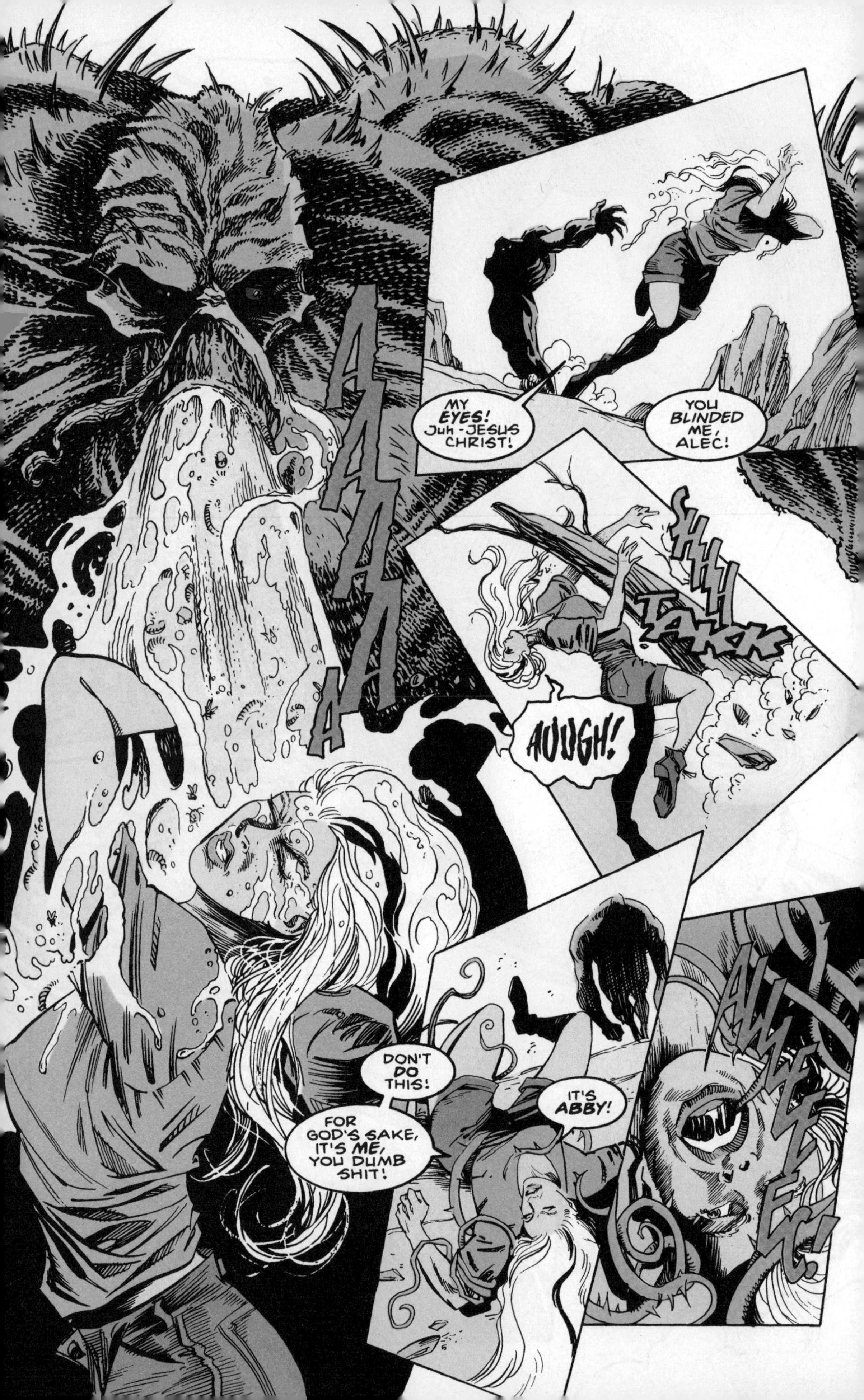

MY EYES! Juh-JESUS CHRIST!
YOU BLINDED ME, ALEC!
AUUGH!
DON'T DO THIS!
FOR GOD'S SAKE, IT'S ME, YOU DUMB SHIT!
IT'S ABBY!

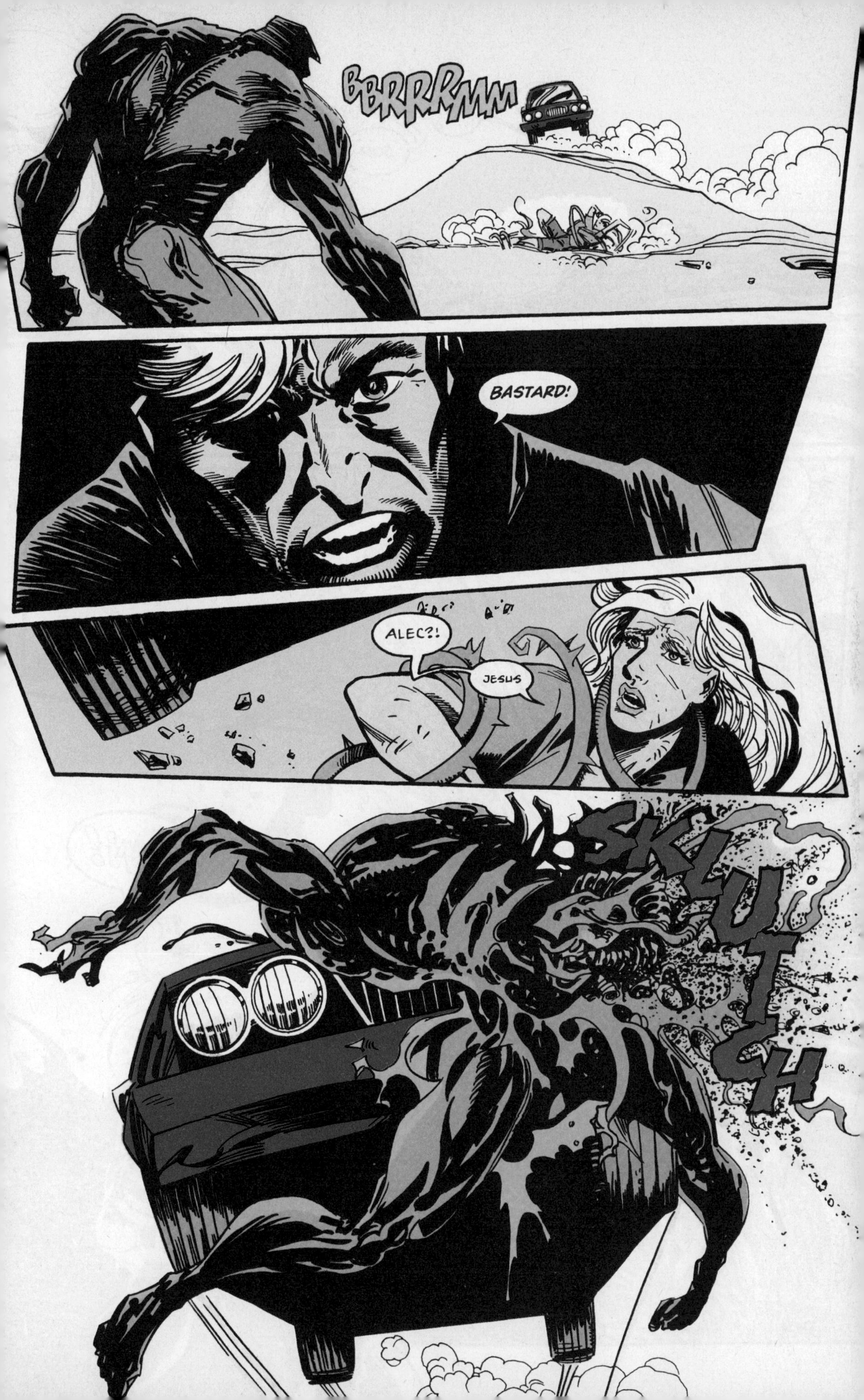
BBRRRMM
BASTARD!
ALEC?!
JESUS
SKLUTCH

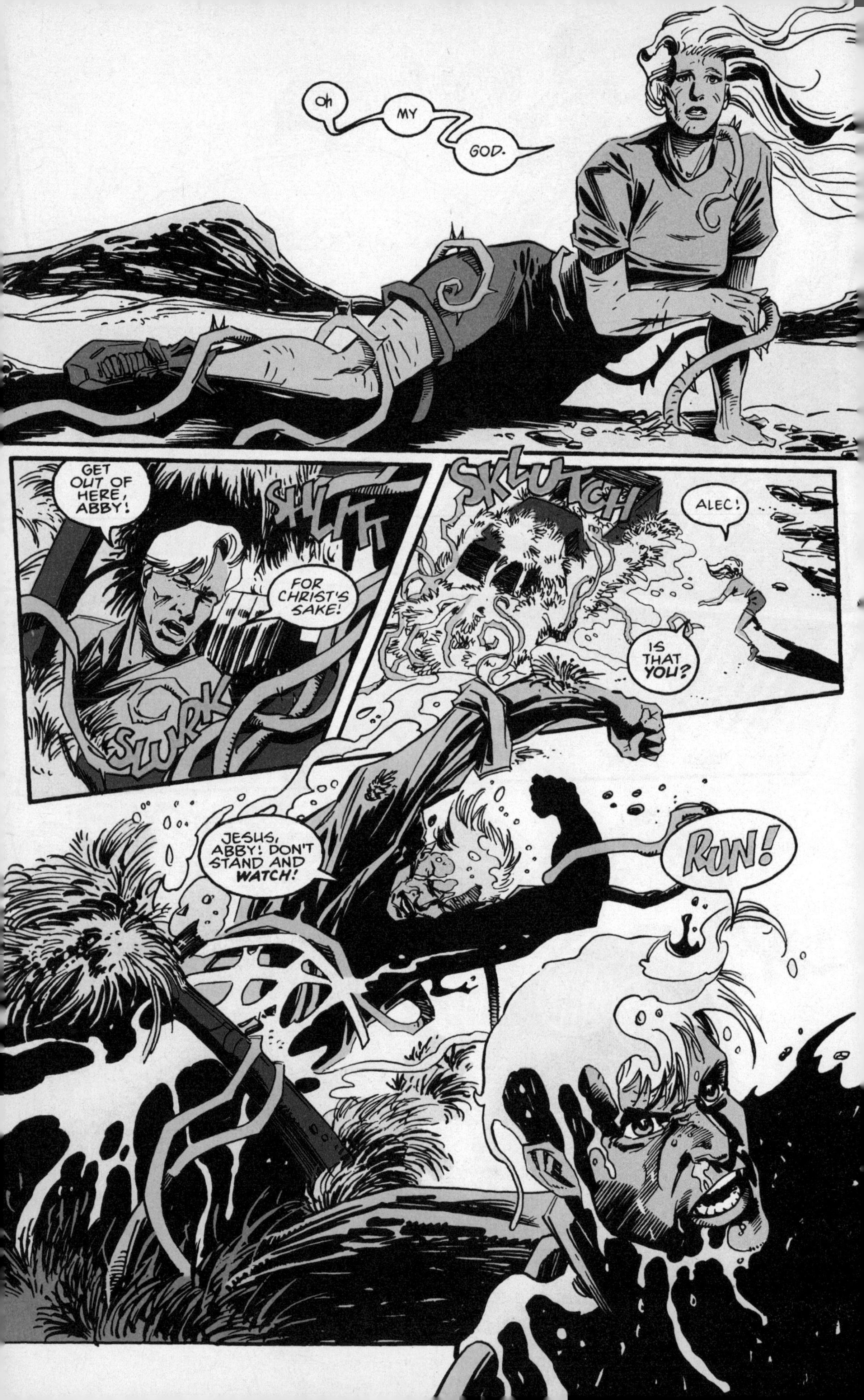
Oh
MY
GOD.
GET OUT OF HERE, ABBY!
SHLITT
FOR CHRIST'S SAKE!
SLURK
SKLUTCH
ALEC!
IS THAT YOU?
JESUS, ABBY! DON'T STAND AND WATCH!
RUN!

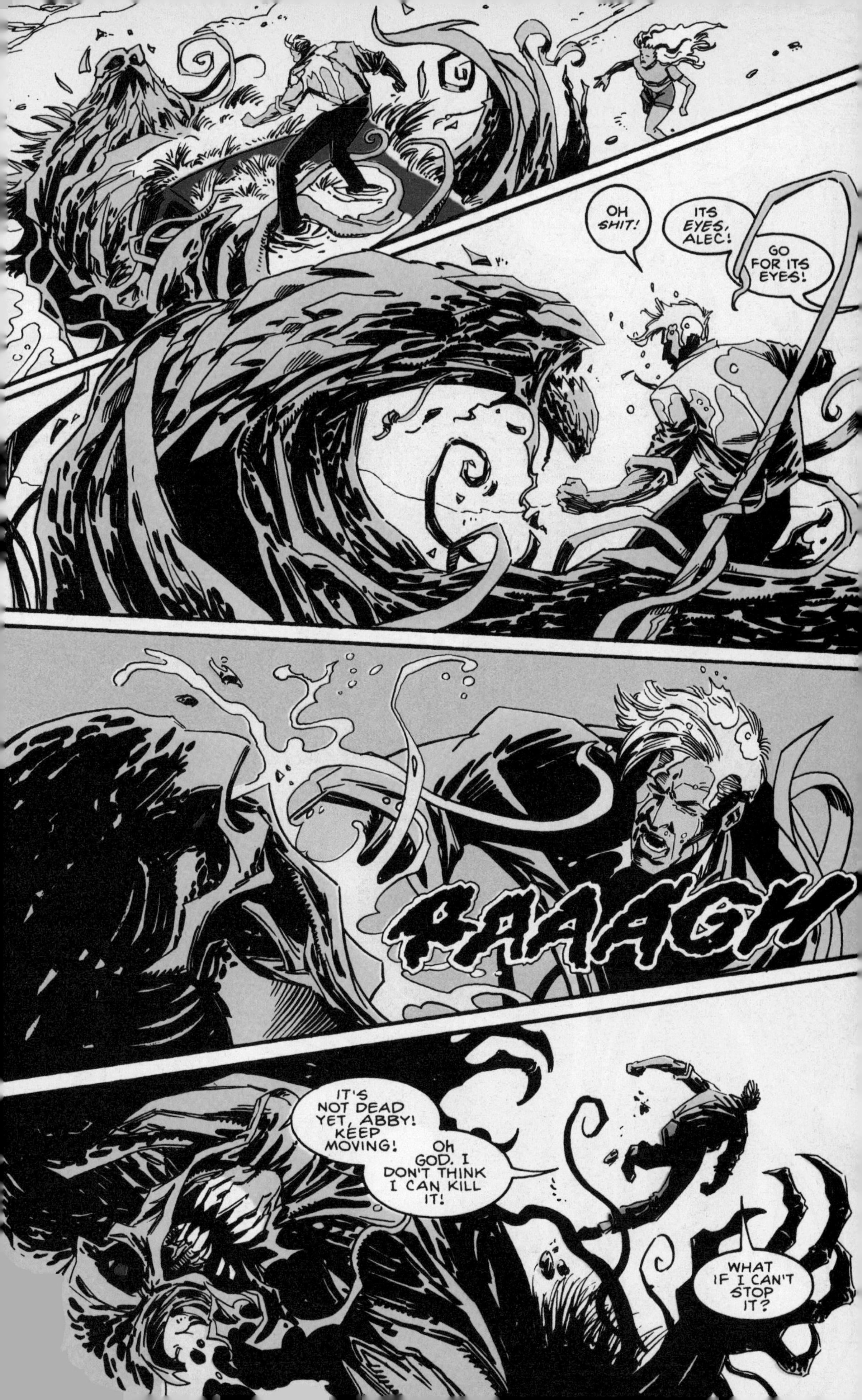
OH SHIT!
ITS EYES, ALEC!
GO FOR ITS EYES!
RAAAGH
IT'S NOT DEAD YET, ABBY! KEEP MOVING!
OH GOD. I DON'T THINK I CAN KILL IT!
WHAT IF I CAN'T STOP IT?

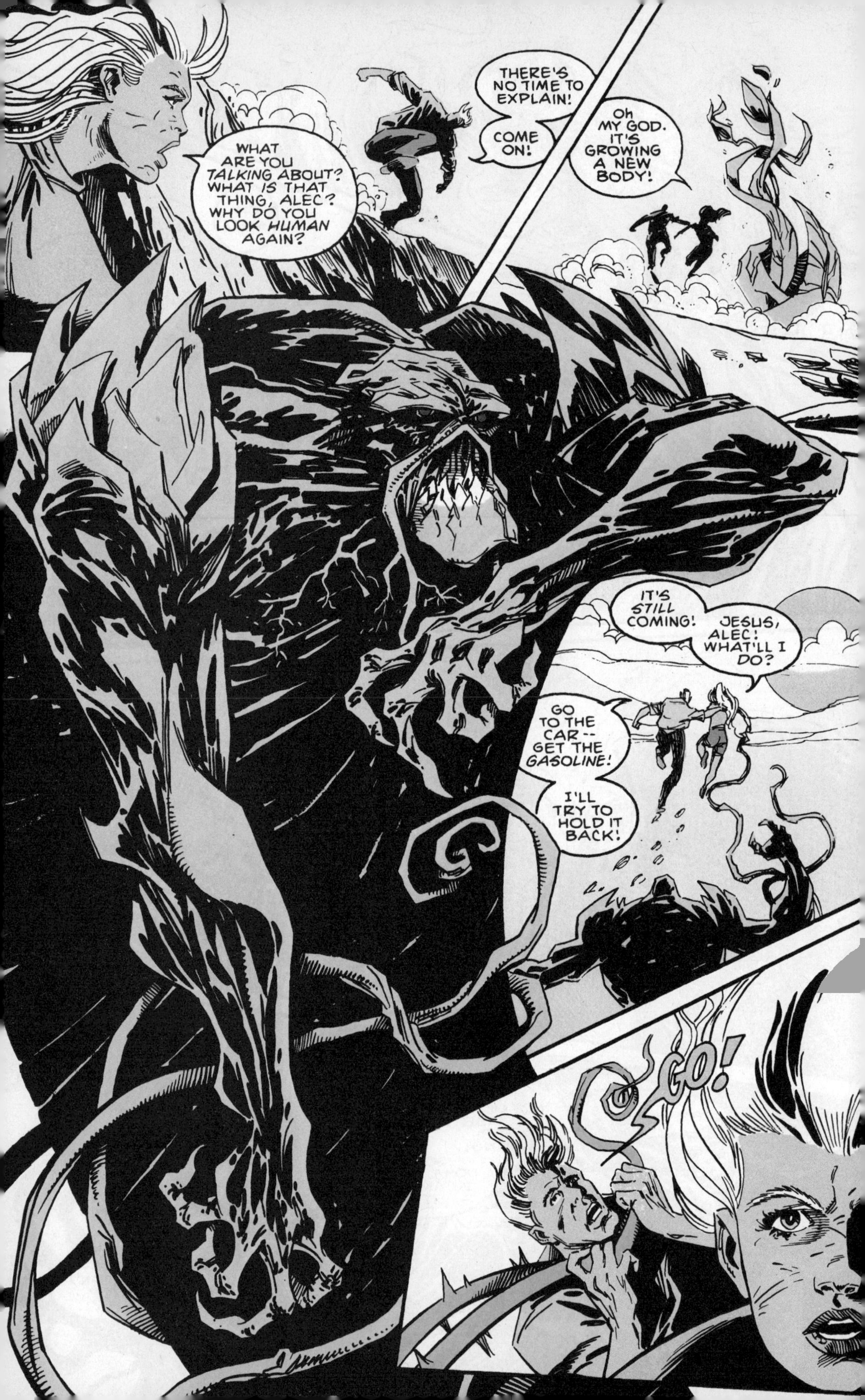
WHAT ARE YOU TALKING ABOUT? WHAT IS THAT THING, ALEC? WHY DO YOU LOOK HUMAN AGAIN?
THERE'S NO TIME TO EXPLAIN!
COME ON!
Oh MY GOD. IT'S GROWING A NEW BODY!
IT'S STILL COMING!
JESUS, ALEC! WHAT'LL I DO?
GO TO THE CAR-- GET THE GASOLINE!
I'LL TRY TO HOLD IT BACK!
GO!

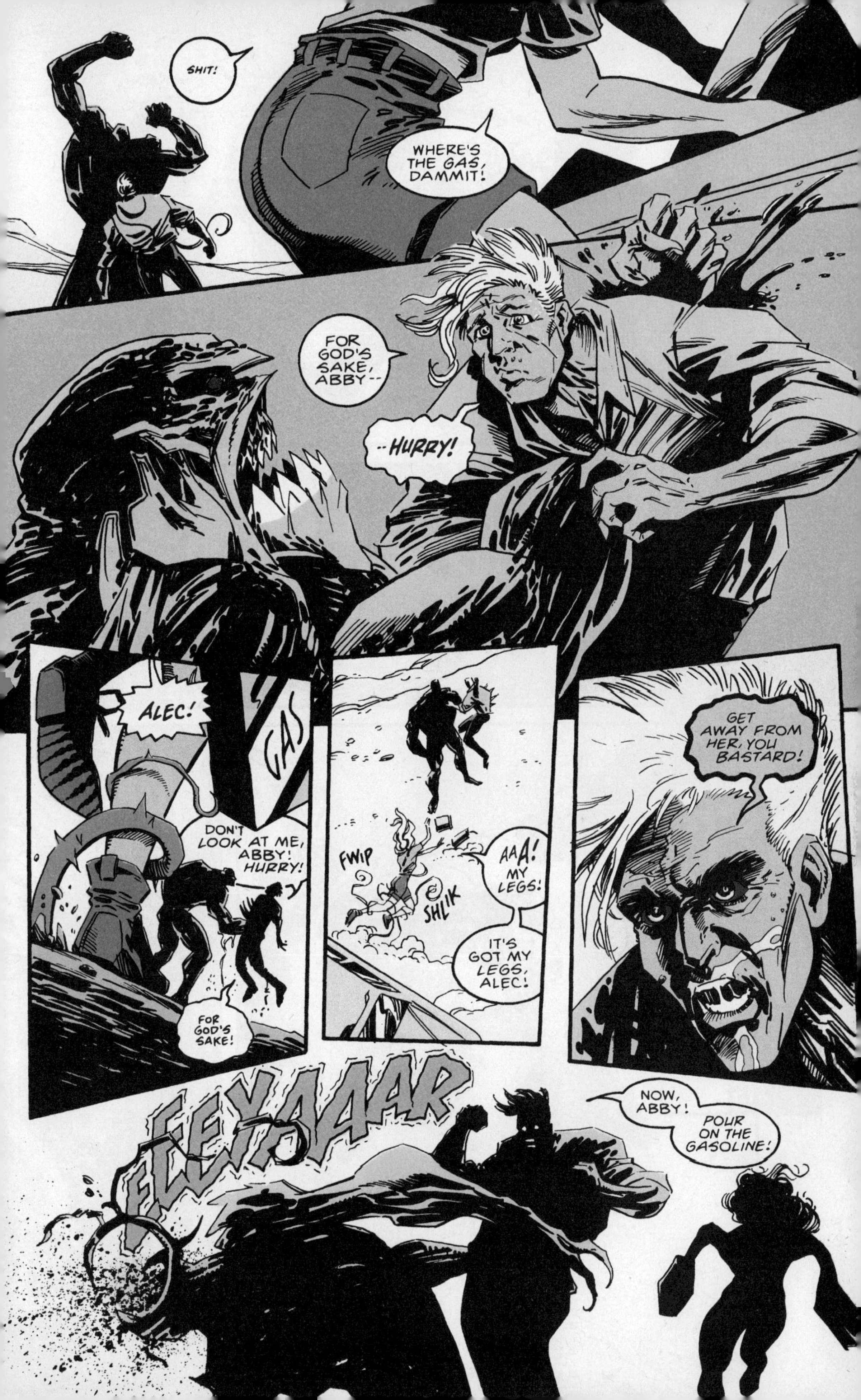
SHIT!
WHERE'S THE GAS, DAMMIT!
FOR GOD'S SAKE, ABBY--
--HURRY!
ALEC!
GAS
DON'T LOOK AT ME, ABBY! HURRY!
FOR GOD'S SAKE!
FWIP
SHLIK
AAA! MY LEGS!
IT'S GOT MY LEGS, ALEC!
GET AWAY FROM HER, YOU BASTARD!
EEEYAAAR
NOW, ABBY!
POUR ON THE GASOLINE!

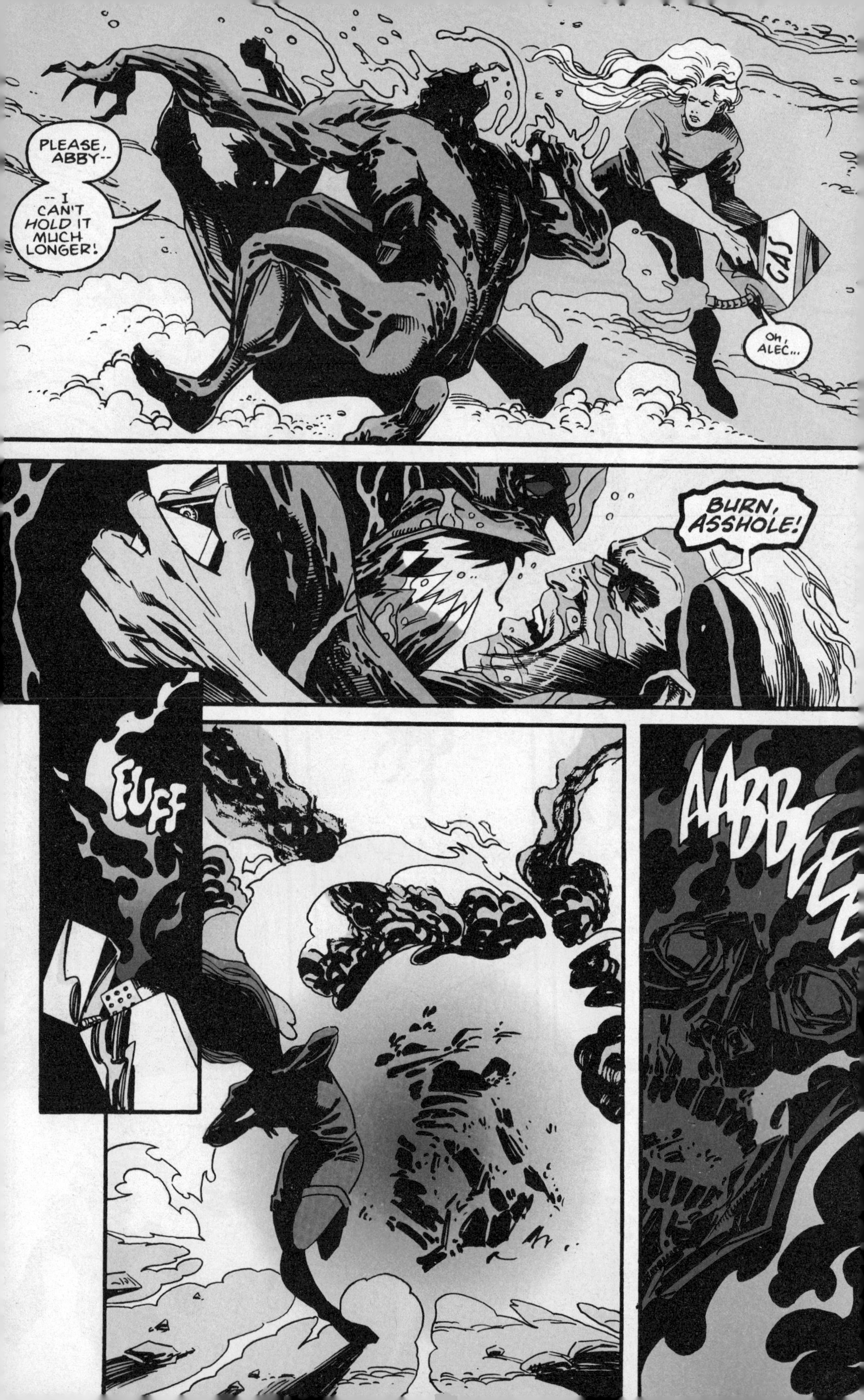
PLEASE, ABBY--
-- I CAN'T HOLD IT MUCH LONGER!
GAS
OH, ALEC...
BURN, ASSHOLE!
FUFF
AABBEEE

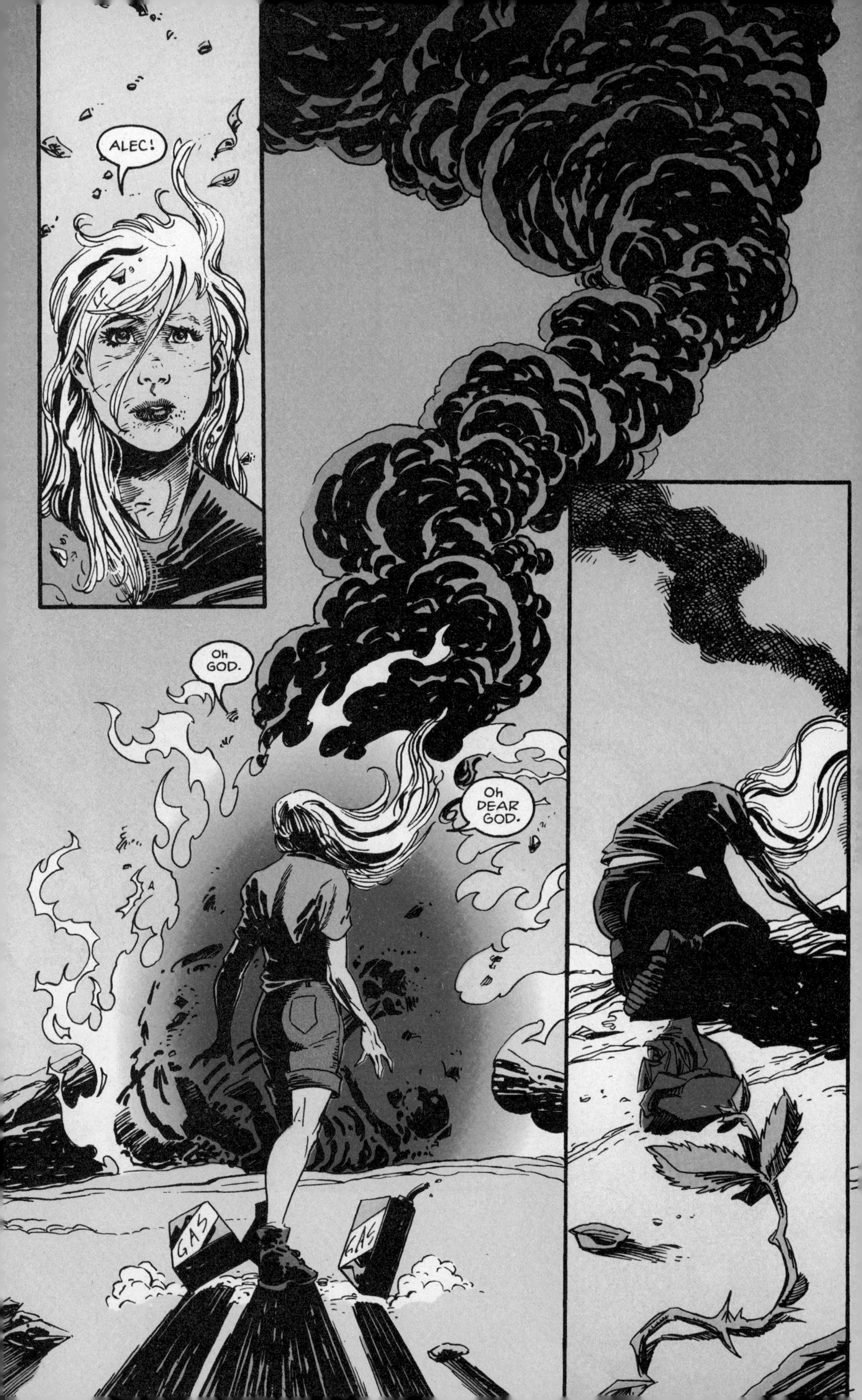
ALEC!
Oh GOD.
Oh DEAR GOD.

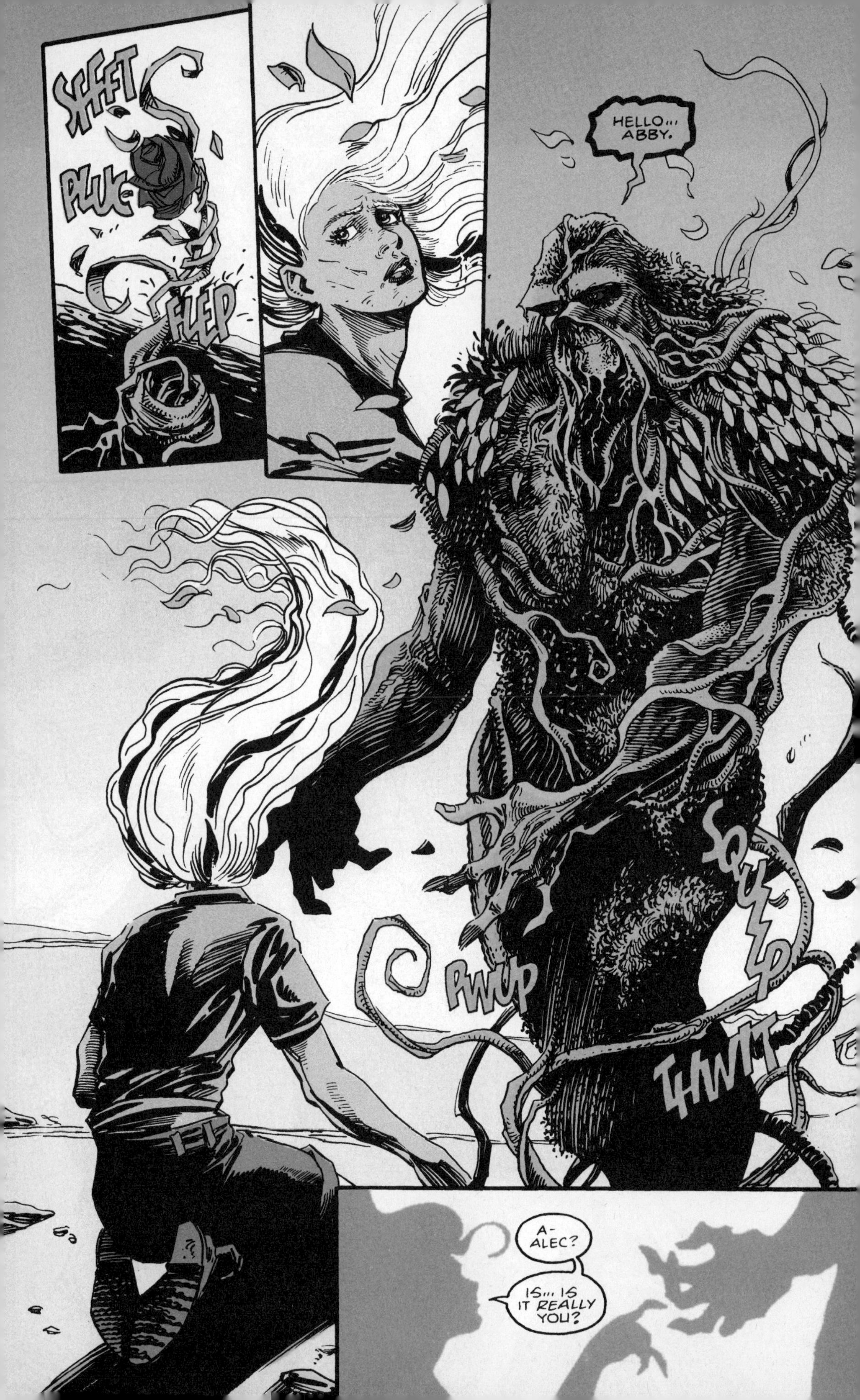
SKFFT
PLUC
FLEP
HELLO... ABBY.
SQUELP
PWUP
THWIT
A- ALEC?
IS... IS IT REALLY YOU?

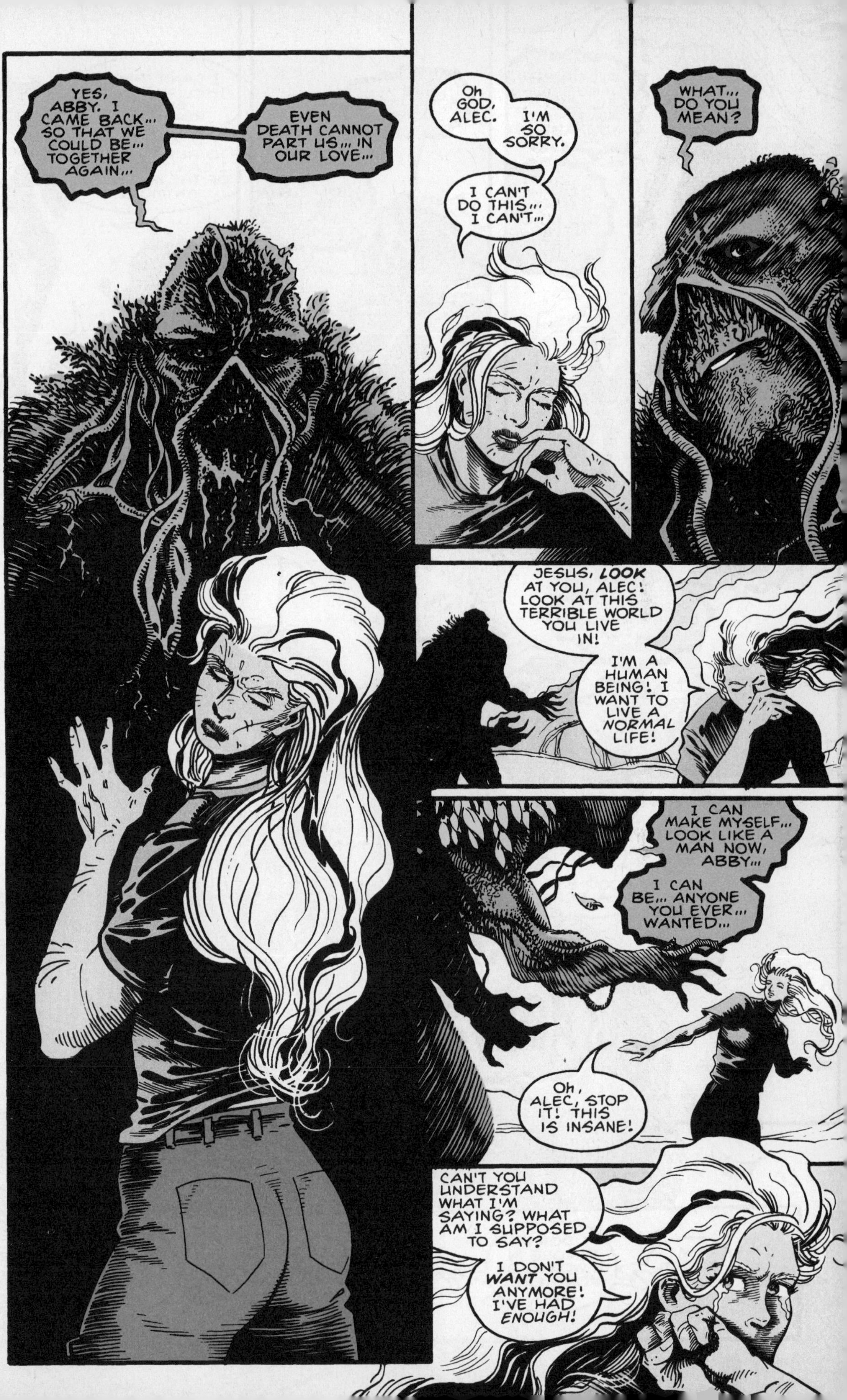
YES, ABBY. I CAME BACK... SO THAT WE COULD BE... TOGETHER AGAIN...
EVEN DEATH CANNOT PART US... IN OUR LOVE...
Oh GOD, ALEC.
I'M SO SORRY.
I CAN'T DO THIS... I CAN'T...
WHAT... DO YOU MEAN?
JESUS, LOOK AT YOU, ALEC! LOOK AT THIS TERRIBLE WORLD YOU LIVE IN!
I'M A HUMAN BEING! I WANT TO LIVE A NORMAL LIFE!
I CAN MAKE MYSELF... LOOK LIKE A MAN NOW, ABBY...
I CAN BE... ANYONE YOU EVER... WANTED...
Oh, ALEC, STOP IT! THIS IS INSANE!
CAN'T YOU UNDERSTAND WHAT I'M SAYING? WHAT AM I SUPPOSED TO SAY?
I DON'T WANT YOU ANYMORE! I'VE HAD ENOUGH!

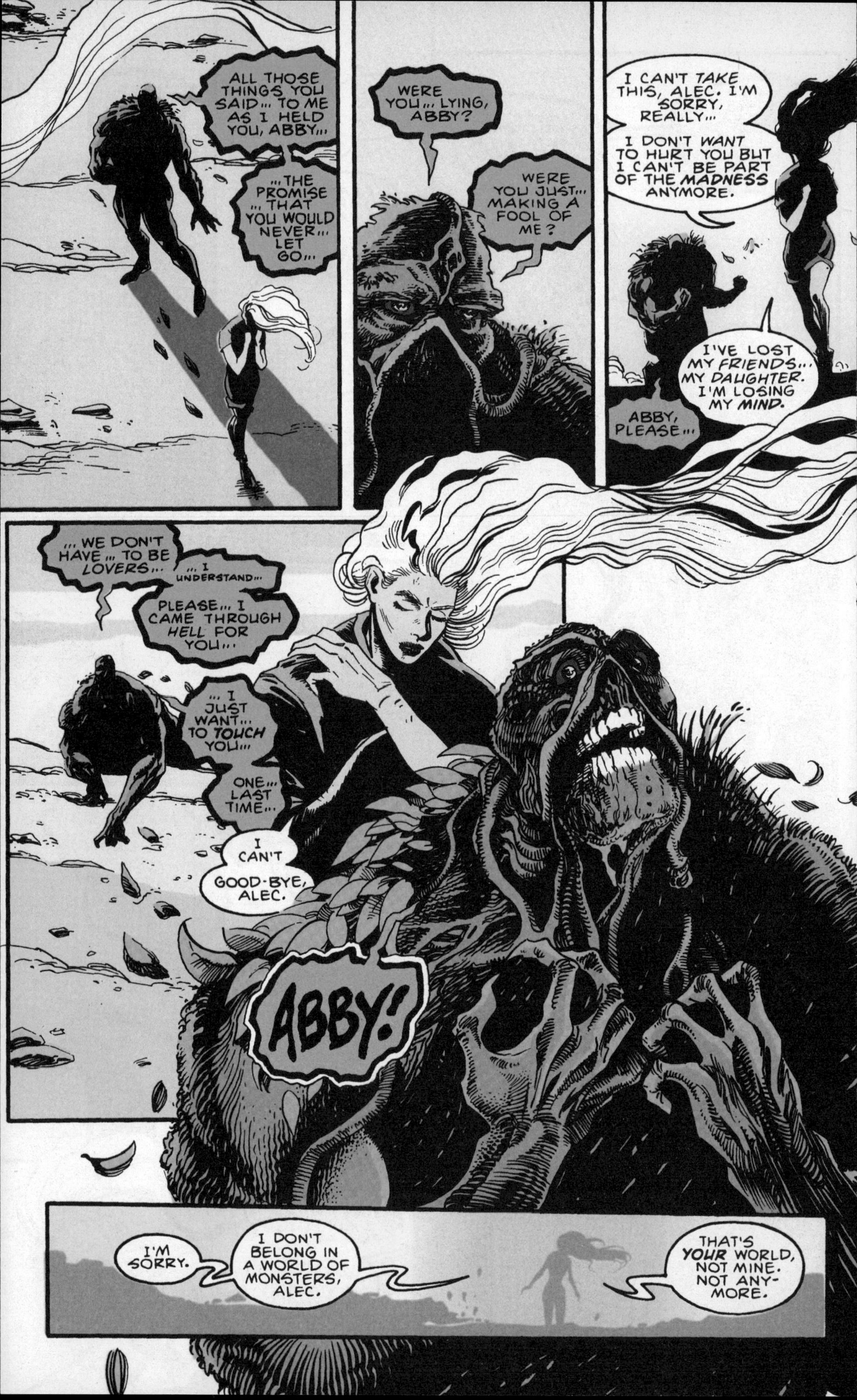
ALL THOSE THINGS YOU SAID... TO ME AS I HELD YOU, ABBY...
...THE PROMISE ...THAT YOU WOULD NEVER... LET GO...
WERE YOU... LYING, ABBY?
WERE YOU JUST... MAKING A FOOL OF ME?
I CAN'T TAKE THIS, ALEC. I'M SORRY, REALLY...
I DON'T WANT TO HURT YOU BUT I CAN'T BE PART OF THE MADNESS ANYMORE.
I'VE LOST MY FRIENDS... MY DAUGHTER. I'M LOSING MY MIND.
ABBY, PLEASE...
...WE DON'T HAVE... TO BE LOVERS...
...I UNDERSTAND...
PLEASE... I CAME THROUGH HELL FOR YOU...
...I JUST WANT... TO TOUCH YOU...
ONE... LAST TIME...
I CAN'T
GOOD-BYE, ALEC.
ABBY!
I'M SORRY.
I DON'T BELONG IN A WORLD OF MONSTERS, ALEC.
THAT'S YOUR WORLD, NOT MINE. NOT ANY-MORE.

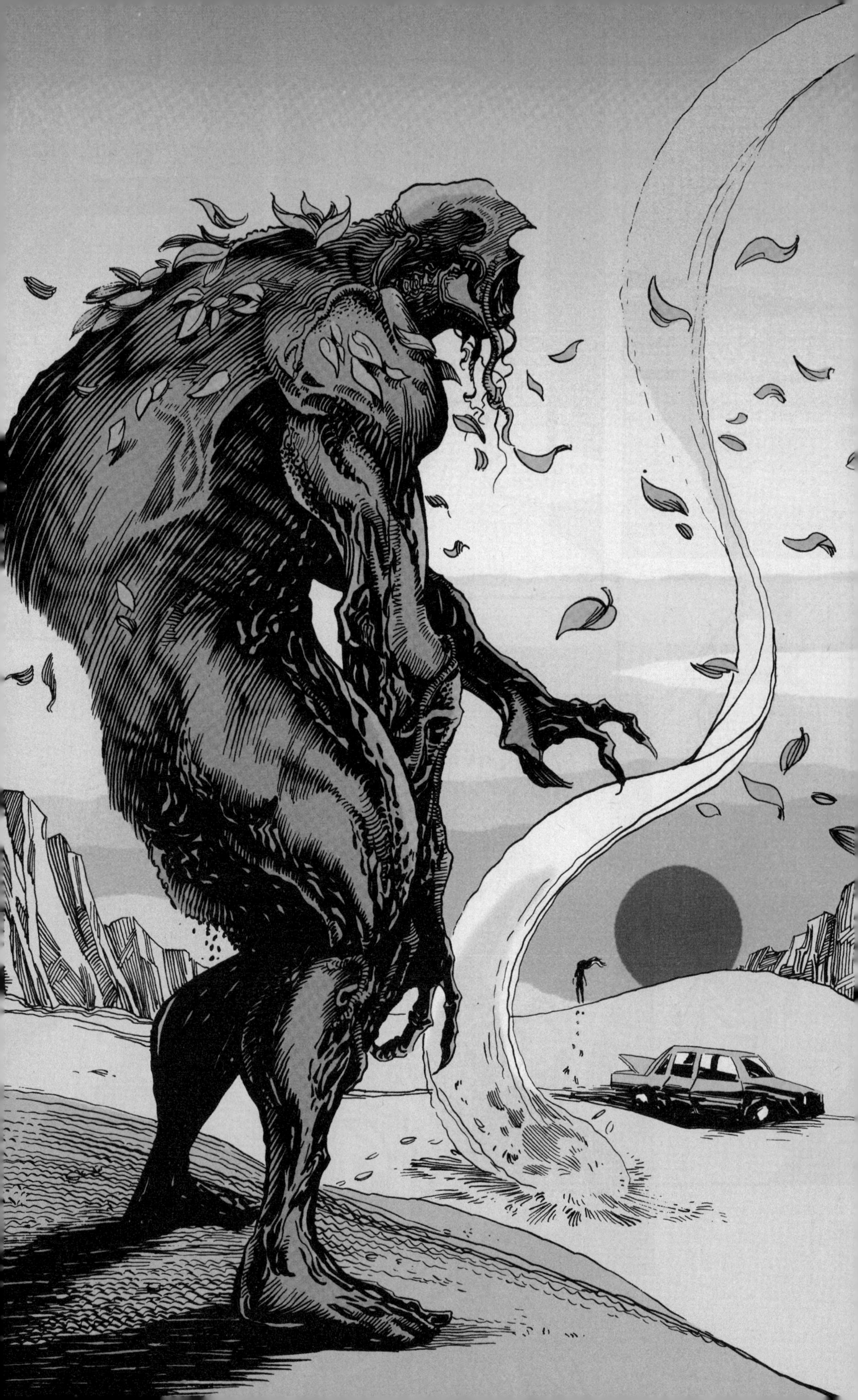

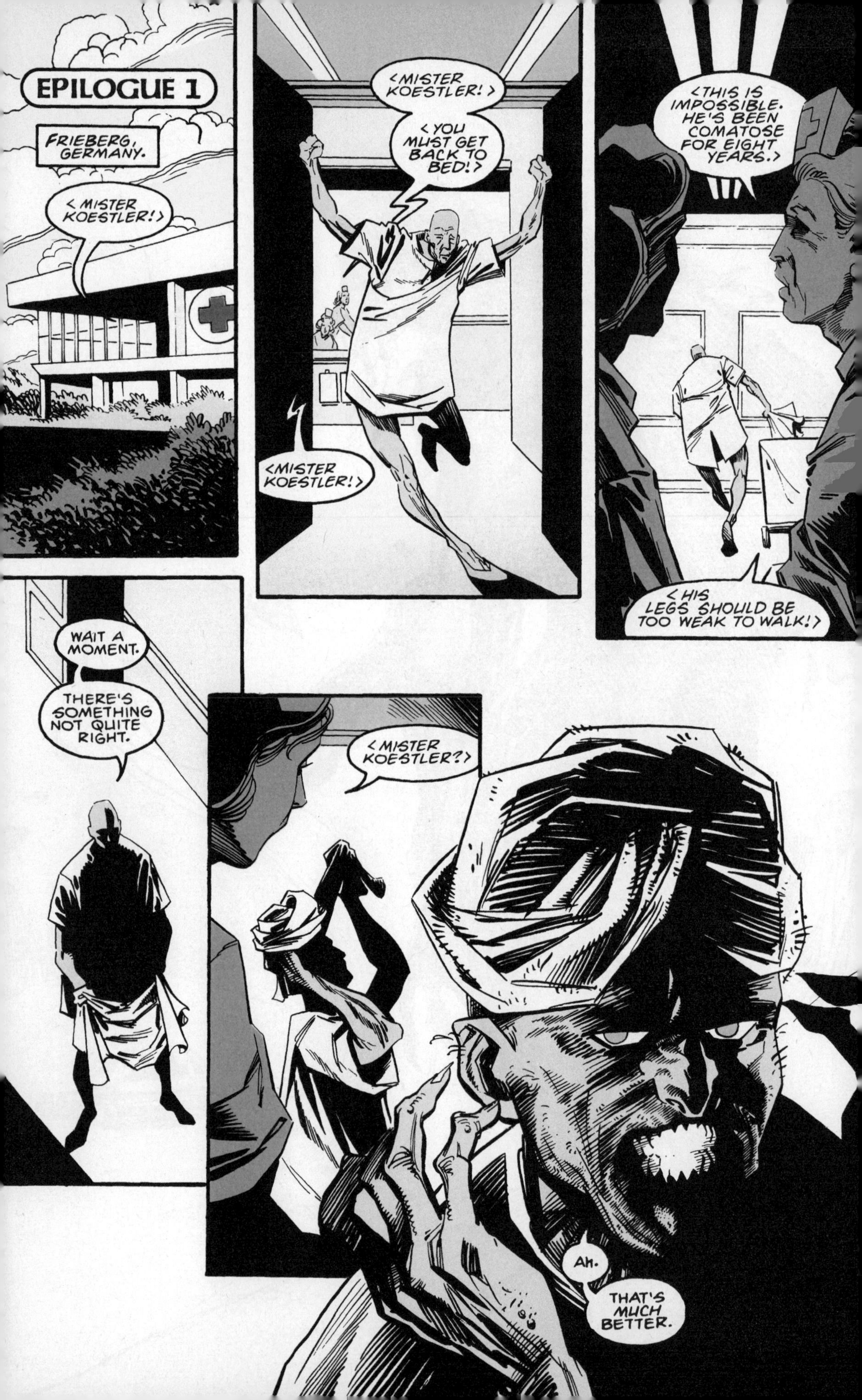
EPILOGUE 1
FRIEBERG, GERMANY.
<MISTER KOESTLER!>
<MISTER KOESTLER!>
<YOU MUST GET BACK TO BED!>
<MISTER KOESTLER!>
<THIS IS IMPOSSIBLE. HE'S BEEN COMATOSE FOR EIGHT YEARS.>
<HIS LEGS SHOULD BE TOO WEAK TO WALK!>
WAIT A MOMENT.
THERE'S SOMETHING NOT QUITE RIGHT.
<MISTER KOESTLER?>
Ah.
THAT'S MUCH BETTER.

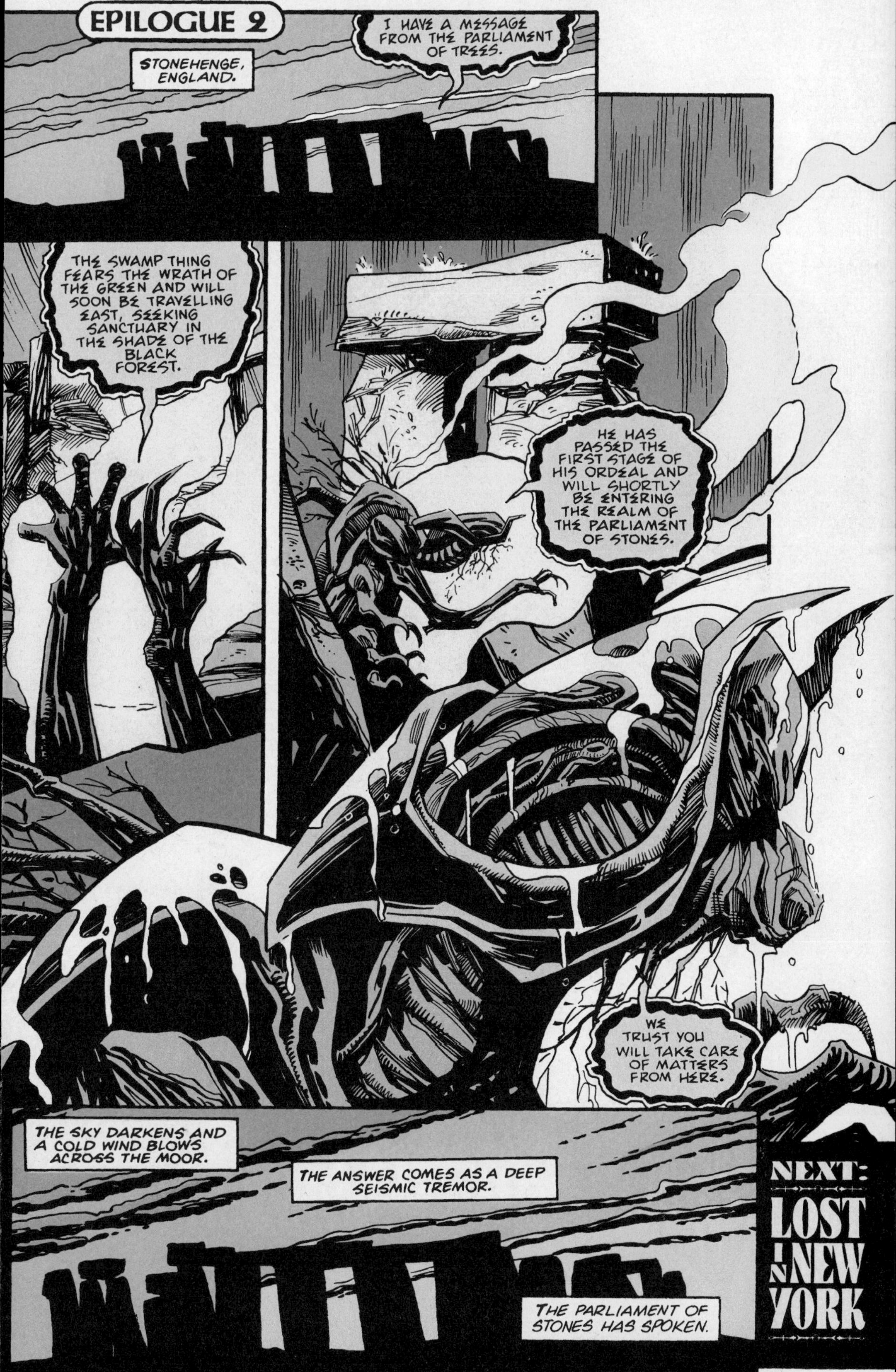
EPILOGUE 2
STONEHENGE, ENGLAND.
I HAVE A MESSAGE FROM THE PARLIAMENT OF TREES.
THE SWAMP THING FEARS THE WRATH OF THE GREEN AND WILL SOON BE TRAVELLING EAST, SEEKING SANCTUARY IN THE SHADE OF THE BLACK FOREST.
HE HAS PASSED THE FIRST STAGE OF HIS ORDEAL AND WILL SHORTLY BE ENTERING THE REALM OF THE PARLIAMENT OF STONES.
WE TRUST YOU WILL TAKE CARE OF MATTERS FROM HERE.
THE SKY DARKENS AND A COLD WIND BLOWS ACROSS THE MOOR.
THE ANSWER COMES AS A DEEP SEISMIC TREMOR.
THE PARLIAMENT OF STONES HAS SPOKEN.
NEXT:
LOST IN NEW YORK

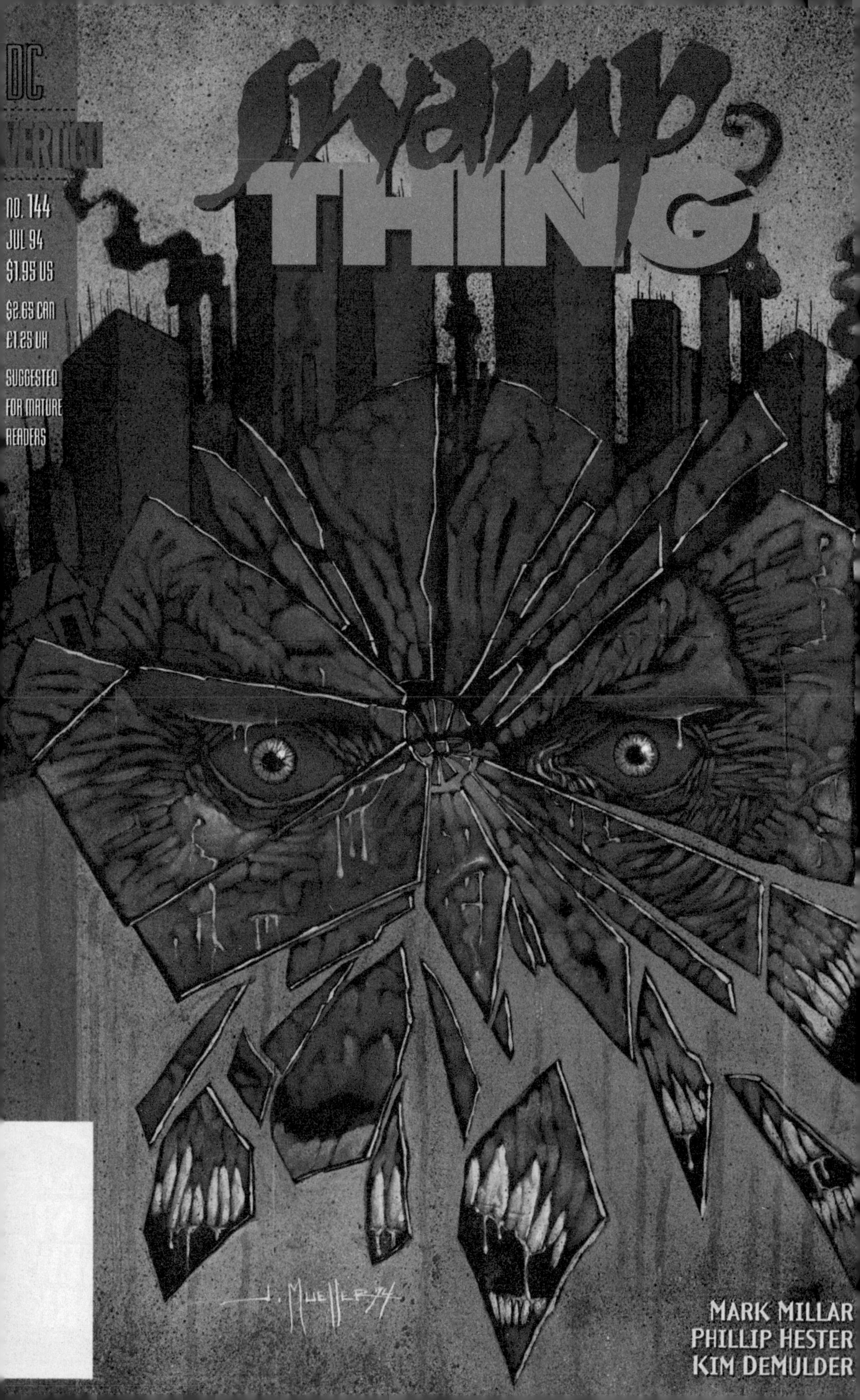
DC
VERTIGO
Swamp
THING
NO. 144
JUL 94
$1.95 US
$2.65 CAN
£1.25 UK
SUGGESTED FOR MATURE READERS
MARK MILLAR
PHILLIP HESTER
KIM DEMULDER

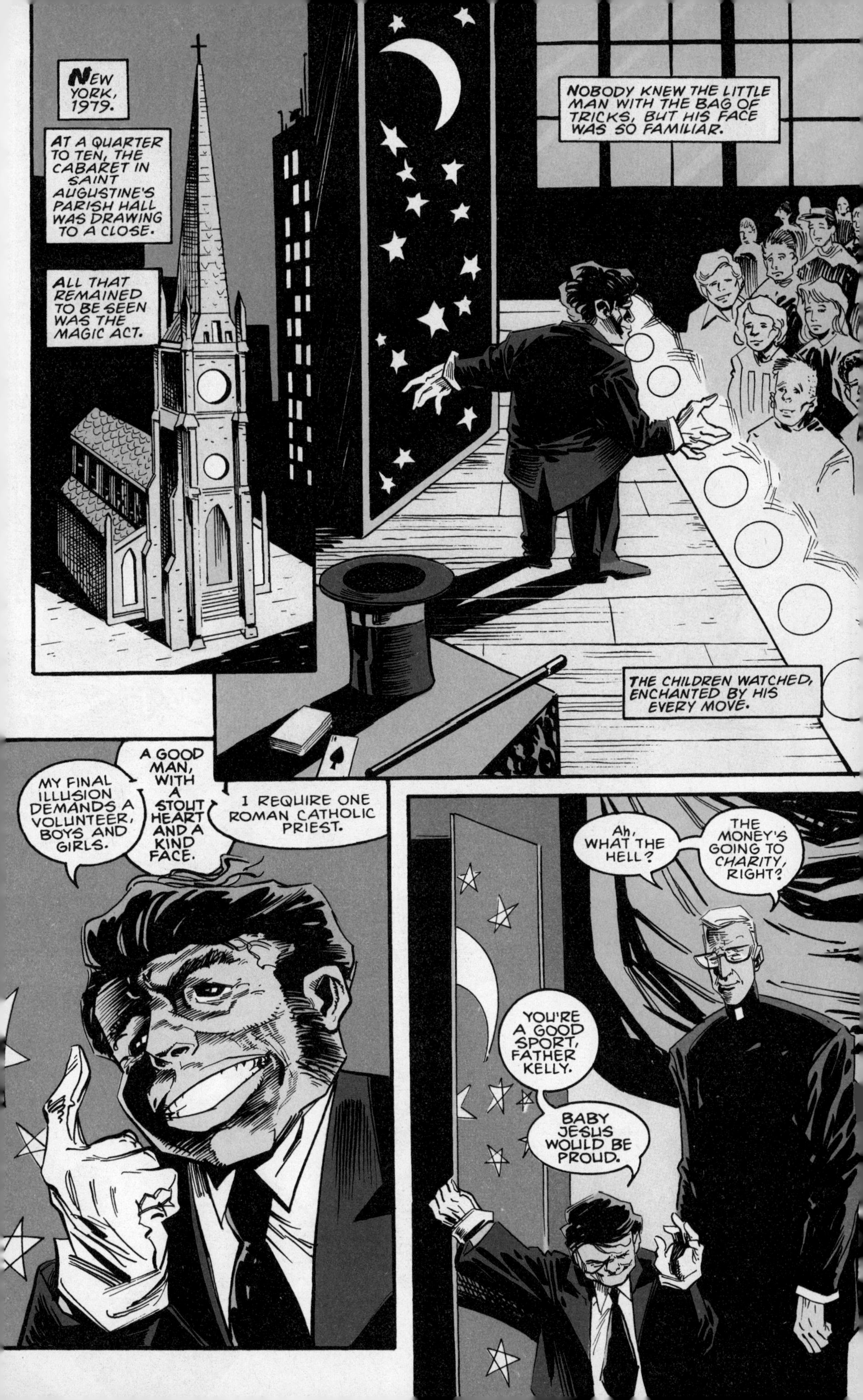
NEW YORK, 1979.
AT A QUARTER TO TEN, THE CABARET IN SAINT AUGUSTINE'S PARISH HALL WAS DRAWING TO A CLOSE.
ALL THAT REMAINED TO BE SEEN WAS THE MAGIC ACT.
NOBODY KNEW THE LITTLE MAN WITH THE BAG OF TRICKS, BUT HIS FACE WAS SO FAMILIAR.
THE CHILDREN WATCHED, ENCHANTED BY HIS EVERY MOVE.
MY FINAL ILLUSION DEMANDS A VOLUNTEER, BOYS AND GIRLS.
A GOOD MAN, WITH A STOUT HEART AND A KIND FACE.
I REQUIRE ONE ROMAN CATHOLIC PRIEST.
Ah, WHAT THE HELL?
THE MONEY'S GOING TO CHARITY, RIGHT?
YOU'RE A GOOD SPORT, FATHER KELLY.
BABY JESUS WOULD BE PROUD.

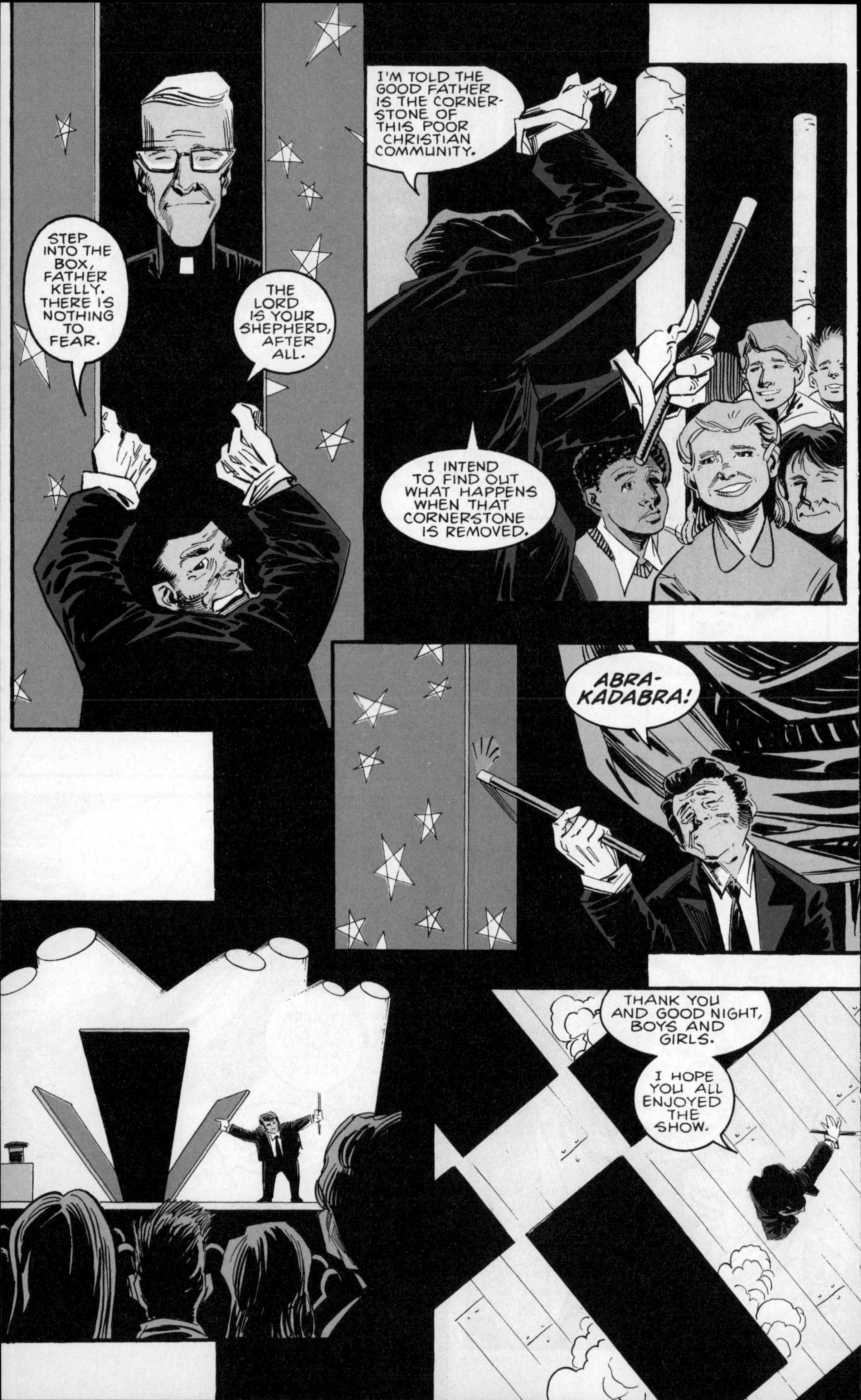
STEP INTO THE BOX, FATHER KELLY. THERE IS NOTHING TO FEAR.
THE LORD IS YOUR SHEPHERD, AFTER ALL.
I'M TOLD THE GOOD FATHER IS THE CORNER-STONE OF THIS POOR CHRISTIAN COMMUNITY.
I INTEND TO FIND OUT WHAT HAPPENS WHEN THAT CORNERSTONE IS REMOVED.
ABRA-KADABRA!
THANK YOU AND GOOD NIGHT, BOYS AND GIRLS.
I HOPE YOU ALL ENJOYED THE SHOW.

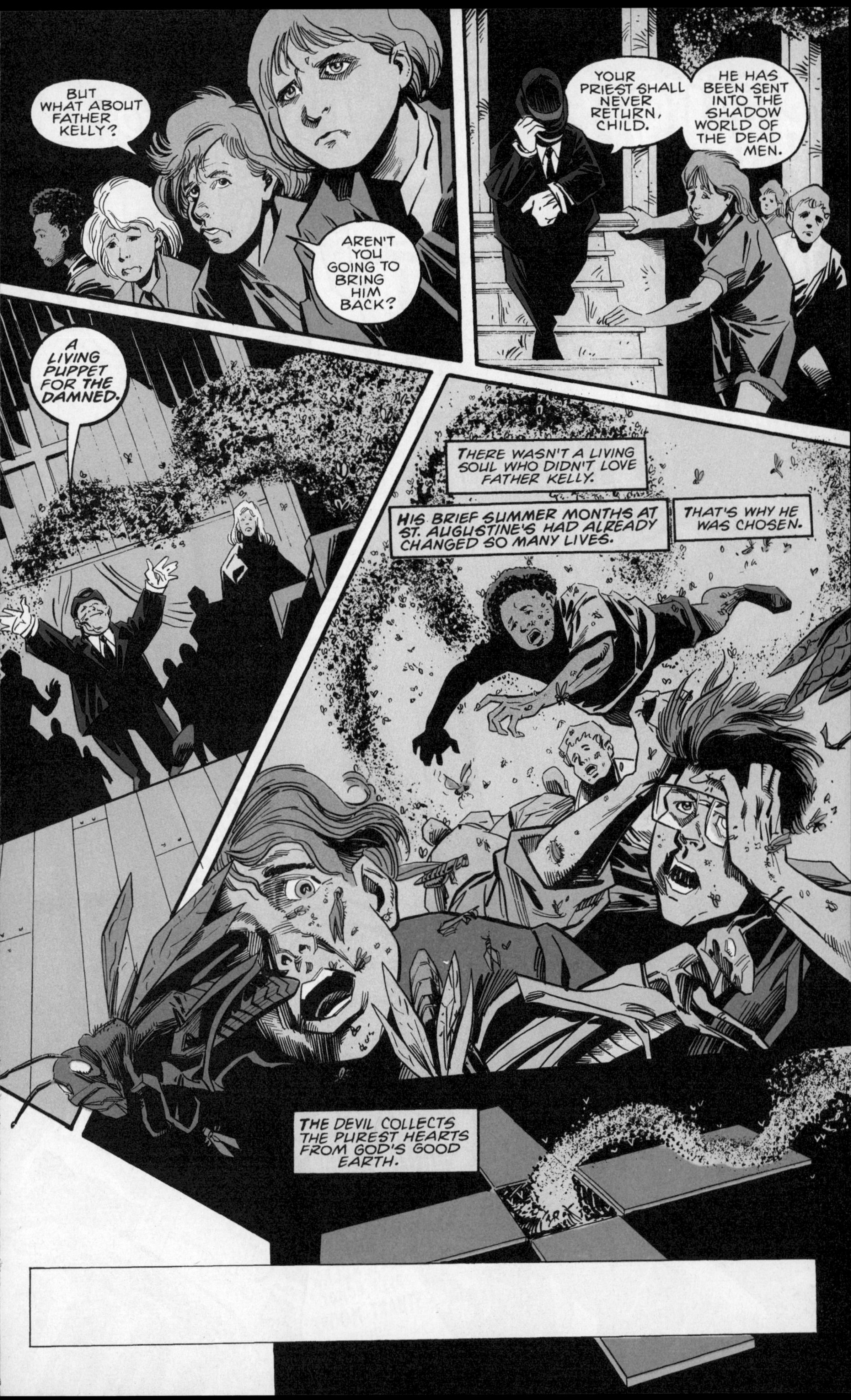
BUT WHAT ABOUT FATHER KELLY?
AREN'T YOU GOING TO BRING HIM BACK?
YOUR PRIEST SHALL NEVER RETURN, CHILD.
HE HAS BEEN SENT INTO THE SHADOW WORLD OF THE DEAD MEN.
A LIVING PUPPET FOR THE DAMNED.
THERE WASN'T A LIVING SOUL WHO DIDN'T LOVE FATHER KELLY.
HIS BRIEF SUMMER MONTHS AT ST. AUGUSTINE'S HAD ALREADY CHANGED SO MANY LIVES.
THAT'S WHY HE WAS CHOSEN.
THE DEVIL COLLECTS THE PUREST HEARTS FROM GOD'S GOOD EARTH.

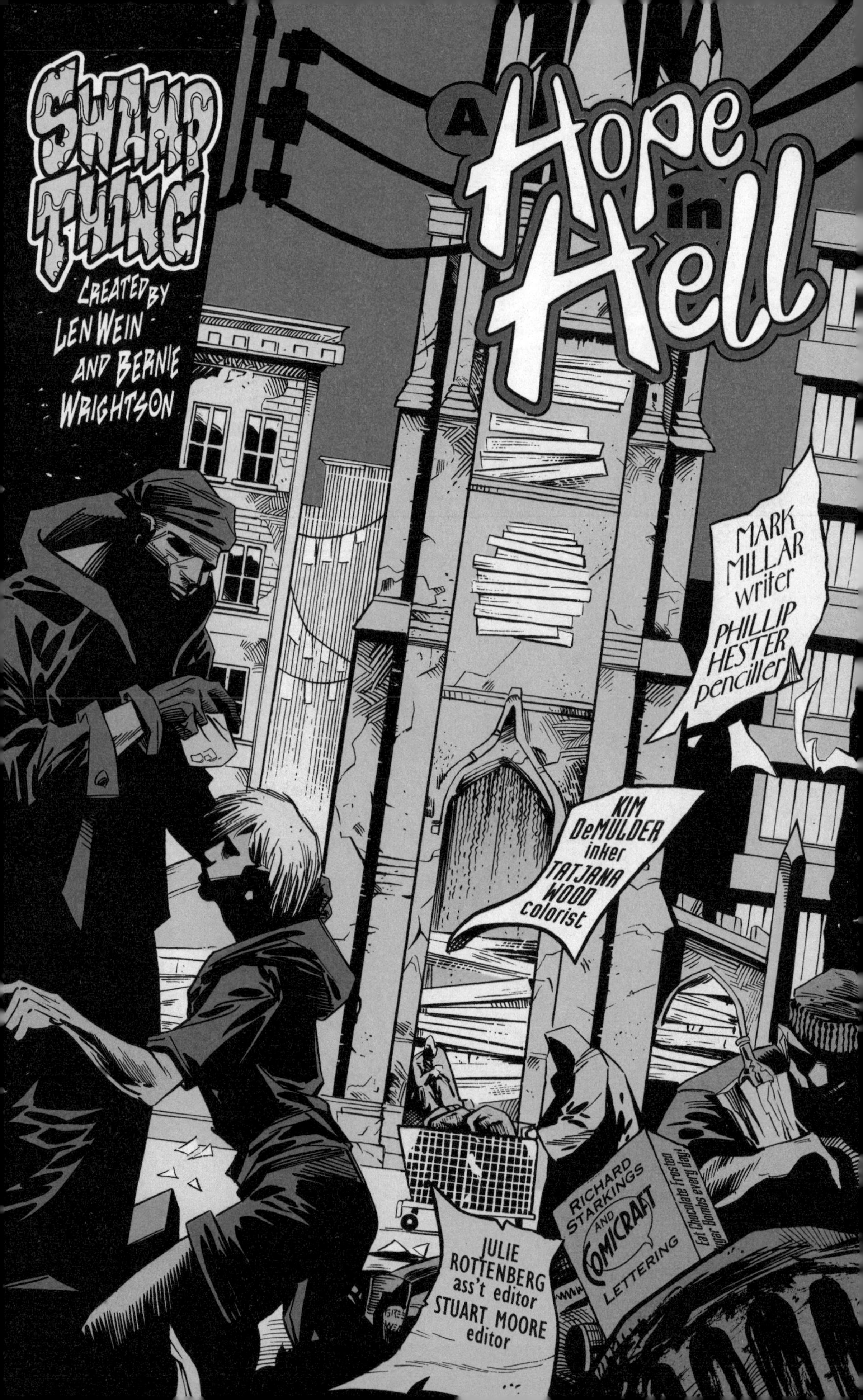

SWAMP THING
CREATED BY LEN WEIN AND BERNIE WRIGHTSON
A Hope in Hell
MARK MILLAR writer
PHILLIP HESTER penciller
KIM DeMULDER inker
TATJANA WOOD colorist
RICHARD STARKINGS AND COMICRAFT LETTERING
Eat Chocolate Frosted Sugar Bombs every day!
JULIE ROTTENBERG ass't editor
STUART MOORE editor

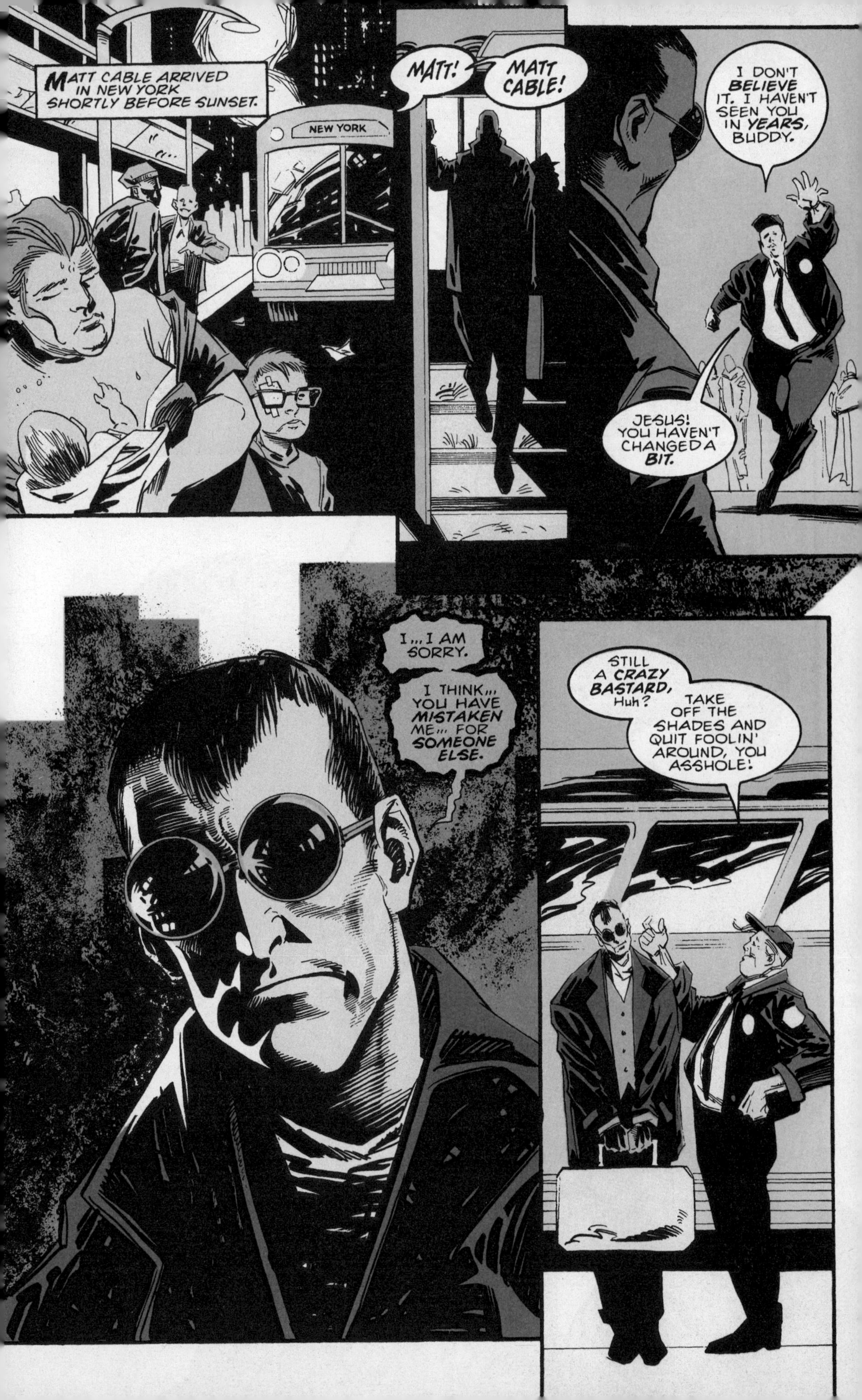
MATT CABLE ARRIVED IN NEW YORK SHORTLY BEFORE SUNSET.
NEW YORK
MATT!
MATT CABLE!
I DON'T BELIEVE IT. I HAVEN'T SEEN YOU IN YEARS, BUDDY.
JESUS! YOU HAVEN'T CHANGED A BIT.
I... I AM SORRY.
I THINK... YOU HAVE MISTAKEN ME... FOR SOMEONE ELSE.
STILL A CRAZY BASTARD, Huh?
TAKE OFF THE SHADES AND QUIT FOOLIN' AROUND, YOU ASSHOLE!

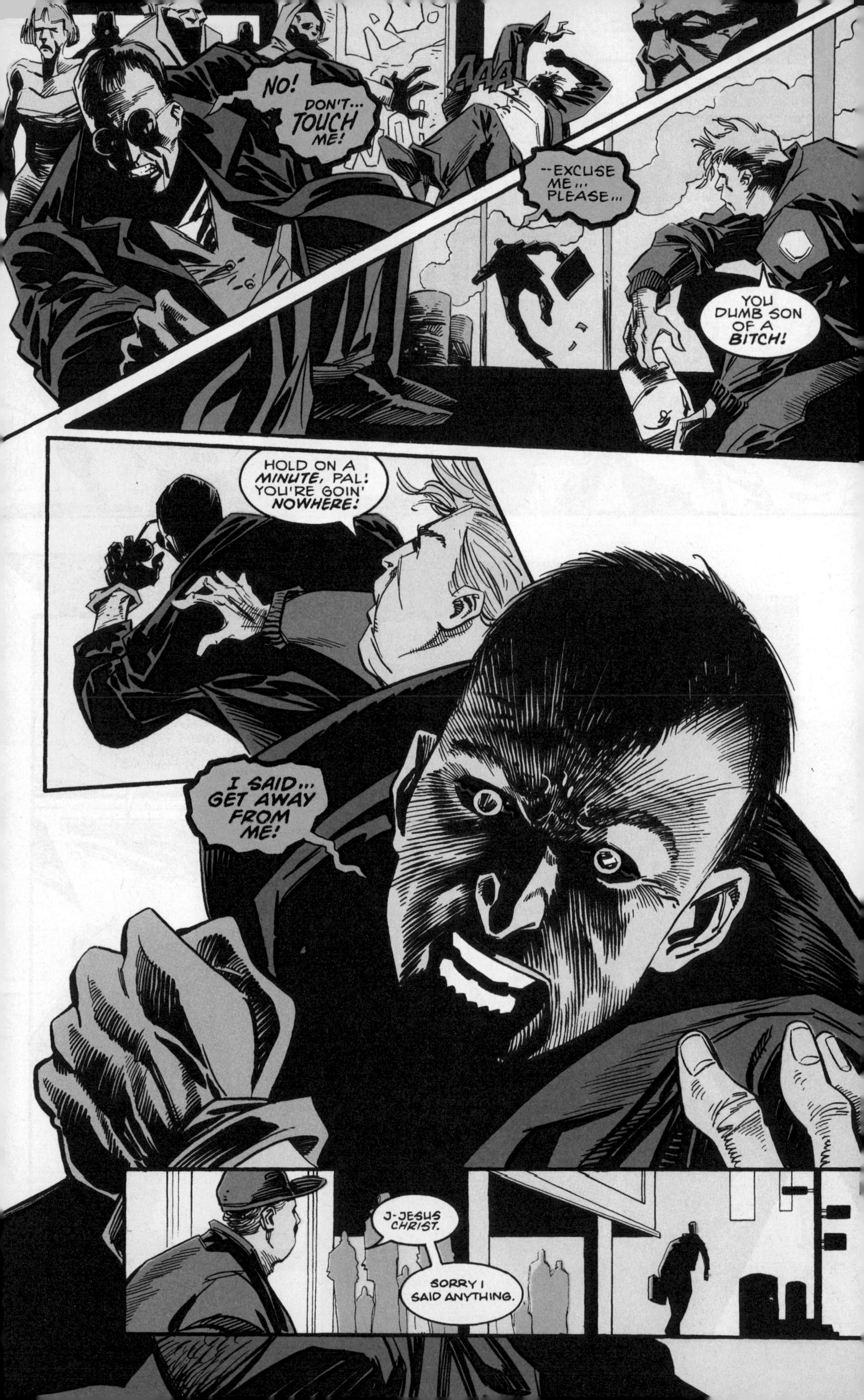
AAA
NO! DON'T... TOUCH ME!
--EXCUSE ME... PLEASE...
YOU DUMB SON OF A BITCH!
HOLD ON A MINUTE, PAL! YOU'RE GOIN' NOWHERE!
I SAID... GET AWAY FROM ME!
J-JESUS CHRIST.
SORRY I SAID ANYTHING.

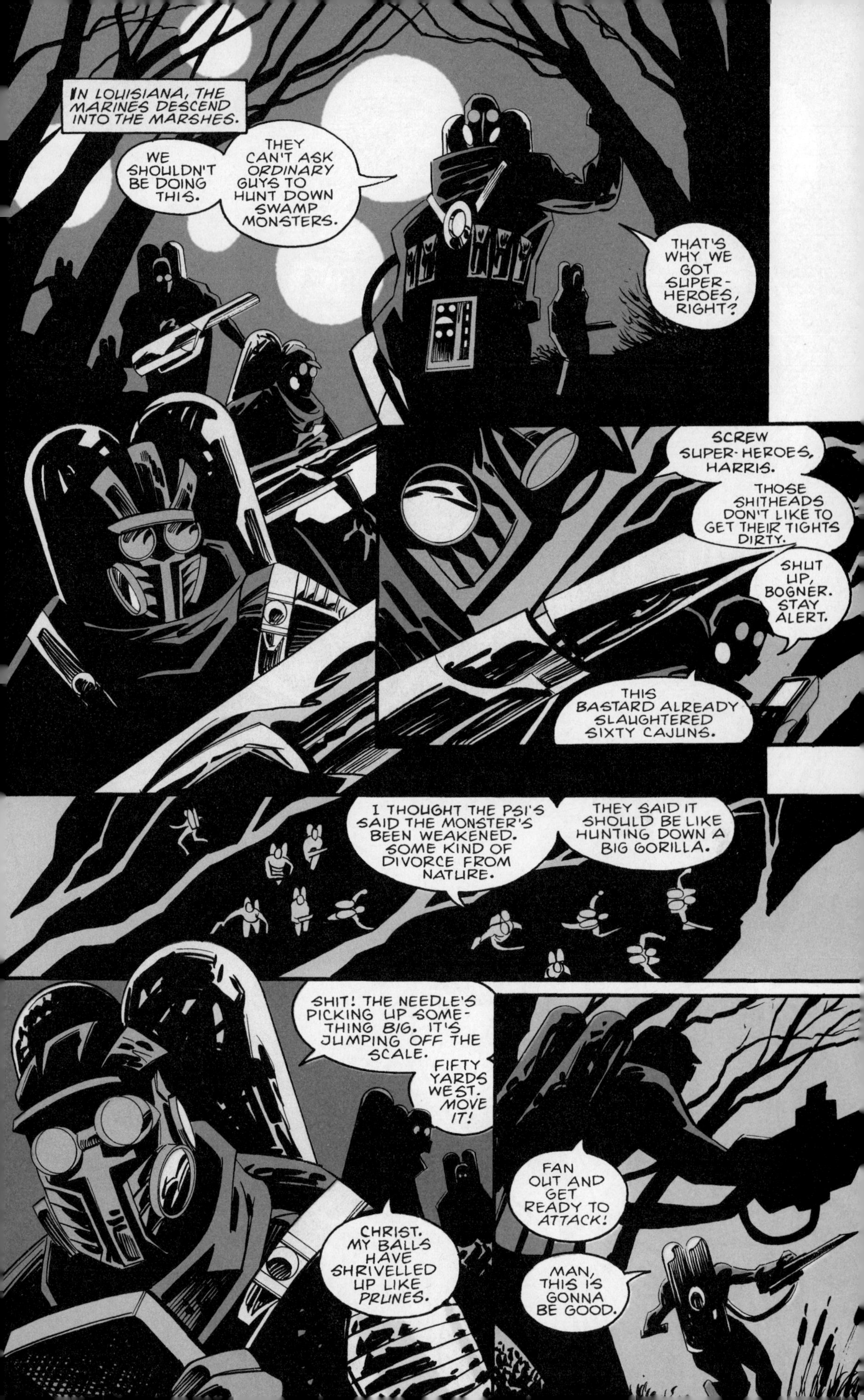
IN LOUISIANA, THE MARINES DESCEND INTO THE MARSHES.
WE SHOULDN'T BE DOING THIS.
THEY CAN'T ASK ORDINARY GUYS TO HUNT DOWN SWAMP MONSTERS.
THAT'S WHY WE GOT SUPER-HEROES, RIGHT?
SCREW SUPER-HEROES, HARRIS.
THOSE SHITHEADS DON'T LIKE TO GET THEIR TIGHTS DIRTY.
SHUT UP, BOGNER. STAY ALERT.
THIS BASTARD ALREADY SLAUGHTERED SIXTY CAJUNS.
I THOUGHT THE PSI'S SAID THE MONSTER'S BEEN WEAKENED. SOME KIND OF DIVORCE FROM NATURE.
THEY SAID IT SHOULD BE LIKE HUNTING DOWN A BIG GORILLA.
SHIT! THE NEEDLE'S PICKING UP SOMETHING BIG. IT'S JUMPING OFF THE SCALE.
FIFTY YARDS WEST. MOVE IT!
CHRIST. MY BALLS HAVE SHRIVELLED UP LIKE PRUNES.
FAN OUT AND GET READY TO ATTACK!
MAN, THIS IS GONNA BE GOOD.

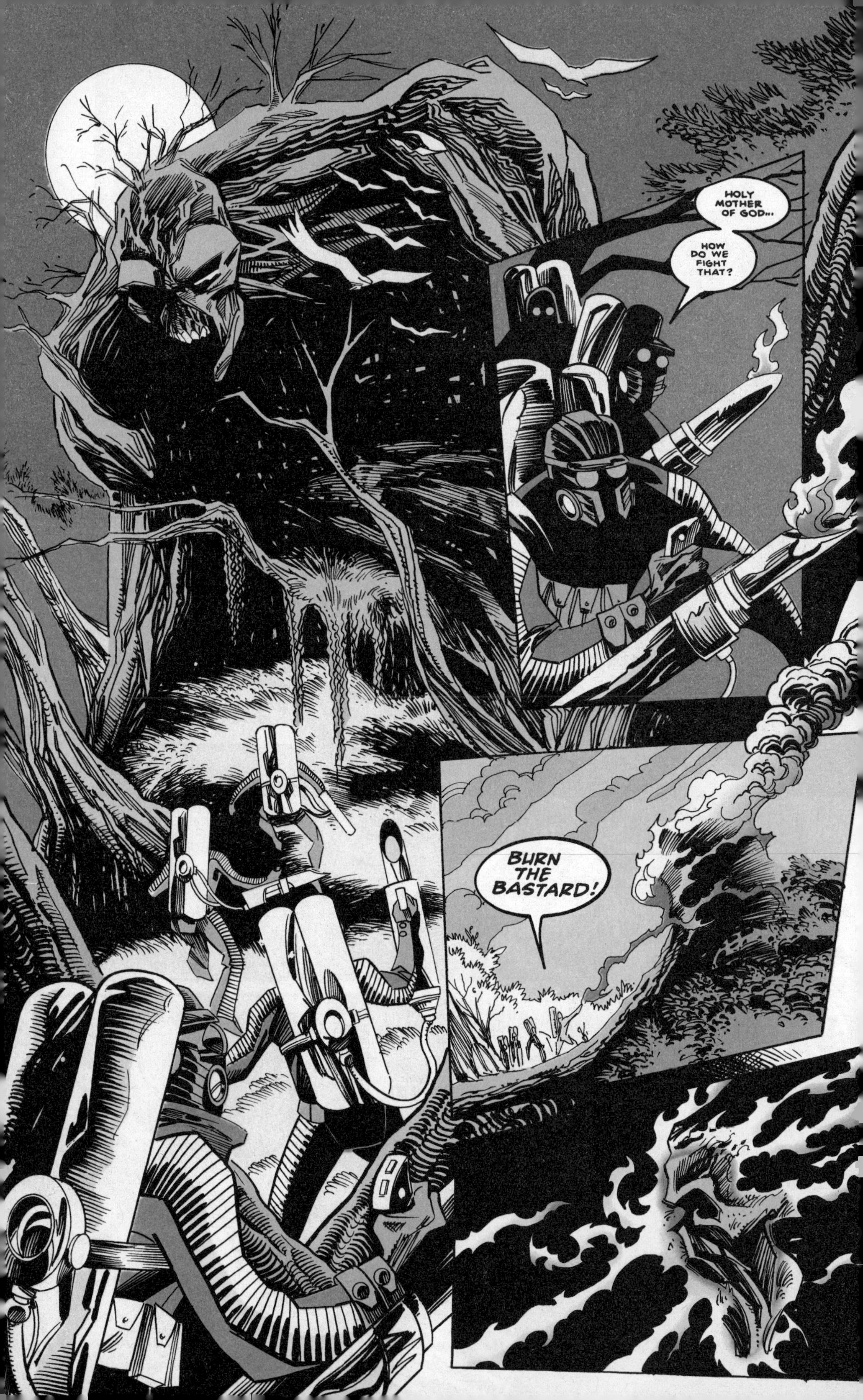
HOLY MOTHER OF GOD...
HOW DO WE FIGHT THAT?
BURN THE BASTARD!

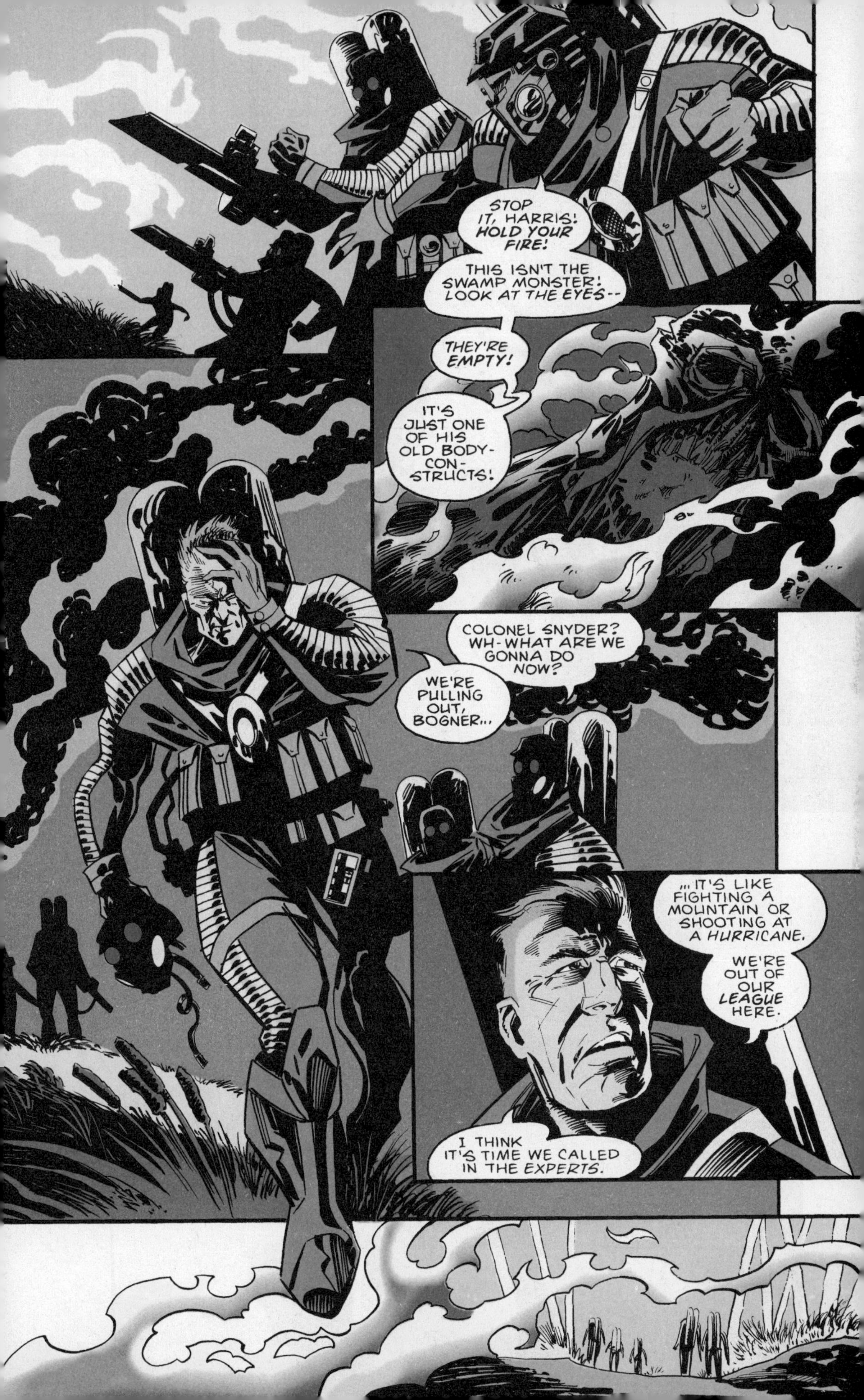
STOP IT, HARRIS! HOLD YOUR FIRE!
THIS ISN'T THE SWAMP MONSTER! LOOK AT THE EYES--
THEY'RE EMPTY!
IT'S JUST ONE OF HIS OLD BODY-CON-STRUCTS!
COLONEL SNYDER? WH-WHAT ARE WE GONNA DO NOW?
WE'RE PULLING OUT, BOGNER...
...IT'S LIKE FIGHTING A MOUNTAIN OR SHOOTING AT A HURRICANE.
WE'RE OUT OF OUR LEAGUE HERE.
I THINK IT'S TIME WE CALLED IN THE EXPERTS.

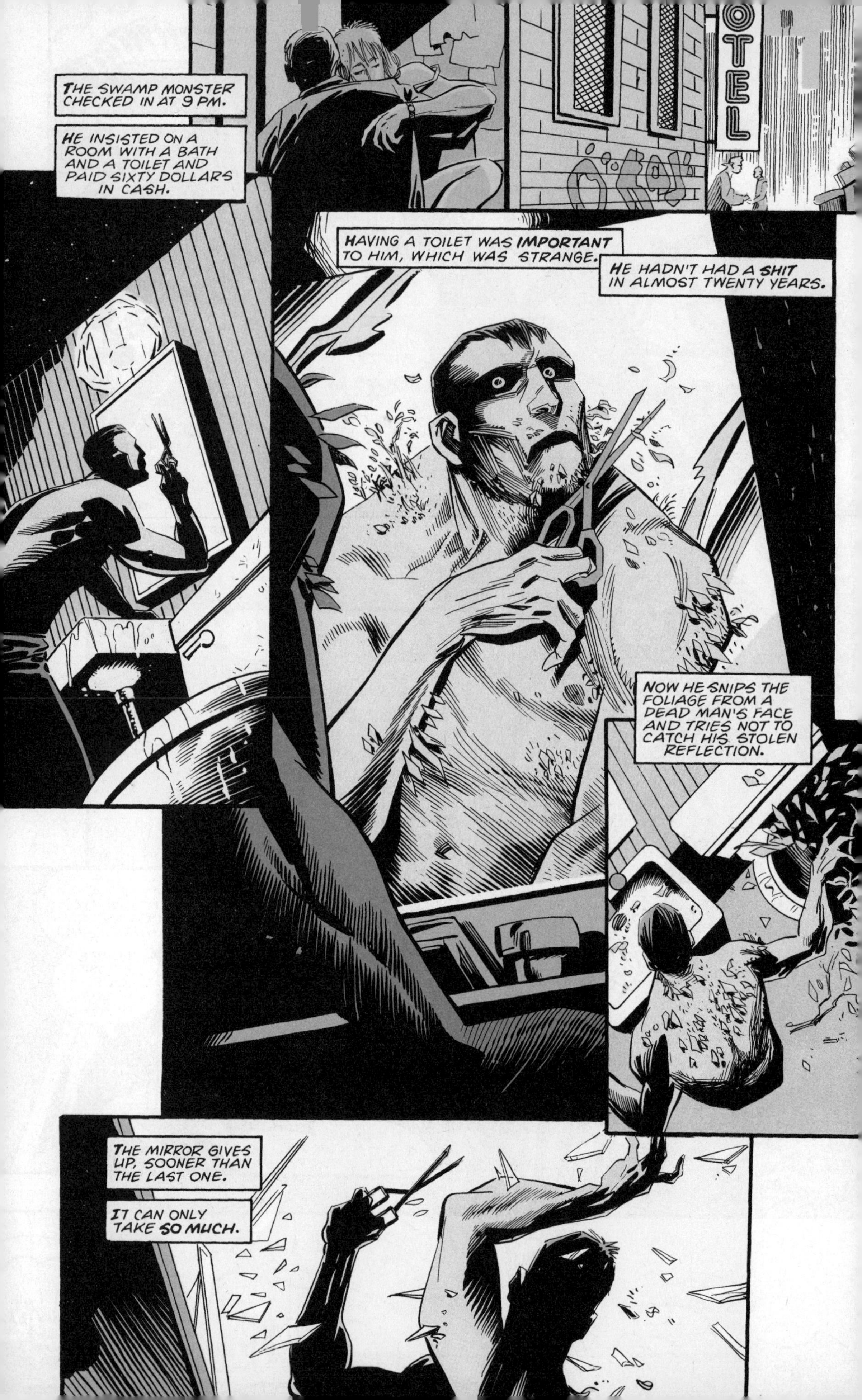
THE SWAMP MONSTER CHECKED IN AT 9 PM.
HE INSISTED ON A ROOM WITH A BATH AND A TOILET AND PAID SIXTY DOLLARS IN CASH.
OTEL
HAVING A TOILET WAS **IMPORTANT** TO HIM, WHICH WAS STRANGE.
HE HADN'T HAD A **SHIT** IN ALMOST TWENTY YEARS.
NOW HE SNIPS THE FOLIAGE FROM A DEAD MAN'S FACE AND TRIES NOT TO CATCH HIS STOLEN REFLECTION.
THE MIRROR GIVES UP, SOONER THAN THE LAST ONE.
IT CAN ONLY TAKE **SO MUCH**.

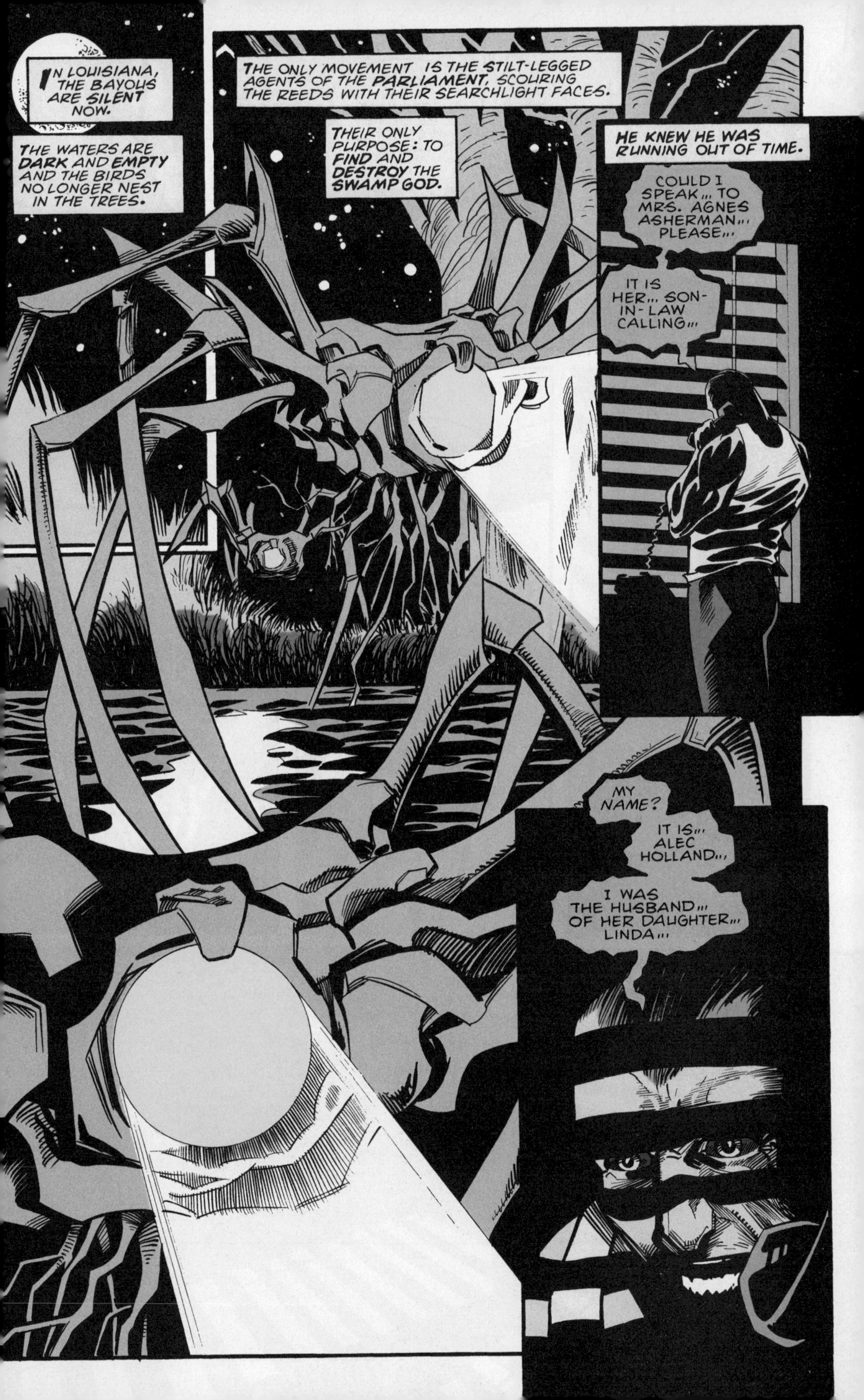
IN LOUISIANA, THE BAYOUS ARE SILENT NOW.
THE WATERS ARE DARK AND EMPTY AND THE BIRDS NO LONGER NEST IN THE TREES.
THE ONLY MOVEMENT IS THE STILT-LEGGED AGENTS OF THE PARLIAMENT, SCOURING THE REEDS WITH THEIR SEARCHLIGHT FACES.
THEIR ONLY PURPOSE: TO FIND AND DESTROY THE SWAMP GOD.
HE KNEW HE WAS RUNNING OUT OF TIME.
COULD I SPEAK... TO MRS. AGNES ASHERMAN... PLEASE...
IT IS HER... SON-IN-LAW CALLING...
MY NAME?
IT IS... ALEC HOLLAND...
I WAS THE HUSBAND... OF HER DAUGHTER... LINDA...

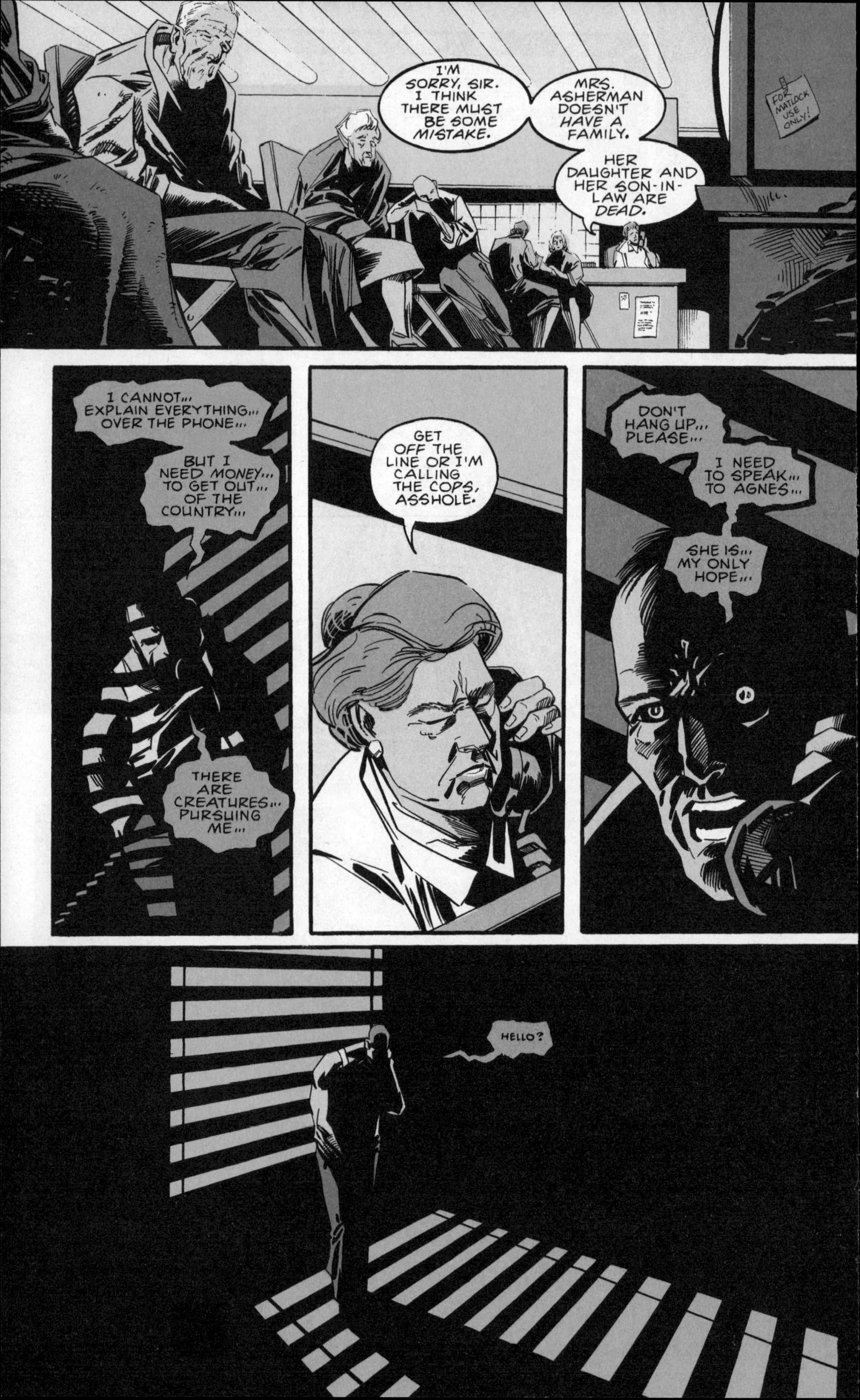
I'M SORRY, SIR. I THINK THERE MUST BE SOME MISTAKE.
MRS. ASHERMAN DOESN'T HAVE A FAMILY.
HER DAUGHTER AND HER SON-IN-LAW ARE DEAD.
FOR MATLOCK USE ONLY!
I CANNOT... EXPLAIN EVERYTHING... OVER THE PHONE...
BUT I NEED MONEY... TO GET OUT... OF THE COUNTRY...
THERE ARE CREATURES... PURSUING ME...
GET OFF THE LINE OR I'M CALLING THE COPS, ASSHOLE.
DON'T HANG UP... PLEASE...
I NEED TO SPEAK... TO AGNES...
SHE IS... MY ONLY HOPE...
HELLO?

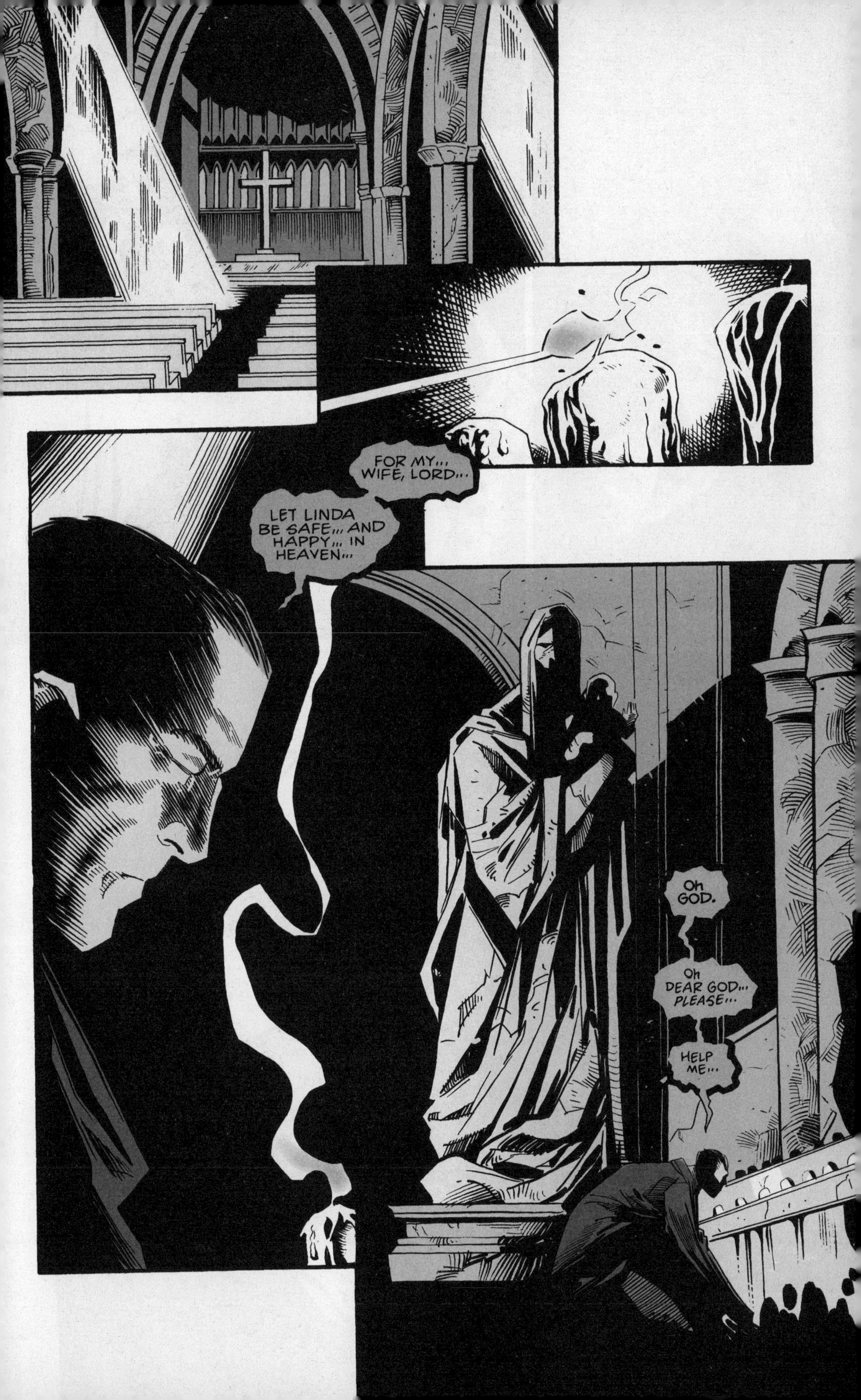
FOR MY... WIFE, LORD...
LET LINDA BE SAFE... AND HAPPY... IN HEAVEN...
Oh GOD.
Oh DEAR GOD... PLEASE...
HELP ME...

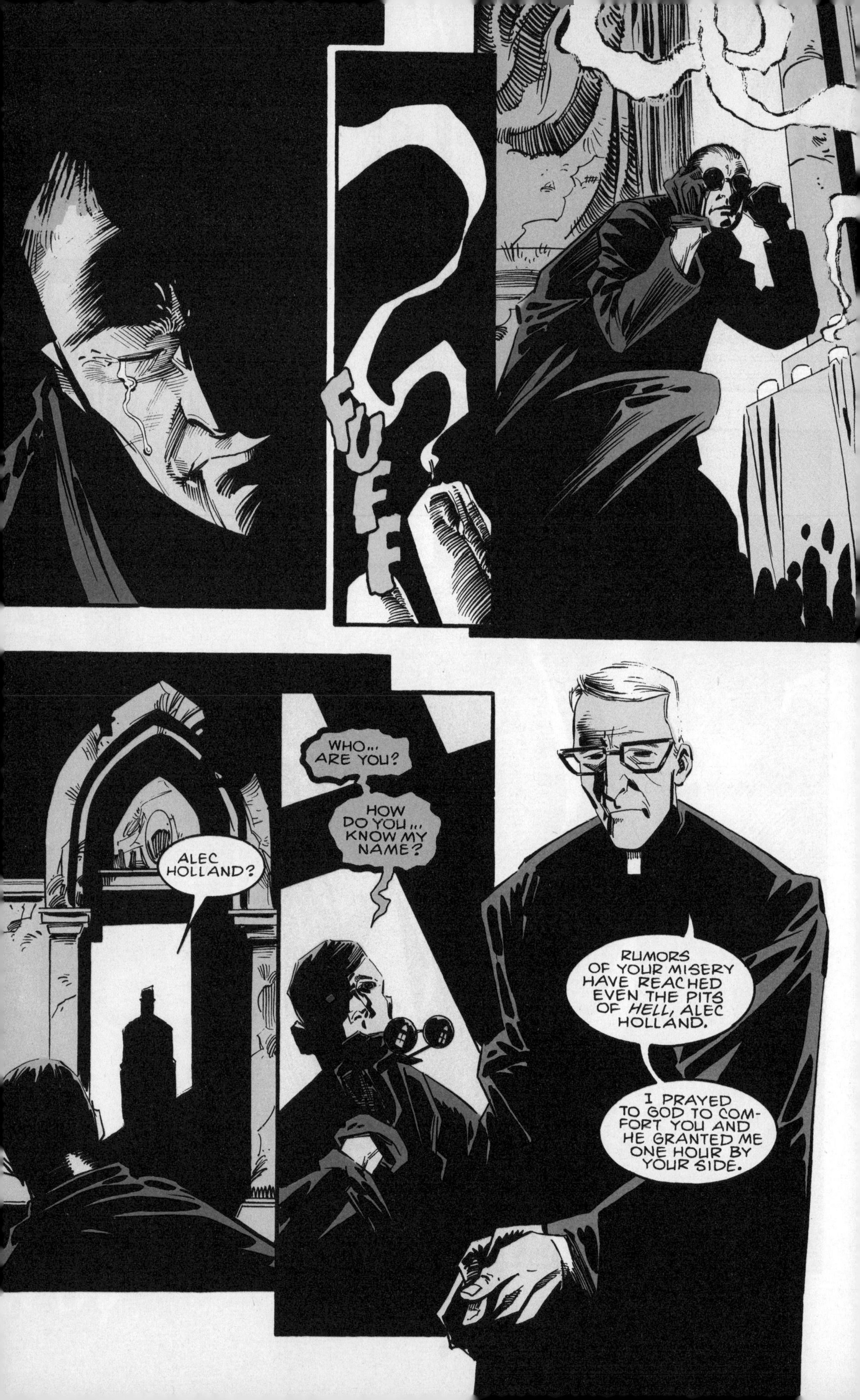
FUFF
ALEC HOLLAND?
WHO... ARE YOU?
HOW DO YOU... KNOW MY NAME?
RUMORS OF YOUR MISERY HAVE REACHED EVEN THE PITS OF *HELL*, ALEC HOLLAND.
I PRAYED TO GOD TO COMFORT YOU AND HE GRANTED ME ONE HOUR BY YOUR SIDE.

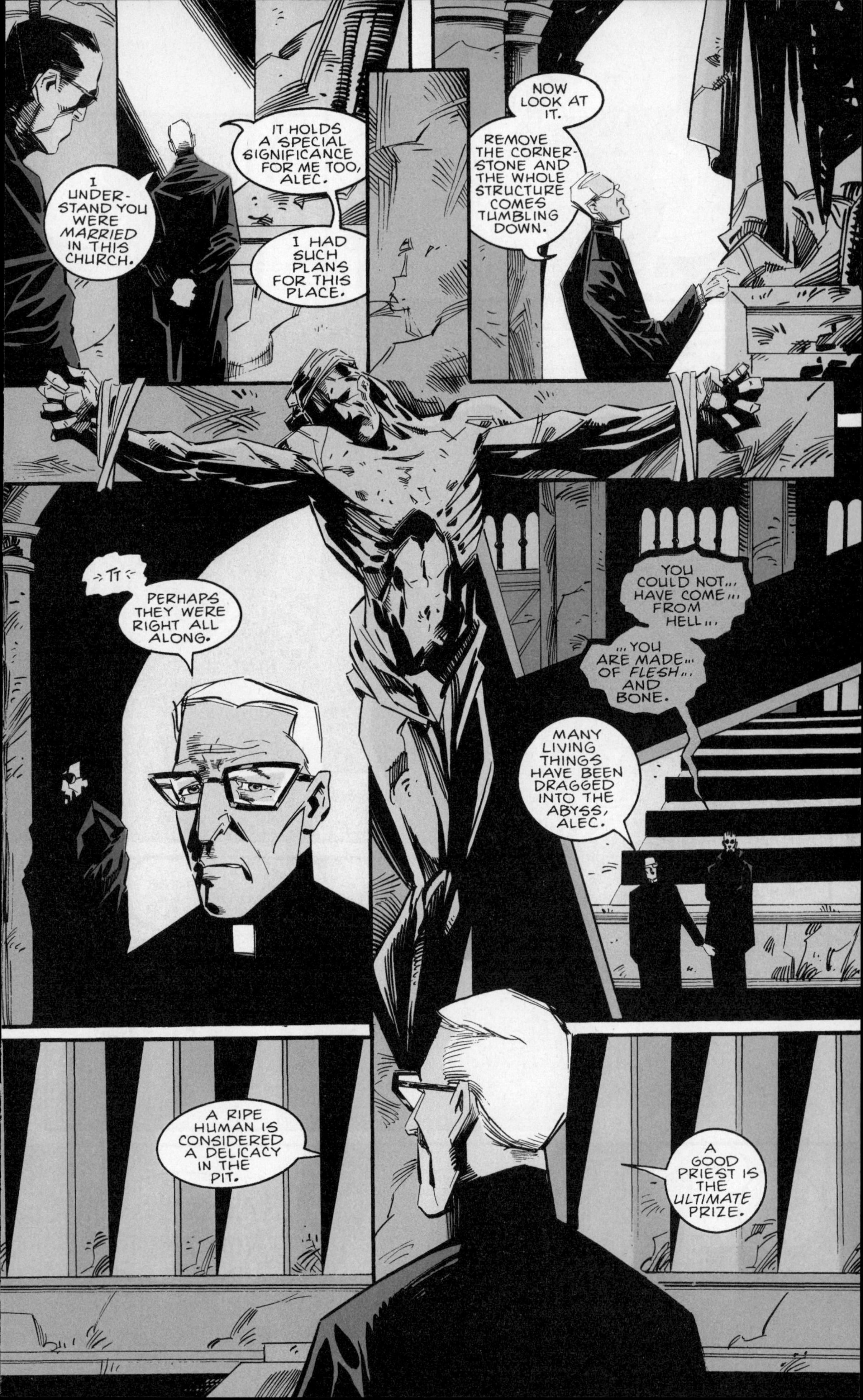
I UNDERSTAND YOU WERE MARRIED IN THIS CHURCH.
IT HOLDS A SPECIAL SIGNIFICANCE FOR ME TOO, ALEC.
I HAD SUCH PLANS FOR THIS PLACE.
NOW LOOK AT IT.
REMOVE THE CORNERSTONE AND THE WHOLE STRUCTURE COMES TUMBLING DOWN.
TT
PERHAPS THEY WERE RIGHT ALL ALONG.
YOU COULD NOT... HAVE COME... FROM HELL...
...YOU ARE MADE... OF FLESH... AND BONE.
MANY LIVING THINGS HAVE BEEN DRAGGED INTO THE ABYSS, ALEC.
A RIPE HUMAN IS CONSIDERED A DELICACY IN THE PIT.
A GOOD PRIEST IS THE ULTIMATE PRIZE.

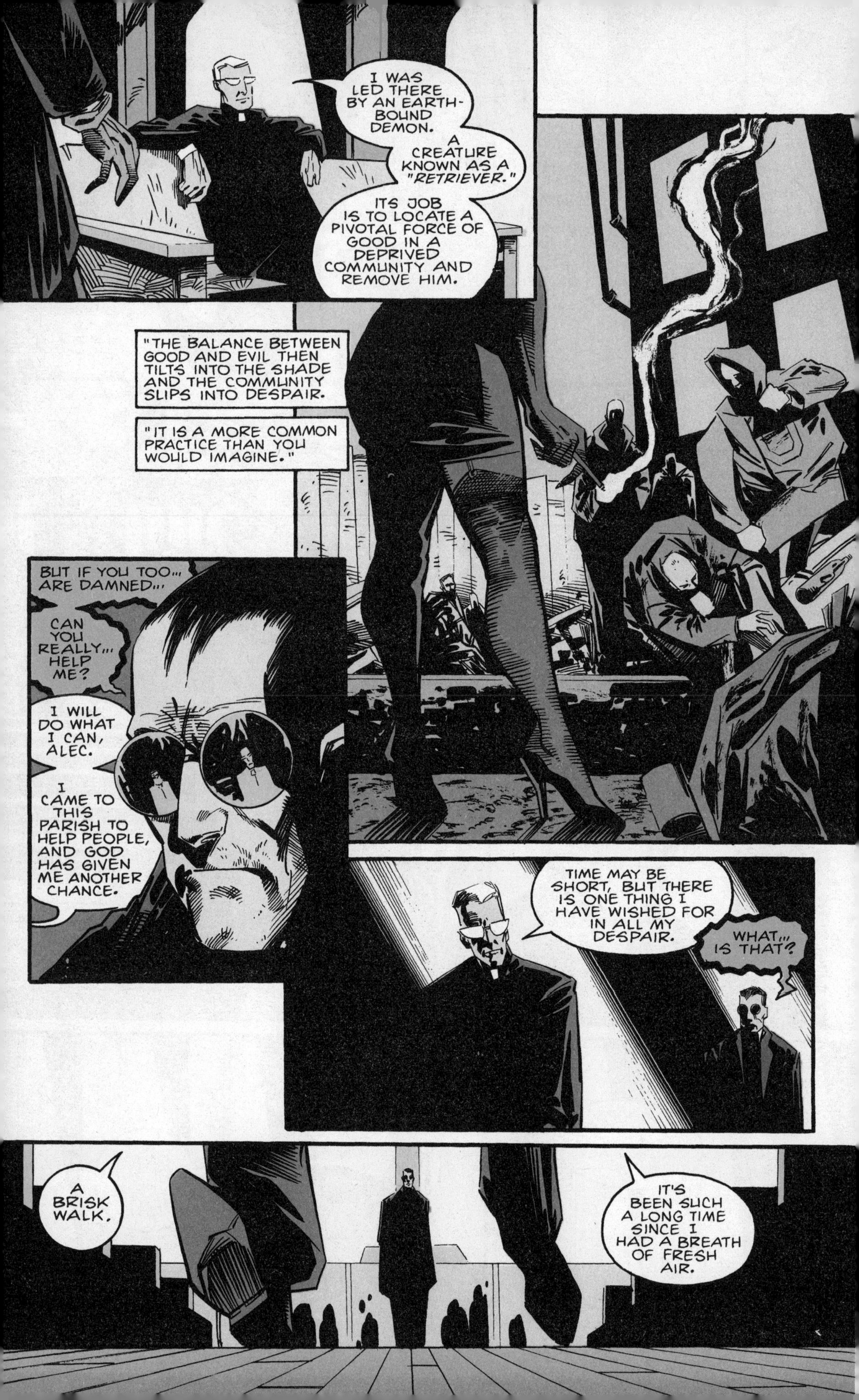
I WAS LED THERE BY AN EARTH-BOUND DEMON.
A CREATURE KNOWN AS A "RETRIEVER."
ITS JOB IS TO LOCATE A PIVOTAL FORCE OF GOOD IN A DEPRIVED COMMUNITY AND REMOVE HIM.
"THE BALANCE BETWEEN GOOD AND EVIL THEN TILTS INTO THE SHADE AND THE COMMUNITY SLIPS INTO DESPAIR.
"IT IS A MORE COMMON PRACTICE THAN YOU WOULD IMAGINE."
BUT IF YOU TOO... ARE DAMNED...
CAN YOU REALLY... HELP ME?
I WILL DO WHAT I CAN, ALEC.
I CAME TO THIS PARISH TO HELP PEOPLE, AND GOD HAS GIVEN ME ANOTHER CHANCE.
TIME MAY BE SHORT, BUT THERE IS ONE THING I HAVE WISHED FOR IN ALL MY DESPAIR.
WHAT... IS THAT?
A BRISK WALK.
IT'S BEEN SUCH A LONG TIME SINCE I HAD A BREATH OF FRESH AIR.

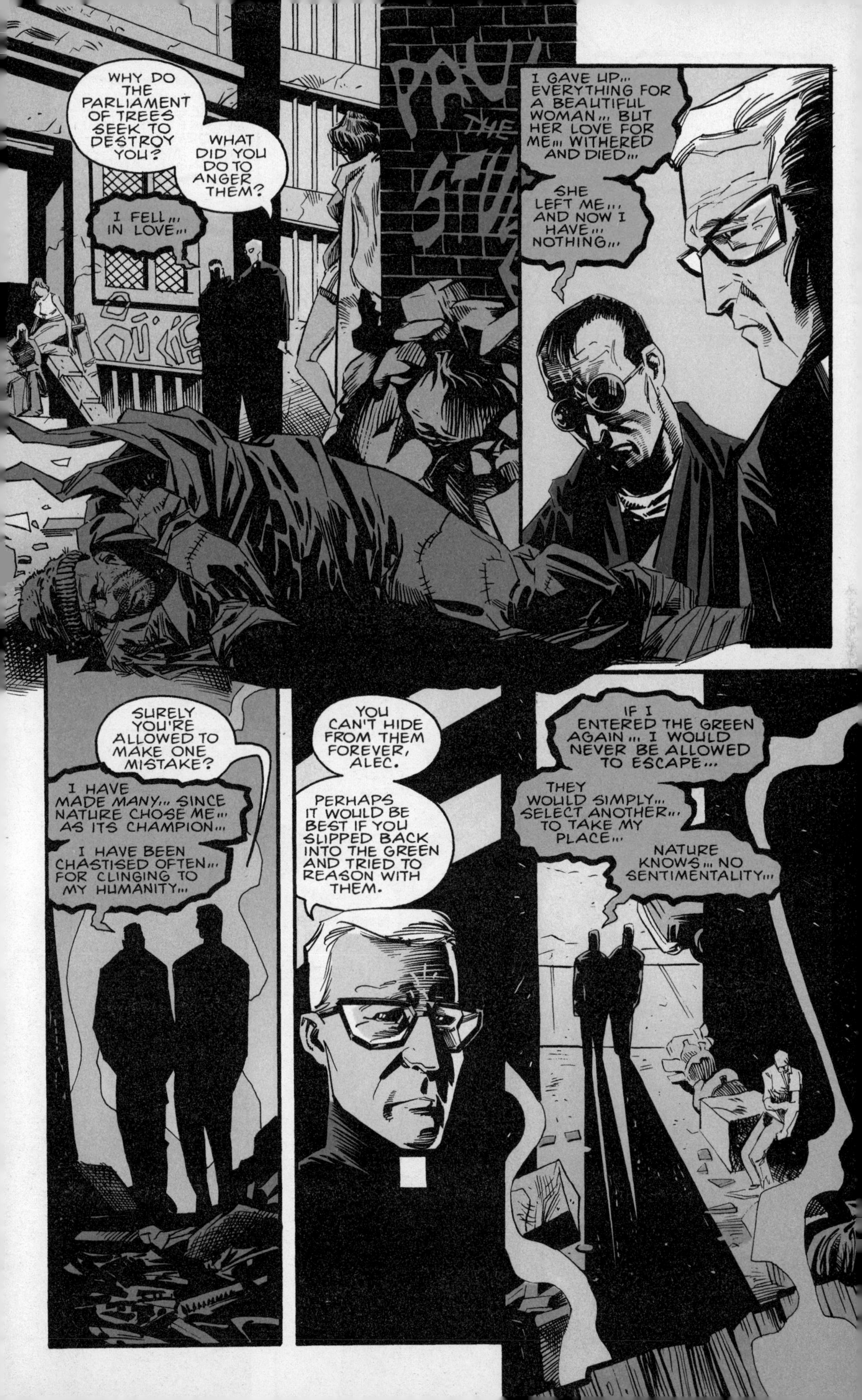
WHY DO THE PARLIAMENT OF TREES SEEK TO DESTROY YOU?
WHAT DID YOU DO TO ANGER THEM?
I FELL... IN LOVE...
I GAVE UP... EVERYTHING FOR A BEAUTIFUL WOMAN... BUT HER LOVE FOR ME... WITHERED AND DIED...
SHE LEFT ME... AND NOW I HAVE... NOTHING...
SURELY YOU'RE ALLOWED TO MAKE ONE MISTAKE?
I HAVE MADE MANY... SINCE NATURE CHOSE ME... AS ITS CHAMPION...
I HAVE BEEN CHASTISED OFTEN... FOR CLINGING TO MY HUMANITY...
YOU CAN'T HIDE FROM THEM FOREVER, ALEC.
PERHAPS IT WOULD BE BEST IF YOU SLIPPED BACK INTO THE GREEN AND TRIED TO REASON WITH THEM.
IF I ENTERED THE GREEN AGAIN... I WOULD NEVER BE ALLOWED TO ESCAPE...
THEY WOULD SIMPLY... SELECT ANOTHER... TO TAKE MY PLACE...
NATURE KNOWS... NO SENTIMENTALITY...

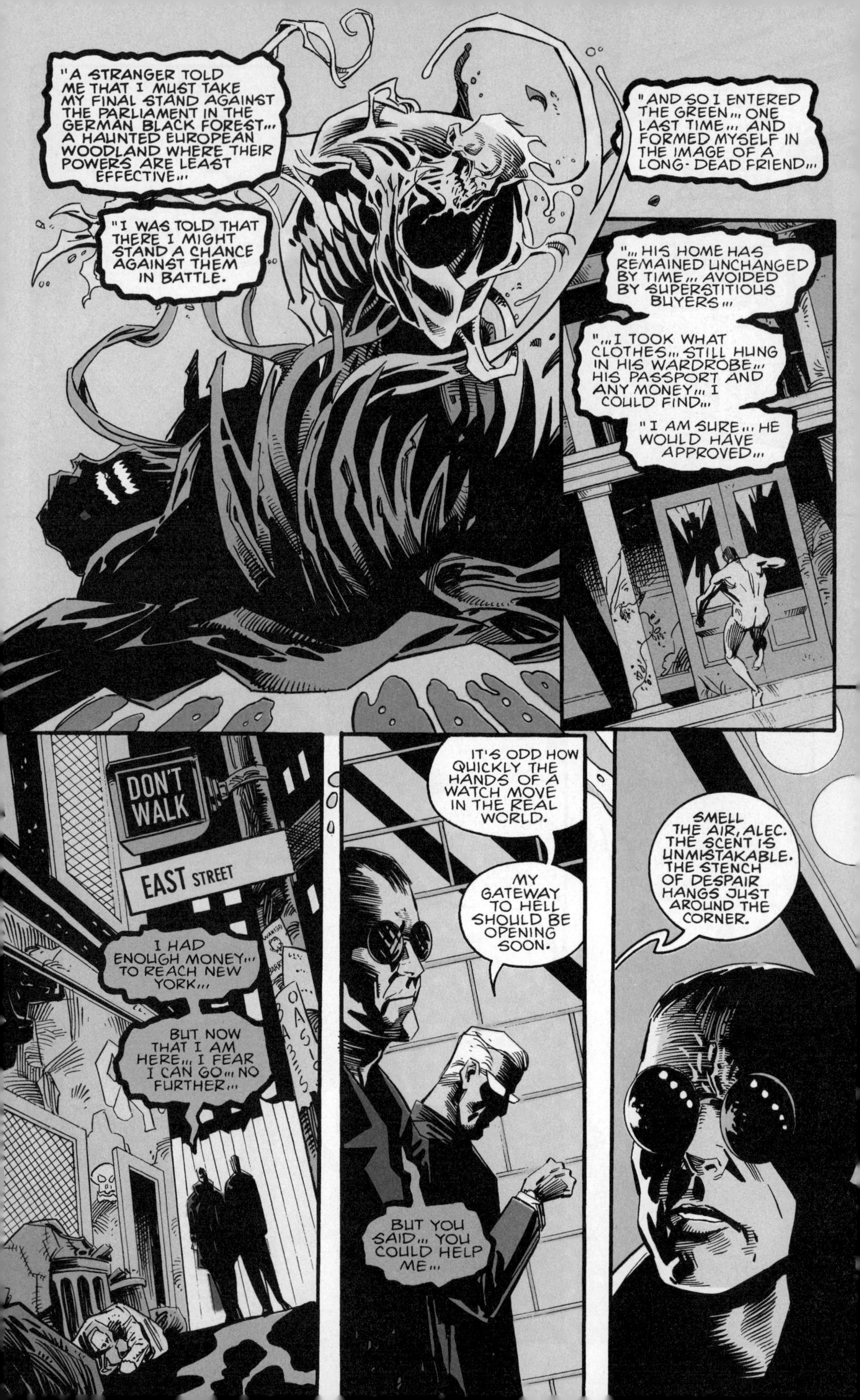
"A STRANGER TOLD ME THAT I MUST TAKE MY FINAL STAND AGAINST THE PARLIAMENT IN THE GERMAN BLACK FOREST... A HAUNTED EUROPEAN WOODLAND WHERE THEIR POWERS ARE LEAST EFFECTIVE...
"I WAS TOLD THAT THERE I MIGHT STAND A CHANCE AGAINST THEM IN BATTLE.
"AND SO I ENTERED THE GREEN... ONE LAST TIME... AND FORMED MYSELF IN THE IMAGE OF A LONG-DEAD FRIEND...
"...HIS HOME HAS REMAINED UNCHANGED BY TIME... AVOIDED BY SUPERSTITIOUS BUYERS...
"...I TOOK WHAT CLOTHES... STILL HUNG IN HIS WARDROBE... HIS PASSPORT AND ANY MONEY... I COULD FIND...
"I AM SURE... HE WOULD HAVE APPROVED...
DON'T WALK
EAST STREET
I HAD ENOUGH MONEY... TO REACH NEW YORK...
BUT NOW THAT I AM HERE... I FEAR I CAN GO... NO FURTHER...
IT'S ODD HOW QUICKLY THE HANDS OF A WATCH MOVE IN THE REAL WORLD.
MY GATEWAY TO HELL SHOULD BE OPENING SOON.
BUT YOU SAID... YOU COULD HELP ME...
SMELL THE AIR, ALEC. THE SCENT IS UNMISTAKABLE. THE STENCH OF DESPAIR HANGS JUST AROUND THE CORNER.

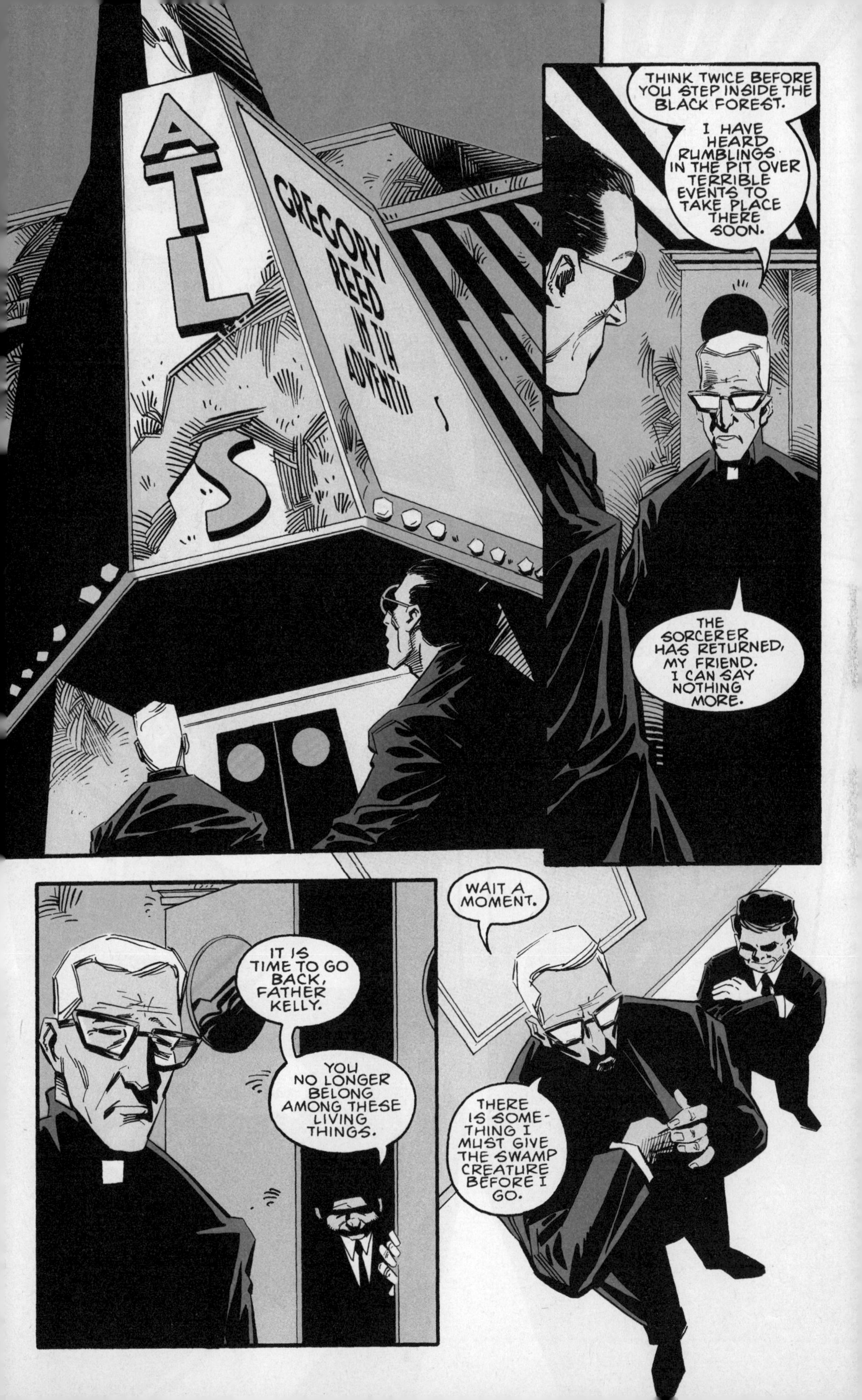
ATL
GREGORY REED IN TH ADVENT
S
THINK TWICE BEFORE YOU STEP INSIDE THE BLACK FOREST.
I HAVE HEARD RUMBLINGS IN THE PIT OVER TERRIBLE EVENTS TO TAKE PLACE THERE SOON.
THE SORCERER HAS RETURNED, MY FRIEND. I CAN SAY NOTHING MORE.
IT IS TIME TO GO BACK, FATHER KELLY.
YOU NO LONGER BELONG AMONG THESE LIVING THINGS.
WAIT A MOMENT.
THERE IS SOME-THING I MUST GIVE THE SWAMP CREATURE BEFORE I GO.

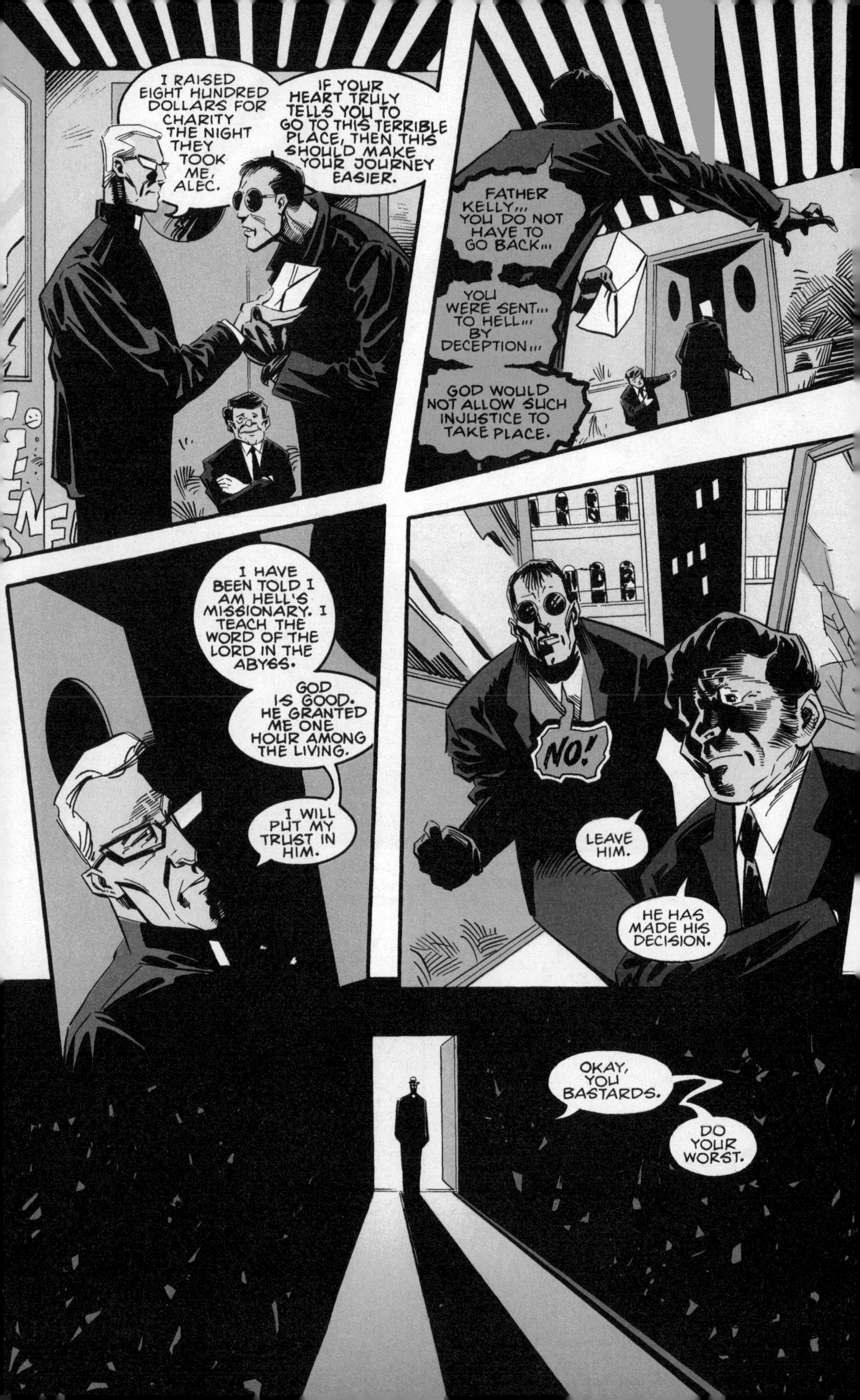
I RAISED EIGHT HUNDRED DOLLARS FOR CHARITY THE NIGHT THEY TOOK ME, ALEC.
IF YOUR HEART TRULY TELLS YOU TO GO TO THIS TERRIBLE PLACE, THEN THIS SHOULD MAKE YOUR JOURNEY EASIER.
FATHER KELLY... YOU DO NOT HAVE TO GO BACK...
YOU WERE SENT... TO HELL... BY DECEPTION...
GOD WOULD NOT ALLOW SUCH INJUSTICE TO TAKE PLACE.
I HAVE BEEN TOLD I AM HELL'S MISSIONARY. I TEACH THE WORD OF THE LORD IN THE ABYSS.
GOD IS GOOD. HE GRANTED ME ONE HOUR AMONG THE LIVING.
I WILL PUT MY TRUST IN HIM.
NO!
LEAVE HIM.
HE HAS MADE HIS DECISION.
OKAY, YOU BASTARDS.
DO YOUR WORST.

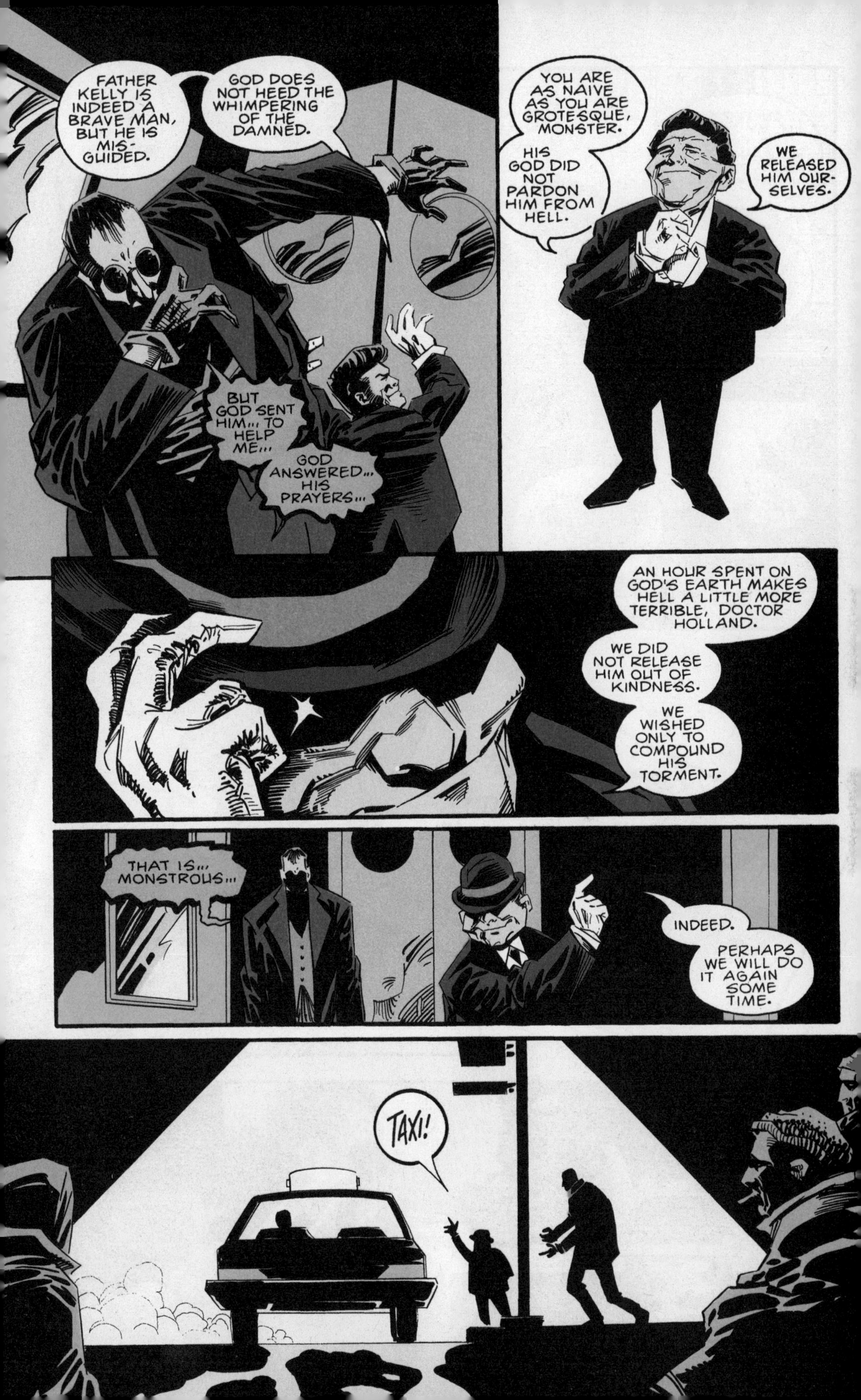
FATHER KELLY IS INDEED A BRAVE MAN, BUT HE IS MIS-GUIDED.
GOD DOES NOT HEED THE WHIMPERING OF THE DAMNED.
BUT GOD SENT HIM... TO HELP ME...
GOD ANSWERED... HIS PRAYERS...
YOU ARE AS NAIVE AS YOU ARE GROTESQUE, MONSTER.
HIS GOD DID NOT PARDON HIM FROM HELL.
WE RELEASED HIM OUR-SELVES.
AN HOUR SPENT ON GOD'S EARTH MAKES HELL A LITTLE MORE TERRIBLE, DOCTOR HOLLAND.
WE DID NOT RELEASE HIM OUT OF KINDNESS.
WE WISHED ONLY TO COMPOUND HIS TORMENT.
THAT IS... MONSTROUS...
INDEED.
PERHAPS WE WILL DO IT AGAIN SOME TIME.
TAXI!

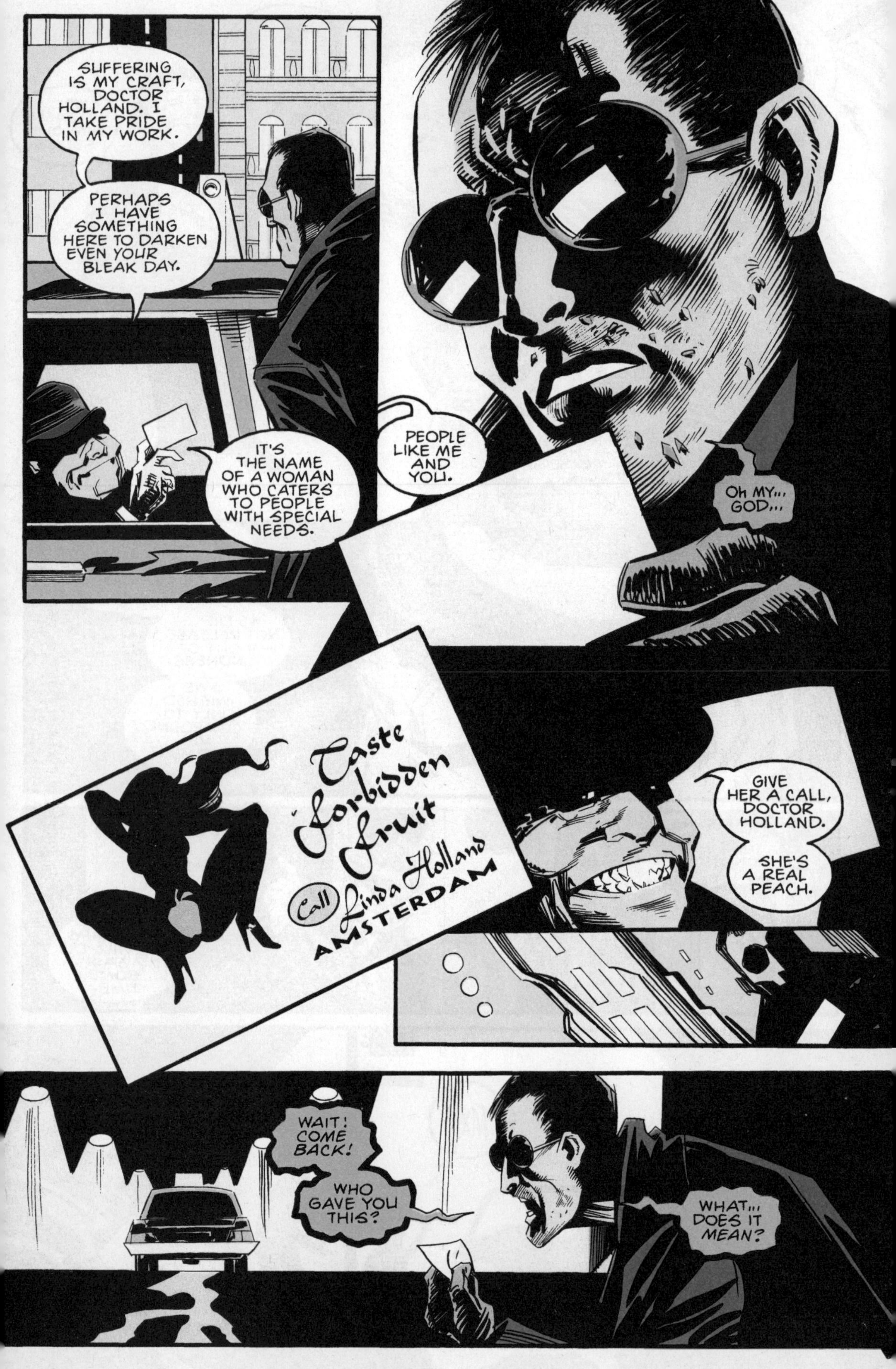
SUFFERING IS MY CRAFT, DOCTOR HOLLAND. I TAKE PRIDE IN MY WORK.
PERHAPS I HAVE SOMETHING HERE TO DARKEN EVEN YOUR BLEAK DAY.
IT'S THE NAME OF A WOMAN WHO CATERS TO PEOPLE WITH SPECIAL NEEDS.
PEOPLE LIKE ME AND YOU.
OH MY... GOD...
Taste Forbidden Fruit
Call Linda Holland
AMSTERDAM
GIVE HER A CALL, DOCTOR HOLLAND.
SHE'S A REAL PEACH.
WAIT! COME BACK!
WHO GAVE YOU THIS?
WHAT... DOES IT MEAN?

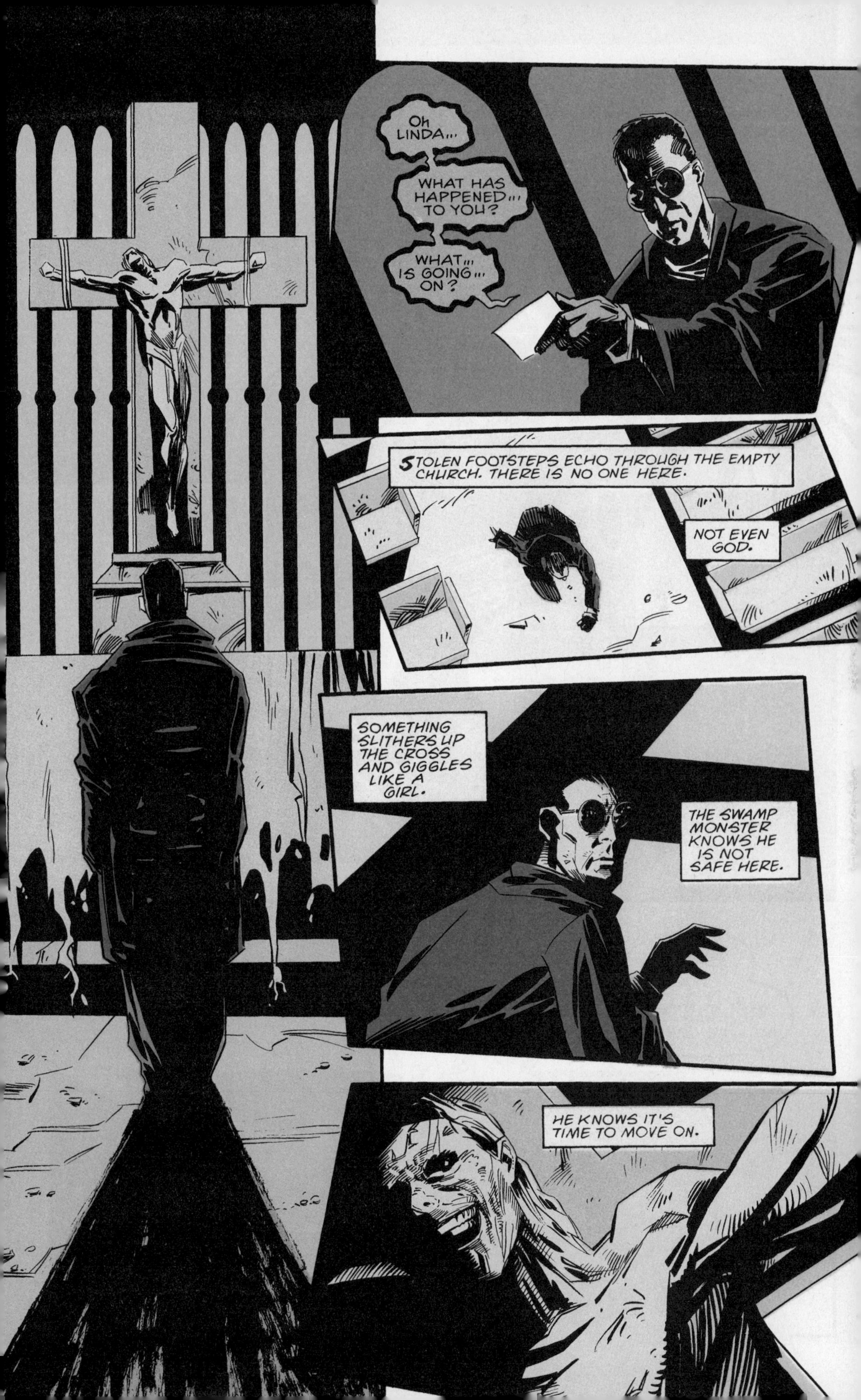

Oh LINDA...
WHAT HAS HAPPENED... TO YOU?
WHAT... IS GOING... ON?
STOLEN FOOTSTEPS ECHO THROUGH THE EMPTY CHURCH. THERE IS NO ONE HERE.
NOT EVEN GOD.
SOMETHING SLITHERS UP THE CROSS AND GIGGLES LIKE A GIRL.
THE SWAMP MONSTER KNOWS HE IS NOT SAFE HERE.
HE KNOWS IT'S TIME TO MOVE ON.

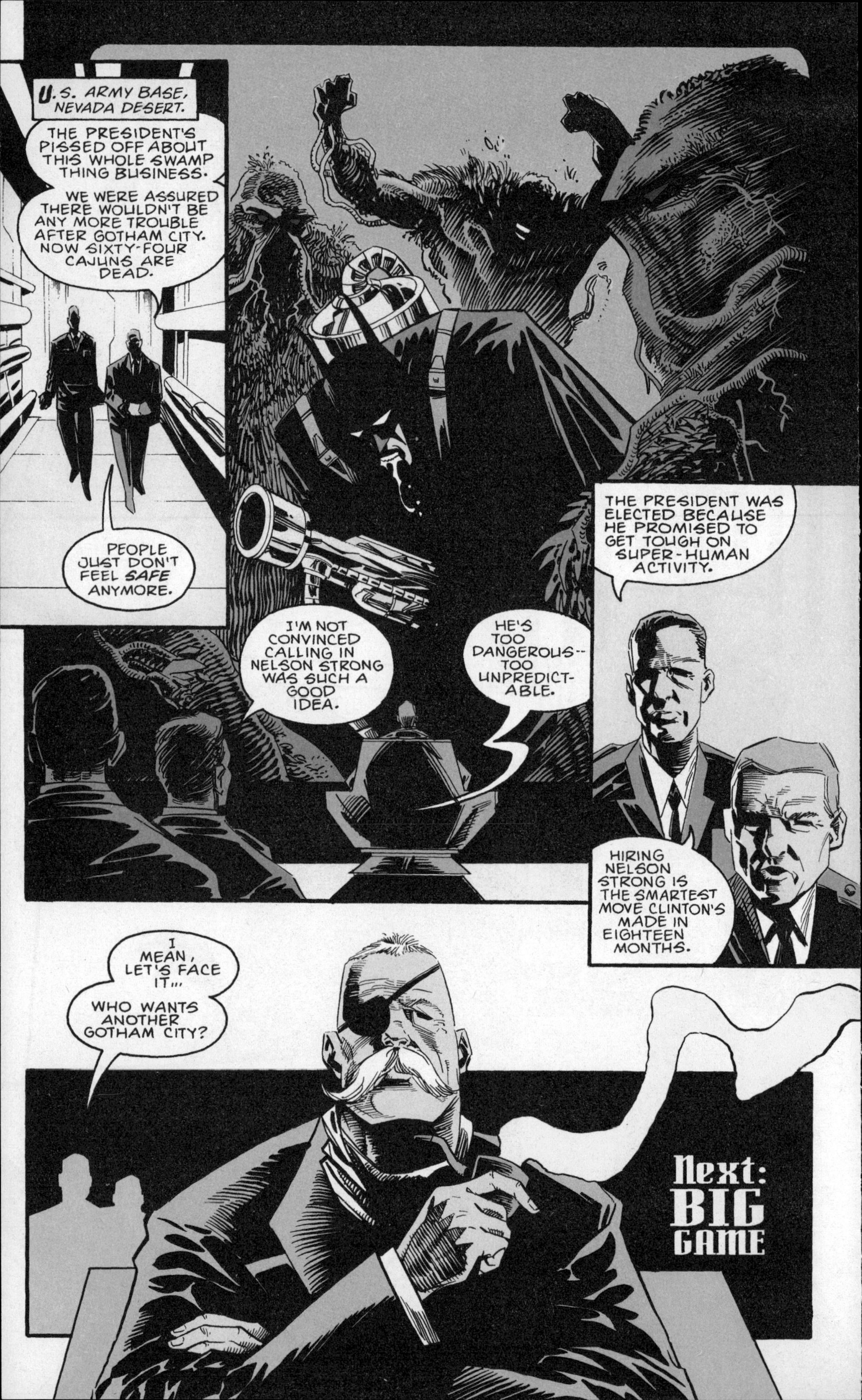
U.S. ARMY BASE, NEVADA DESERT.
THE PRESIDENT'S PISSED OFF ABOUT THIS WHOLE SWAMP THING BUSINESS.
WE WERE ASSURED THERE WOULDN'T BE ANY MORE TROUBLE AFTER GOTHAM CITY. NOW SIXTY-FOUR CAJUNS ARE DEAD.
PEOPLE JUST DON'T FEEL SAFE ANYMORE.
THE PRESIDENT WAS ELECTED BECAUSE HE PROMISED TO GET TOUGH ON SUPER-HUMAN ACTIVITY.
I'M NOT CONVINCED CALLING IN NELSON STRONG WAS SUCH A GOOD IDEA.
HE'S TOO DANGEROUS-- TOO UNPREDICTABLE.
HIRING NELSON STRONG IS THE SMARTEST MOVE CLINTON'S MADE IN EIGHTEEN MONTHS.
I MEAN, LET'S FACE IT...
WHO WANTS ANOTHER GOTHAM CITY?
Next: BIG GAME

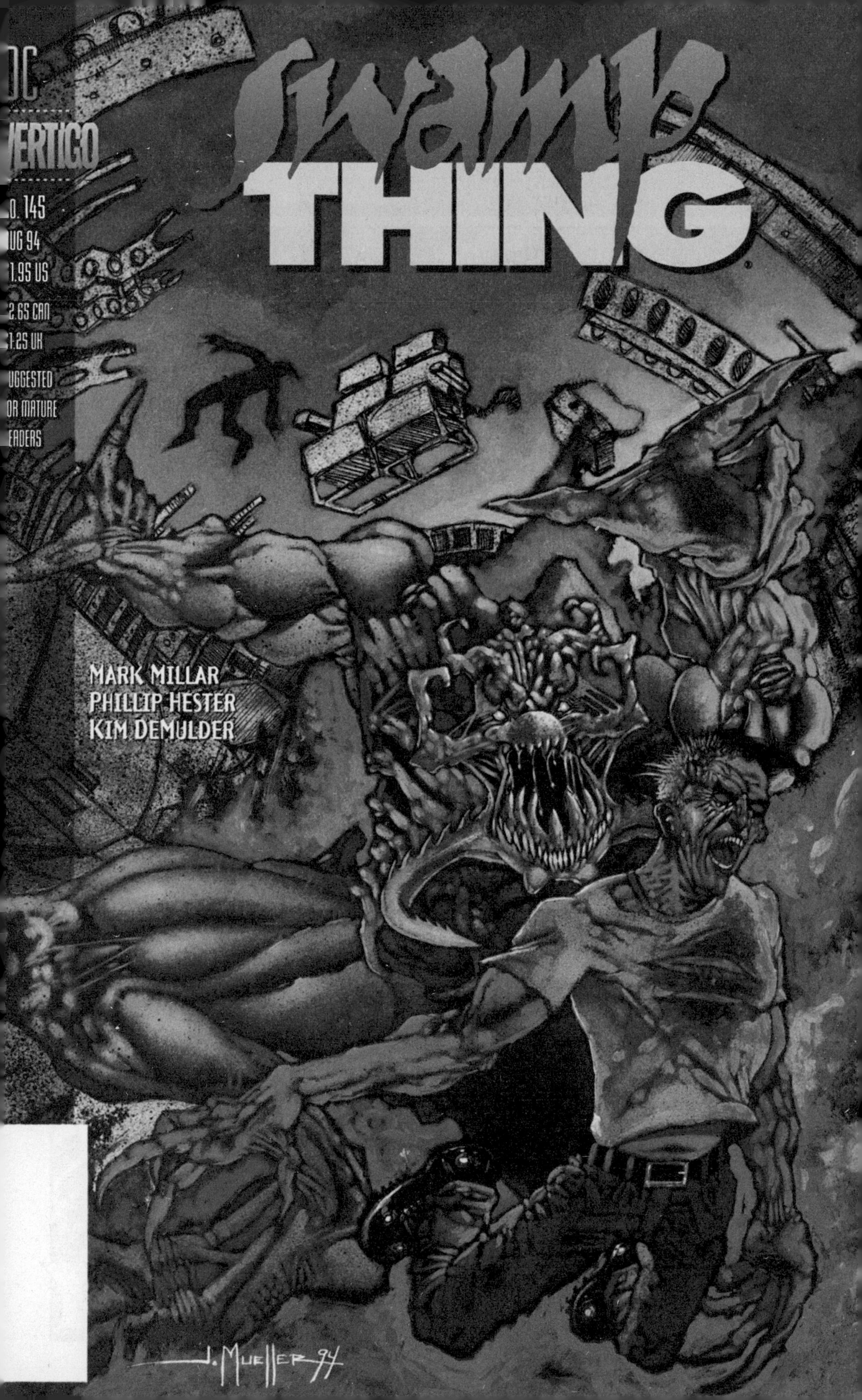
DC
VERTIGO
0. 145
UG 94
1.95 US
2.65 CAN
1.25 UK
UGGESTED
OR MATURE
EADERS
Swamp
THING
MARK MILLAR
PHILLIP HESTER
KIM DEMULDER
J. Mueller 94

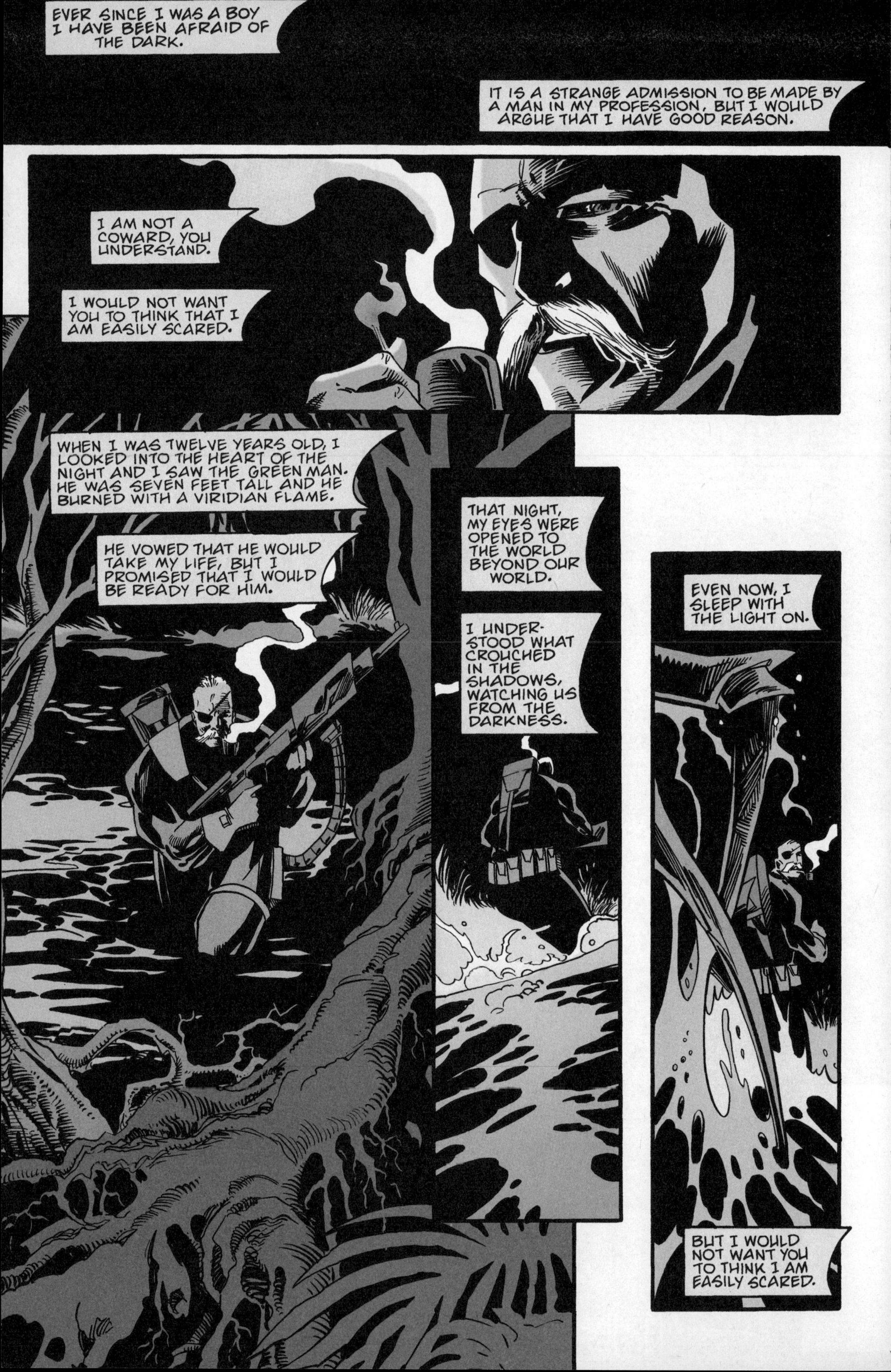
EVER SINCE I WAS A BOY I HAVE BEEN AFRAID OF THE DARK.
IT IS A STRANGE ADMISSION TO BE MADE BY A MAN IN MY PROFESSION, BUT I WOULD ARGUE THAT I HAVE GOOD REASON.
I AM NOT A COWARD, YOU UNDERSTAND.
I WOULD NOT WANT YOU TO THINK THAT I AM EASILY SCARED.
WHEN I WAS TWELVE YEARS OLD, I LOOKED INTO THE HEART OF THE NIGHT AND I SAW THE GREEN MAN. HE WAS SEVEN FEET TALL AND HE BURNED WITH A VIRIDIAN FLAME.
HE VOWED THAT HE WOULD TAKE MY LIFE, BUT I PROMISED THAT I WOULD BE READY FOR HIM.
THAT NIGHT, MY EYES WERE OPENED TO THE WORLD BEYOND OUR WORLD.
I UNDERSTOOD WHAT CROUCHED IN THE SHADOWS, WATCHING US FROM THE DARKNESS.
EVEN NOW, I SLEEP WITH THE LIGHT ON.
BUT I WOULD NOT WANT YOU TO THINK I AM EASILY SCARED.

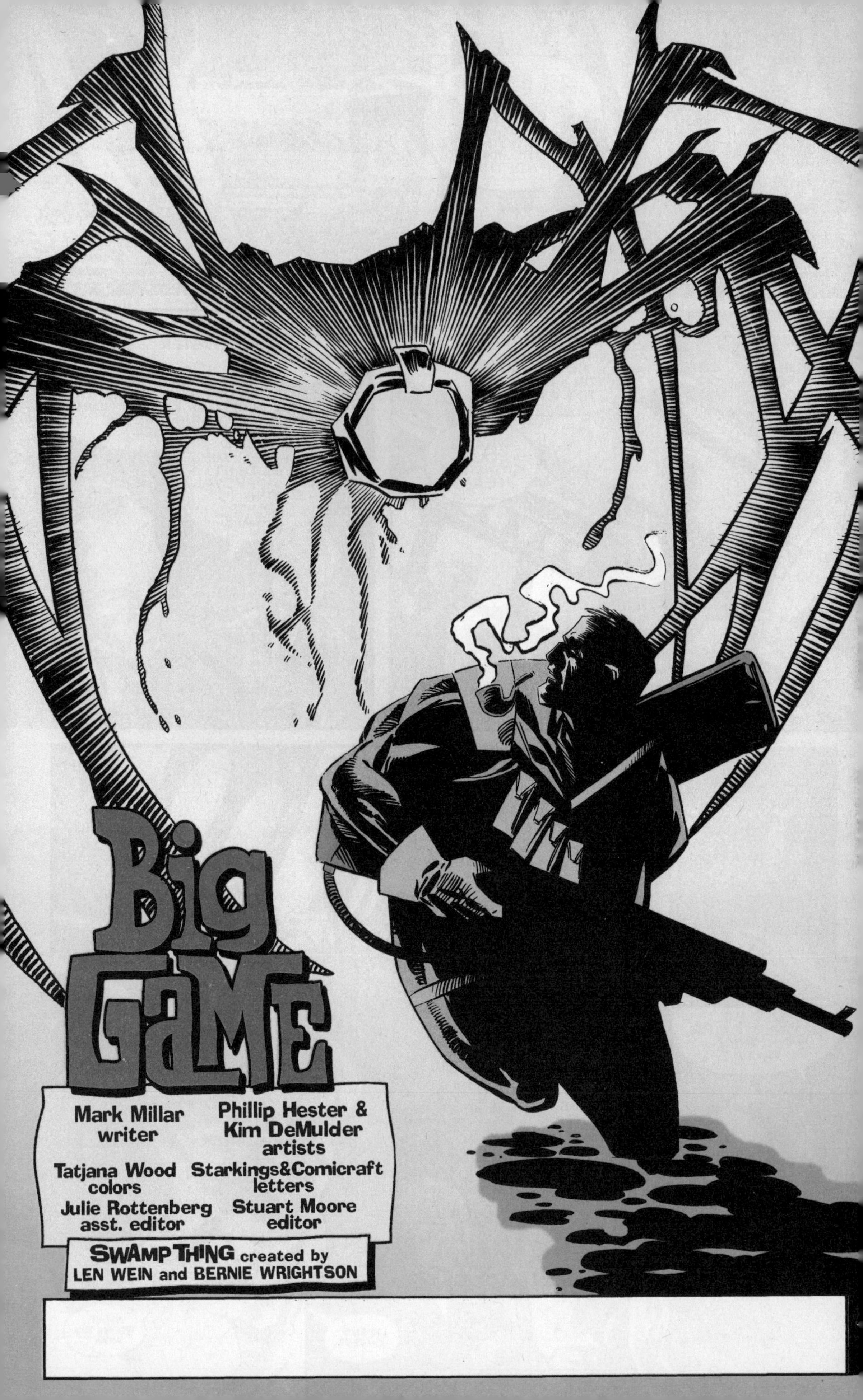
Big Game
Mark Millar writer
Phillip Hester & Kim DeMulder artists
Tatjana Wood colors
Starkings&Comicraft letters
Julie Rottenberg asst. editor
Stuart Moore editor
SWAMP THING created by LEN WEIN and BERNIE WRIGHTSON

THE PAPERS ARE ALREADY COMPARING THE CAJUN SLAUGHTER TO GOTHAM CITY, MAJOR NORTH.

REAGAN'S POLL RATING DROPPED THIRTY POINTS AFTER THAT LITTLE FIASCO. NOW CLINTON'S GETTING PRETTY NERVOUS.

WHAT'S YOUR SITUATION HERE?

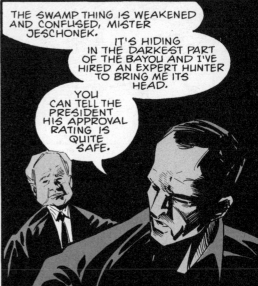

THE SWAMP THING IS WEAKENED AND CONFUSED, MISTER JESCHONEK.

IT'S HIDING IN THE DARKEST PART OF THE BAYOU AND I'VE HIRED AN EXPERT HUNTER TO BRING ME ITS HEAD.

YOU CAN TELL THE PRESIDENT HIS APPROVAL RATING IS QUITE SAFE.

DISTURBANCE IN SECTOR G, MAJOR NORTH.

NELSON STRONG HAS LAUNCHED SOME KIND OF ATTACK.

IT COULD BE ANOTHER 'GATOR. ANY OTHER DATA?

COORDINATES MATCH THE FLORAL INTELLIGENCE WE PICKED UP EARLIER, SIR.

THIS MIGHT BE OUR MONSTER.

JESUS CHRIST.

WHAT DO WE DO NOW?

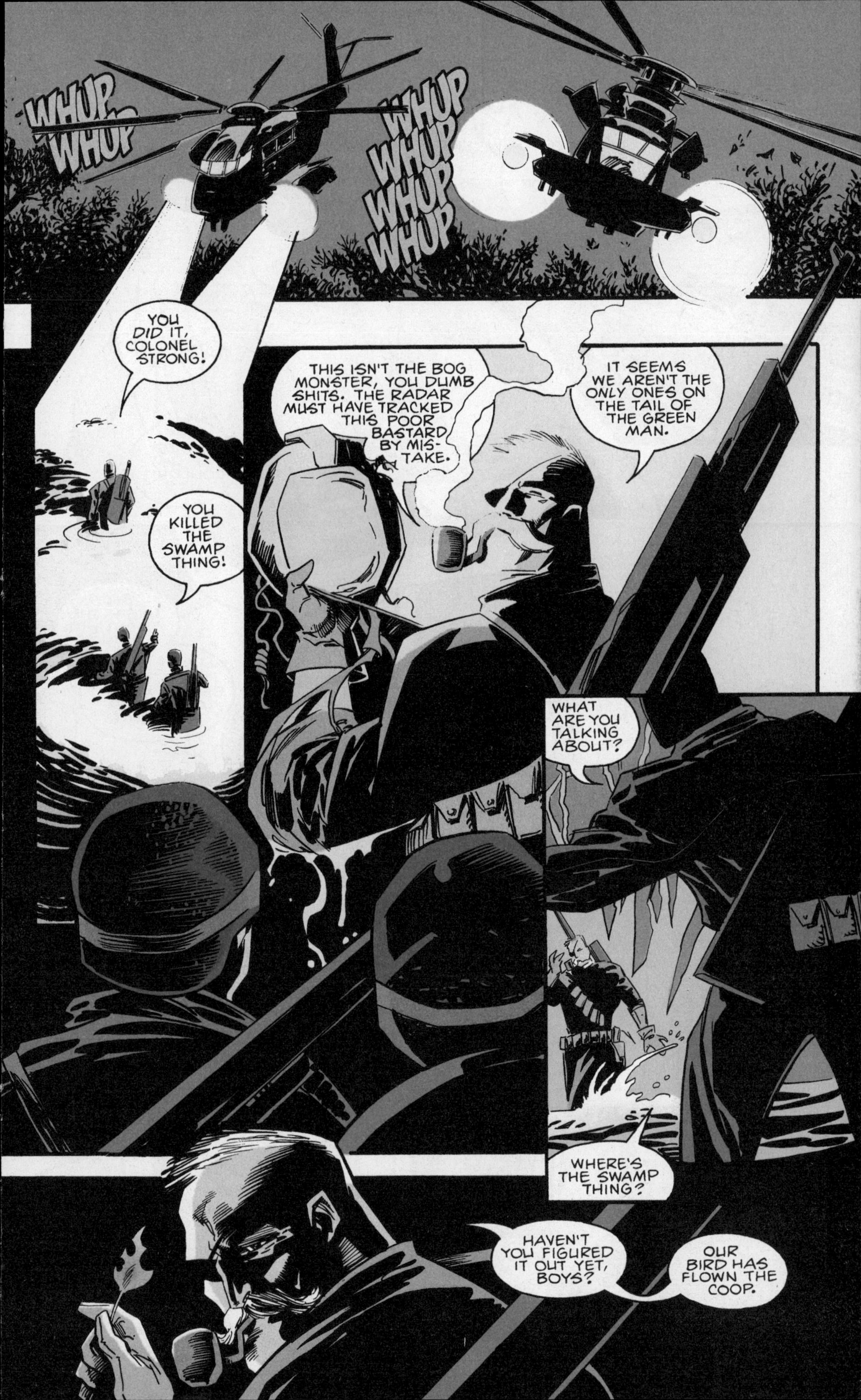
WHUP WHUP
WHUP WHUP WHUP WHUP
YOU DID IT, COLONEL STRONG!
YOU KILLED THE SWAMP THING!
THIS ISN'T THE BOG MONSTER, YOU DUMB SHITS. THE RADAR MUST HAVE TRACKED THIS POOR BASTARD BY MIS-TAKE.
IT SEEMS WE AREN'T THE ONLY ONES ON THE TAIL OF THE GREEN MAN.
WHAT ARE YOU TALKING ABOUT?
WHERE'S THE SWAMP THING?
HAVEN'T YOU FIGURED IT OUT YET, BOYS?
OUR BIRD HAS FLOWN THE COOP.

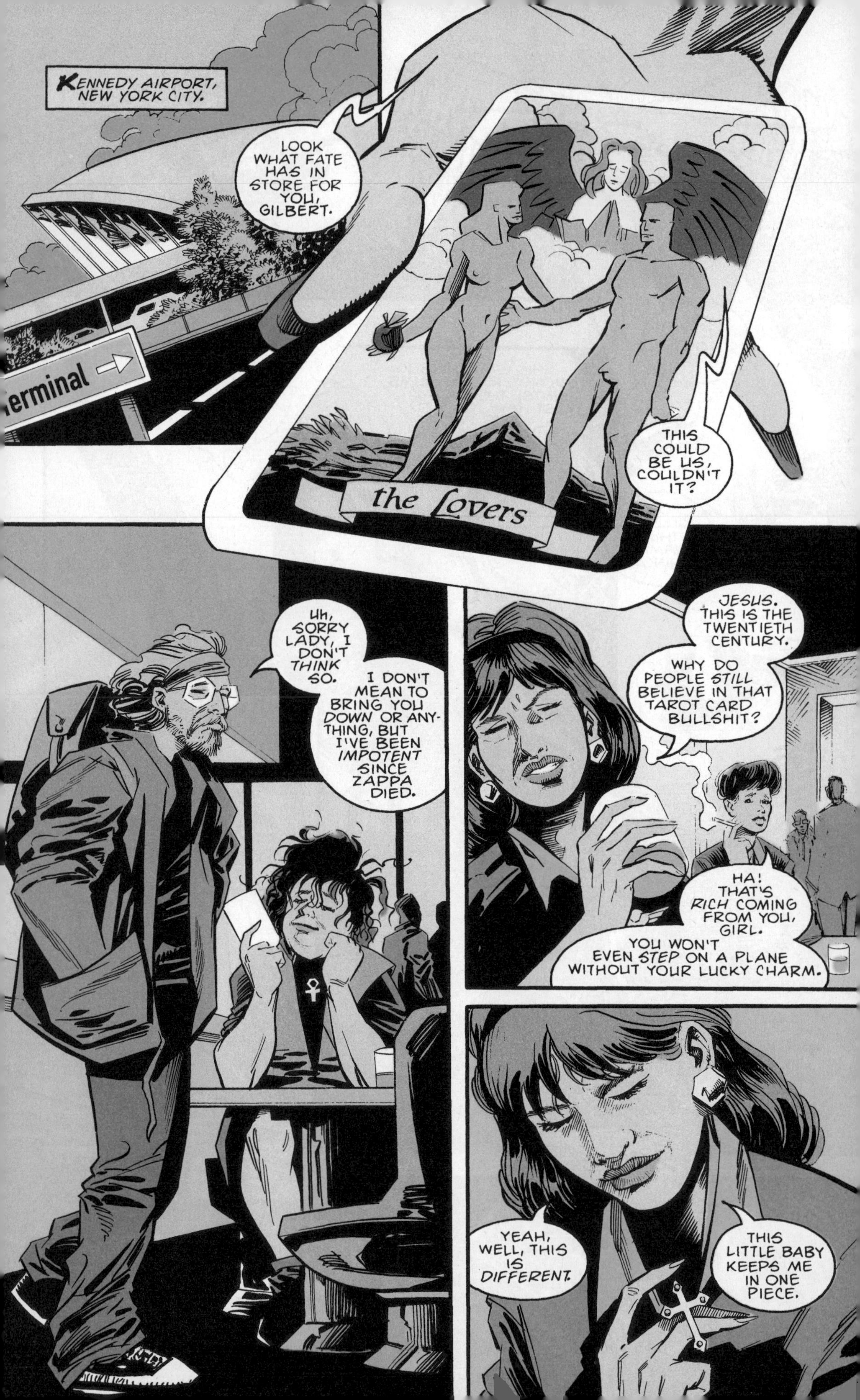
KENNEDY AIRPORT, NEW YORK CITY.
erminal
LOOK WHAT FATE HAS IN STORE FOR YOU, GILBERT.
the Lovers
THIS COULD BE US, COULDN'T IT?
uh, SORRY LADY, I DON'T THINK SO.
I DON'T MEAN TO BRING YOU DOWN OR ANYTHING, BUT I'VE BEEN IMPOTENT SINCE ZAPPA DIED.
JESUS. THIS IS THE TWENTIETH CENTURY.
WHY DO PEOPLE STILL BELIEVE IN THAT TAROT CARD BULLSHIT?
HA! THAT'S RICH COMING FROM YOU, GIRL.
YOU WON'T EVEN STEP ON A PLANE WITHOUT YOUR LUCKY CHARM.
YEAH, WELL, THIS IS DIFFERENT.
THIS LITTLE BABY KEEPS ME IN ONE PIECE.

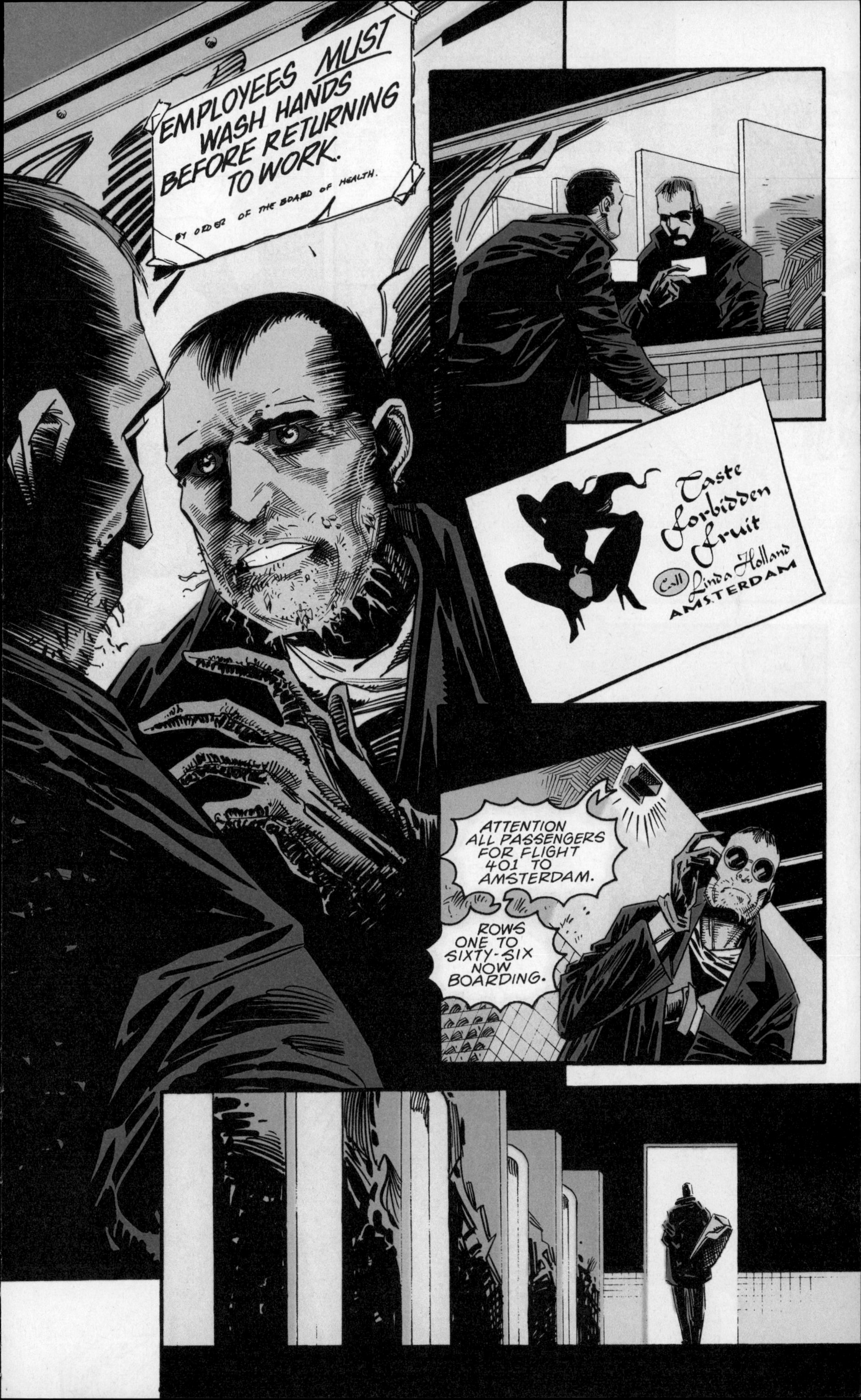
EMPLOYEES MUST WASH HANDS BEFORE RETURNING TO WORK.
BY ORDER OF THE BOARD OF HEALTH.
Taste Forbidden Fruit
Call Linda Holland
AMSTERDAM
ATTENTION ALL PASSENGERS FOR FLIGHT 401 TO AMSTERDAM.
ROWS ONE TO SIXTY-SIX NOW BOARDING.

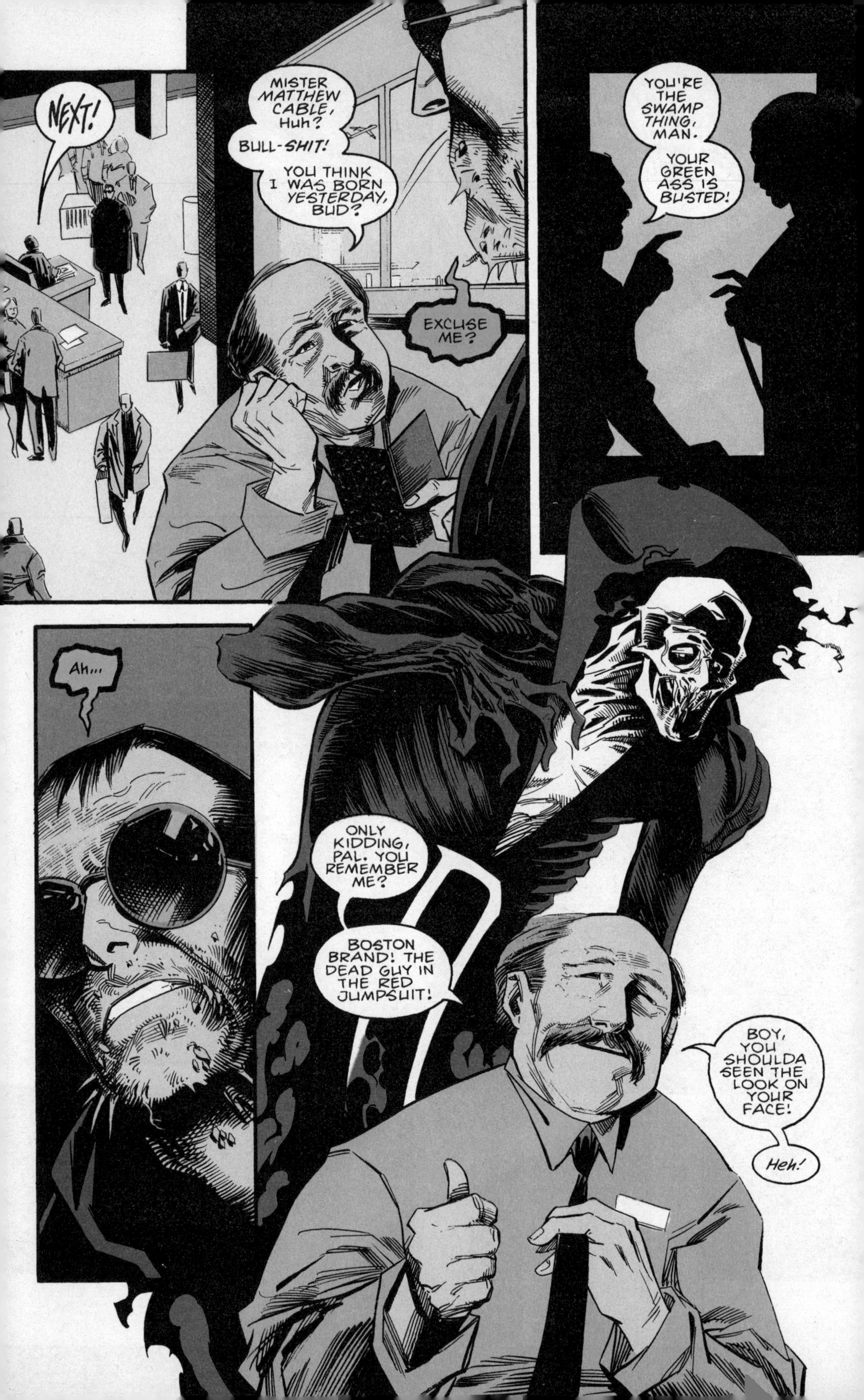
NEXT!
MISTER MATTHEW CABLE, Huh?
BULL-SHIT!
YOU THINK I WAS BORN YESTERDAY, BUD?
EXCUSE ME?
YOU'RE THE SWAMP THING, MAN.
YOUR GREEN ASS IS BUSTED!
Ah...
ONLY KIDDING, PAL. YOU REMEMBER ME?
BOSTON BRAND! THE DEAD GUY IN THE RED JUMPSUIT!
BOY, YOU SHOULDA SEEN THE LOOK ON YOUR FACE!
Heh!

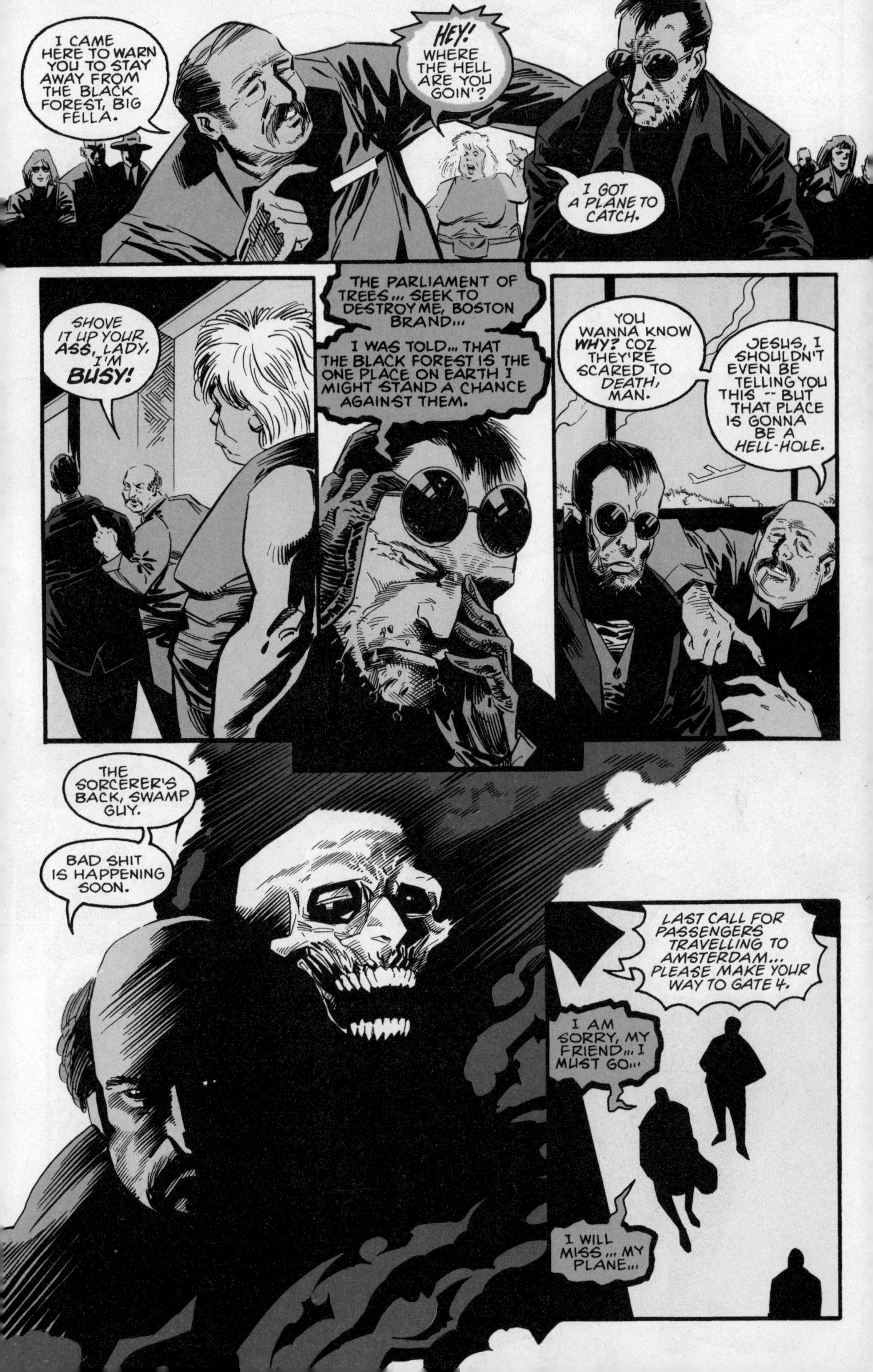
I CAME HERE TO WARN YOU TO STAY AWAY FROM THE BLACK FOREST, BIG FELLA.
HEY! WHERE THE HELL ARE YOU GOIN'?
I GOT A PLANE TO CATCH.
SHOVE IT UP YOUR ASS, LADY, I'M BUSY!
THE PARLIAMENT OF TREES... SEEK TO DESTROY ME, BOSTON BRAND...
I WAS TOLD... THAT THE BLACK FOREST IS THE ONE PLACE ON EARTH I MIGHT STAND A CHANCE AGAINST THEM.
YOU WANNA KNOW WHY? COZ THEY'RE SCARED TO DEATH, MAN.
JESUS, I SHOULDN'T EVEN BE TELLING YOU THIS -- BUT THAT PLACE IS GONNA BE A HELL-HOLE.
THE SORCERER'S BACK, SWAMP GUY.
BAD SHIT IS HAPPENING SOON.
LAST CALL FOR PASSENGERS TRAVELLING TO AMSTERDAM... PLEASE MAKE YOUR WAY TO GATE 4.
I AM SORRY, MY FRIEND... I MUST GO...
I WILL MISS... MY PLANE...

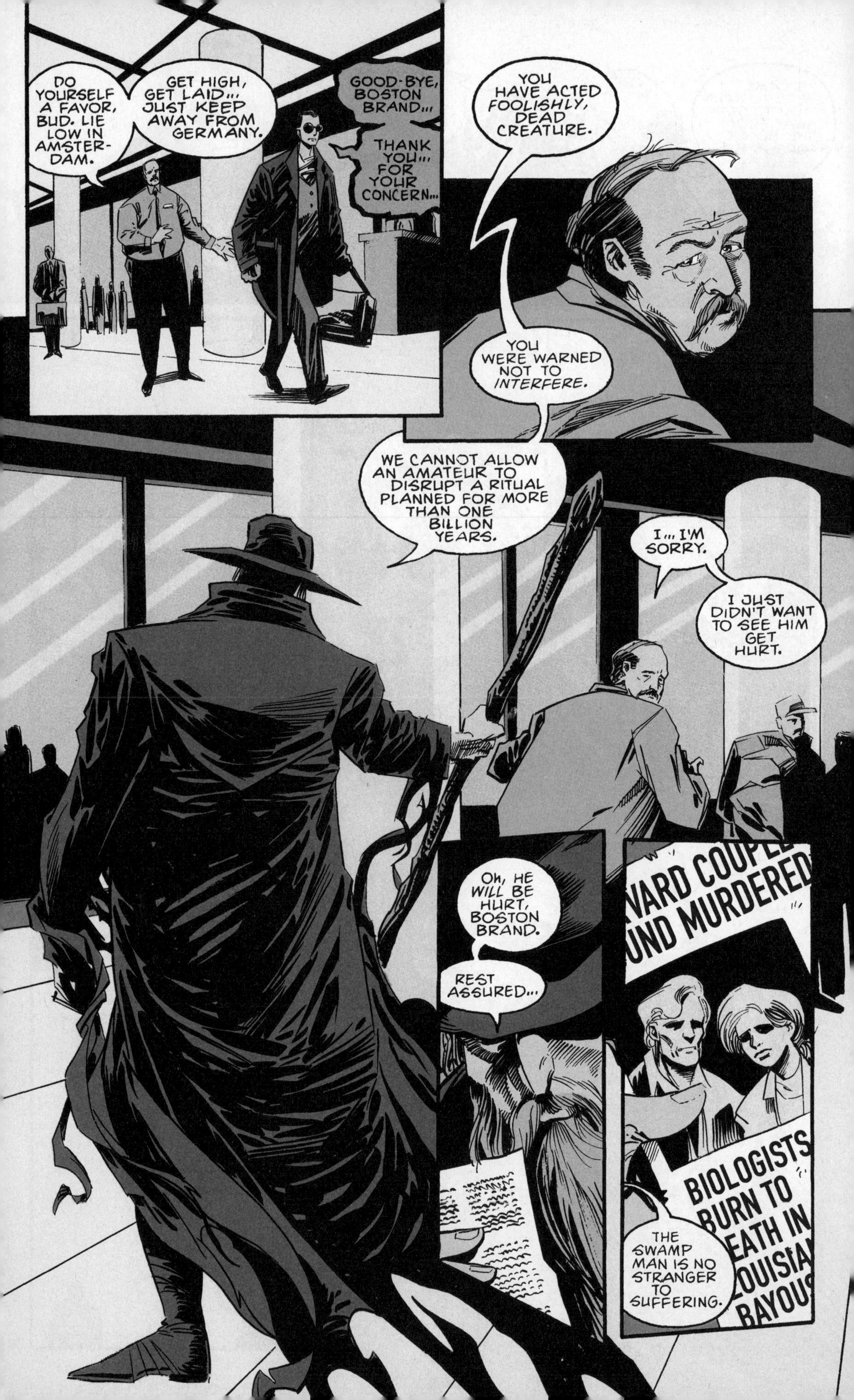

DO YOURSELF A FAVOR, BUD. LIE LOW IN AMSTER-DAM.
GET HIGH, GET LAID... JUST KEEP AWAY FROM GERMANY.
GOOD-BYE, BOSTON BRAND...
THANK YOU... FOR YOUR CONCERN...
YOU HAVE ACTED FOOLISHLY, DEAD CREATURE.
YOU WERE WARNED NOT TO INTERFERE.
WE CANNOT ALLOW AN AMATEUR TO DISRUPT A RITUAL PLANNED FOR MORE THAN ONE BILLION YEARS.
I... I'M SORRY.
I JUST DIDN'T WANT TO SEE HIM GET HURT.
Oh, HE WILL BE HURT, BOSTON BRAND.
REST ASSURED...
VARD COUPLE
UND MURDERED
BIOLOGISTS BURN TO EATH IN OUISIAN BAYOUS
THE SWAMP MAN IS NO STRANGER TO SUFFERING.

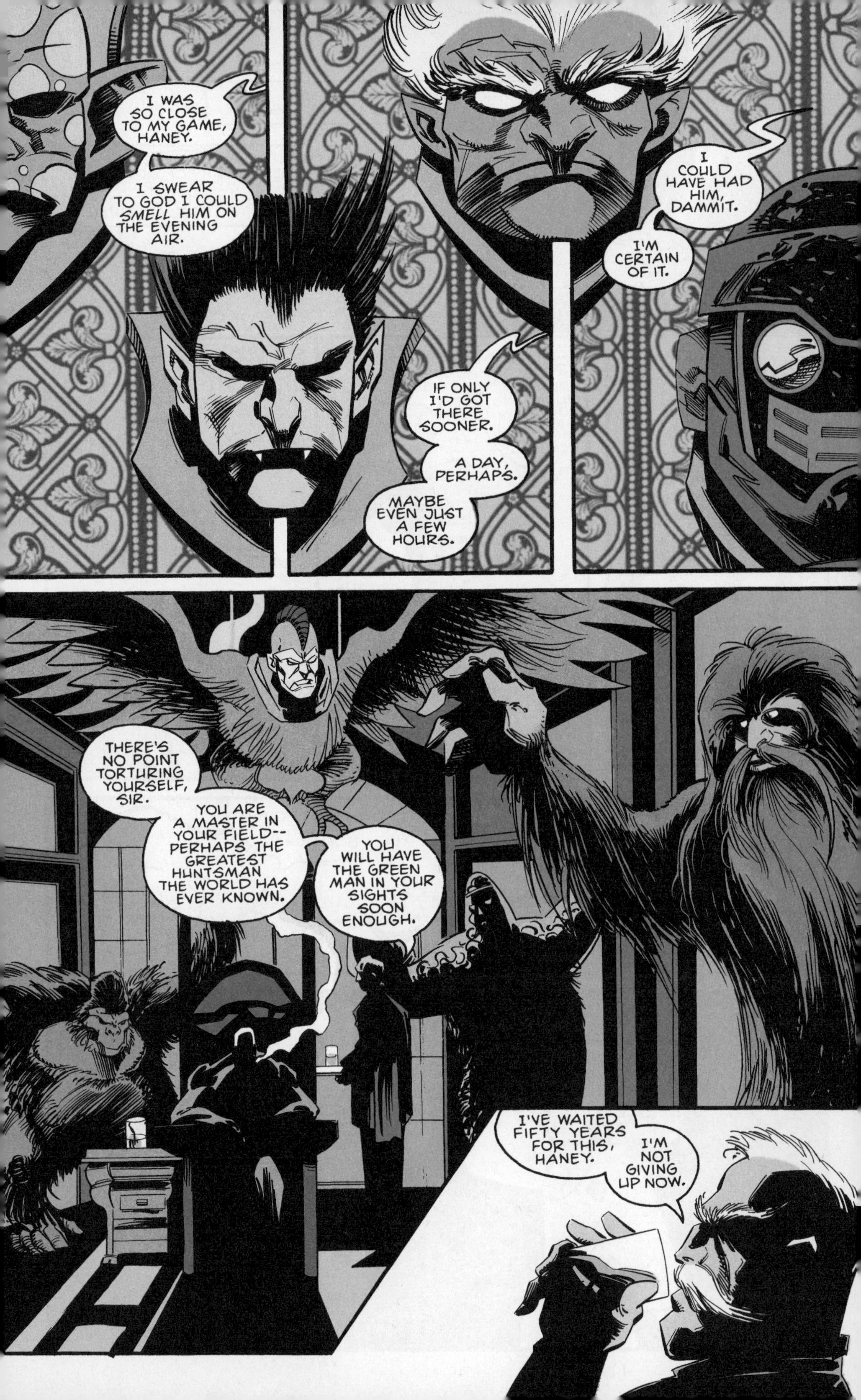
I WAS SO CLOSE TO MY GAME, HANEY.
I SWEAR TO GOD I COULD SMELL HIM ON THE EVENING AIR.
I COULD HAVE HAD HIM, DAMMIT.
I'M CERTAIN OF IT.
IF ONLY I'D GOT THERE SOONER.
A DAY, PERHAPS.
MAYBE EVEN JUST A FEW HOURS.
THERE'S NO POINT TORTURING YOURSELF, SIR.
YOU ARE A MASTER IN YOUR FIELD-- PERHAPS THE GREATEST HUNTSMAN THE WORLD HAS EVER KNOWN.
YOU WILL HAVE THE GREEN MAN IN YOUR SIGHTS SOON ENOUGH.
I'VE WAITED FIFTY YEARS FOR THIS, HANEY.
I'M NOT GIVING UP NOW.

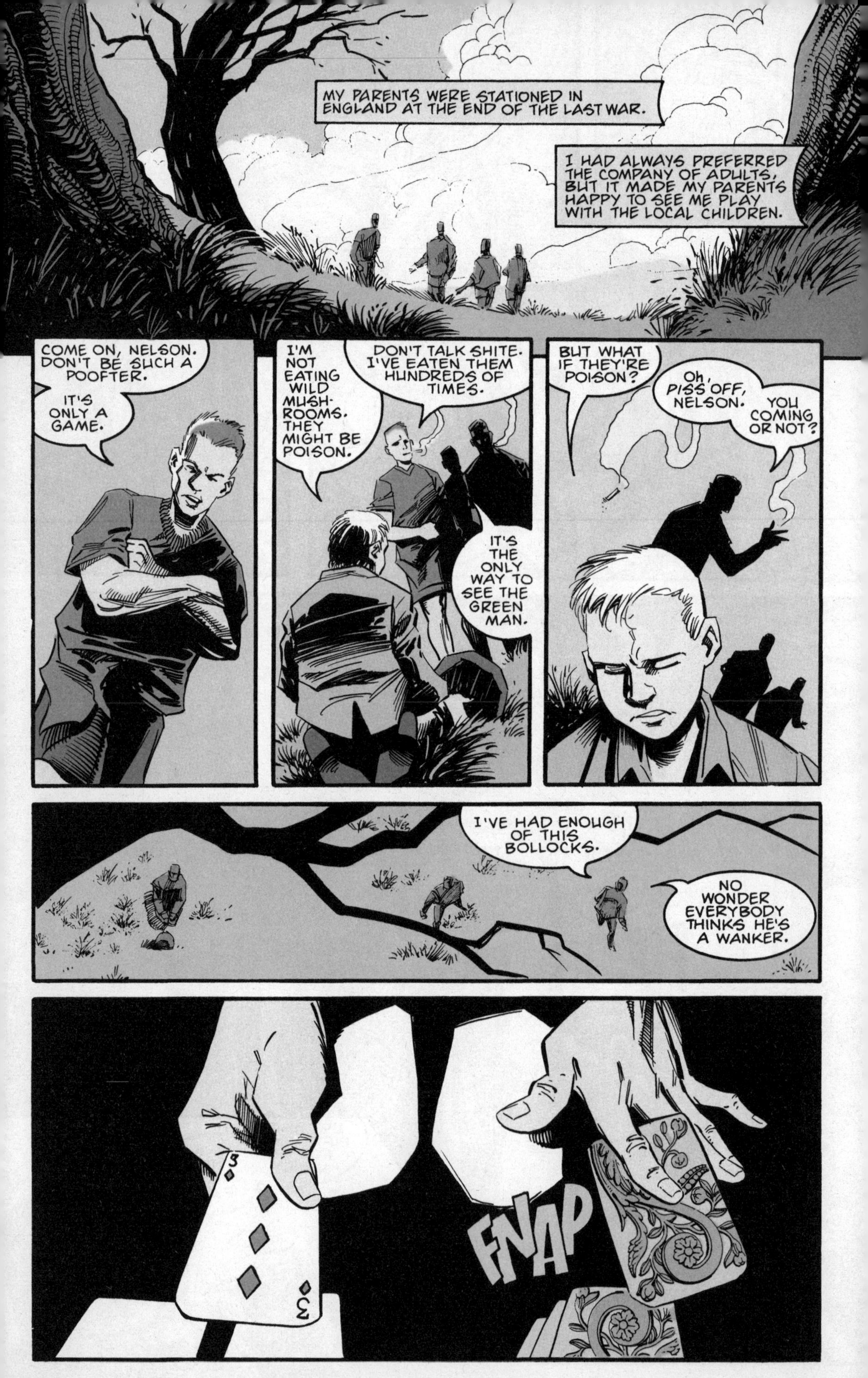
MY PARENTS WERE STATIONED IN ENGLAND AT THE END OF THE LAST WAR.
I HAD ALWAYS PREFERRED THE COMPANY OF ADULTS, BUT IT MADE MY PARENTS HAPPY TO SEE ME PLAY WITH THE LOCAL CHILDREN.
COME ON, NELSON. DON'T BE SUCH A POOFTER.
IT'S ONLY A GAME.
I'M NOT EATING WILD MUSH-ROOMS. THEY MIGHT BE POISON.
DON'T TALK SHITE. I'VE EATEN THEM HUNDREDS OF TIMES.
IT'S THE ONLY WAY TO SEE THE GREEN MAN.
BUT WHAT IF THEY'RE POISON?
Oh, PISS OFF, NELSON.
YOU COMING OR NOT?
I'VE HAD ENOUGH OF THIS BOLLOCKS.
NO WONDER EVERYBODY THINKS HE'S A WANKER.
FNAP

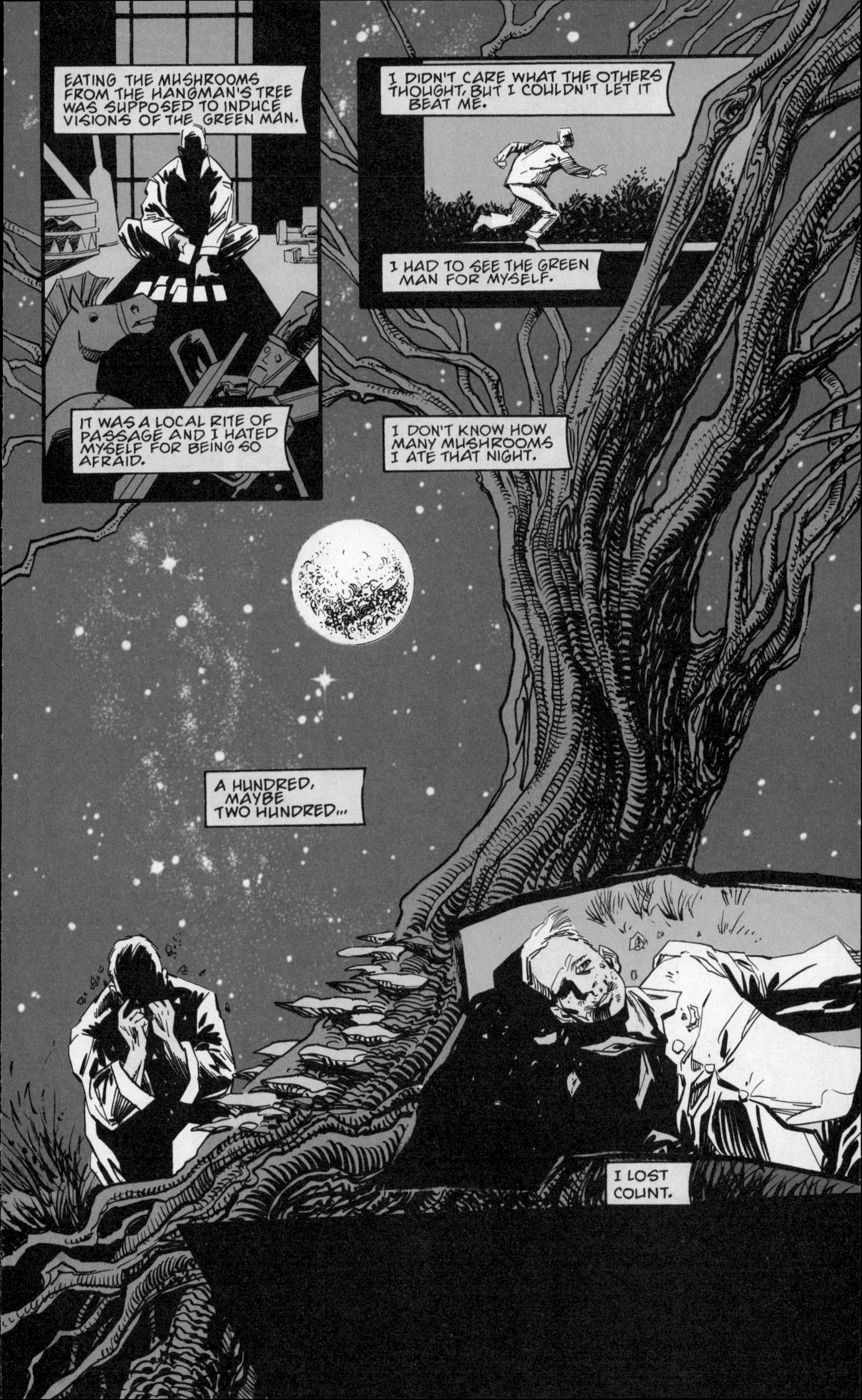
EATING THE MUSHROOMS FROM THE HANGMAN'S TREE WAS SUPPOSED TO INDUCE VISIONS OF THE GREEN MAN.
IT WAS A LOCAL RITE OF PASSAGE AND I HATED MYSELF FOR BEING SO AFRAID.
I DIDN'T CARE WHAT THE OTHERS THOUGHT, BUT I COULDN'T LET IT BEAT ME.
I HAD TO SEE THE GREEN MAN FOR MYSELF.
I DON'T KNOW HOW MANY MUSHROOMS I ATE THAT NIGHT.
A HUNDRED, MAYBE TWO HUNDRED...
I LOST COUNT.

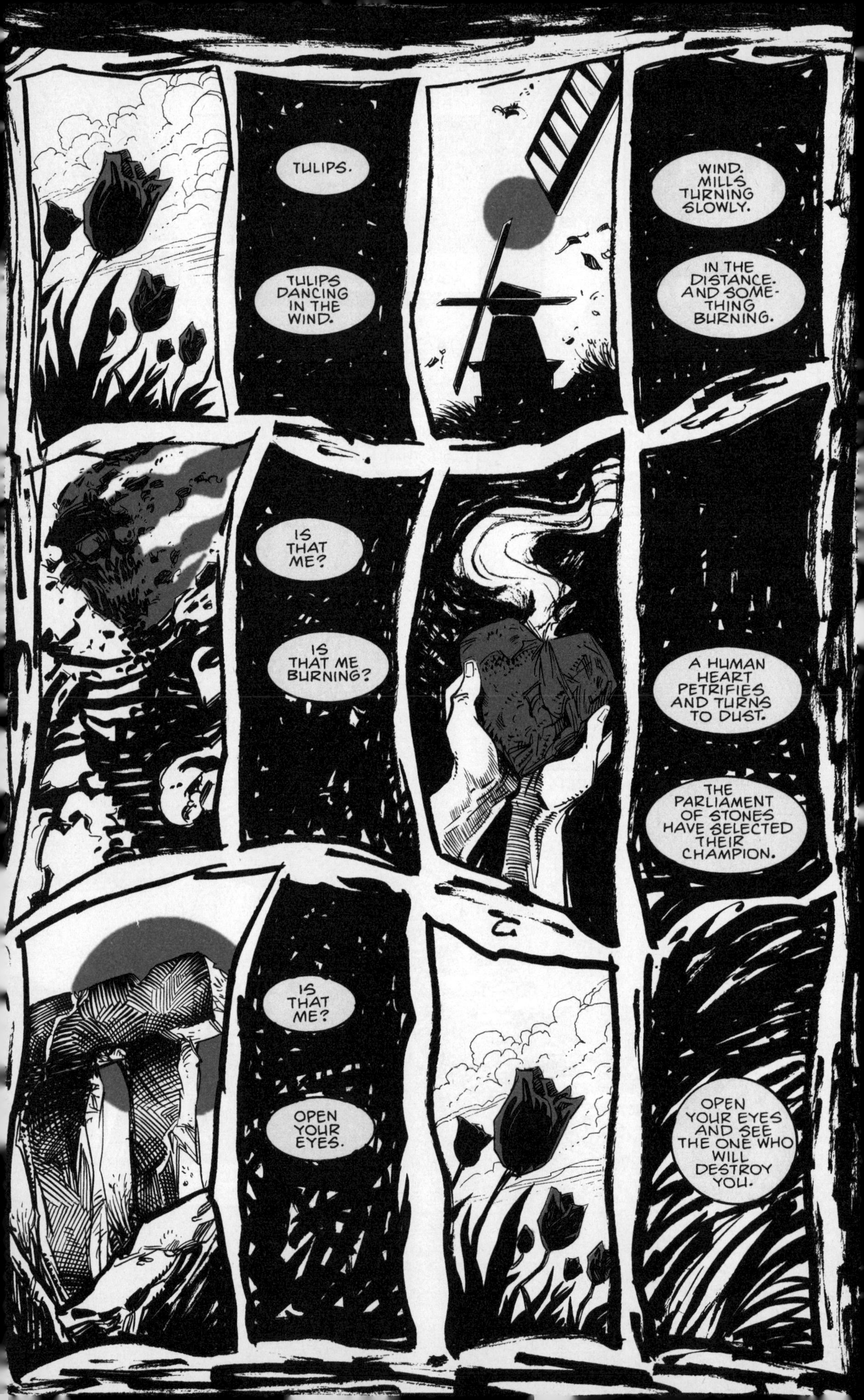
TULIPS.
TULIPS DANCING IN THE WIND.
WIND. MILLS TURNING SLOWLY.
IN THE DISTANCE. AND SOME-THING BURNING.
IS THAT ME?
IS THAT ME BURNING?
A HUMAN HEART PETRIFIES AND TURNS TO DUST.
THE PARLIAMENT OF STONES HAVE SELECTED THEIR CHAMPION.
IS THAT ME?
OPEN YOUR EYES.
OPEN YOUR EYES AND SEE THE ONE WHO WILL DESTROY YOU.

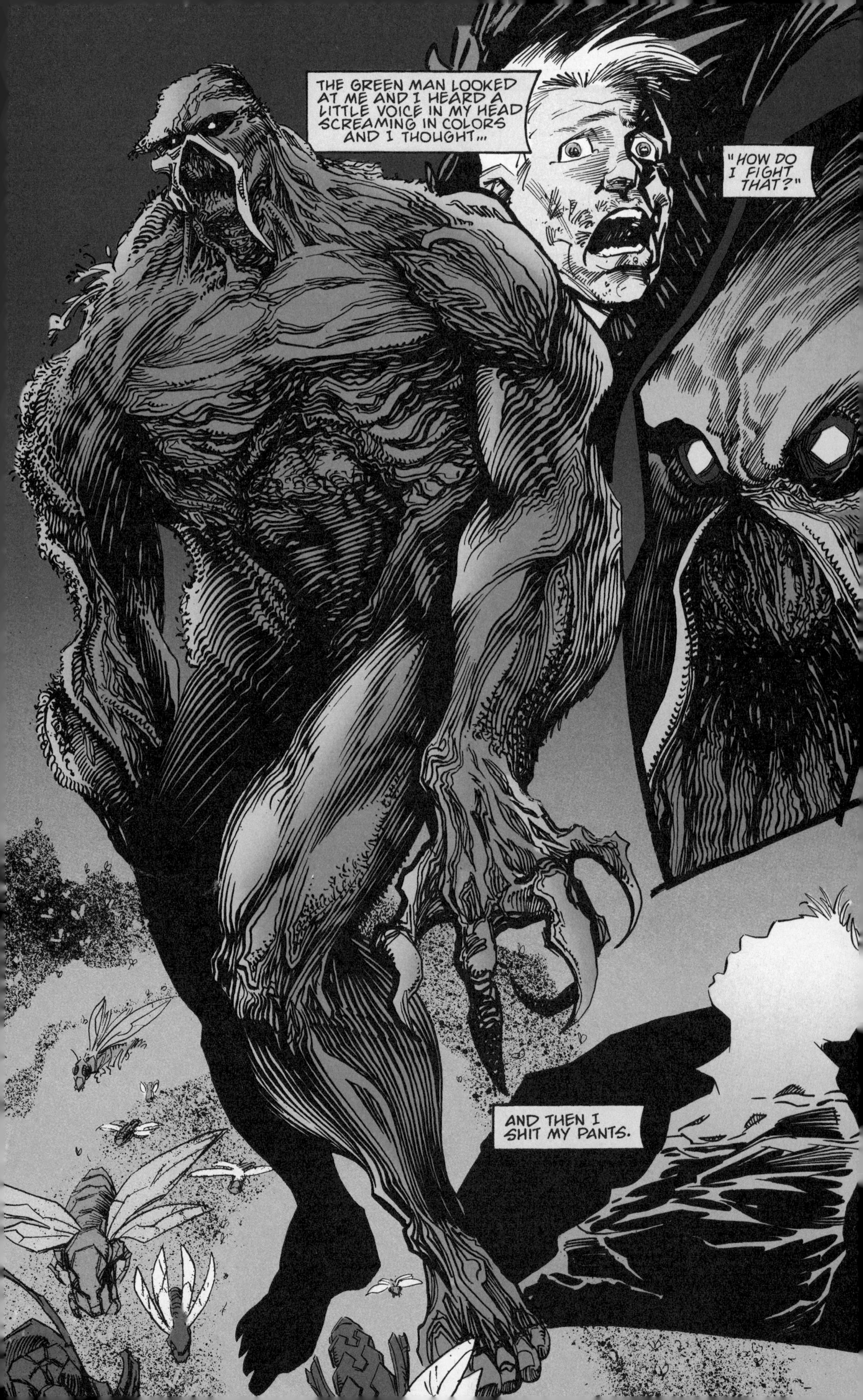
THE GREEN MAN LOOKED AT ME AND I HEARD A LITTLE VOICE IN MY HEAD SCREAMING IN COLORS AND I THOUGHT...
"HOW DO I FIGHT THAT?"
AND THEN I SHIT MY PANTS.

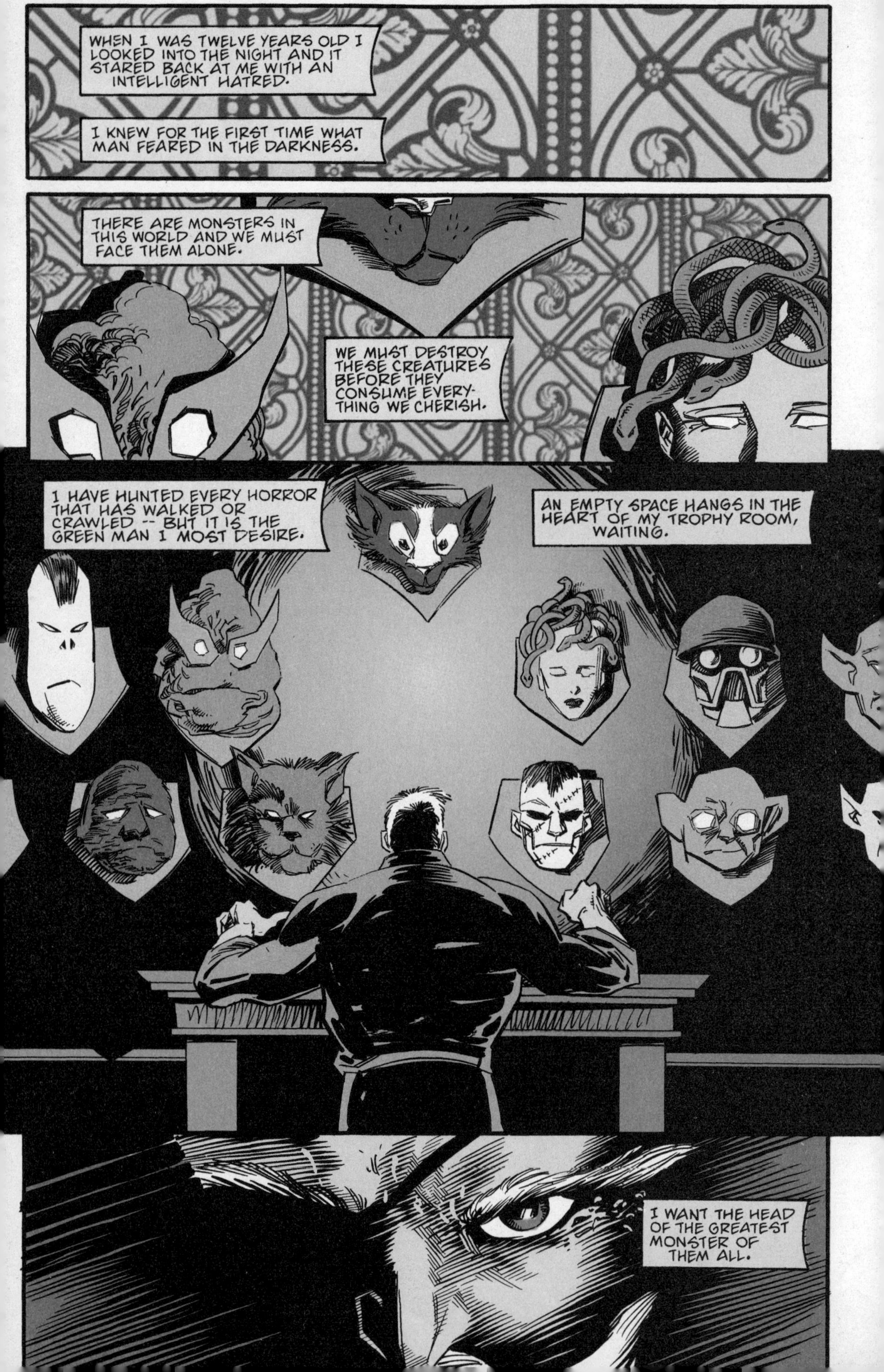
WHEN I WAS TWELVE YEARS OLD I LOOKED INTO THE NIGHT AND IT STARED BACK AT ME WITH AN INTELLIGENT HATRED.
I KNEW FOR THE FIRST TIME WHAT MAN FEARED IN THE DARKNESS.
THERE ARE MONSTERS IN THIS WORLD AND WE MUST FACE THEM ALONE.
WE MUST DESTROY THESE CREATURES BEFORE THEY CONSUME EVERY-THING WE CHERISH.
I HAVE HUNTED EVERY HORROR THAT HAS WALKED OR CRAWLED -- BUT IT IS THE GREEN MAN I MOST DESIRE.
AN EMPTY SPACE HANGS IN THE HEART OF MY TROPHY ROOM, WAITING.
I WANT THE HEAD OF THE GREATEST MONSTER OF THEM ALL.

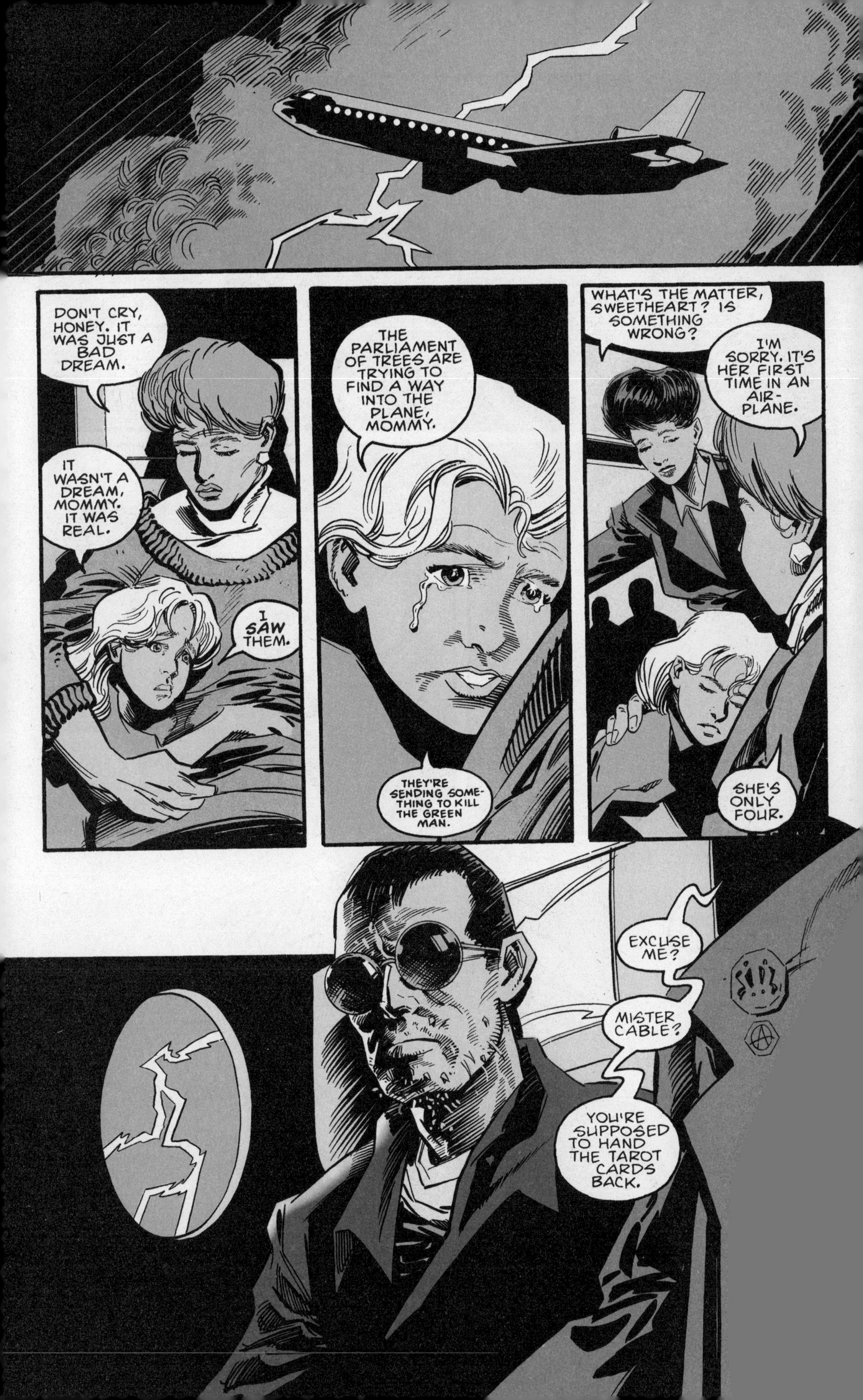

DON'T CRY, HONEY. IT WAS JUST A BAD DREAM.
IT WASN'T A DREAM, MOMMY. IT WAS REAL.
I SAW THEM.
THE PARLIAMENT OF TREES ARE TRYING TO FIND A WAY INTO THE PLANE, MOMMY.
THEY'RE SENDING SOMETHING TO KILL THE GREEN MAN.
WHAT'S THE MATTER, SWEETHEART? IS SOMETHING WRONG?
I'M SORRY. IT'S HER FIRST TIME IN AN AIRPLANE.
SHE'S ONLY FOUR.
EXCUSE ME?
MISTER CABLE?
YOU'RE SUPPOSED TO HAND THE TAROT CARDS BACK.

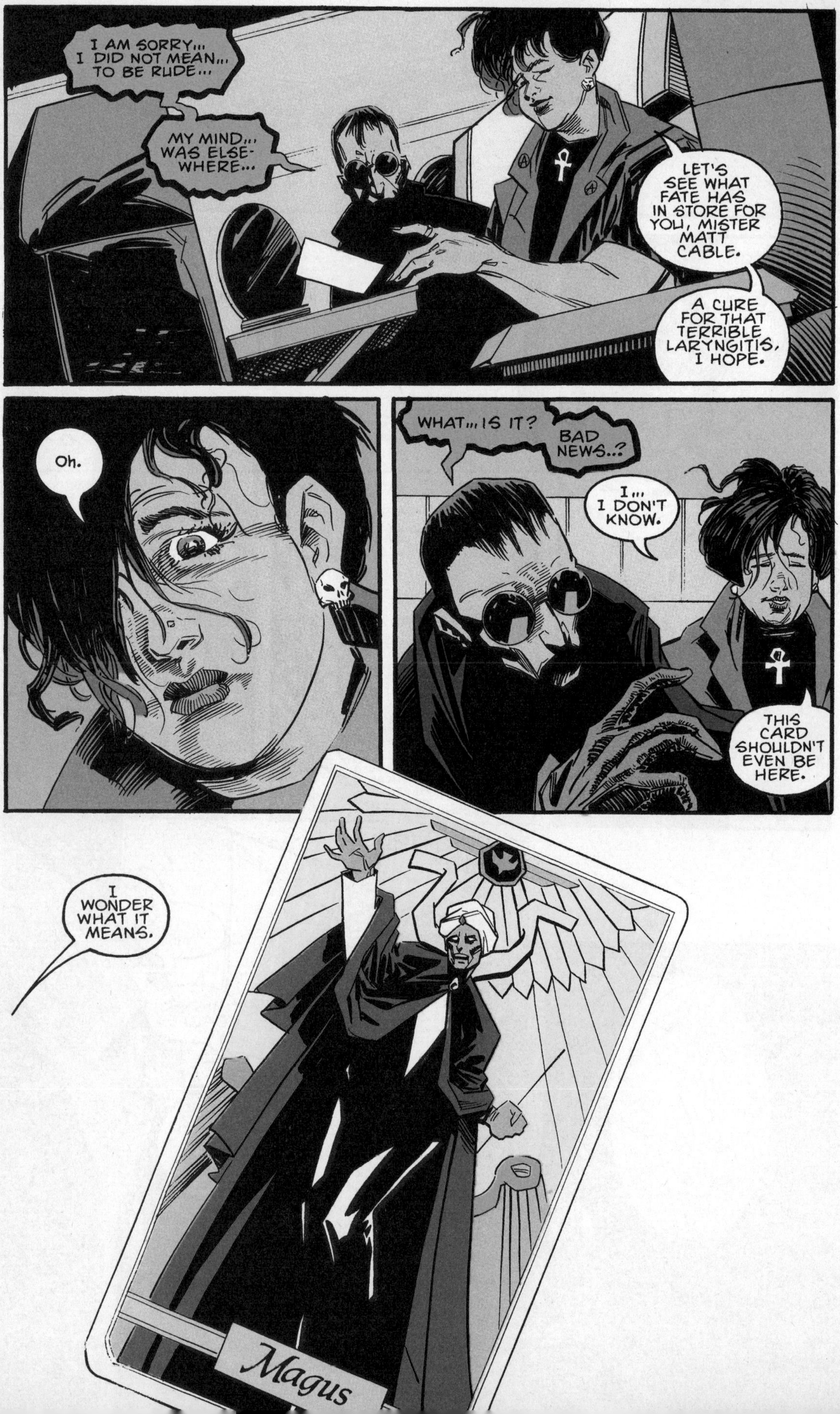
I AM SORRY... I DID NOT MEAN... TO BE RUDE...
MY MIND... WAS ELSE-WHERE...
LET'S SEE WHAT FATE HAS IN STORE FOR YOU, MISTER MATT CABLE.
A CURE FOR THAT TERRIBLE LARYNGITIS, I HOPE.
Oh.
WHAT... IS IT?
BAD NEWS..?
I... I DON'T KNOW.
THIS CARD SHOULDN'T EVEN BE HERE.
I WONDER WHAT IT MEANS.
Magus

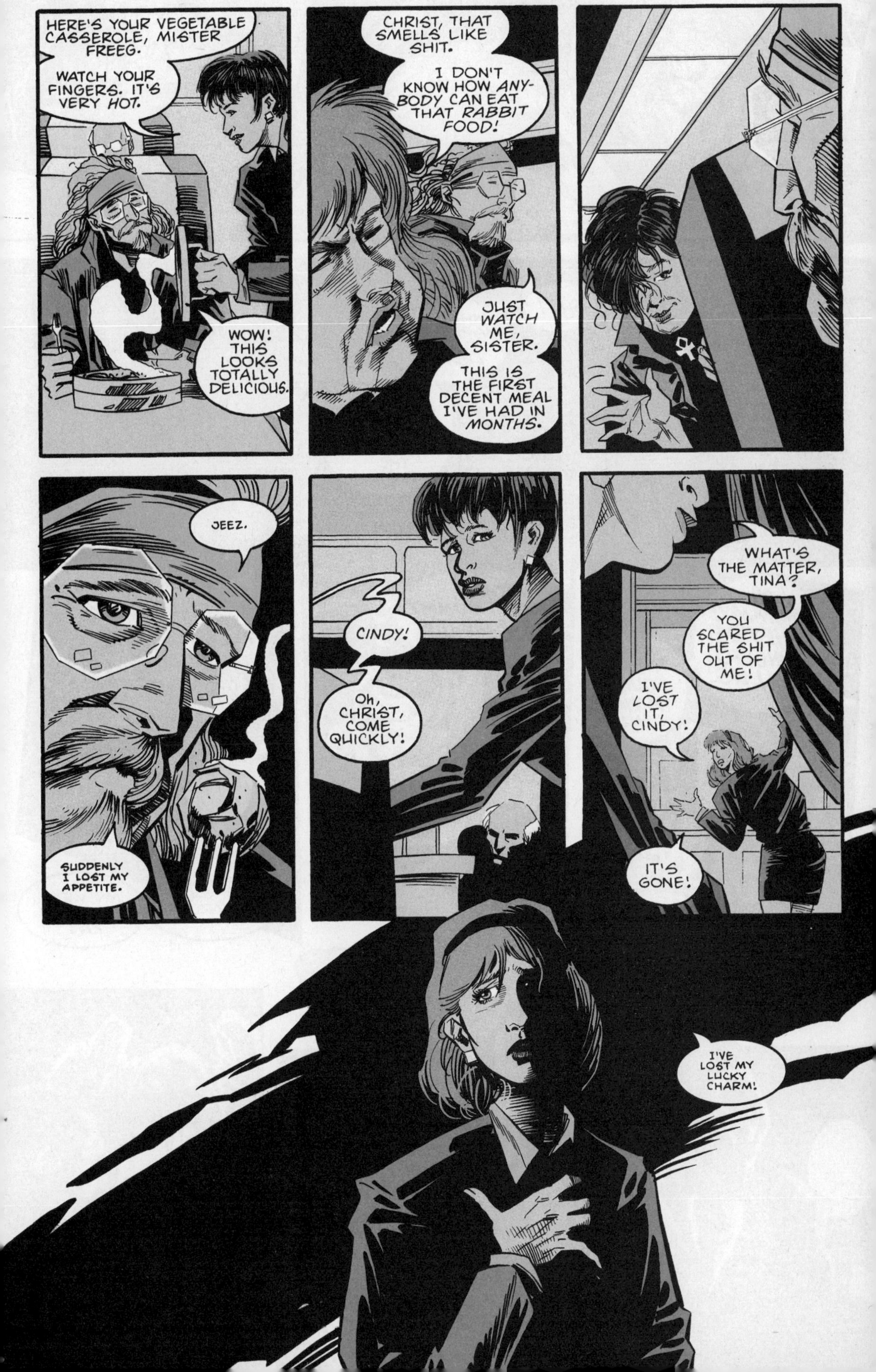

HERE'S YOUR VEGETABLE CASSEROLE, MISTER FREEG.
WATCH YOUR FINGERS. IT'S VERY HOT.
WOW! THIS LOOKS TOTALLY DELICIOUS.
CHRIST, THAT SMELLS LIKE SHIT.
I DON'T KNOW HOW ANYBODY CAN EAT THAT RABBIT FOOD!
JUST WATCH ME, SISTER.
THIS IS THE FIRST DECENT MEAL I'VE HAD IN MONTHS.
JEEZ.
SUDDENLY I LOST MY APPETITE.
CINDY!
Oh, CHRIST, COME QUICKLY!
WHAT'S THE MATTER, TINA?
YOU SCARED THE SHIT OUT OF ME!
I'VE LOST IT, CINDY!
IT'S GONE!
I'VE LOST MY LUCKY CHARM!

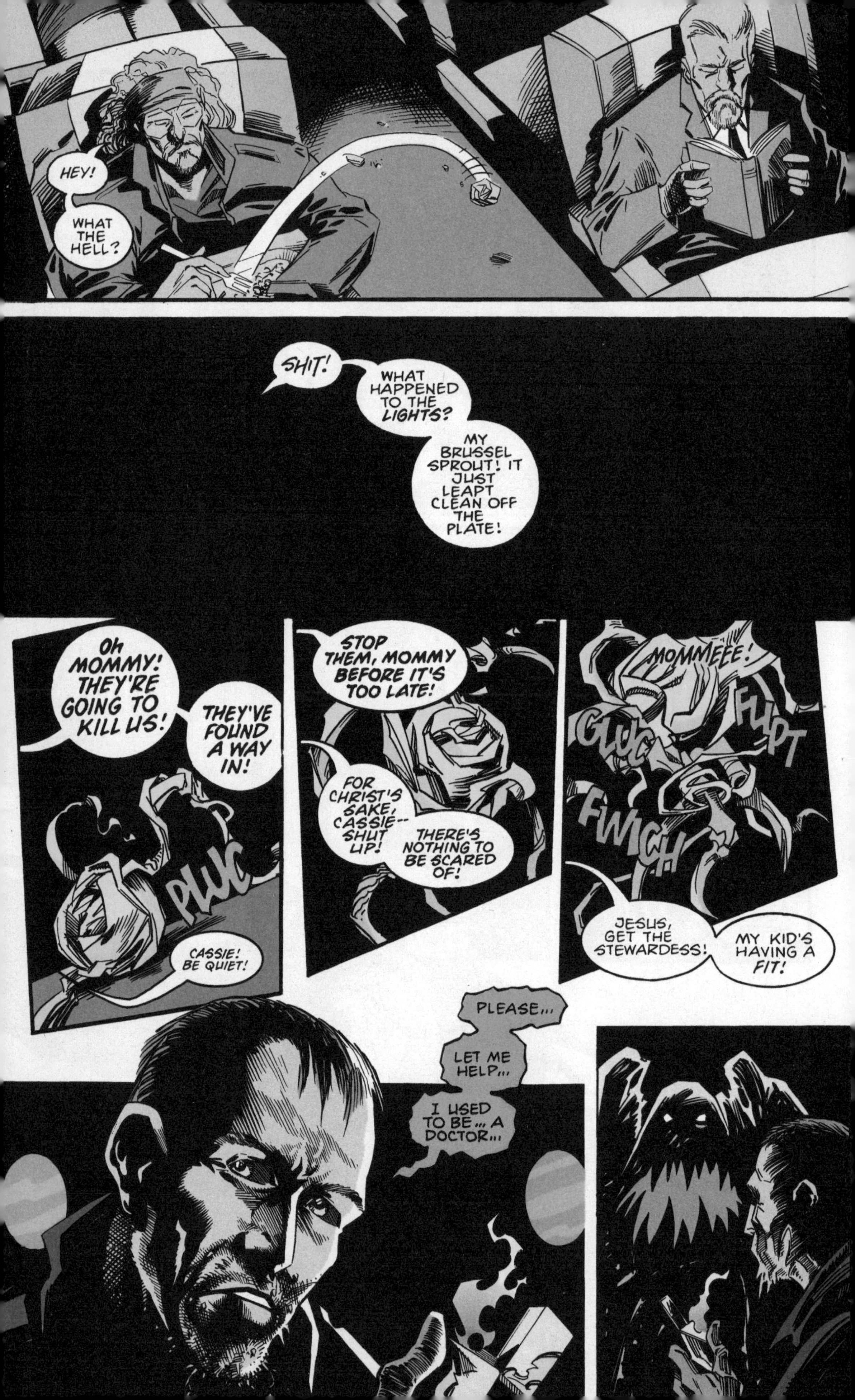
HEY!
WHAT THE HELL?
SHIT!
WHAT HAPPENED TO THE LIGHTS?
MY BRUSSEL SPROUT! IT JUST LEAPT CLEAN OFF THE PLATE!
Oh MOMMY! THEY'RE GOING TO KILL US!
THEY'VE FOUND A WAY IN!
PLUC
CASSIE! BE QUIET!
STOP THEM, MOMMY BEFORE IT'S TOO LATE!
FOR CHRIST'S SAKE, CASSIE-- SHUT UP!
THERE'S NOTHING TO BE SCARED OF!
MOMMEEE!
GLUC
FLUPT
FWICH
JESUS, GET THE STEWARDESS!
MY KID'S HAVING A FIT!
PLEASE...
LET ME HELP...
I USED TO BE... A DOCTOR...

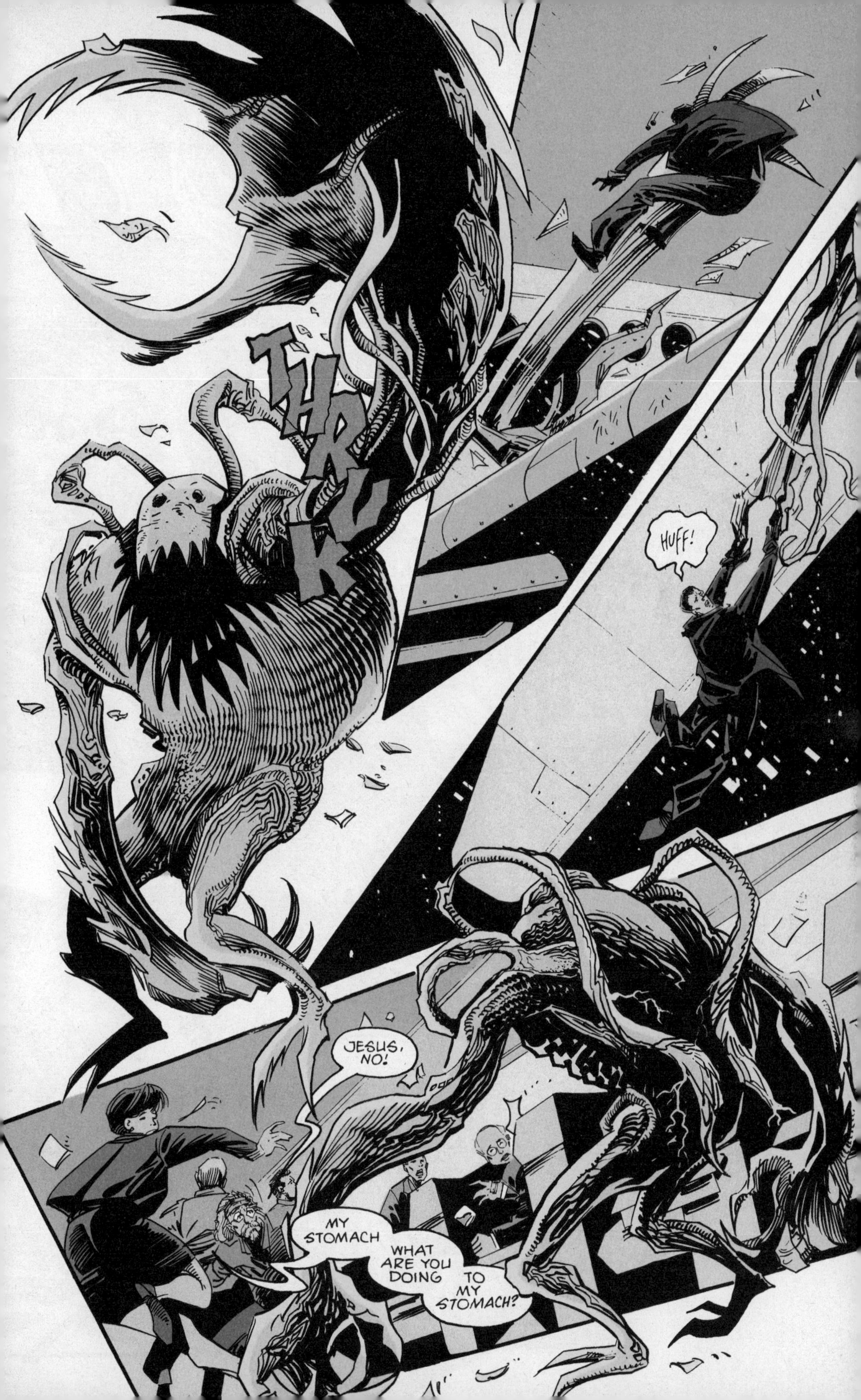
THRUK
HUFF!
JESUS, NO!
MY STOMACH
WHAT ARE YOU DOING TO MY STOMACH?

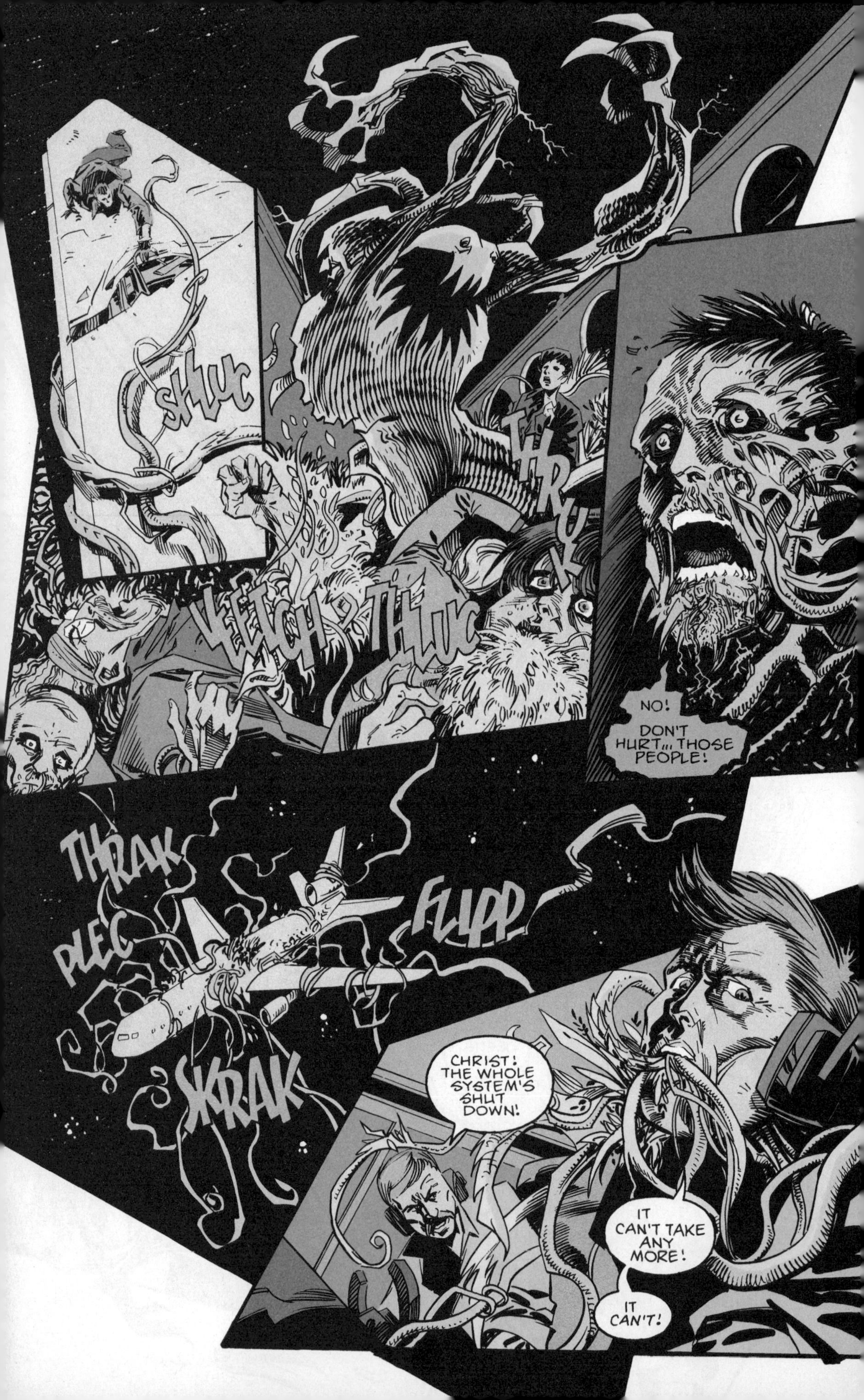
SHUC
THRUK
VLECH
THUC
NO! DON'T HURT... THOSE PEOPLE!
THRAK
PLEC
FLIPP
SKRAK
CHRIST! THE WHOLE SYSTEM'S SHUT DOWN!
IT CAN'T TAKE ANY MORE!
IT CAN'T!

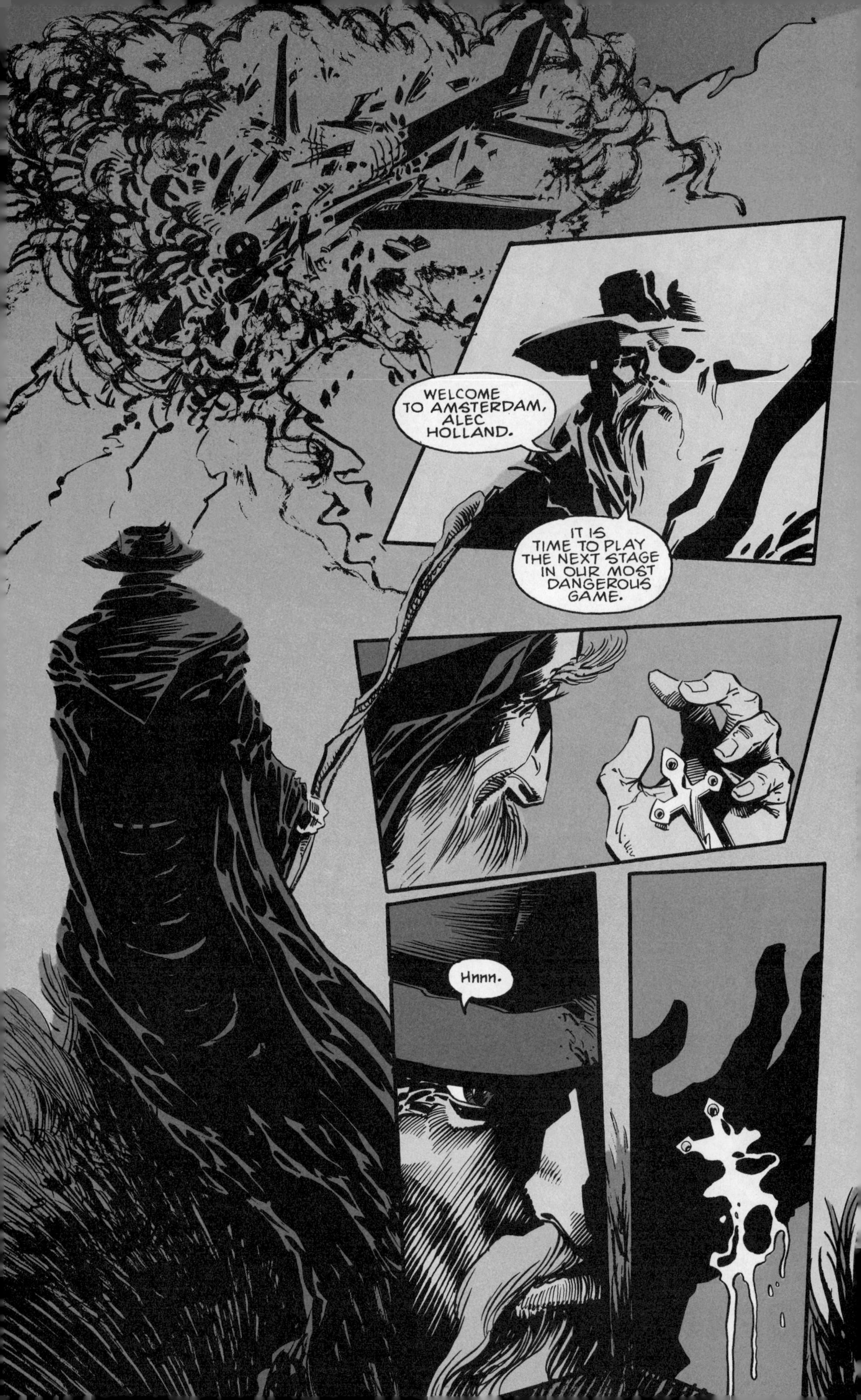
WELCOME TO AMSTERDAM, ALEC HOLLAND.
IT IS TIME TO PLAY THE NEXT STAGE IN OUR MOST DANGEROUS GAME.
Hnnn.

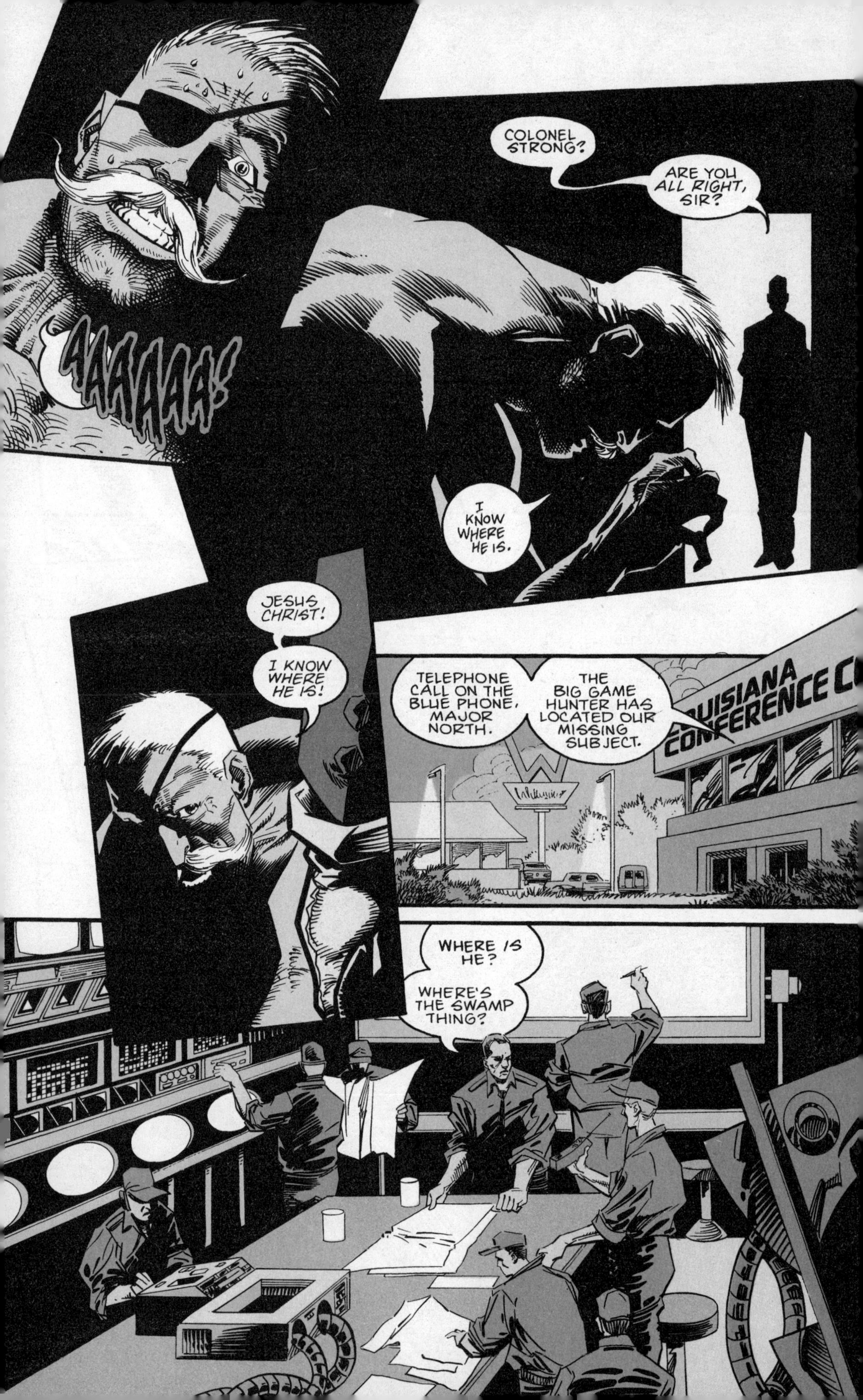

AAAAAA!
COLONEL STRONG?
ARE YOU ALL RIGHT, SIR?
I KNOW WHERE HE IS.
JESUS CHRIST!
I KNOW WHERE HE IS!
TELEPHONE CALL ON THE BLUE PHONE, MAJOR NORTH.
THE BIG GAME HUNTER HAS LOCATED OUR MISSING SUBJECT.
LOUISIANA CONFERENCE C
WHERE IS HE?
WHERE'S THE SWAMP THING?

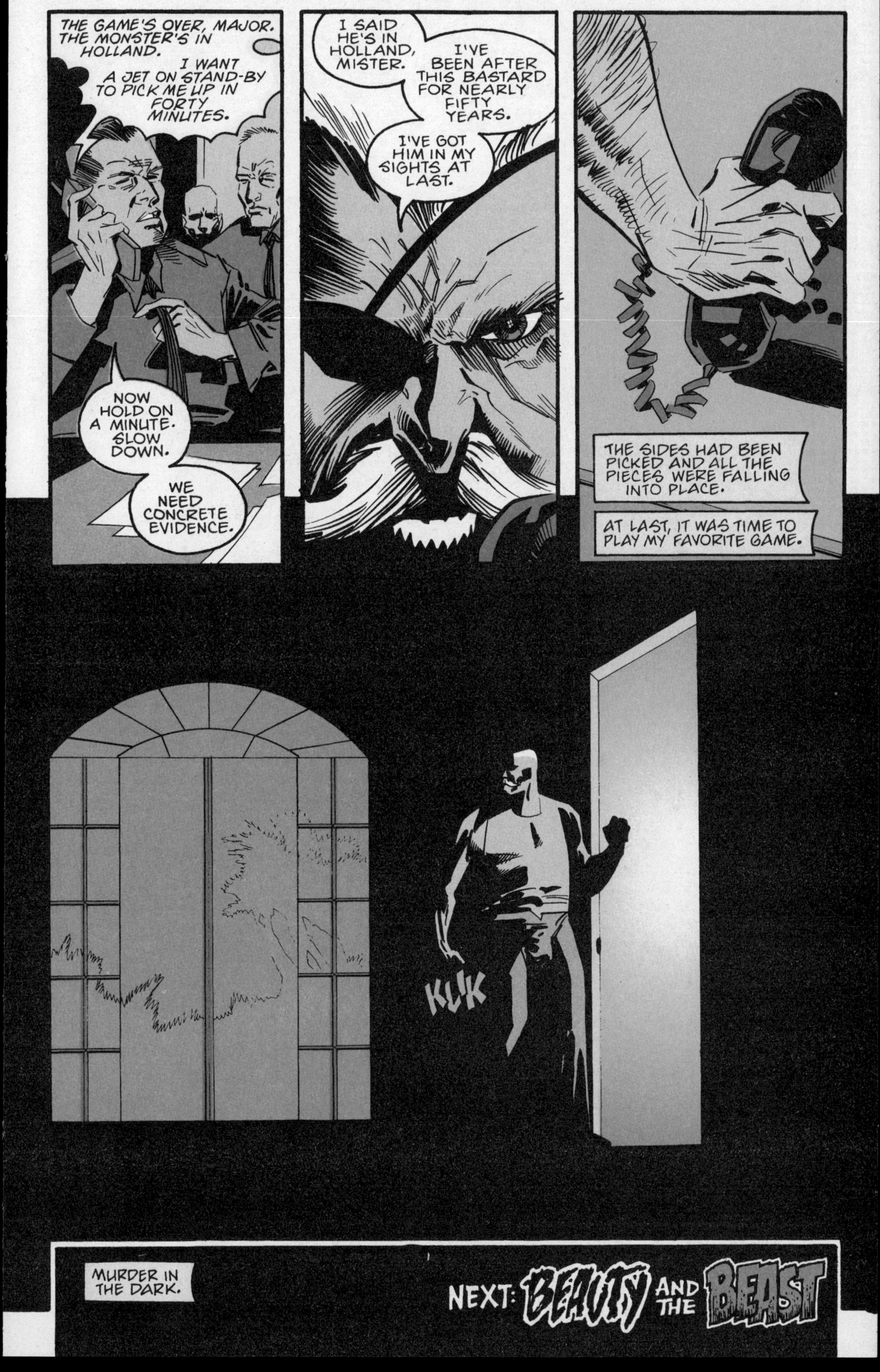
THE GAME'S OVER, MAJOR. THE MONSTER'S IN HOLLAND.
I WANT A JET ON STAND-BY TO PICK ME UP IN FORTY MINUTES.
NOW HOLD ON A MINUTE. SLOW DOWN.
WE NEED CONCRETE EVIDENCE.
I SAID HE'S IN HOLLAND, MISTER.
I'VE BEEN AFTER THIS BASTARD FOR NEARLY FIFTY YEARS.
I'VE GOT HIM IN MY SIGHTS AT LAST.
THE SIDES HAD BEEN PICKED AND ALL THE PIECES WERE FALLING INTO PLACE.
AT LAST, IT WAS TIME TO PLAY MY FAVORITE GAME.
KLIK
MURDER IN THE DARK.
NEXT: BEAUTY AND THE BEAST

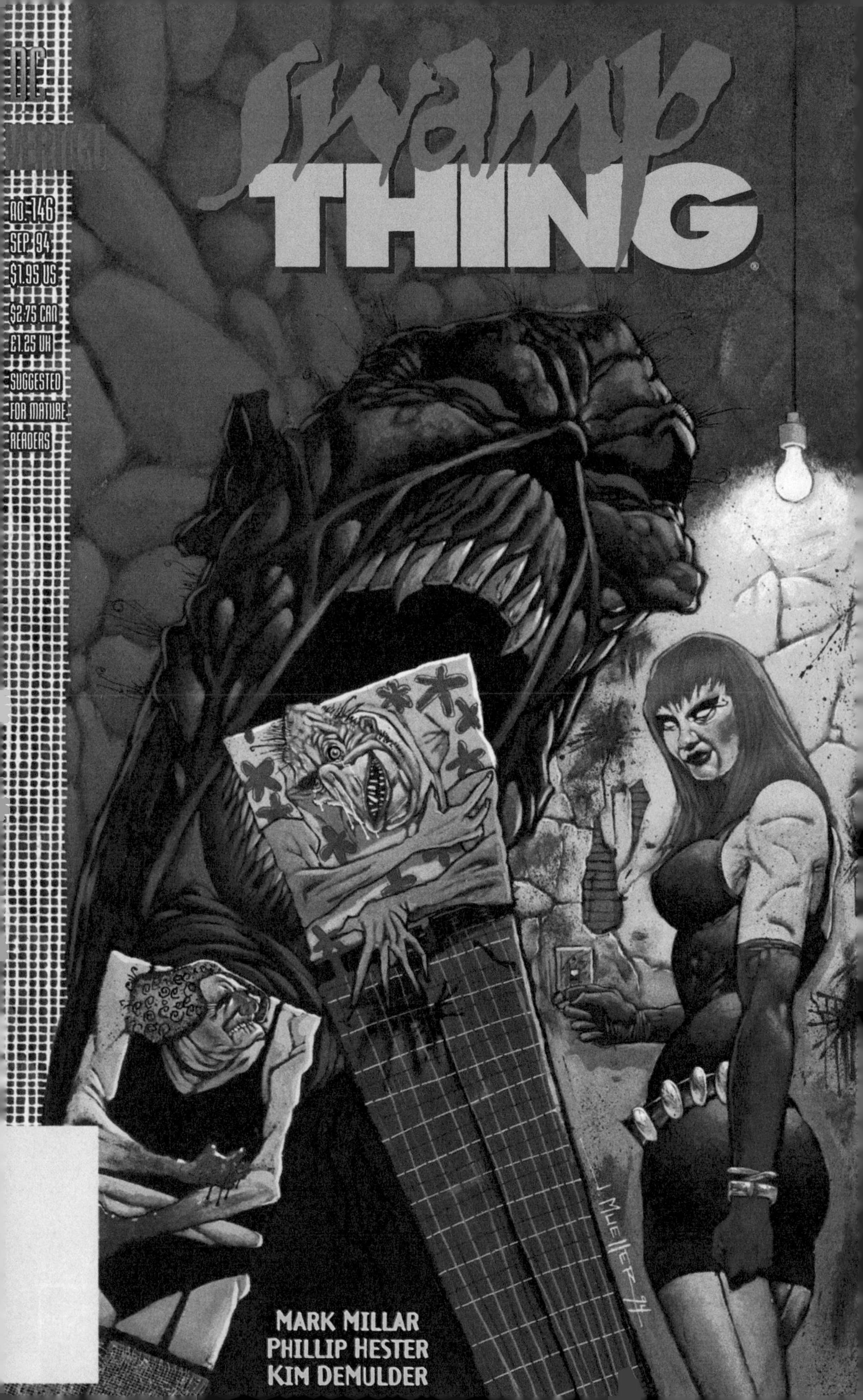
DC
SWAMP THING
NO. 146
SEP 94
$1.95 US
$2.75 CAN
£1.25 UK
SUGGESTED FOR MATURE READERS
MARK MILLAR
PHILLIP HESTER
KIM DEMULDER

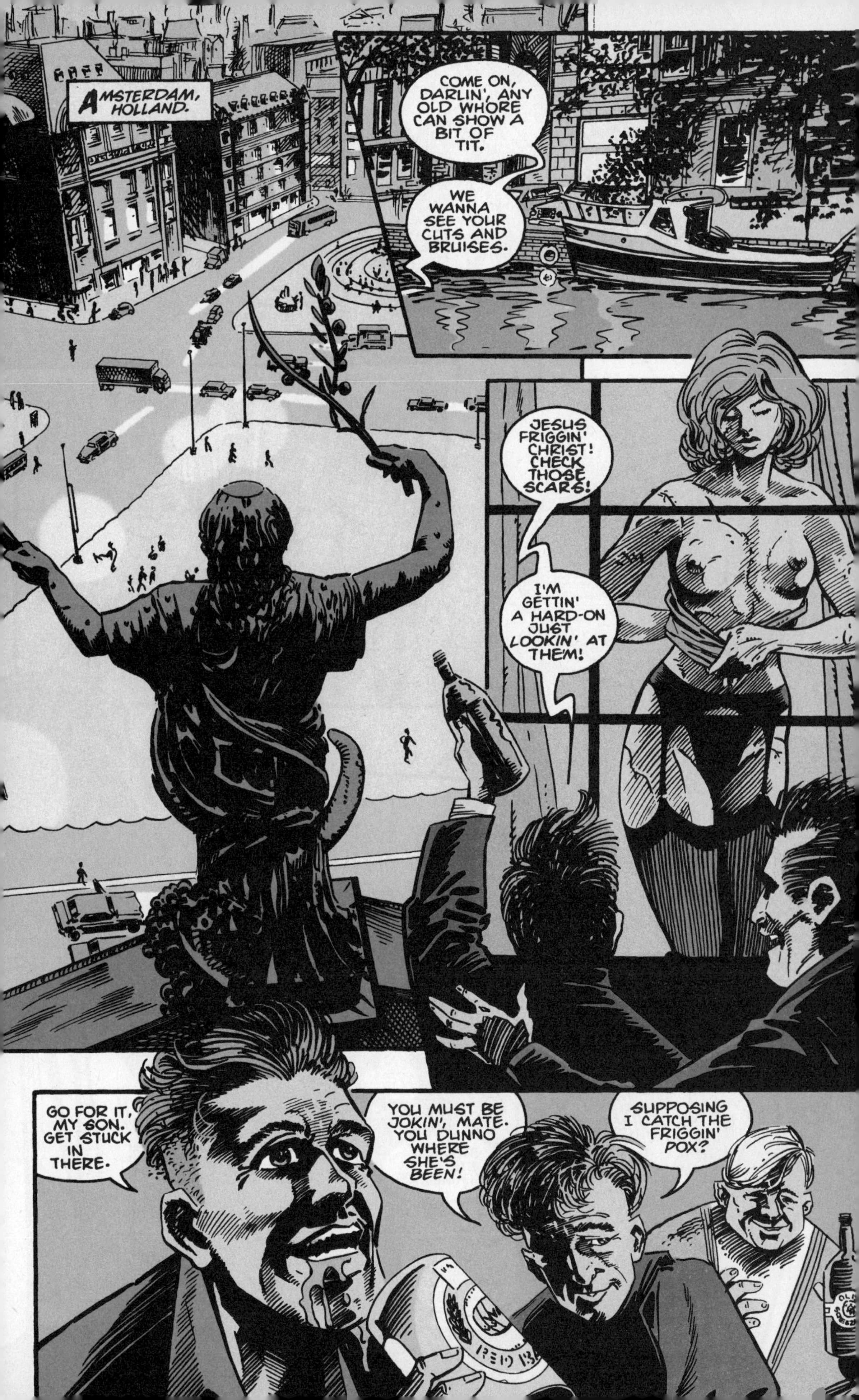
AMSTERDAM, HOLLAND.
COME ON, DARLIN', ANY OLD WHORE CAN SHOW A BIT OF TIT.
WE WANNA SEE YOUR CUTS AND BRUISES.
JESUS FRIGGIN' CHRIST! CHECK THOSE SCARS!
I'M GETTIN' A HARD-ON JUST LOOKIN' AT THEM!
GO FOR IT, MY SON. GET STUCK IN THERE.
YOU MUST BE JOKIN', MATE. YOU DUNNO WHERE SHE'S BEEN!
SUPPOSING I CATCH THE FRIGGIN' POX?

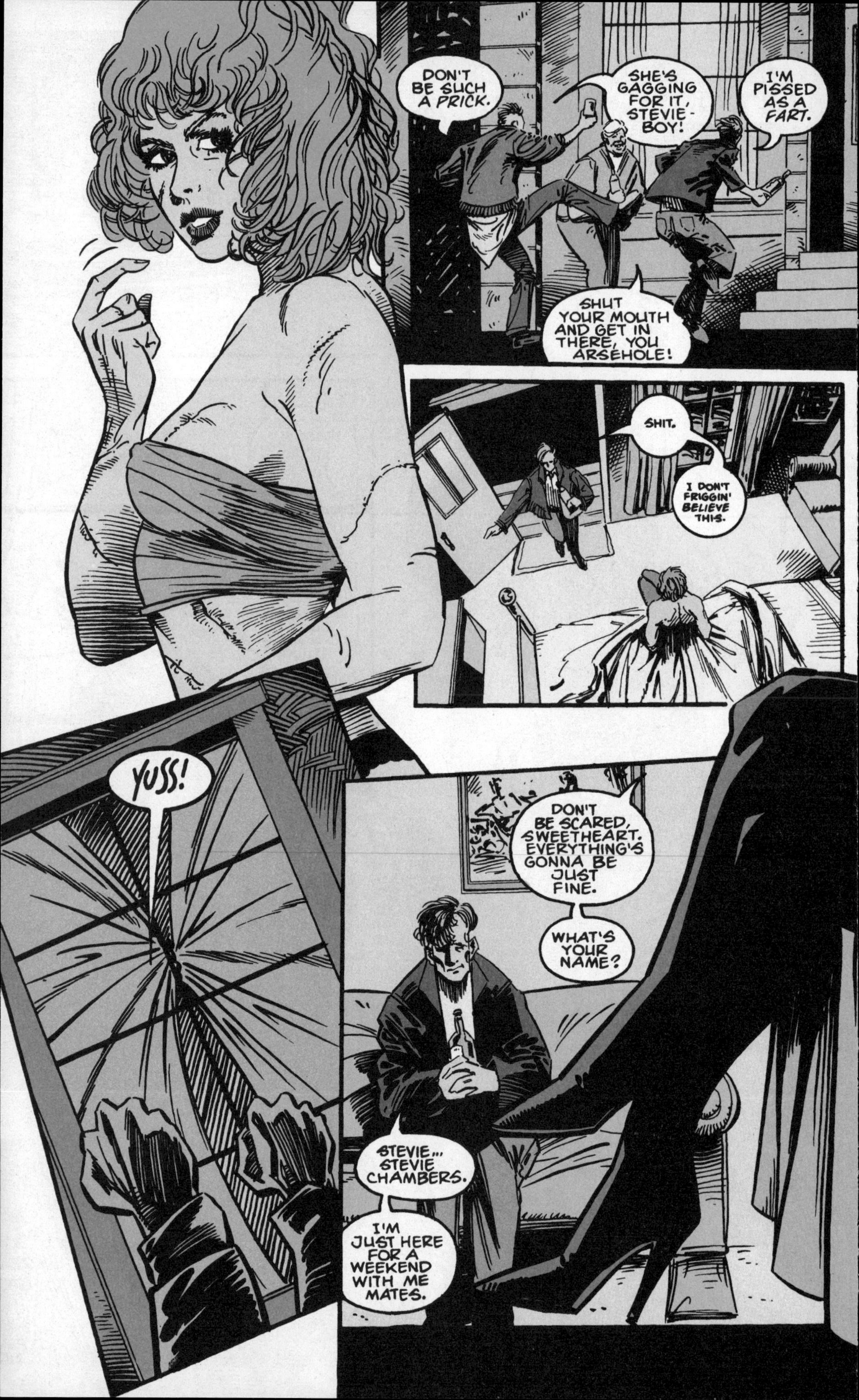
DON'T BE SUCH A PRICK.
SHE'S GAGGING FOR IT, STEVIE-BOY!
I'M PISSED AS A FART.
SHUT YOUR MOUTH AND GET IN THERE, YOU ARSEHOLE!
SHIT.
I DON'T FRIGGIN' BELIEVE THIS.
YUSS!
DON'T BE SCARED, SWEETHEART. EVERYTHING'S GONNA BE JUST FINE.
WHAT'S YOUR NAME?
STEVIE... STEVIE CHAMBERS.
I'M JUST HERE FOR A WEEKEND WITH ME MATES.

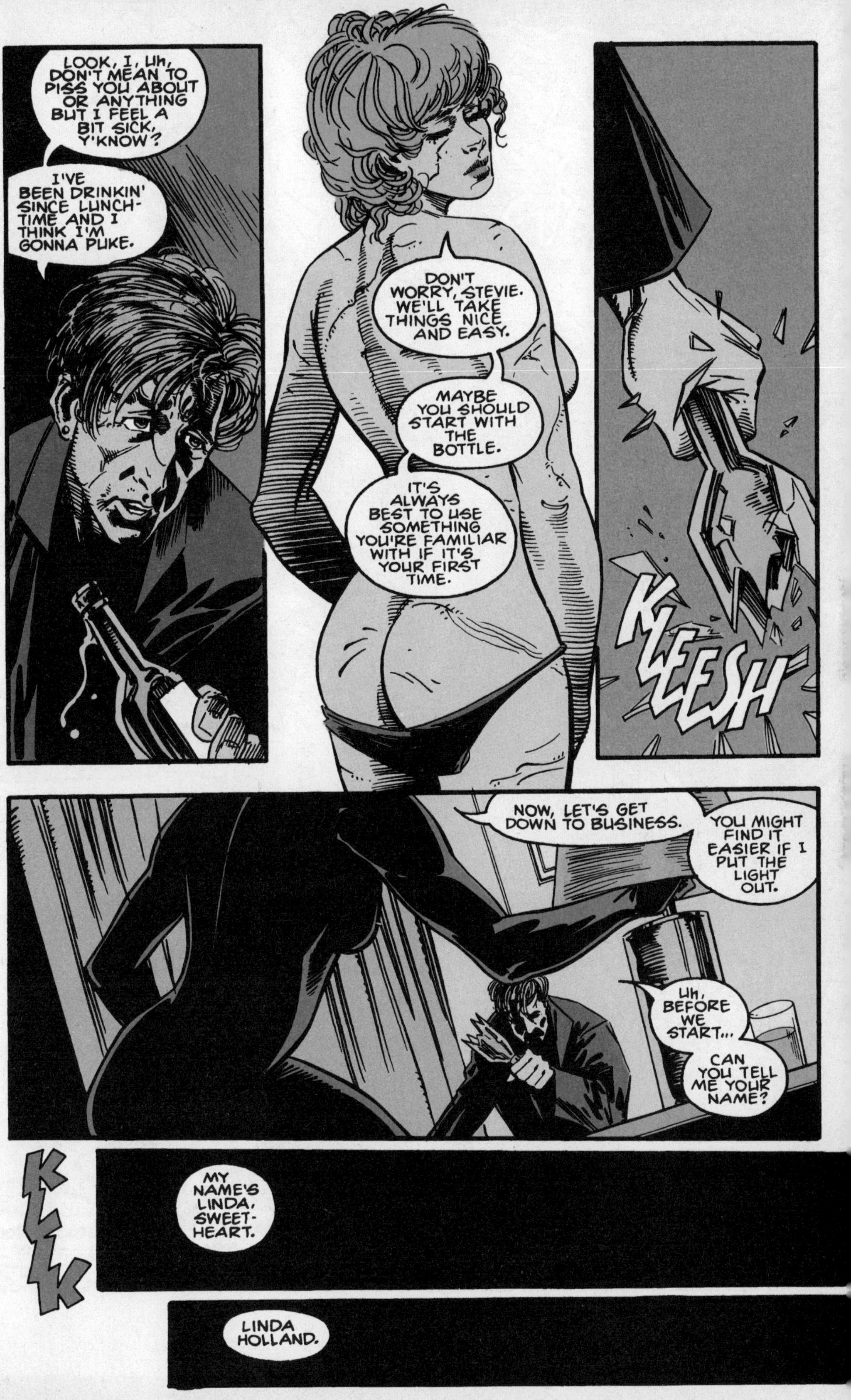
LOOK, I, UH, DON'T MEAN TO PISS YOU ABOUT OR ANYTHING BUT I FEEL A BIT SICK, Y'KNOW?
I'VE BEEN DRINKIN' SINCE LUNCH-TIME AND I THINK I'M GONNA PUKE.
DON'T WORRY, STEVIE. WE'LL TAKE THINGS NICE AND EASY.
MAYBE YOU SHOULD START WITH THE BOTTLE.
IT'S ALWAYS BEST TO USE SOMETHING YOU'RE FAMILIAR WITH IF IT'S YOUR FIRST TIME.
KLEESH
NOW, LET'S GET DOWN TO BUSINESS.
YOU MIGHT FIND IT EASIER IF I PUT THE LIGHT OUT.
UH, BEFORE WE START...
CAN YOU TELL ME YOUR NAME?
KLIK
MY NAME'S LINDA, SWEET-HEART.
LINDA HOLLAND.

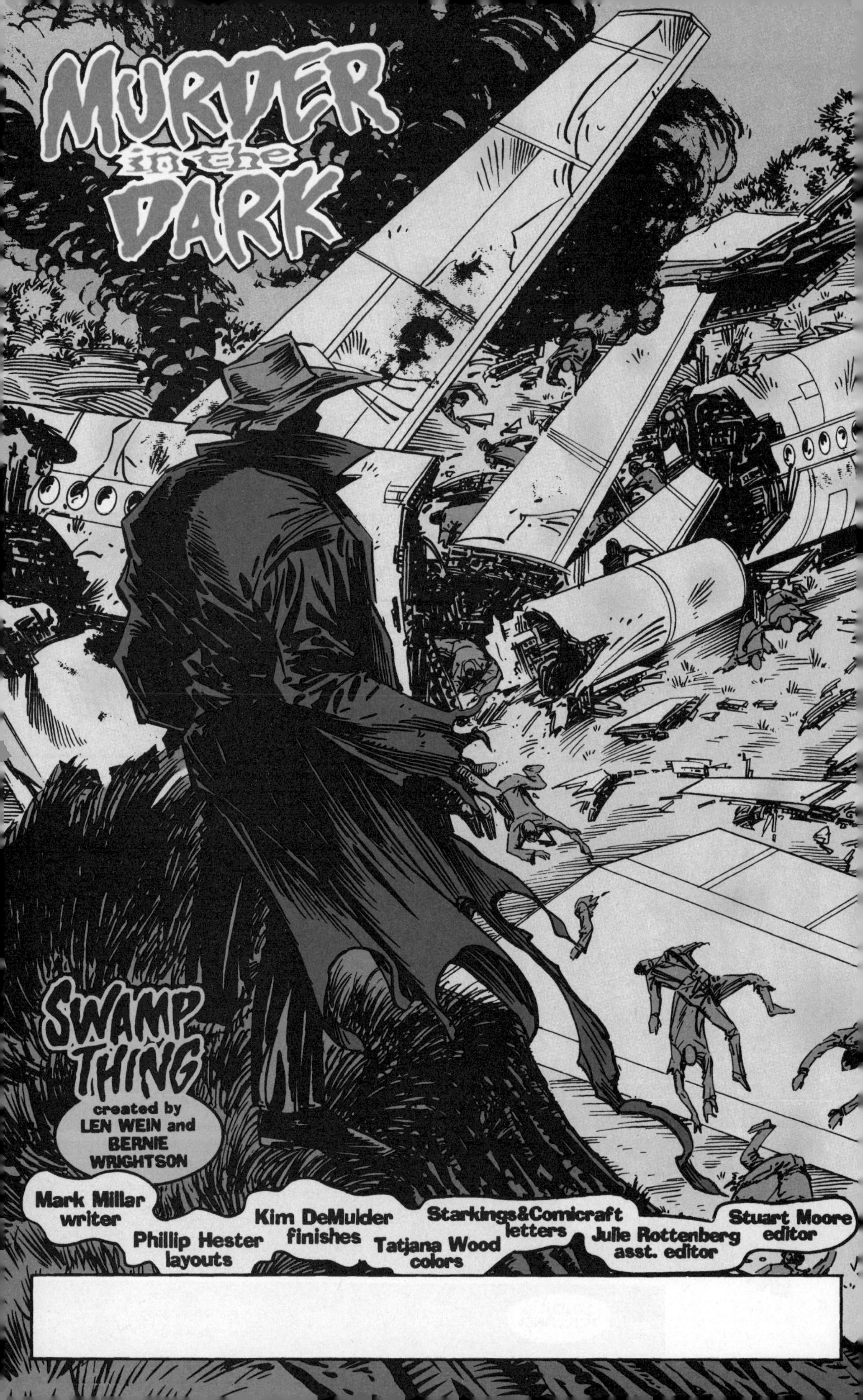

MURDER in the DARK
SWAMP THING
created by LEN WEIN and BERNIE WRIGHTSON
Mark Millar writer
Phillip Hester layouts
Kim DeMulder finishes
Tatjana Wood colors
Starkings&Comicraft letters
Julie Rottenberg asst. editor
Stuart Moore editor

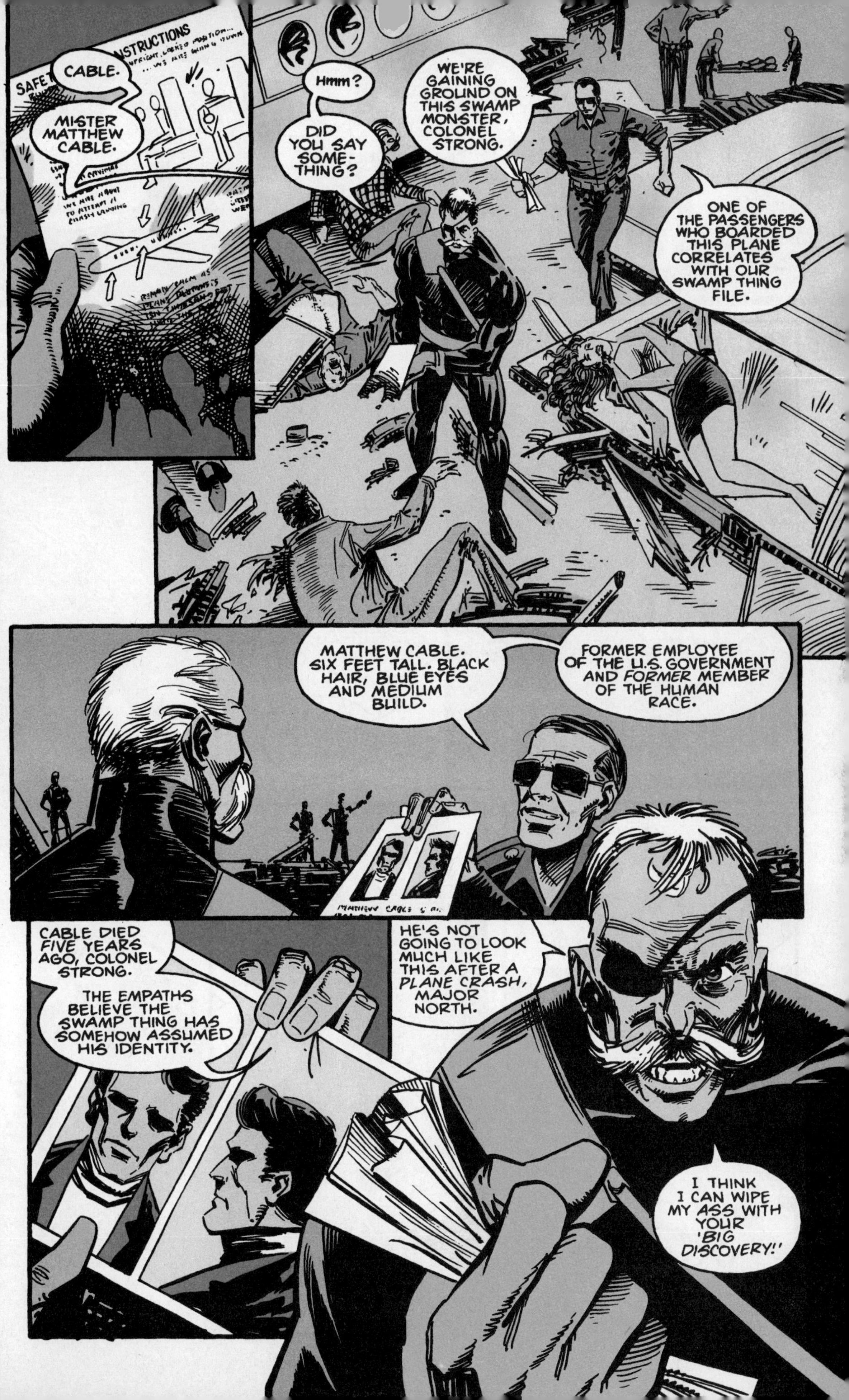
SAFETY INSTRUCTIONS
CABLE.
MISTER MATTHEW CABLE.
Hmm?
DID YOU SAY SOME-THING?
WE'RE GAINING GROUND ON THIS SWAMP MONSTER, COLONEL STRONG.
ONE OF THE PASSENGERS WHO BOARDED THIS PLANE CORRELATES WITH OUR SWAMP THING FILE.
MATTHEW CABLE. SIX FEET TALL. BLACK HAIR, BLUE EYES AND MEDIUM BUILD.
FORMER EMPLOYEE OF THE U.S. GOVERNMENT AND FORMER MEMBER OF THE HUMAN RACE.
CABLE DIED FIVE YEARS AGO, COLONEL STRONG.
THE EMPATHS BELIEVE THE SWAMP THING HAS SOMEHOW ASSUMED HIS IDENTITY.
HE'S NOT GOING TO LOOK MUCH LIKE THIS AFTER A PLANE CRASH, MAJOR NORTH.
I THINK I CAN WIPE MY ASS WITH YOUR 'BIG DISCOVERY!'

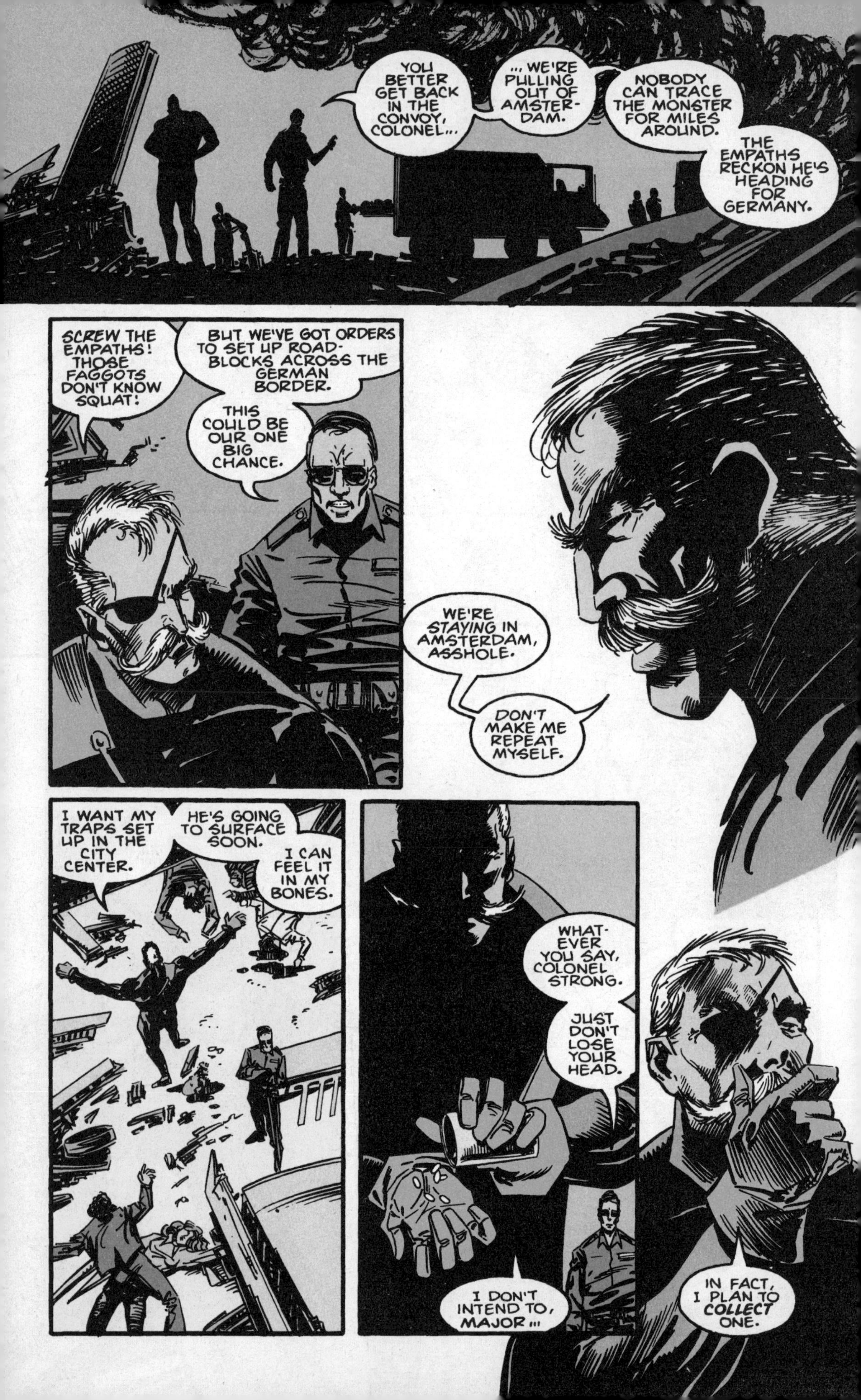

YOU BETTER GET BACK IN THE CONVOY, COLONEL...
... WE'RE PULLING OUT OF AMSTER-DAM.
NOBODY CAN TRACE THE MONSTER FOR MILES AROUND.
THE EMPATHS RECKON HE'S HEADING FOR GERMANY.
SCREW THE EMPATHS! THOSE FAGGOTS DON'T KNOW SQUAT!
BUT WE'VE GOT ORDERS TO SET UP ROAD-BLOCKS ACROSS THE GERMAN BORDER.
THIS COULD BE OUR ONE BIG CHANCE.
WE'RE STAYING IN AMSTERDAM, ASSHOLE.
DON'T MAKE ME REPEAT MYSELF.
I WANT MY TRAPS SET UP IN THE CITY CENTER.
HE'S GOING TO SURFACE SOON.
I CAN FEEL IT IN MY BONES.
WHAT-EVER YOU SAY, COLONEL STRONG.
JUST DON'T LOSE YOUR HEAD.
I DON'T INTEND TO, MAJOR...
IN FACT, I PLAN TO COLLECT ONE.

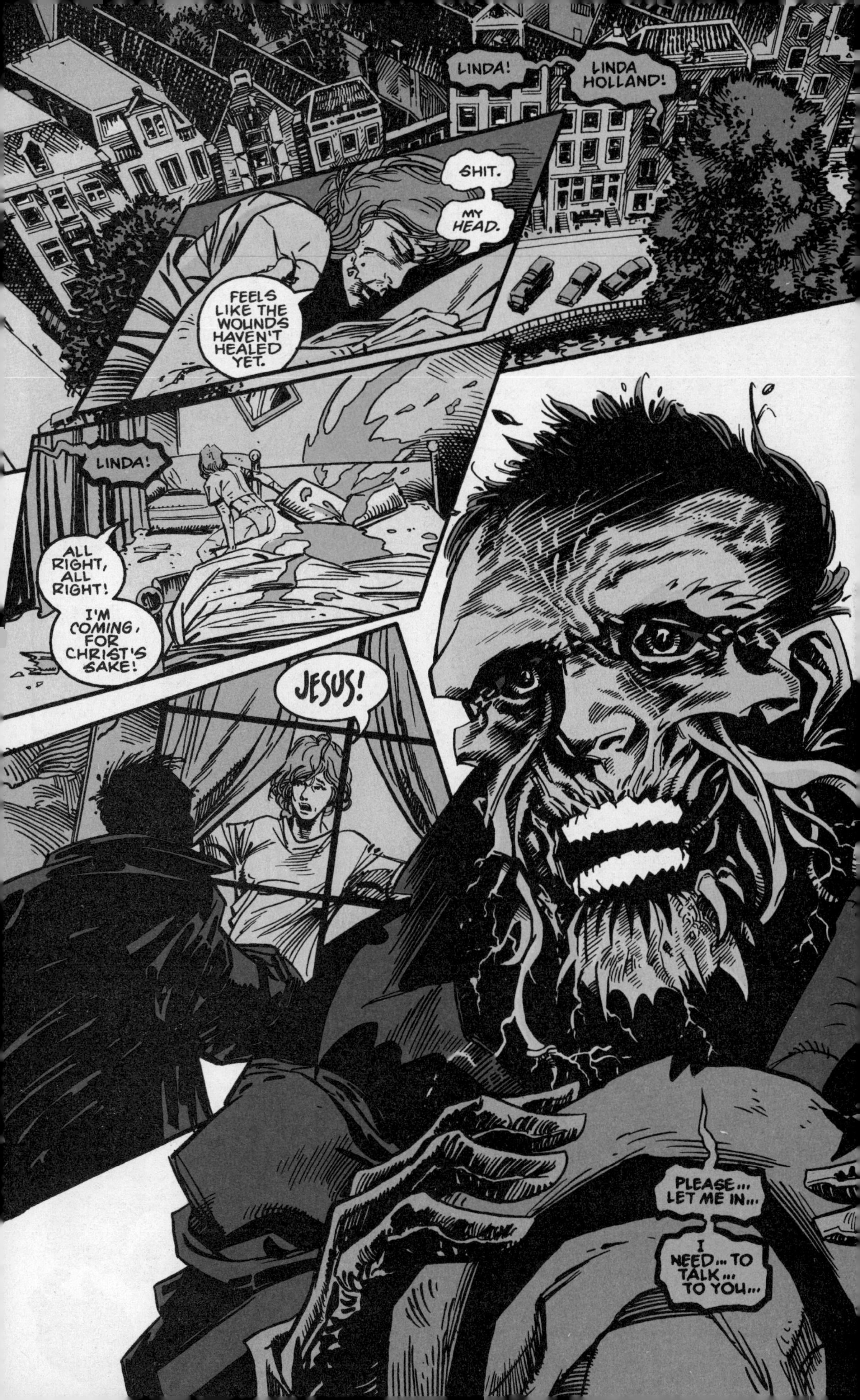
LINDA!
LINDA HOLLAND!
SHIT.
MY HEAD.
FEELS LIKE THE WOUNDS HAVEN'T HEALED YET.
LINDA!
ALL RIGHT, ALL RIGHT!
I'M COMING, FOR CHRIST'S SAKE!
JESUS!
PLEASE... LET ME IN...
I NEED... TO TALK... TO YOU...

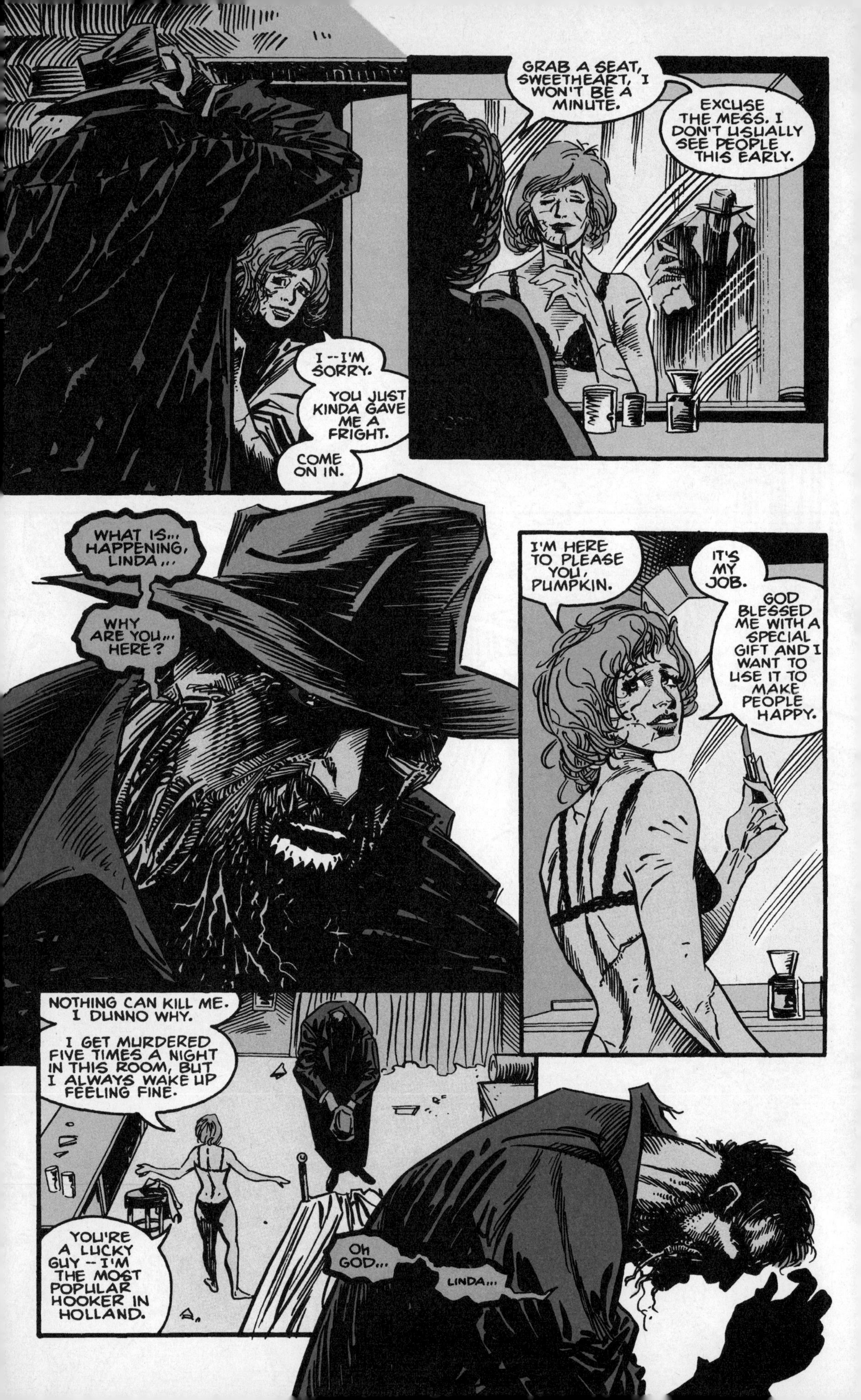

I --I'M SORRY.
YOU JUST KINDA GAVE ME A FRIGHT.
COME ON IN.
GRAB A SEAT, SWEETHEART, I WON'T BE A MINUTE.
EXCUSE THE MESS. I DON'T USUALLY SEE PEOPLE THIS EARLY.
WHAT IS... HAPPENING, LINDA...
WHY ARE YOU... HERE?
I'M HERE TO PLEASE YOU, PUMPKIN.
IT'S MY JOB.
GOD BLESSED ME WITH A SPECIAL GIFT AND I WANT TO USE IT TO MAKE PEOPLE HAPPY.
NOTHING CAN KILL ME. I DUNNO WHY.
I GET MURDERED FIVE TIMES A NIGHT IN THIS ROOM, BUT I ALWAYS WAKE UP FEELING FINE.
YOU'RE A LUCKY GUY -- I'M THE MOST POPULAR HOOKER IN HOLLAND.
Oh GOD...
LINDA...

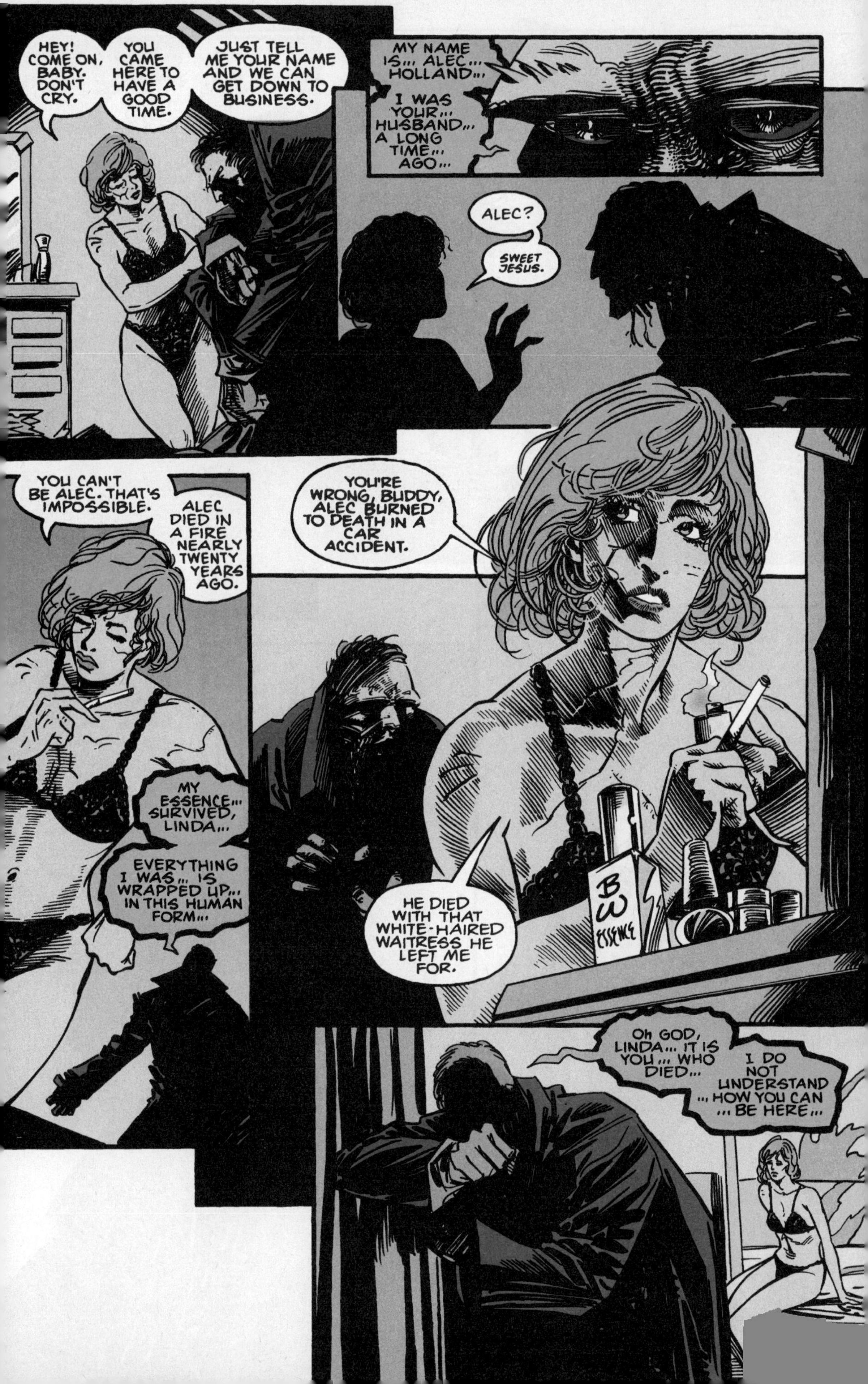
HEY! COME ON, BABY. DON'T CRY.
YOU CAME HERE TO HAVE A GOOD TIME.
JUST TELL ME YOUR NAME AND WE CAN GET DOWN TO BUSINESS.
MY NAME IS... ALEC... HOLLAND...
I WAS YOUR... HUSBAND... A LONG TIME... AGO...
ALEC?
SWEET JESUS.
YOU CAN'T BE ALEC. THAT'S IMPOSSIBLE.
ALEC DIED IN A FIRE NEARLY TWENTY YEARS AGO.
MY ESSENCE... SURVIVED, LINDA...
EVERYTHING I WAS... IS WRAPPED UP... IN THIS HUMAN FORM...
YOU'RE WRONG, BUDDY. ALEC BURNED TO DEATH IN A CAR ACCIDENT.
HE DIED WITH THAT WHITE-HAIRED WAITRESS HE LEFT ME FOR.
BW
ESSENCE
Oh GOD, LINDA... IT IS YOU... WHO DIED...
I DO NOT UNDERSTAND ... HOW YOU CAN ... BE HERE...

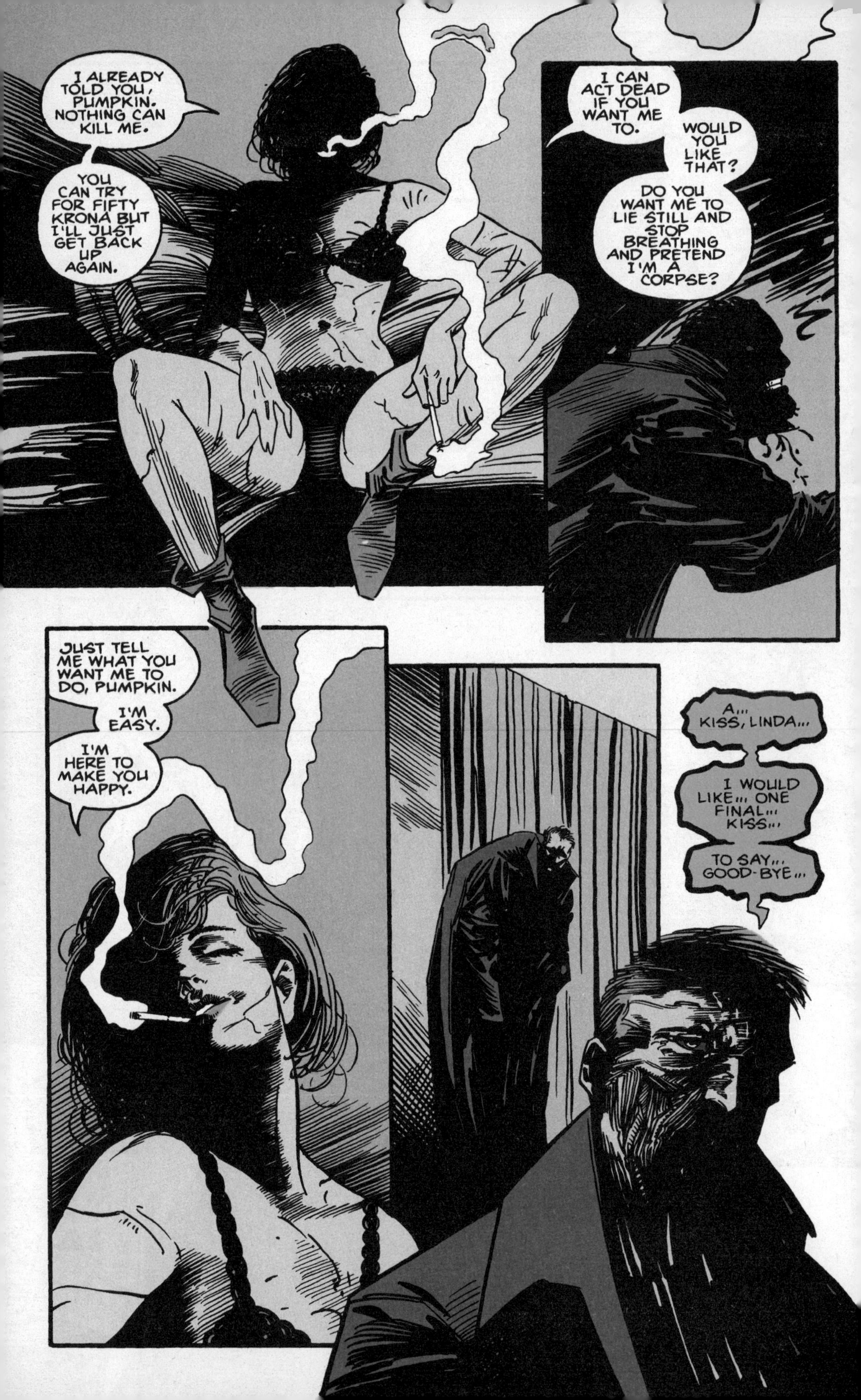
I ALREADY TOLD YOU, PUMPKIN. NOTHING CAN KILL ME.
YOU CAN TRY FOR FIFTY KRONA BUT I'LL JUST GET BACK UP AGAIN.
I CAN ACT DEAD IF YOU WANT ME TO.
WOULD YOU LIKE THAT?
DO YOU WANT ME TO LIE STILL AND STOP BREATHING AND PRETEND I'M A CORPSE?
JUST TELL ME WHAT YOU WANT ME TO DO, PUMPKIN.
I'M EASY.
I'M HERE TO MAKE YOU HAPPY.
A... KISS, LINDA...
I WOULD LIKE... ONE FINAL... KISS...
TO SAY... GOOD-BYE...

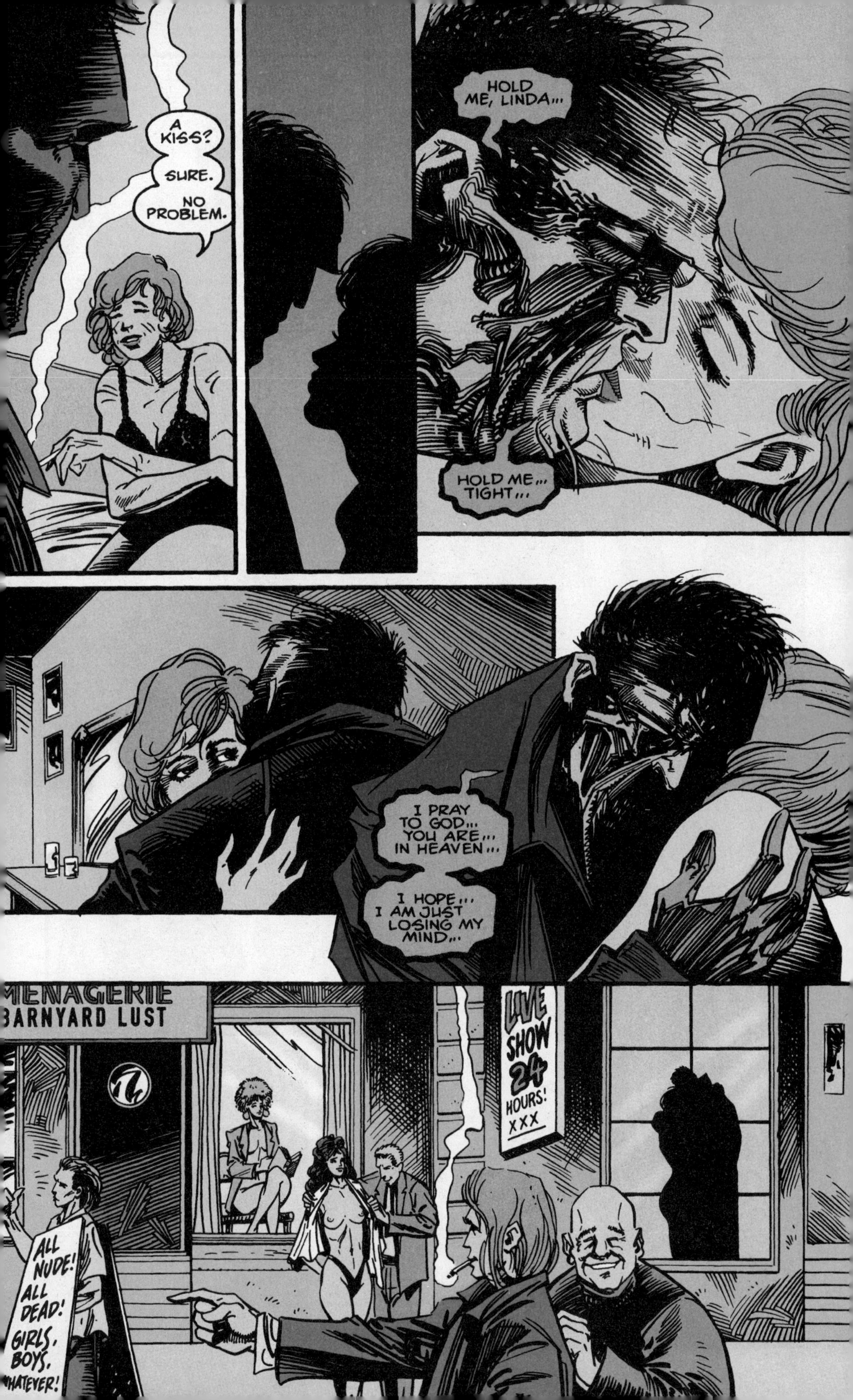
A KISS? SURE. NO PROBLEM.
HOLD ME, LINDA...
HOLD ME... TIGHT...
I PRAY TO GOD... YOU ARE... IN HEAVEN...
I HOPE... I AM JUST LOSING MY MIND...
MENAGERIE
BARNYARD LUST
LIVE SHOW 24 HOURS! XXX
ALL NUDE! ALL DEAD! GIRLS. BOYS. WHATEVER!

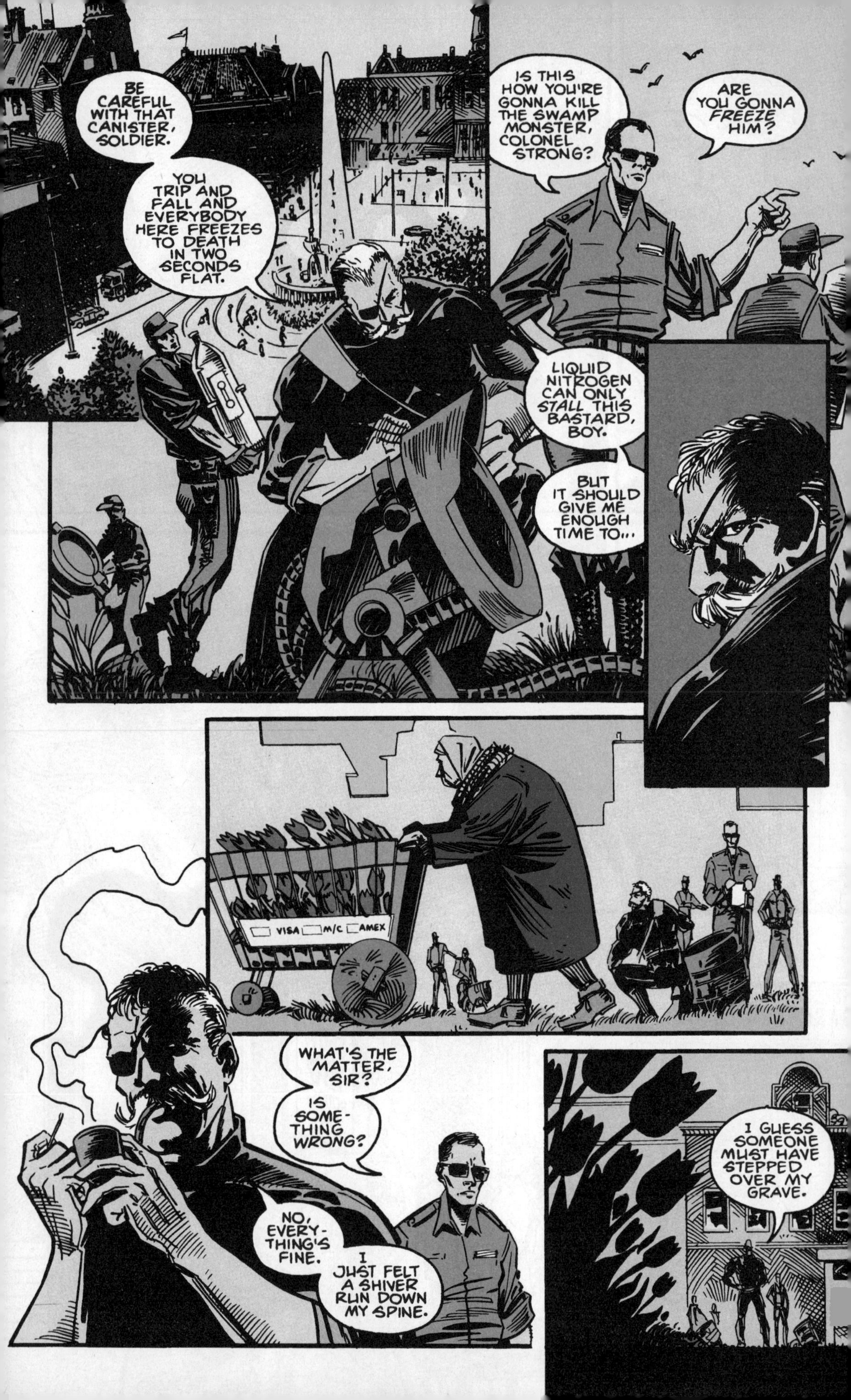
BE CAREFUL WITH THAT CANISTER, SOLDIER.
YOU TRIP AND FALL AND EVERYBODY HERE FREEZES TO DEATH IN TWO SECONDS FLAT.
IS THIS HOW YOU'RE GONNA KILL THE SWAMP MONSTER, COLONEL STRONG?
ARE YOU GONNA FREEZE HIM?
LIQUID NITROGEN CAN ONLY STALL THIS BASTARD, BOY.
BUT IT SHOULD GIVE ME ENOUGH TIME TO...
VISA M/C AMEX
WHAT'S THE MATTER, SIR?
IS SOMETHING WRONG?
NO, EVERYTHING'S FINE.
I JUST FELT A SHIVER RUN DOWN MY SPINE.
I GUESS SOMEONE MUST HAVE STEPPED OVER MY GRAVE.

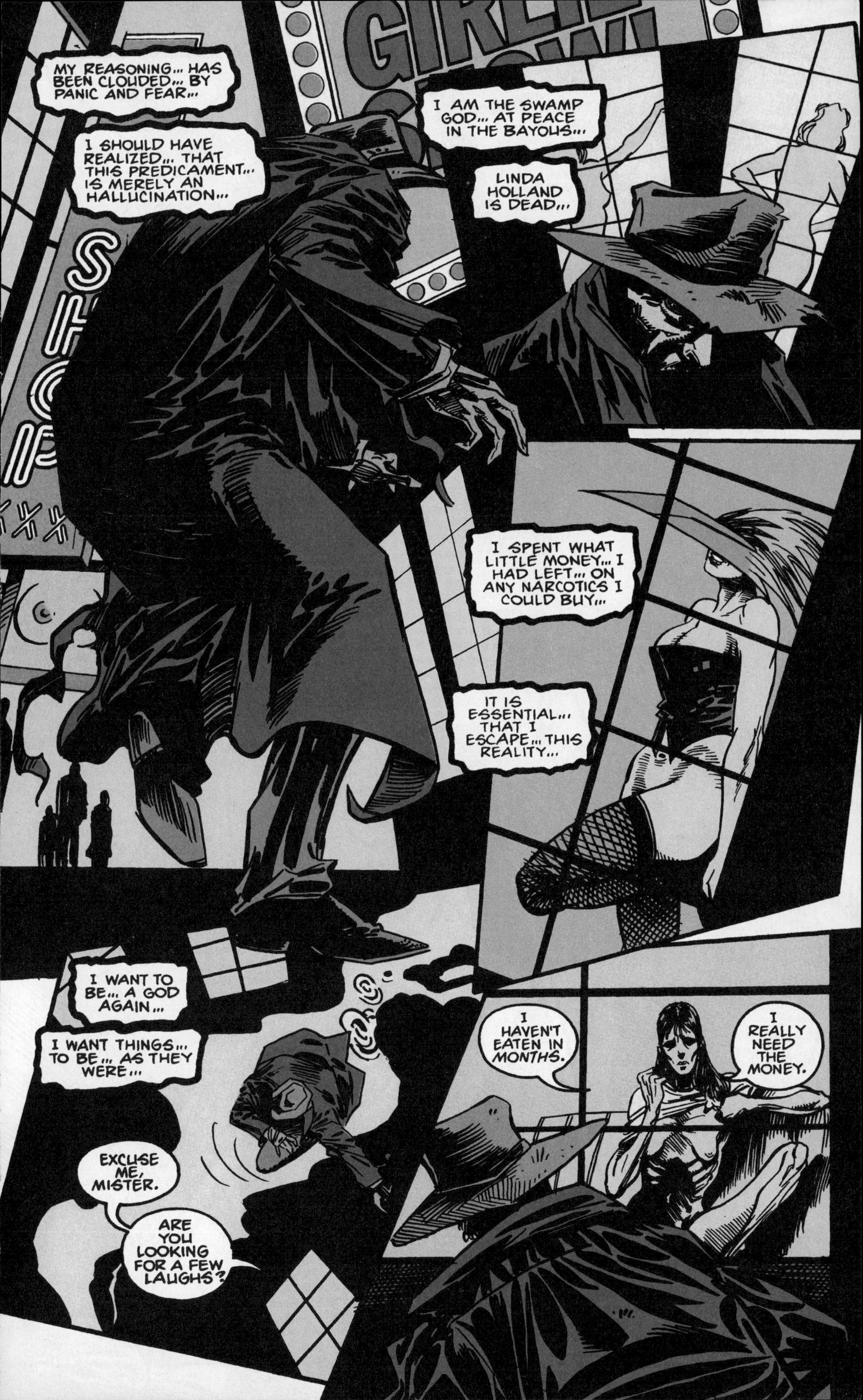

MY REASONING... HAS BEEN CLOUDED... BY PANIC AND FEAR...
I SHOULD HAVE REALIZED... THAT THIS PREDICAMENT... IS MERELY AN HALLUCINATION...
I AM THE SWAMP GOD... AT PEACE IN THE BAYOUS...
LINDA HOLLAND IS DEAD...
I SPENT WHAT LITTLE MONEY... I HAD LEFT... ON ANY NARCOTICS I COULD BUY...
IT IS ESSENTIAL... THAT I ESCAPE... THIS REALITY...
I WANT TO BE... A GOD AGAIN...
I WANT THINGS... TO BE... AS THEY WERE...
EXCUSE ME, MISTER.
ARE YOU LOOKING FOR A FEW LAUGHS?
I HAVEN'T EATEN IN MONTHS.
I REALLY NEED THE MONEY.

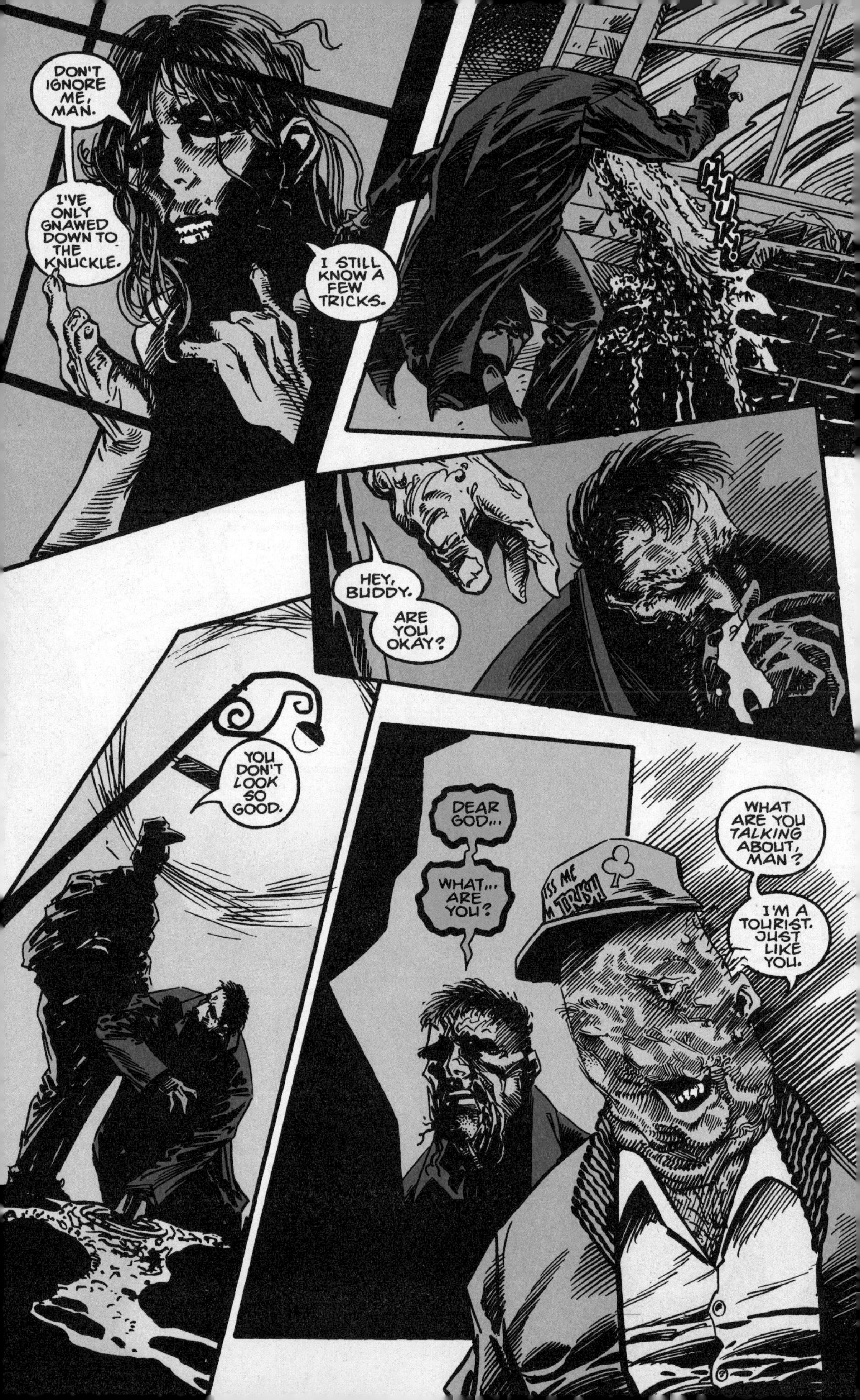
DON'T IGNORE ME, MAN.
I'VE ONLY GNAWED DOWN TO THE KNUCKLE.
I STILL KNOW A FEW TRICKS.
HUUK!
HEY, BUDDY.
ARE YOU OKAY?
YOU DON'T LOOK SO GOOD.
DEAR GOD...
WHAT... ARE YOU?
WHAT ARE YOU TALKING ABOUT, MAN?
I'M A TOURIST. JUST LIKE YOU.

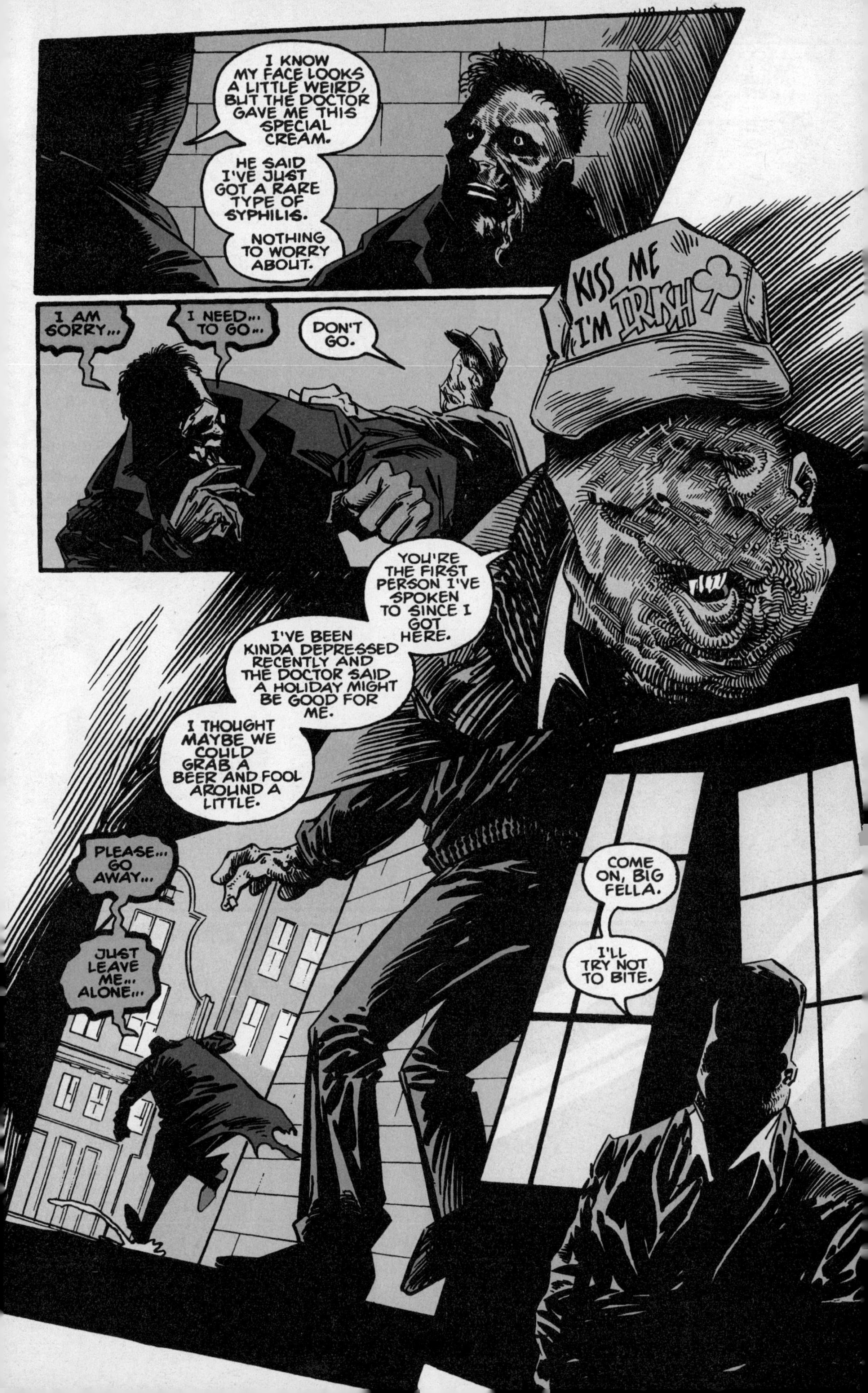
I KNOW MY FACE LOOKS A LITTLE WEIRD, BUT THE DOCTOR GAVE ME THIS SPECIAL CREAM.
HE SAID I'VE JUST GOT A RARE TYPE OF SYPHILIS.
NOTHING TO WORRY ABOUT.
KISS ME I'M IRISH
I AM SORRY...
I NEED... TO GO...
DON'T GO.
YOU'RE THE FIRST PERSON I'VE SPOKEN TO SINCE I GOT HERE.
I'VE BEEN KINDA DEPRESSED RECENTLY AND THE DOCTOR SAID A HOLIDAY MIGHT BE GOOD FOR ME.
I THOUGHT MAYBE WE COULD GRAB A BEER AND FOOL AROUND A LITTLE.
PLEASE... GO AWAY...
JUST LEAVE ME... ALONE...
COME ON, BIG FELLA.
I'LL TRY NOT TO BITE.

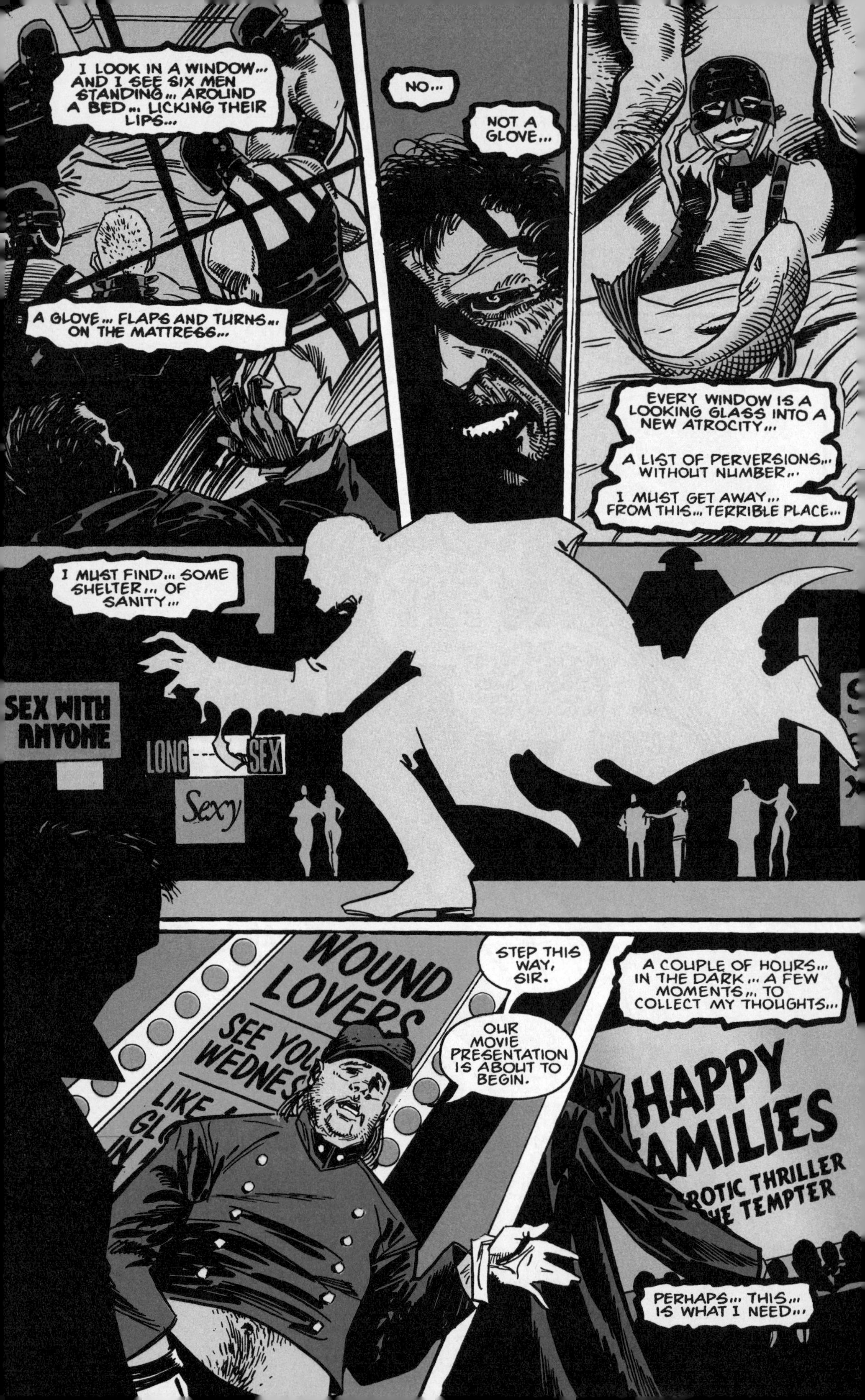
I LOOK IN A WINDOW... AND I SEE SIX MEN STANDING... AROUND A BED... LICKING THEIR LIPS...
A GLOVE... FLAPS AND TURNS... ON THE MATTRESS...
NO...
NOT A GLOVE...
EVERY WINDOW IS A LOOKING GLASS INTO A NEW ATROCITY...
A LIST OF PERVERSIONS... WITHOUT NUMBER...
I MUST GET AWAY... FROM THIS... TERRIBLE PLACE...
I MUST FIND... SOME SHELTER... OF SANITY...
SEX WITH ANYONE
LONG SEX
Sexy
WOUND LOVERS
SEE YOU WEDNES
STEP THIS WAY, SIR.
OUR MOVIE PRESENTATION IS ABOUT TO BEGIN.
A COUPLE OF HOURS... IN THE DARK... A FEW MOMENTS... TO COLLECT MY THOUGHTS...
HAPPY AMILIES
ROTIC THRILLER
HE TEMPTER
PERHAPS... THIS... IS WHAT I NEED...

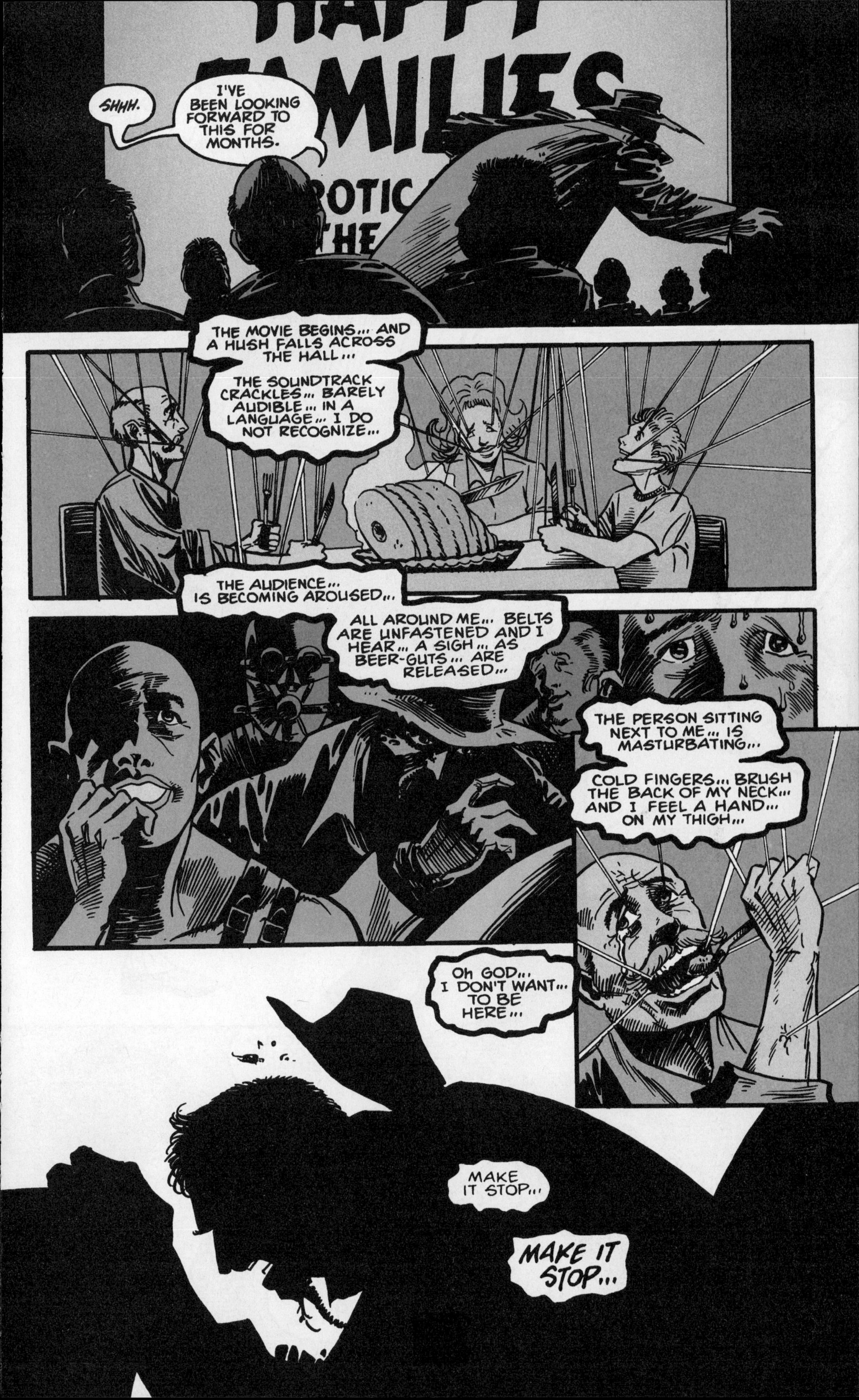
HAPPY FAMILIES
EROTIC
THE
SHHH.
I'VE BEEN LOOKING FORWARD TO THIS FOR MONTHS.
THE MOVIE BEGINS... AND A HUSH FALLS ACROSS THE HALL...
THE SOUNDTRACK CRACKLES... BARELY AUDIBLE... IN A LANGUAGE... I DO NOT RECOGNIZE...
THE AUDIENCE... IS BECOMING AROUSED...
ALL AROUND ME... BELTS ARE UNFASTENED AND I HEAR... A SIGH... AS BEER-GUTS... ARE RELEASED...
THE PERSON SITTING NEXT TO ME... IS MASTURBATING...
COLD FINGERS... BRUSH THE BACK OF MY NECK... AND I FEEL A HAND... ON MY THIGH...
Oh GOD... I DON'T WANT... TO BE HERE...
MAKE IT STOP...
MAKE IT STOP...

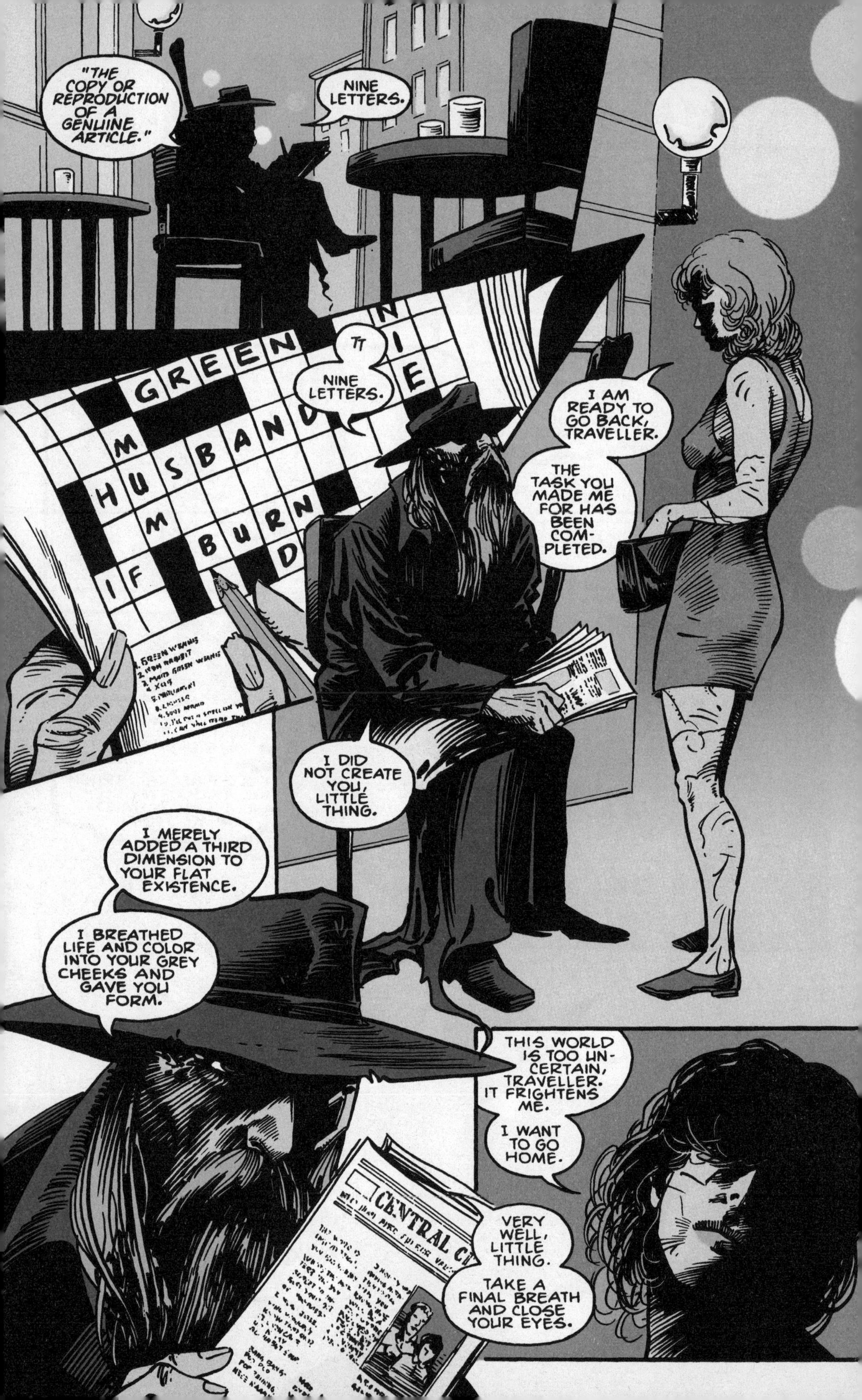
"THE COPY OR REPRODUCTION OF A GENUINE ARTICLE."
NINE LETTERS.
NINE LETTERS.
I AM READY TO GO BACK, TRAVELLER.
THE TASK YOU MADE ME FOR HAS BEEN COM-PLETED.
I DID NOT CREATE YOU, LITTLE THING.
I MERELY ADDED A THIRD DIMENSION TO YOUR FLAT EXISTENCE.
I BREATHED LIFE AND COLOR INTO YOUR GREY CHEEKS AND GAVE YOU FORM.
THIS WORLD IS TOO UN-CERTAIN, TRAVELLER. IT FRIGHTENS ME.
I WANT TO GO HOME.
VERY WELL, LITTLE THING.
TAKE A FINAL BREATH AND CLOSE YOUR EYES.

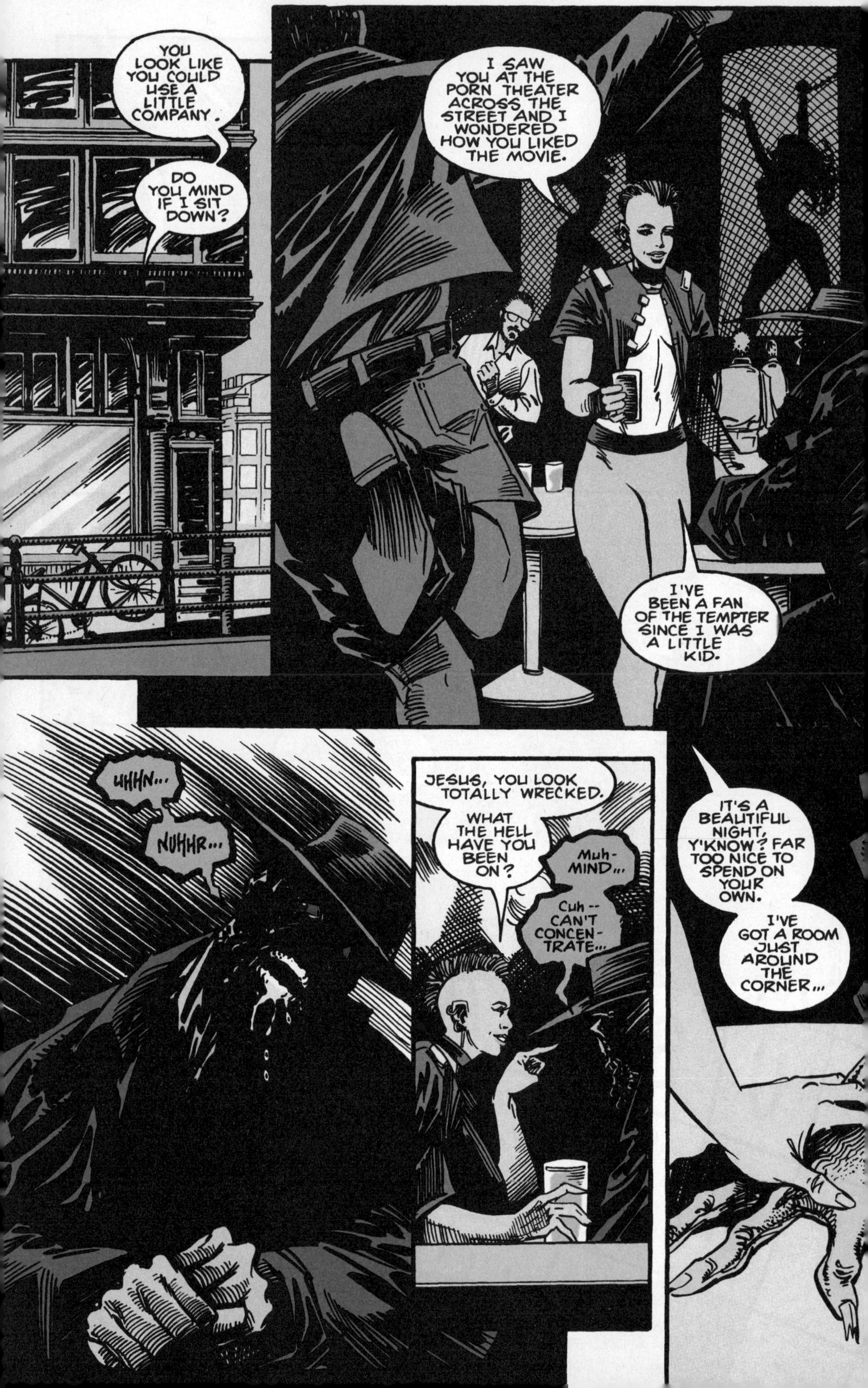
YOU LOOK LIKE YOU COULD USE A LITTLE COMPANY.
DO YOU MIND IF I SIT DOWN?
I SAW YOU AT THE PORN THEATER ACROSS THE STREET AND I WONDERED HOW YOU LIKED THE MOVIE.
I'VE BEEN A FAN OF THE TEMPTER SINCE I WAS A LITTLE KID.
UHHN...
NUHHR...
JESUS, YOU LOOK TOTALLY WRECKED.
WHAT THE HELL HAVE YOU BEEN ON?
Muh-MIND...
Cuh-- CAN'T CONCEN-TRATE...
IT'S A BEAUTIFUL NIGHT, Y'KNOW? FAR TOO NICE TO SPEND ON YOUR OWN.
I'VE GOT A ROOM JUST AROUND THE CORNER...

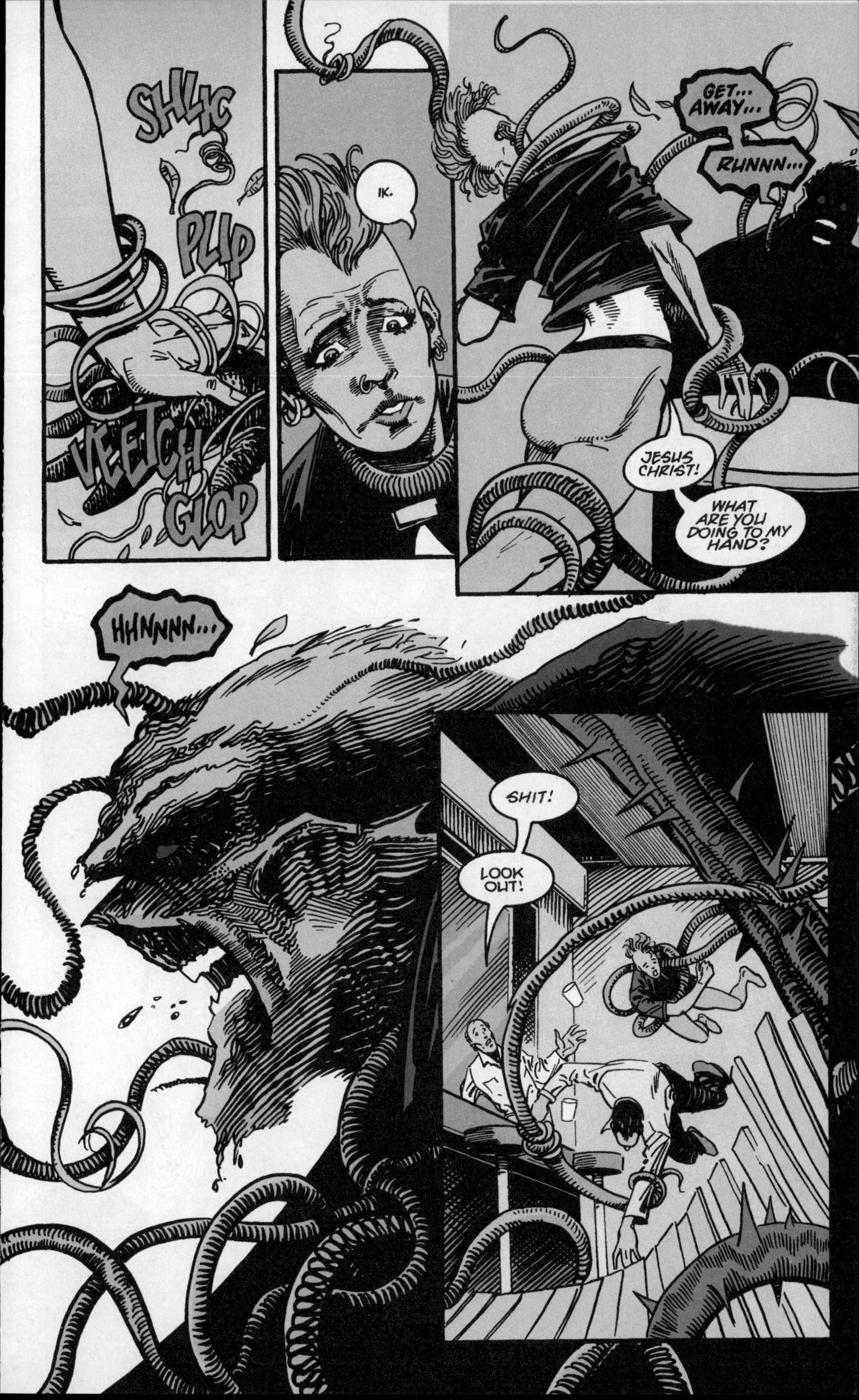
SHLIC
PLIP
VEETCH
GLOP
IK.
GET... AWAY...
RUNNN...
JESUS CHRIST!
WHAT ARE YOU DOING TO MY HAND?
HHNNNN...
SHIT!
LOOK OUT!

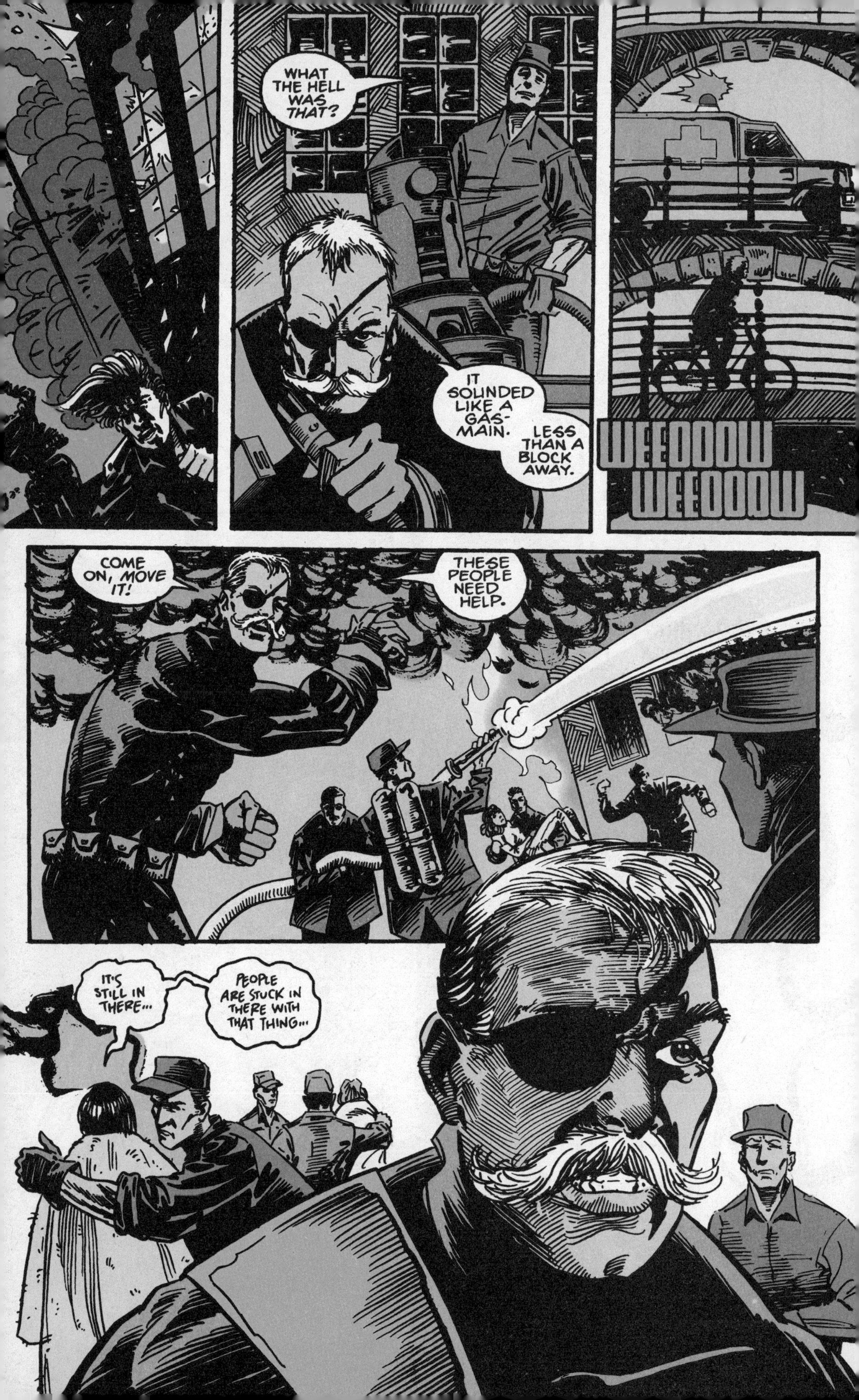
WHAT THE HELL WAS THAT?
IT SOUNDED LIKE A GAS-MAIN.
LESS THAN A BLOCK AWAY.
WEEOOOW WEEOOOW
COME ON, MOVE IT!
THESE PEOPLE NEED HELP.
IT'S STILL IN THERE...
PEOPLE ARE STUCK IN THERE WITH THAT THING...

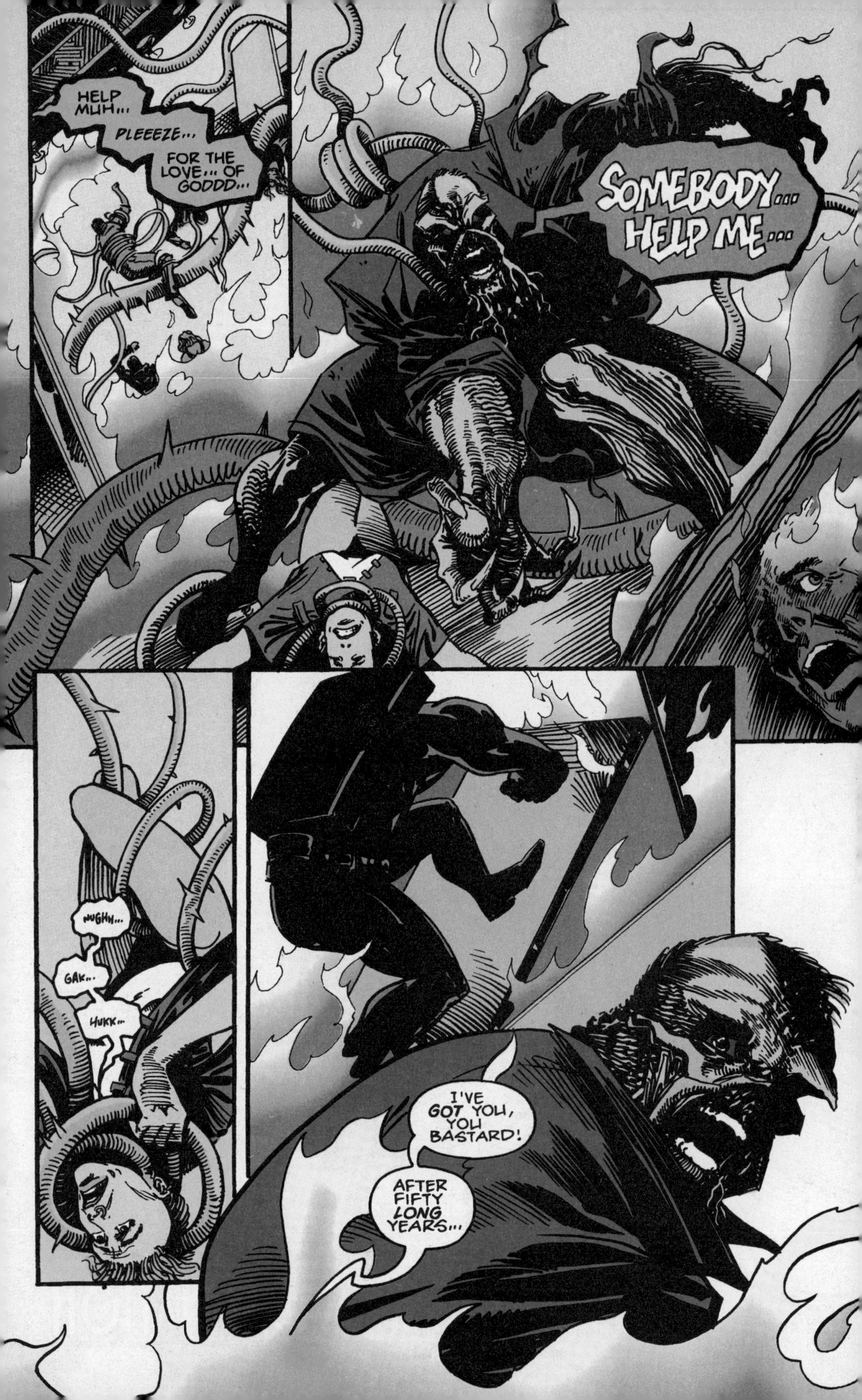
HELP MUH...
PLEEEZE...
FOR THE LOVE... OF GODDD...
SOMEBODY... HELP ME...
NUGHH...
GAK...
HUKK...
I'VE GOT YOU, YOU BASTARD!
AFTER FIFTY LONG YEARS...

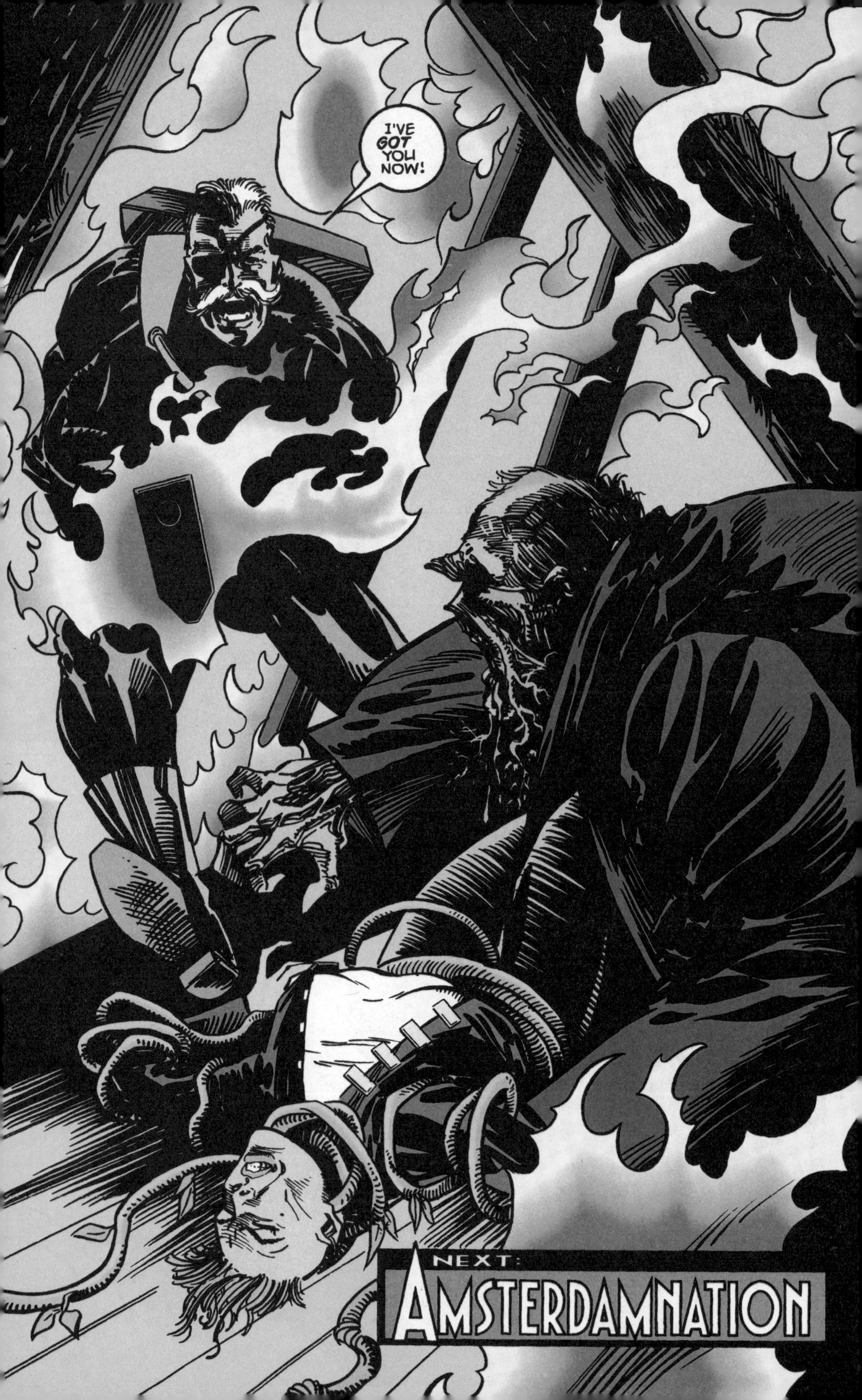
I'VE GOT YOU NOW!
NEXT:
AMSTERDAMNATION

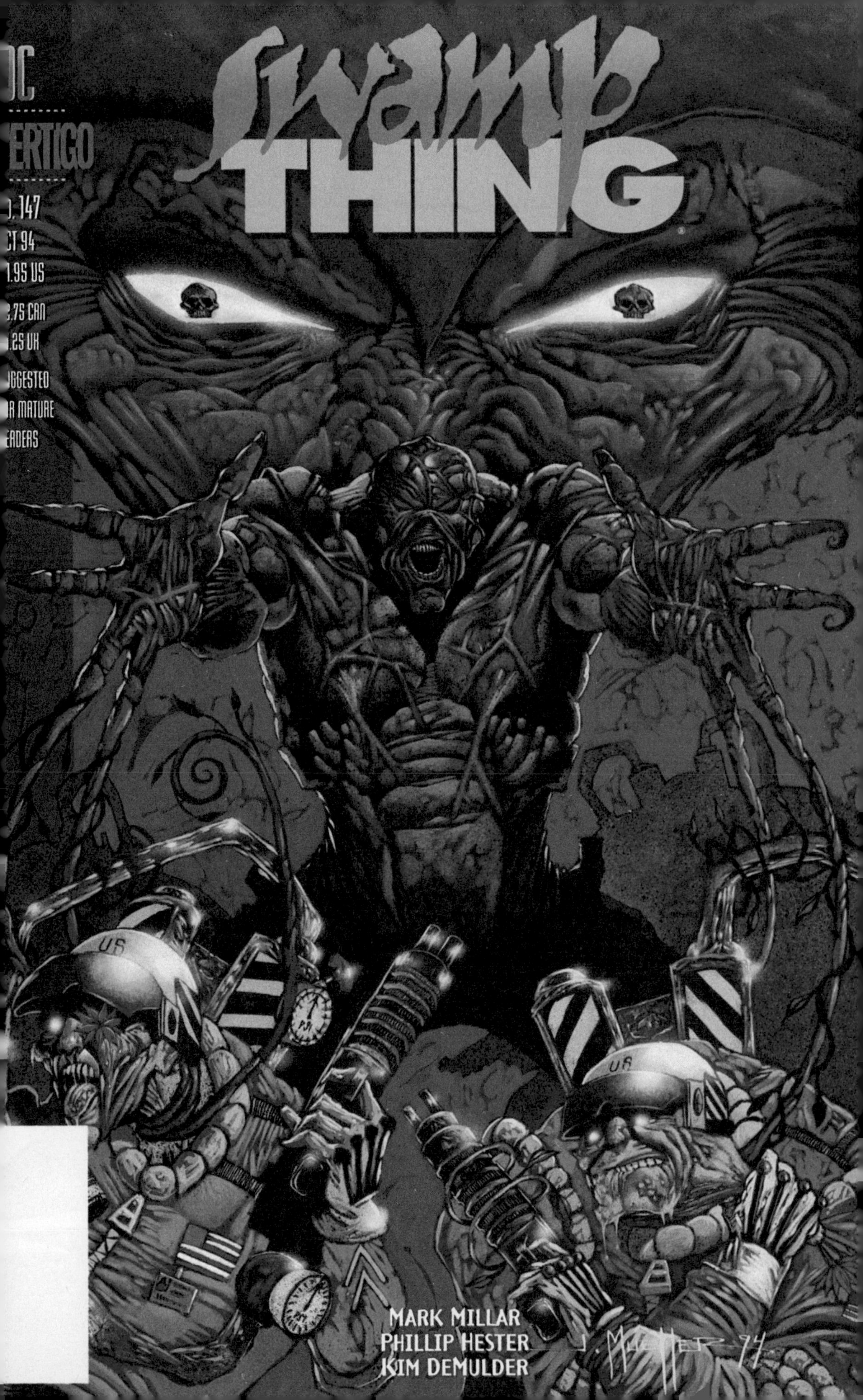
Swamp
THING
MARK MILLAR
PHILLIP HESTER
KIM DEMULDER

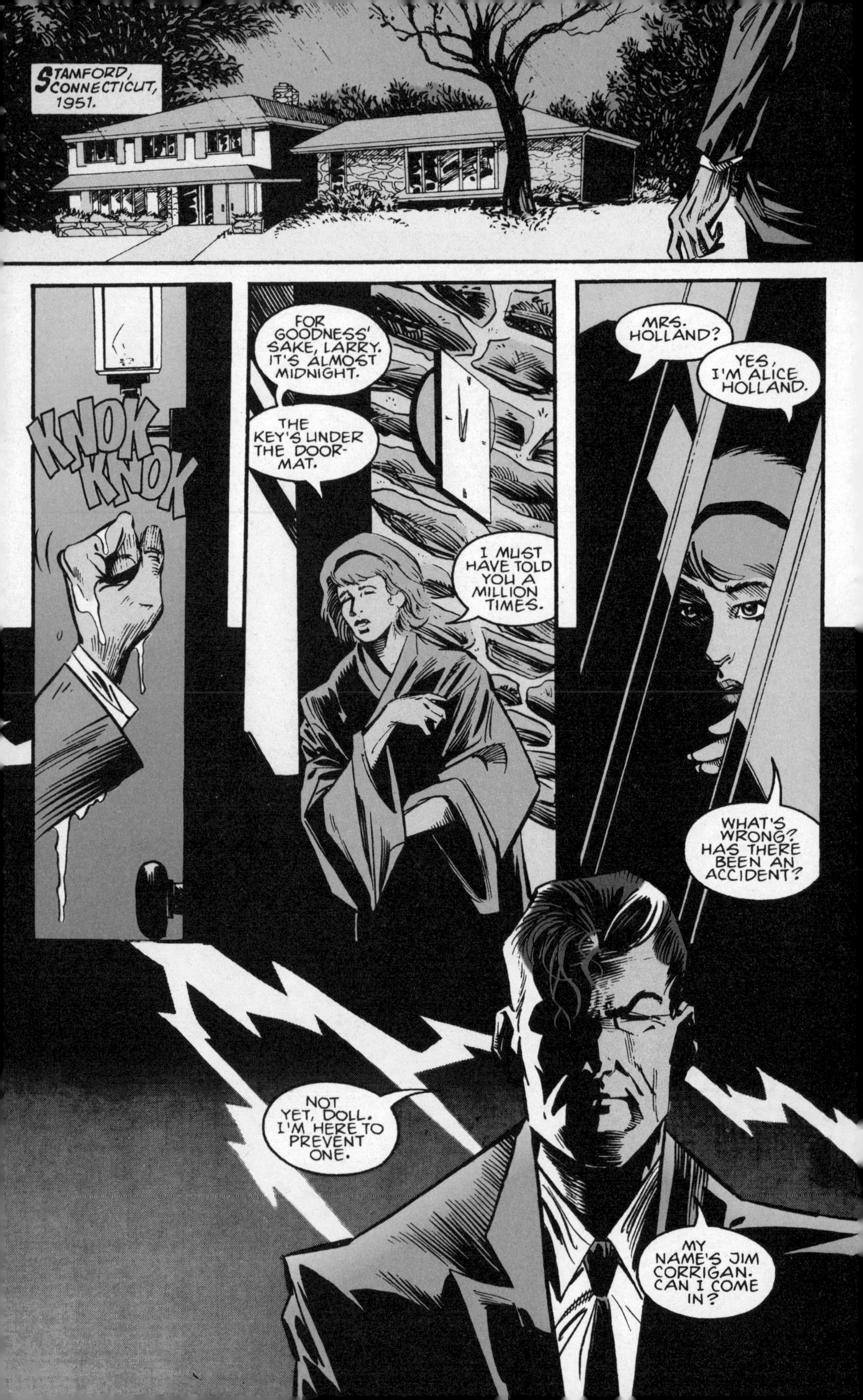
STAMFORD, CONNECTICUT, 1951.
KNOK KNOK
FOR GOODNESS' SAKE, LARRY. IT'S ALMOST MIDNIGHT.
THE KEY'S UNDER THE DOOR-MAT.
I MUST HAVE TOLD YOU A MILLION TIMES.
MRS. HOLLAND?
YES, I'M ALICE HOLLAND.
WHAT'S WRONG? HAS THERE BEEN AN ACCIDENT?
NOT YET, DOLL. I'M HERE TO PREVENT ONE.
MY NAME'S JIM CORRIGAN. CAN I COME IN?

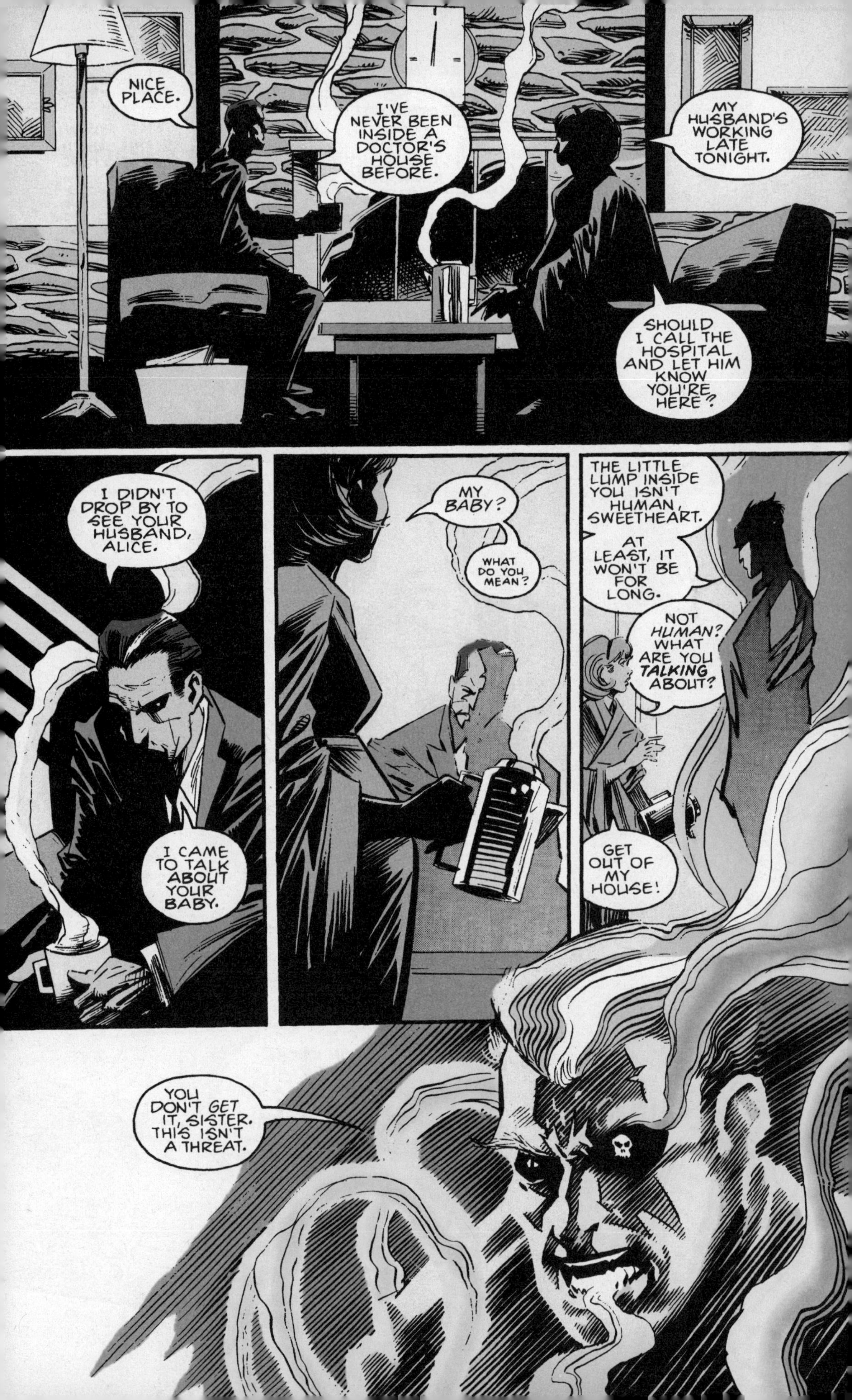
NICE PLACE.
I'VE NEVER BEEN INSIDE A DOCTOR'S HOUSE BEFORE.
MY HUSBAND'S WORKING LATE TONIGHT.
SHOULD I CALL THE HOSPITAL AND LET HIM KNOW YOU'RE HERE?
I DIDN'T DROP BY TO SEE YOUR HUSBAND, ALICE.
I CAME TO TALK ABOUT YOUR BABY.
MY BABY?
WHAT DO YOU MEAN?
THE LITTLE LUMP INSIDE YOU ISN'T HUMAN, SWEETHEART.
AT LEAST, IT WON'T BE FOR LONG.
NOT *HUMAN*? WHAT ARE YOU ***TALKING*** ABOUT?
GET OUT OF MY HOUSE!
YOU DON'T GET IT, SISTER. THIS ISN'T A THREAT.

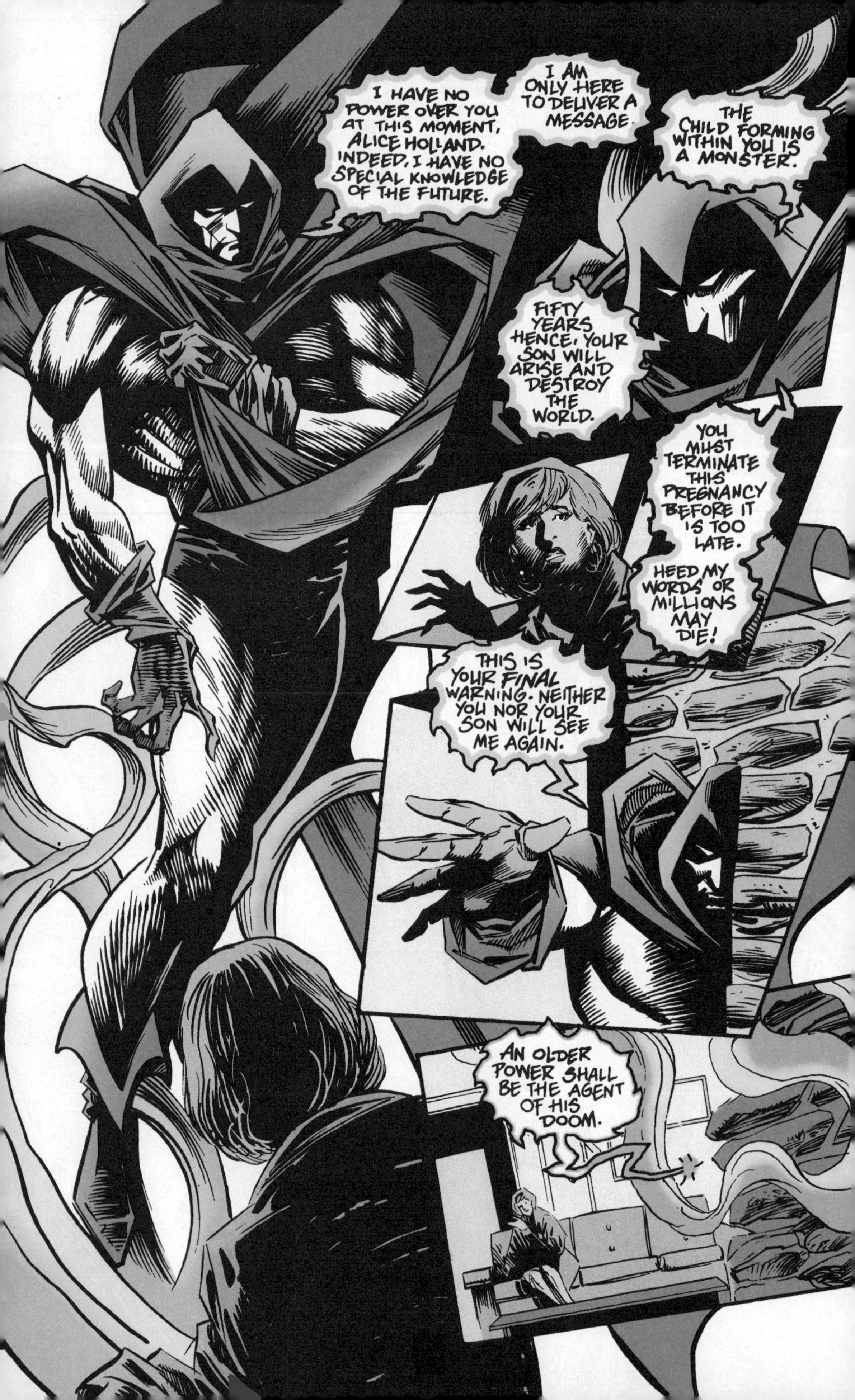
I HAVE NO POWER OVER YOU AT THIS MOMENT, ALICE HOLLAND. INDEED, I HAVE NO SPECIAL KNOWLEDGE OF THE FUTURE.
I AM ONLY HERE TO DELIVER A MESSAGE.
THE CHILD FORMING WITHIN YOU IS A MONSTER.
FIFTY YEARS HENCE, YOUR SON WILL ARISE AND DESTROY THE WORLD.
YOU MUST TERMINATE THIS PREGNANCY BEFORE IT IS TOO LATE.
HEED MY WORDS OR MILLIONS MAY DIE!
THIS IS YOUR FINAL WARNING. NEITHER YOU NOR YOUR SON WILL SEE ME AGAIN.
AN OLDER POWER SHALL BE THE AGENT OF HIS DOOM.

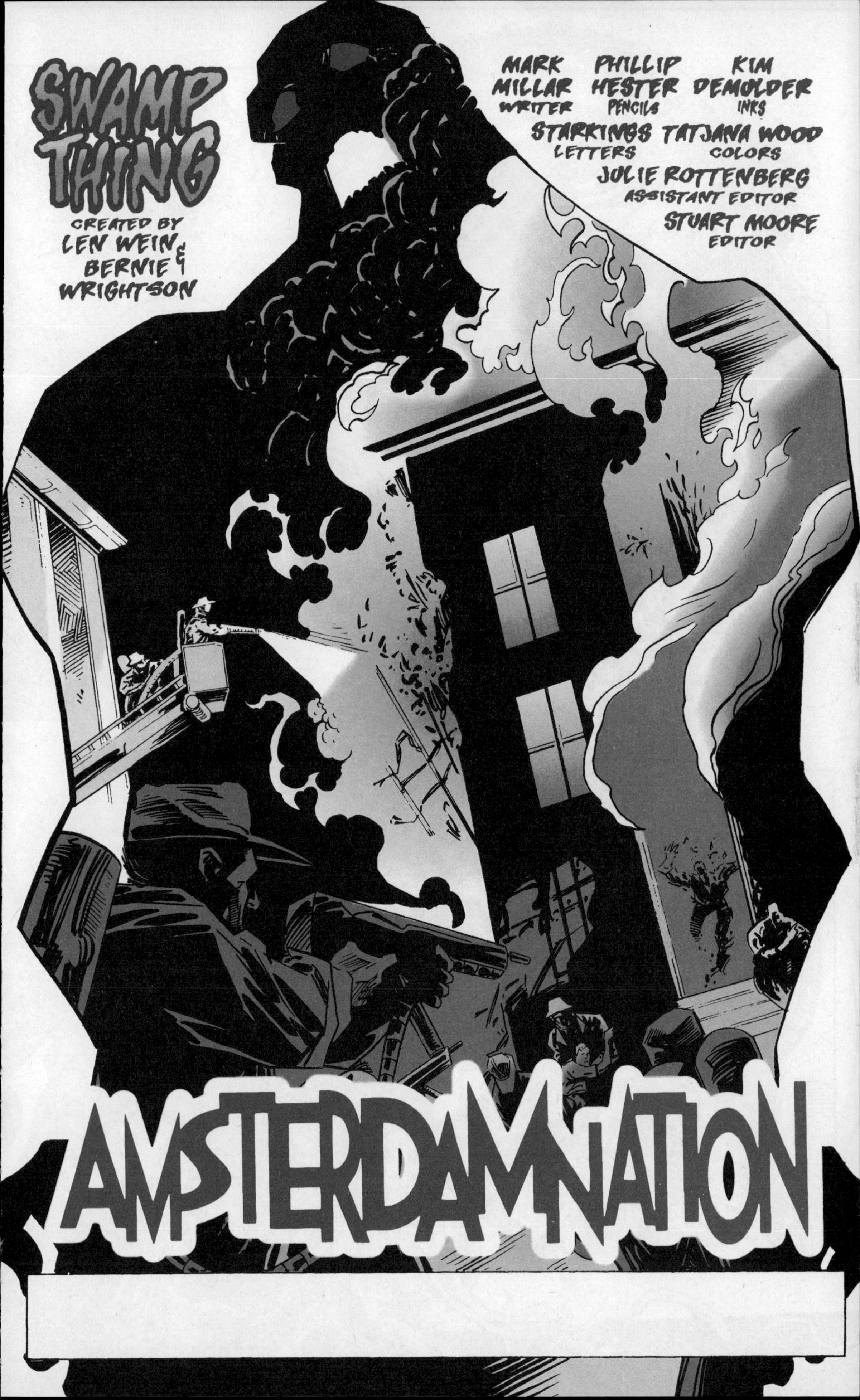
SWAMP THING
CREATED BY LEN WEIN & BERNIE WRIGHTSON
MARK MILLAR WRITER
PHILLIP HESTER PENCILS
KIM DEMULDER INKS
STARKINGS LETTERS
TATJANA WOOD COLORS
JULIE ROTTENBERG ASSISTANT EDITOR
STUART MOORE EDITOR
AMSTERDAMNATION

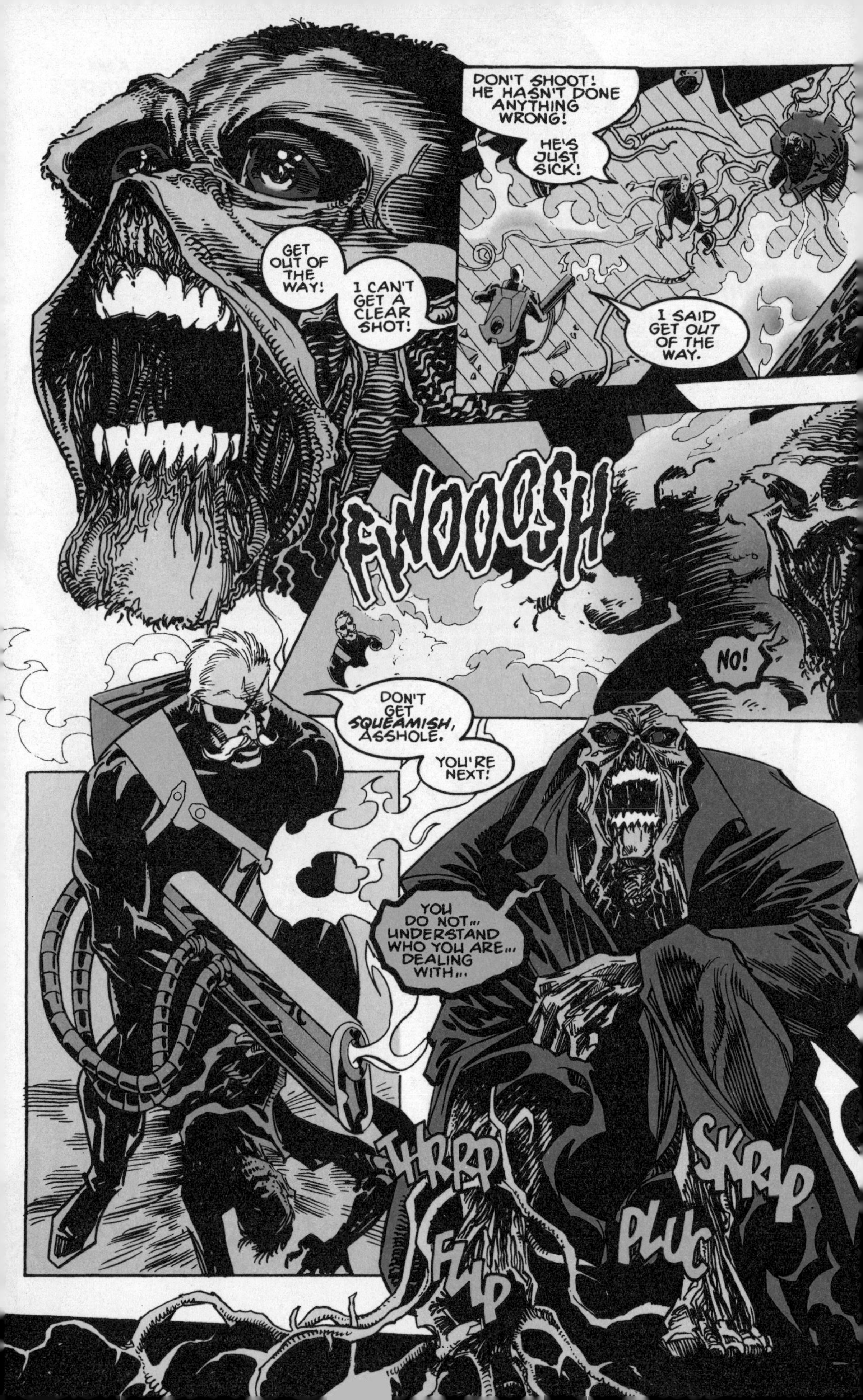

GET OUT OF THE WAY!
I CAN'T GET A CLEAR SHOT!
DON'T SHOOT! HE HASN'T DONE ANYTHING WRONG!
HE'S JUST SICK!
I SAID GET OUT OF THE WAY.
FWOOOSH
NO!
DON'T GET SQUEAMISH, ASSHOLE.
YOU'RE NEXT!
YOU DO NOT... UNDERSTAND WHO YOU ARE... DEALING WITH...
THRRP
SKRAP
PLUC
FLUP

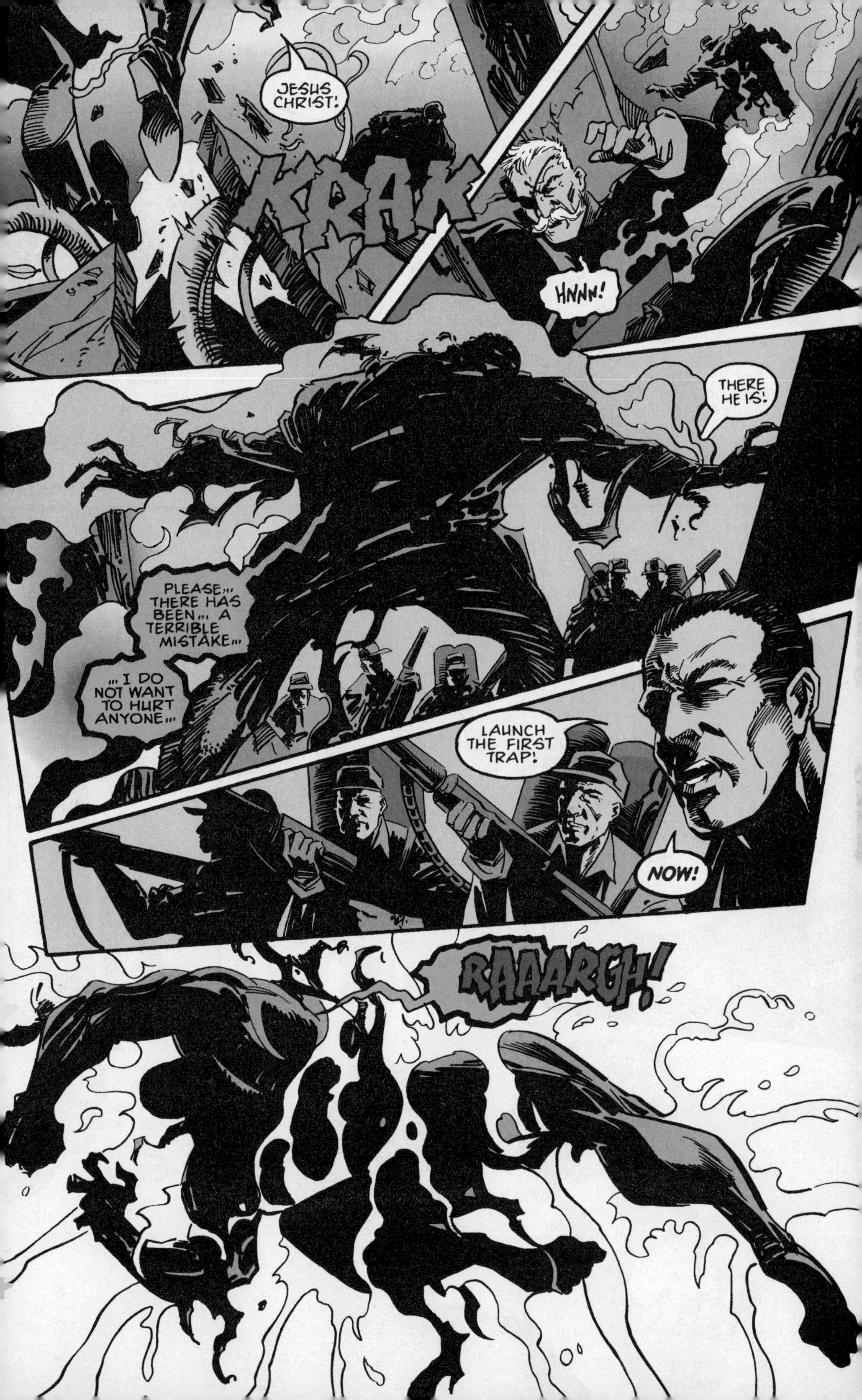
JESUS CHRIST!
KRAK
HNNN!
THERE HE IS!
PLEASE... THERE HAS BEEN... A TERRIBLE MISTAKE...
...I DO NOT WANT TO HURT ANYONE...
LAUNCH THE FIRST TRAP!
NOW!
RAAARGH!

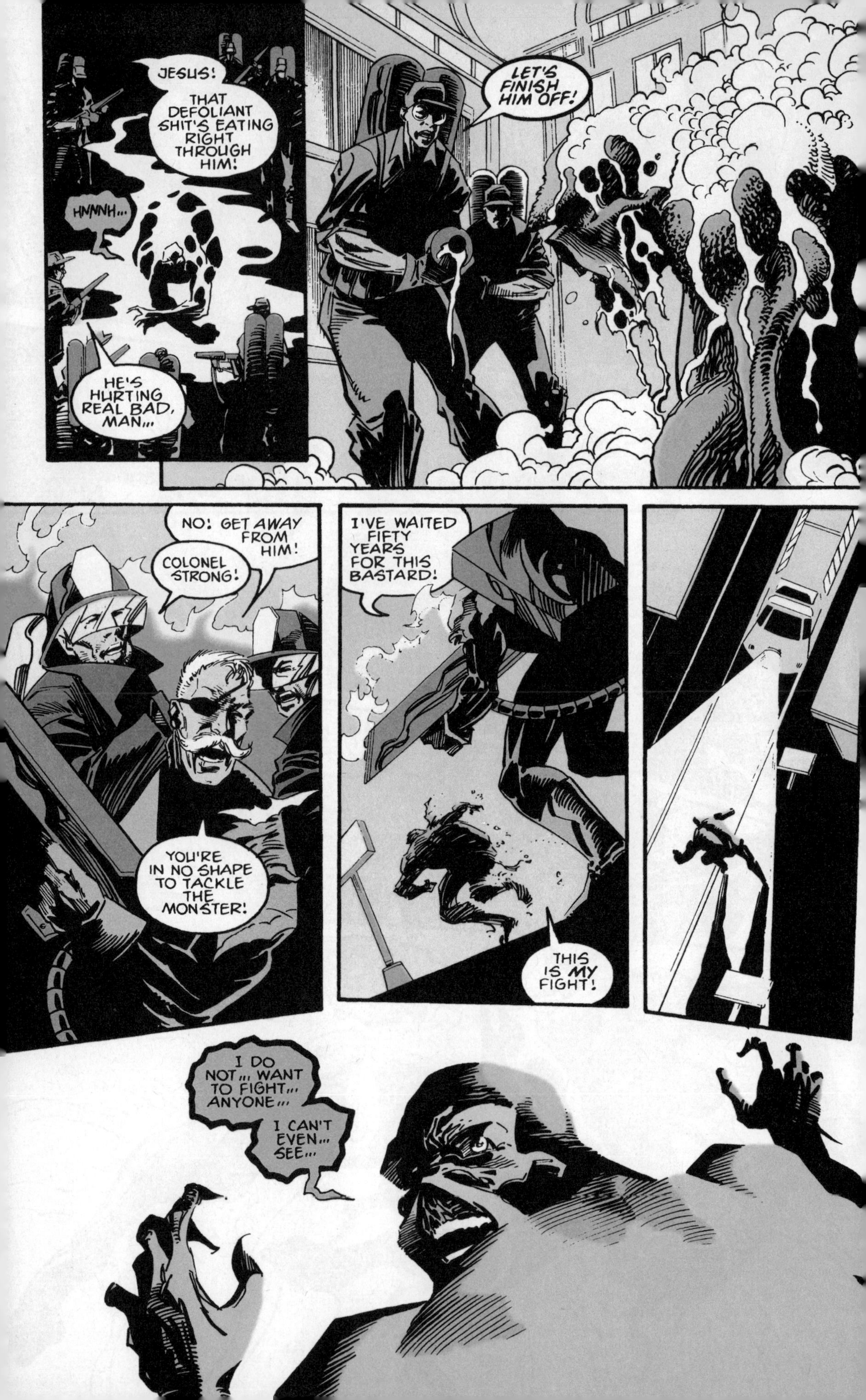
JESUS!
THAT DEFOLIANT SHIT'S EATING RIGHT THROUGH HIM!
HNNNH...
HE'S HURTING REAL BAD, MAN...
LET'S FINISH HIM OFF!
NO: GET AWAY FROM HIM!
COLONEL STRONG!
YOU'RE IN NO SHAPE TO TACKLE THE MONSTER!
I'VE WAITED FIFTY YEARS FOR THIS BASTARD!
THIS IS MY FIGHT!
I DO NOT... WANT TO FIGHT... ANYONE...
I CAN'T EVEN... SEE...

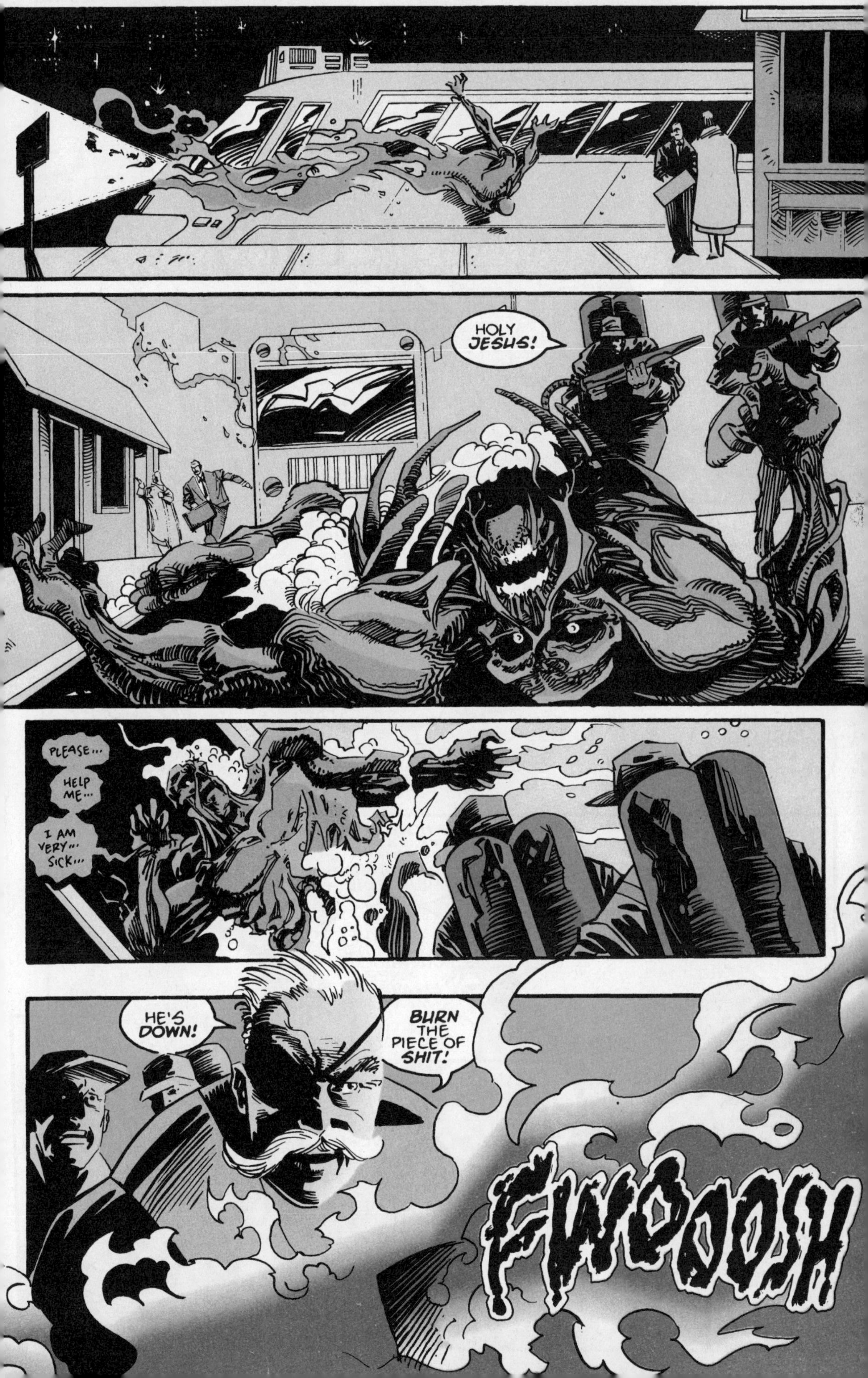
HOLY JESUS!
PLEASE...
HELP ME...
I AM VERY... SICK...
HE'S DOWN!
BURN THE PIECE OF SHIT!
FWOOOSH

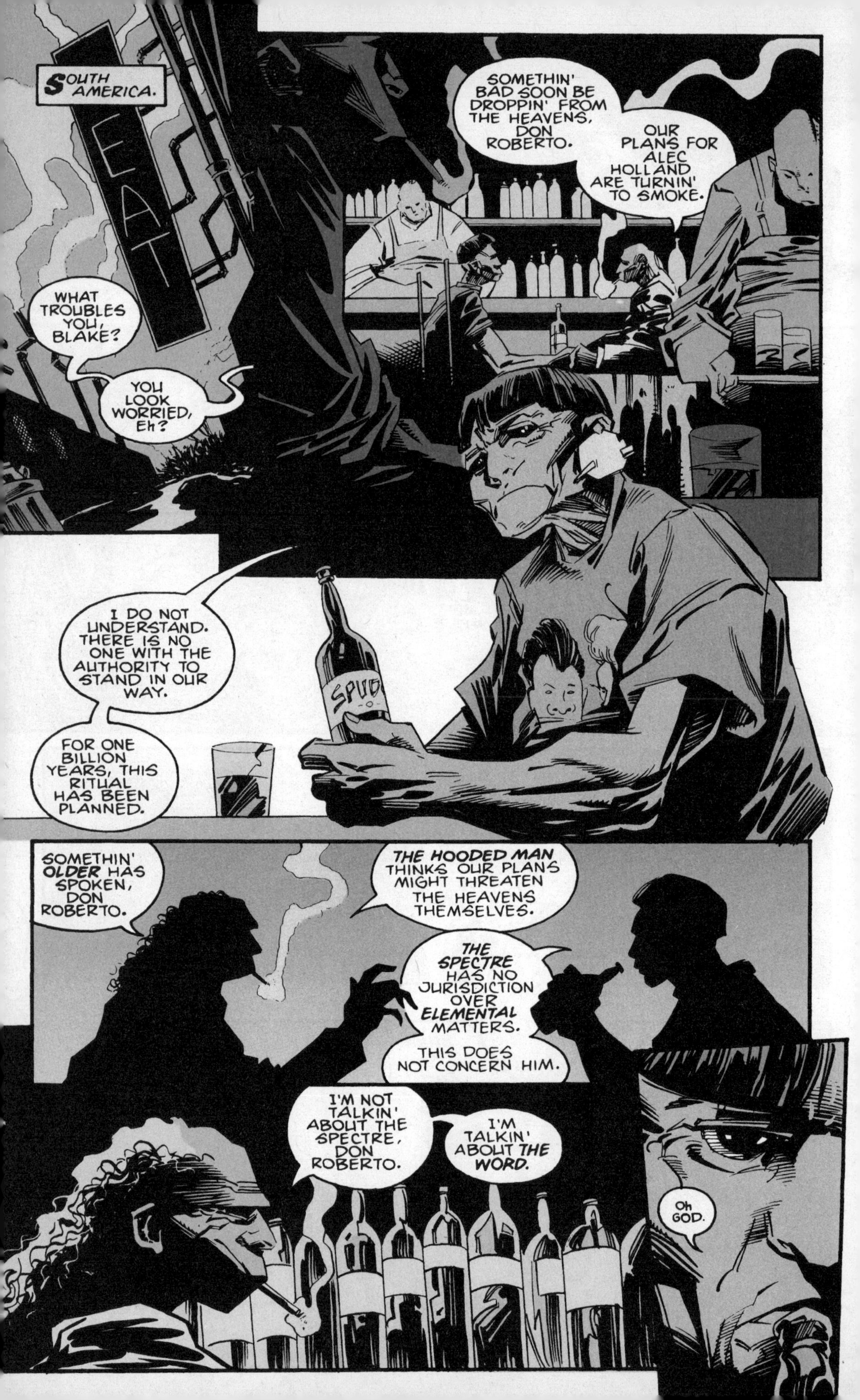
SOUTH AMERICA.
EAT
SOMETHIN' BAD SOON BE DROPPIN' FROM THE HEAVENS, DON ROBERTO.
OUR PLANS FOR ALEC HOLLAND ARE TURNIN' TO SMOKE.
WHAT TROUBLES YOU, BLAKE?
YOU LOOK WORRIED, Eh?
I DO NOT UNDERSTAND. THERE IS NO ONE WITH THE AUTHORITY TO STAND IN OUR WAY.
FOR ONE BILLION YEARS, THIS RITUAL HAS BEEN PLANNED.
SOMETHIN' OLDER HAS SPOKEN, DON ROBERTO.
THE HOODED MAN THINKS OUR PLANS MIGHT THREATEN THE HEAVENS THEMSELVES.
THE SPECTRE HAS NO JURISDICTION OVER ELEMENTAL MATTERS.
THIS DOES NOT CONCERN HIM.
I'M NOT TALKIN' ABOUT THE SPECTRE, DON ROBERTO.
I'M TALKIN' ABOUT THE WORD.
Oh GOD.

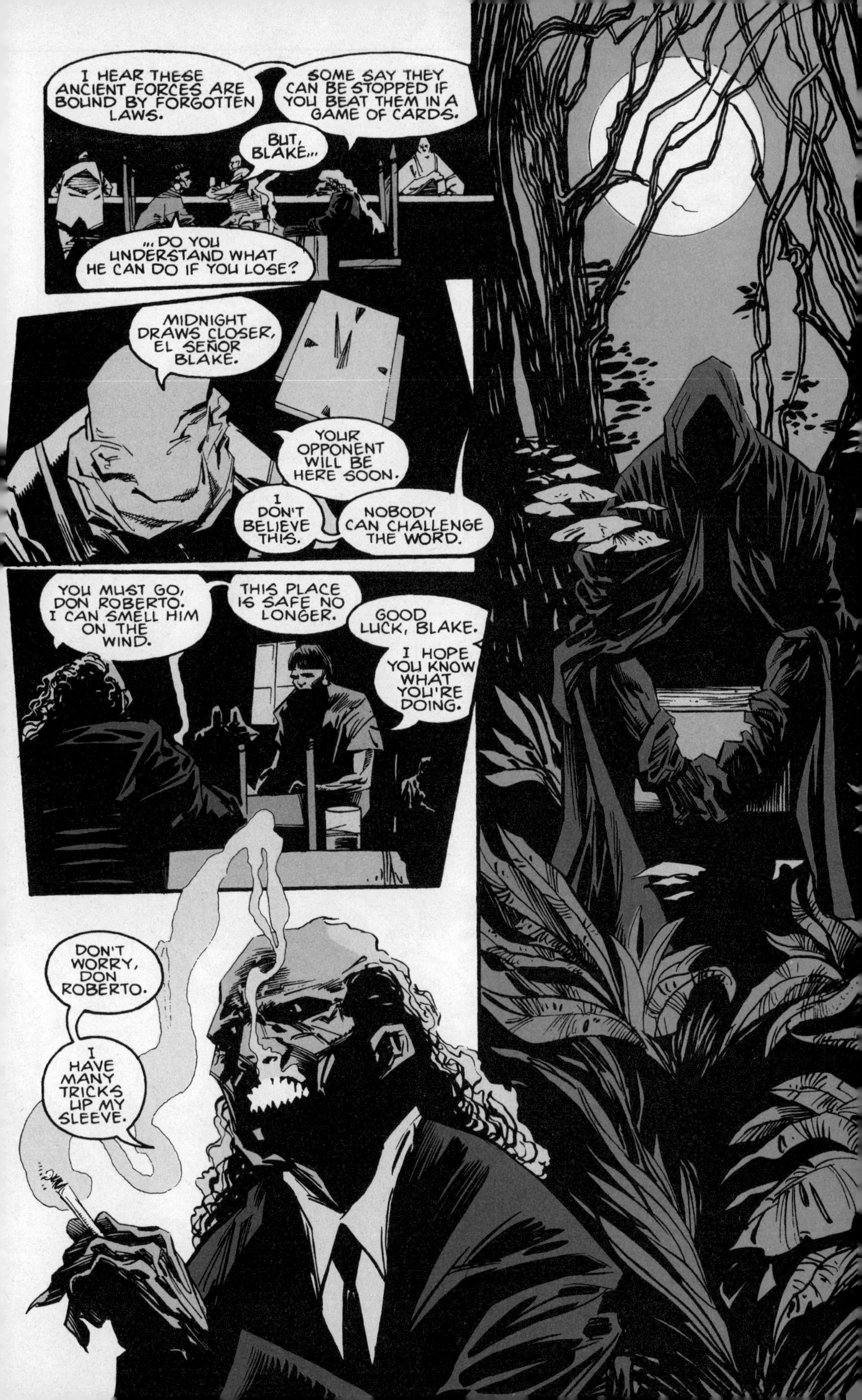
I HEAR THESE ANCIENT FORCES ARE BOUND BY FORGOTTEN LAWS.
SOME SAY THEY CAN BE STOPPED IF YOU BEAT THEM IN A GAME OF CARDS.
BUT, BLAKE...
...DO YOU UNDERSTAND WHAT HE CAN DO IF YOU LOSE?
MIDNIGHT DRAWS CLOSER, EL SEÑOR BLAKE.
YOUR OPPONENT WILL BE HERE SOON.
I DON'T BELIEVE THIS.
NOBODY CAN CHALLENGE THE WORD.
YOU MUST GO, DON ROBERTO. I CAN SMELL HIM ON THE WIND.
THIS PLACE IS SAFE NO LONGER.
GOOD LUCK, BLAKE.
I HOPE YOU KNOW WHAT YOU'RE DOING.
DON'T WORRY, DON ROBERTO.
I HAVE MANY TRICKS UP MY SLEEVE.

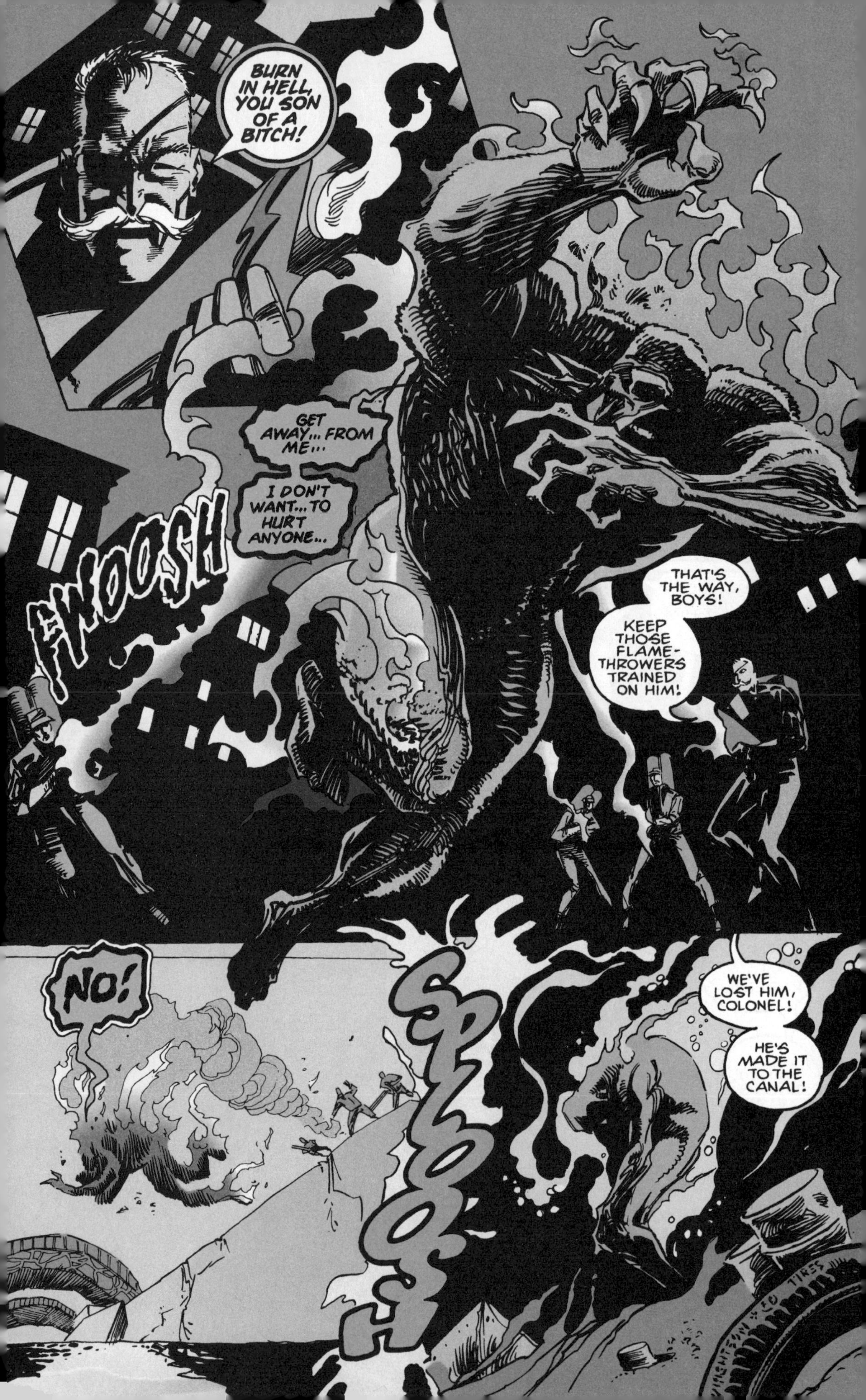
BURN IN HELL, YOU SON OF A BITCH!
GET AWAY... FROM ME...
I DON'T WANT... TO HURT ANYONE...
FWOOSH
THAT'S THE WAY, BOYS!
KEEP THOSE FLAME-THROWERS TRAINED ON HIM!
NO!
SPLOOSH
WE'VE LOST HIM, COLONEL!
HE'S MADE IT TO THE CANAL!

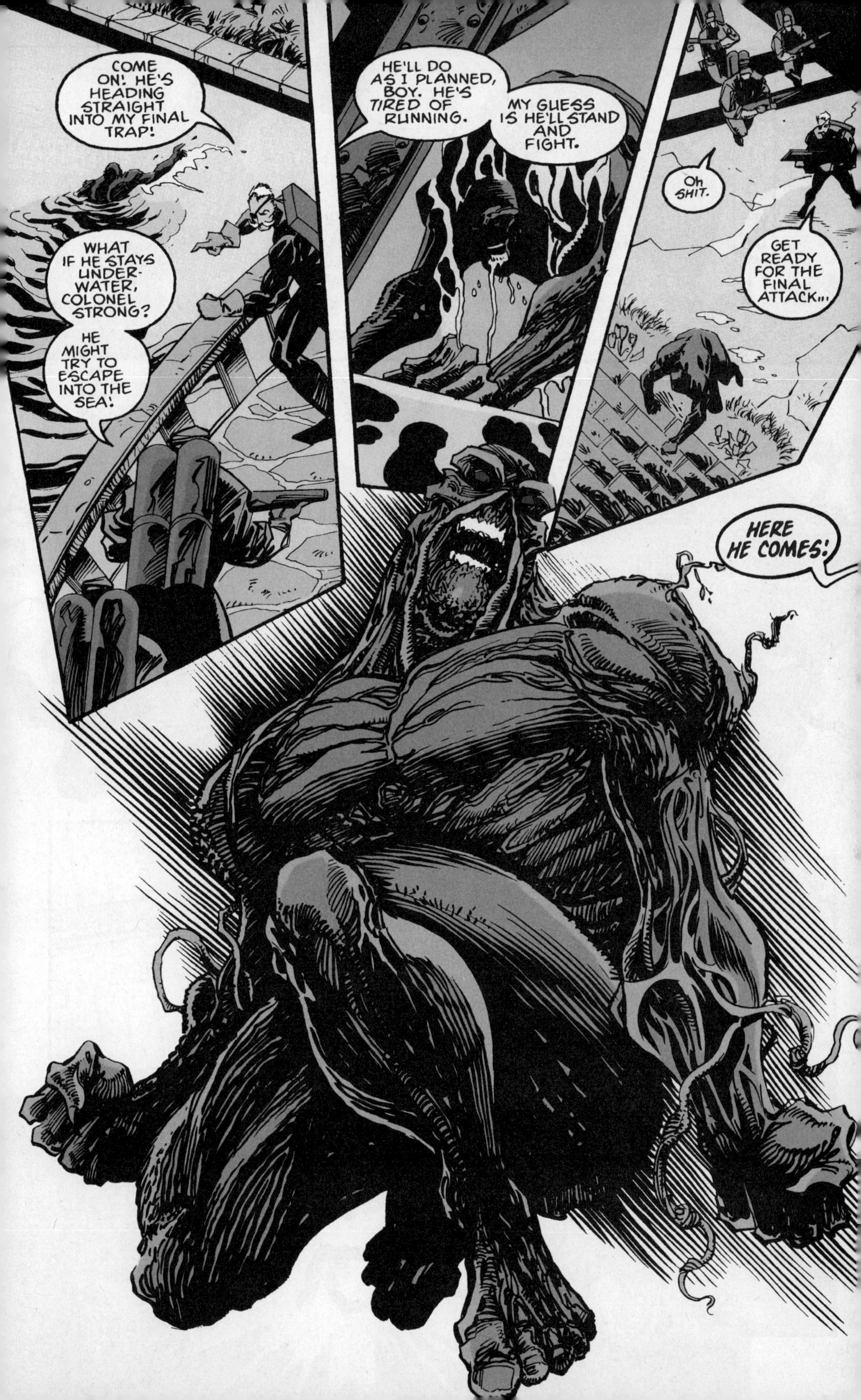
COME ON! HE'S HEADING STRAIGHT INTO MY FINAL TRAP!
WHAT IF HE STAYS UNDER-WATER, COLONEL STRONG?
HE MIGHT TRY TO ESCAPE INTO THE SEA!
HE'LL DO AS I PLANNED, BOY. HE'S TIRED OF RUNNING.
MY GUESS IS HE'LL STAND AND FIGHT.
Oh SHIT.
GET READY FOR THE FINAL ATTACK...
HERE HE COMES!

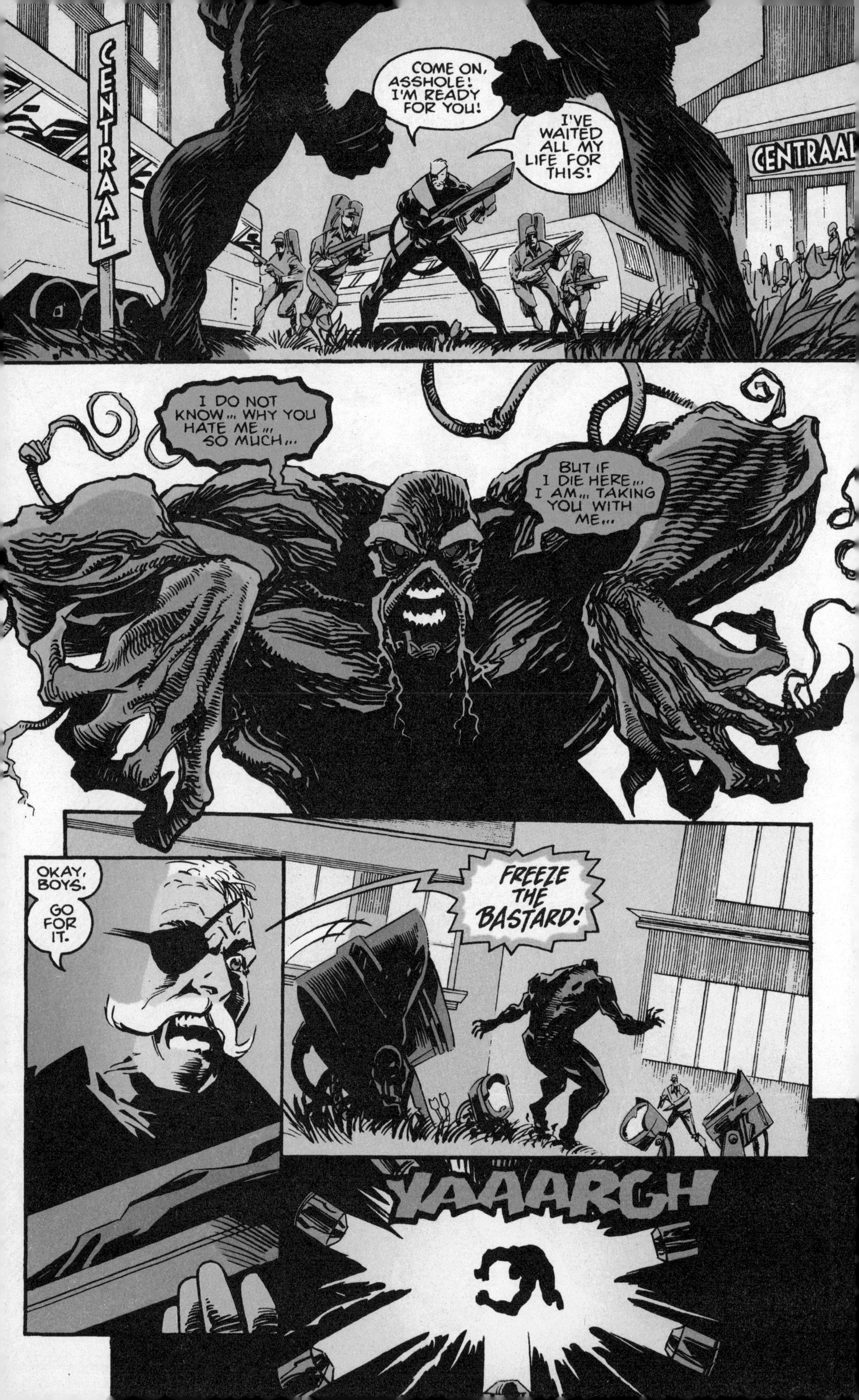
CENTRAAL
COME ON, ASSHOLE! I'M READY FOR YOU!
I'VE WAITED ALL MY LIFE FOR THIS!
CENTRAAL
I DO NOT KNOW... WHY YOU HATE ME... SO MUCH...
BUT IF I DIE HERE... I AM... TAKING YOU WITH ME...
OKAY, BOYS. GO FOR IT.
FREEZE THE BASTARD!
YAAARGH

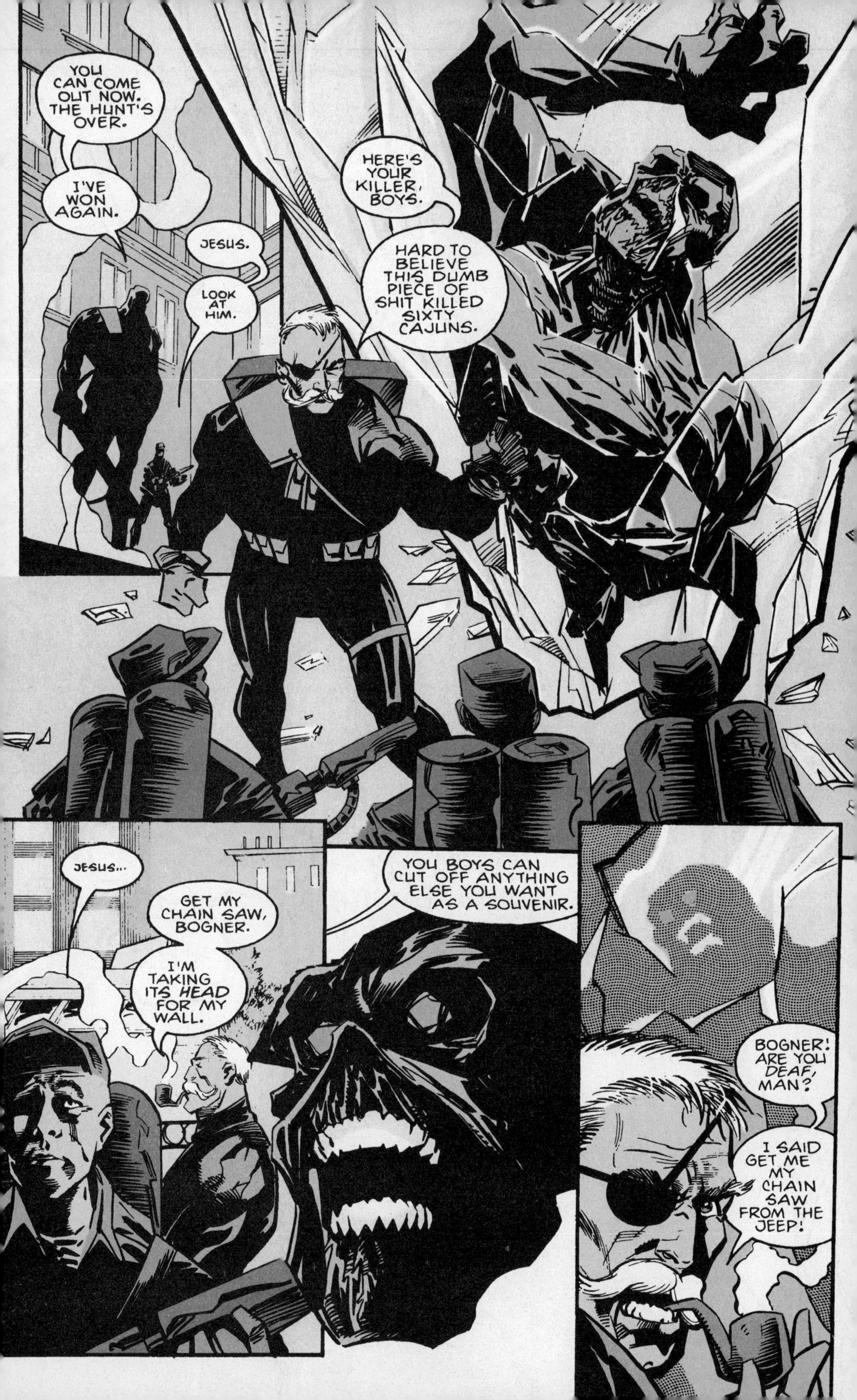
YOU CAN COME OUT NOW. THE HUNT'S OVER.
I'VE WON AGAIN.
HERE'S YOUR KILLER, BOYS.
JESUS.
LOOK AT HIM.
HARD TO BELIEVE THIS DUMB PIECE OF SHIT KILLED SIXTY CAJUNS.
JESUS...
GET MY CHAIN SAW, BOGNER.
I'M TAKING ITS *HEAD* FOR MY WALL.
YOU BOYS CAN CUT OFF ANYTHING ELSE YOU WANT AS A SOUVENIR.
BOGNER! ARE YOU *DEAF,* MAN?
I SAID GET ME MY CHAIN SAW FROM THE JEEP!

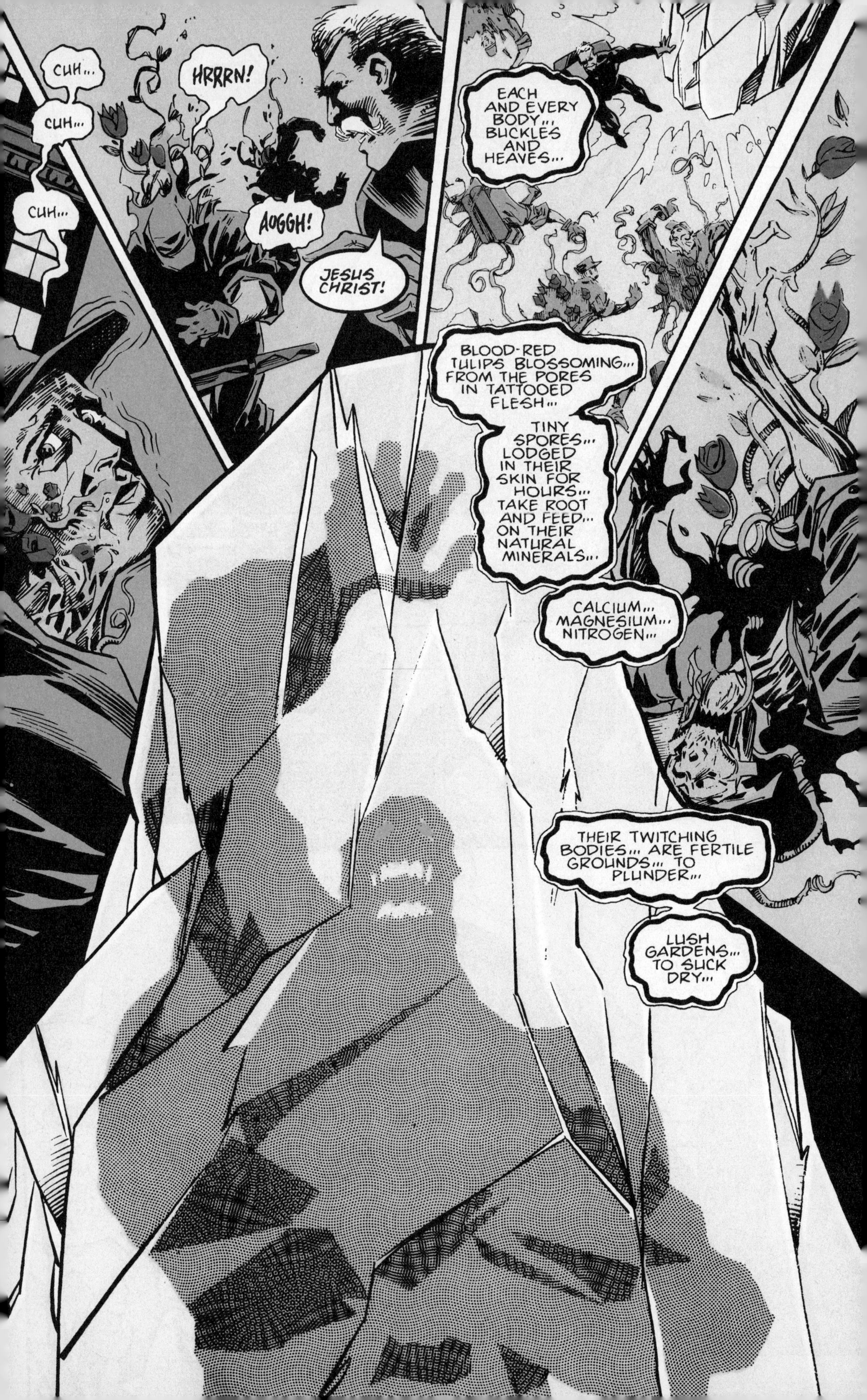
CUH...
CUH...
CUH...
HRRRN!
AUGGH!
JESUS CHRIST!
EACH AND EVERY BODY... BUCKLES AND HEAVES...
BLOOD-RED TULIPS BLOSSOMING... FROM THE PORES IN TATTOOED FLESH...
TINY SPORES... LODGED IN THEIR SKIN FOR HOURS... TAKE ROOT AND FEED... ON THEIR NATURAL MINERALS...
CALCIUM... MAGNESIUM... NITROGEN...
THEIR TWITCHING BODIES... ARE FERTILE GROUNDS... TO PLUNDER...
LUSH GARDENS... TO SUCK DRY...

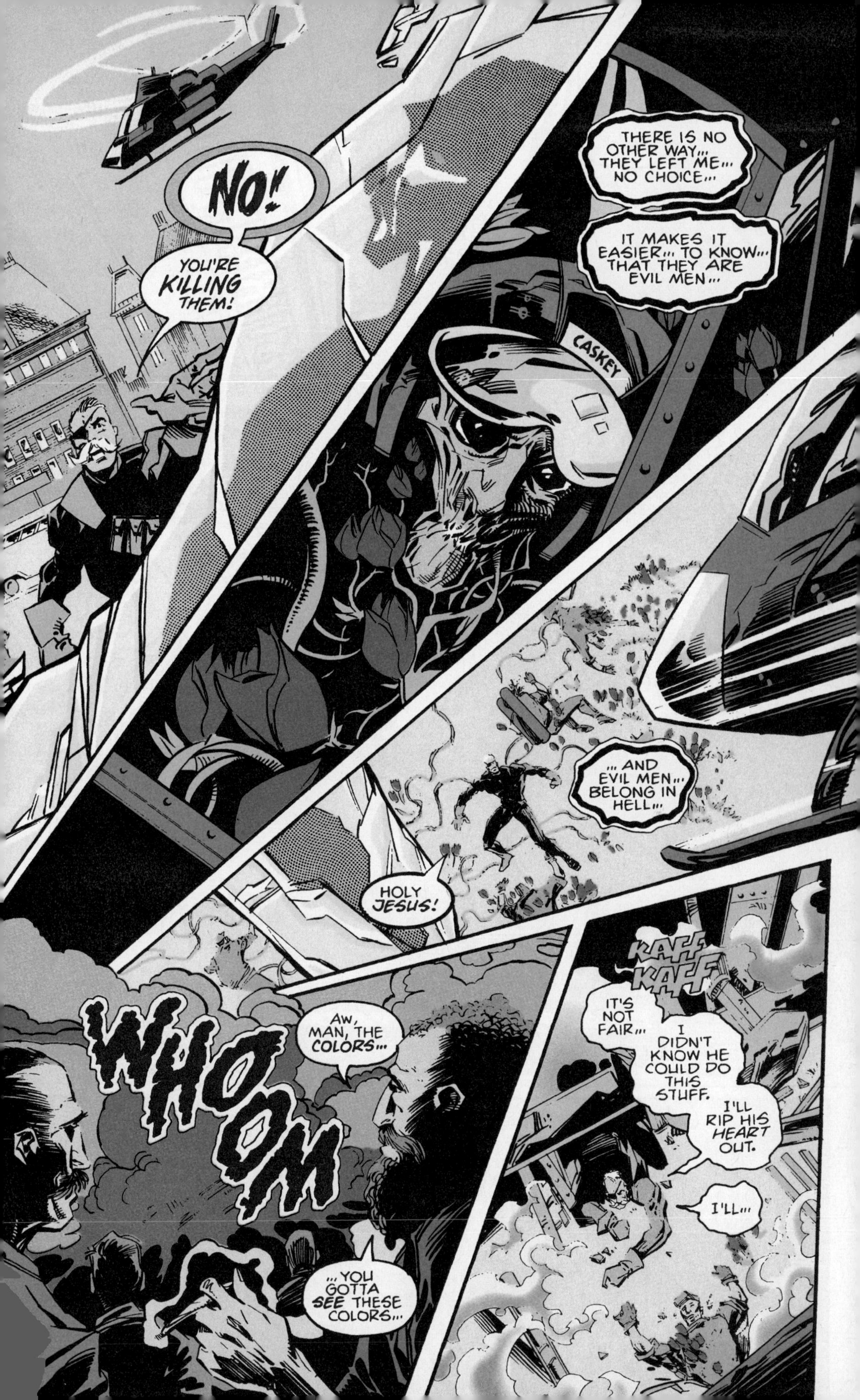
NO!
YOU'RE KILLING THEM!
THERE IS NO OTHER WAY... THEY LEFT ME... NO CHOICE...
IT MAKES IT EASIER... TO KNOW... THAT THEY ARE EVIL MEN...
CASKEY
...AND EVIL MEN... BELONG IN HELL...
HOLY JESUS!
WHOOM
AW, MAN, THE COLORS...
...YOU GOTTA SEE THESE COLORS...
KAFF KAFF
IT'S NOT FAIR...
I DIDN'T KNOW HE COULD DO THIS STUFF.
I'LL RIP HIS HEART OUT.
I'LL...

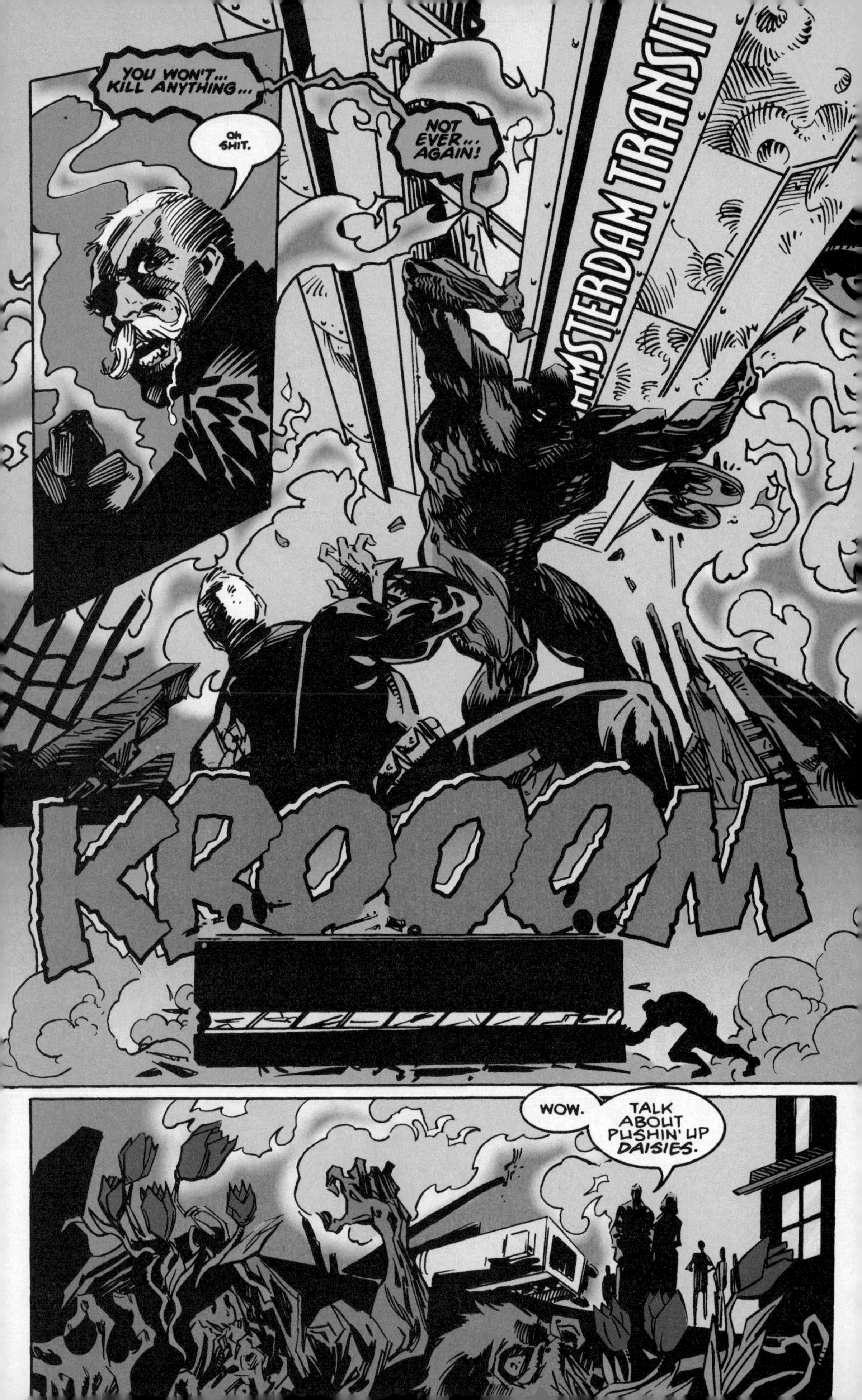
YOU WON'T... KILL ANYTHING...
Oh SHIT.
NOT EVER... AGAIN!
AMSTERDAM TRANSIT
KROOM
WOW.
TALK ABOUT PUSHIN' UP DAISIES.

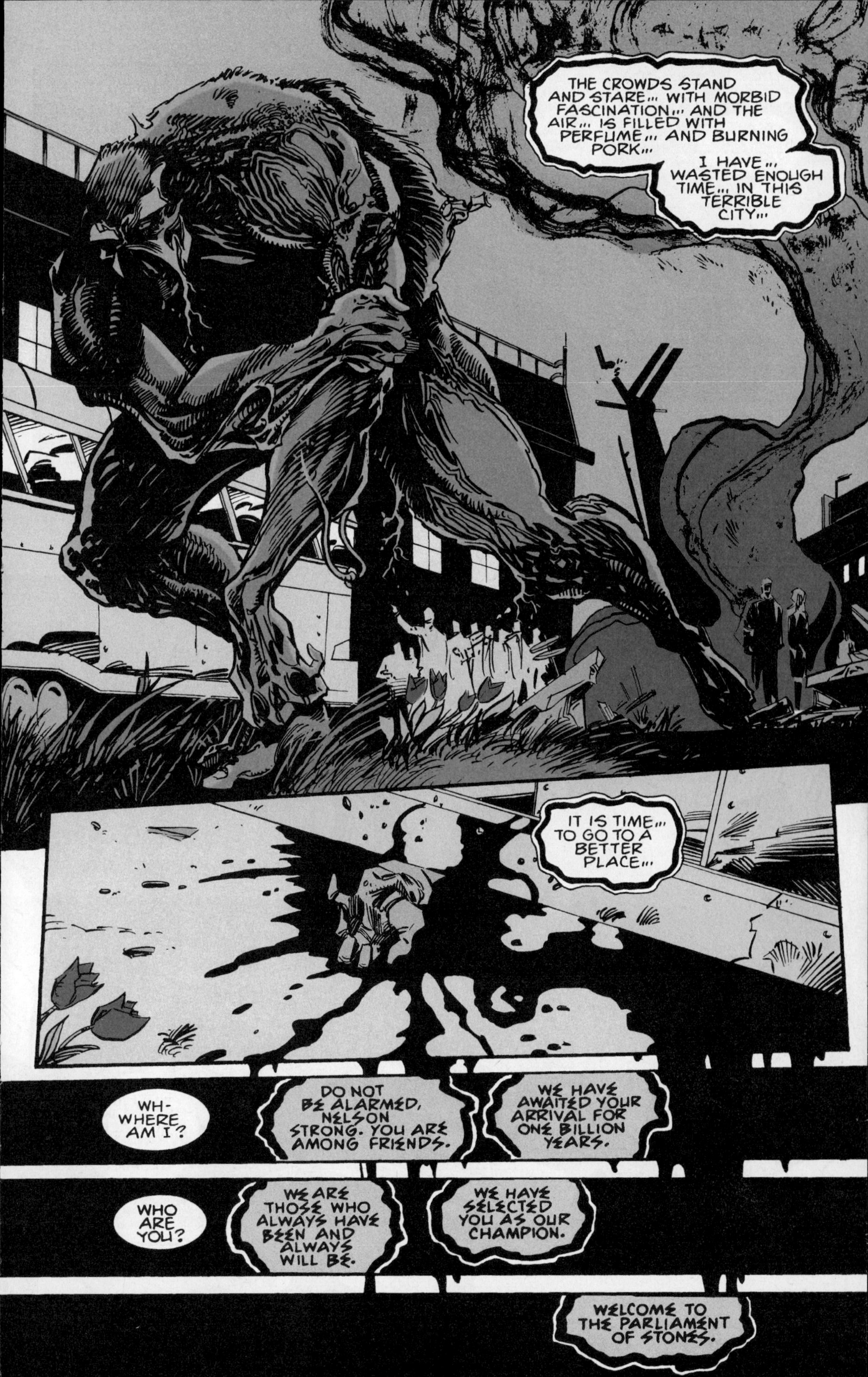
THE CROWDS STAND AND STARE... WITH MORBID FASCINATION... AND THE AIR... IS FILLED WITH PERFUME... AND BURNING PORK...
I HAVE... WASTED ENOUGH TIME... IN THIS TERRIBLE CITY...
IT IS TIME... TO GO TO A BETTER PLACE...
WH-WHERE AM I?
DO NOT BE ALARMED, NELSON STRONG. YOU ARE AMONG FRIENDS.
WE HAVE AWAITED YOUR ARRIVAL FOR ONE BILLION YEARS.
WHO ARE YOU?
WE ARE THOSE WHO ALWAYS HAVE BEEN AND ALWAYS WILL BE.
WE HAVE SELECTED YOU AS OUR CHAMPION.
WELCOME TO THE PARLIAMENT OF STONES.

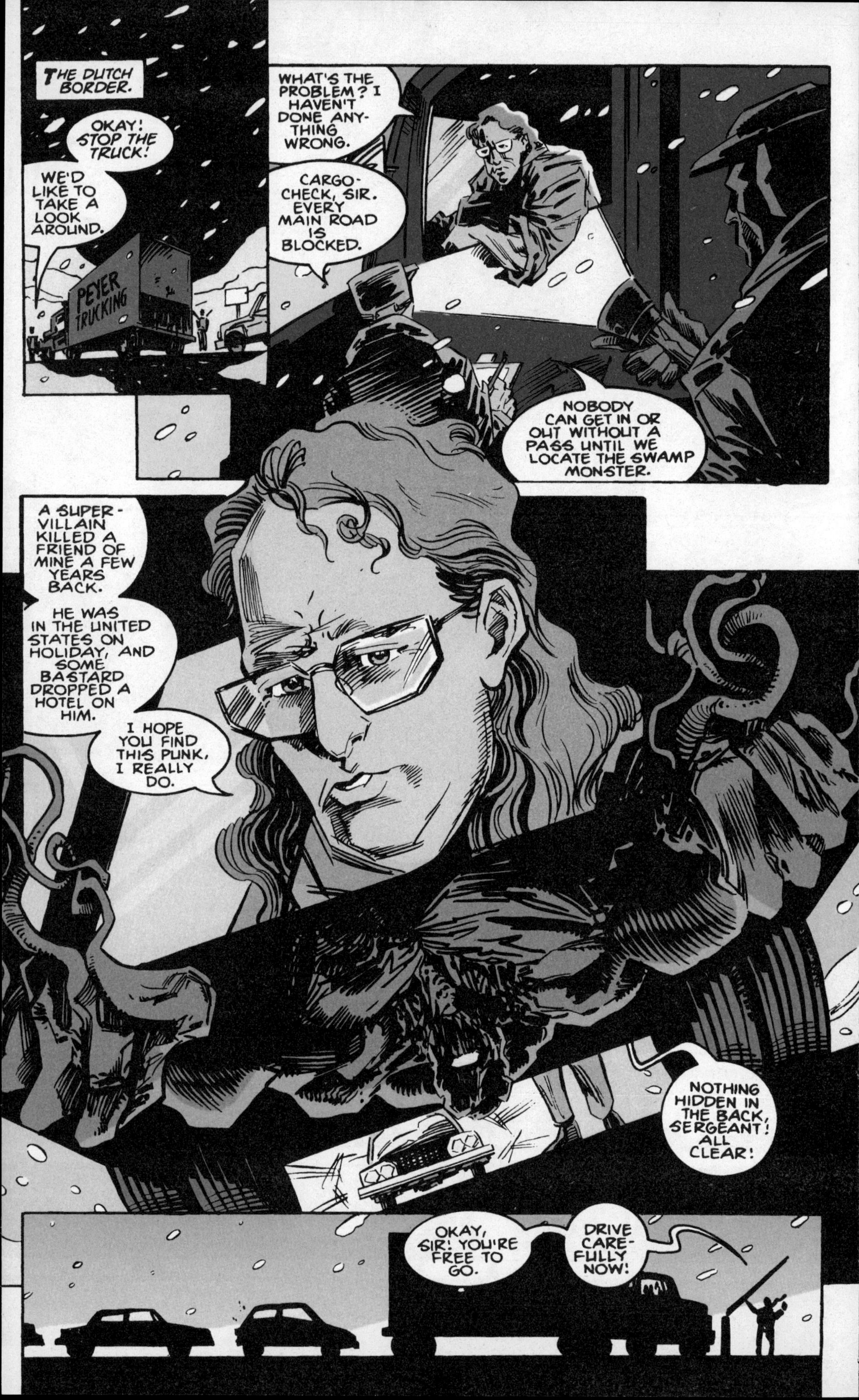
THE DUTCH BORDER.
OKAY! STOP THE TRUCK!
WE'D LIKE TO TAKE A LOOK AROUND.
PEYER TRUCKING
WHAT'S THE PROBLEM? I HAVEN'T DONE ANYTHING WRONG.
CARGO-CHECK, SIR. EVERY MAIN ROAD IS BLOCKED.
NOBODY CAN GET IN OR OUT WITHOUT A PASS UNTIL WE LOCATE THE SWAMP MONSTER.
A SUPER-VILLAIN KILLED A FRIEND OF MINE A FEW YEARS BACK.
HE WAS IN THE UNITED STATES ON HOLIDAY, AND SOME BASTARD DROPPED A HOTEL ON HIM.
I HOPE YOU FIND THIS PUNK, I REALLY DO.
NOTHING HIDDEN IN THE BACK, SERGEANT! ALL CLEAR!
OKAY, SIR: YOU'RE FREE TO GO.
DRIVE CAREFULLY NOW!

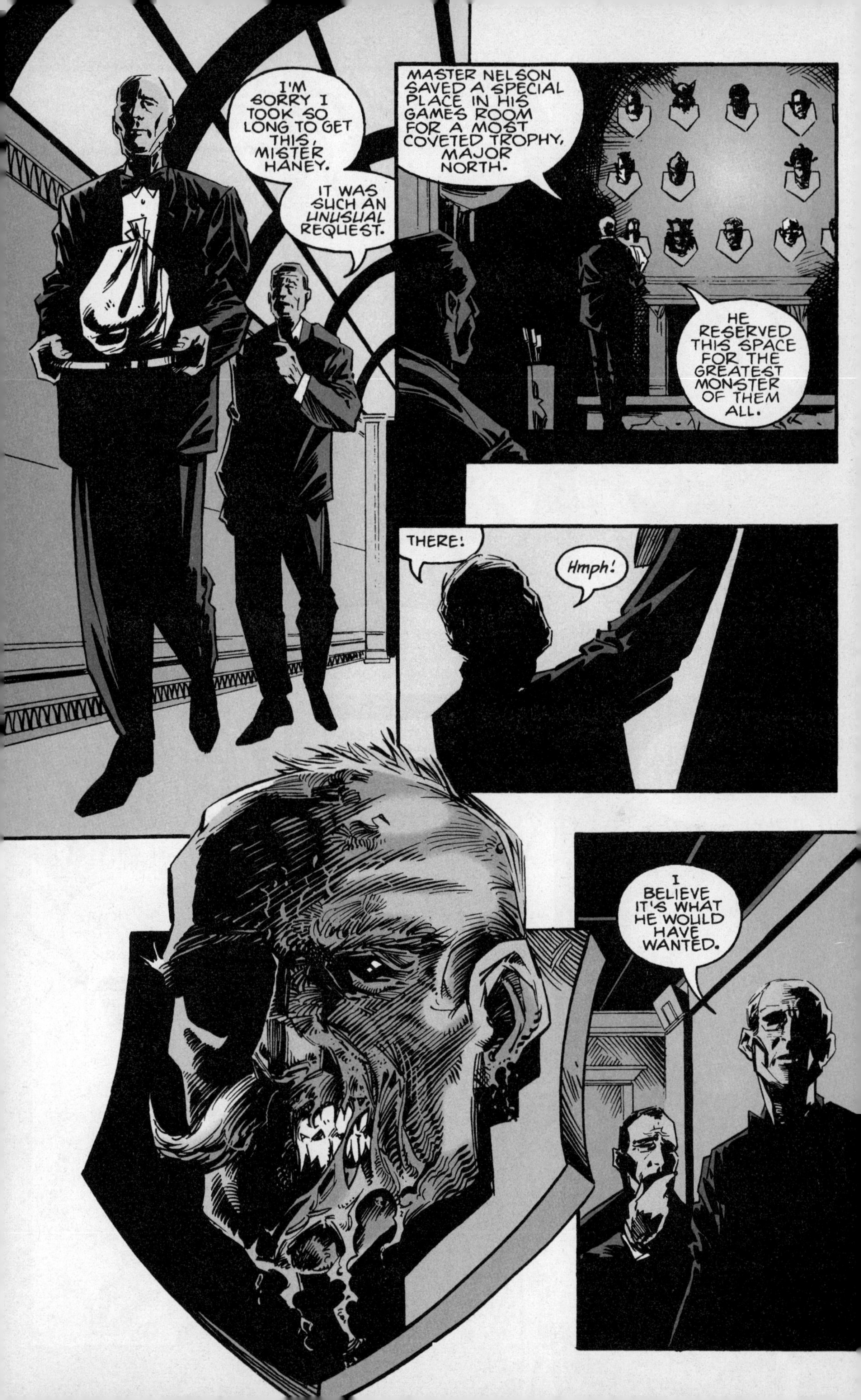
I'M SORRY I TOOK SO LONG TO GET THIS, MISTER HANEY.
IT WAS SUCH AN *UNUSUAL* REQUEST.
MASTER NELSON SAVED A SPECIAL PLACE IN HIS GAMES ROOM FOR A MOST COVETED TROPHY, MAJOR NORTH.
HE RESERVED THIS SPACE FOR THE GREATEST MONSTER OF THEM ALL.
THERE!
Hmph!
I BELIEVE IT'S WHAT HE WOULD HAVE WANTED.

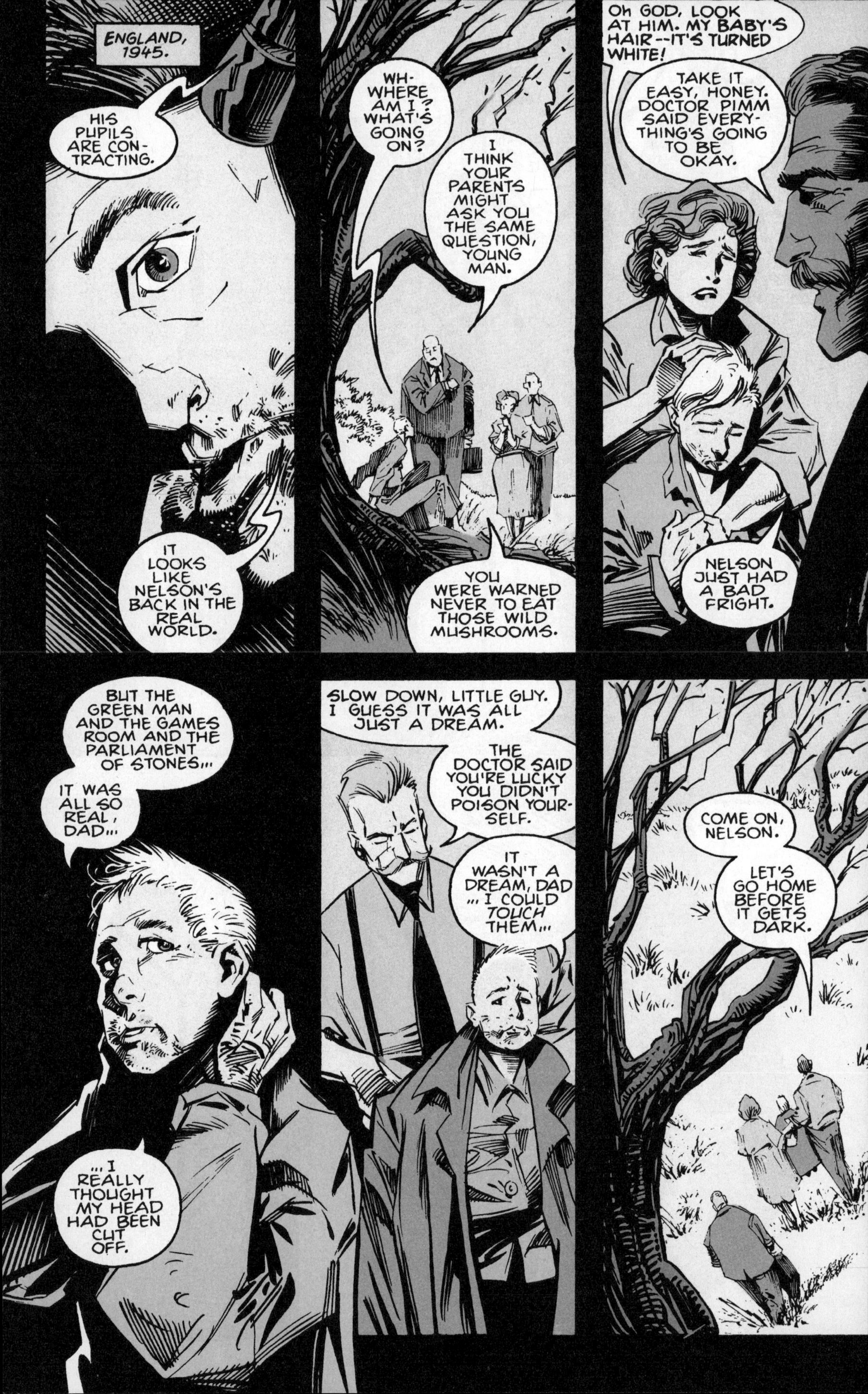
ENGLAND, 1945.
HIS PUPILS ARE CONTRACTING.
IT LOOKS LIKE NELSON'S BACK IN THE REAL WORLD.
WH- WHERE AM I? WHAT'S GOING ON?
I THINK YOUR PARENTS MIGHT ASK YOU THE SAME QUESTION, YOUNG MAN.
YOU WERE WARNED NEVER TO EAT THOSE WILD MUSHROOMS.
Oh GOD, LOOK AT HIM. MY BABY'S HAIR--IT'S TURNED WHITE!
TAKE IT EASY, HONEY. DOCTOR PIMM SAID EVERYTHING'S GOING TO BE OKAY.
NELSON JUST HAD A BAD FRIGHT.
BUT THE GREEN MAN AND THE GAMES ROOM AND THE PARLIAMENT OF STONES...
IT WAS ALL SO REAL, DAD...
...I REALLY THOUGHT MY HEAD HAD BEEN CUT OFF.
SLOW DOWN, LITTLE GUY. I GUESS IT WAS ALL JUST A DREAM.
THE DOCTOR SAID YOU'RE LUCKY YOU DIDN'T POISON YOURSELF.
IT WASN'T A DREAM, DAD ... I COULD TOUCH THEM...
COME ON, NELSON.
LET'S GO HOME BEFORE IT GETS DARK.

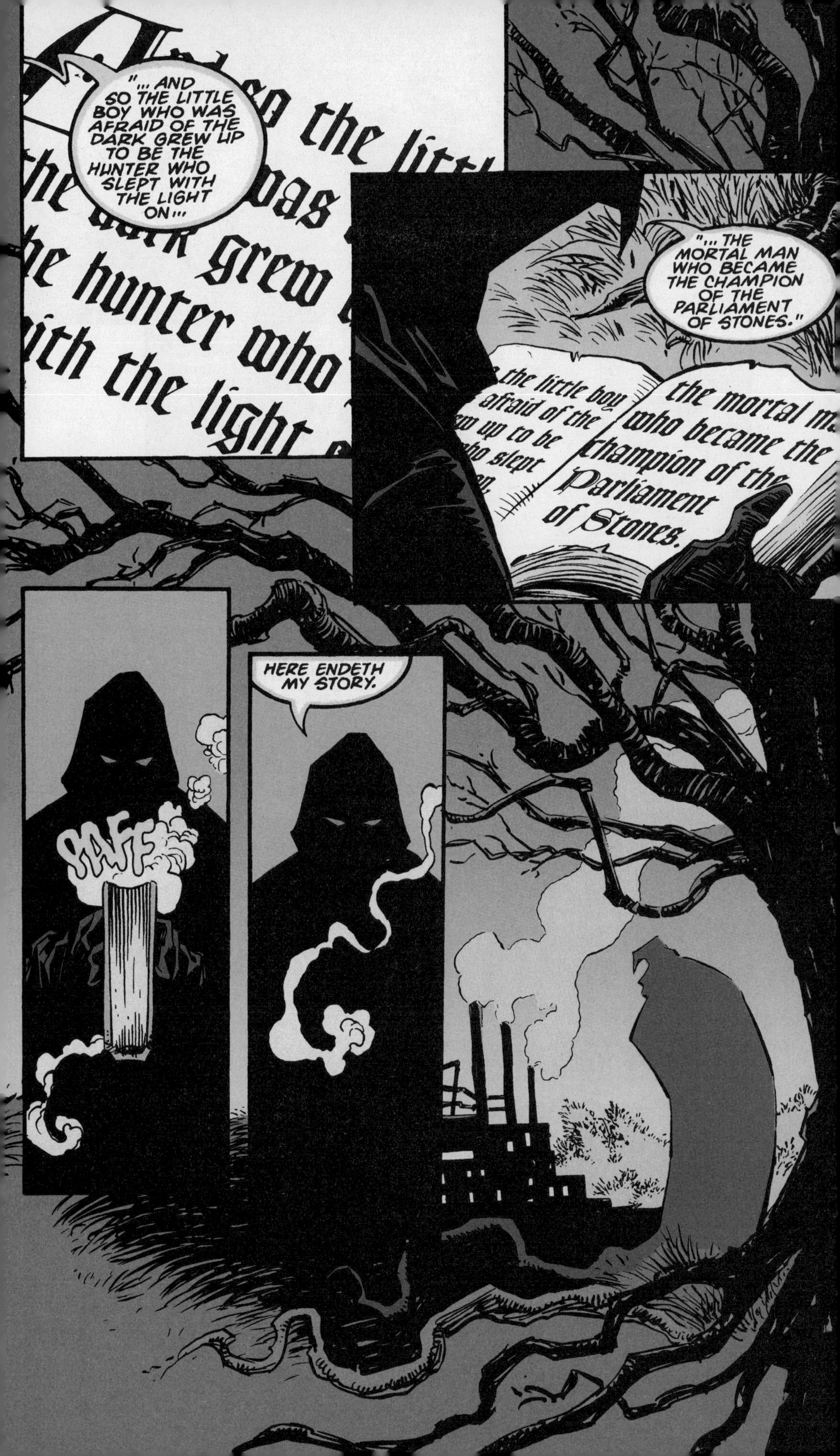
"... AND SO THE LITTLE BOY WHO WAS AFRAID OF THE DARK GREW UP TO BE THE HUNTER WHO SLEPT WITH THE LIGHT ON...
"... THE MORTAL MAN WHO BECAME THE CHAMPION OF THE PARLIAMENT OF STONES."
HERE ENDETH MY STORY.

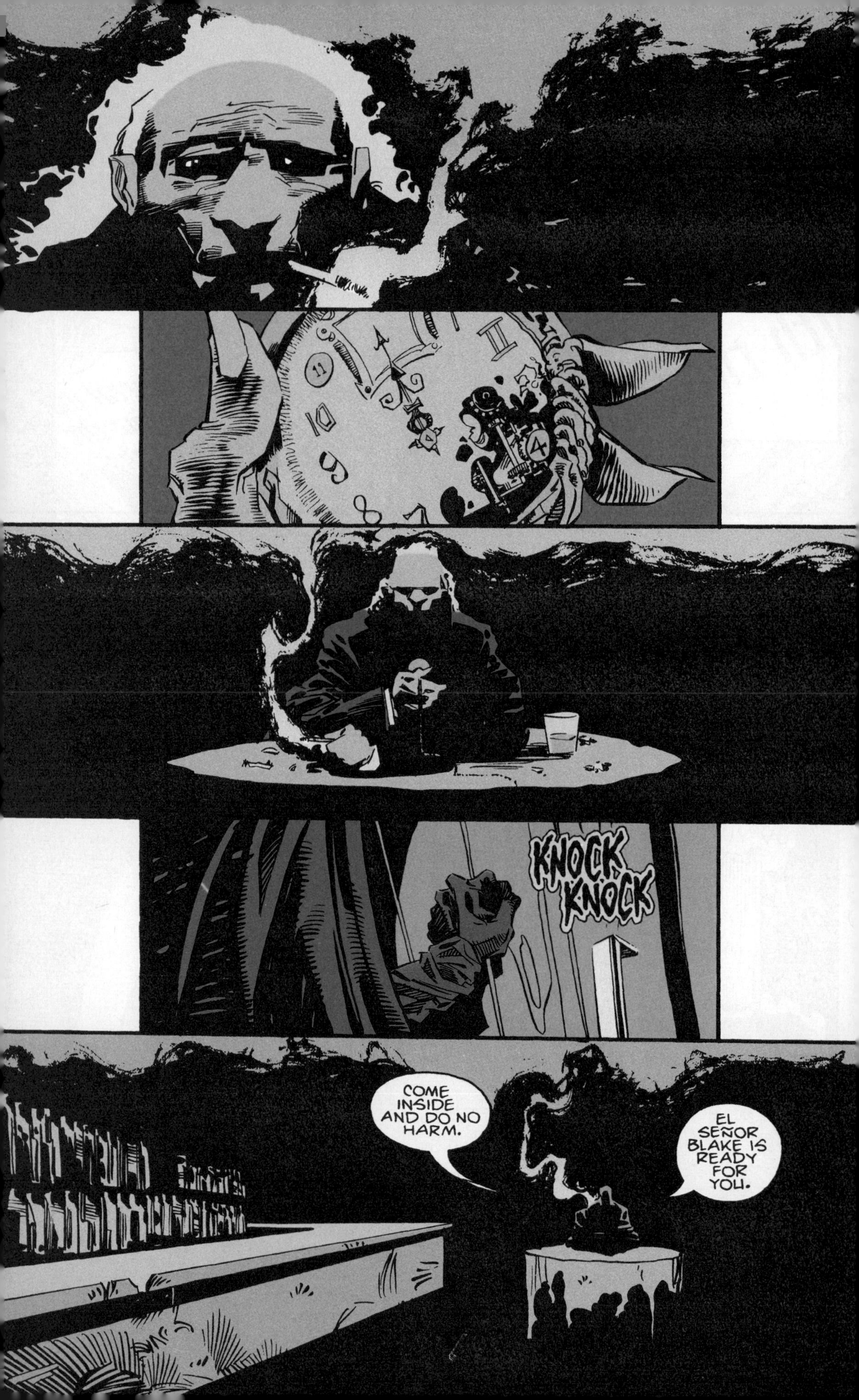
KNOCK KNOCK
COME INSIDE AND DO NO HARM.
EL SEÑOR BLAKE IS READY FOR YOU.

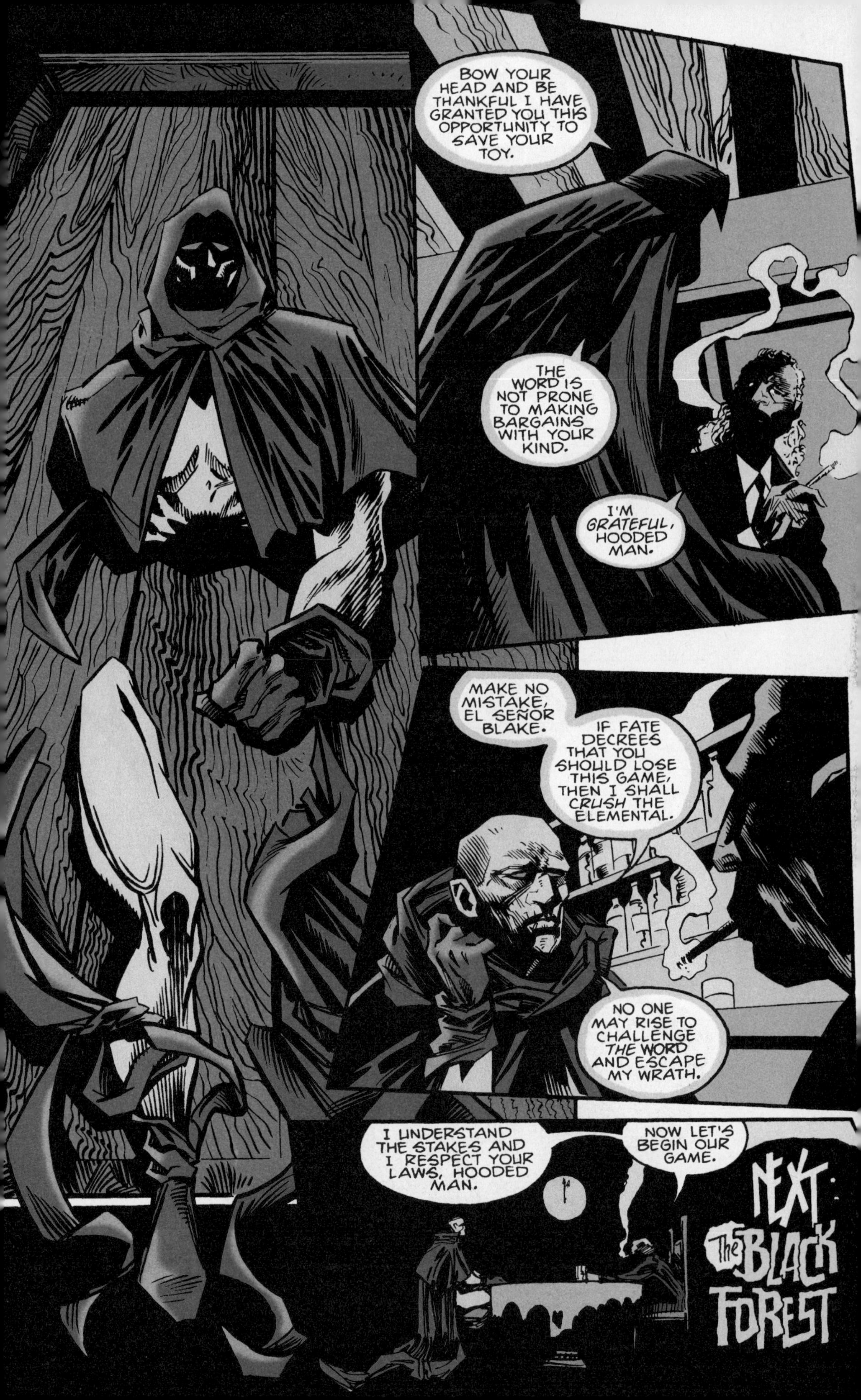
BOW YOUR HEAD AND BE THANKFUL I HAVE GRANTED YOU THIS OPPORTUNITY TO SAVE YOUR TOY.
THE WORD IS NOT PRONE TO MAKING BARGAINS WITH YOUR KIND.
I'M GRATEFUL, HOODED MAN.
MAKE NO MISTAKE, EL SEÑOR BLAKE.
IF FATE DECREES THAT YOU SHOULD LOSE THIS GAME, THEN I SHALL CRUSH THE ELEMENTAL.
NO ONE MAY RISE TO CHALLENGE THE WORD AND ESCAPE MY WRATH.
I UNDERSTAND THE STAKES AND I RESPECT YOUR LAWS, HOODED MAN.
NOW LET'S BEGIN OUR GAME.
NEXT: The BLACK FOREST

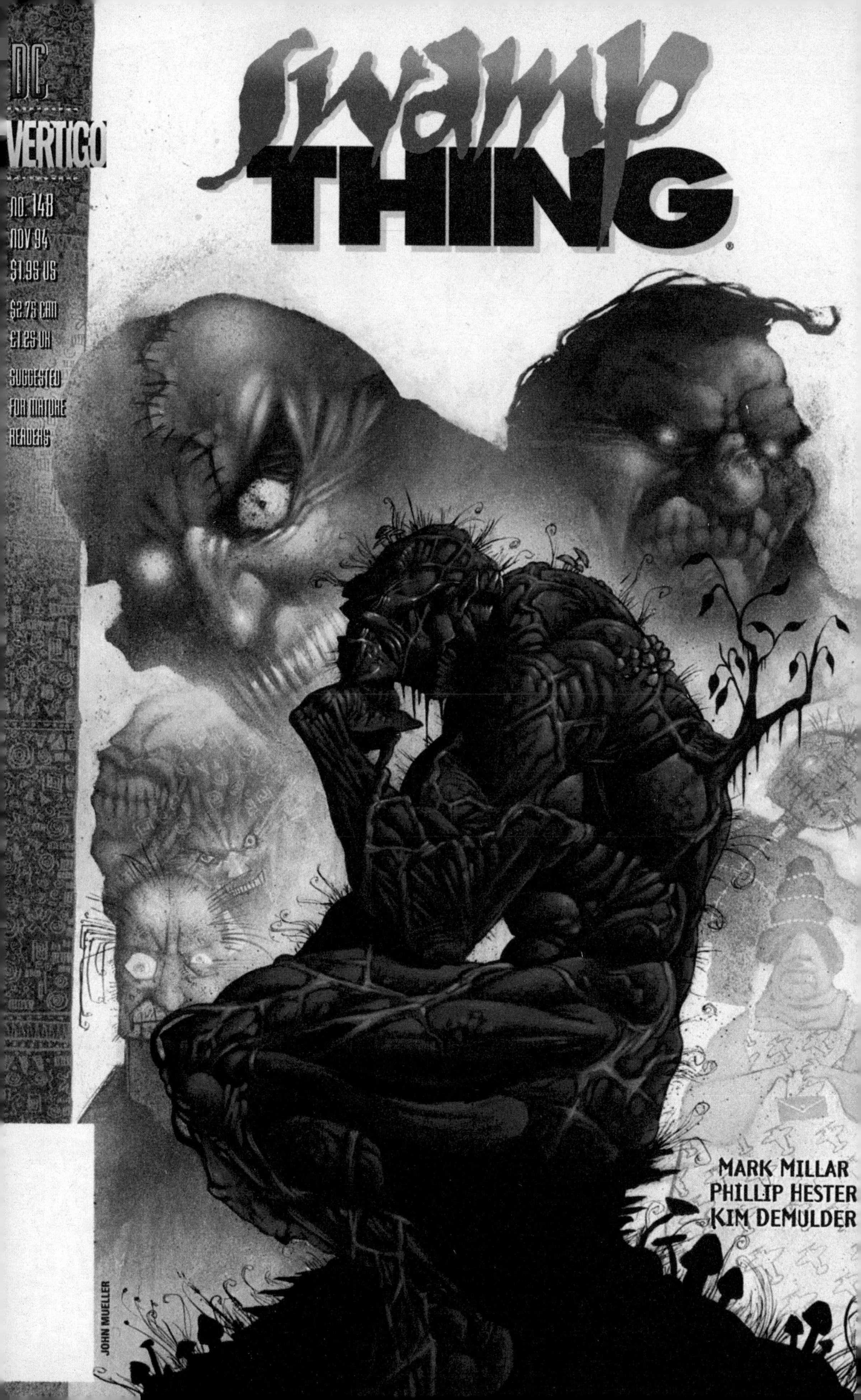
DC
VERTIGO
no. 148
NOV 94
$1.95 US
$2.75 CAN
£1.25 UK
SUGGESTED FOR MATURE READERS
Swamp THING
MARK MILLAR
PHILLIP HESTER
KIM DEMULDER
JOHN MUELLER

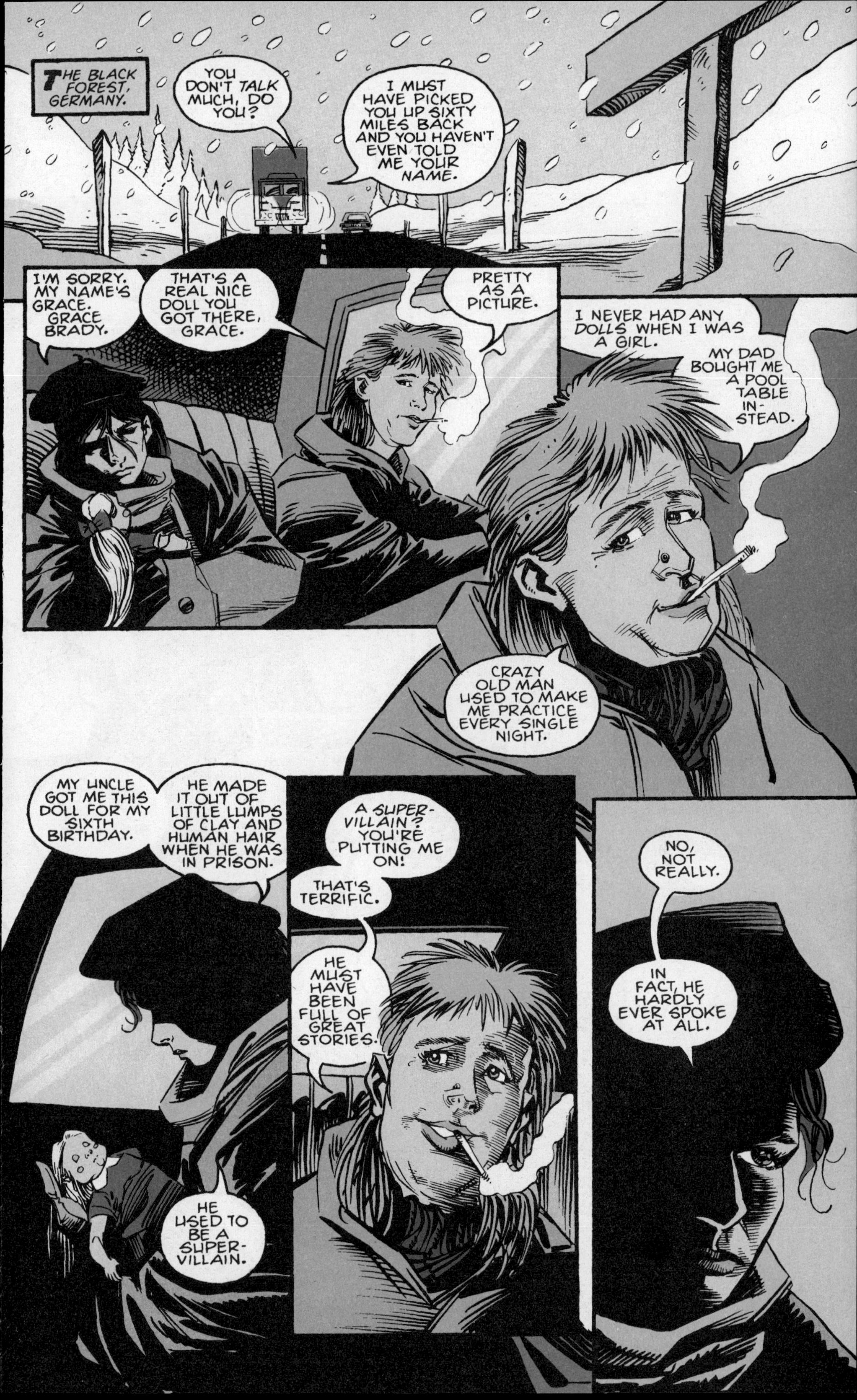
THE BLACK FOREST, GERMANY.
YOU DON'T TALK MUCH, DO YOU?
I MUST HAVE PICKED YOU UP SIXTY MILES BACK AND YOU HAVEN'T EVEN TOLD ME YOUR NAME.
I'M SORRY. MY NAME'S GRACE. GRACE BRADY.
THAT'S A REAL NICE DOLL YOU GOT THERE, GRACE.
PRETTY AS A PICTURE.
I NEVER HAD ANY DOLLS WHEN I WAS A GIRL.
MY DAD BOUGHT ME A POOL TABLE IN-STEAD.
CRAZY OLD MAN USED TO MAKE ME PRACTICE EVERY SINGLE NIGHT.
MY UNCLE GOT ME THIS DOLL FOR MY SIXTH BIRTHDAY.
HE MADE IT OUT OF LITTLE LUMPS OF CLAY AND HUMAN HAIR WHEN HE WAS IN PRISON.
HE USED TO BE A SUPER-VILLAIN.
A SUPER-VILLAIN? YOU'RE PUTTING ME ON!
THAT'S TERRIFIC.
HE MUST HAVE BEEN FULL OF GREAT STORIES.
NO, NOT REALLY.
IN FACT, HE HARDLY EVER SPOKE AT ALL.

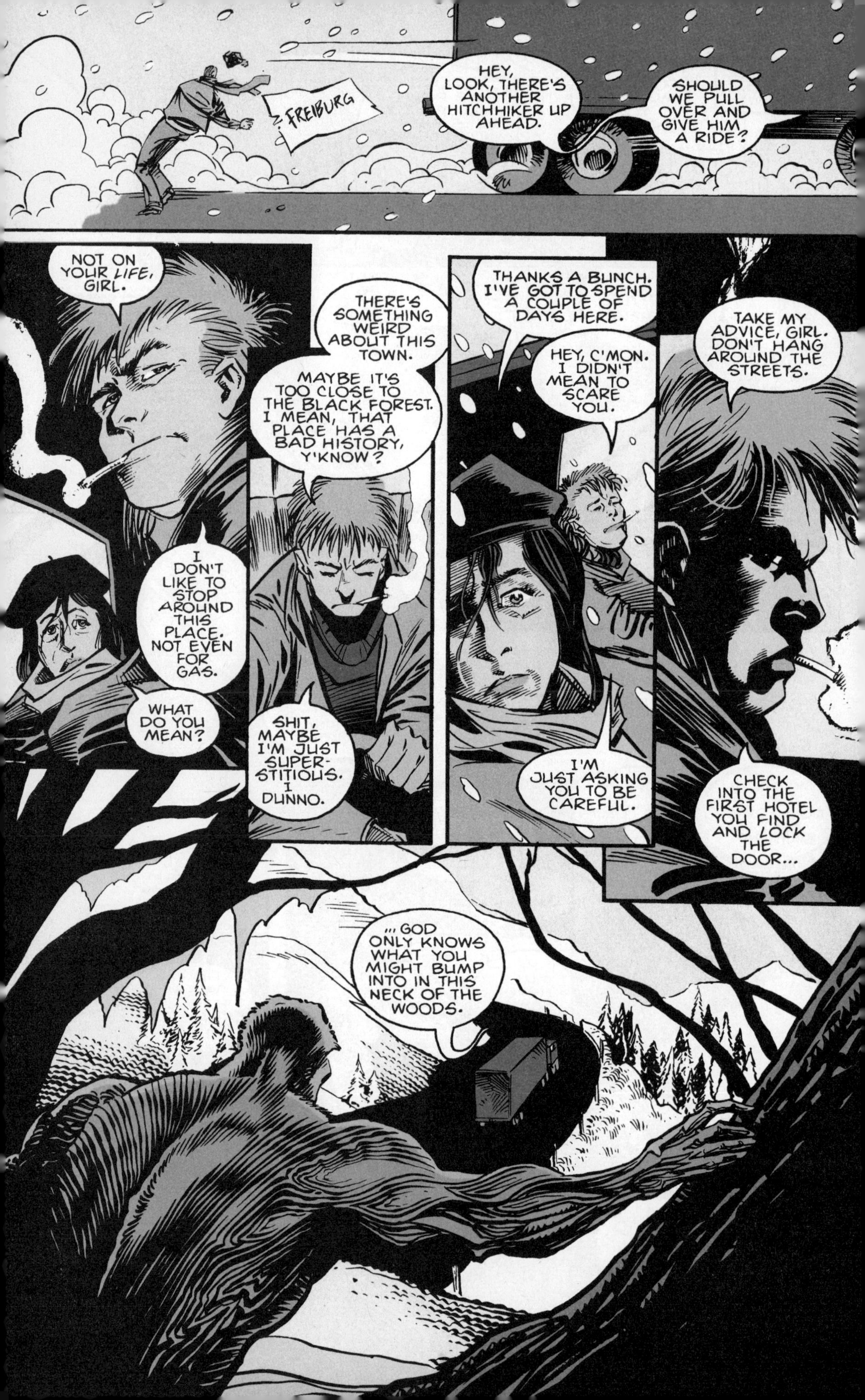

FREIBURG
HEY, LOOK, THERE'S ANOTHER HITCHHIKER UP AHEAD.
SHOULD WE PULL OVER AND GIVE HIM A RIDE?
NOT ON YOUR LIFE, GIRL.
I DON'T LIKE TO STOP AROUND THIS PLACE. NOT EVEN FOR GAS.
WHAT DO YOU MEAN?
THERE'S SOMETHING WEIRD ABOUT THIS TOWN.
MAYBE IT'S TOO CLOSE TO THE BLACK FOREST. I MEAN, THAT PLACE HAS A BAD HISTORY, Y'KNOW?
SHIT, MAYBE I'M JUST SUPER-STITIOUS. I DUNNO.
THANKS A BUNCH. I'VE GOT TO SPEND A COUPLE OF DAYS HERE.
HEY, C'MON. I DIDN'T MEAN TO SCARE YOU.
I'M JUST ASKING YOU TO BE CAREFUL.
TAKE MY ADVICE, GIRL. DON'T HANG AROUND THE STREETS.
CHECK INTO THE FIRST HOTEL YOU FIND AND LOCK THE DOOR...
...GOD ONLY KNOWS WHAT YOU MIGHT BUMP INTO IN THIS NECK OF THE WOODS.

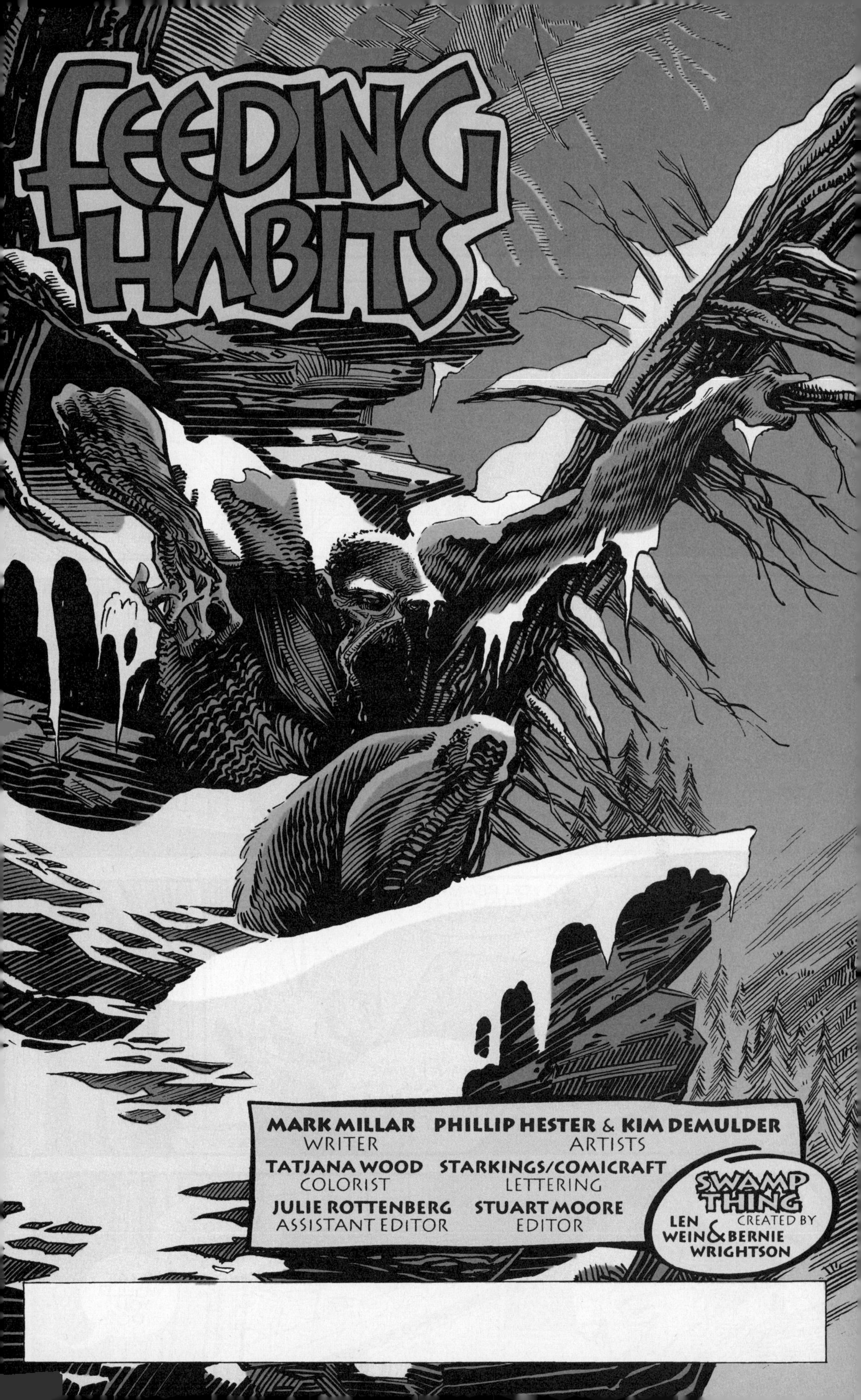
FEEDING HABITS
MARK MILLAR WRITER
PHILLIP HESTER & KIM DEMULDER ARTISTS
TATJANA WOOD COLORIST
STARKINGS/COMICRAFT LETTERING
JULIE ROTTENBERG ASSISTANT EDITOR
STUART MOORE EDITOR
SWAMP THING CREATED BY LEN WEIN & BERNIE WRIGHTSON

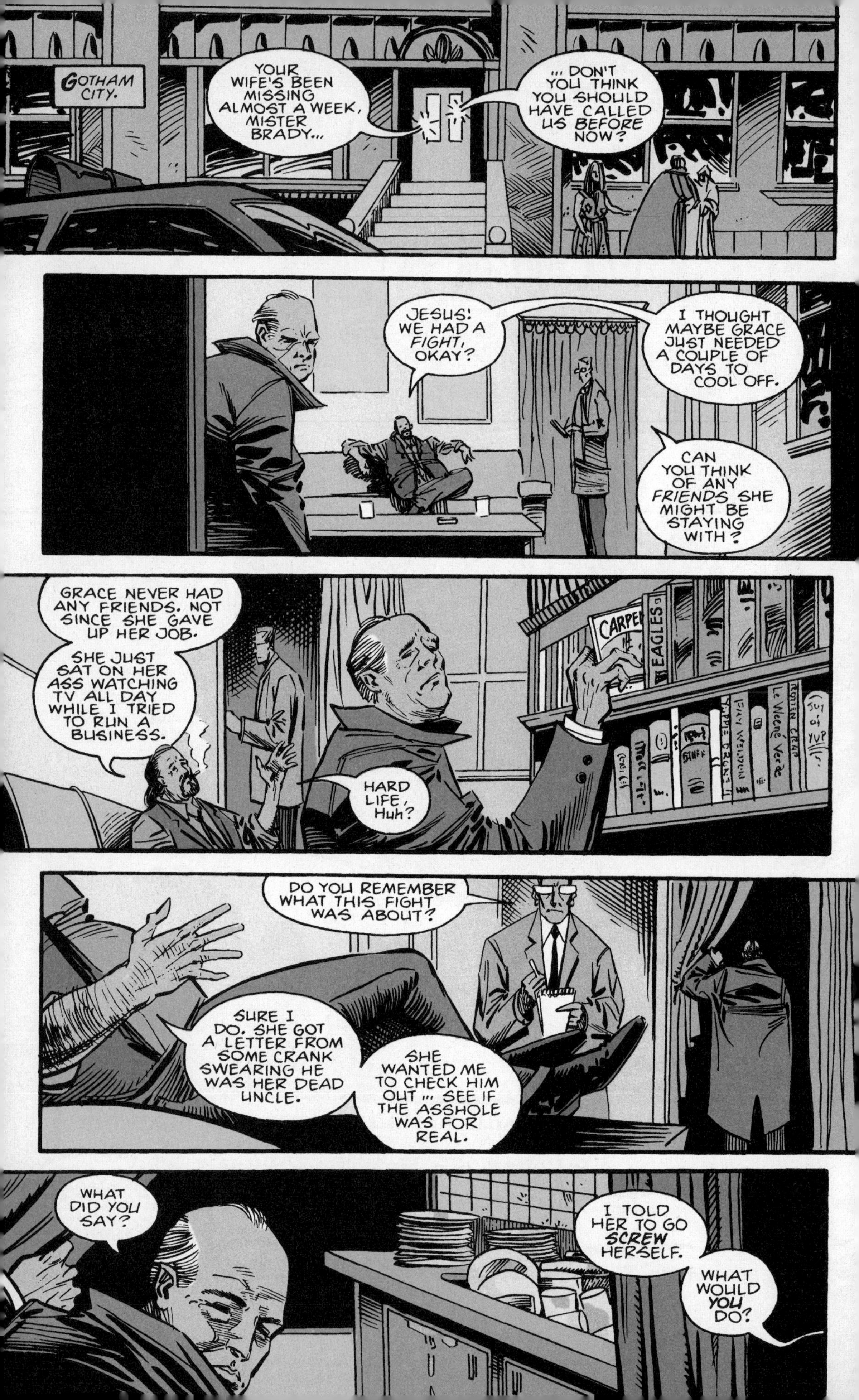
GOTHAM CITY.
YOUR WIFE'S BEEN MISSING ALMOST A WEEK, MISTER BRADY...
... DON'T YOU THINK YOU SHOULD HAVE CALLED US BEFORE NOW?
JESUS! WE HAD A FIGHT, OKAY?
I THOUGHT MAYBE GRACE JUST NEEDED A COUPLE OF DAYS TO COOL OFF.
CAN YOU THINK OF ANY FRIENDS SHE MIGHT BE STAYING WITH?
GRACE NEVER HAD ANY FRIENDS. NOT SINCE SHE GAVE UP HER JOB.
SHE JUST SAT ON HER ASS WATCHING TV ALL DAY WHILE I TRIED TO RUN A BUSINESS.
CARPE
EAGLES
HARD LIFE, Huh?
DO YOU REMEMBER WHAT THIS FIGHT WAS ABOUT?
SURE I DO. SHE GOT A LETTER FROM SOME CRANK SWEARING HE WAS HER DEAD UNCLE.
SHE WANTED ME TO CHECK HIM OUT ... SEE IF THE ASSHOLE WAS FOR REAL.
WHAT DID YOU SAY?
I TOLD HER TO GO SCREW HERSELF.
WHAT WOULD YOU DO?

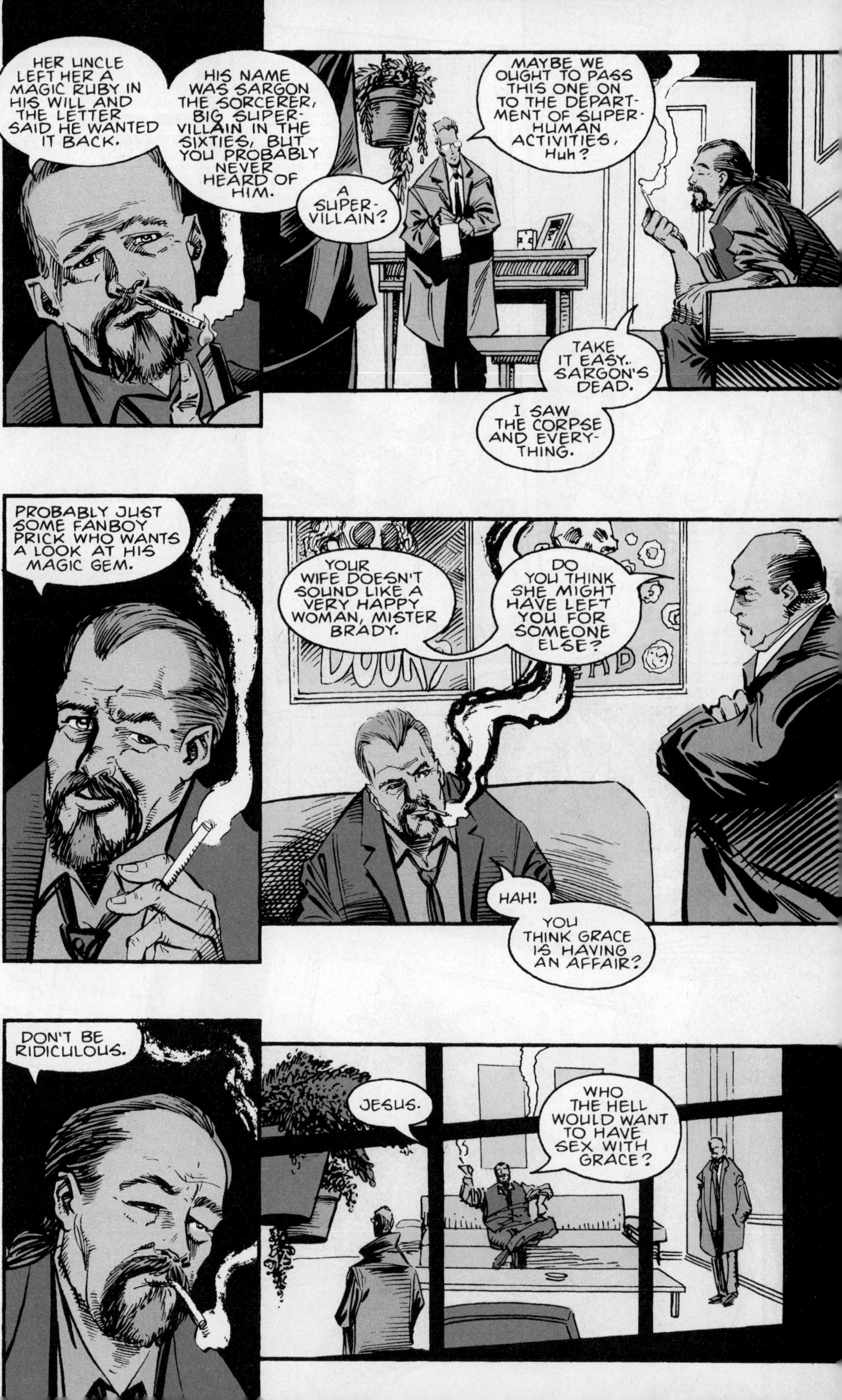
HER UNCLE LEFT HER A MAGIC RUBY IN HIS WILL AND THE LETTER SAID HE WANTED IT BACK.
HIS NAME WAS SARGON THE SORCERER, BIG SUPER-VILLAIN IN THE SIXTIES, BUT YOU PROBABLY NEVER HEARD OF HIM.
A SUPER-VILLAIN?
MAYBE WE OUGHT TO PASS THIS ONE ON TO THE DEPART-MENT OF SUPER-HUMAN ACTIVITIES, Huh?
TAKE IT EASY.. SARGON'S DEAD.
I SAW THE CORPSE AND EVERY-THING.
PROBABLY JUST SOME FANBOY PRICK WHO WANTS A LOOK AT HIS MAGIC GEM.
YOUR WIFE DOESN'T SOUND LIKE A VERY HAPPY WOMAN, MISTER BRADY.
DO YOU THINK SHE MIGHT HAVE LEFT YOU FOR SOMEONE ELSE?
HAH!
YOU THINK GRACE IS HAVING AN AFFAIR?
DON'T BE RIDICULOUS.
JESUS.
WHO THE HELL WOULD WANT TO HAVE SEX WITH GRACE?

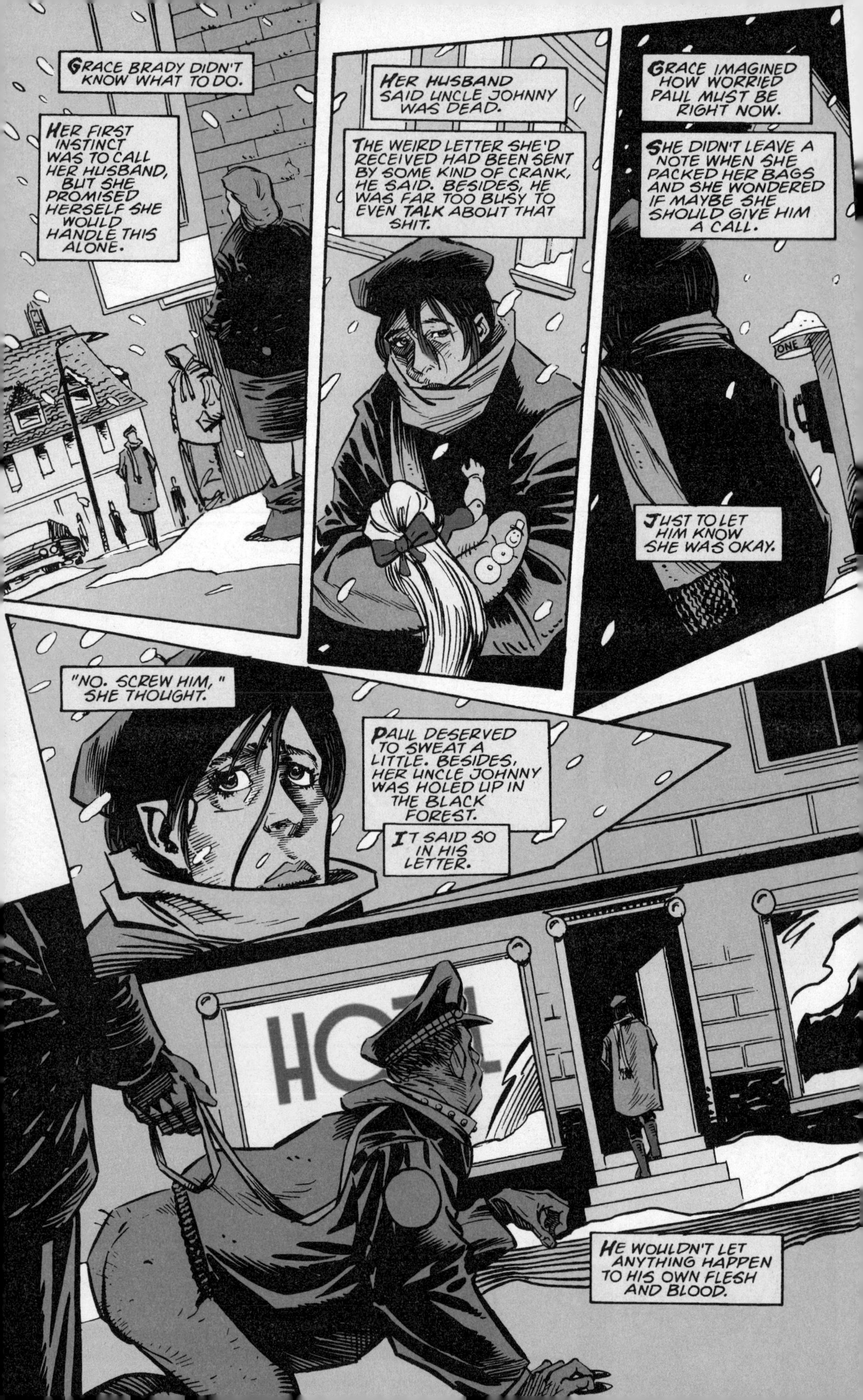
GRACE BRADY DIDN'T KNOW WHAT TO DO.
HER FIRST INSTINCT WAS TO CALL HER HUSBAND, BUT SHE PROMISED HERSELF SHE WOULD HANDLE THIS ALONE.
HER HUSBAND SAID UNCLE JOHNNY WAS DEAD.
THE WEIRD LETTER SHE'D RECEIVED HAD BEEN SENT BY SOME KIND OF CRANK, HE SAID. BESIDES, HE WAS FAR TOO BUSY TO EVEN TALK ABOUT THAT SHIT.
GRACE IMAGINED HOW WORRIED PAUL MUST BE RIGHT NOW.
SHE DIDN'T LEAVE A NOTE WHEN SHE PACKED HER BAGS AND SHE WONDERED IF MAYBE SHE SHOULD GIVE HIM A CALL.
ONE
JUST TO LET HIM KNOW SHE WAS OKAY.
"NO. SCREW HIM," SHE THOUGHT.
PAUL DESERVED TO SWEAT A LITTLE. BESIDES, HER UNCLE JOHNNY WAS HOLED UP IN THE BLACK FOREST.
IT SAID SO IN HIS LETTER.
HE WOULDN'T LET ANYTHING HAPPEN TO HIS OWN FLESH AND BLOOD.

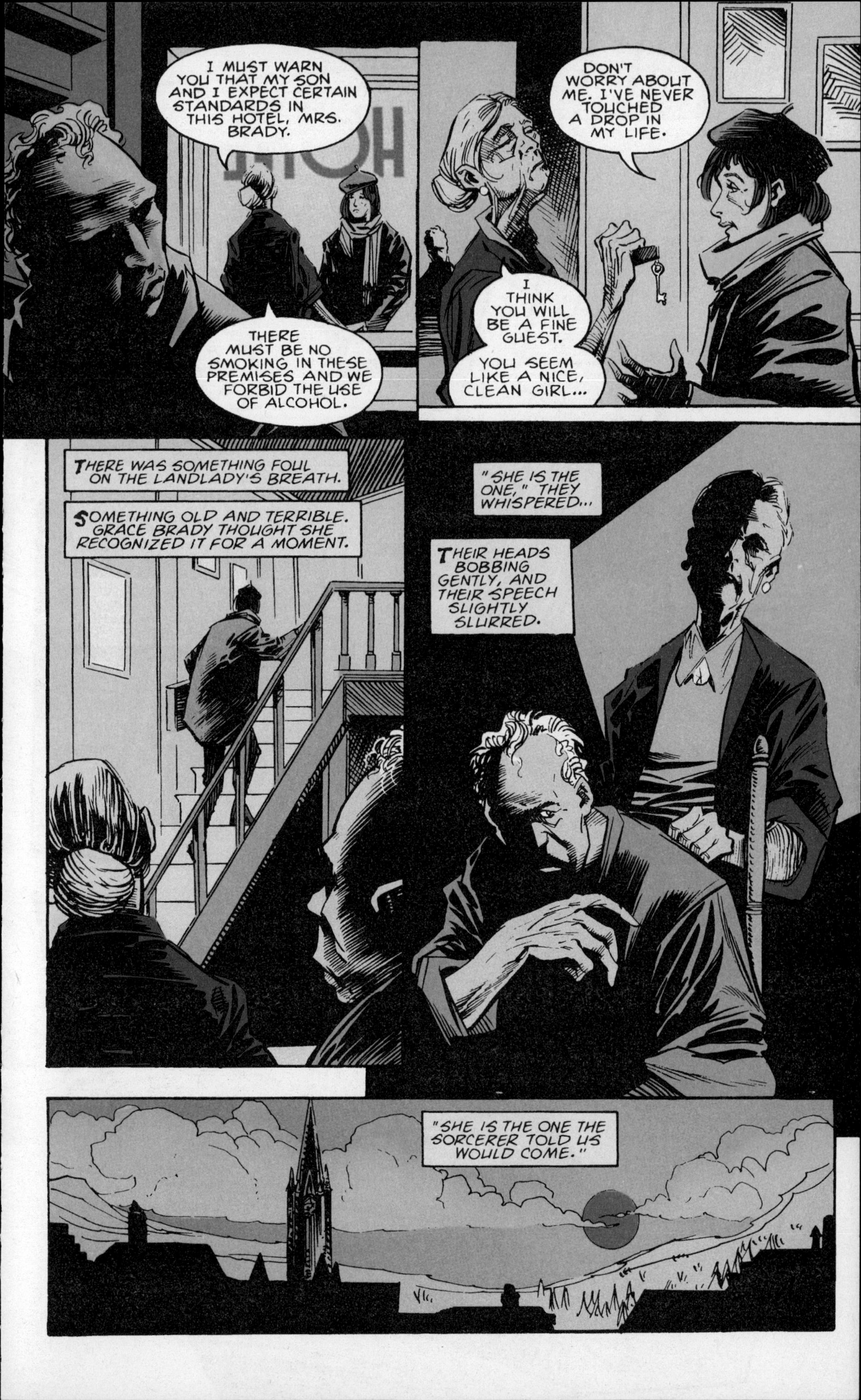
I MUST WARN YOU THAT MY SON AND I EXPECT CERTAIN STANDARDS IN THIS HOTEL, MRS. BRADY.
THERE MUST BE NO SMOKING IN THESE PREMISES AND WE FORBID THE USE OF ALCOHOL.
DON'T WORRY ABOUT ME. I'VE NEVER TOUCHED A DROP IN MY LIFE.
I THINK YOU WILL BE A FINE GUEST.
YOU SEEM LIKE A NICE, CLEAN GIRL...
THERE WAS SOMETHING FOUL ON THE LANDLADY'S BREATH.
SOMETHING OLD AND TERRIBLE. GRACE BRADY THOUGHT SHE RECOGNIZED IT FOR A MOMENT.
"SHE IS THE ONE," THEY WHISPERED...
THEIR HEADS BOBBING GENTLY, AND THEIR SPEECH SLIGHTLY SLURRED.
"SHE IS THE ONE THE SORCERER TOLD US WOULD COME."

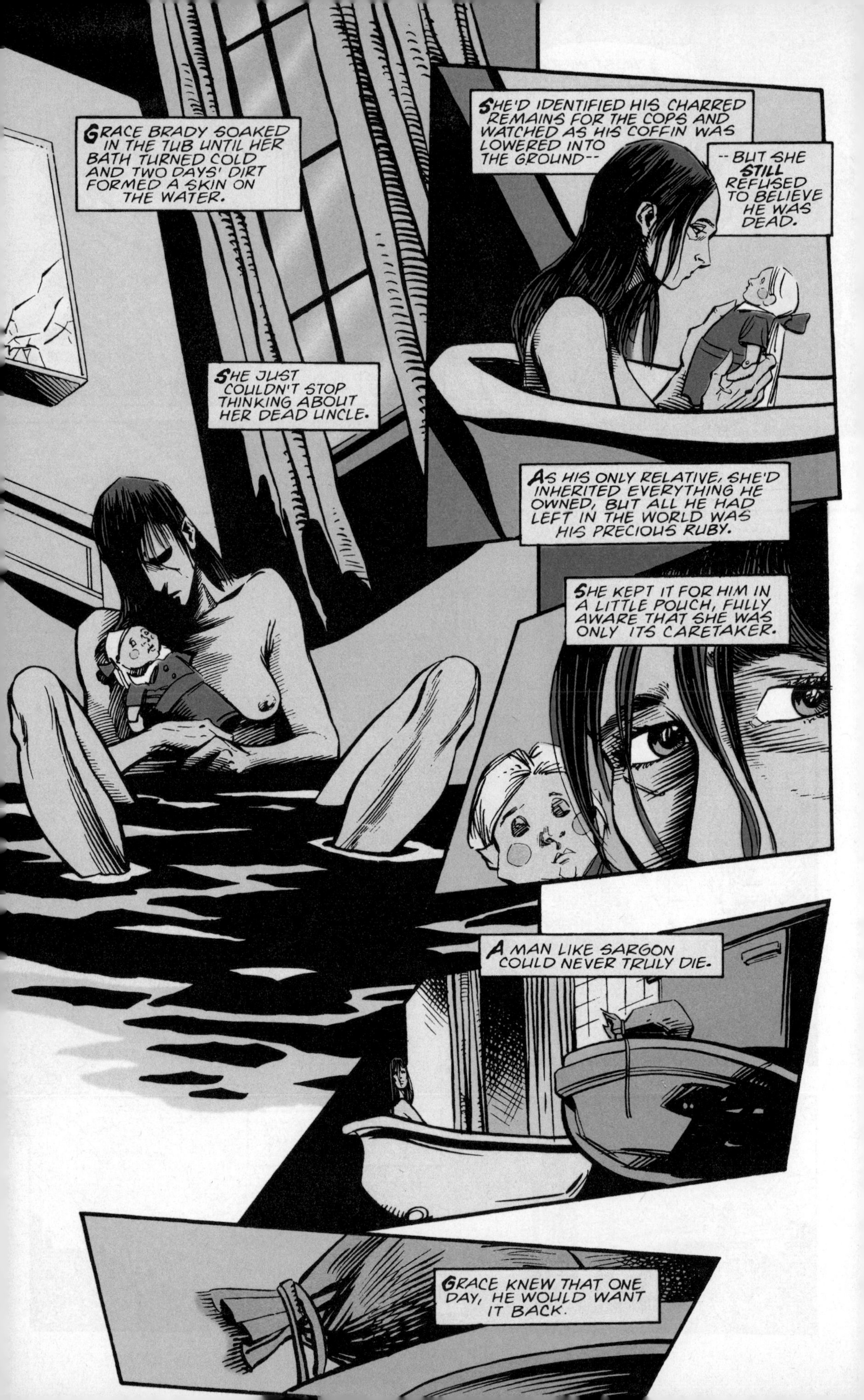
GRACE BRADY SOAKED IN THE TUB UNTIL HER BATH TURNED COLD AND TWO DAYS' DIRT FORMED A SKIN ON THE WATER.
SHE JUST COULDN'T STOP THINKING ABOUT HER DEAD UNCLE.
SHE'D IDENTIFIED HIS CHARRED REMAINS FOR THE COPS AND WATCHED AS HIS COFFIN WAS LOWERED INTO THE GROUND--
--BUT SHE STILL REFUSED TO BELIEVE HE WAS DEAD.
AS HIS ONLY RELATIVE, SHE'D INHERITED EVERYTHING HE OWNED, BUT ALL HE HAD LEFT IN THE WORLD WAS HIS PRECIOUS RUBY.
SHE KEPT IT FOR HIM IN A LITTLE POUCH, FULLY AWARE THAT SHE WAS ONLY ITS CARETAKER.
A MAN LIKE SARGON COULD NEVER TRULY DIE.
GRACE KNEW THAT ONE DAY, HE WOULD WANT IT BACK.

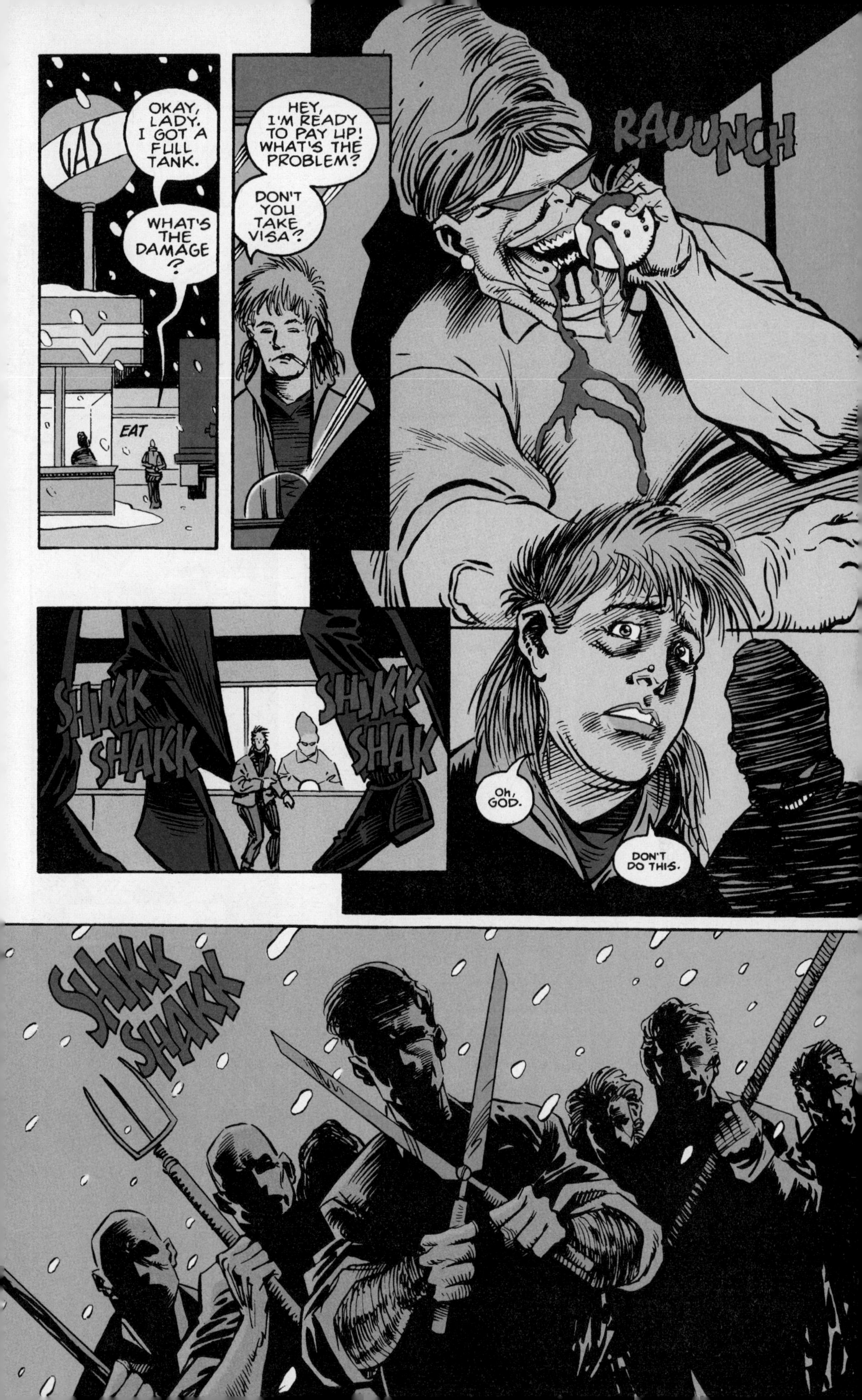
GAS
OKAY, LADY. I GOT A FULL TANK.
WHAT'S THE DAMAGE?
EAT
HEY, I'M READY TO PAY UP! WHAT'S THE PROBLEM?
DON'T YOU TAKE VISA?
RAUUNCH
SHIKK SHAKK
SHIKK SHAK
OH, GOD.
DON'T DO THIS.
SHIKK SHAKK

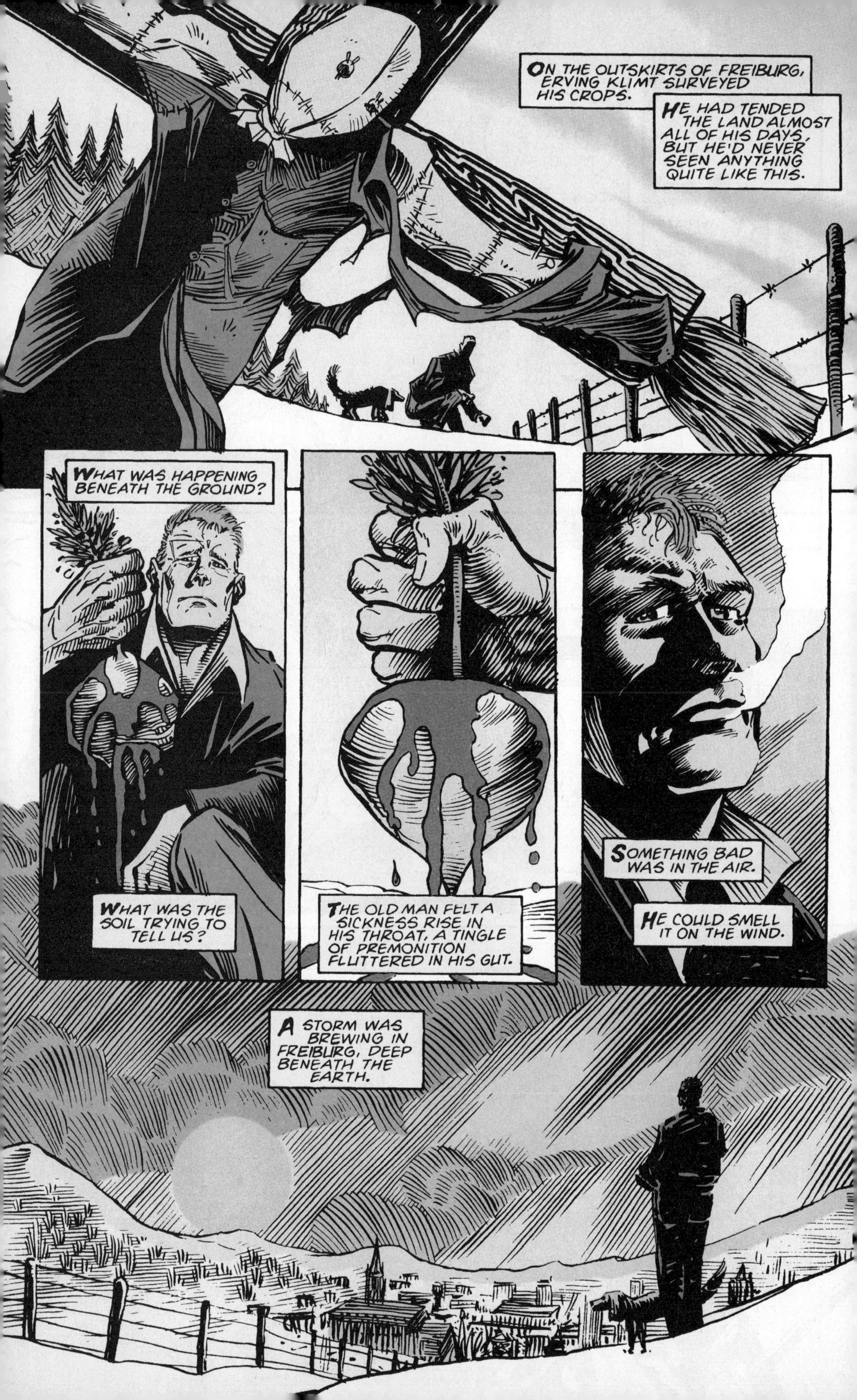
ON THE OUTSKIRTS OF FREIBURG, ERVING KLIMT SURVEYED HIS CROPS.
HE HAD TENDED THE LAND ALMOST ALL OF HIS DAYS, BUT HE'D NEVER SEEN ANYTHING QUITE LIKE THIS.
WHAT WAS HAPPENING BENEATH THE GROUND?
WHAT WAS THE SOIL TRYING TO TELL US?
THE OLD MAN FELT A SICKNESS RISE IN HIS THROAT, A TINGLE OF PREMONITION FLUTTERED IN HIS GUT.
SOMETHING BAD WAS IN THE AIR.
HE COULD SMELL IT ON THE WIND.
A STORM WAS BREWING IN FREIBURG, DEEP BENEATH THE EARTH.

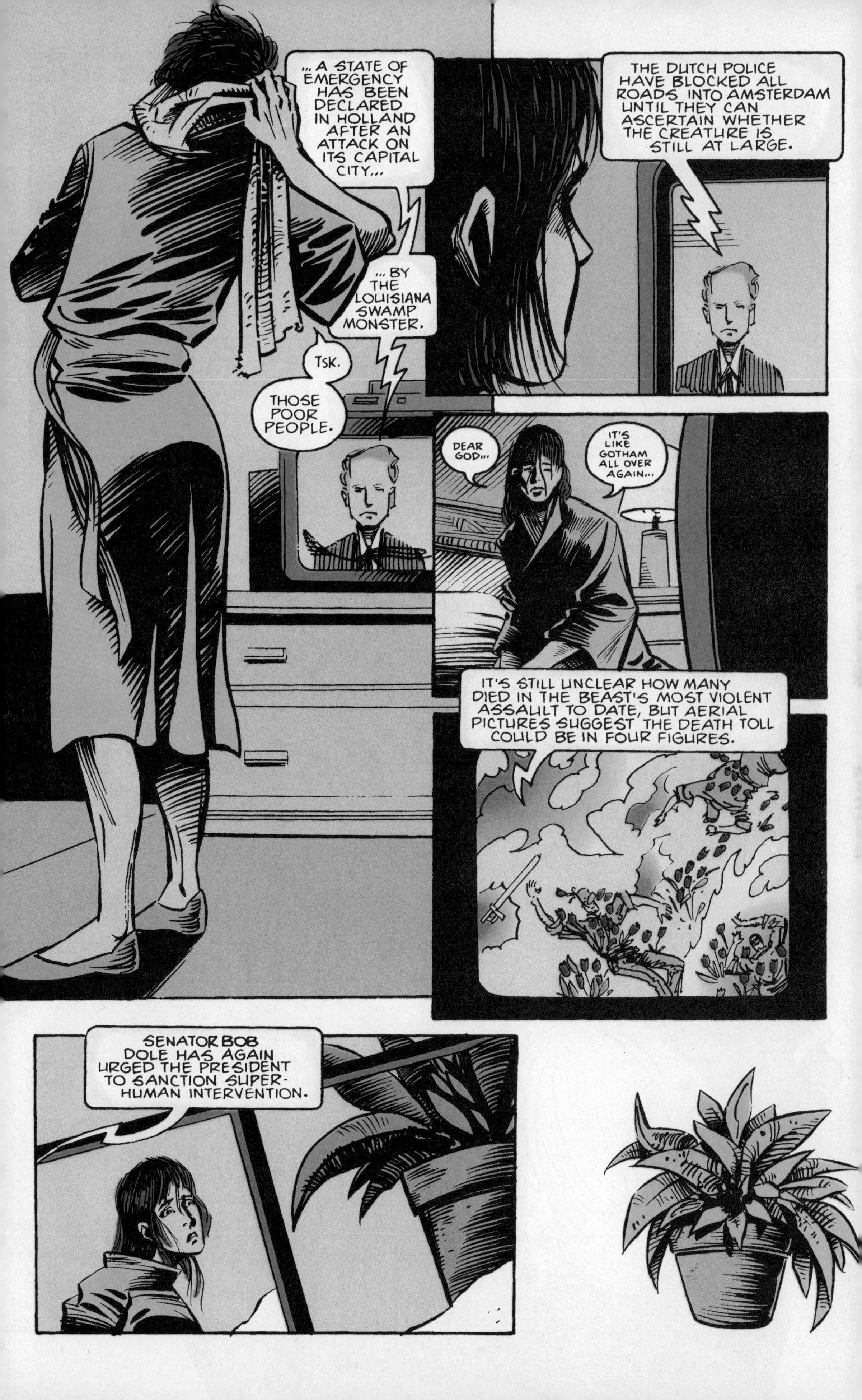
...A STATE OF EMERGENCY HAS BEEN DECLARED IN HOLLAND AFTER AN ATTACK ON ITS CAPITAL CITY...
...BY THE LOUISIANA SWAMP MONSTER.
TSK.
THOSE POOR PEOPLE.
THE DUTCH POLICE HAVE BLOCKED ALL ROADS INTO AMSTERDAM UNTIL THEY CAN ASCERTAIN WHETHER THE CREATURE IS STILL AT LARGE.
DEAR GOD...
IT'S LIKE GOTHAM ALL OVER AGAIN...
IT'S STILL UNCLEAR HOW MANY DIED IN THE BEAST'S MOST VIOLENT ASSAULT TO DATE, BUT AERIAL PICTURES SUGGEST THE DEATH TOLL COULD BE IN FOUR FIGURES.
SENATOR BOB DOLE HAS AGAIN URGED THE PRESIDENT TO SANCTION SUPER-HUMAN INTERVENTION.

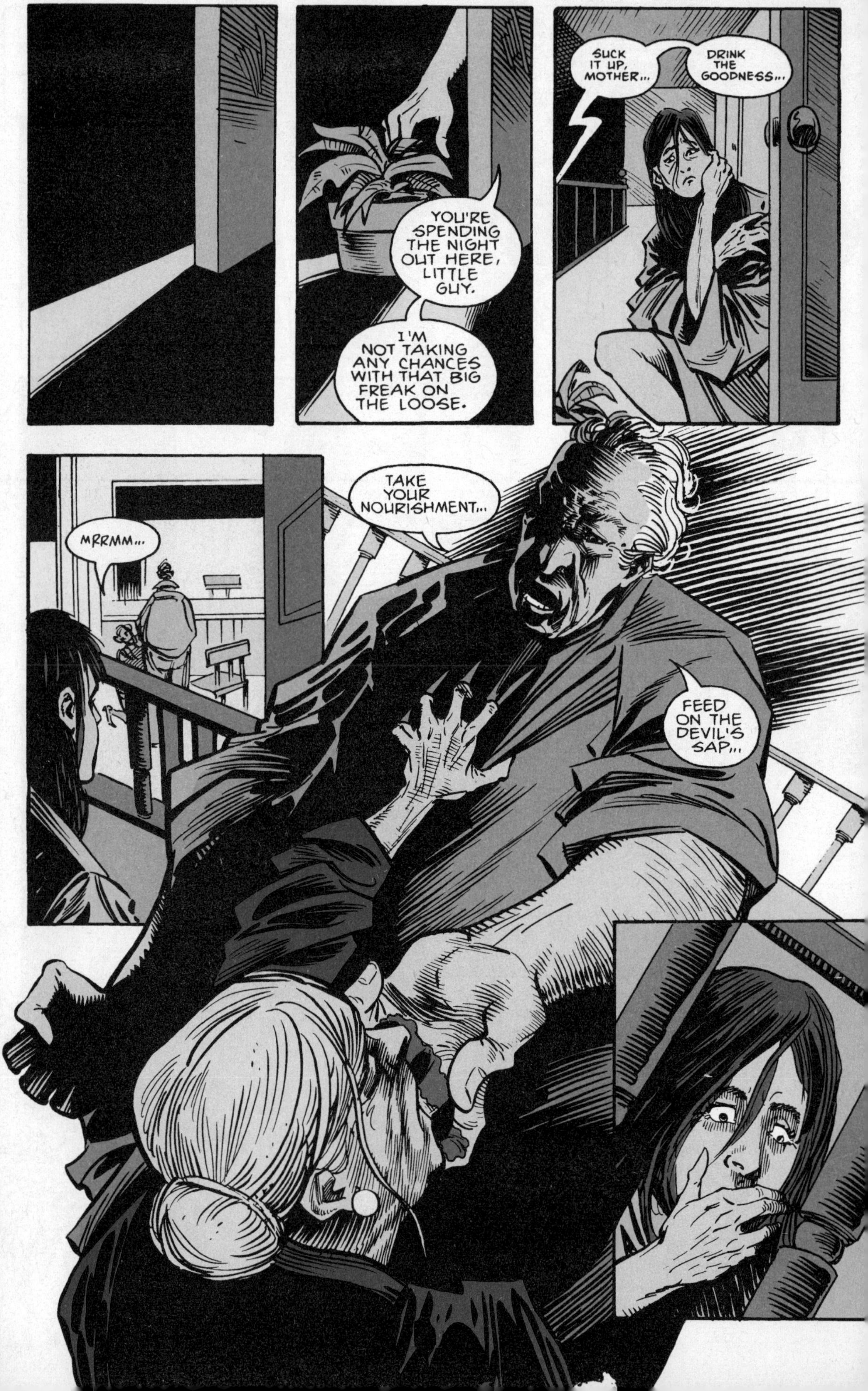
YOU'RE SPENDING THE NIGHT OUT HERE, LITTLE GUY.
I'M NOT TAKING ANY CHANCES WITH THAT BIG FREAK ON THE LOOSE.
SUCK IT UP, MOTHER...
DRINK THE GOODNESS...
MRRMM...
TAKE YOUR NOURISHMENT...
FEED ON THE DEVIL'S SAP...

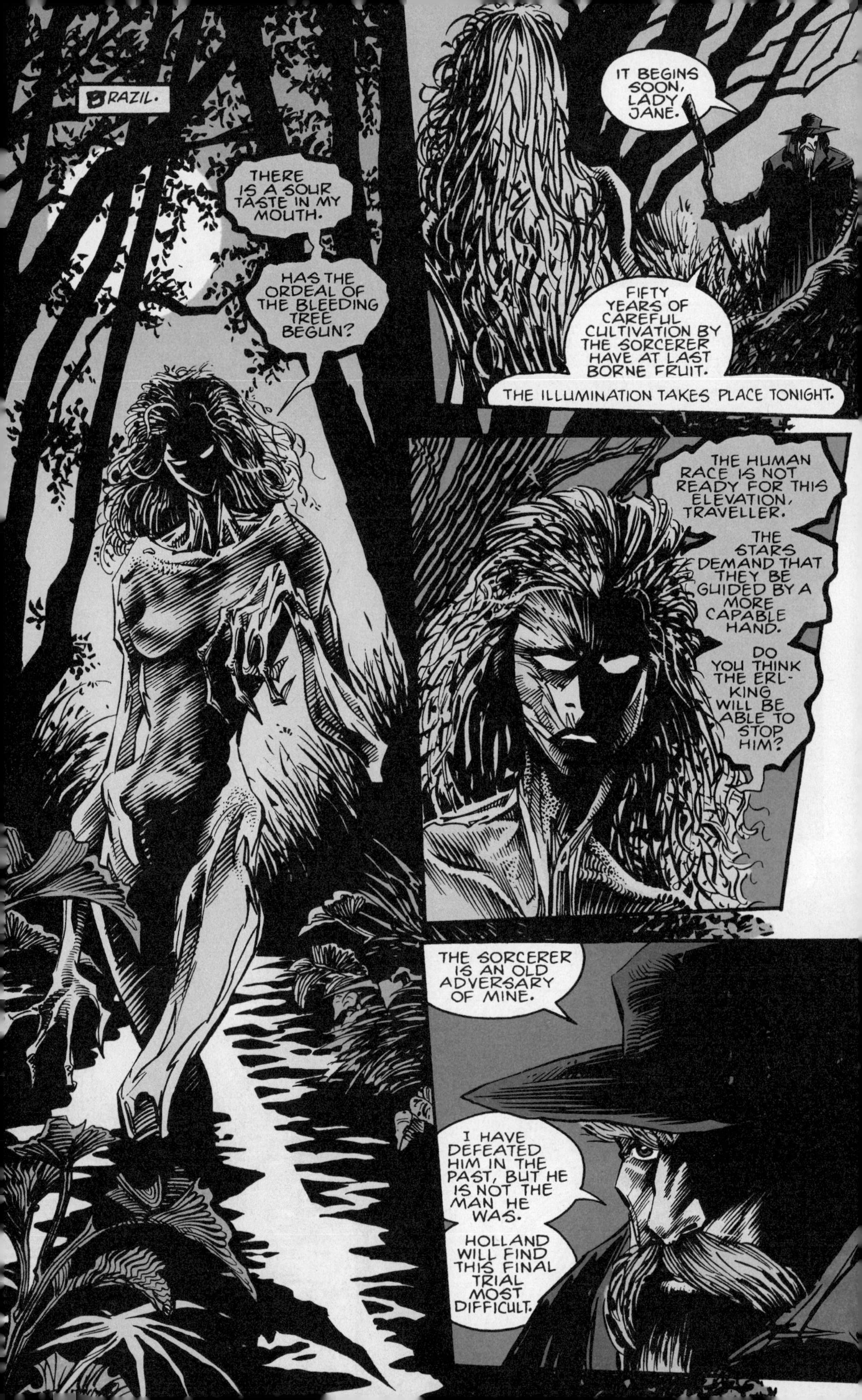
BRAZIL.
THERE IS A SOUR TASTE IN MY MOUTH.
HAS THE ORDEAL OF THE BLEEDING TREE BEGUN?
IT BEGINS SOON, LADY JANE.
FIFTY YEARS OF CAREFUL CULTIVATION BY THE SORCERER HAVE AT LAST BORNE FRUIT.
THE ILLUMINATION TAKES PLACE TONIGHT.
THE HUMAN RACE IS NOT READY FOR THIS ELEVATION, TRAVELLER.
THE STARS DEMAND THAT THEY BE GUIDED BY A MORE CAPABLE HAND.
DO YOU THINK THE ERL-KING WILL BE ABLE TO STOP HIM?
THE SORCERER IS AN OLD ADVERSARY OF MINE.
I HAVE DEFEATED HIM IN THE PAST, BUT HE IS NOT THE MAN HE WAS.
HOLLAND WILL FIND THIS FINAL TRIAL MOST DIFFICULT.

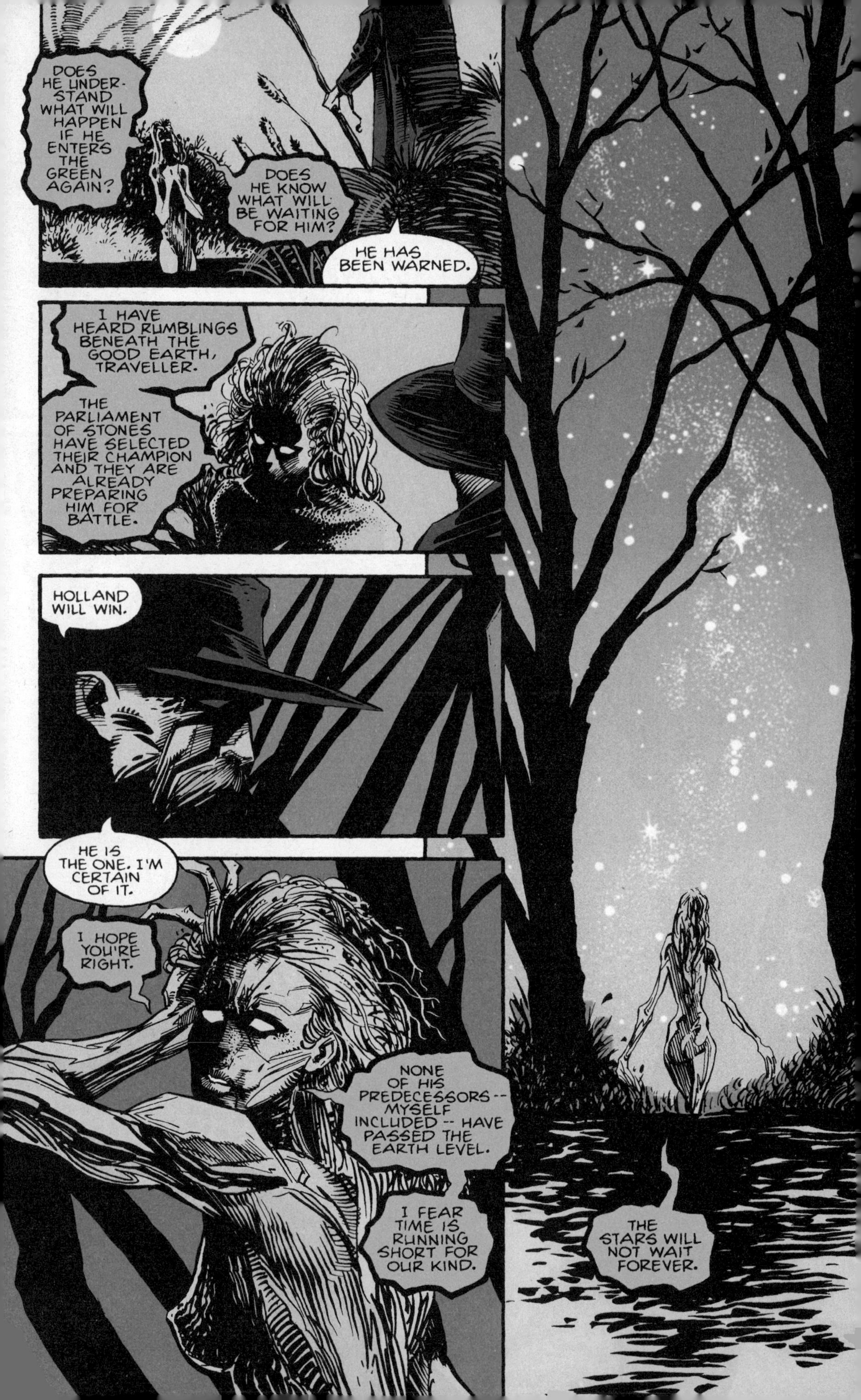
DOES HE UNDERSTAND WHAT WILL HAPPEN IF HE ENTERS THE GREEN AGAIN?
DOES HE KNOW WHAT WILL BE WAITING FOR HIM?
HE HAS BEEN WARNED.
I HAVE HEARD RUMBLINGS BENEATH THE GOOD EARTH, TRAVELLER.
THE PARLIAMENT OF STONES HAVE SELECTED THEIR CHAMPION AND THEY ARE ALREADY PREPARING HIM FOR BATTLE.
HOLLAND WILL WIN.
HE IS THE ONE. I'M CERTAIN OF IT.
I HOPE YOU'RE RIGHT.
NONE OF HIS PREDECESSORS -- MYSELF INCLUDED -- HAVE PASSED THE EARTH LEVEL.
I FEAR TIME IS RUNNING SHORT FOR OUR KIND.
THE STARS WILL NOT WAIT FOREVER.

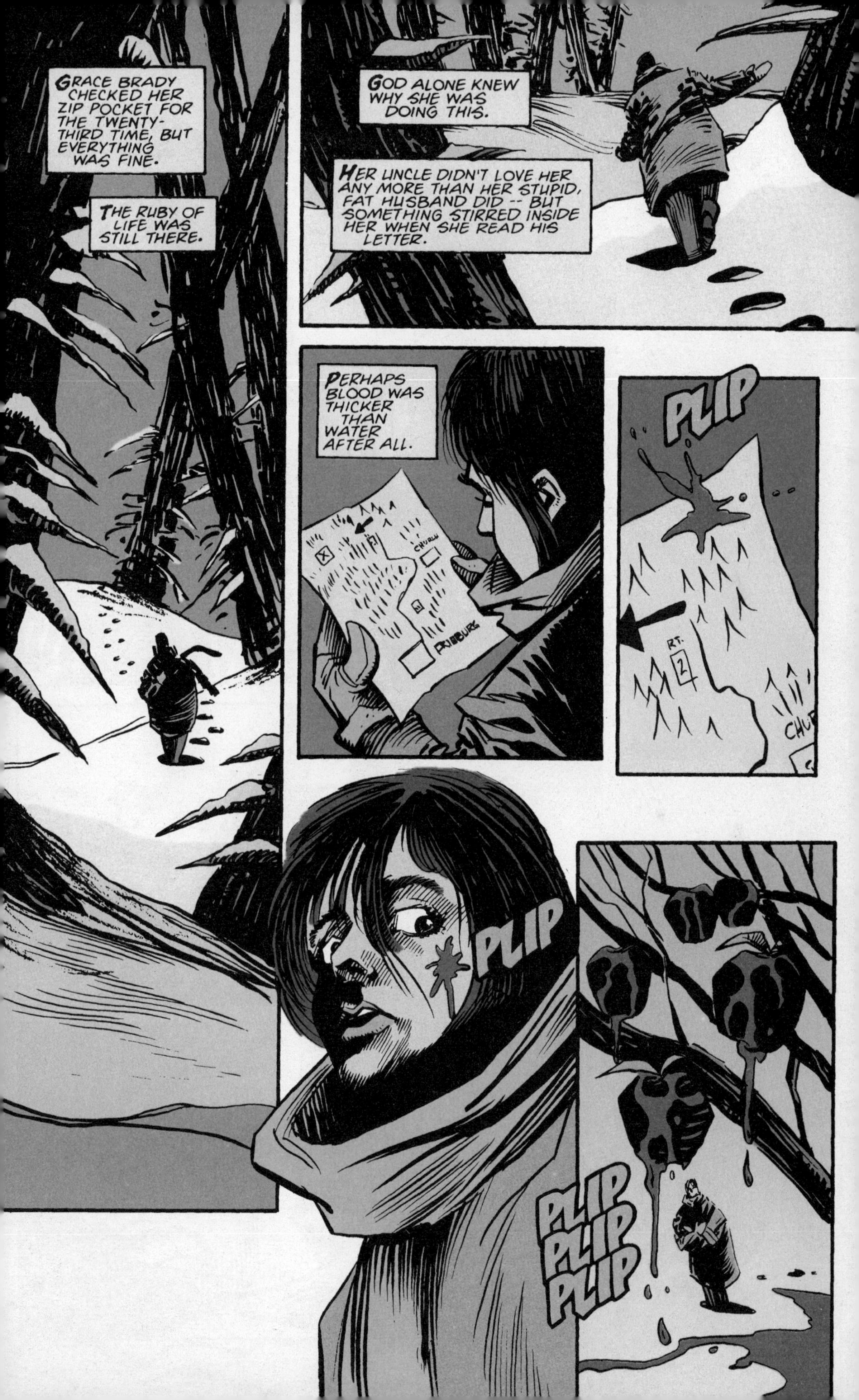
GRACE BRADY CHECKED HER ZIP POCKET FOR THE TWENTY-THIRD TIME, BUT EVERYTHING WAS FINE.
THE RUBY OF LIFE WAS STILL THERE.
GOD ALONE KNEW WHY SHE WAS DOING THIS.
HER UNCLE DIDN'T LOVE HER ANY MORE THAN HER STUPID, FAT HUSBAND DID -- BUT SOMETHING STIRRED INSIDE HER WHEN SHE READ HIS LETTER.
PERHAPS BLOOD WAS THICKER THAN WATER AFTER ALL.
CHURCH
PRIBURG
PLIP
RT.
2
PLIP
PLIP
PLIP
PLIP

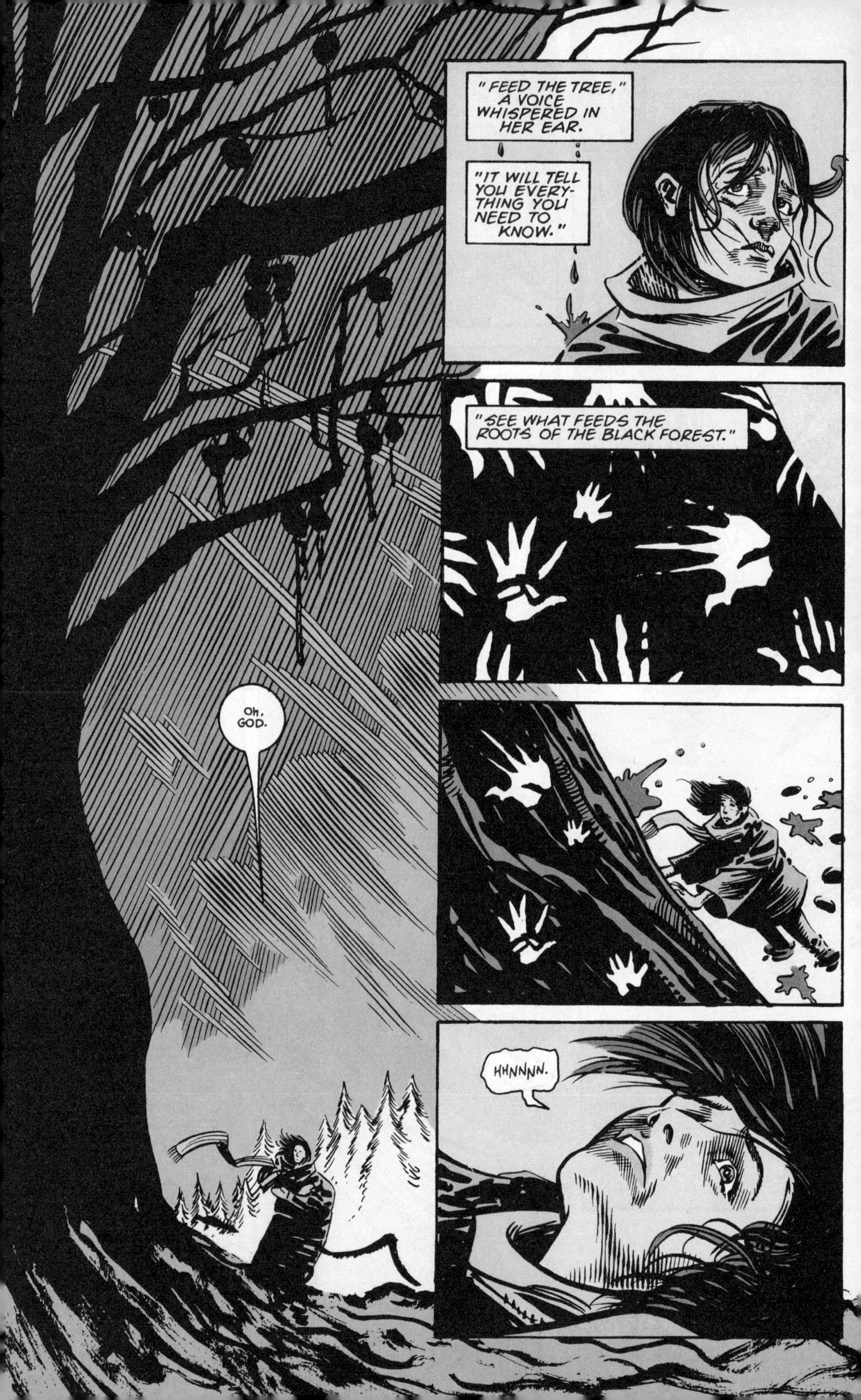
"FEED THE TREE," A VOICE WHISPERED IN HER EAR.
"IT WILL TELL YOU EVERYTHING YOU NEED TO KNOW."
"SEE WHAT FEEDS THE ROOTS OF THE BLACK FOREST."
OH, GOD.
HHNNNN.

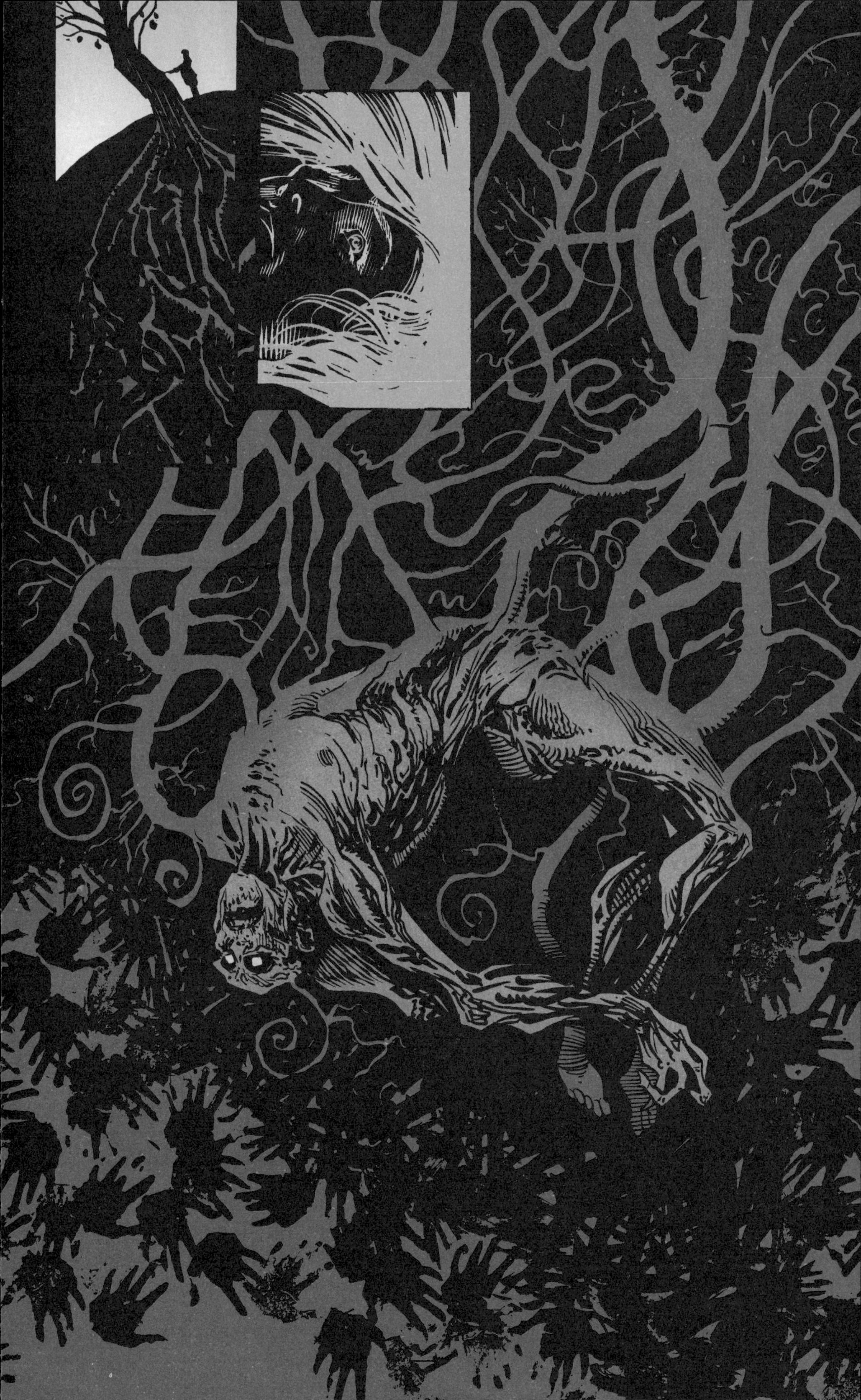

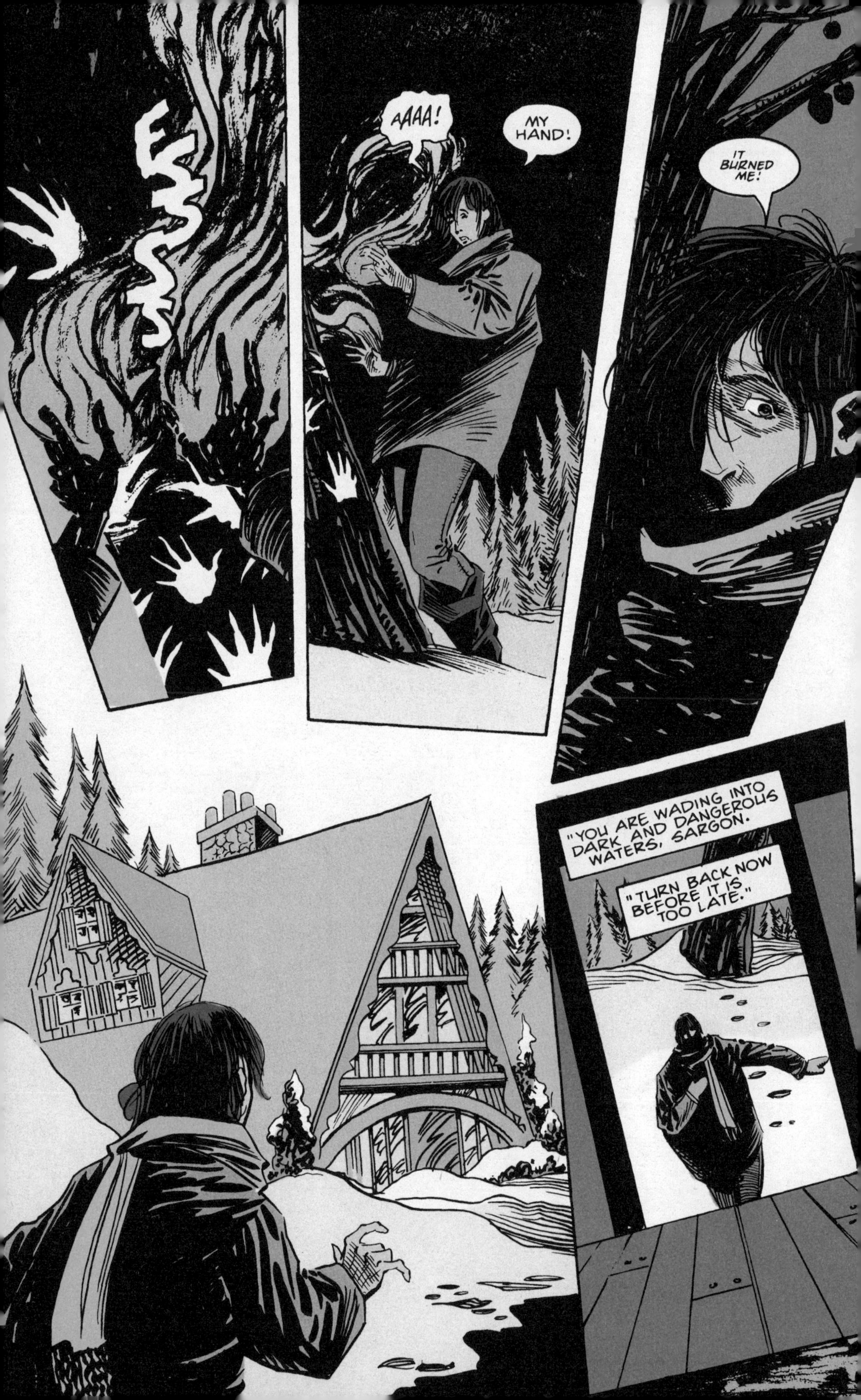
AAAA!
MY HAND!
IT BURNED ME!
"YOU ARE WADING INTO DARK AND DANGEROUS WATERS, SARGON.
"TURN BACK NOW BEFORE IT IS TOO LATE."

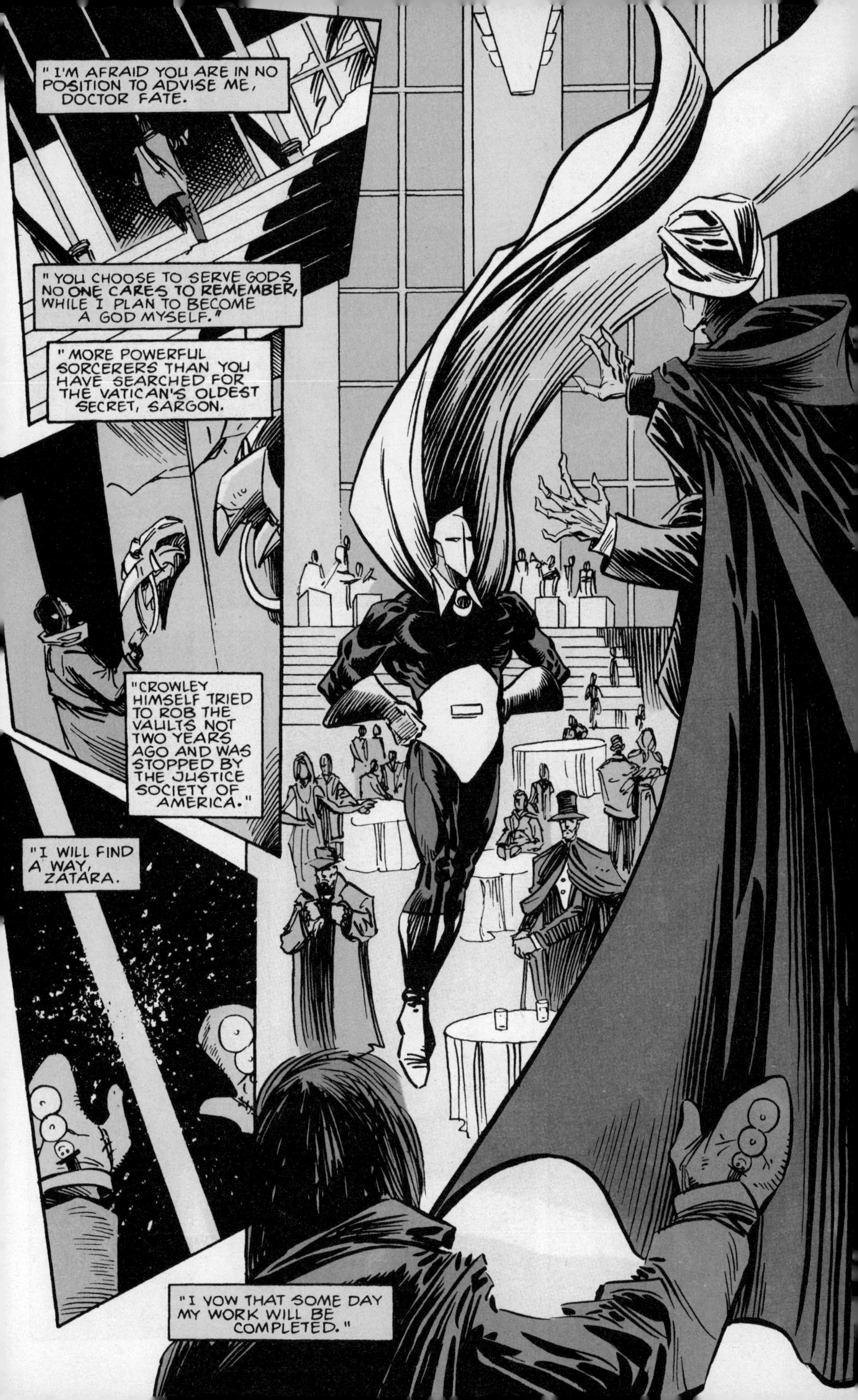
"I'M AFRAID YOU ARE IN NO POSITION TO ADVISE ME, DOCTOR FATE.
"YOU CHOOSE TO SERVE GODS NO ONE CARES TO REMEMBER, WHILE I PLAN TO BECOME A GOD MYSELF."
"MORE POWERFUL SORCERERS THAN YOU HAVE SEARCHED FOR THE VATICAN'S OLDEST SECRET, SARGON.
"CROWLEY HIMSELF TRIED TO ROB THE VAULTS NOT TWO YEARS AGO AND WAS STOPPED BY THE JUSTICE SOCIETY OF AMERICA."
"I WILL FIND A WAY, ZATARA.
"I VOW THAT SOME DAY MY WORK WILL BE COMPLETED."

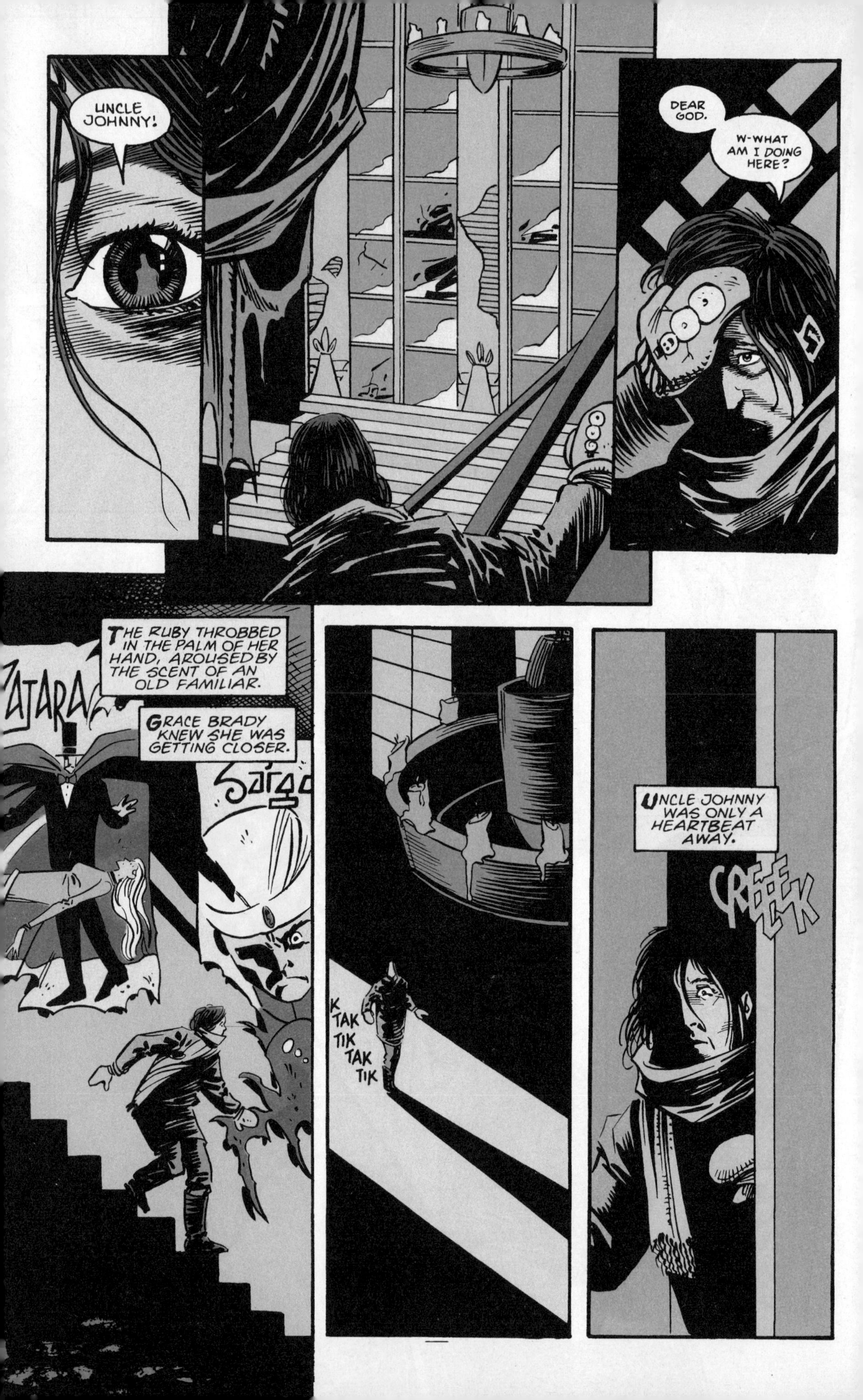
UNCLE JOHNNY!
DEAR GOD.
W-WHAT AM I DOING HERE?
THE RUBY THROBBED IN THE PALM OF HER HAND, AROUSED BY THE SCENT OF AN OLD FAMILIAR.
GRACE BRADY KNEW SHE WAS GETTING CLOSER.
K TAK TIK TAK TIK
UNCLE JOHNNY WAS ONLY A HEARTBEAT AWAY.
CREEEK

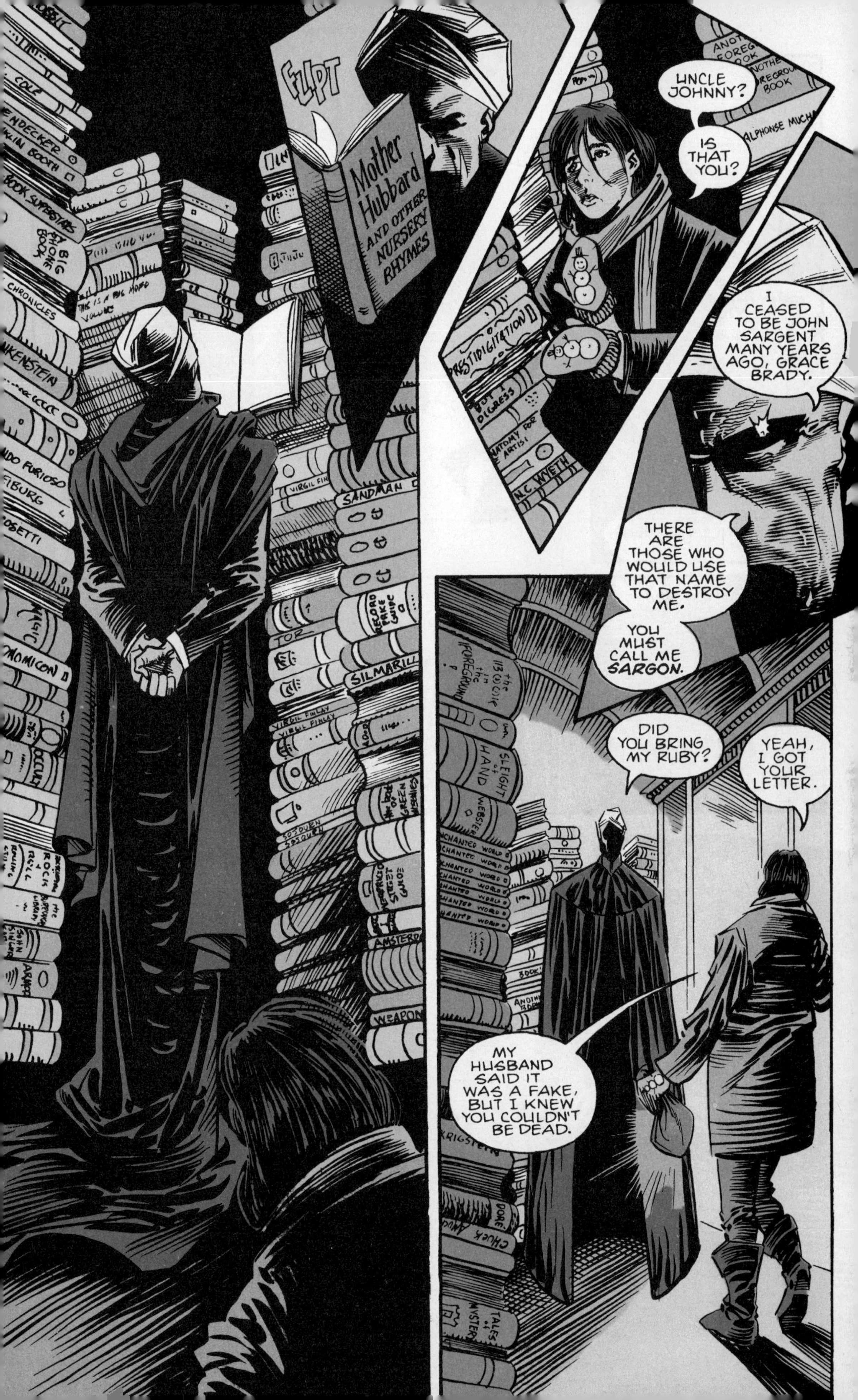
UNCLE JOHNNY?
IS THAT YOU?
I CEASED TO BE JOHN SARGENT MANY YEARS AGO, GRACE BRADY.
THERE ARE THOSE WHO WOULD USE THAT NAME TO DESTROY ME.
YOU MUST CALL ME SARGON.
DID YOU BRING MY RUBY?
YEAH, I GOT YOUR LETTER.
MY HUSBAND SAID IT WAS A FAKE, BUT I KNEW YOU COULDN'T BE DEAD.

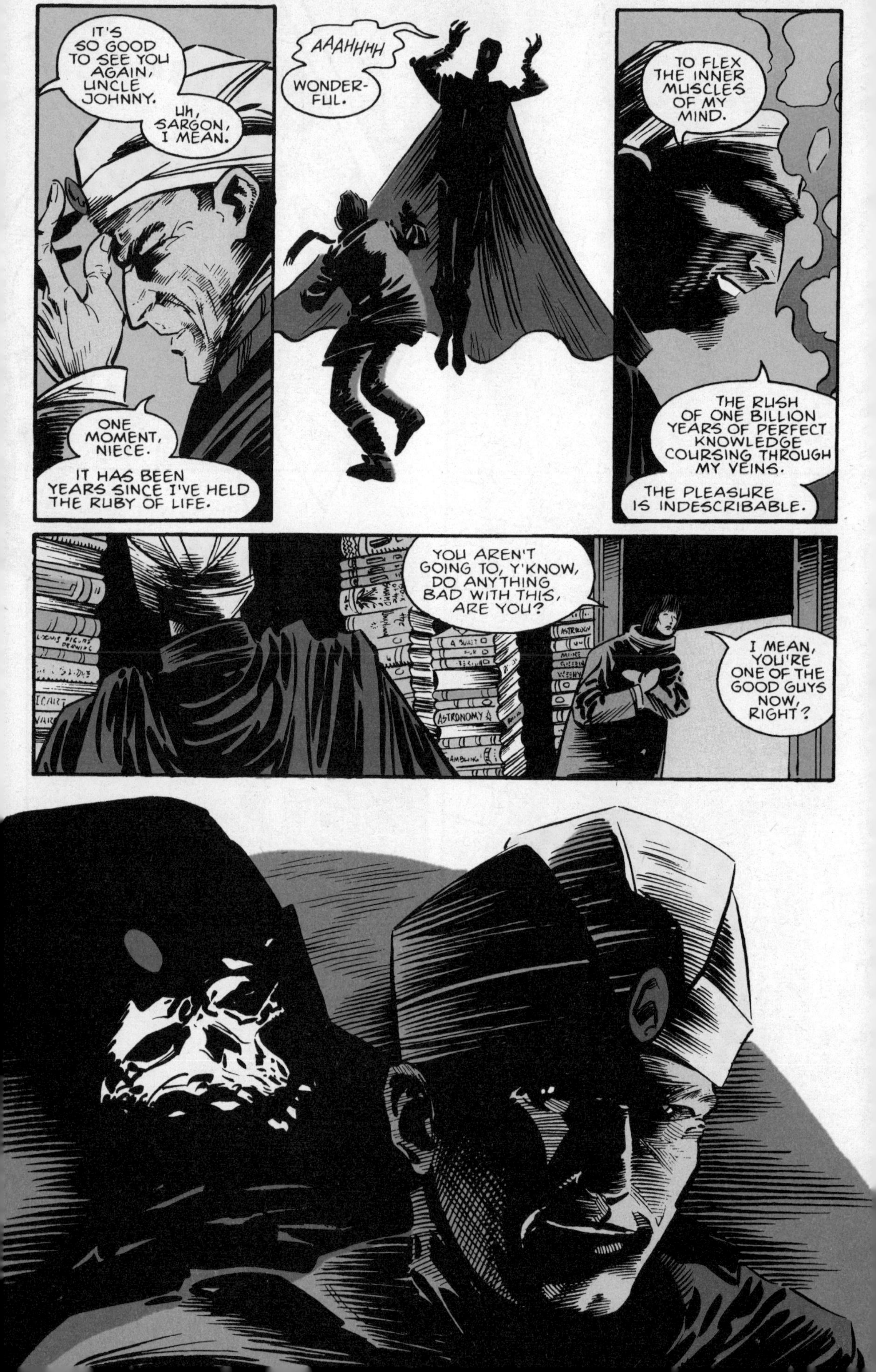
IT'S SO GOOD TO SEE YOU AGAIN, UNCLE JOHNNY.
UH, SARGON, I MEAN.
ONE MOMENT, NIECE.
IT HAS BEEN YEARS SINCE I'VE HELD THE RUBY OF LIFE.
AAAHHHH
WONDER-FUL.
TO FLEX THE INNER MUSCLES OF MY MIND.
THE RUSH OF ONE BILLION YEARS OF PERFECT KNOWLEDGE COURSING THROUGH MY VEINS.
THE PLEASURE IS INDESCRIBABLE.
YOU AREN'T GOING TO, Y'KNOW, DO ANYTHING BAD WITH THIS, ARE YOU?
I MEAN, YOU'RE ONE OF THE GOOD GUYS NOW, RIGHT?
ASTRONOMY

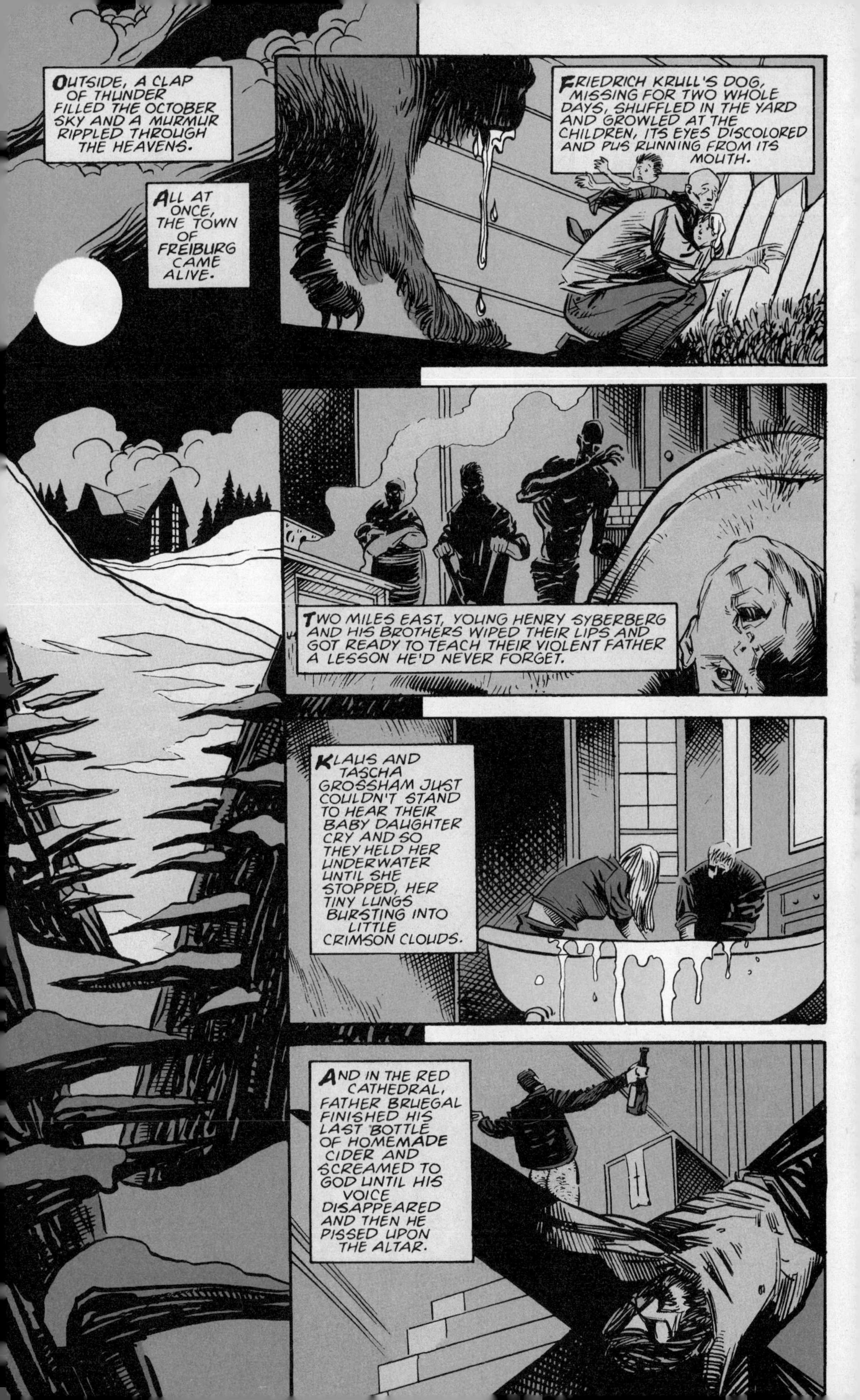
OUTSIDE, A CLAP OF THUNDER FILLED THE OCTOBER SKY AND A MURMUR RIPPLED THROUGH THE HEAVENS.
ALL AT ONCE, THE TOWN OF FREIBURG CAME ALIVE.
FRIEDRICH KRULL'S DOG, MISSING FOR TWO WHOLE DAYS, SHUFFLED IN THE YARD AND GROWLED AT THE CHILDREN, ITS EYES DISCOLORED AND PUS RUNNING FROM ITS MOUTH.
TWO MILES EAST, YOUNG HENRY SYBERBERG AND HIS BROTHERS WIPED THEIR LIPS AND GOT READY TO TEACH THEIR VIOLENT FATHER A LESSON HE'D NEVER FORGET.
KLAUS AND TASCHA GROSSHAM JUST COULDN'T STAND TO HEAR THEIR BABY DAUGHTER CRY AND SO THEY HELD HER UNDERWATER UNTIL SHE STOPPED, HER TINY LUNGS BURSTING INTO LITTLE CRIMSON CLOUDS.
AND IN THE RED CATHEDRAL, FATHER BRUEGAL FINISHED HIS LAST BOTTLE OF HOMEMADE CIDER AND SCREAMED TO GOD UNTIL HIS VOICE DISAPPEARED AND THEN HE PISSED UPON THE ALTAR.

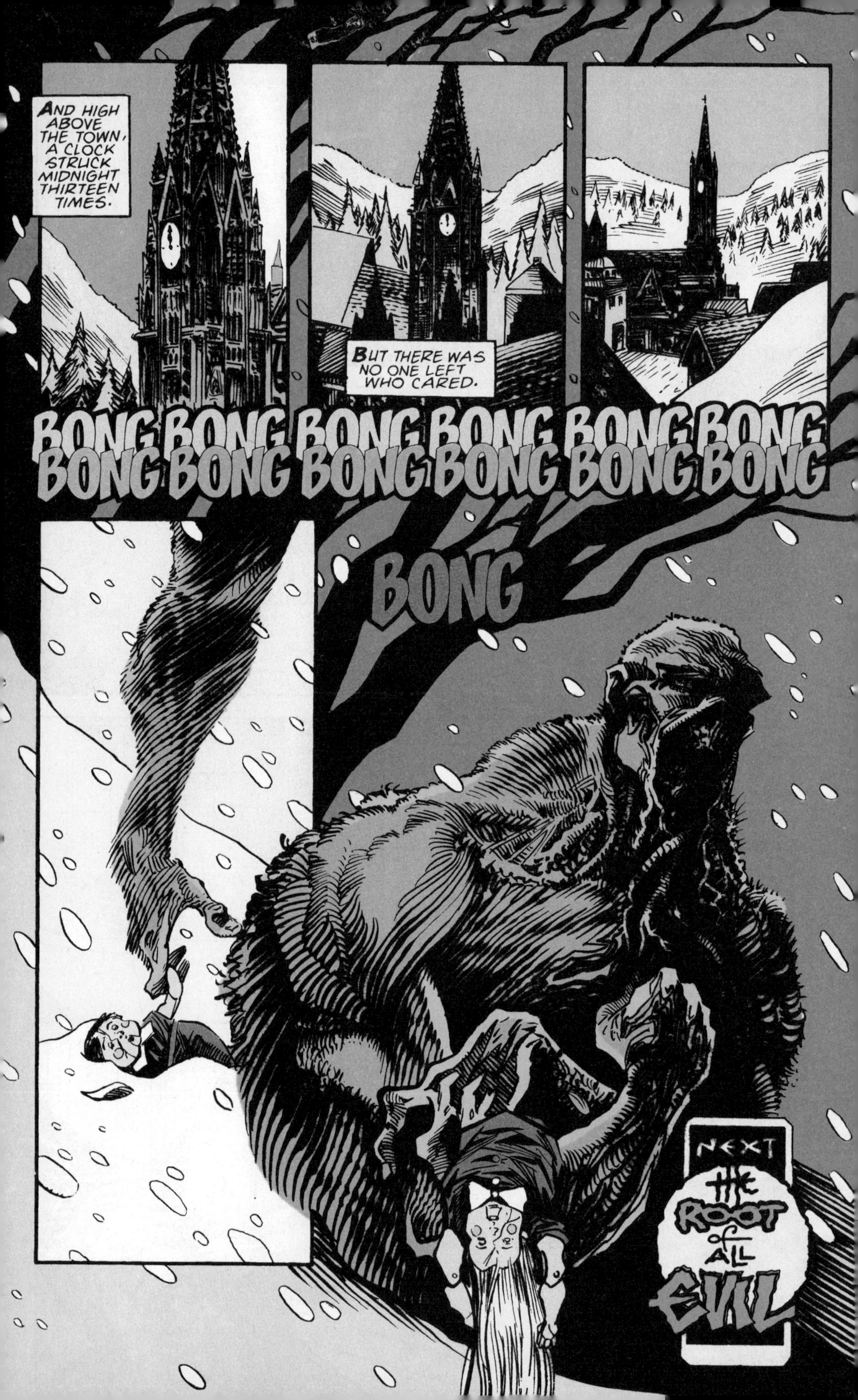

AND HIGH ABOVE THE TOWN, A CLOCK STRUCK MIDNIGHT THIRTEEN TIMES.
BUT THERE WAS NO ONE LEFT WHO CARED.
BONG BONG BONG BONG BONG BONG
BONG BONG BONG BONG BONG BONG
BONG
NEXT
THE ROOT of ALL EVIL

DC
VERTIGO
Swamp
THING
0. 149
EC 94
1.95 US
2.75 CAN
1.25 UK
UGGESTED
OR MATURE
EADERS
J. Mueller 94
Joker
GRAVE
DIGGER
OLD
666
GOOD OL'
WHISKEY
MARK MILLAR
PHILLIP HESTER
KIM DEMULDER

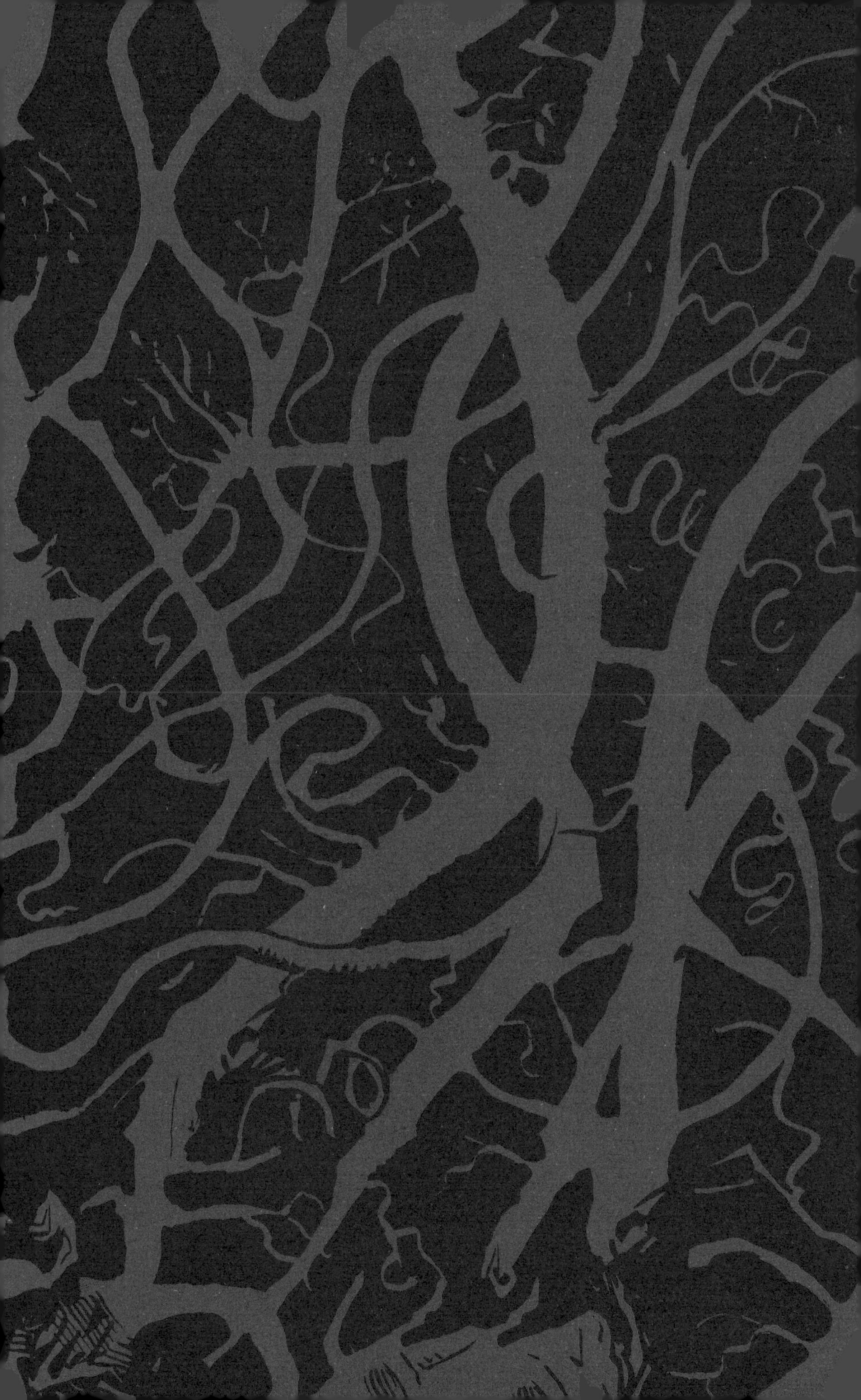

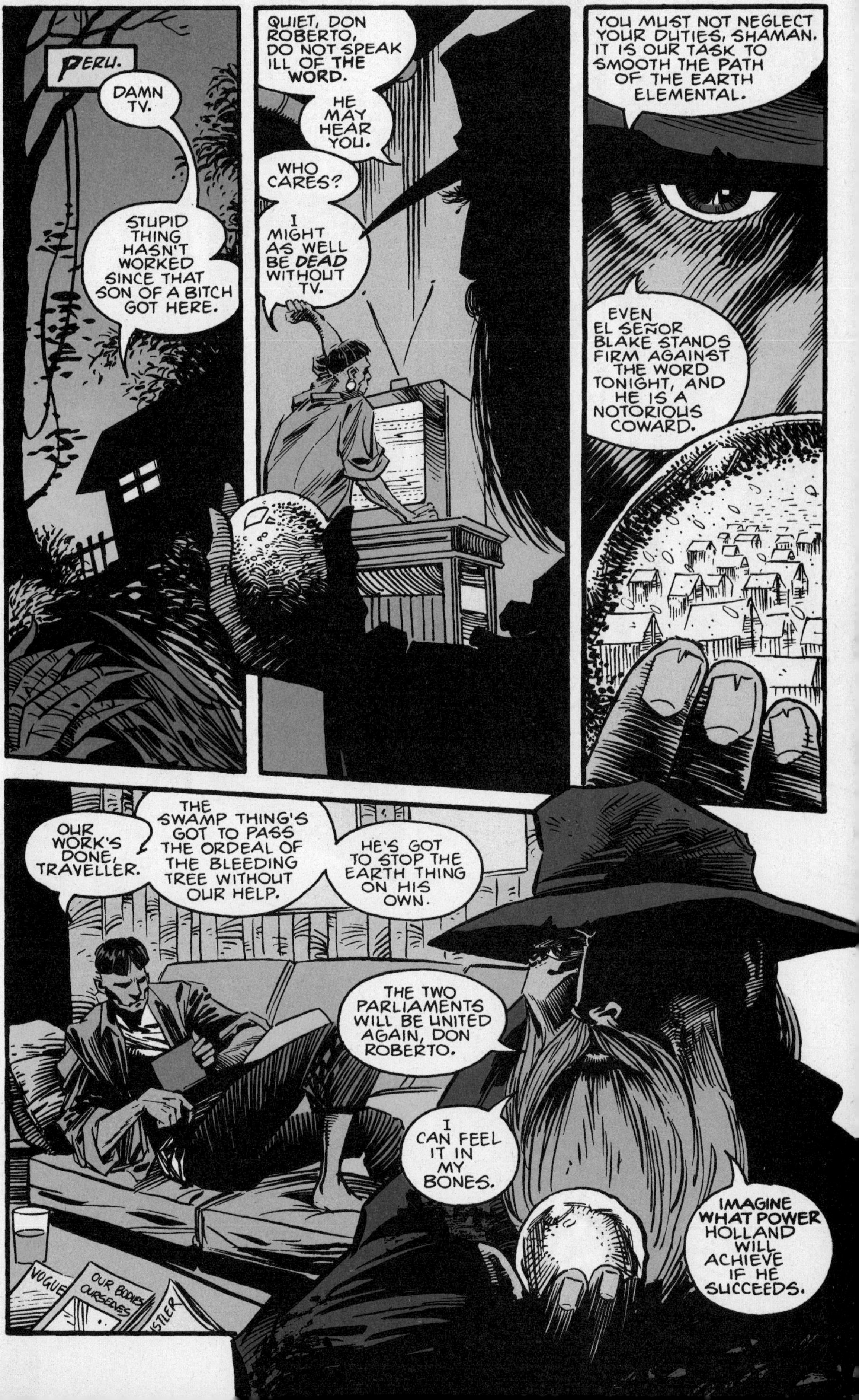
PERU.
DAMN TV.
STUPID THING HASN'T WORKED SINCE THAT SON OF A BITCH GOT HERE.
QUIET, DON ROBERTO, DO NOT SPEAK ILL OF THE WORD.
HE MAY HEAR YOU.
WHO CARES?
I MIGHT AS WELL BE DEAD WITHOUT TV.
YOU MUST NOT NEGLECT YOUR DUTIES, SHAMAN. IT IS OUR TASK TO SMOOTH THE PATH OF THE EARTH ELEMENTAL.
EVEN EL SEÑOR BLAKE STANDS FIRM AGAINST THE WORD TONIGHT, AND HE IS A NOTORIOUS COWARD.
OUR WORK'S DONE, TRAVELLER.
THE SWAMP THING'S GOT TO PASS THE ORDEAL OF THE BLEEDING TREE WITHOUT OUR HELP.
HE'S GOT TO STOP THE EARTH THING ON HIS OWN.
THE TWO PARLIAMENTS WILL BE UNITED AGAIN, DON ROBERTO.
I CAN FEEL IT IN MY BONES.
IMAGINE WHAT POWER HOLLAND WILL ACHIEVE IF HE SUCCEEDS.
VOGUE
OUR BODIES OURSELVES

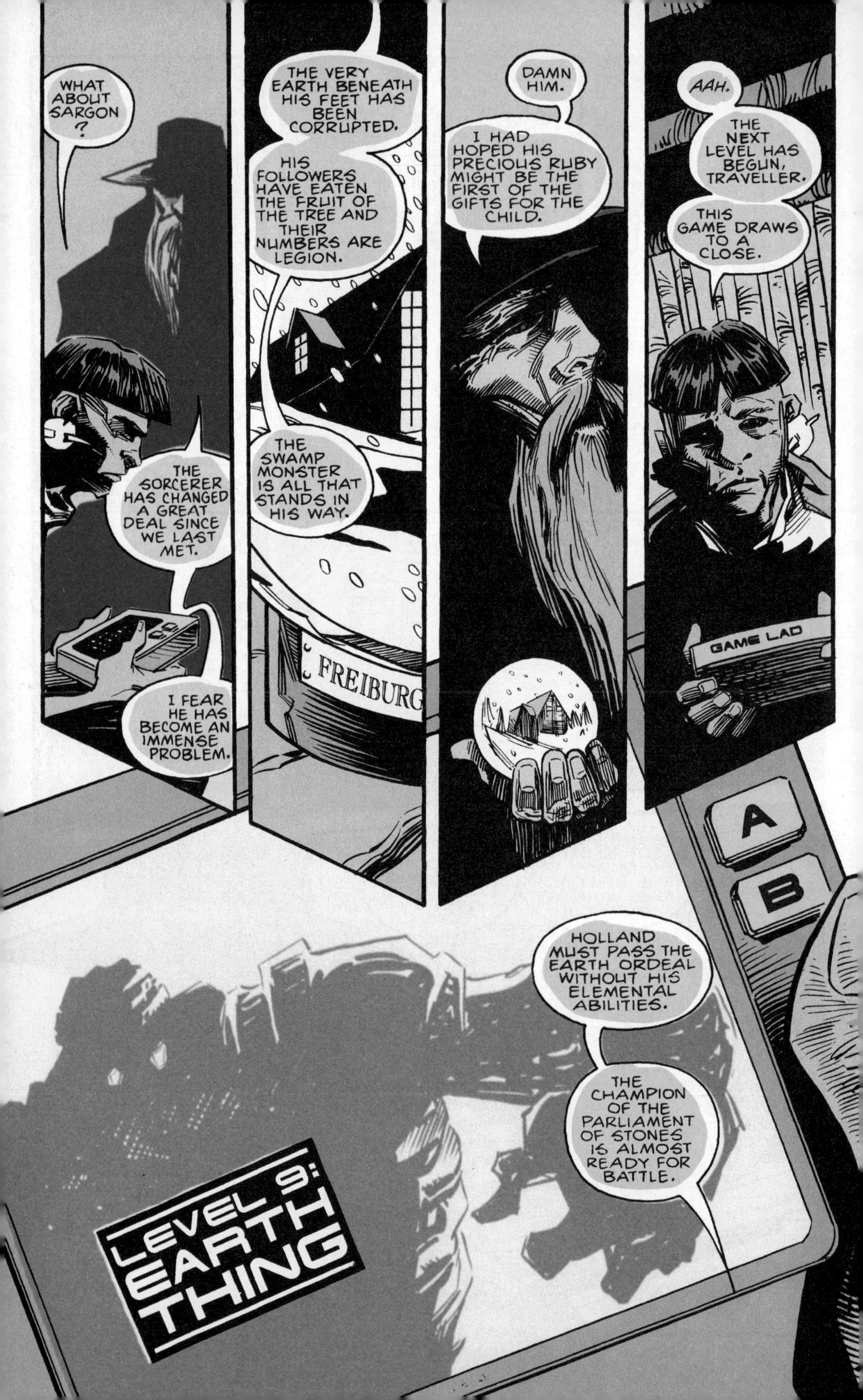
WHAT ABOUT SARGON?
THE SORCERER HAS CHANGED A GREAT DEAL SINCE WE LAST MET.
I FEAR HE HAS BECOME AN IMMENSE PROBLEM.
THE VERY EARTH BENEATH HIS FEET HAS BEEN CORRUPTED.
HIS FOLLOWERS HAVE EATEN THE FRUIT OF THE TREE AND THEIR NUMBERS ARE LEGION.
THE SWAMP MONSTER IS ALL THAT STANDS IN HIS WAY.
FREIBURG
DAMN HIM.
I HAD HOPED HIS PRECIOUS RUBY MIGHT BE THE FIRST OF THE GIFTS FOR THE CHILD.
AAH.
THE NEXT LEVEL HAS BEGUN, TRAVELLER.
THIS GAME DRAWS TO A CLOSE.
GAME LAD
A
B
HOLLAND MUST PASS THE EARTH ORDEAL WITHOUT HIS ELEMENTAL ABILITIES.
THE CHAMPION OF THE PARLIAMENT OF STONES IS ALMOST READY FOR BATTLE.
LEVEL 9: EARTH THING

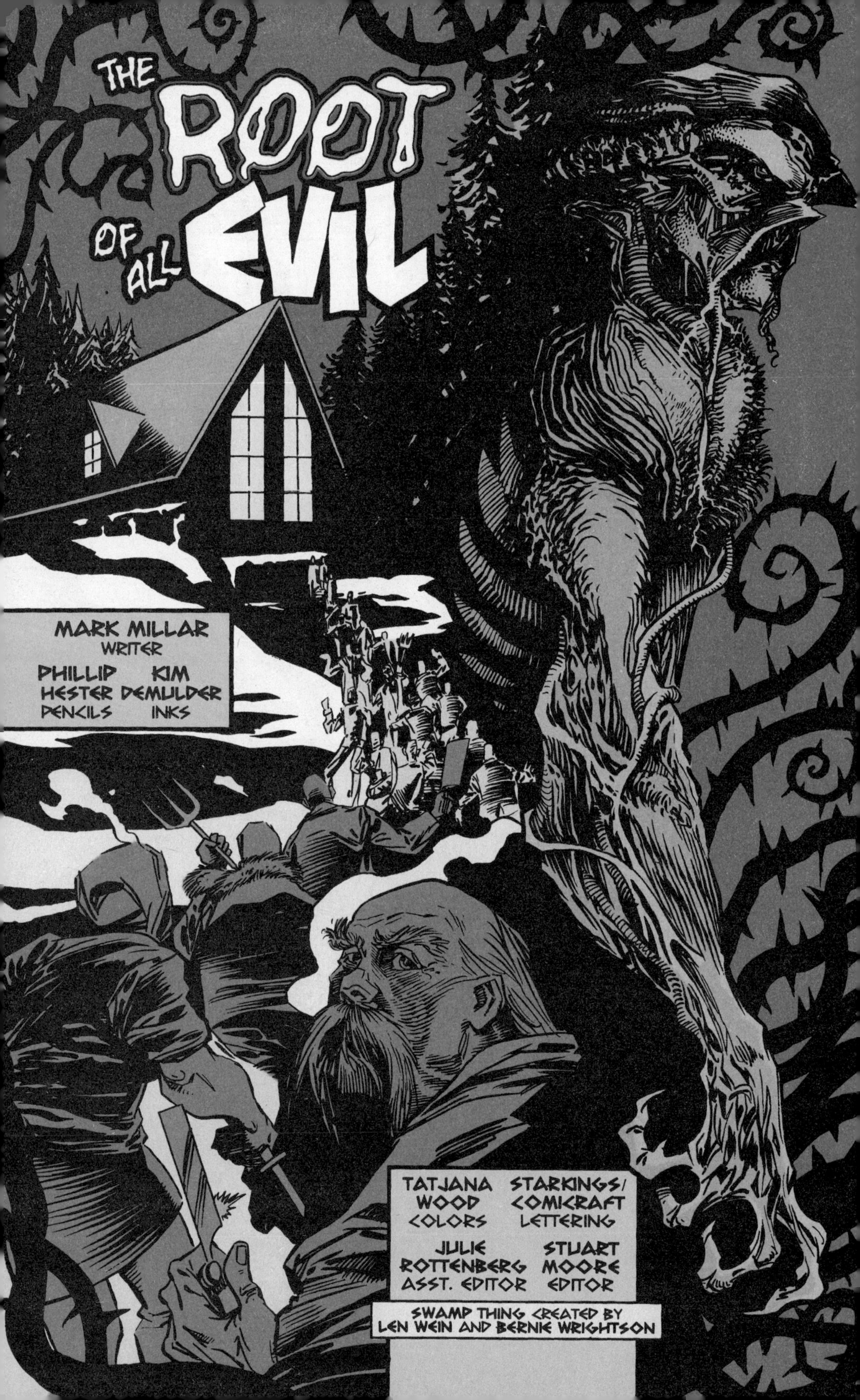
THE ROOT OF ALL EVIL
MARK MILLAR WRITER
PHILLIP HESTER PENCILS
KIM DEMULDER INKS
TATJANA WOOD COLORS
STARKINGS/ COMICRAFT LETTERING
JULIE ROTTENBERG ASST. EDITOR
STUART MOORE EDITOR
SWAMP THING CREATED BY LEN WEIN AND BERNIE WRIGHTSON

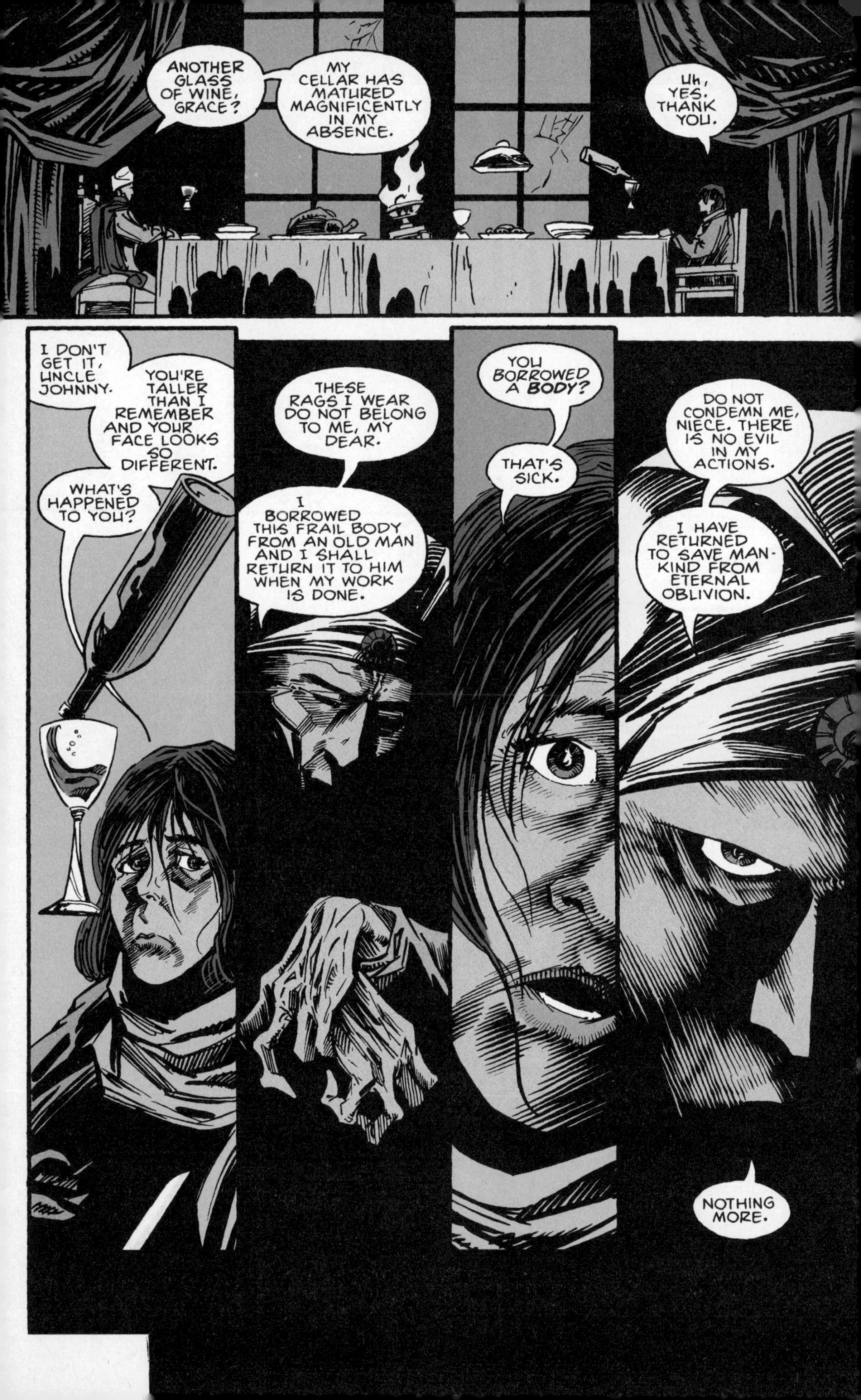
ANOTHER GLASS OF WINE, GRACE?
MY CELLAR HAS MATURED MAGNIFICENTLY IN MY ABSENCE.
UH, YES. THANK YOU.
I DON'T GET IT, UNCLE JOHNNY.
YOU'RE TALLER THAN I REMEMBER AND YOUR FACE LOOKS SO DIFFERENT.
WHAT'S HAPPENED TO YOU?
THESE RAGS I WEAR DO NOT BELONG TO ME, MY DEAR.
I BORROWED THIS FRAIL BODY FROM AN OLD MAN AND I SHALL RETURN IT TO HIM WHEN MY WORK IS DONE.
YOU BORROWED A BODY?
THAT'S SICK.
DO NOT CONDEMN ME, NIECE. THERE IS NO EVIL IN MY ACTIONS.
I HAVE RETURNED TO SAVE MAN-KIND FROM ETERNAL OBLIVION.
NOTHING MORE.

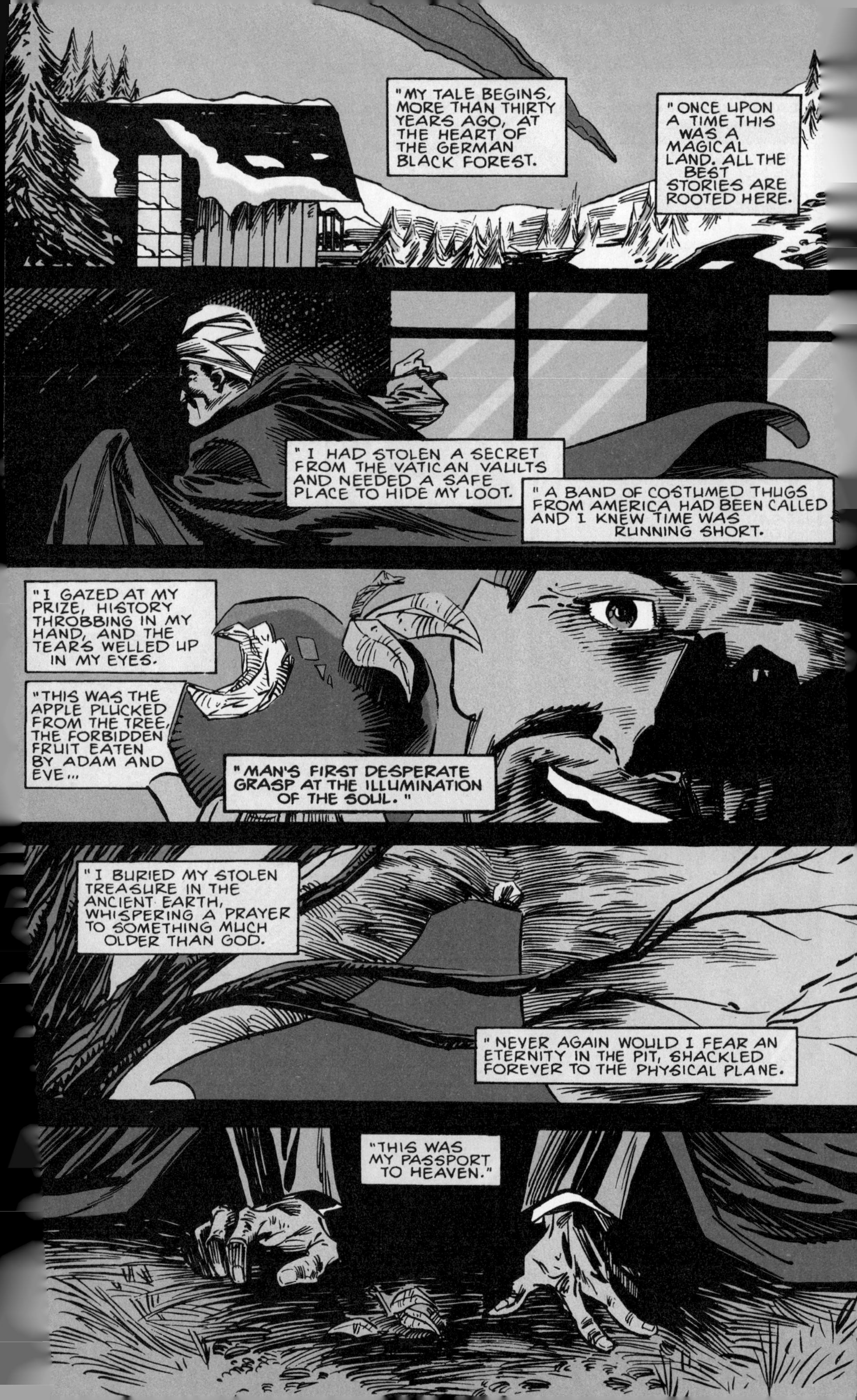
"MY TALE BEGINS, MORE THAN THIRTY YEARS AGO, AT THE HEART OF THE GERMAN BLACK FOREST.
"ONCE UPON A TIME THIS WAS A MAGICAL LAND. ALL THE BEST STORIES ARE ROOTED HERE.
"I HAD STOLEN A SECRET FROM THE VATICAN VAULTS AND NEEDED A SAFE PLACE TO HIDE MY LOOT.
"A BAND OF COSTUMED THUGS FROM AMERICA HAD BEEN CALLED AND I KNEW TIME WAS RUNNING SHORT.
"I GAZED AT MY PRIZE, HISTORY THROBBING IN MY HAND, AND THE TEARS WELLED UP IN MY EYES.
"THIS WAS THE APPLE PLUCKED FROM THE TREE, THE FORBIDDEN FRUIT EATEN BY ADAM AND EVE...
"MAN'S FIRST DESPERATE GRASP AT THE ILLUMINATION OF THE SOUL."
"I BURIED MY STOLEN TREASURE IN THE ANCIENT EARTH, WHISPERING A PRAYER TO SOMETHING MUCH OLDER THAN GOD.
"NEVER AGAIN WOULD I FEAR AN ETERNITY IN THE PIT, SHACKLED FOREVER TO THE PHYSICAL PLANE.
"THIS WAS MY PASSPORT TO HEAVEN."

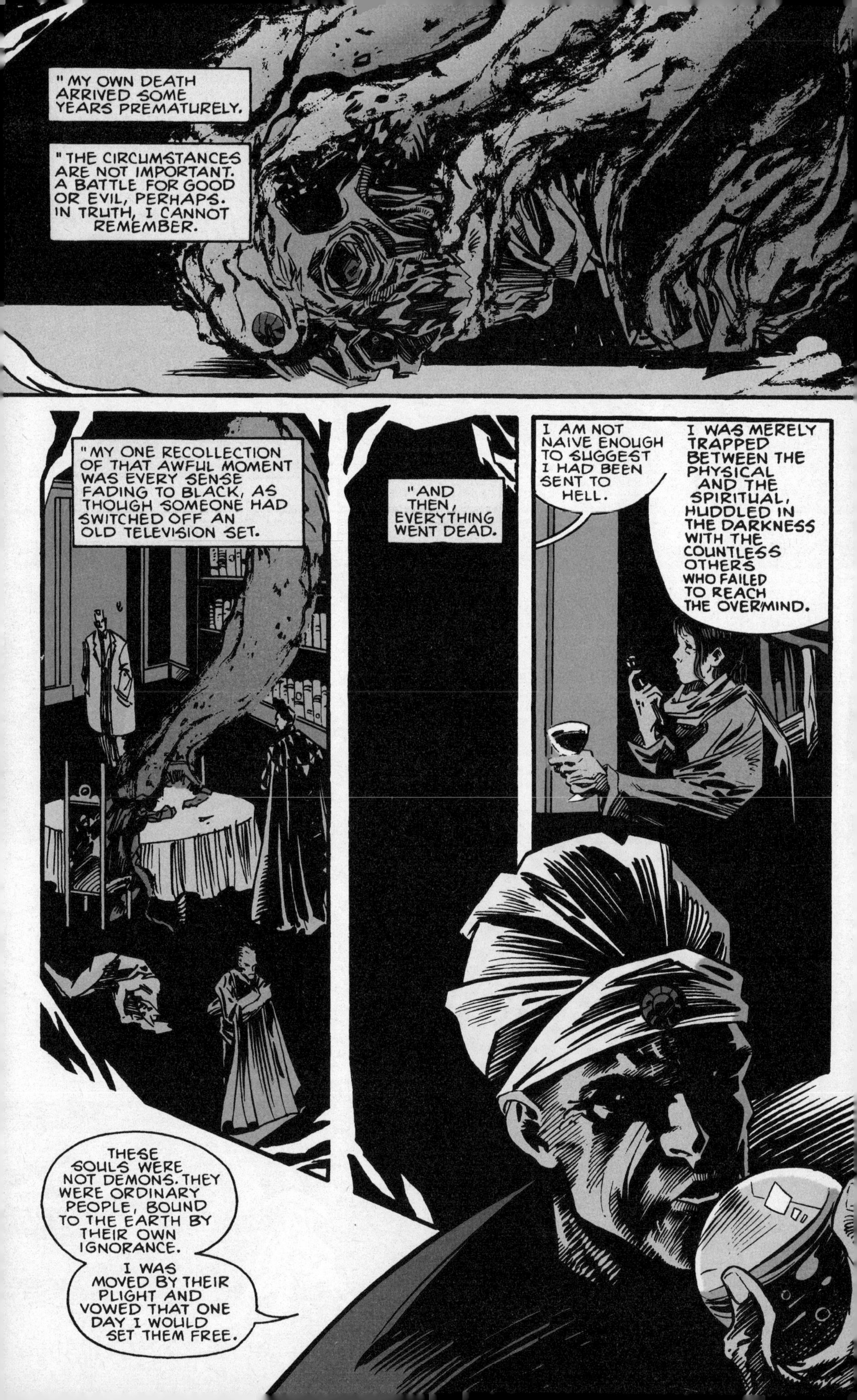
"MY OWN DEATH ARRIVED SOME YEARS PREMATURELY.
"THE CIRCUMSTANCES ARE NOT IMPORTANT. A BATTLE FOR GOOD OR EVIL, PERHAPS. IN TRUTH, I CANNOT REMEMBER.
"MY ONE RECOLLECTION OF THAT AWFUL MOMENT WAS EVERY SENSE FADING TO BLACK, AS THOUGH SOMEONE HAD SWITCHED OFF AN OLD TELEVISION SET.
"AND THEN, EVERYTHING WENT DEAD.
I AM NOT NAIVE ENOUGH TO SUGGEST I HAD BEEN SENT TO HELL.
I WAS MERELY TRAPPED BETWEEN THE PHYSICAL AND THE SPIRITUAL, HUDDLED IN THE DARKNESS WITH THE COUNTLESS OTHERS WHO FAILED TO REACH THE OVERMIND.
THESE SOULS WERE NOT DEMONS. THEY WERE ORDINARY PEOPLE, BOUND TO THE EARTH BY THEIR OWN IGNORANCE.
I WAS MOVED BY THEIR PLIGHT AND VOWED THAT ONE DAY I WOULD SET THEM FREE.

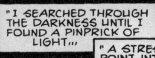

"I SEARCHED THROUGH THE DARKNESS UNTIL I FOUND A PINPRICK OF LIGHT...

" A STRESS POINT INTO THE NATURAL WORLD.

"FOCUSING ON THE CIRCLE, I MADE IT BIGGER, UNTIL I COULD SMELL THE SCENT OF HOSPITAL BLEACH...

"THE INSECT BUZZ OF CONVERSATION, GETTING LOUDER AND LOUDER, UNTIL...

"I SAT UP AND LOOKED AROUND THE WARD, AMUSED BY THE FLUTTERING OF THE NURSES, LIKE BRIGHT LITTLE BIRDS.

"MY HOST WAS WEAK AND EASY TO MANIPULATE, HAVING LAIN COMATOSE FOR A NUMBER OF YEARS.

"OUTSIDE, I COULD SMELL THE FRESH PINE OF THE BLACK FOREST AND I WAS OLD ENOUGH TO KNOW THERE IS NO SUCH THING IN THE WORLD AS COINCIDENCE.

"I KNEW I HAD BEEN SENT BACK HERE FOR A VERY SIMPLE REASON."

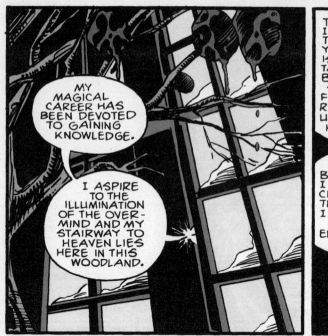

MY MAGICAL CAREER HAS BEEN DEVOTED TO GAINING KNOWLEDGE.

I ASPIRE TO THE ILLUMINATION OF THE OVER-MIND AND MY STAIRWAY TO HEAVEN LIES HERE IN THIS WOODLAND.

THE APPLE I PLANTED THIRTY YEARS AGO IS NOW A TALL TREE, BEARING STRANGE FRUIT AND REACHING UP INTO THE HEAVENS.

BRANCH BY BRANCH, I PLAN TO CLIMB THAT TREE UNTIL I REACH TRUE ENLIGHTEN-MENT.

MY VISIT TO THE HELL-WORLD TAUGHT ME ONE THING, GRACE.

I HAVE LEARNED THAT I AM THE NEW MESSIAH.

HE WHO DIED AND ROSE AGAIN.

JESUS CHRIST.

THE DEAD HAVE SHIVERED IN THE DARKNESS TOO LONG, MY DEAR.

I'M FORCING OPEN THE GATES OF PARADISE.

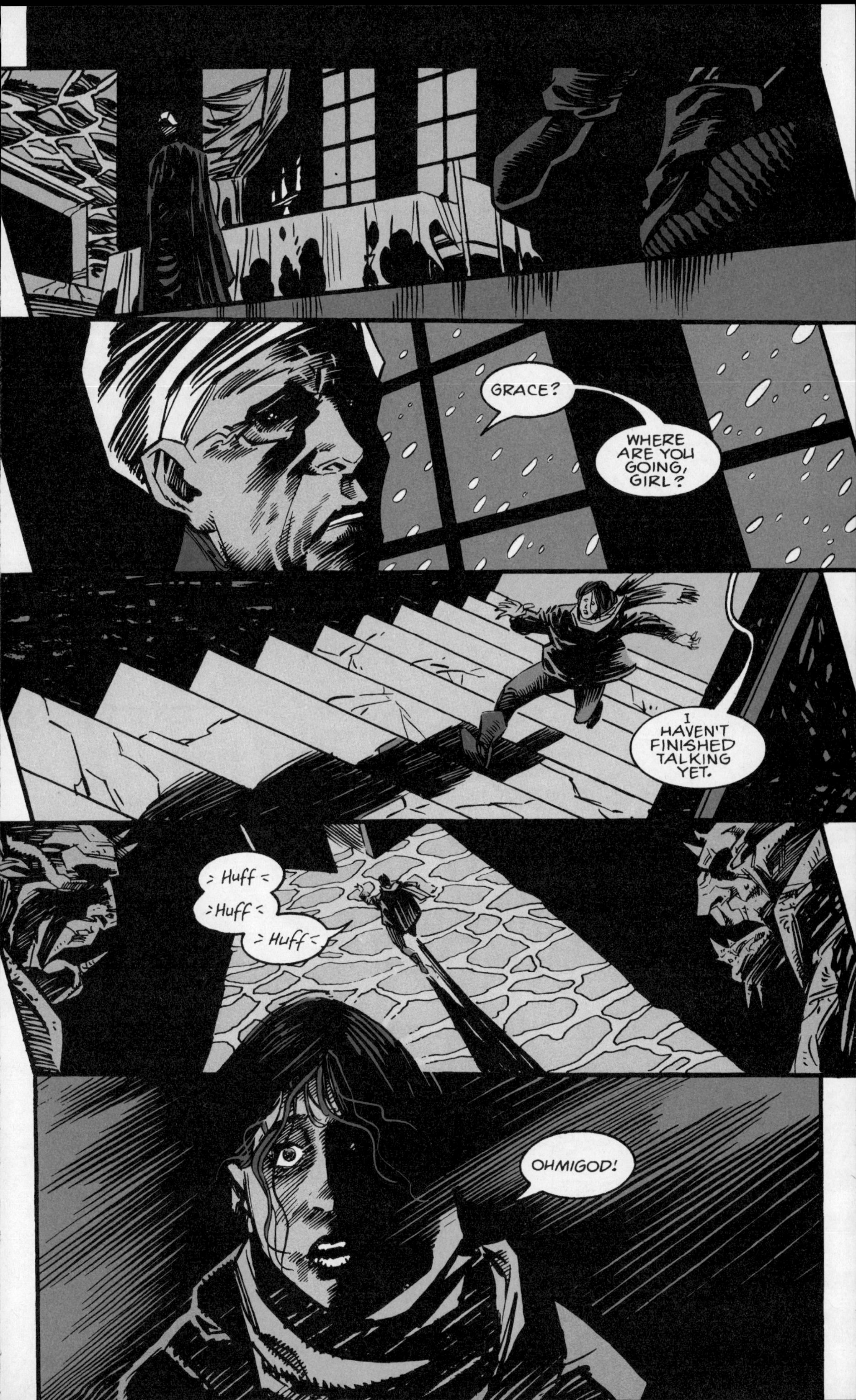
GRACE?
WHERE ARE YOU GOING, GIRL?
I HAVEN'T FINISHED TALKING YET.
> Huff <
> Huff <
> Huff <
OHMIGOD!

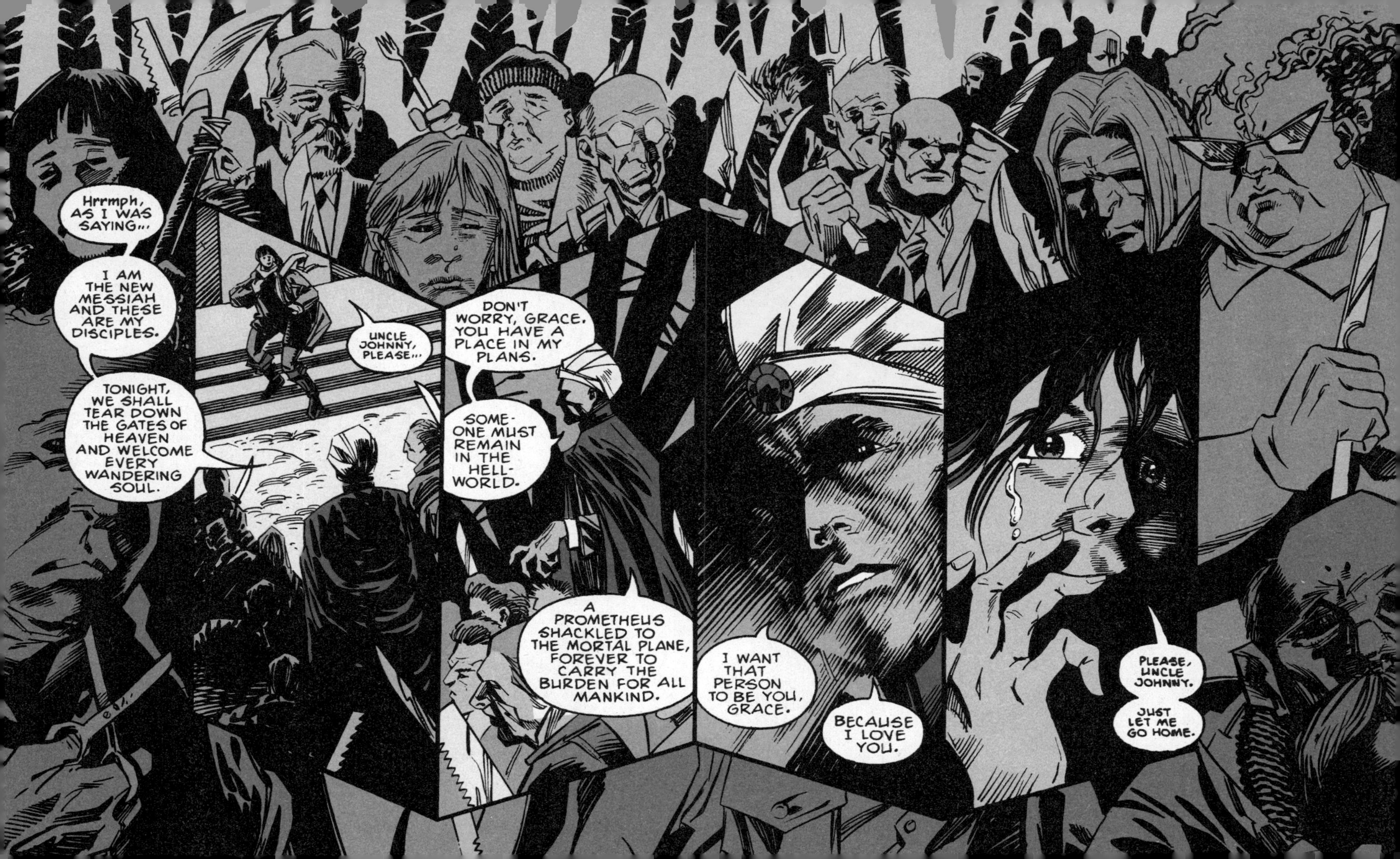
Hrrmph, AS I WAS SAYING...
I AM THE NEW MESSIAH AND THESE ARE MY DISCIPLES.
TONIGHT, WE SHALL TEAR DOWN THE GATES OF HEAVEN AND WELCOME EVERY WANDERING SOUL.
UNCLE JOHNNY, PLEASE...
DON'T WORRY, GRACE. YOU HAVE A PLACE IN MY PLANS.
SOME-ONE MUST REMAIN IN THE HELL-WORLD.
A PROMETHEUS SHACKLED TO THE MORTAL PLANE, FOREVER TO CARRY THE BURDEN FOR ALL MANKIND.
I WANT THAT PERSON TO BE YOU, GRACE.
BECAUSE I LOVE YOU.
PLEASE, UNCLE JOHNNY.
JUST LET ME GO HOME.

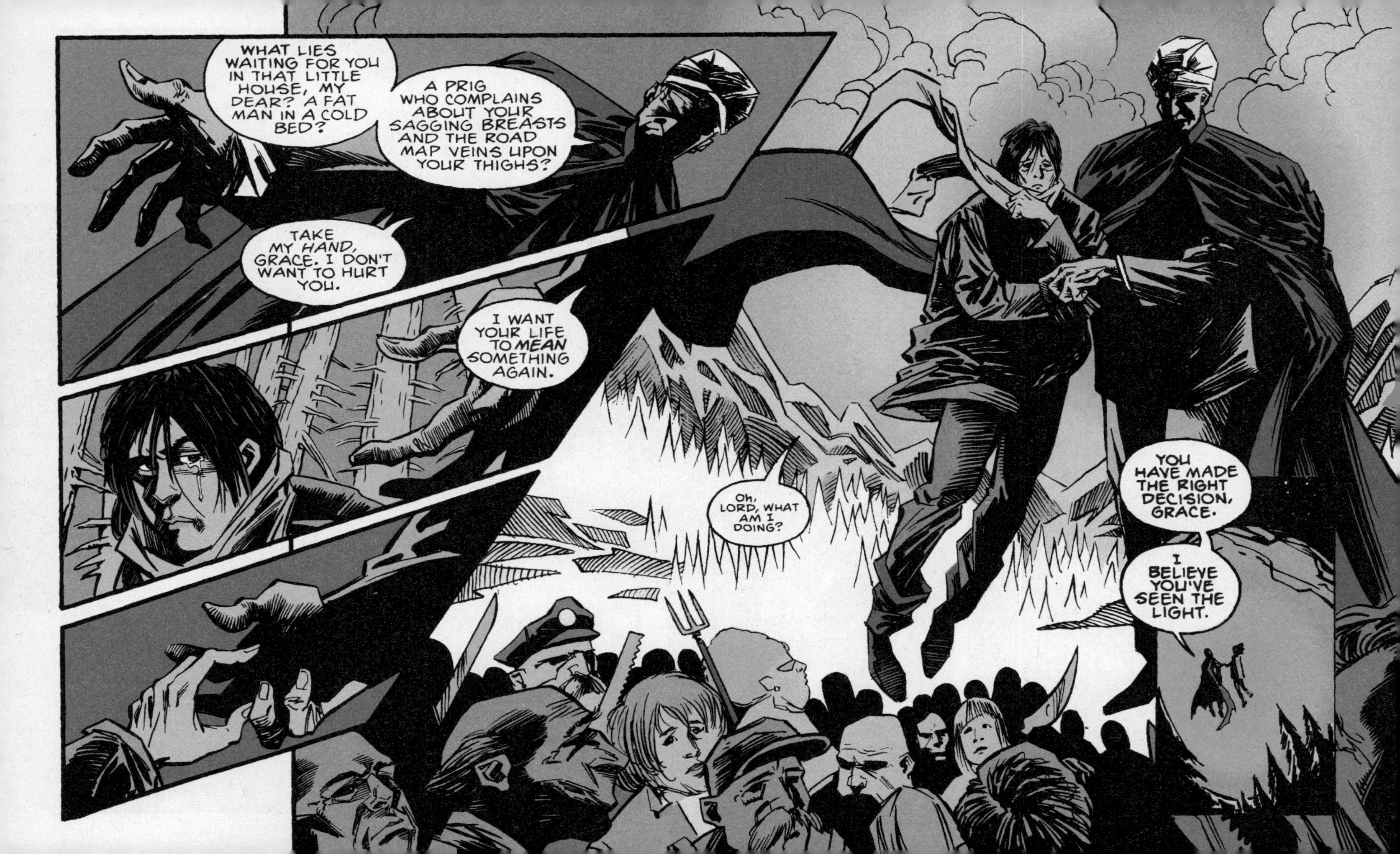
WHAT LIES WAITING FOR YOU IN THAT LITTLE HOUSE, MY DEAR? A FAT MAN IN A COLD BED?
A PRIG WHO COMPLAINS ABOUT YOUR SAGGING BREASTS AND THE ROAD MAP VEINS UPON YOUR THIGHS?
TAKE MY HAND, GRACE. I DON'T WANT TO HURT YOU.
I WANT YOUR LIFE TO MEAN SOMETHING AGAIN.
Oh, LORD, WHAT AM I DOING?
YOU HAVE MADE THE RIGHT DECISION, GRACE.
I BELIEVE YOU'VE SEEN THE LIGHT.

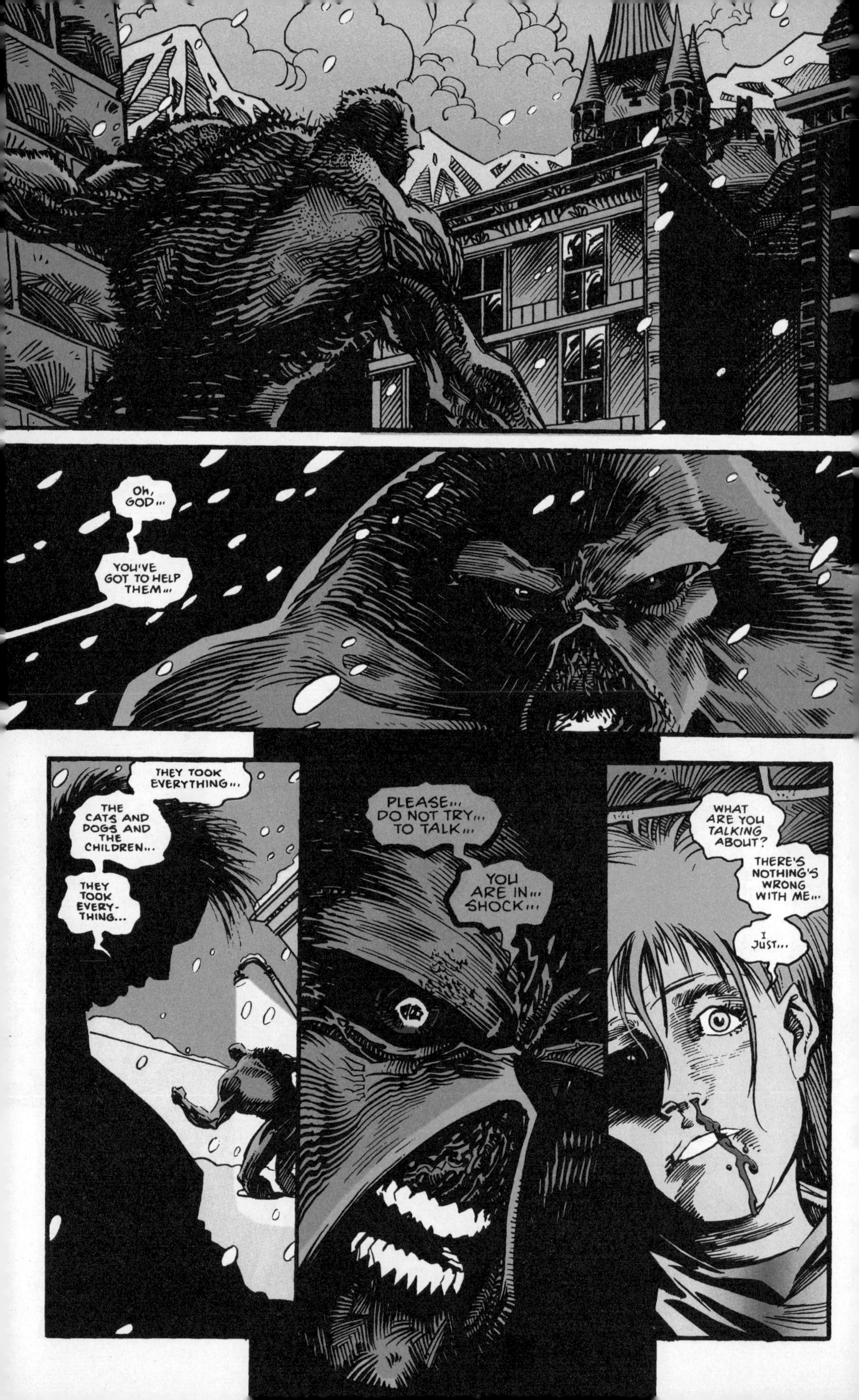

OH, GOD...
YOU'VE GOT TO HELP THEM...
THEY TOOK EVERYTHING...
THE CATS AND DOGS AND THE CHILDREN...
THEY TOOK EVERY-THING...
PLEASE... DO NOT TRY... TO TALK...
YOU ARE IN... SHOCK...
WHAT ARE YOU TALKING ABOUT?
THERE'S NOTHING'S WRONG WITH ME...
I JUST...

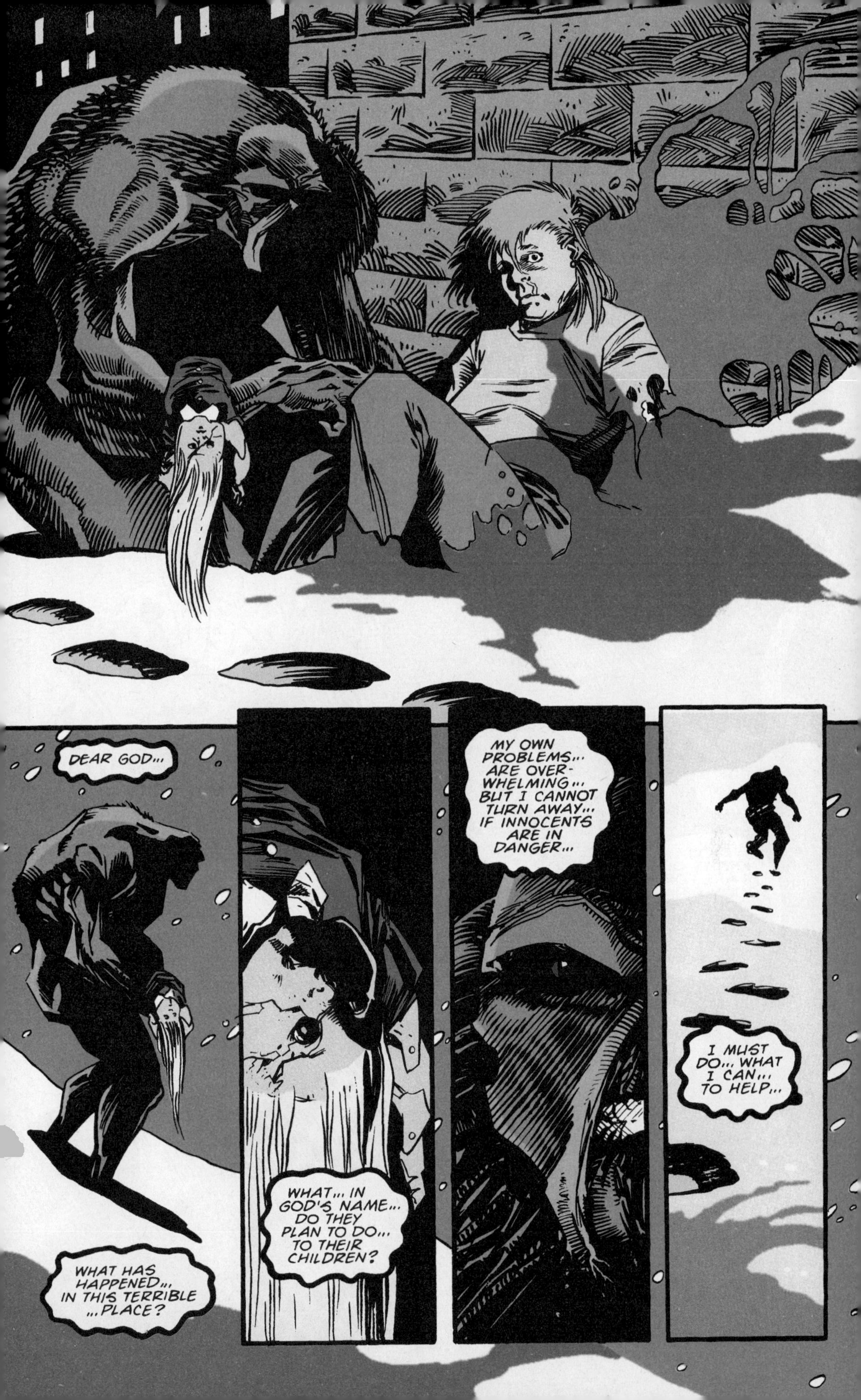
DEAR GOD...
WHAT HAS HAPPENED... IN THIS TERRIBLE ...PLACE?
WHAT... IN GOD'S NAME... DO THEY PLAN TO DO... TO THEIR CHILDREN?
MY OWN PROBLEMS... ARE OVER-WHELMING... BUT I CANNOT TURN AWAY... IF INNOCENTS ARE IN DANGER...
I MUST DO... WHAT I CAN... TO HELP...

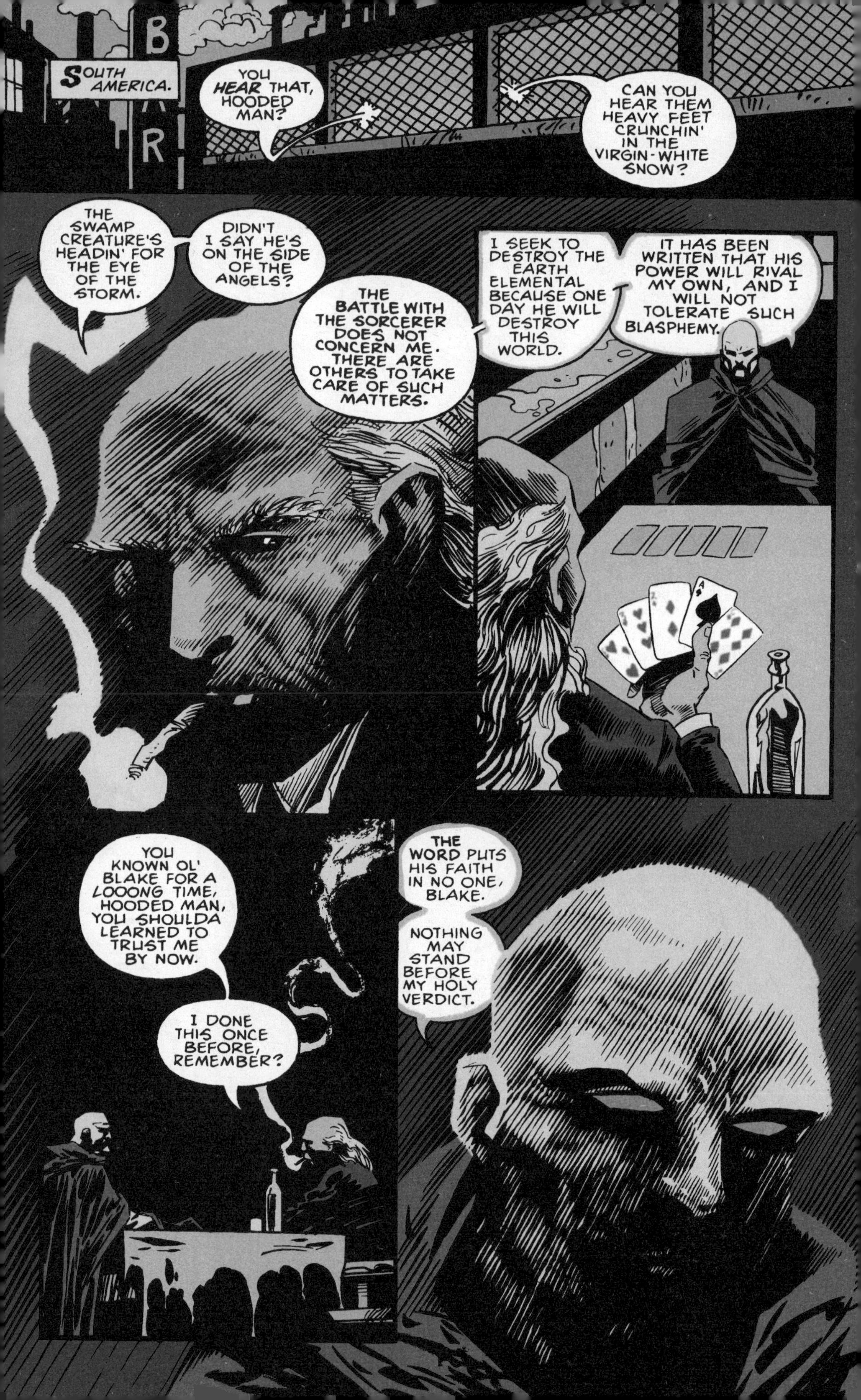
B
A
R
SOUTH AMERICA.
YOU HEAR THAT, HOODED MAN?
CAN YOU HEAR THEM HEAVY FEET CRUNCHIN' IN THE VIRGIN-WHITE SNOW?
THE SWAMP CREATURE'S HEADIN' FOR THE EYE OF THE STORM.
DIDN'T I SAY HE'S ON THE SIDE OF THE ANGELS?
THE BATTLE WITH THE SORCERER DOES NOT CONCERN ME. THERE ARE OTHERS TO TAKE CARE OF SUCH MATTERS.
I SEEK TO DESTROY THE EARTH ELEMENTAL BECAUSE ONE DAY HE WILL DESTROY THIS WORLD.
IT HAS BEEN WRITTEN THAT HIS POWER WILL RIVAL MY OWN, AND I WILL NOT TOLERATE SUCH BLASPHEMY.
YOU KNOWN OL' BLAKE FOR A LOOOONG TIME, HOODED MAN, YOU SHOULDA LEARNED TO TRUST ME BY NOW.
I DONE THIS ONCE BEFORE, REMEMBER?
THE WORD PUTS HIS FAITH IN NO ONE, BLAKE.
NOTHING MAY STAND BEFORE MY HOLY VERDICT.

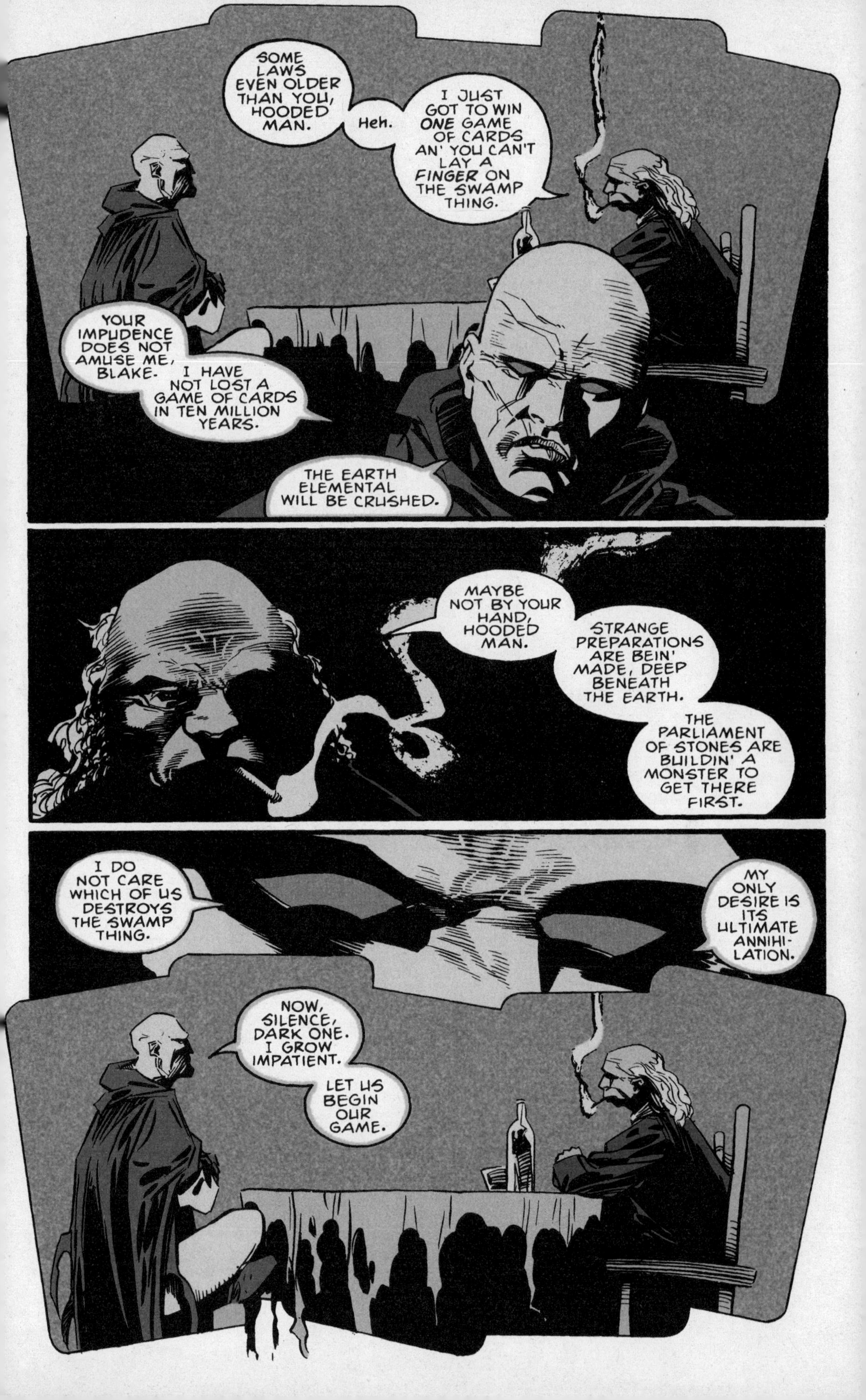
SOME LAWS EVEN OLDER THAN YOU, HOODED MAN.
Heh.
I JUST GOT TO WIN ONE GAME OF CARDS AN' YOU CAN'T LAY A FINGER ON THE SWAMP THING.
YOUR IMPUDENCE DOES NOT AMUSE ME, BLAKE.
I HAVE NOT LOST A GAME OF CARDS IN TEN MILLION YEARS.
THE EARTH ELEMENTAL WILL BE CRUSHED.
MAYBE NOT BY YOUR HAND, HOODED MAN.
STRANGE PREPARATIONS ARE BEIN' MADE, DEEP BENEATH THE EARTH.
THE PARLIAMENT OF STONES ARE BUILDIN' A MONSTER TO GET THERE FIRST.
I DO NOT CARE WHICH OF US DESTROYS THE SWAMP THING.
MY ONLY DESIRE IS ITS ULTIMATE ANNIHI-LATION.
NOW, SILENCE, DARK ONE. I GROW IMPATIENT.
LET US BEGIN OUR GAME.

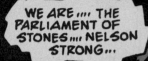

WE ARE .... THE PARLIAMENT OF STONES .... NELSON STRONG ...

THE ELDER OF THE TWO BODIES .... WHICH PRESIDE OVER ALL .... THAT IS OF .... THE EARTH ...

WE HAVE WAITED ...

SINCE THE FIRST SIGNS .... OF NATURAL LIFE .... APPEARED ON THE PEACEFUL ROCK .... AND OUR SISTER PARLIAMENT .... WAS FORMED.

LIKE .... THE PARLIAMENT OF TREES .... WE TOO DESIRE .... AN ELEMENTAL CHAMPION.

IT IS TIME TO DECIDE .... WHO SHOULD REPRESENT .... THE EARTH IN THE NEW AGE .... WHICH WILL SOON BE UPON US ....

WE HAVE .... SELECTED YOU TO BATTLE THE PLANT GOD .... NELSON STRONG ....

.... EVERYTHING YOU ONCE WERE .... IS NOW DEAD AND WRITHING .... WITH MAGGOTS.

ONLY THE HATRED .... HAS SURVIVED ....

YOU MUST USE THIS HATRED .... TO DESTROY .... THE SWAMP THING ....

WE DEMAND A VICTORY .... FOR THE .... PARLIAMENT OF STONES.

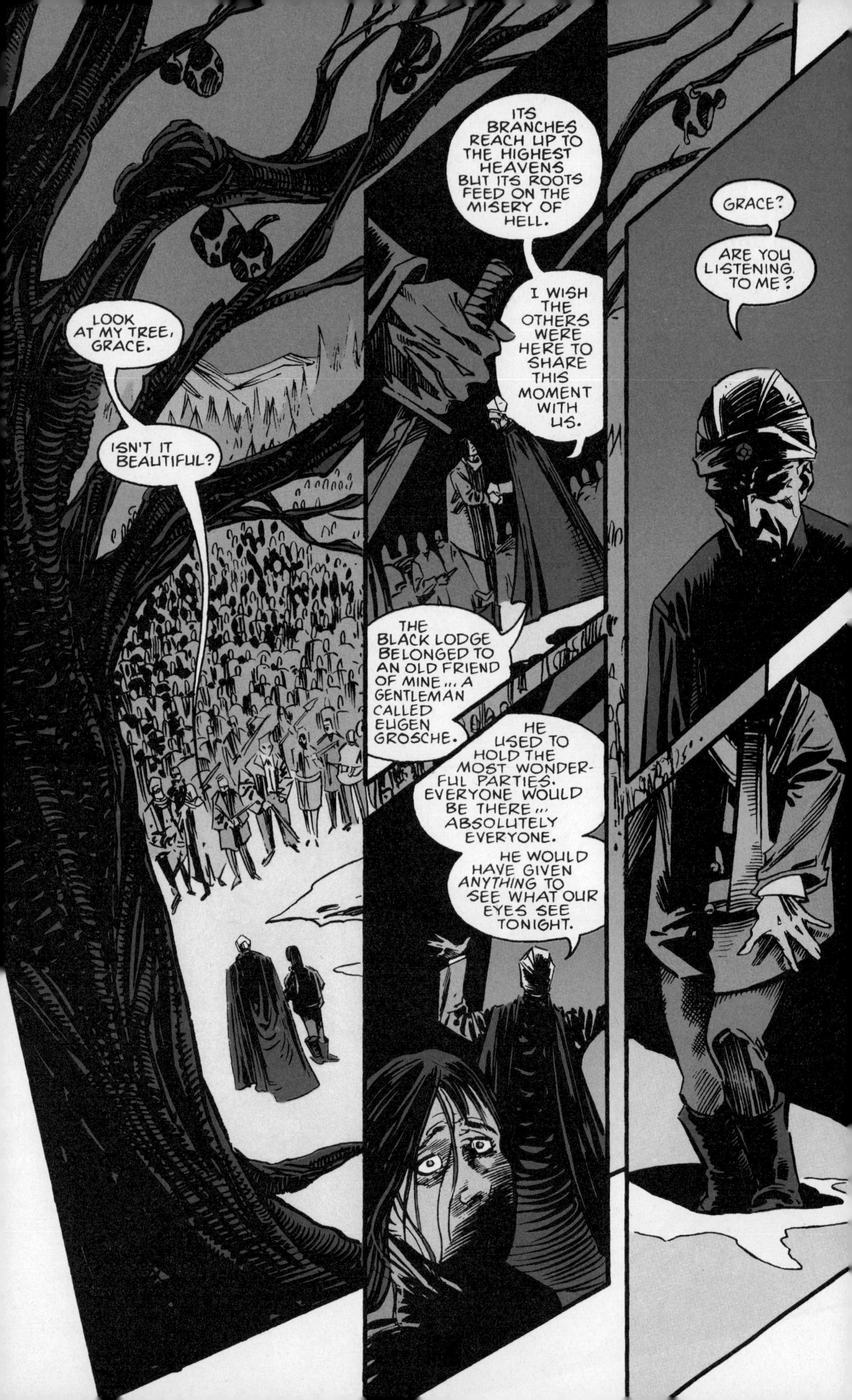
LOOK AT MY TREE, GRACE.
ISN'T IT BEAUTIFUL?
ITS BRANCHES REACH UP TO THE HIGHEST HEAVENS BUT ITS ROOTS FEED ON THE MISERY OF HELL.
I WISH THE OTHERS WERE HERE TO SHARE THIS MOMENT WITH US.
THE BLACK LODGE BELONGED TO AN OLD FRIEND OF MINE... A GENTLEMAN CALLED EUGEN GROSCHE.
HE USED TO HOLD THE MOST WONDERFUL PARTIES. EVERYONE WOULD BE THERE... ABSOLUTELY EVERYONE.
HE WOULD HAVE GIVEN ANYTHING TO SEE WHAT OUR EYES SEE TONIGHT.
GRACE?
ARE YOU LISTENING TO ME?

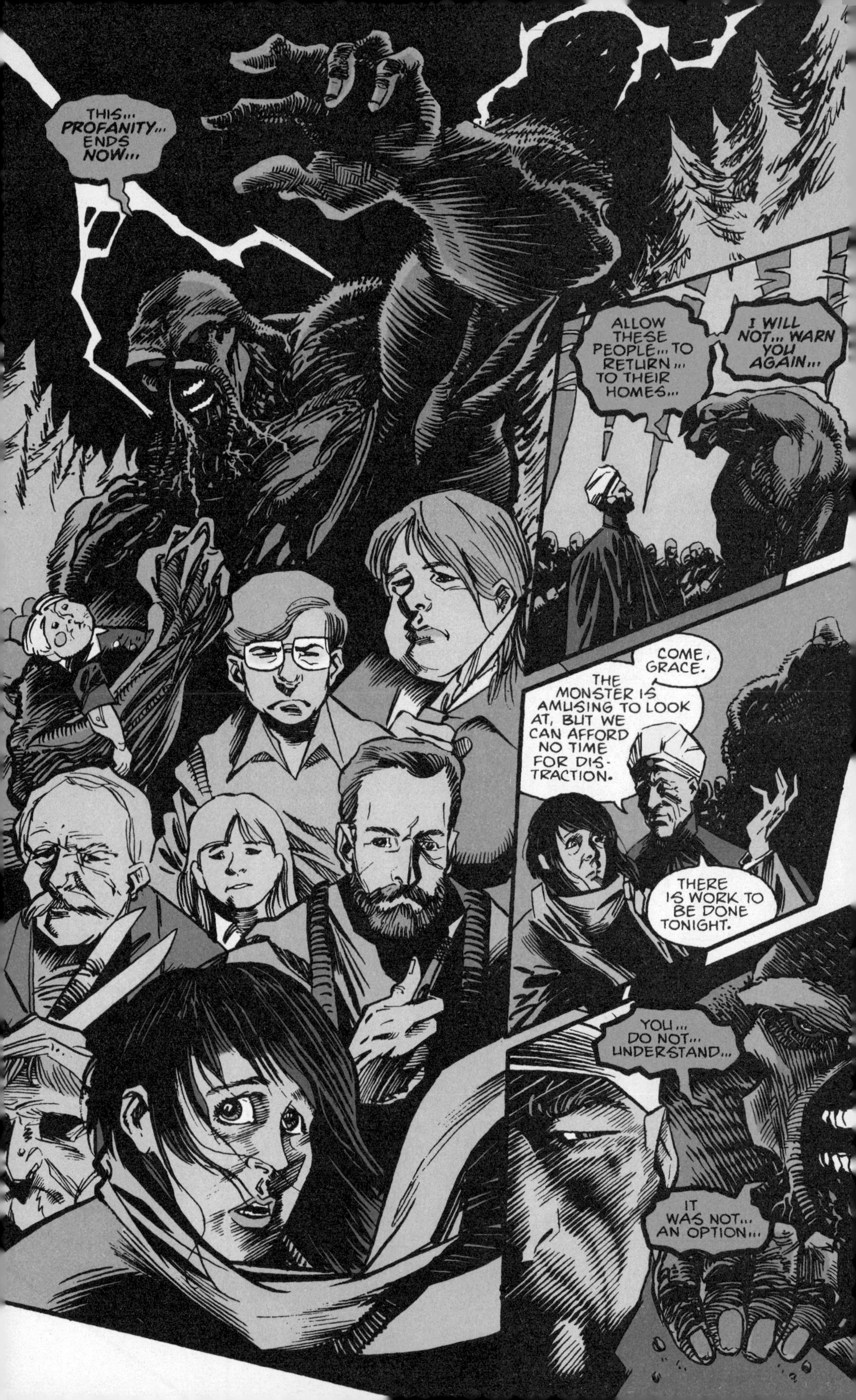
THIS... PROFANITY... ENDS NOW...
ALLOW THESE PEOPLE... TO RETURN... TO THEIR HOMES...
I WILL NOT... WARN YOU AGAIN...
COME, GRACE.
THE MONSTER IS AMUSING TO LOOK AT, BUT WE CAN AFFORD NO TIME FOR DIS-TRACTION.
THERE IS WORK TO BE DONE TONIGHT.
YOU... DO NOT... UNDERSTAND...
IT WAS NOT... AN OPTION...

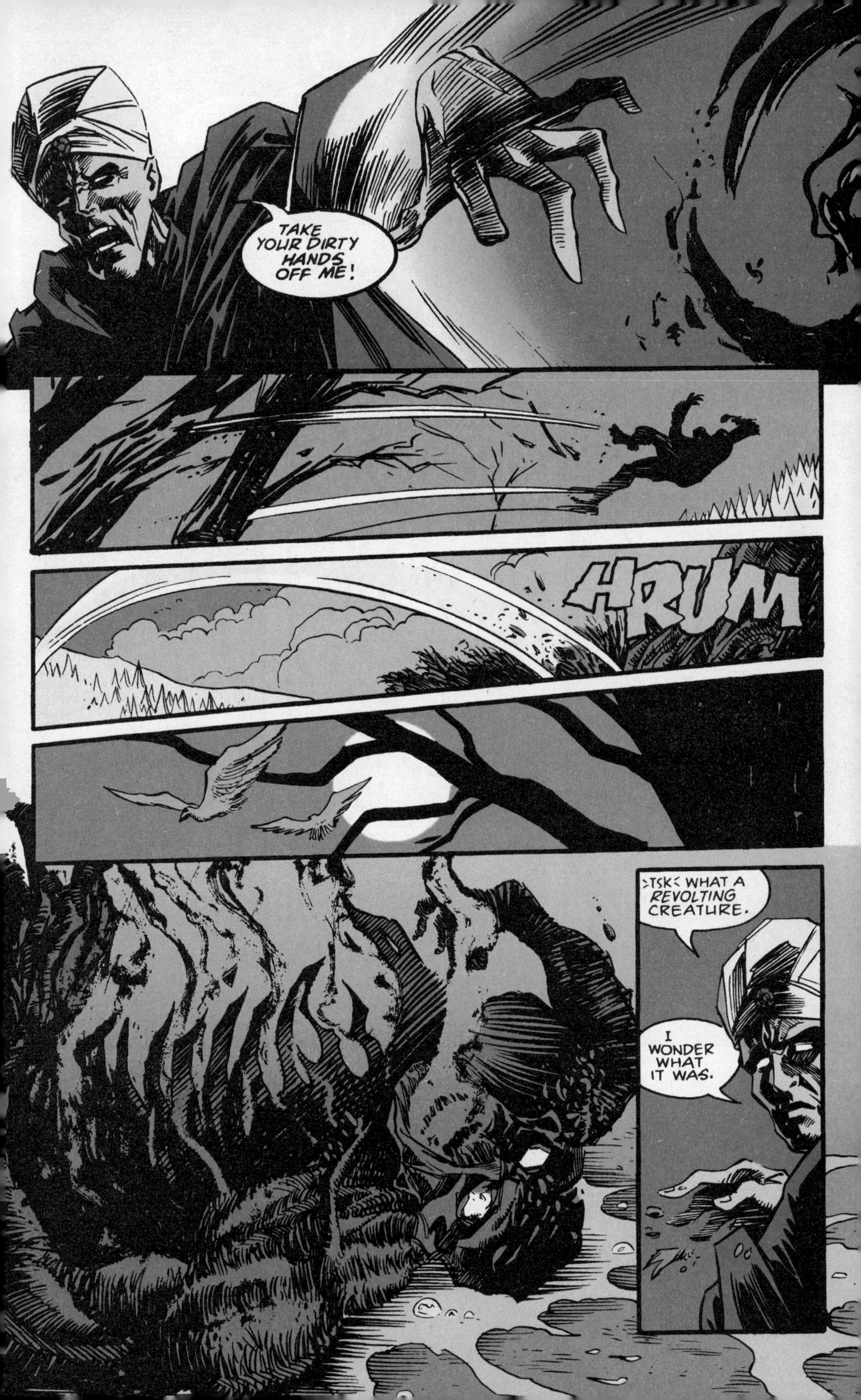
TAKE YOUR DIRTY HANDS OFF ME!
HRUM
>TSK< WHAT A *REVOLTING* CREATURE.
I WONDER WHAT IT WAS.

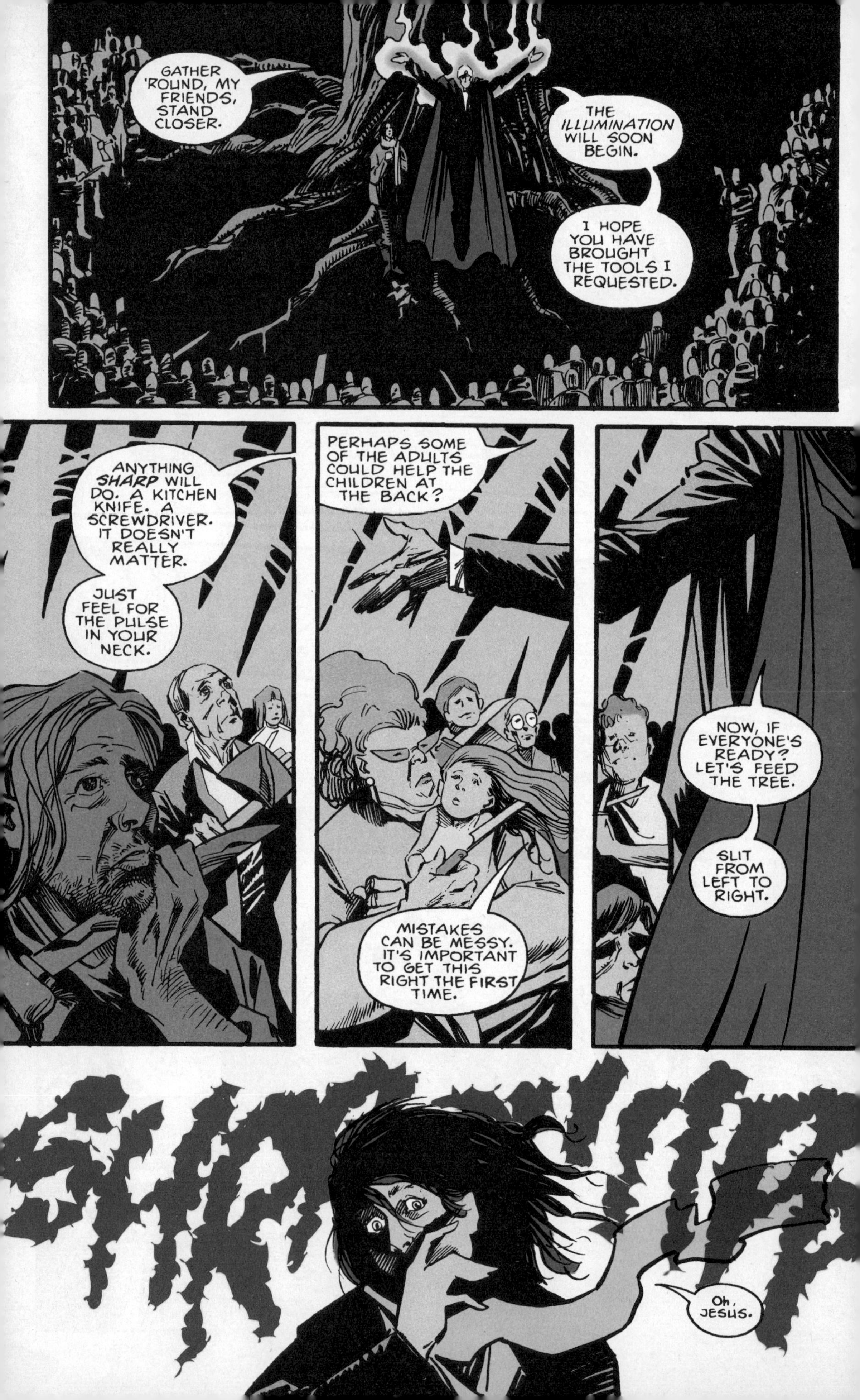
GATHER 'ROUND, MY FRIENDS, STAND CLOSER.
THE *ILLUMINATION* WILL SOON BEGIN.
I HOPE YOU HAVE BROUGHT THE TOOLS I REQUESTED.
ANYTHING *SHARP* WILL DO. A KITCHEN KNIFE. A SCREWDRIVER. IT DOESN'T REALLY MATTER.
JUST FEEL FOR THE PULSE IN YOUR NECK.
PERHAPS SOME OF THE ADULTS COULD HELP THE CHILDREN AT THE BACK?
MISTAKES CAN BE MESSY. IT'S IMPORTANT TO GET THIS RIGHT THE FIRST TIME.
NOW, IF EVERYONE'S READY? LET'S FEED THE TREE.
SLIT FROM LEFT TO RIGHT.
Oh, JESUS.

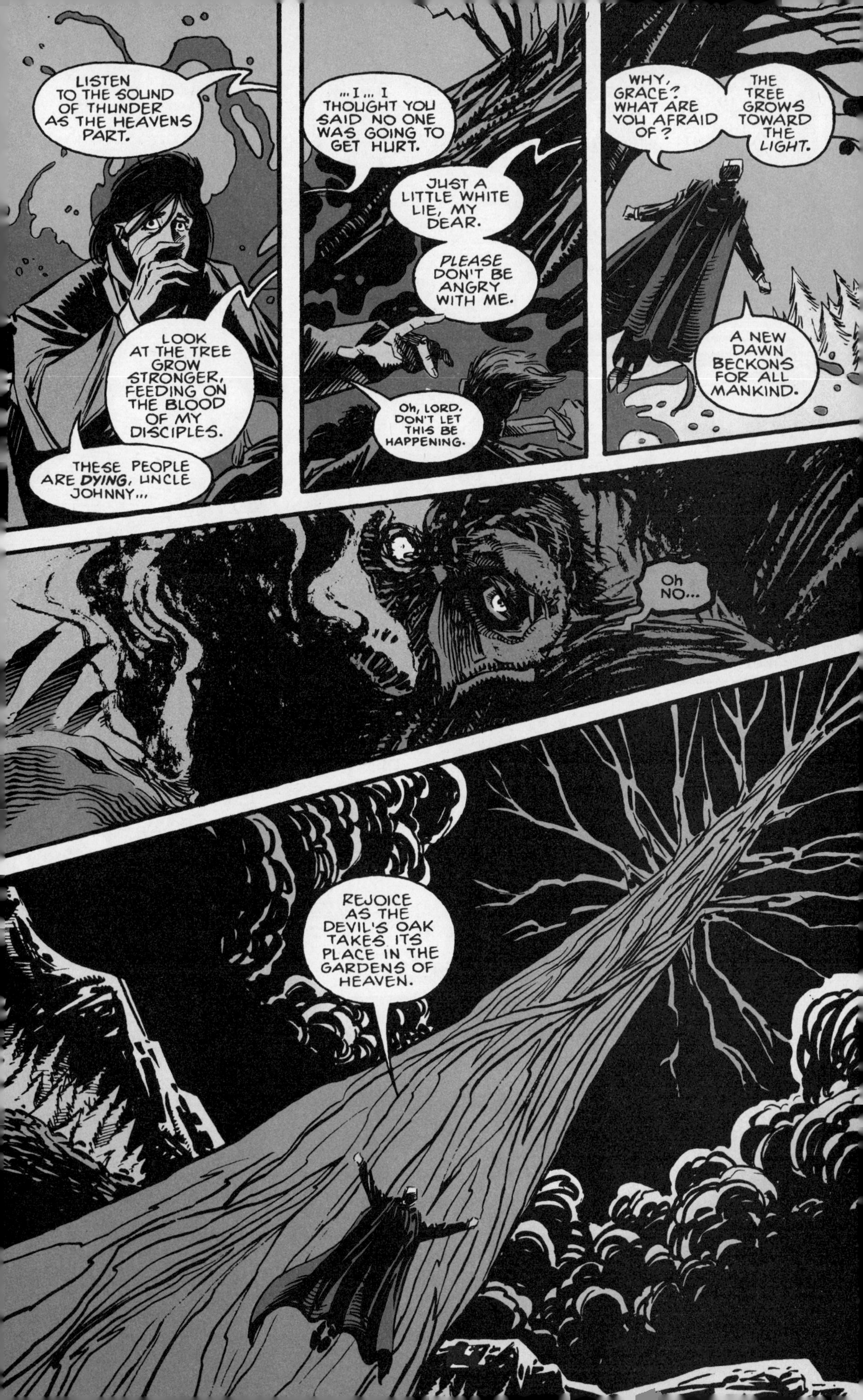
LISTEN TO THE SOUND OF THUNDER AS THE HEAVENS PART.
LOOK AT THE TREE GROW STRONGER, FEEDING ON THE BLOOD OF MY DISCIPLES.
THESE PEOPLE ARE DYING, UNCLE JOHNNY...
...I... I THOUGHT YOU SAID NO ONE WAS GOING TO GET HURT.
JUST A LITTLE WHITE LIE, MY DEAR.
PLEASE DON'T BE ANGRY WITH ME.
Oh, LORD. DON'T LET THIS BE HAPPENING.
WHY, GRACE? WHAT ARE YOU AFRAID OF?
THE TREE GROWS TOWARD THE LIGHT.
A NEW DAWN BECKONS FOR ALL MANKIND.
Oh NO...
REJOICE AS THE DEVIL'S OAK TAKES ITS PLACE IN THE GARDENS OF HEAVEN.

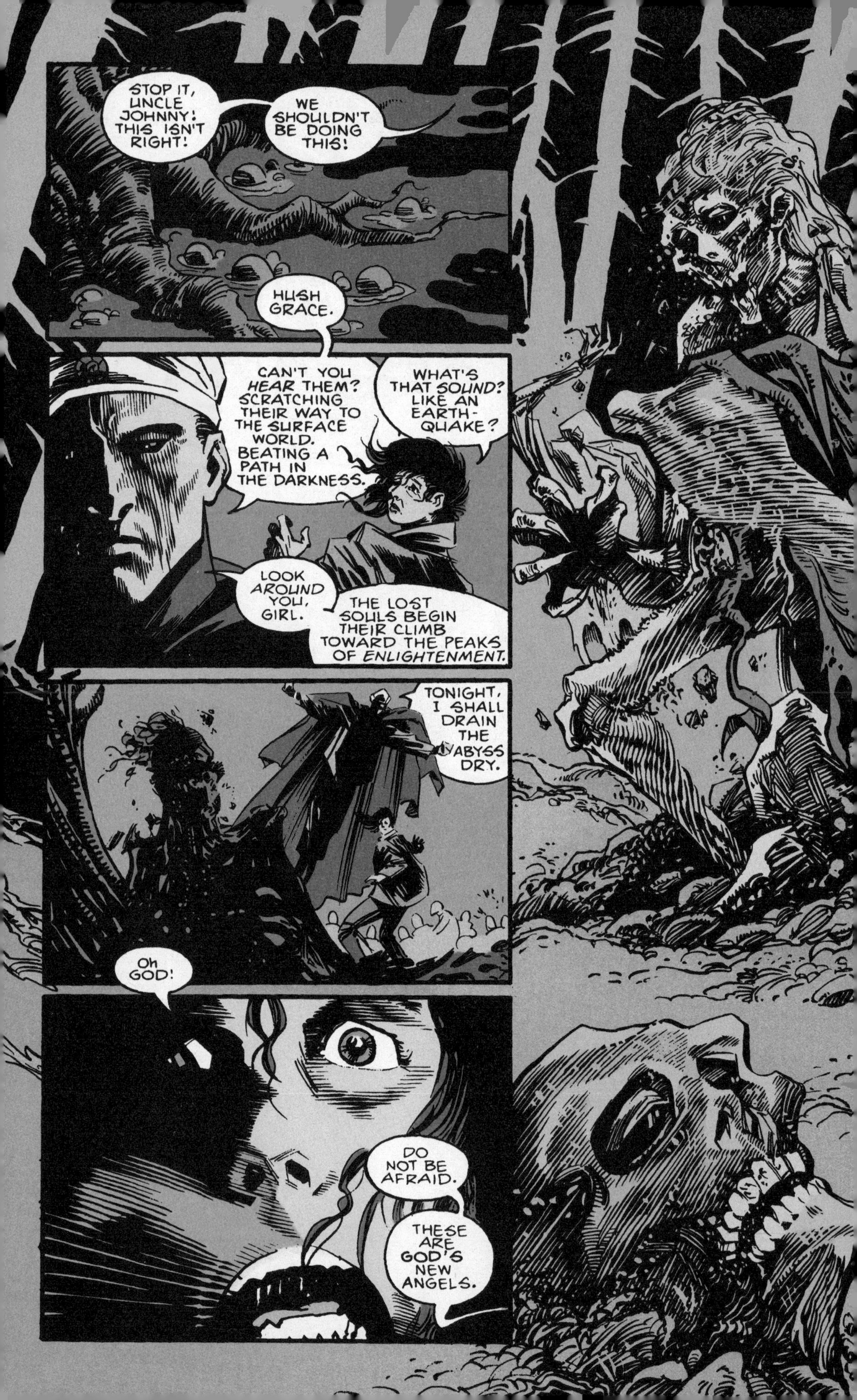
STOP IT, UNCLE JOHNNY! THIS ISN'T RIGHT!
WE SHOULDN'T BE DOING THIS!
HUSH GRACE.
CAN'T YOU *HEAR* THEM? SCRATCHING THEIR WAY TO THE SURFACE WORLD. BEATING A PATH IN THE DARKNESS.
WHAT'S THAT *SOUND*? LIKE AN EARTH-QUAKE?
LOOK *AROUND* YOU, GIRL.
THE LOST SOULS BEGIN THEIR CLIMB TOWARD THE PEAKS OF *ENLIGHTENMENT*.
TONIGHT, I SHALL DRAIN THE ABYSS DRY.
Oh GOD!
DO NOT BE AFRAID.
THESE ARE **GOD'S** NEW ANGELS.

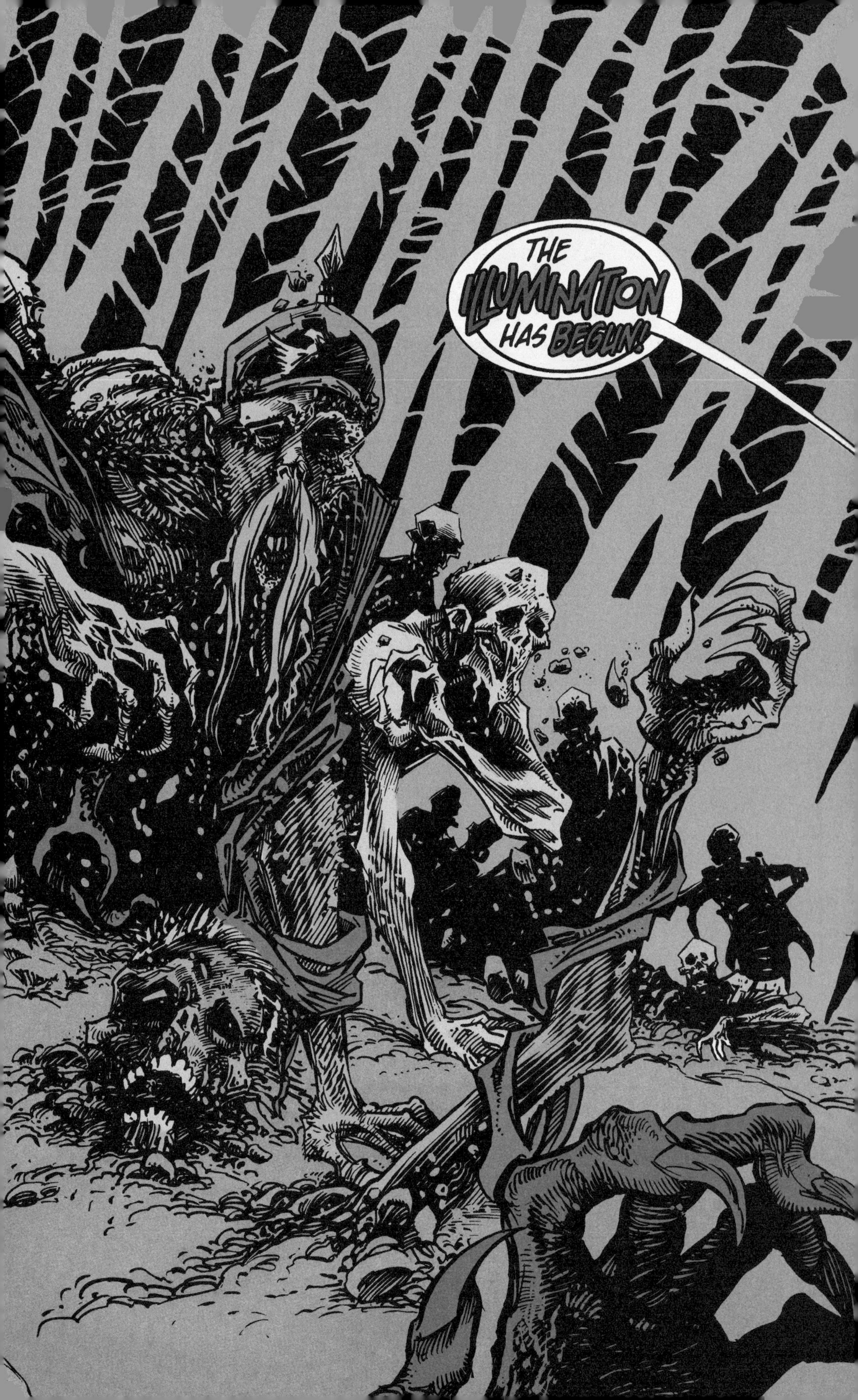
THE ILLUMINATION HAS BEGUN!

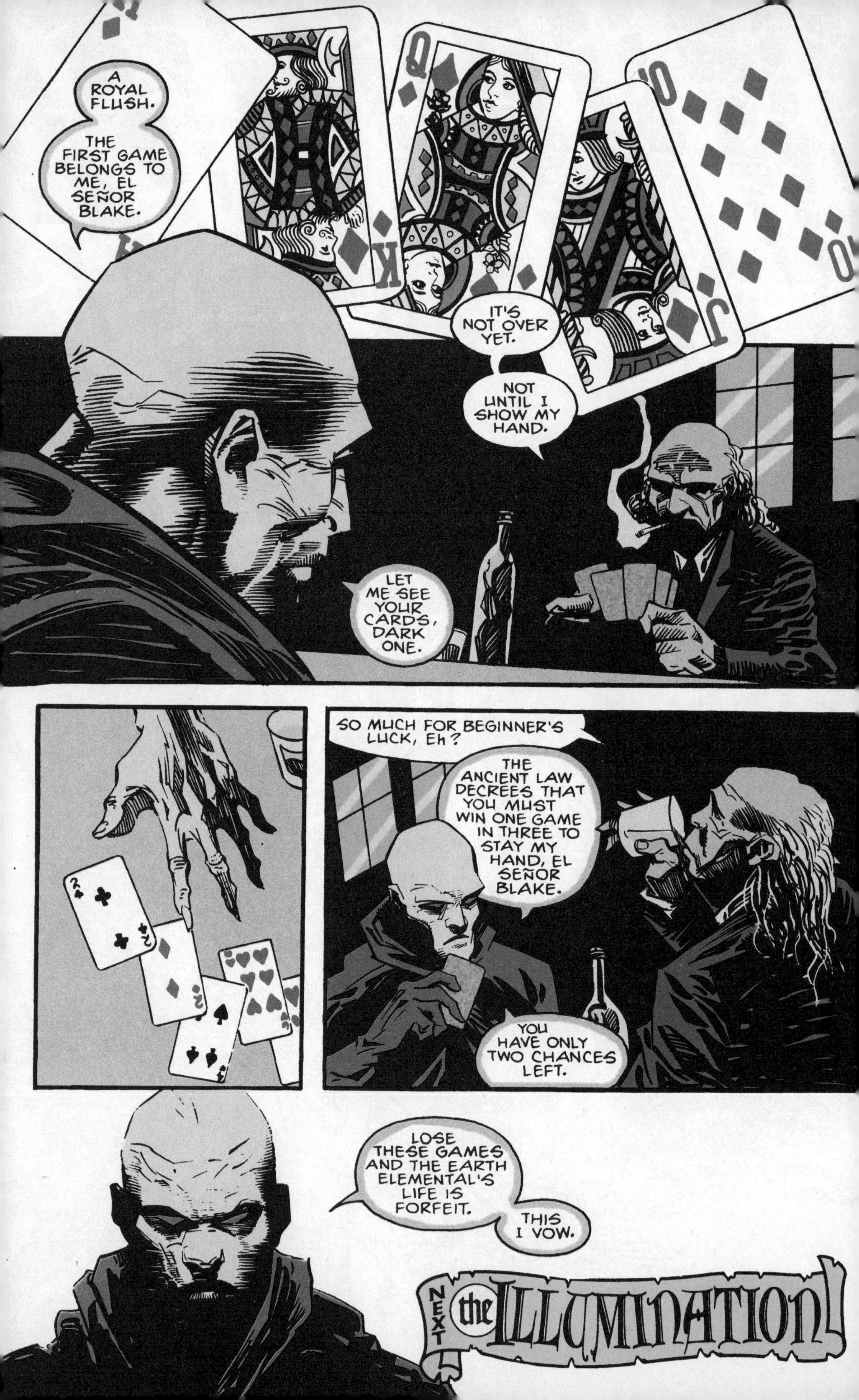
A ROYAL FLUSH.
THE FIRST GAME BELONGS TO ME, EL SEÑOR BLAKE.
IT'S NOT OVER YET.
NOT UNTIL I SHOW MY HAND.
LET ME SEE YOUR CARDS, DARK ONE.
SO MUCH FOR BEGINNER'S LUCK, EH?
THE ANCIENT LAW DECREES THAT YOU MUST WIN ONE GAME IN THREE TO STAY MY HAND, EL SEÑOR BLAKE.
YOU HAVE ONLY TWO CHANCES LEFT.
LOSE THESE GAMES AND THE EARTH ELEMENTAL'S LIFE IS FORFEIT.
THIS I VOW.
NEXT the ILLUMINATION!

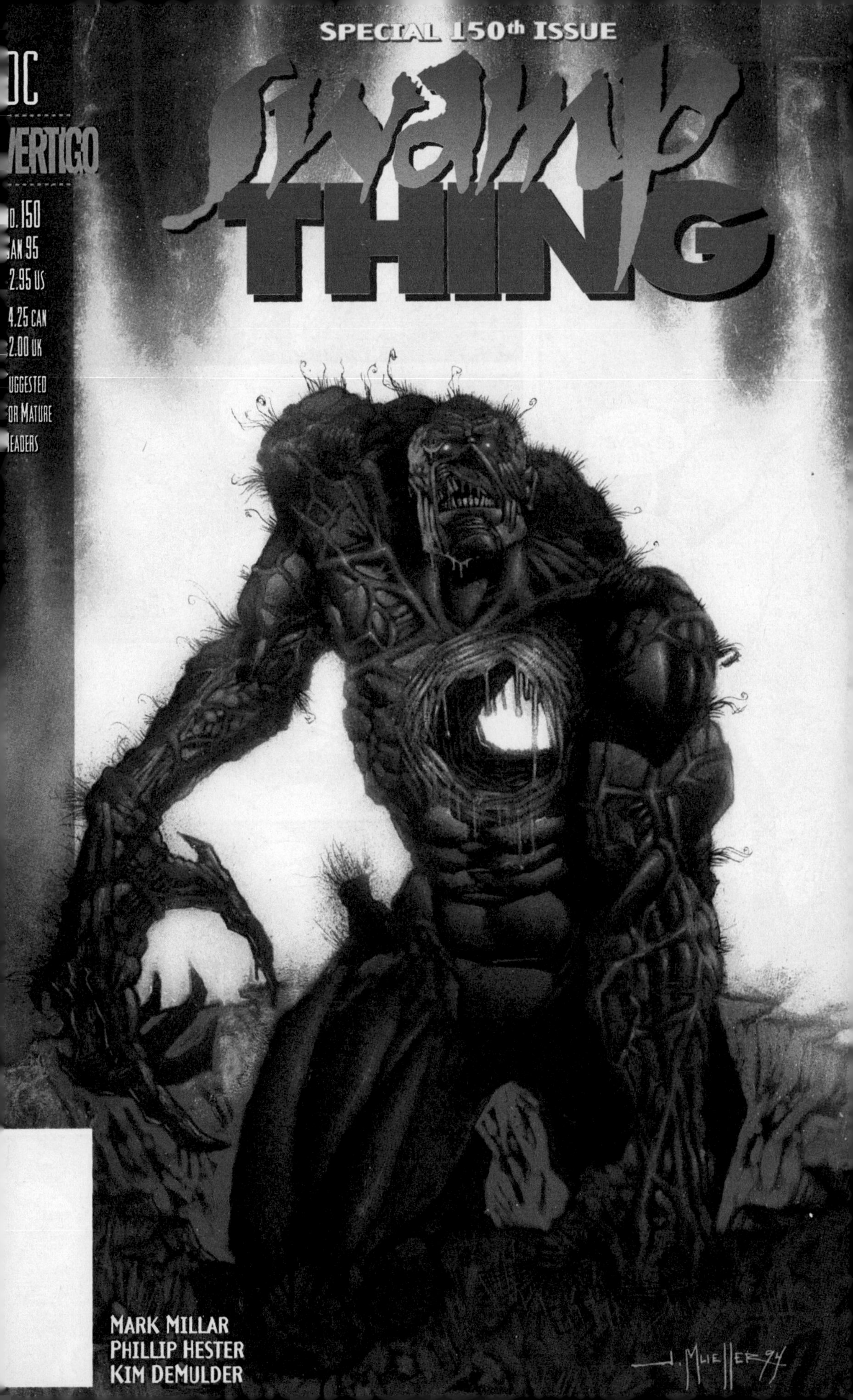
SPECIAL 150th ISSUE
SWAMP THING
VERTIGO
2.95 US
4.25 CAN
2.00 UK
MARK MILLAR
PHILLIP HESTER
KIM DEMULDER

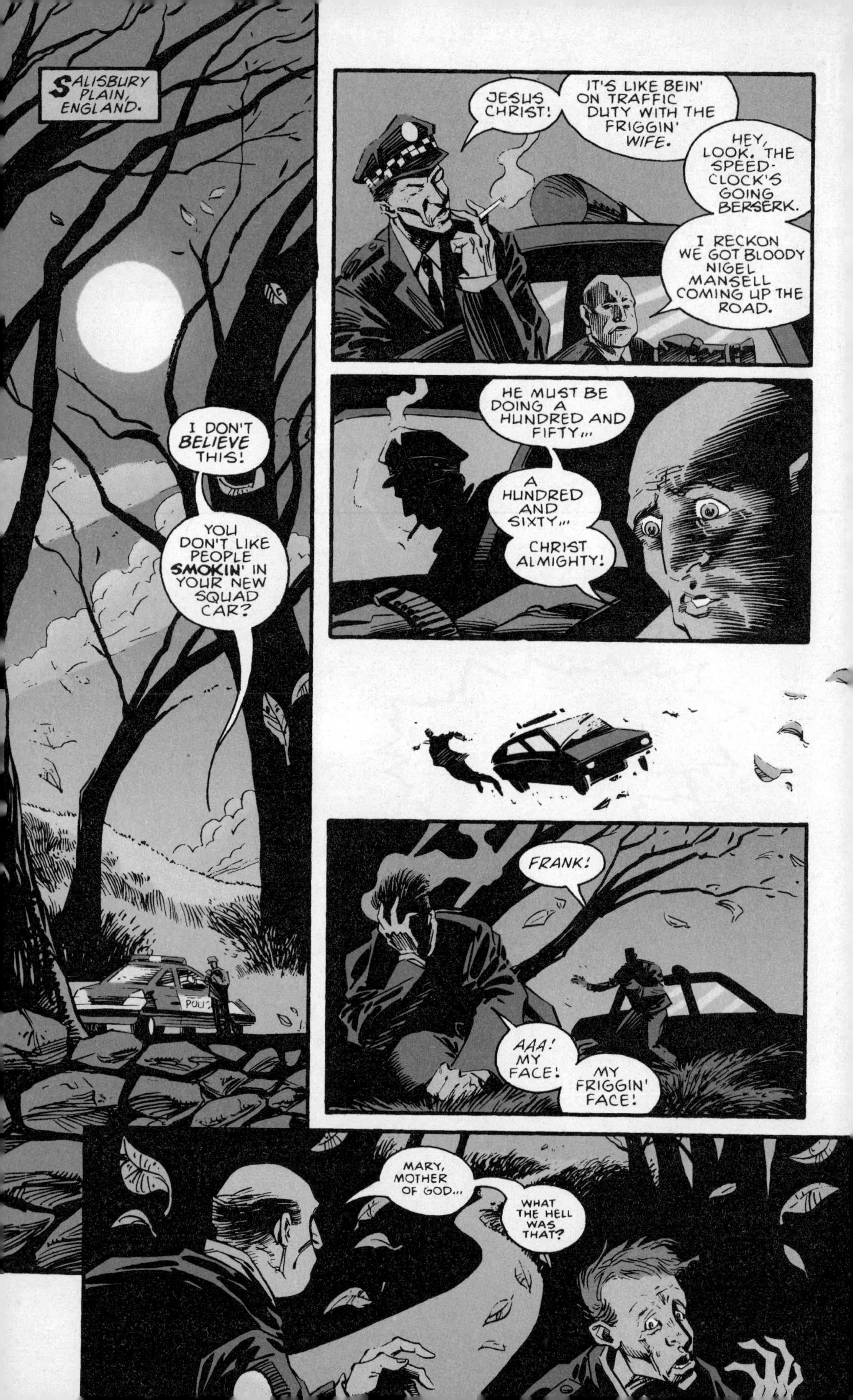
SALISBURY PLAIN, ENGLAND.
JESUS CHRIST!
IT'S LIKE BEIN' ON TRAFFIC DUTY WITH THE FRIGGIN' WIFE.
HEY, LOOK. THE SPEED-CLOCK'S GOING BERSERK.
I RECKON WE GOT BLOODY NIGEL MANSELL COMING UP THE ROAD.
I DON'T BELIEVE THIS!
YOU DON'T LIKE PEOPLE SMOKIN' IN YOUR NEW SQUAD CAR?
HE MUST BE DOING A HUNDRED AND FIFTY...
A HUNDRED AND SIXTY...
CHRIST ALMIGHTY!
FRANK!
AAA! MY FACE!
MY FRIGGIN' FACE!
MARY, MOTHER OF GOD...
WHAT THE HELL WAS THAT?

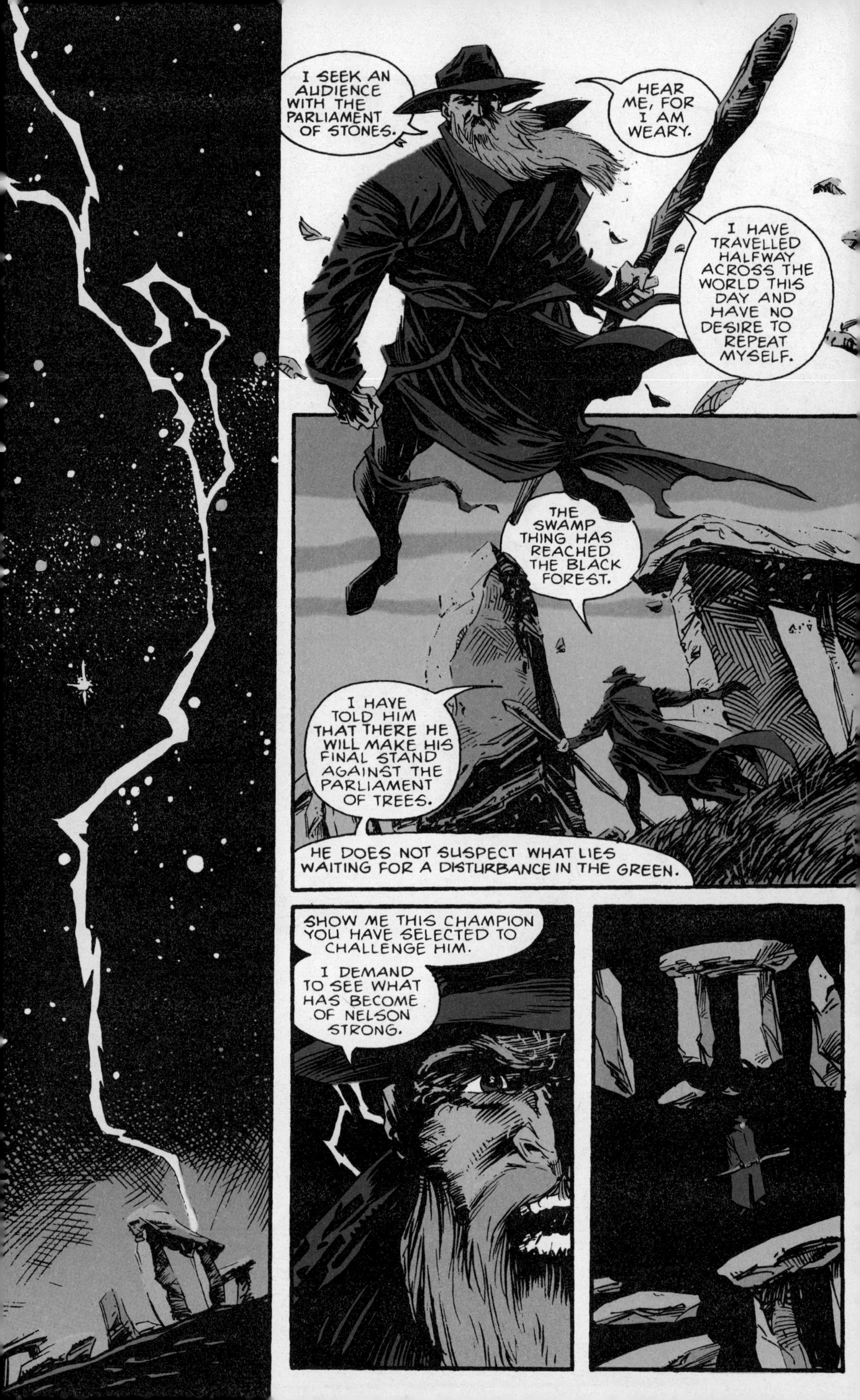
I SEEK AN AUDIENCE WITH THE PARLIAMENT OF STONES.
HEAR ME, FOR I AM WEARY.
I HAVE TRAVELLED HALFWAY ACROSS THE WORLD THIS DAY AND HAVE NO DESIRE TO REPEAT MYSELF.
THE SWAMP THING HAS REACHED THE BLACK FOREST.
I HAVE TOLD HIM THAT THERE HE WILL MAKE HIS FINAL STAND AGAINST THE PARLIAMENT OF TREES.
HE DOES NOT SUSPECT WHAT LIES WAITING FOR A DISTURBANCE IN THE GREEN.
SHOW ME THIS CHAMPION YOU HAVE SELECTED TO CHALLENGE HIM.
I DEMAND TO SEE WHAT HAS BECOME OF NELSON STRONG.

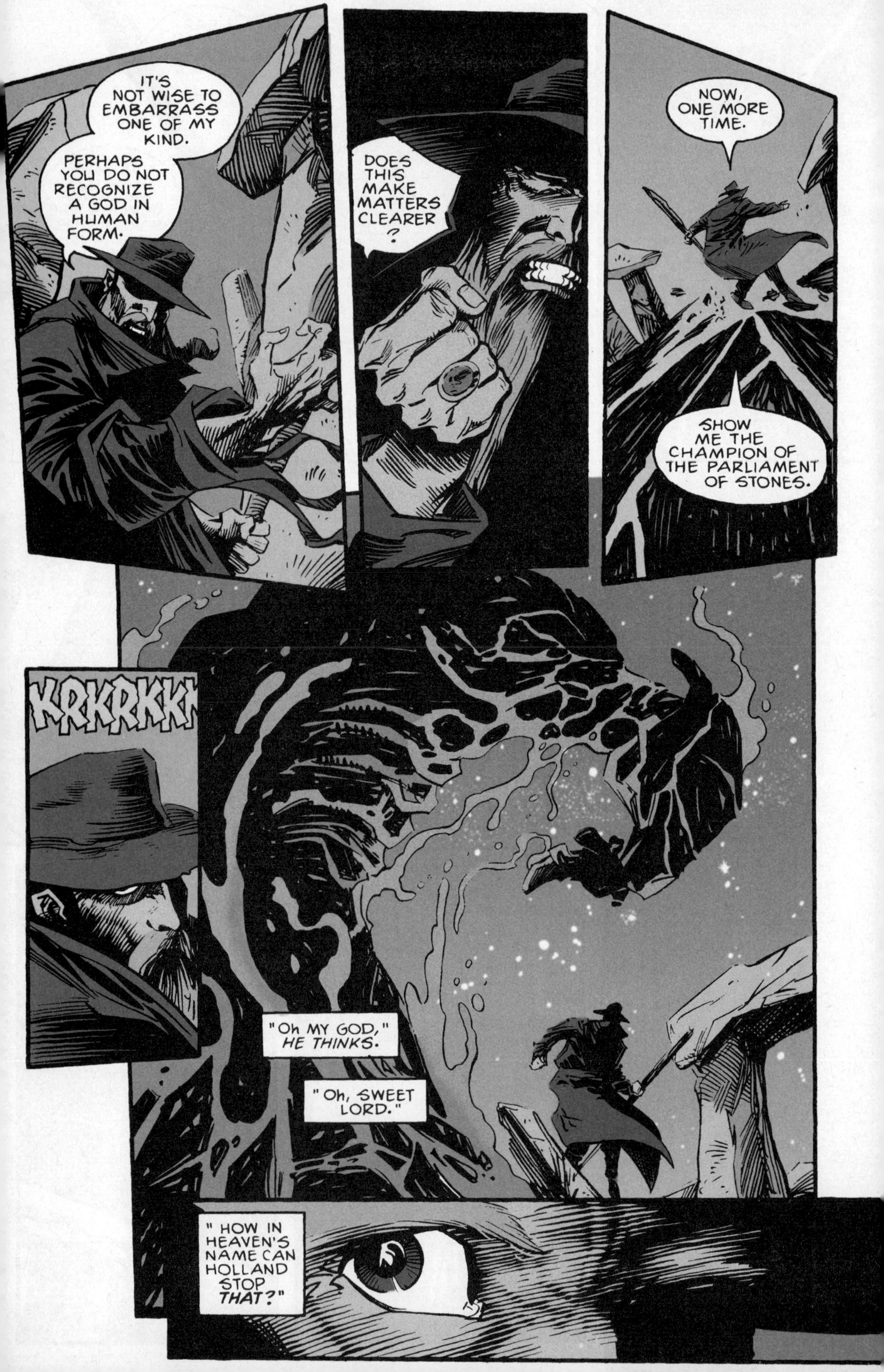
IT'S NOT WISE TO EMBARRASS ONE OF MY KIND.
PERHAPS YOU DO NOT RECOGNIZE A GOD IN HUMAN FORM.
DOES THIS MAKE MATTERS CLEARER?
NOW, ONE MORE TIME.
SHOW ME THE CHAMPION OF THE PARLIAMENT OF STONES.
KRKRKKK
"Oh MY GOD," HE THINKS.
"Oh, SWEET LORD."
"HOW IN HEAVEN'S NAME CAN HOLLAND STOP THAT?"

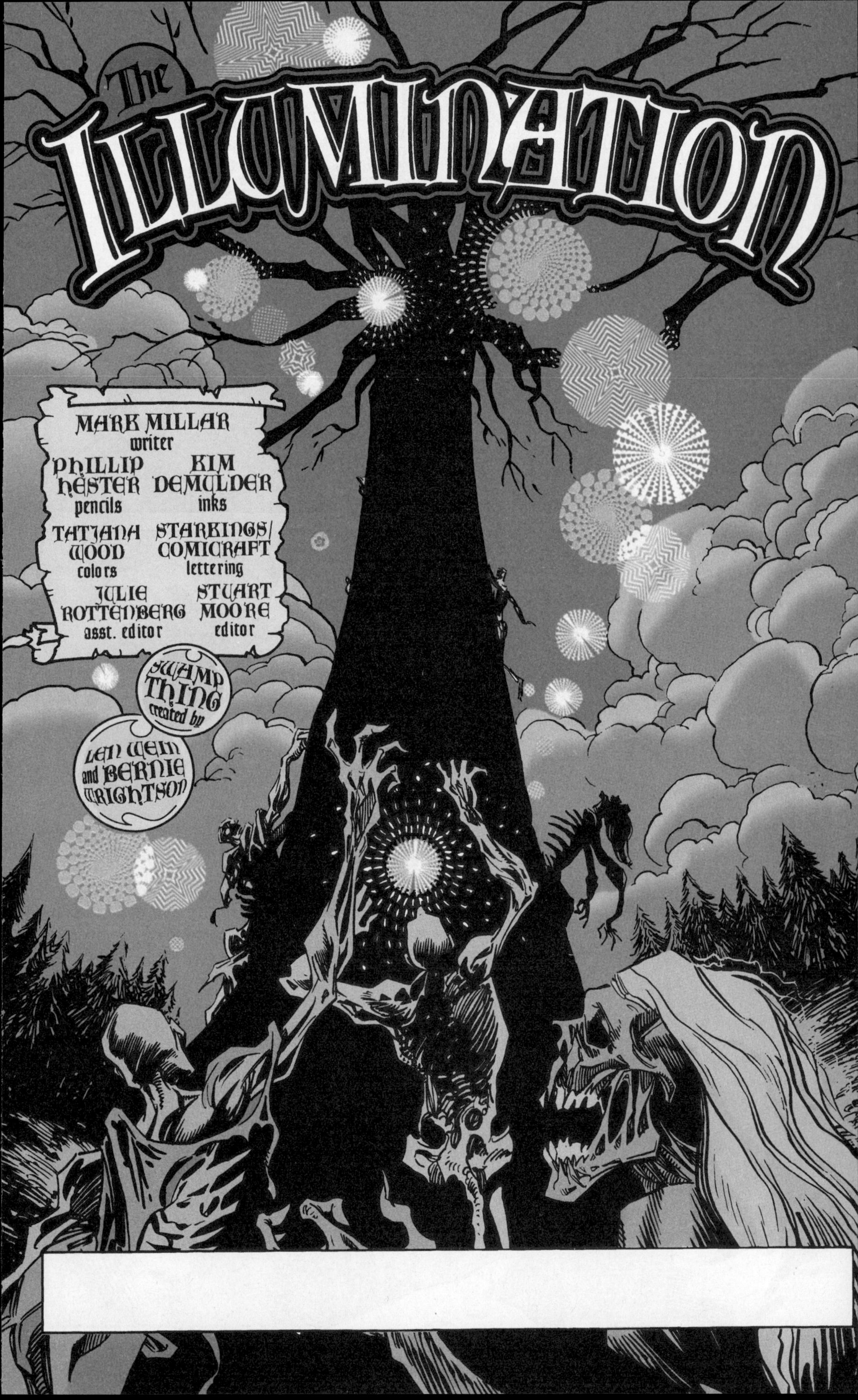
The ILLUMINATION
MARK MILLAR writer
PHILLIP HESTER pencils
KIM DEMULDER inks
TATJANA WOOD colors
STARKINGS/COMICRAFT lettering
JULIE ROTTENBERG asst. editor
STUART MOORE editor
SWAMP THING created by
LEN WEIN and BERNIE WRIGHTSON

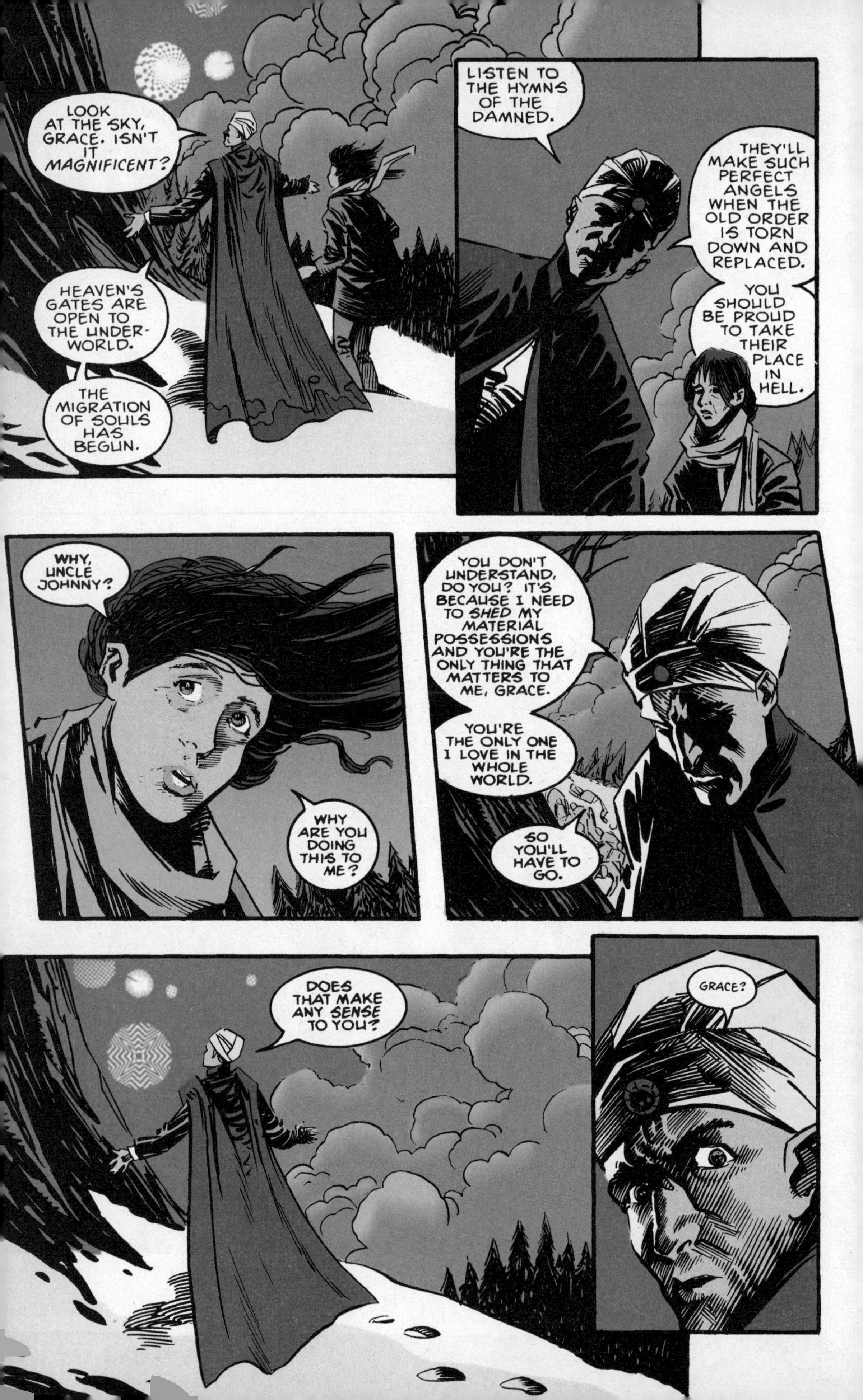
LOOK AT THE SKY, GRACE. ISN'T IT MAGNIFICENT?
HEAVEN'S GATES ARE OPEN TO THE UNDER-WORLD.
THE MIGRATION OF SOULS HAS BEGUN.
LISTEN TO THE HYMNS OF THE DAMNED.
THEY'LL MAKE SUCH PERFECT ANGELS WHEN THE OLD ORDER IS TORN DOWN AND REPLACED.
YOU SHOULD BE PROUD TO TAKE THEIR PLACE IN HELL.
WHY, UNCLE JOHNNY?
WHY ARE YOU DOING THIS TO ME?
YOU DON'T UNDERSTAND, DO YOU? IT'S BECAUSE I NEED TO SHED MY MATERIAL POSSESSIONS AND YOU'RE THE ONLY THING THAT MATTERS TO ME, GRACE.
YOU'RE THE ONLY ONE I LOVE IN THE WHOLE WORLD.
SO YOU'LL HAVE TO GO.
DOES THAT MAKE ANY SENSE TO YOU?
GRACE?

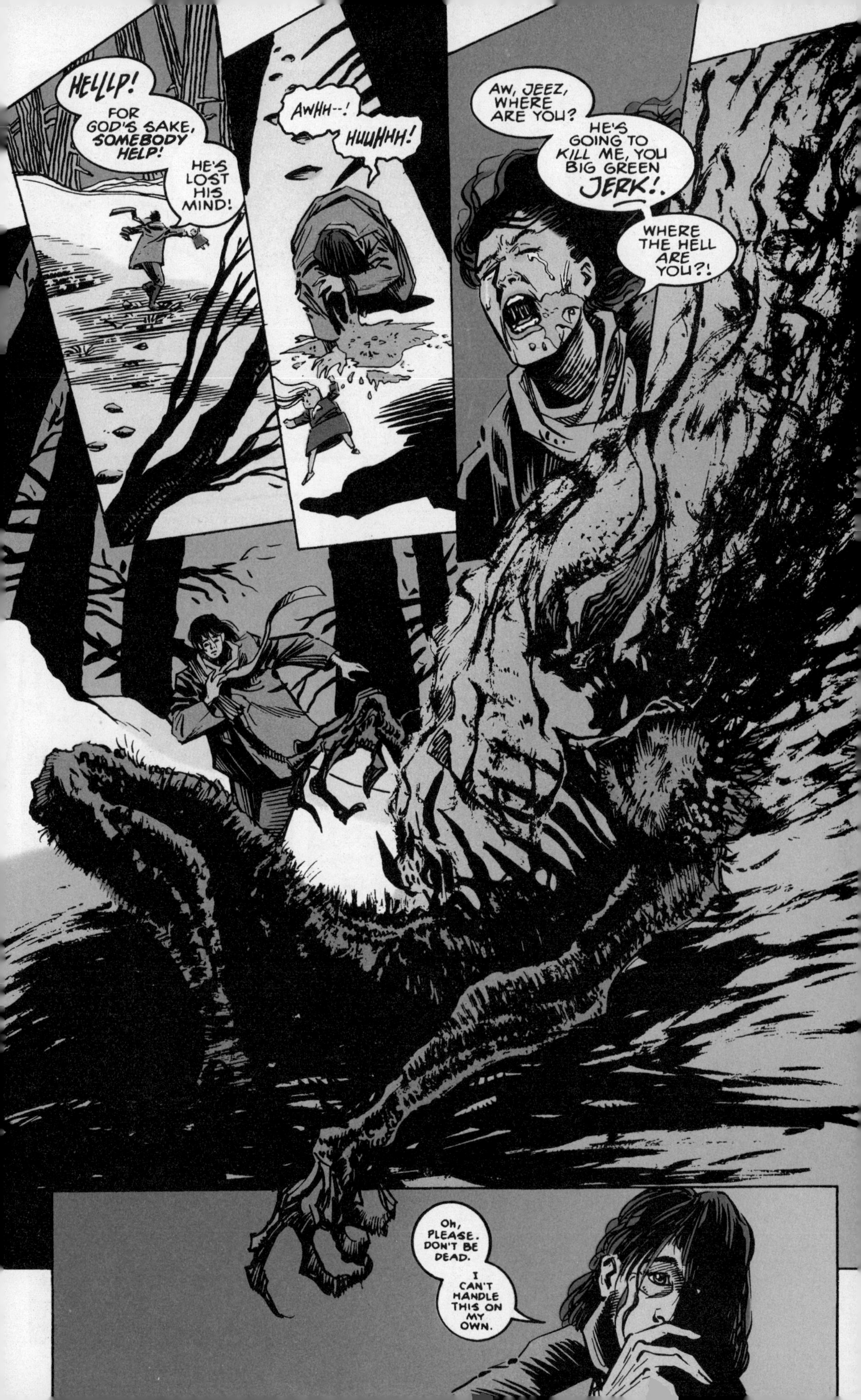

HELLLP!
FOR GOD'S SAKE, SOMEBODY HELP!
HE'S LOST HIS MIND!
AWHH--!
HUUHHH!
AW, JEEZ, WHERE ARE YOU?
HE'S GOING TO KILL ME, YOU BIG GREEN JERK!.
WHERE THE HELL ARE YOU?!
Oh, PLEASE. DON'T BE DEAD.
I CAN'T HANDLE THIS ON MY OWN.

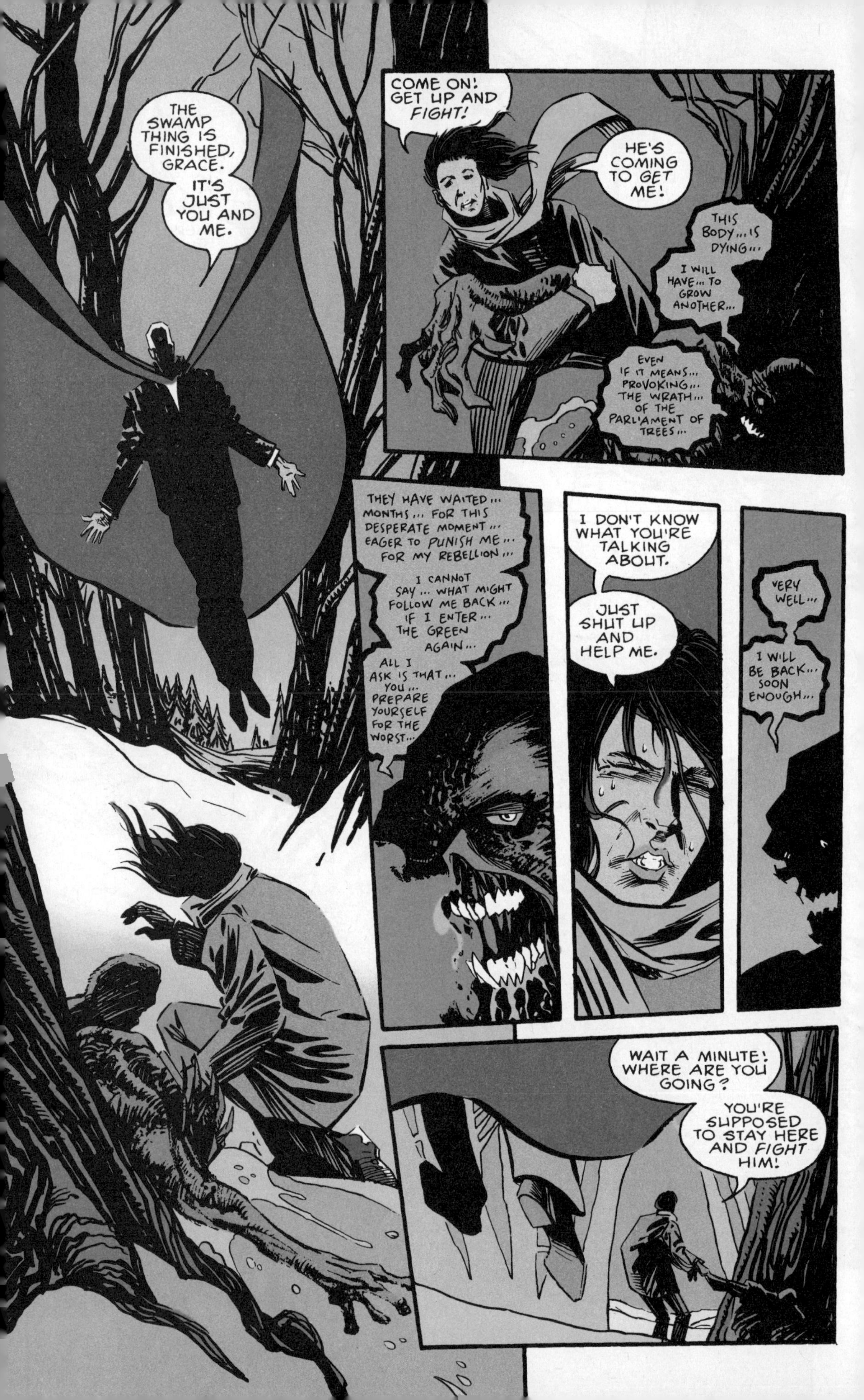
THE SWAMP THING IS FINISHED, GRACE.
IT'S JUST YOU AND ME.
COME ON! GET UP AND FIGHT!
HE'S COMING TO GET ME!
THIS BODY... IS DYING...
I WILL HAVE... TO GROW ANOTHER...
EVEN IF IT MEANS... PROVOKING... THE WRATH... OF THE PARLIAMENT OF TREES...
THEY HAVE WAITED... MONTHS... FOR THIS DESPERATE MOMENT... EAGER TO PUNISH ME... FOR MY REBELLION...
I CANNOT SAY... WHAT MIGHT FOLLOW ME BACK... IF I ENTER... THE GREEN AGAIN...
ALL I ASK IS THAT... YOU... PREPARE YOURSELF FOR THE WORST...
I DON'T KNOW WHAT YOU'RE TALKING ABOUT.
JUST SHUT UP AND HELP ME.
VERY WELL...
I WILL BE BACK... SOON ENOUGH...
WAIT A MINUTE! WHERE ARE YOU GOING?
YOU'RE SUPPOSED TO STAY HERE AND FIGHT HIM!

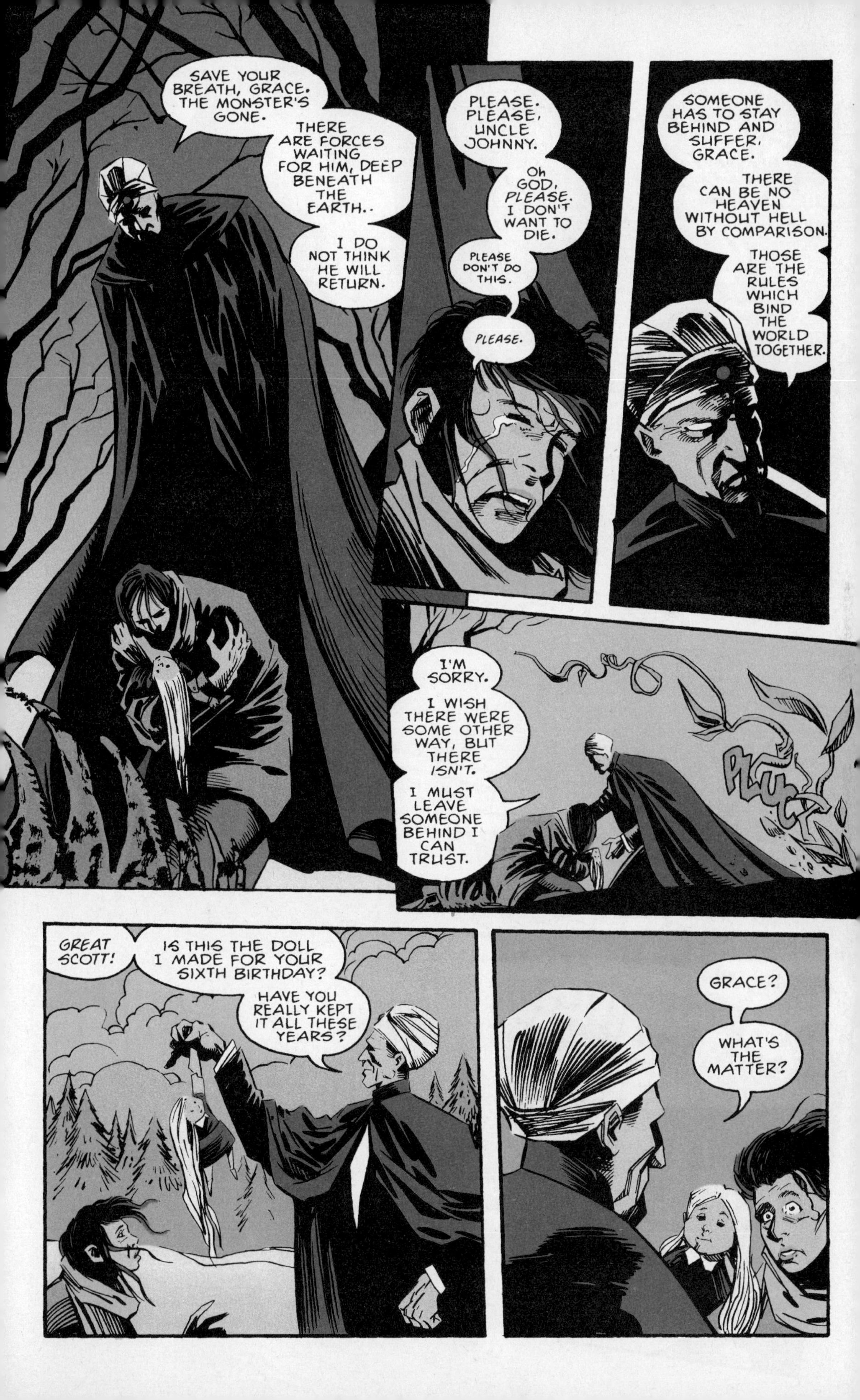
SAVE YOUR BREATH, GRACE. THE MONSTER'S GONE.
THERE ARE FORCES WAITING FOR HIM, DEEP BENEATH THE EARTH..
I DO NOT THINK HE WILL RETURN.
PLEASE. PLEASE, UNCLE JOHNNY.
Oh GOD, PLEASE. I DON'T WANT TO DIE.
PLEASE DON'T DO THIS.
PLEASE.
SOMEONE HAS TO STAY BEHIND AND SUFFER, GRACE.
THERE CAN BE NO HEAVEN WITHOUT HELL BY COMPARISON.
THOSE ARE THE RULES WHICH BIND THE WORLD TOGETHER.
I'M SORRY.
I WISH THERE WERE SOME OTHER WAY, BUT THERE ISN'T.
I MUST LEAVE SOMEONE BEHIND I CAN TRUST.
PLUCK
GREAT SCOTT!
IS THIS THE DOLL I MADE FOR YOUR SIXTH BIRTHDAY?
HAVE YOU REALLY KEPT IT ALL THESE YEARS?
GRACE?
WHAT'S THE MATTER?

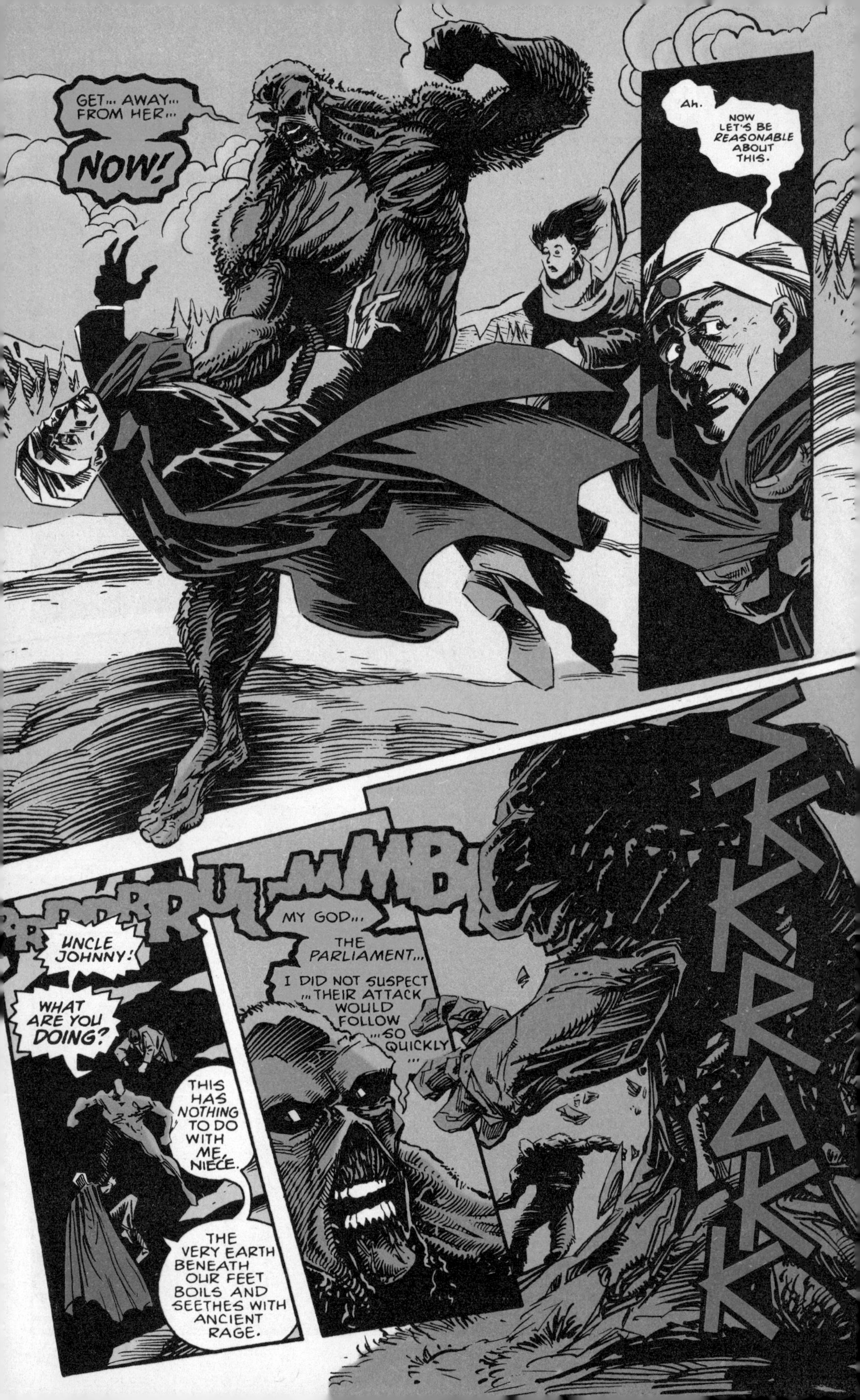
GET... AWAY... FROM HER...
NOW!
Ah.
NOW LET'S BE REASONABLE ABOUT THIS.
SKRAKK
RRRRRUMMB
UNCLE JOHNNY!
WHAT ARE YOU DOING?
MY GOD...
THE PARLIAMENT...
I DID NOT SUSPECT ...THEIR ATTACK WOULD FOLLOW ...SO QUICKLY ...
THIS HAS NOTHING TO DO WITH ME, NIECE.
THE VERY EARTH BENEATH OUR FEET BOILS AND SEETHES WITH ANCIENT RAGE.

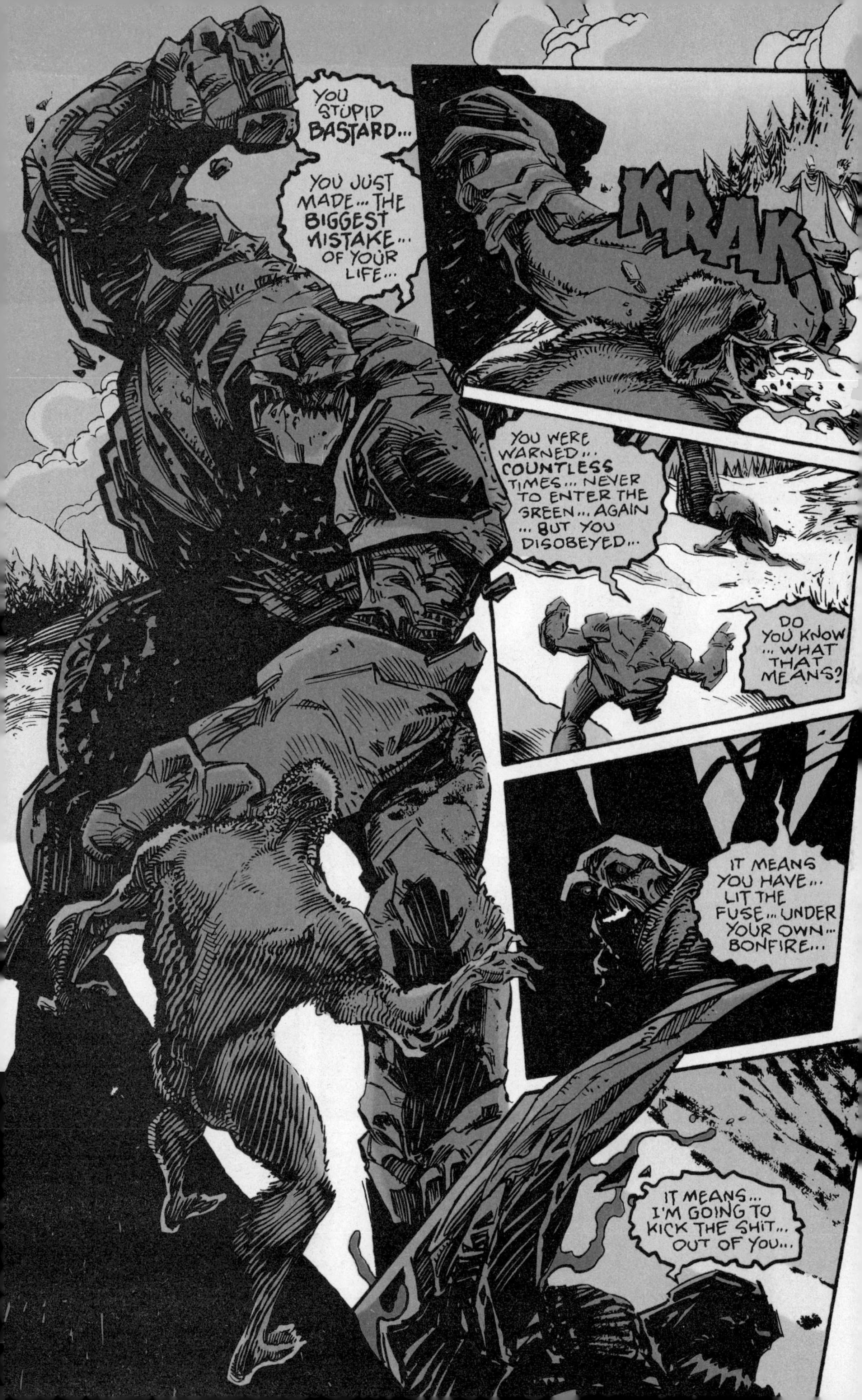
YOU STUPID BASTARD...
YOU JUST MADE... THE BIGGEST MISTAKE... OF YOUR LIFE...
KRAK
YOU WERE WARNED... COUNTLESS TIMES... NEVER TO ENTER THE GREEN... AGAIN ... BUT YOU DISOBEYED...
DO YOU KNOW ... WHAT THAT MEANS?
IT MEANS YOU HAVE... LIT THE FUSE... UNDER YOUR OWN... BONFIRE...
IT MEANS... I'M GOING TO KICK THE SHIT... OUT OF YOU...

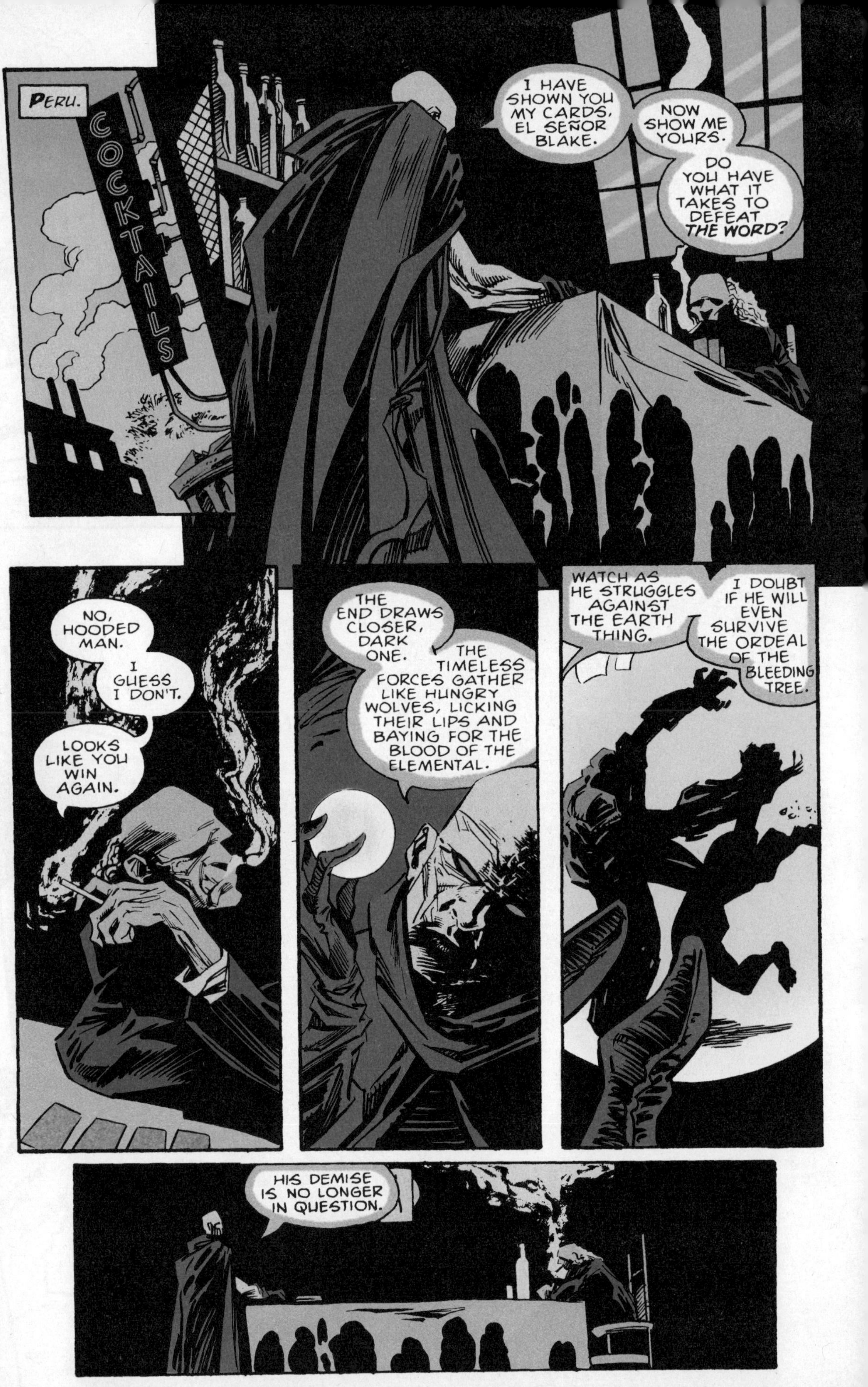
PERU.
COCKTAILS
I HAVE SHOWN YOU MY CARDS, EL SEÑOR BLAKE.
NOW SHOW ME YOURS.
DO YOU HAVE WHAT IT TAKES TO DEFEAT THE WORD?
NO, HOODED MAN.
I GUESS I DON'T.
LOOKS LIKE YOU WIN AGAIN.
THE END DRAWS CLOSER, DARK ONE.
THE TIMELESS FORCES GATHER LIKE HUNGRY WOLVES, LICKING THEIR LIPS AND BAYING FOR THE BLOOD OF THE ELEMENTAL.
WATCH AS HE STRUGGLES AGAINST THE EARTH THING.
I DOUBT IF HE WILL EVEN SURVIVE THE ORDEAL OF THE BLEEDING TREE.
HIS DEMISE IS NO LONGER IN QUESTION.

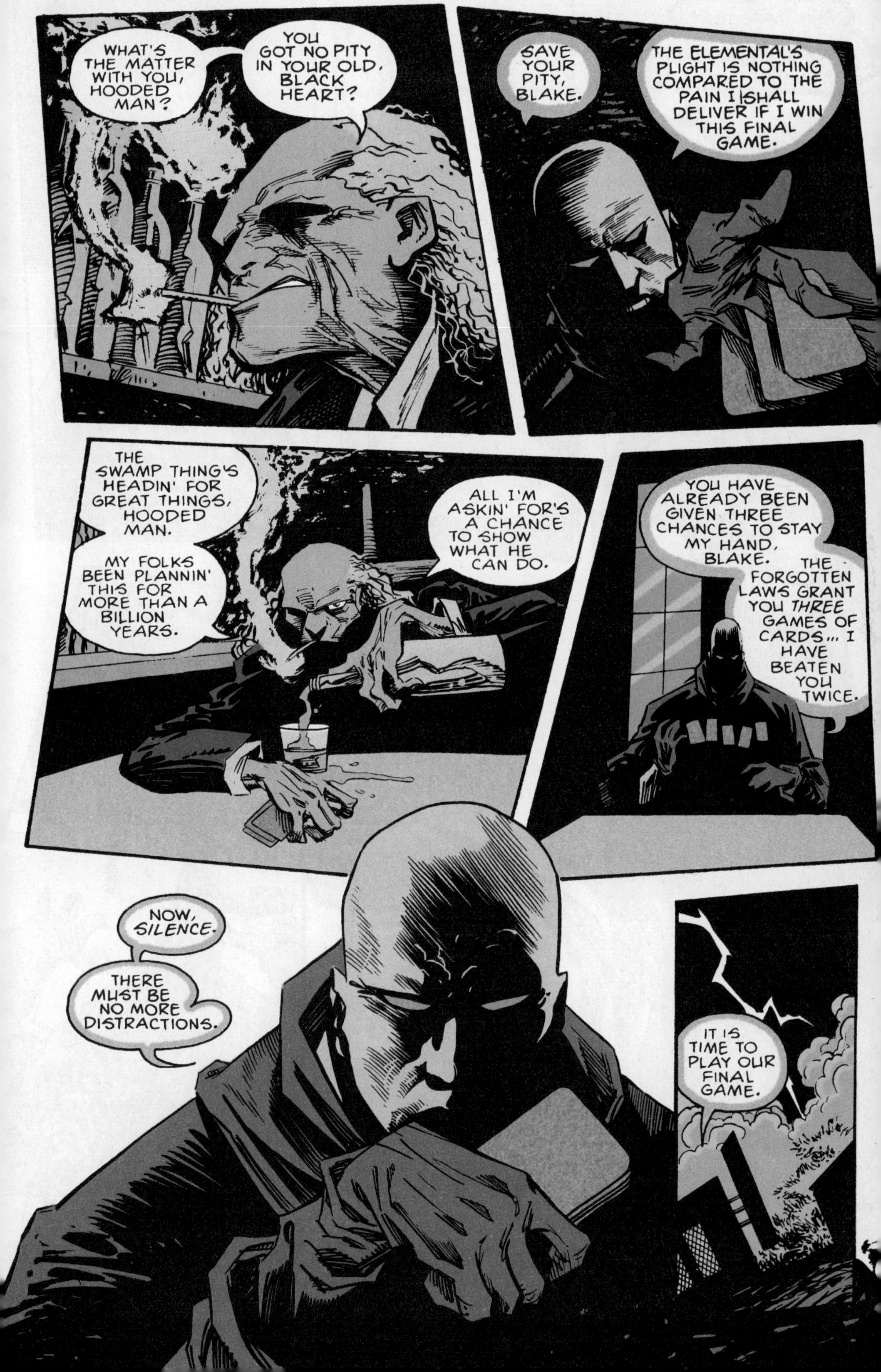
WHAT'S THE MATTER WITH YOU, HOODED MAN?
YOU GOT NO PITY IN YOUR OLD, BLACK HEART?
SAVE YOUR PITY, BLAKE.
THE ELEMENTAL'S PLIGHT IS NOTHING COMPARED TO THE PAIN I SHALL DELIVER IF I WIN THIS FINAL GAME.
THE SWAMP THING'S HEADIN' FOR GREAT THINGS, HOODED MAN.
MY FOLKS BEEN PLANNIN' THIS FOR MORE THAN A BILLION YEARS.
ALL I'M ASKIN' FOR'S A CHANCE TO SHOW WHAT HE CAN DO.
YOU HAVE ALREADY BEEN GIVEN THREE CHANCES TO STAY MY HAND, BLAKE.
THE FORGOTTEN LAWS GRANT YOU *THREE* GAMES OF CARDS... I HAVE BEATEN YOU TWICE.
NOW, *SILENCE*.
THERE MUST BE NO MORE DISTRACTIONS.
IT IS TIME TO PLAY OUR FINAL GAME.

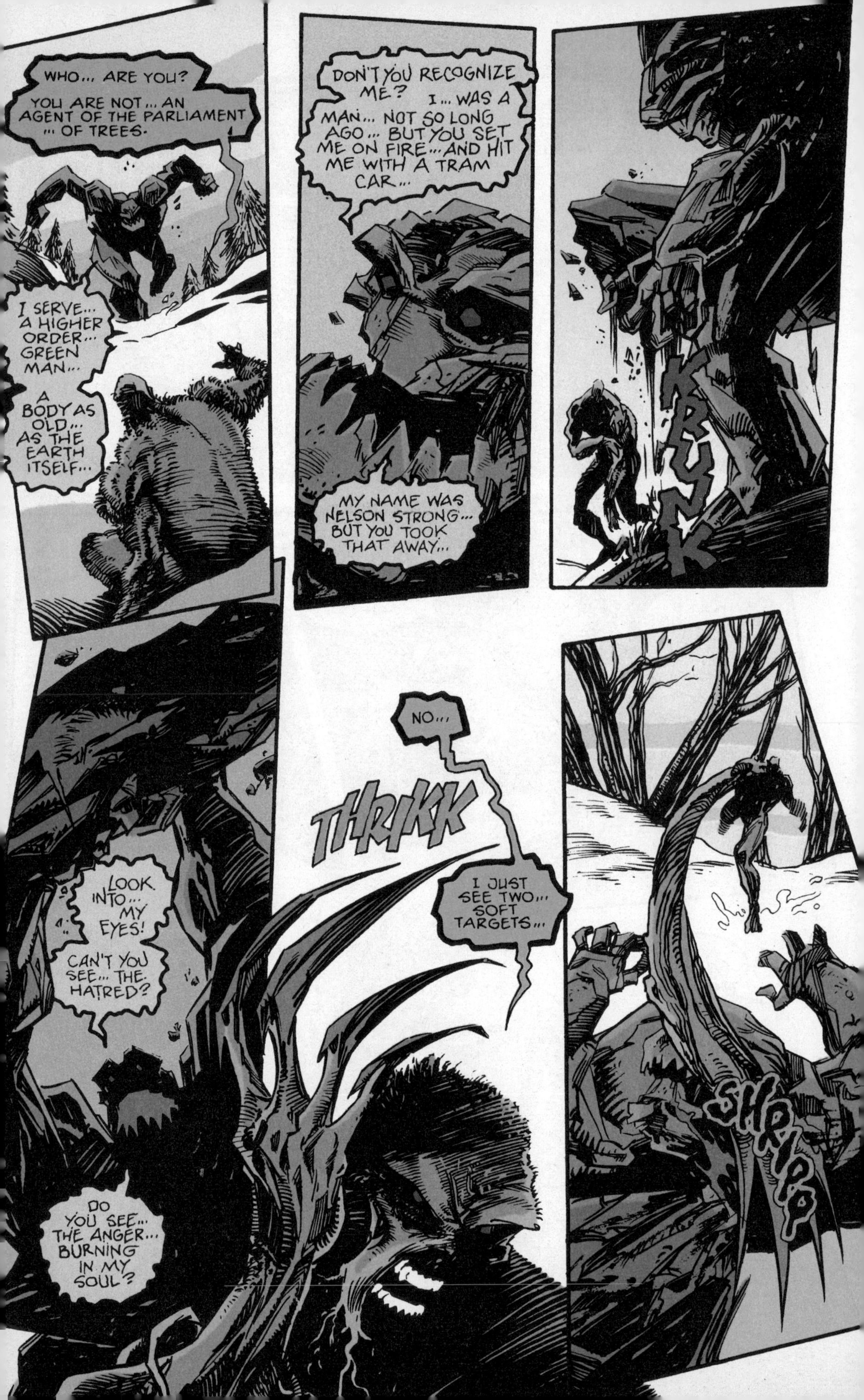
WHO... ARE YOU?
YOU ARE NOT... AN AGENT OF THE PARLIAMENT ... OF TREES.
I SERVE... A HIGHER ORDER... GREEN MAN...
A BODY AS OLD... AS THE EARTH ITSELF...
DON'T YOU RECOGNIZE ME? I... WAS A MAN... NOT SO LONG AGO... BUT YOU SET ME ON FIRE... AND HIT ME WITH A TRAM CAR...
MY NAME WAS NELSON STRONG... BUT YOU TOOK THAT AWAY...
KRUNK
LOOK INTO... MY EYES!
CAN'T YOU SEE... THE HATRED?
DO YOU SEE... THE ANGER... BURNING IN MY SOUL?
NO...
THRIKK
I JUST SEE TWO... SOFT TARGETS...
SHRAPP

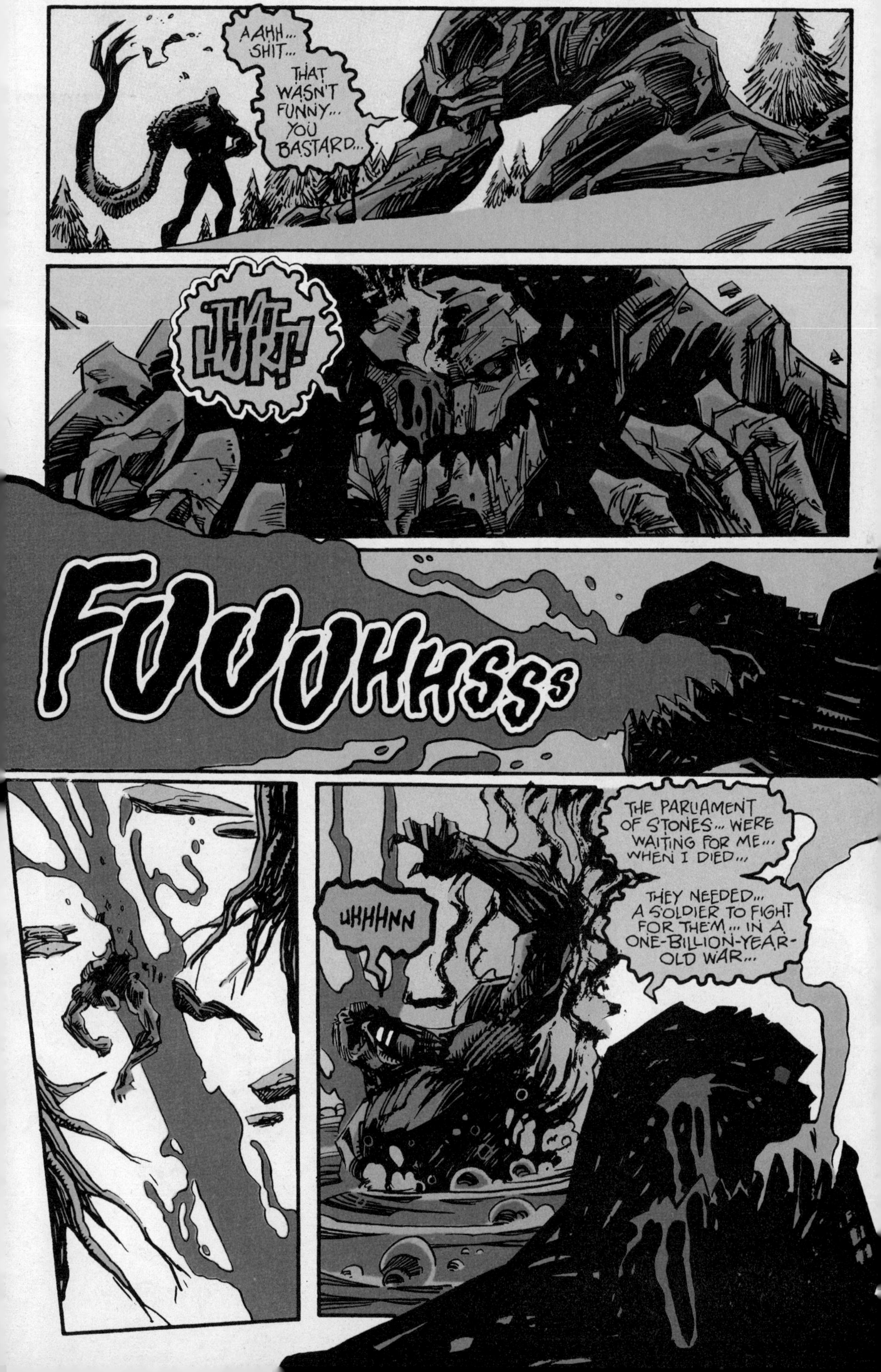
AAHH... SHIT...
THAT WASN'T FUNNY... YOU BASTARD...
THAT HURT!
FOOOHHSSS
UHHHNN
THE PARLIAMENT OF STONES... WERE WAITING FOR ME... WHEN I DIED...
THEY NEEDED... A SOLDIER TO FIGHT FOR THEM... IN A ONE-BILLION-YEAR-OLD WAR...

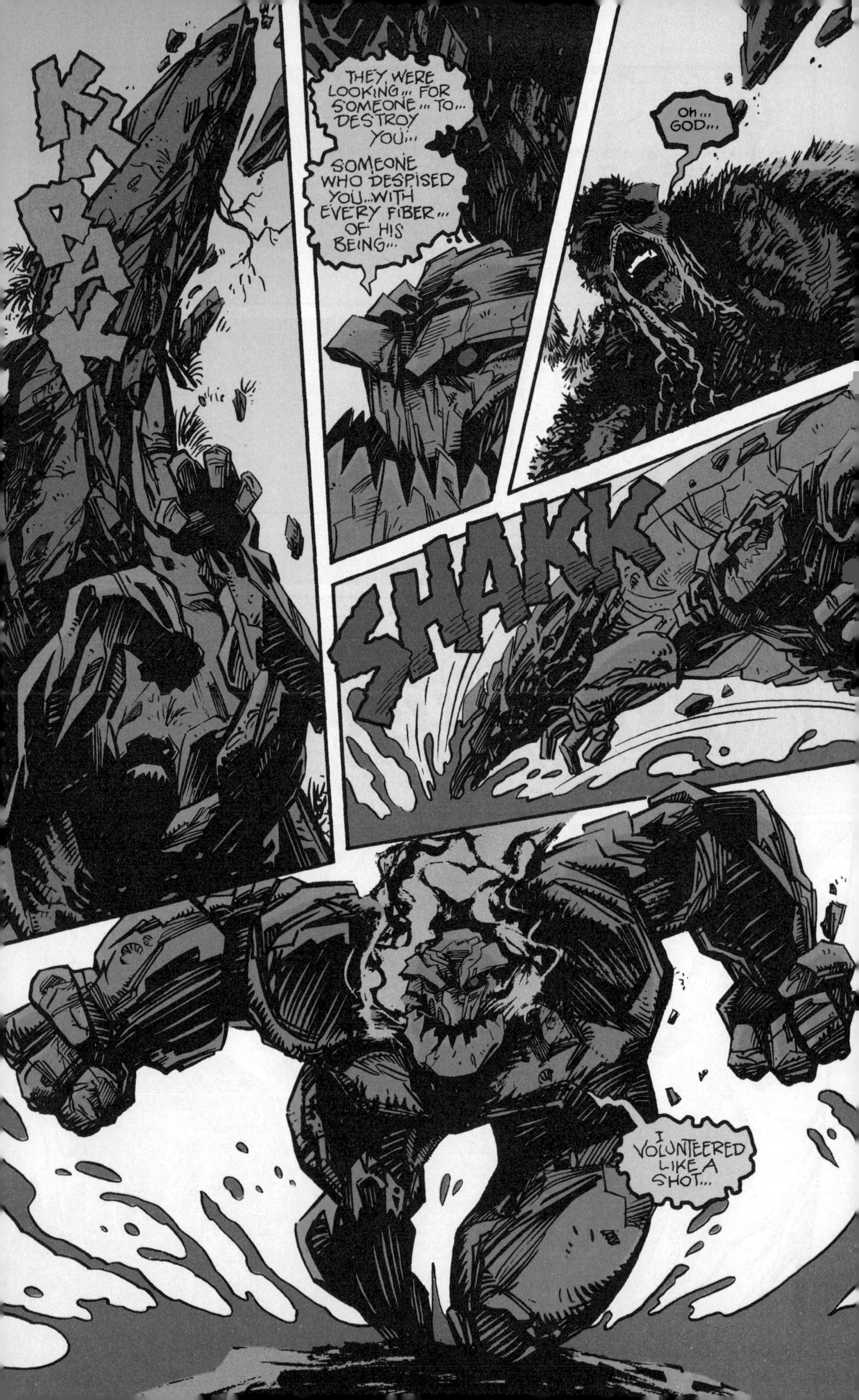
KRAK
THEY WERE LOOKING... FOR SOMEONE... TO... DESTROY YOU...
SOMEONE WHO DESPISED YOU...WITH EVERY FIBER... OF HIS BEING...
Oh... GOD...
SHAKK
I VOLUNTEERED LIKE A SHOT...

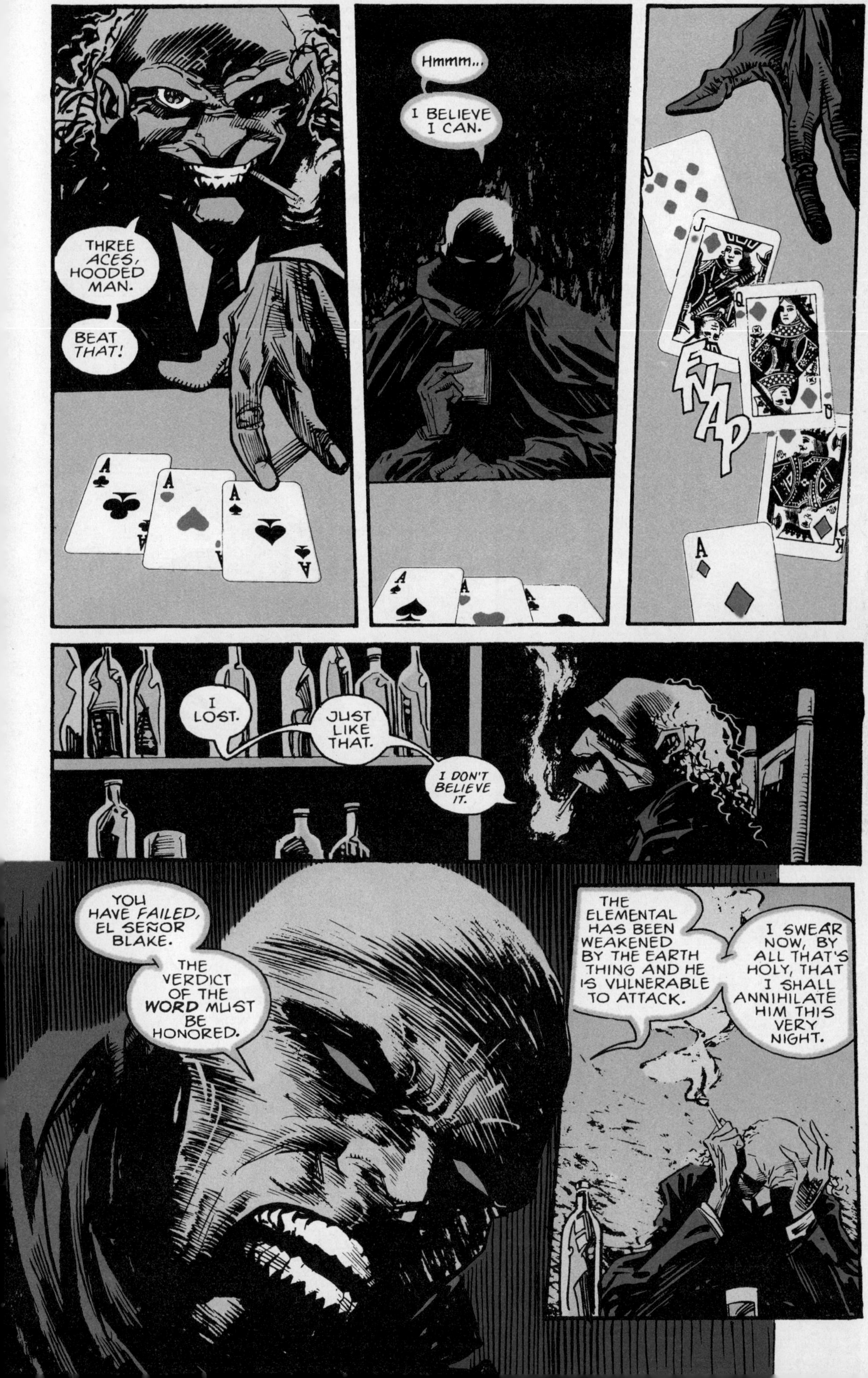
THREE ACES, HOODED MAN.
BEAT THAT!
Hmmm...
I BELIEVE I CAN.
SNAP
I LOST.
JUST LIKE THAT.
I DON'T BELIEVE IT.
YOU HAVE FAILED, EL SEÑOR BLAKE.
THE VERDICT OF THE WORD MUST BE HONORED.
THE ELEMENTAL HAS BEEN WEAKENED BY THE EARTH THING AND HE IS VULNERABLE TO ATTACK.
I SWEAR NOW, BY ALL THAT'S HOLY, THAT I SHALL ANNIHILATE HIM THIS VERY NIGHT.

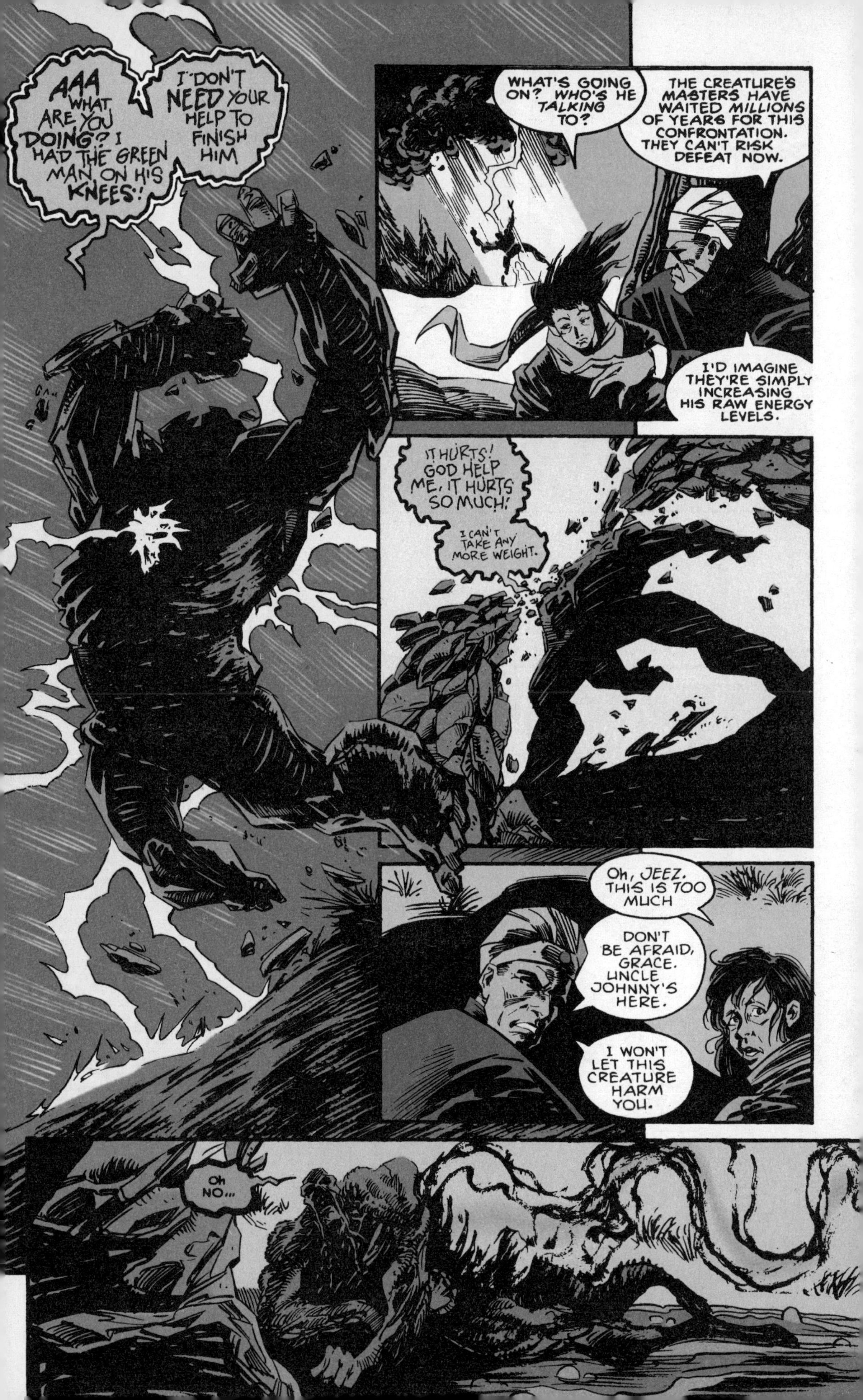
AAA WHAT ARE YOU DOING? I HAD THE GREEN MAN ON HIS KNEES!
I DON'T NEED YOUR HELP TO FINISH HIM
WHAT'S GOING ON? WHO'S HE TALKING TO?
THE CREATURE'S MASTERS HAVE WAITED MILLIONS OF YEARS FOR THIS CONFRONTATION. THEY CAN'T RISK DEFEAT NOW.
I'D IMAGINE THEY'RE SIMPLY INCREASING HIS RAW ENERGY LEVELS.
IT HURTS! GOD HELP ME, IT HURTS SO MUCH!
I CAN'T TAKE ANY MORE WEIGHT.
Oh, JEEZ. THIS IS TOO MUCH
DON'T BE AFRAID, GRACE. UNCLE JOHNNY'S HERE.
I WON'T LET THIS CREATURE HARM YOU.
Oh NO...

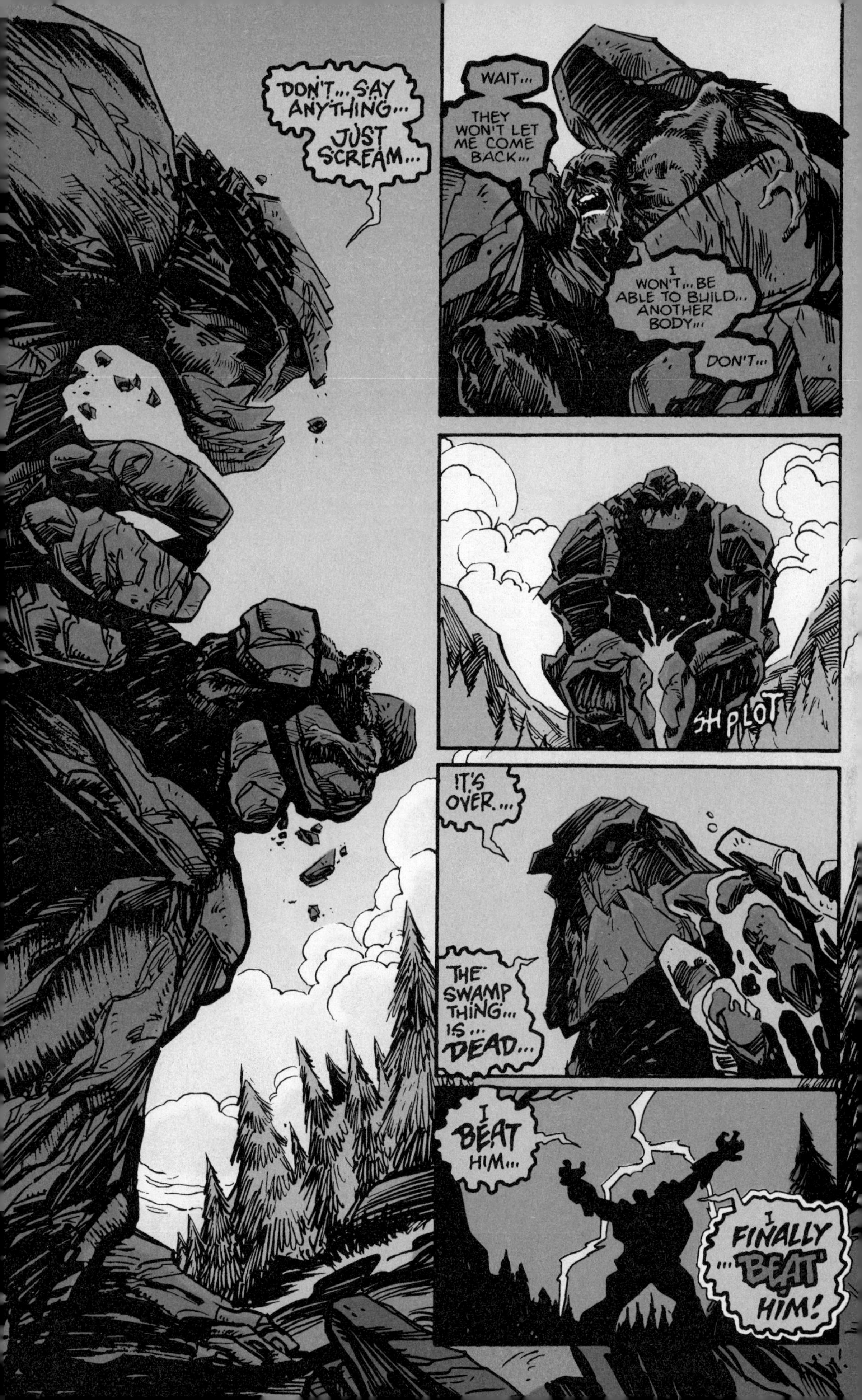
DON'T... SAY ANYTHING... JUST SCREAM...
WAIT...
THEY WON'T LET ME COME BACK...
I WON'T... BE ABLE TO BUILD... ANOTHER BODY...
DON'T...
SHPLOT
IT'S OVER...
THE SWAMP THING... IS... DEAD...
I BEAT HIM...
I FINALLY ...BEAT HIM!

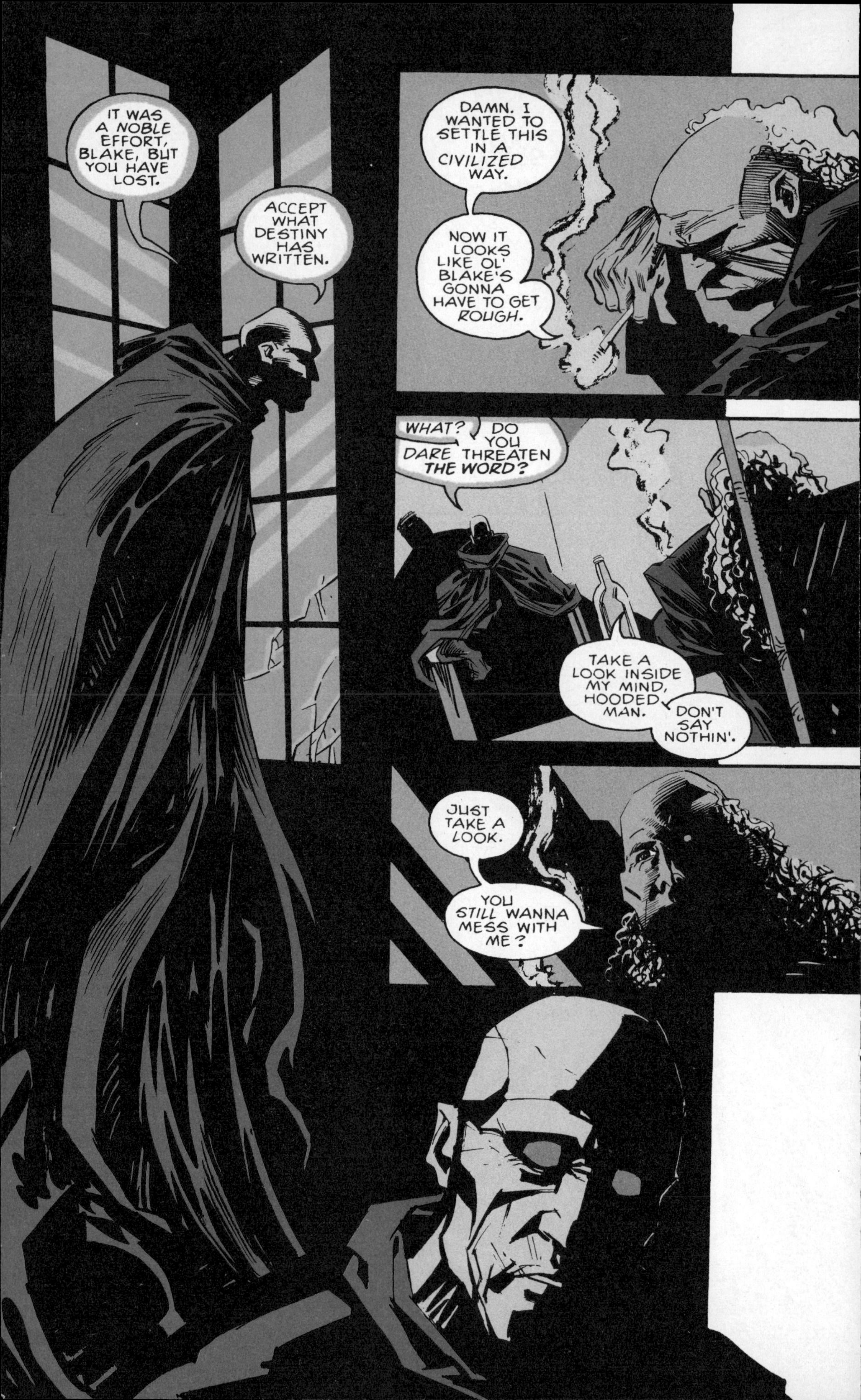
IT WAS A NOBLE EFFORT, BLAKE, BUT YOU HAVE LOST.
ACCEPT WHAT DESTINY HAS WRITTEN.
DAMN. I WANTED TO SETTLE THIS IN A CIVILIZED WAY.
NOW IT LOOKS LIKE OL' BLAKE'S GONNA HAVE TO GET ROUGH.
WHAT? DO YOU DARE THREATEN THE WORD?
TAKE A LOOK INSIDE MY MIND, HOODED MAN.
DON'T SAY NOTHIN'.
JUST TAKE A LOOK.
YOU STILL WANNA MESS WITH ME?

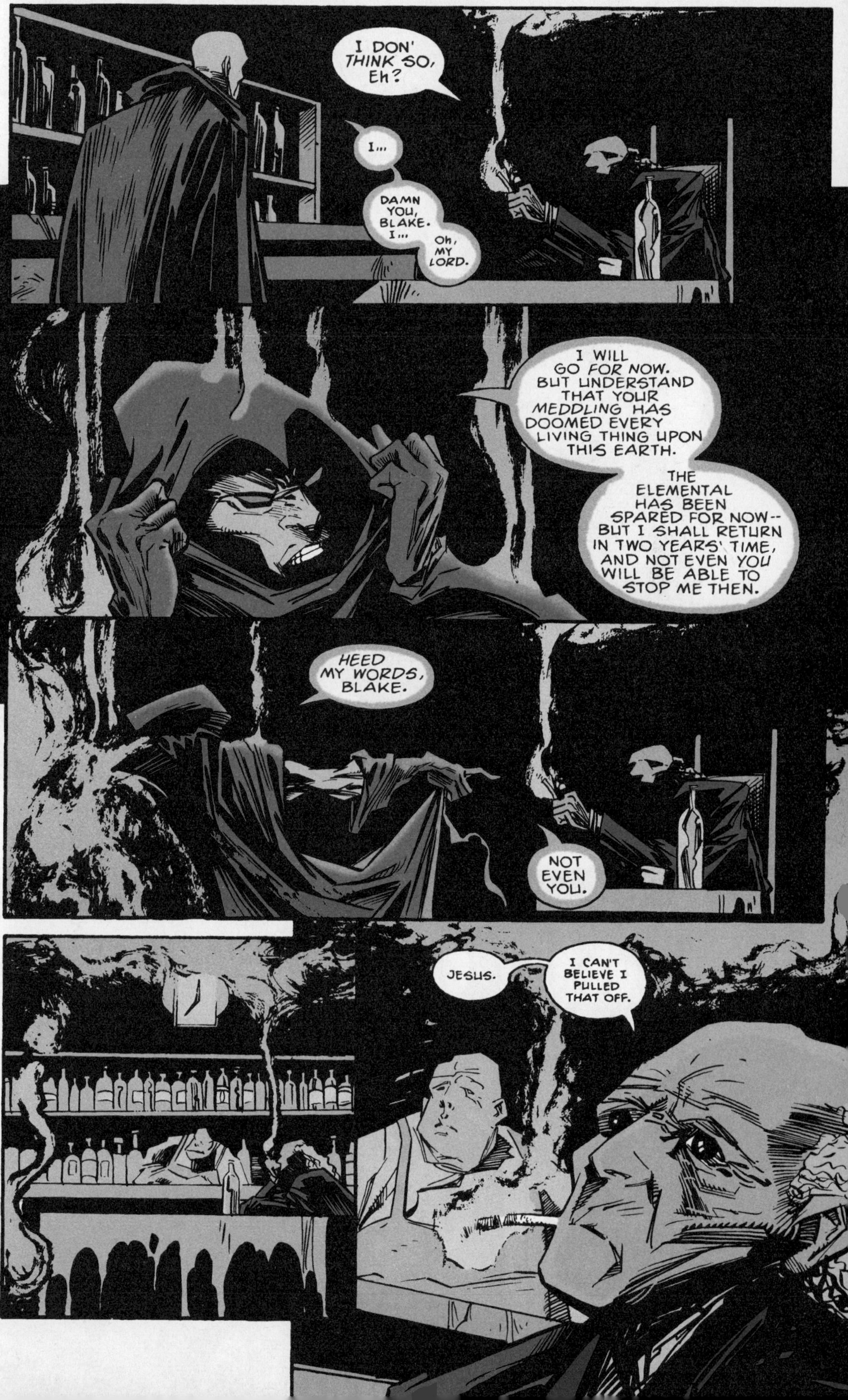
I DON' THINK SO, Eh?
I...
DAMN YOU, BLAKE. I...
Oh, MY LORD.
I WILL GO FOR NOW. BUT UNDERSTAND THAT YOUR MEDDLING HAS DOOMED EVERY LIVING THING UPON THIS EARTH.
THE ELEMENTAL HAS BEEN SPARED FOR NOW-- BUT I SHALL RETURN IN TWO YEARS' TIME, AND NOT EVEN YOU WILL BE ABLE TO STOP ME THEN.
HEED MY WORDS, BLAKE.
NOT EVEN YOU.
JESUS.
I CAN'T BELIEVE I PULLED THAT OFF.

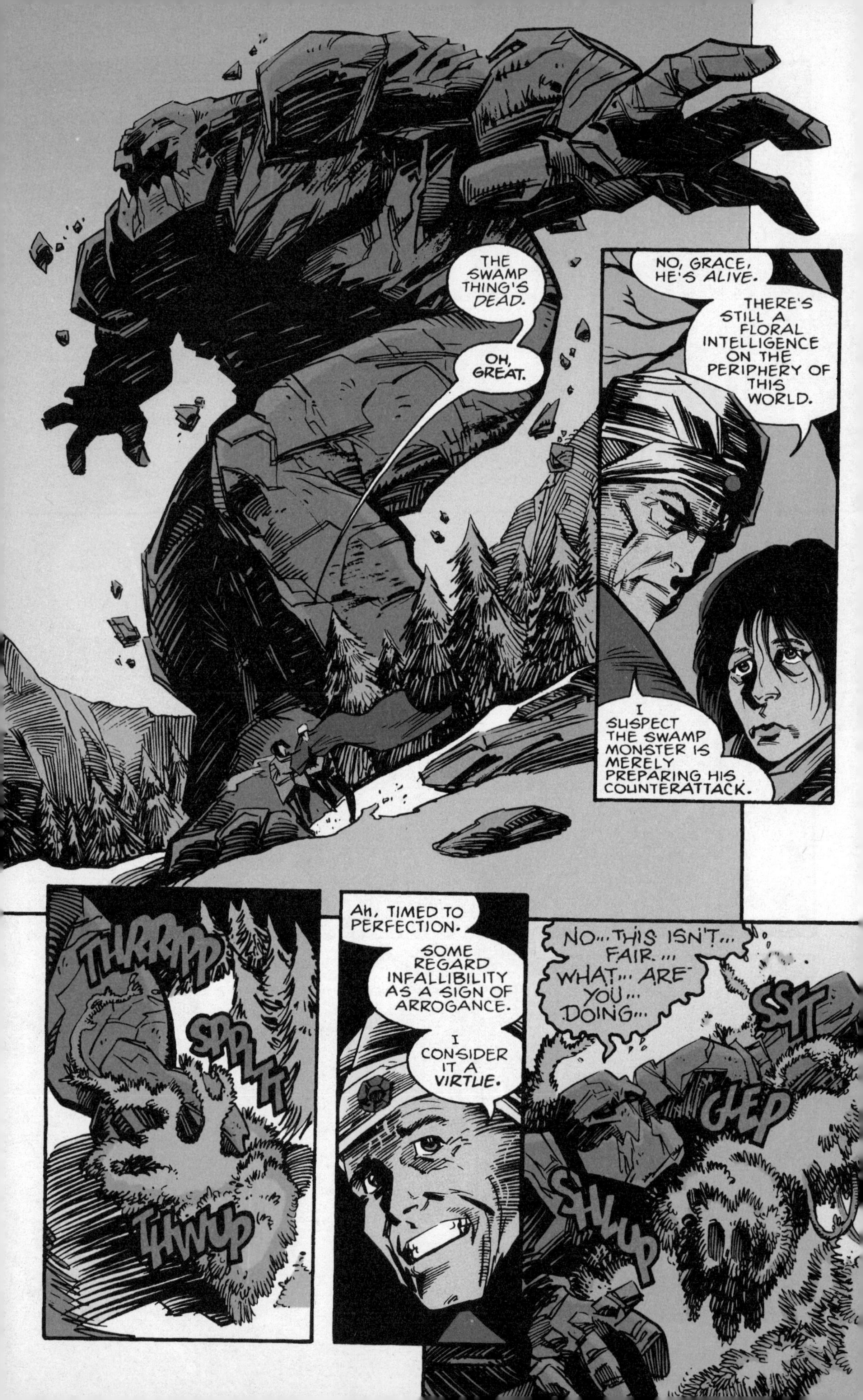
THE SWAMP THING'S DEAD.
OH, GREAT.
NO, GRACE, HE'S ALIVE.
THERE'S STILL A FLORAL INTELLIGENCE ON THE PERIPHERY OF THIS WORLD.
I SUSPECT THE SWAMP MONSTER IS MERELY PREPARING HIS COUNTERATTACK.
THRRAPP
SPPLTT
THWUP
Ah, TIMED TO PERFECTION.
SOME REGARD INFALLIBILITY AS A SIGN OF ARROGANCE.
I CONSIDER IT A VIRTUE.
NO... THIS ISN'T... FAIR.... WHAT... ARE YOU... DOING...
SSFT
GLEP
SHLUP

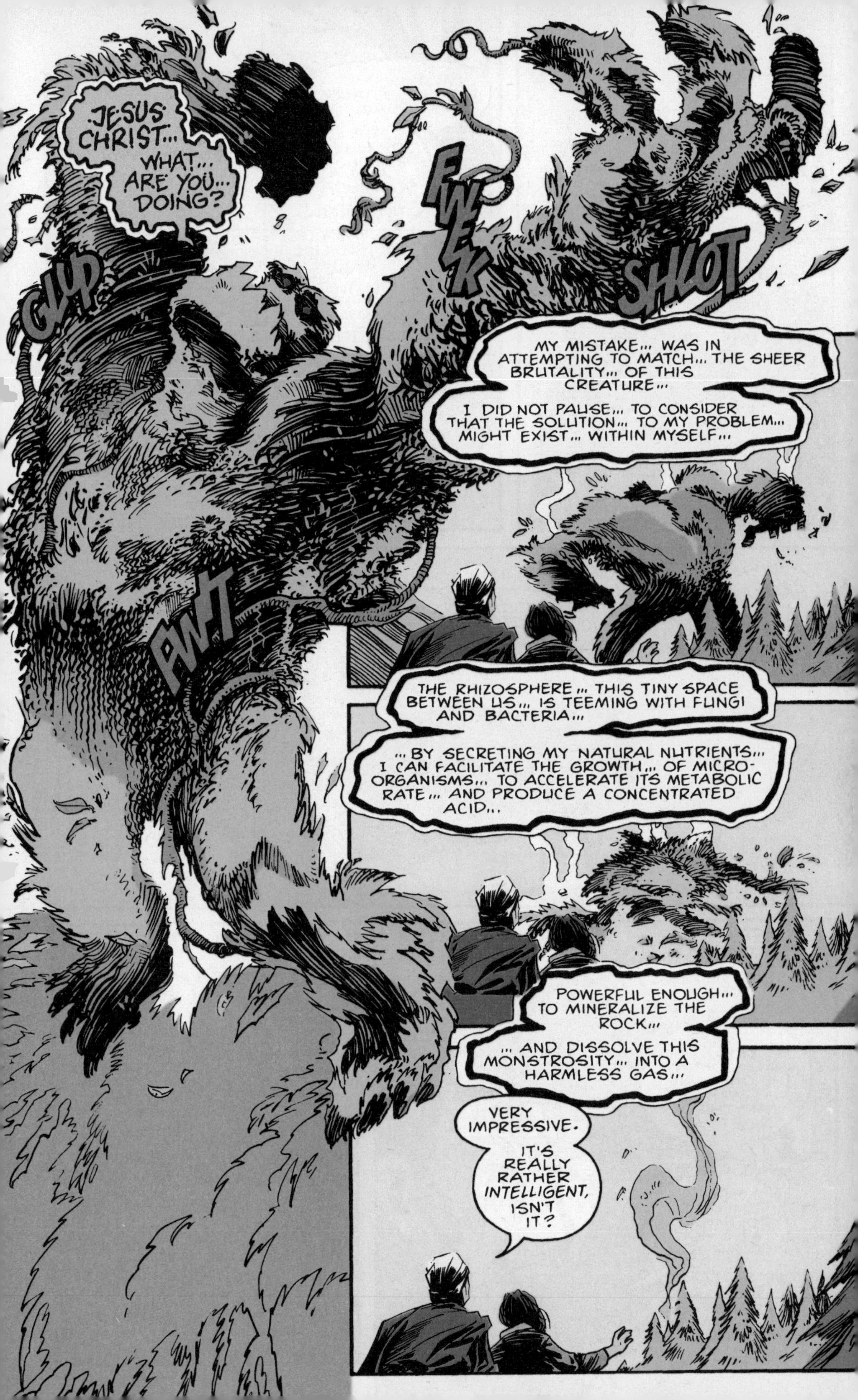
JESUS CHRIST... WHAT... ARE YOU... DOING?
GLUP
FWEK
SHLOT
AWT
MY MISTAKE... WAS IN ATTEMPTING TO MATCH... THE SHEER BRUTALITY... OF THIS CREATURE...
I DID NOT PAUSE... TO CONSIDER THAT THE SOLUTION... TO MY PROBLEM... MIGHT EXIST... WITHIN MYSELF...
THE RHIZOSPHERE... THIS TINY SPACE BETWEEN US... IS TEEMING WITH FUNGI AND BACTERIA...
...BY SECRETING MY NATURAL NUTRIENTS... I CAN FACILITATE THE GROWTH... OF MICRO-ORGANISMS... TO ACCELERATE ITS METABOLIC RATE... AND PRODUCE A CONCENTRATED ACID...
POWERFUL ENOUGH... TO MINERALIZE THE ROCK...
...AND DISSOLVE THIS MONSTROSITY... INTO A HARMLESS GAS...
VERY IMPRESSIVE.
IT'S REALLY RATHER INTELLIGENT, ISN'T IT?

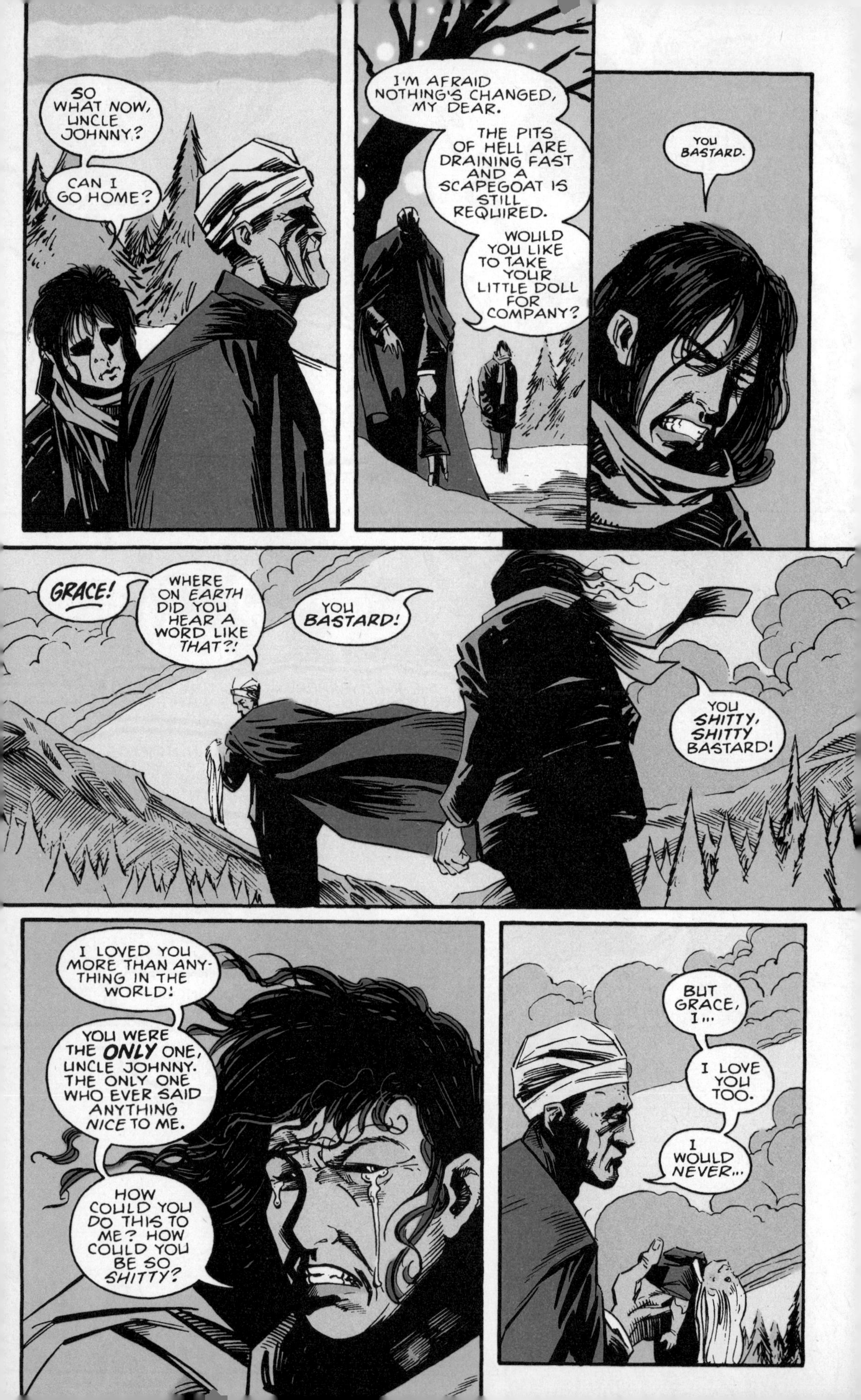
SO WHAT NOW, UNCLE JOHNNY?
CAN I GO HOME?
I'M AFRAID NOTHING'S CHANGED, MY DEAR.
THE PITS OF HELL ARE DRAINING FAST AND A SCAPEGOAT IS STILL REQUIRED.
WOULD YOU LIKE TO TAKE YOUR LITTLE DOLL FOR COMPANY?
YOU BASTARD.
GRACE!
WHERE ON EARTH DID YOU HEAR A WORD LIKE THAT?!
YOU BASTARD!
YOU SHITTY, SHITTY BASTARD!
I LOVED YOU MORE THAN ANYTHING IN THE WORLD!
YOU WERE THE ONLY ONE, UNCLE JOHNNY. THE ONLY ONE WHO EVER SAID ANYTHING NICE TO ME.
HOW COULD YOU DO THIS TO ME? HOW COULD YOU BE SO SHITTY?
BUT GRACE, I...
I LOVE YOU TOO.
I WOULD NEVER...

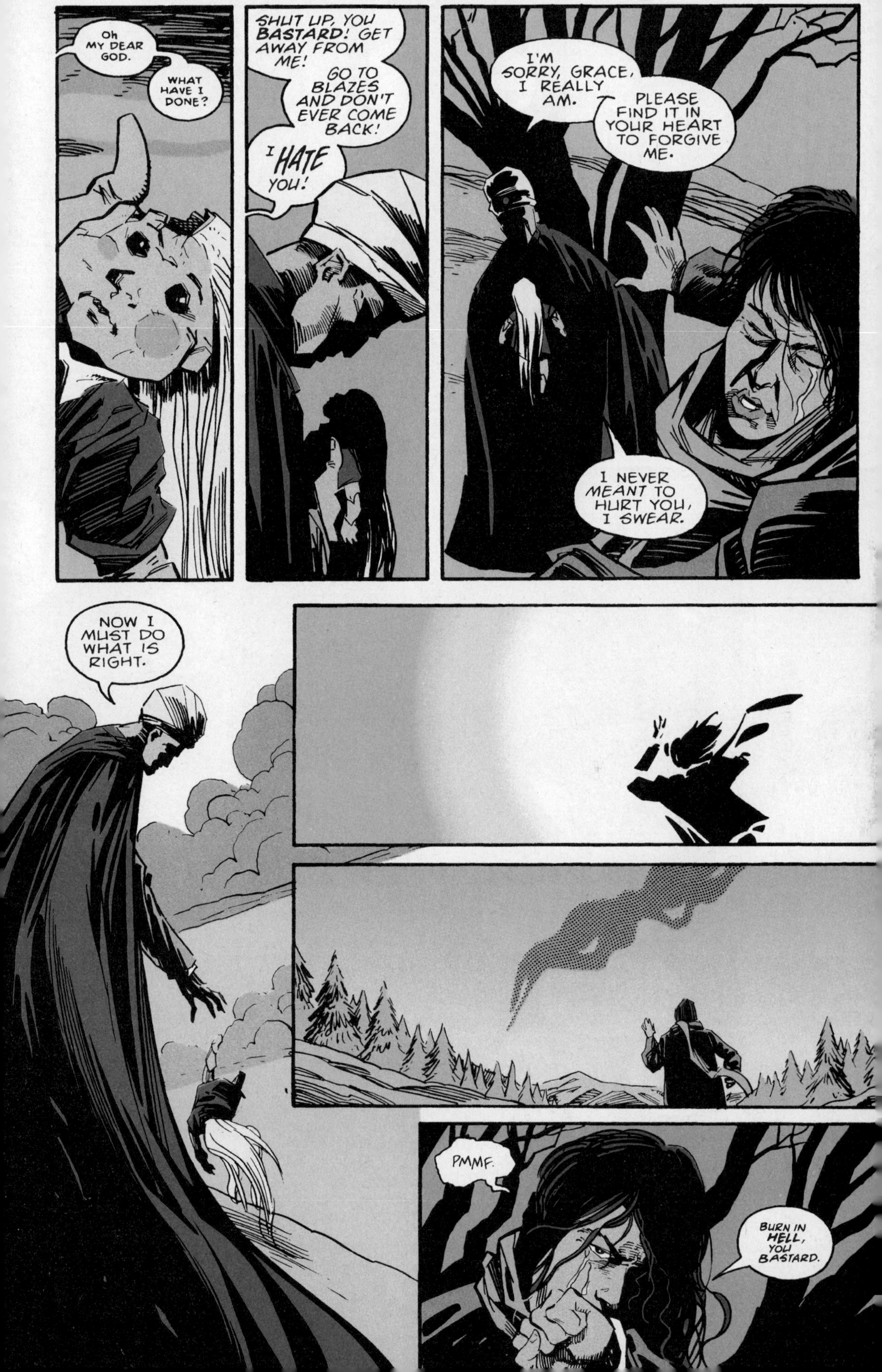

Oh MY DEAR GOD.
WHAT HAVE I DONE?
SHUT UP, YOU BASTARD! GET AWAY FROM ME!
GO TO BLAZES AND DON'T EVER COME BACK!
I HATE YOU!
I'M SORRY, GRACE, I REALLY AM.
PLEASE FIND IT IN YOUR HEART TO FORGIVE ME.
I NEVER MEANT TO HURT YOU, I SWEAR.
NOW I MUST DO WHAT IS RIGHT.
PMMF.
BURN IN HELL, YOU BASTARD.

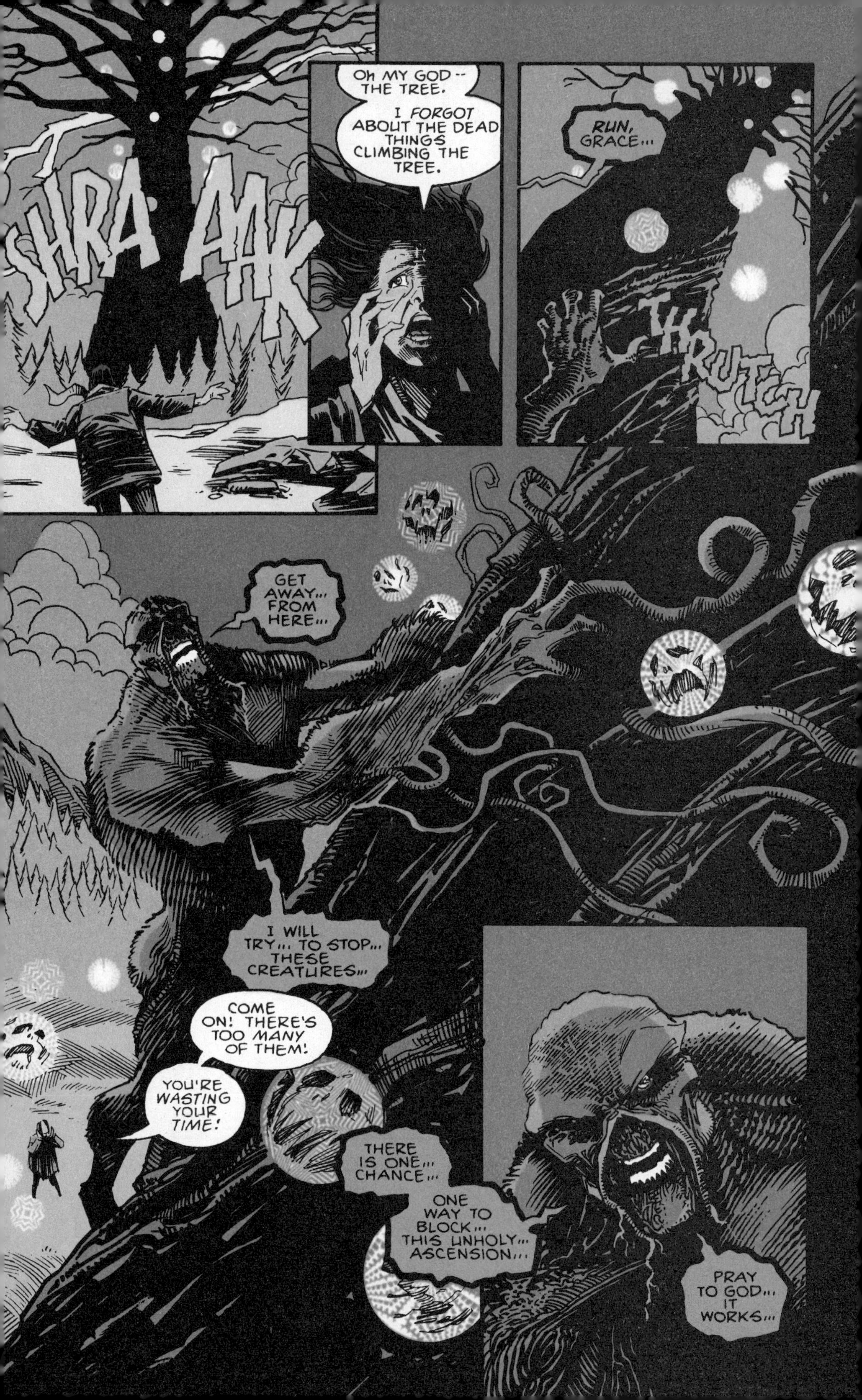

SHRAAAK
Oh MY GOD -- THE TREE.
I FORGOT ABOUT THE DEAD THINGS CLIMBING THE TREE.
RUN, GRACE...
THRUTCH
GET AWAY... FROM HERE...
I WILL TRY... TO STOP... THESE CREATURES...
COME ON! THERE'S TOO MANY OF THEM!
YOU'RE WASTING YOUR TIME!
THERE IS ONE... CHANCE...
ONE WAY TO BLOCK... THIS UNHOLY... ASCENSION...
PRAY TO GOD... IT WORKS...

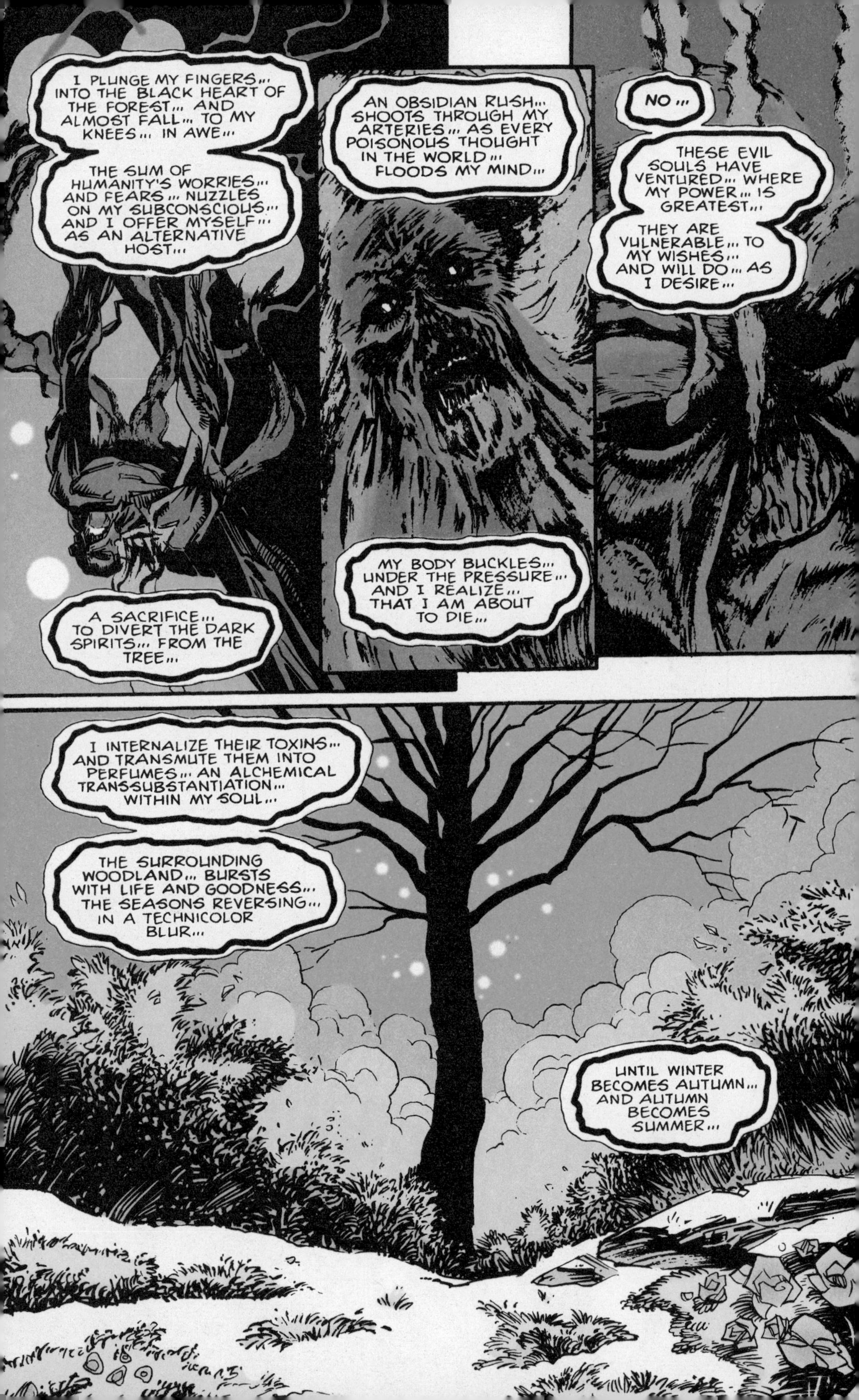
I PLUNGE MY FINGERS... INTO THE BLACK HEART OF THE FOREST... AND ALMOST FALL... TO MY KNEES... IN AWE...
THE SUM OF HUMANITY'S WORRIES... AND FEARS... NUZZLES ON MY SUBCONSCIOUS... AND I OFFER MYSELF... AS AN ALTERNATIVE HOST...
A SACRIFICE... TO DIVERT THE DARK SPIRITS... FROM THE TREE...
AN OBSIDIAN RUSH... SHOOTS THROUGH MY ARTERIES... AS EVERY POISONOUS THOUGHT IN THE WORLD... FLOODS MY MIND...
MY BODY BUCKLES... UNDER THE PRESSURE... AND I REALIZE... THAT I AM ABOUT TO DIE...
NO...
THESE EVIL SOULS HAVE VENTURED... WHERE MY POWER... IS GREATEST...
THEY ARE VULNERABLE... TO MY WISHES... AND WILL DO... AS I DESIRE...
I INTERNALIZE THEIR TOXINS... AND TRANSMUTE THEM INTO PERFUMES... AN ALCHEMICAL TRANSSUBSTANTIATION... WITHIN MY SOUL...
THE SURROUNDING WOODLAND... BURSTS WITH LIFE AND GOODNESS... THE SEASONS REVERSING... IN A TECHNICOLOR BLUR...
UNTIL WINTER BECOMES AUTUMN... AND AUTUMN BECOMES SUMMER...

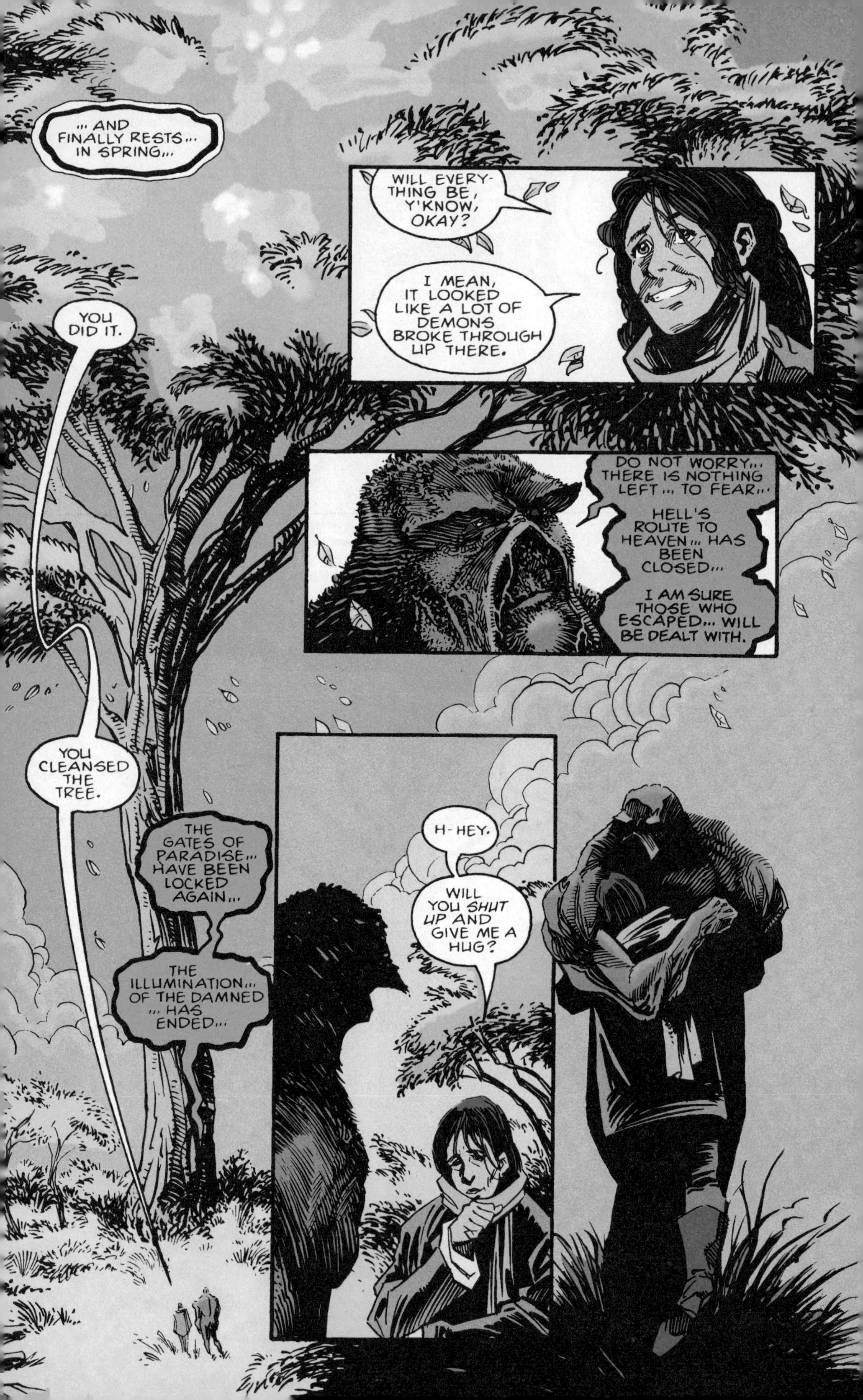
...AND FINALLY RESTS... IN SPRING...
WILL EVERYTHING BE, Y'KNOW, OKAY?
I MEAN, IT LOOKED LIKE A LOT OF DEMONS BROKE THROUGH UP THERE.
YOU DID IT.
DO NOT WORRY... THERE IS NOTHING LEFT... TO FEAR...
HELL'S ROUTE TO HEAVEN... HAS BEEN CLOSED...
I AM SURE THOSE WHO ESCAPED... WILL BE DEALT WITH.
YOU CLEANSED THE TREE.
THE GATES OF PARADISE... HAVE BEEN LOCKED AGAIN...
THE ILLUMINATION... OF THE DAMNED ...HAS ENDED...
H-HEY.
WILL YOU SHUT UP AND GIVE ME A HUG?

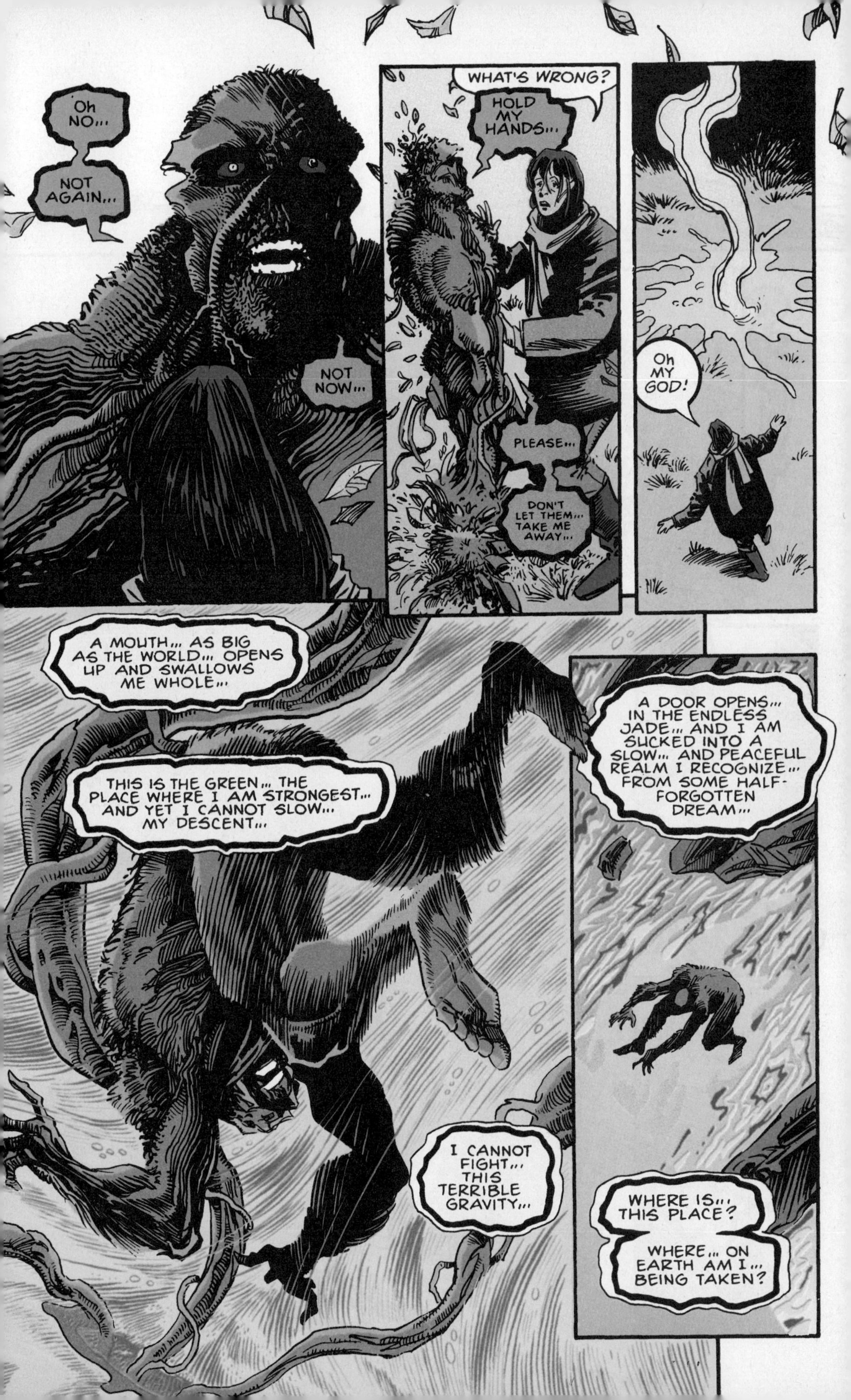
Oh NO...
NOT AGAIN...
NOT NOW...
WHAT'S WRONG?
HOLD MY HANDS...
PLEASE...
DON'T LET THEM... TAKE ME AWAY...
Oh MY GOD!
A MOUTH... AS BIG AS THE WORLD... OPENS UP AND SWALLOWS ME WHOLE...
THIS IS THE GREEN... THE PLACE WHERE I AM STRONGEST... AND YET I CANNOT SLOW... MY DESCENT...
A DOOR OPENS... IN THE ENDLESS JADE... AND I AM SUCKED INTO A SLOW... AND PEACEFUL REALM I RECOGNIZE... FROM SOME HALF-FORGOTTEN DREAM...
I CANNOT FIGHT... THIS TERRIBLE GRAVITY...
WHERE IS... THIS PLACE?
WHERE... ON EARTH AM I... BEING TAKEN?

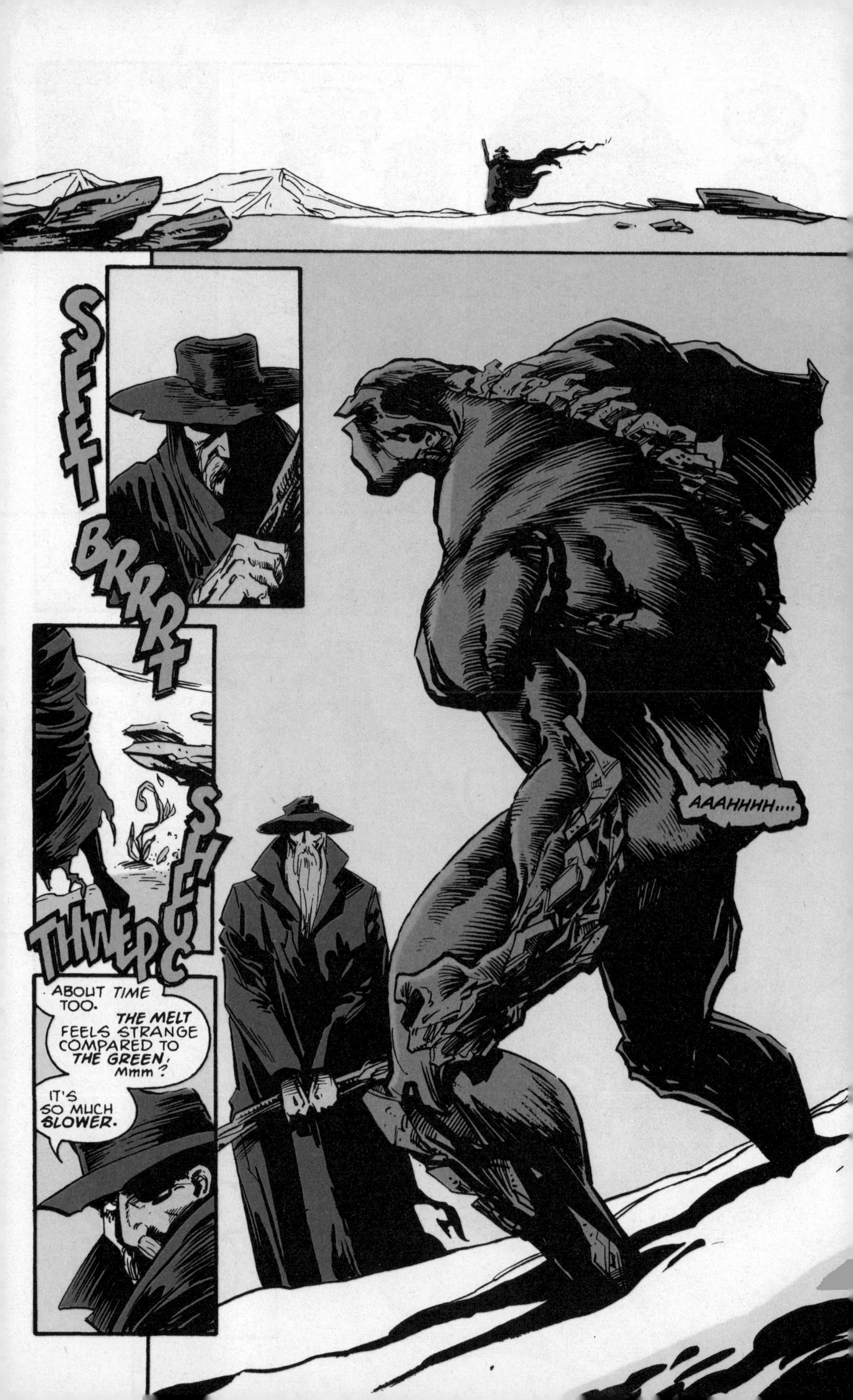
SFFT
BRRRRT
SHLUC
THWEP
AAAHHHH....
ABOUT TIME TOO. THE MELT FEELS STRANGE COMPARED TO THE GREEN, Mmm?
IT'S SO MUCH SLOWER.

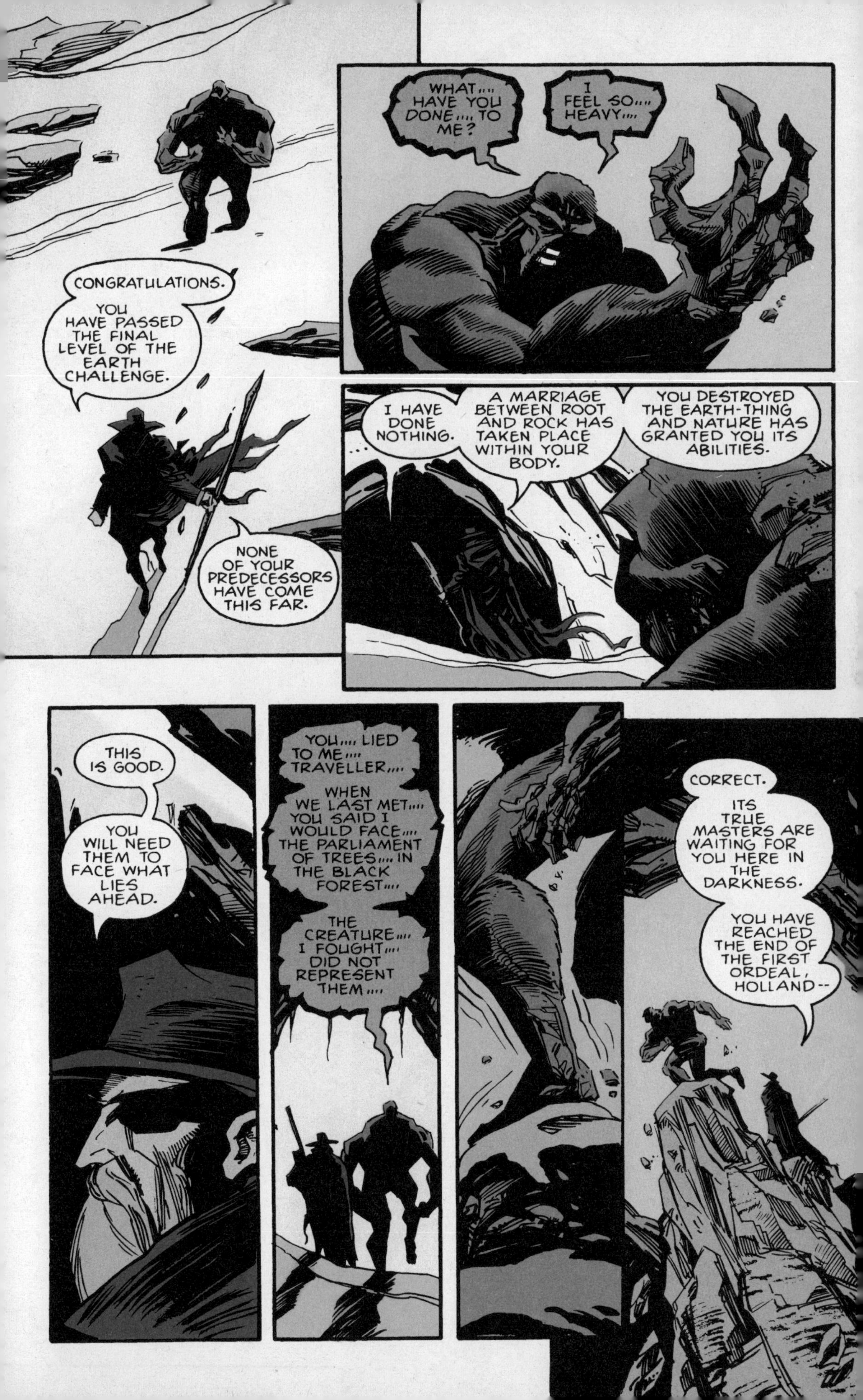
WHAT.... HAVE YOU DONE.... TO ME?
I FEEL SO.... HEAVY....
CONGRATULATIONS.
YOU HAVE PASSED THE FINAL LEVEL OF THE EARTH CHALLENGE.
NONE OF YOUR PREDECESSORS HAVE COME THIS FAR.
I HAVE DONE NOTHING.
A MARRIAGE BETWEEN ROOT AND ROCK HAS TAKEN PLACE WITHIN YOUR BODY.
YOU DESTROYED THE EARTH-THING AND NATURE HAS GRANTED YOU ITS ABILITIES.
THIS IS GOOD.
YOU WILL NEED THEM TO FACE WHAT LIES AHEAD.
YOU.... LIED TO ME.... TRAVELLER....
WHEN WE LAST MET.... YOU SAID I WOULD FACE.... THE PARLIAMENT OF TREES.... IN THE BLACK FOREST....
THE CREATURE.... I FOUGHT.... DID NOT REPRESENT THEM....
CORRECT.
ITS TRUE MASTERS ARE WAITING FOR YOU HERE IN THE DARKNESS.
YOU HAVE REACHED THE END OF THE FIRST ORDEAL, HOLLAND--

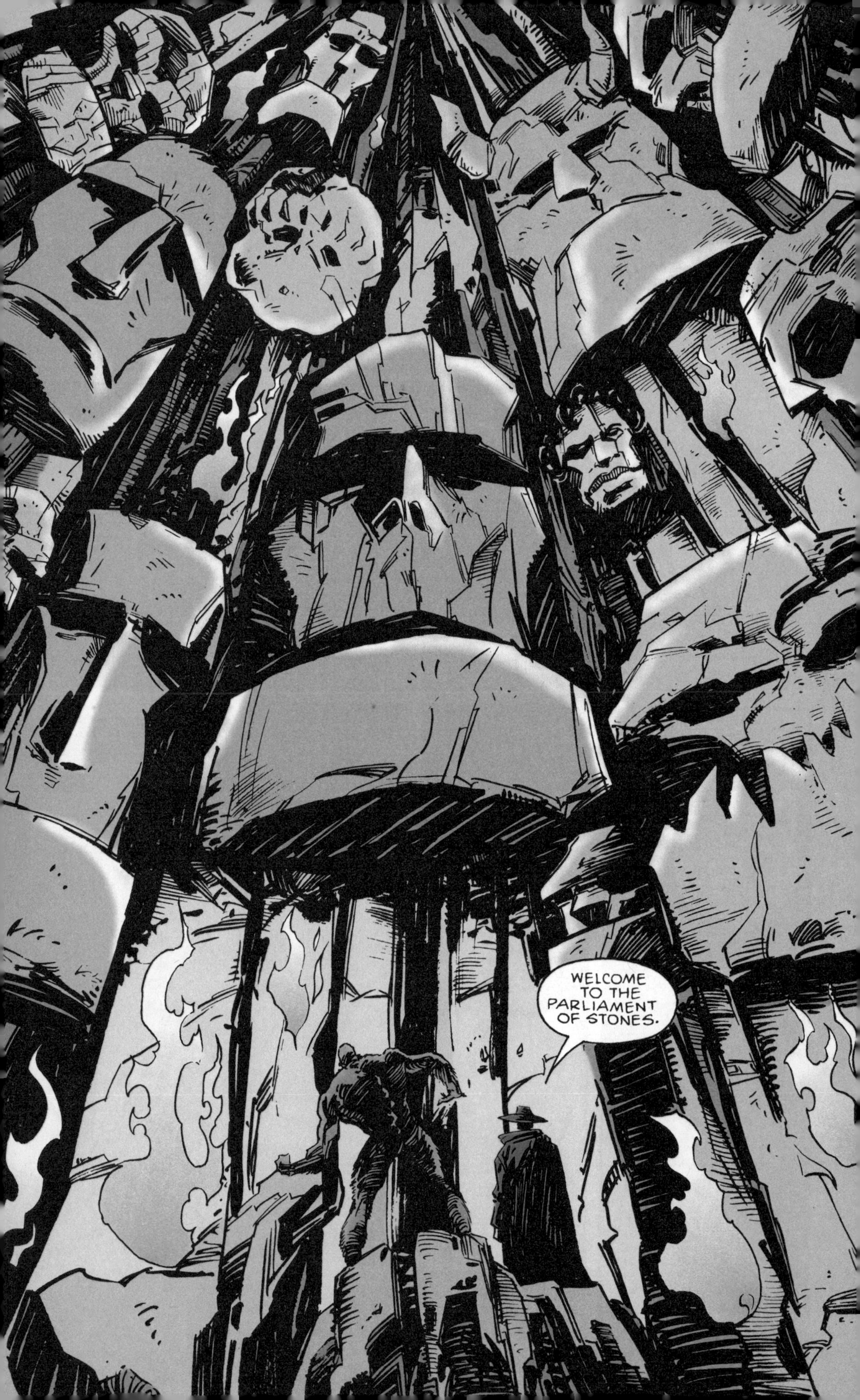
WELCOME TO THE PARLIAMENT OF STONES.

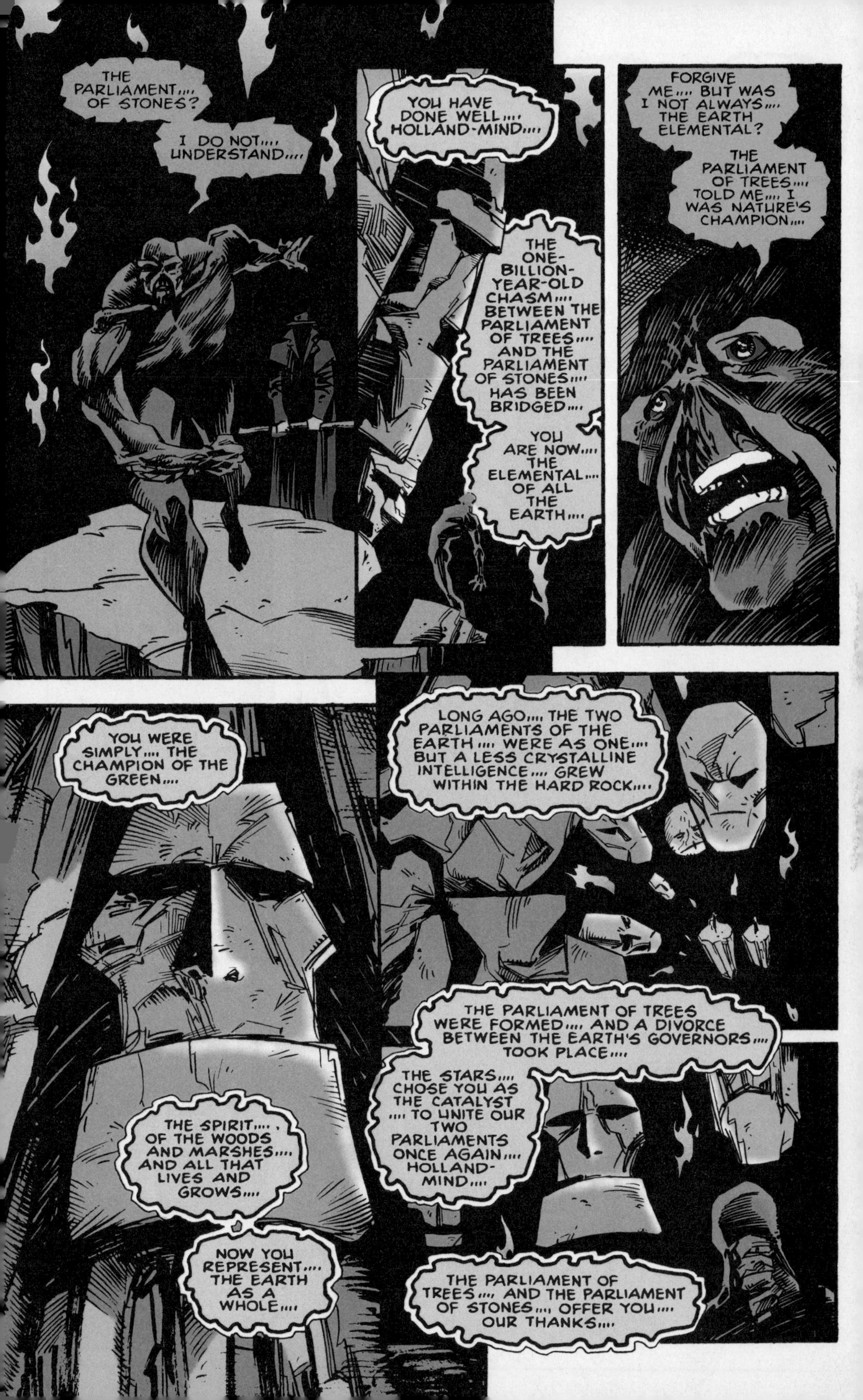
THE PARLIAMENT.... OF STONES?
I DO NOT.... UNDERSTAND....
YOU HAVE DONE WELL.... HOLLAND-MIND....
THE ONE-BILLION-YEAR-OLD CHASM.... BETWEEN THE PARLIAMENT OF TREES.... AND THE PARLIAMENT OF STONES.... HAS BEEN BRIDGED....
YOU ARE NOW.... THE ELEMENTAL.... OF ALL THE EARTH....
FORGIVE ME.... BUT WAS I NOT ALWAYS.... THE EARTH ELEMENTAL?
THE PARLIAMENT OF TREES.... TOLD ME.... I WAS NATURE'S CHAMPION....
YOU WERE SIMPLY.... THE CHAMPION OF THE GREEN....
THE SPIRIT.... OF THE WOODS AND MARSHES.... AND ALL THAT LIVES AND GROWS....
NOW YOU REPRESENT.... THE EARTH AS A WHOLE....
LONG AGO.... THE TWO PARLIAMENTS OF THE EARTH .... WERE AS ONE.... BUT A LESS CRYSTALLINE INTELLIGENCE.... GREW WITHIN THE HARD ROCK....
THE PARLIAMENT OF TREES WERE FORMED.... AND A DIVORCE BETWEEN THE EARTH'S GOVERNORS.... TOOK PLACE....
THE STARS.... CHOSE YOU AS THE CATALYST .... TO UNITE OUR TWO PARLIAMENTS ONCE AGAIN.... HOLLAND-MIND....
THE PARLIAMENT OF TREES.... AND THE PARLIAMENT OF STONES.... OFFER YOU.... OUR THANKS....

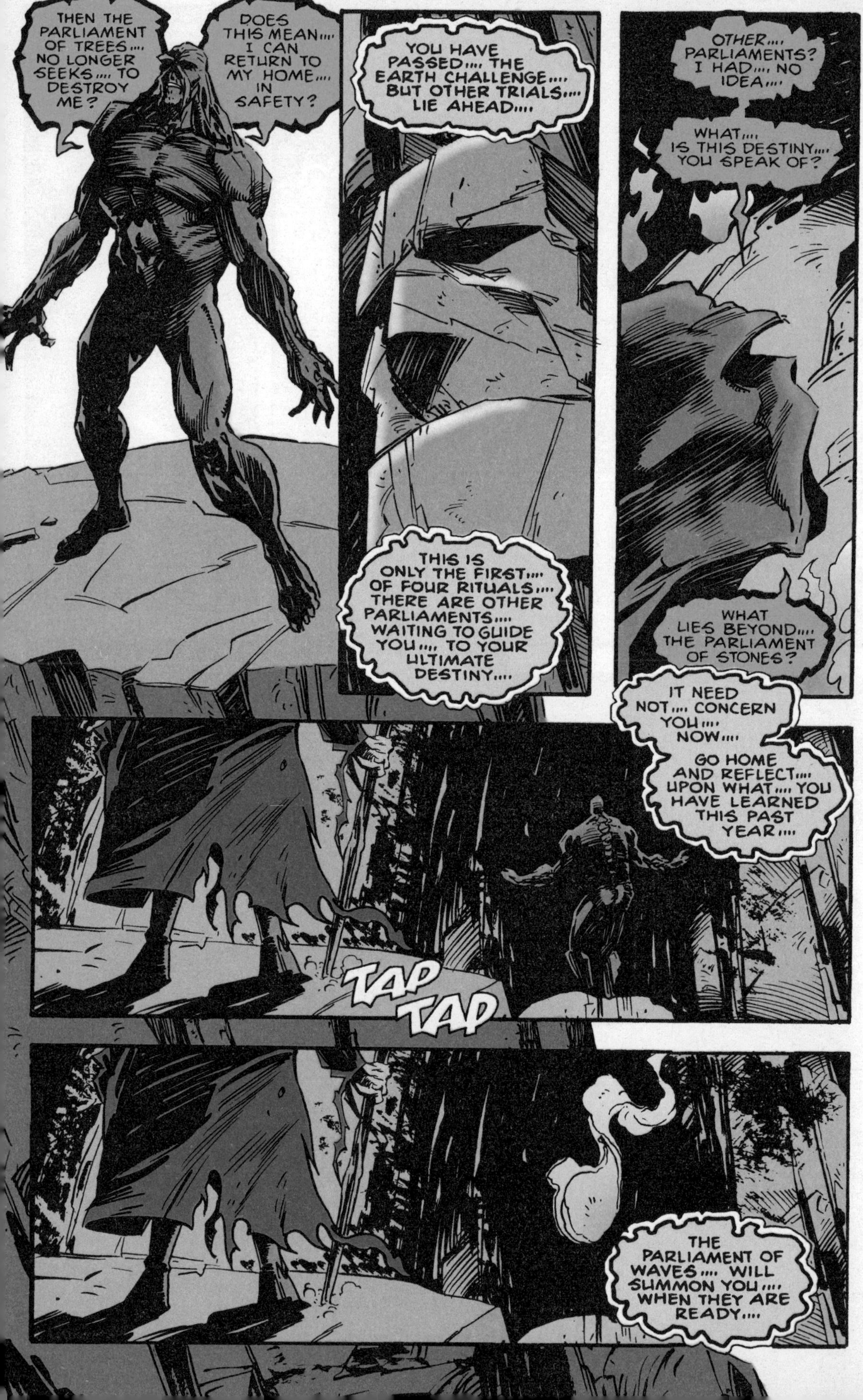
THEN THE PARLIAMENT OF TREES.... NO LONGER SEEKS.... TO DESTROY ME?
DOES THIS MEAN.... I CAN RETURN TO MY HOME.... IN SAFETY?
YOU HAVE PASSED.... THE EARTH CHALLENGE.... BUT OTHER TRIALS.... LIE AHEAD....
THIS IS ONLY THE FIRST.... OF FOUR RITUALS.... THERE ARE OTHER PARLIAMENTS.... WAITING TO GUIDE YOU.... TO YOUR ULTIMATE DESTINY....
OTHER.... PARLIAMENTS? I HAD.... NO IDEA....
WHAT.... IS THIS DESTINY.... YOU SPEAK OF?
WHAT LIES BEYOND.... THE PARLIAMENT OF STONES?
IT NEED NOT.... CONCERN YOU.... NOW....
GO HOME AND REFLECT.... UPON WHAT.... YOU HAVE LEARNED THIS PAST YEAR....
TAP TAP
THE PARLIAMENT OF WAVES.... WILL SUMMON YOU.... WHEN THEY ARE READY....

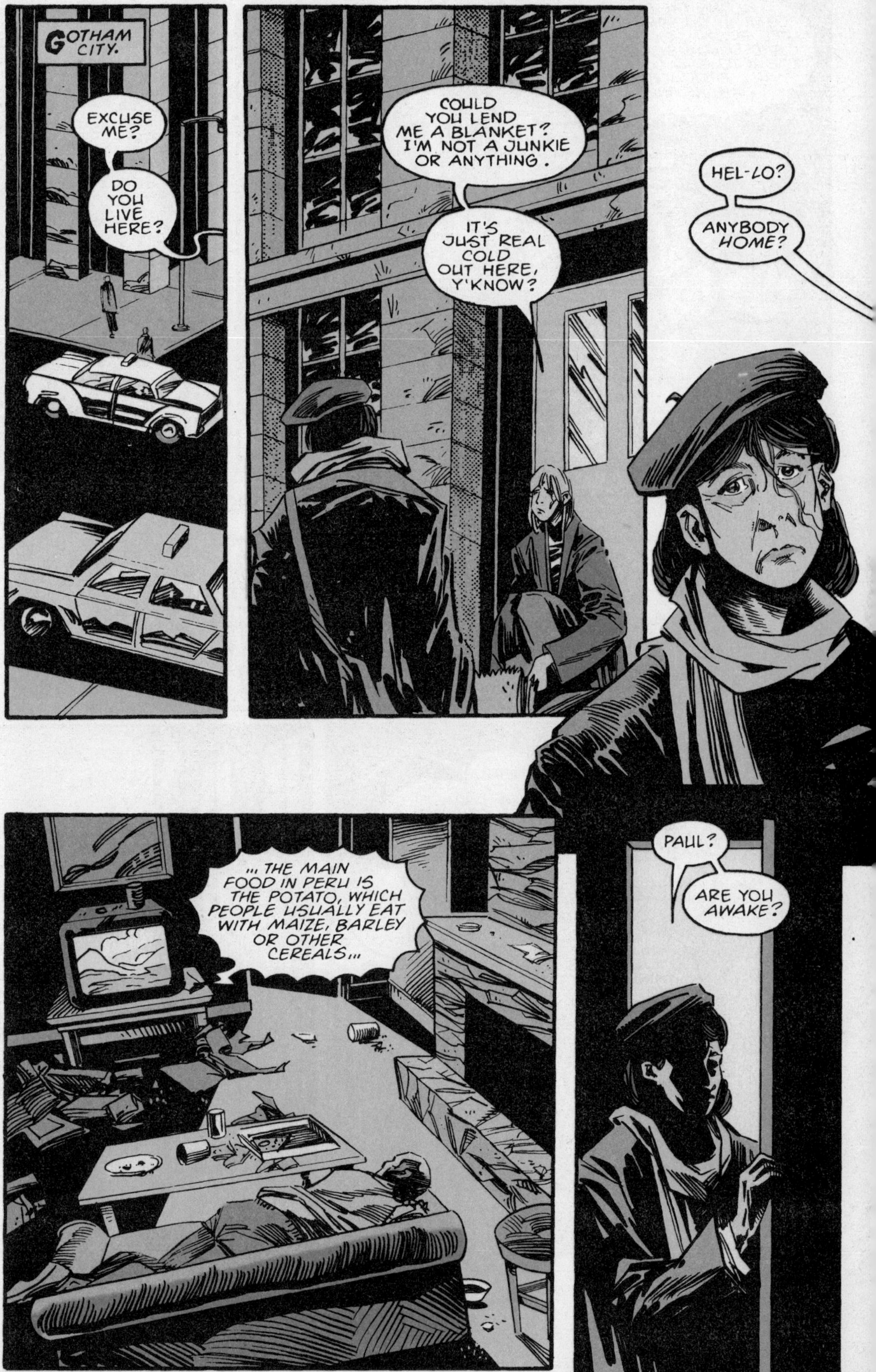
GOTHAM CITY.
EXCUSE ME?
DO YOU LIVE HERE?
COULD YOU LEND ME A BLANKET? I'M NOT A JUNKIE OR ANYTHING.
IT'S JUST REAL COLD OUT HERE, Y'KNOW?
HEL-LO?
ANYBODY HOME?
...THE MAIN FOOD IN PERU IS THE POTATO, WHICH PEOPLE USUALLY EAT WITH MAIZE, BARLEY OR OTHER CEREALS...
PAUL?
ARE YOU AWAKE?

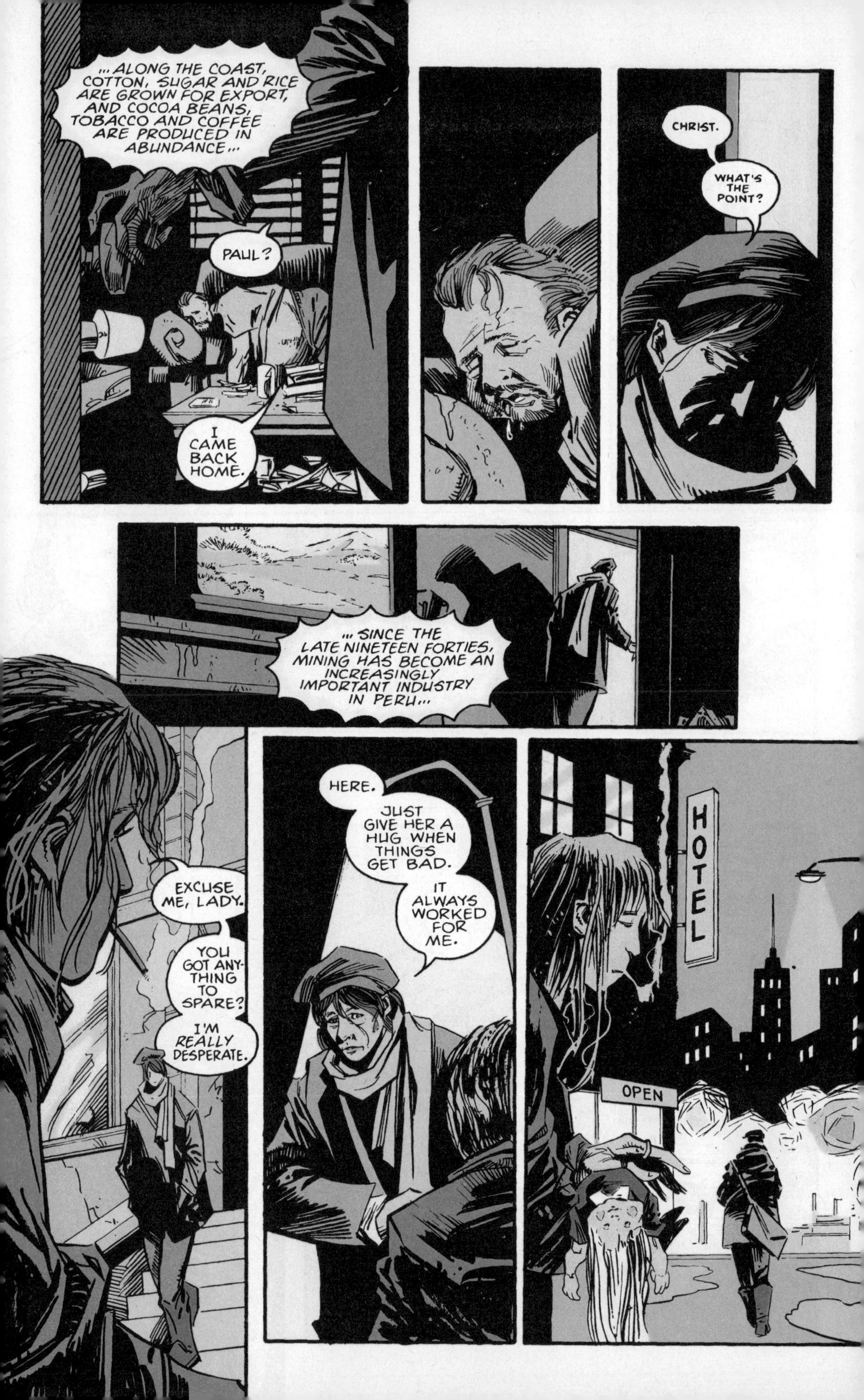
...ALONG THE COAST, COTTON, SUGAR AND RICE ARE GROWN FOR EXPORT, AND COCOA BEANS, TOBACCO AND COFFEE ARE PRODUCED IN ABUNDANCE...
PAUL?
I CAME BACK HOME.
CHRIST.
WHAT'S THE POINT?
...SINCE THE LATE NINETEEN FORTIES, MINING HAS BECOME AN INCREASINGLY IMPORTANT INDUSTRY IN PERU...
EXCUSE ME, LADY.
YOU GOT ANY-THING TO SPARE?
I'M REALLY DESPERATE.
HERE.
JUST GIVE HER A HUG WHEN THINGS GET BAD.
IT ALWAYS WORKED FOR ME.
HOTEL
OPEN

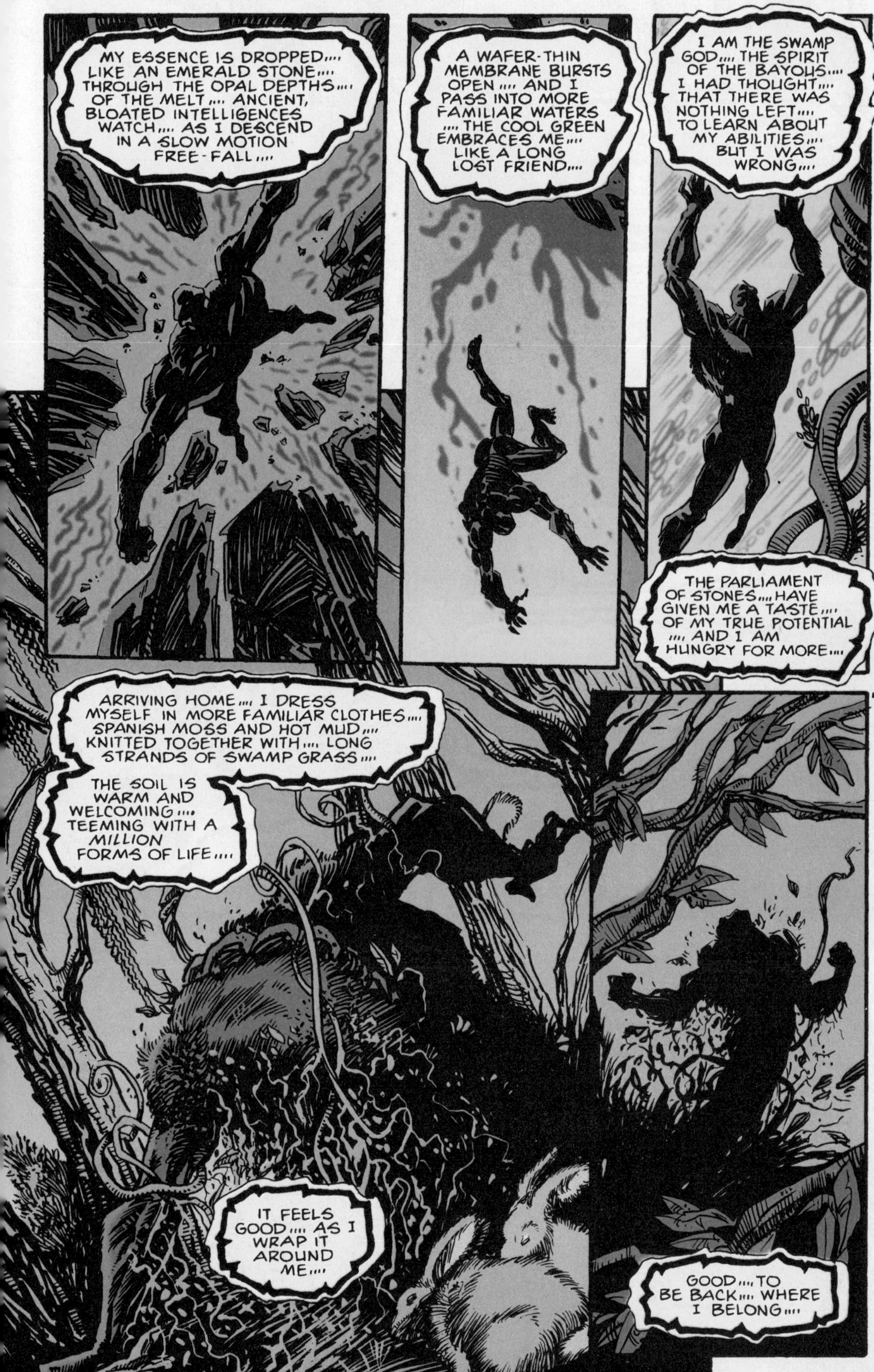
MY ESSENCE IS DROPPED.... LIKE AN EMERALD STONE.... THROUGH THE OPAL DEPTHS.... OF THE MELT.... ANCIENT, BLOATED INTELLIGENCES WATCH.... AS I DESCEND IN A SLOW MOTION FREE-FALL....
A WAFER-THIN MEMBRANE BURSTS OPEN.... AND I PASS INTO MORE FAMILIAR WATERS .... THE COOL GREEN EMBRACES ME.... LIKE A LONG LOST FRIEND....
I AM THE SWAMP GOD.... THE SPIRIT OF THE BAYOUS.... I HAD THOUGHT.... THAT THERE WAS NOTHING LEFT.... TO LEARN ABOUT MY ABILITIES.... BUT I WAS WRONG....
THE PARLIAMENT OF STONES.... HAVE GIVEN ME A TASTE.... OF MY TRUE POTENTIAL .... AND I AM HUNGRY FOR MORE....
ARRIVING HOME.... I DRESS MYSELF IN MORE FAMILIAR CLOTHES.... SPANISH MOSS AND HOT MUD.... KNITTED TOGETHER WITH.... LONG STRANDS OF SWAMP GRASS....
THE SOIL IS WARM AND WELCOMING.... TEEMING WITH A MILLION FORMS OF LIFE....
IT FEELS GOOD.... AS I WRAP IT AROUND ME....
GOOD.... TO BE BACK.... WHERE I BELONG....

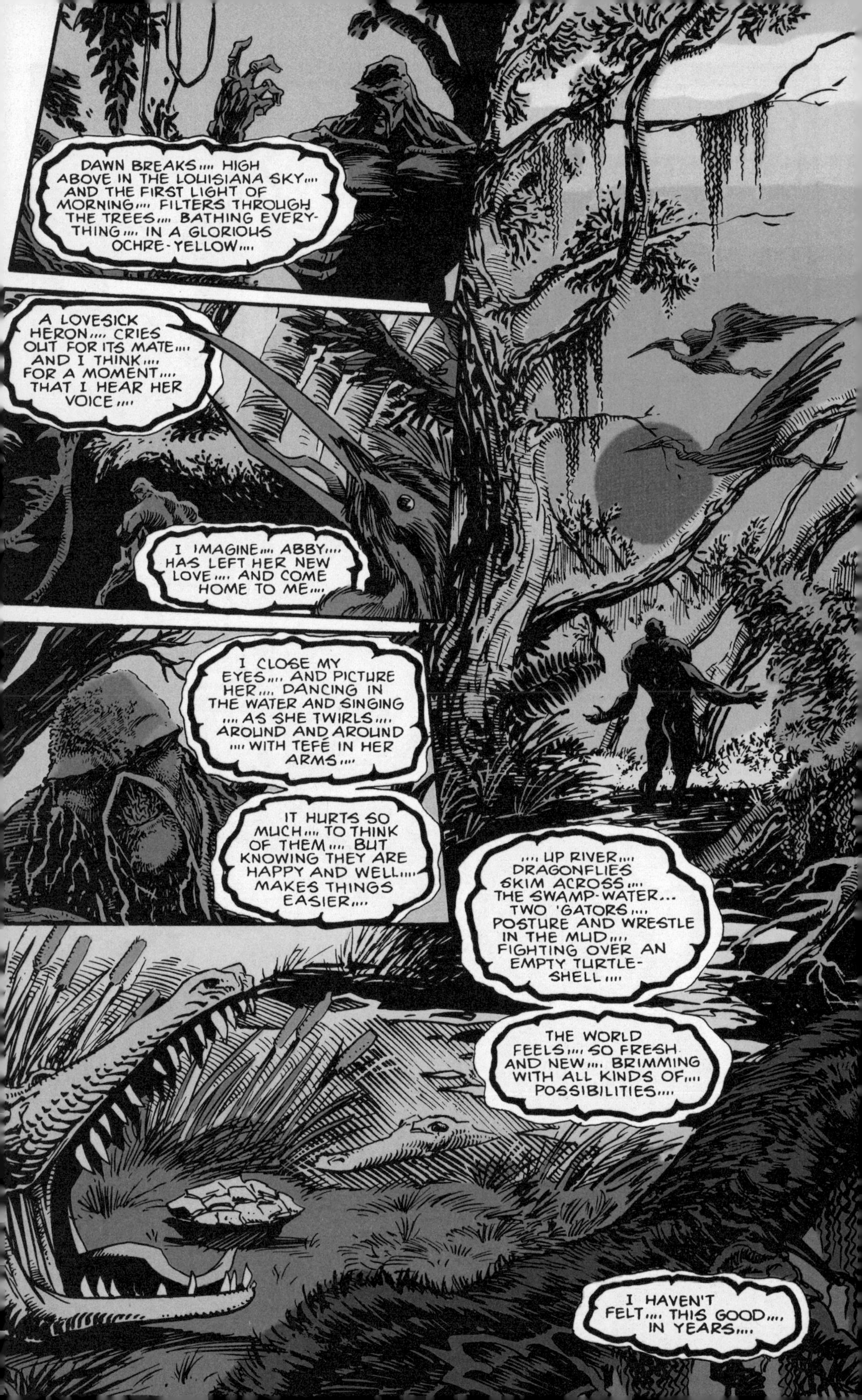
DAWN BREAKS.... HIGH ABOVE IN THE LOUISIANA SKY.... AND THE FIRST LIGHT OF MORNING.... FILTERS THROUGH THE TREES.... BATHING EVERY-THING.... IN A GLORIOUS OCHRE-YELLOW....
A LOVESICK HERON.... CRIES OUT FOR ITS MATE.... AND I THINK.... FOR A MOMENT.... THAT I HEAR HER VOICE....
I IMAGINE.... ABBY.... HAS LEFT HER NEW LOVE.... AND COME HOME TO ME....
I CLOSE MY EYES.... AND PICTURE HER.... DANCING IN THE WATER AND SINGING .... AS SHE TWIRLS.... AROUND AND AROUND .... WITH TEFÉ IN HER ARMS....
IT HURTS SO MUCH.... TO THINK OF THEM.... BUT KNOWING THEY ARE HAPPY AND WELL.... MAKES THINGS EASIER....
.... UP RIVER.... DRAGONFLIES SKIM ACROSS.... THE SWAMP-WATER... TWO 'GATORS.... POSTURE AND WRESTLE IN THE MUD.... FIGHTING OVER AN EMPTY TURTLE-SHELL....
THE WORLD FEELS.... SO FRESH AND NEW.... BRIMMING WITH ALL KINDS OF.... POSSIBILITIES....
I HAVEN'T FELT.... THIS GOOD.... IN YEARS....

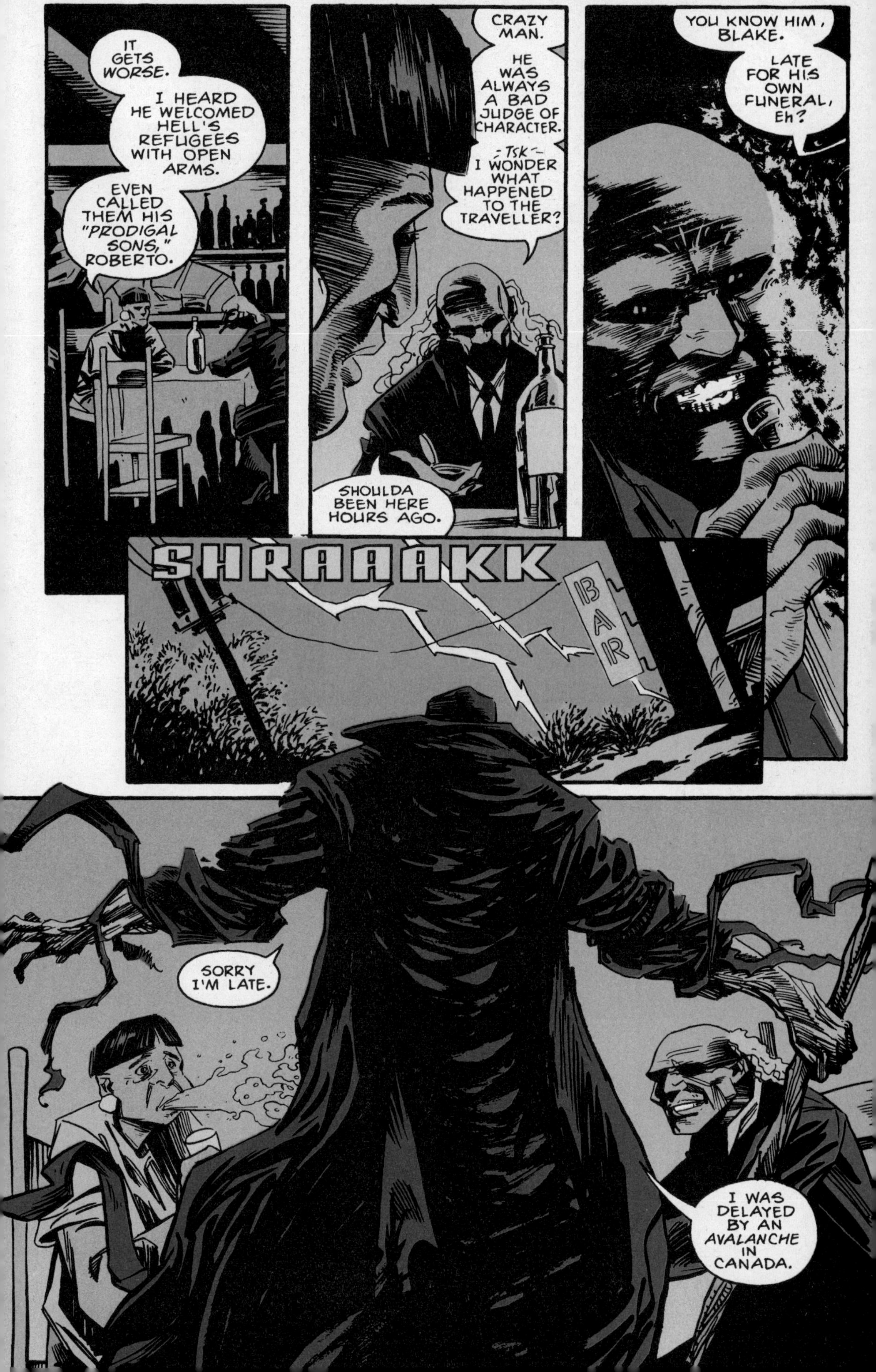

IT GETS WORSE.
I HEARD HE WELCOMED HELL'S REFUGEES WITH OPEN ARMS.
EVEN CALLED THEM HIS "PRODIGAL SONS," ROBERTO.
CRAZY MAN.
HE WAS ALWAYS A BAD JUDGE OF CHARACTER.
-TSK- I WONDER WHAT HAPPENED TO THE TRAVELLER?
SHOULDA BEEN HERE HOURS AGO.
YOU KNOW HIM, BLAKE.
LATE FOR HIS OWN FUNERAL, EH?
SHRAAAKK
BAR
SORRY I'M LATE.
I WAS DELAYED BY AN AVALANCHE IN CANADA.

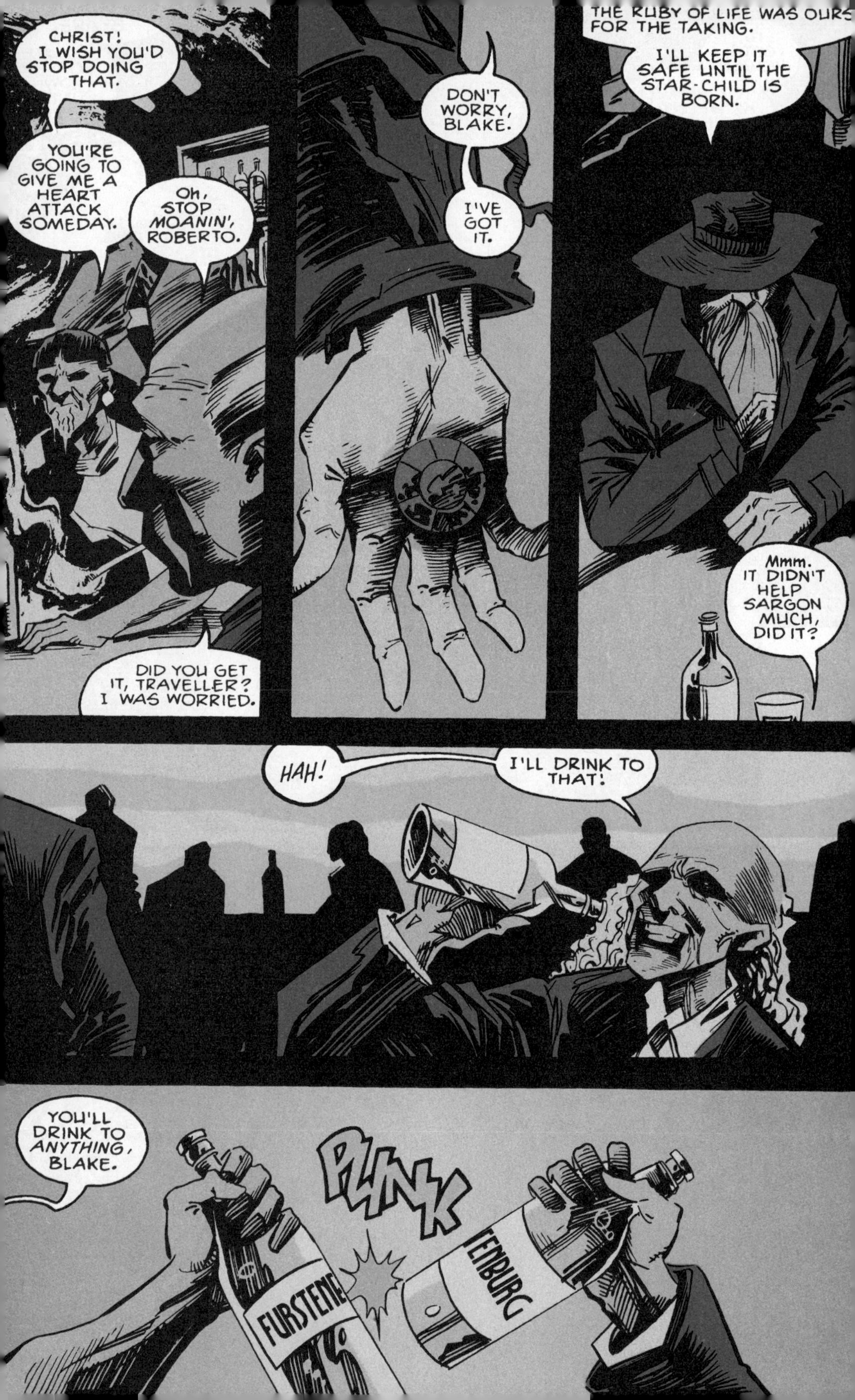
CHRIST! I WISH YOU'D STOP DOING THAT.
YOU'RE GOING TO GIVE ME A HEART ATTACK SOMEDAY.
Oh, STOP MOANIN', ROBERTO.
DID YOU GET IT, TRAVELLER? I WAS WORRIED.
DON'T WORRY, BLAKE.
I'VE GOT IT.
THE RUBY OF LIFE WAS OURS FOR THE TAKING.
I'LL KEEP IT SAFE UNTIL THE STAR-CHILD IS BORN.
Mmm. IT DIDN'T HELP SARGON MUCH, DID IT?
HAH!
I'LL DRINK TO THAT!
YOU'LL DRINK TO ANYTHING, BLAKE.
PLINK
FURSTENE
TENBURG

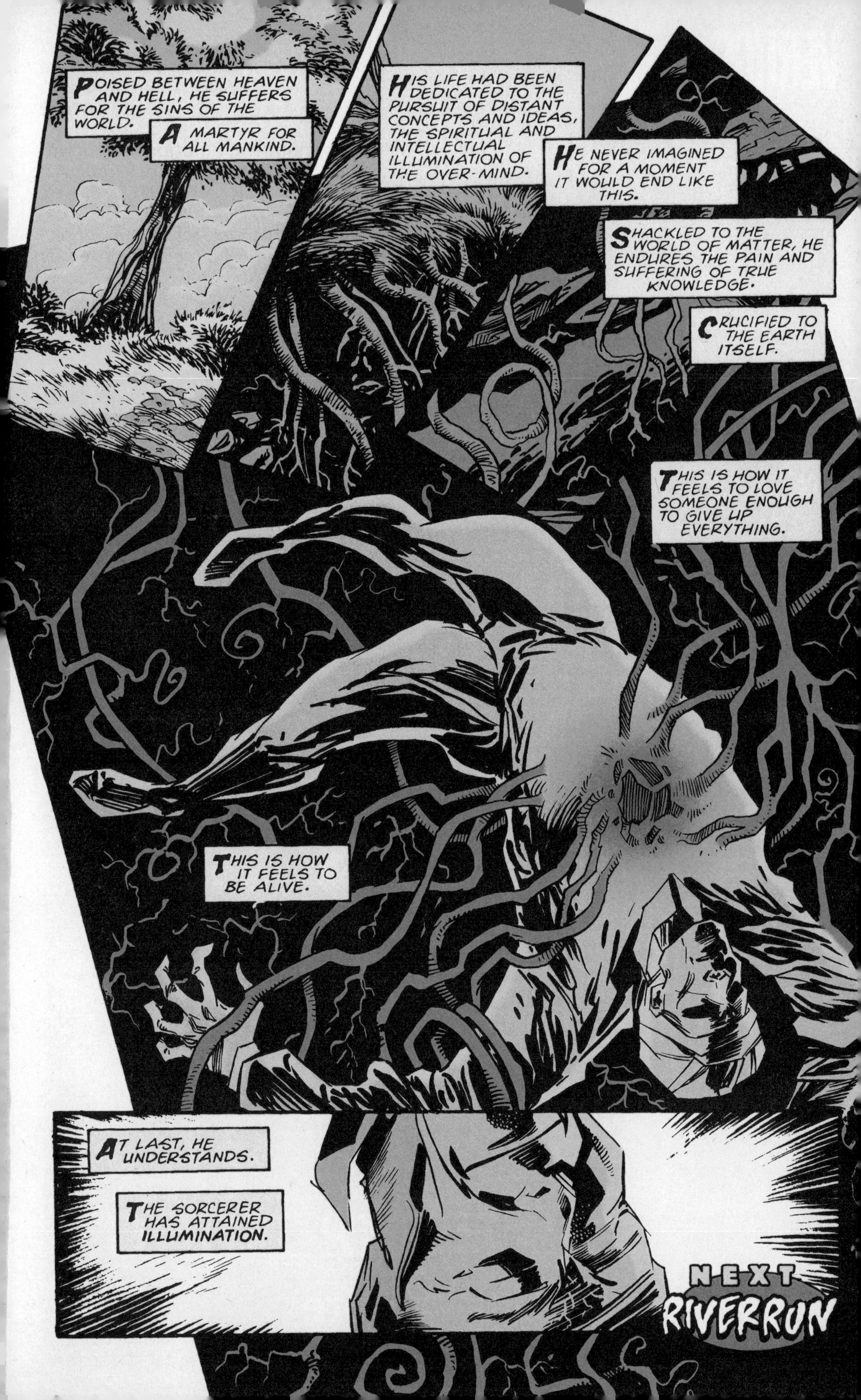
POISED BETWEEN HEAVEN AND HELL, HE SUFFERS FOR THE SINS OF THE WORLD.
A MARTYR FOR ALL MANKIND.
HIS LIFE HAD BEEN DEDICATED TO THE PURSUIT OF DISTANT CONCEPTS AND IDEAS, THE SPIRITUAL AND INTELLECTUAL ILLUMINATION OF THE OVER-MIND.
HE NEVER IMAGINED FOR A MOMENT IT WOULD END LIKE THIS.
SHACKLED TO THE WORLD OF MATTER, HE ENDURES THE PAIN AND SUFFERING OF TRUE KNOWLEDGE.
CRUCIFIED TO THE EARTH ITSELF.
THIS IS HOW IT FEELS TO LOVE SOMEONE ENOUGH TO GIVE UP EVERYTHING.
THIS IS HOW IT FEELS TO BE ALIVE.
AT LAST, HE UNDERSTANDS.
THE SORCERER HAS ATTAINED ILLUMINATION.
NEXT
RIVERRUN